Kant's Methodology

Kant's Methodology

An Essay in Philosophical Archeology

Charles P. Bigger

OHIO UNIVERSITY PRESS

Athens

Ohio University Press, Athens, Ohio 45701
© 1996 by Charles P. Bigger
Printed in the United States of America

00 99 98 97 96   5 4 3 2 1

Ohio University Press books are printed on acid-free paper ∞

Library of Congress Cataloging-in-Publication Data

Bigger, Charles P.
    Kant's methodology : an essay in philosophical archeology /
Charles P. Bigger.
        p.   cm. — (Series in Continental thought ; 23)
    Includes bibliographical references and index.
    ISBN 0-8214-1124-1 (alk. paper)
    1. Kant, Immanuel, 1724-1804—Contributions in methodology.
2. Methodology.   I. Title.   II. Series
B2799.M514B54   1995
193—dc20   95-9639
                                        CIP

In grateful memory

EDWARD G. BALLARD AND W. H. WALSH

Contents

....

CONTENTS   ix

....

ACKNOWLEDGEMENTS

....

MANY HAVE HELPED ME arrive at this version of Kant. My greatest debt is to the late Edward Goodwin Ballard whose chance remark in 1961 that he did not understand Kant's thesis that time is self-affection (B 68) reminded me that I did not understand it either. This set me on a road that began with an analytic and epistemological approach to Kant which led hither and yon to "archeology." Though my approach is so different from his own, the gracious hospitality and the inspiration of working at Edinburgh with the late W. H. "Richard" Walsh inspired me to take up Kant within phenomenology. His unfailing wisdom, courtesy, and tact led me to take Kant seriously, something that had eluded me in graduate school and in twenty years of teaching Kant. I dedicate this book to their memory.

This study was begun many years ago with an attempt to situate the reader in the dead time between the 1770 *Inaugural Dissertation* and the 1781 first edition of the *Critique of Pure Reason,* and to see it take shape in this gap. I had hoped to show how the two major contemporary Kantian traditions, analytic philosophy and the various Continental schools, shared a common root. This wasn't my calling, as I discovered when an editor at the Center for Advanced Studies in Phenomenology invited me to revise and resubmit the manuscript. Two versions and many years later, thanks to the patient advice and helpful scrutiny of many readers, my constantly shifting interest, and the always helpful guidance of a succession of editors, Lester Embree, J. N. Mohanty, and Claude Evans, I have something different, if not true, to offer the reader. The constant battle to extract something presumed to lodge within the interstices of my computer taxed every one's patience, including the experts at the Word Perfect Corporation; but now thanks to the Ohio University Press, especially to Helen Gawthrop, Holly Panich, and Mary Gillis, it is to see daylight in their Continental Philosophy Series. To all who in good will faced a difficult text I express the deepest appreciation.

The late David Cornay, among the most gifted young philosophers I have known, taught me to appreciate Husserl's rigor and Heidegger's writings on early Greek philosophy and was an incisive critic of earlier versions. I was also the beneficiary of Kenneth Smith's wise and sympathetic advice on Hegel and post-Hegelian German philosophy. David Stern also gave this a very careful reading and suggested how it might be brought into greater conformity with the judgment theory of the second edition. To my former wife and collaborator, Dr. Anita Bigger, a molecular biologist, I owe my interest in non-conceptual recognition in molecular phenomena and help with the chemical details of an essentially Aristotelian model of living systems. A very special thanks goes to that best and most generous of philosophers, John Llewelyn, who awakened my interest in the middle voice and its role in recent European philosophy and who was kind enough to suffer through several versions of this text. I am also grateful to Jacques Derrida for acknowledging my presumption of his debt to the *Timaeus* and to Charles Taylor for reading portions of the text on the book of nature. Gerd Buchdahl was especially encouraging. He read and incisively critized several versions of my chapter on Objects; what is of value in my treatment will surely bear the mark of his considerable authority. I am also the beneficiary of wise advice from younger colleagues from various disciplines. Bainard Cowan, Robert Chumbley, and Joseph Kronick shared some of my seminars with me, provided many sources, and read parts of this manuscript. Among my own colleagues past and present who have been willing to respond to a dull text with generous advice are Mary Sirridge, Edward Shirley, Edward Henderson, Tina Chanter, Greg Schufreider, Glen Mazis, John Protevi, and John Baker. Among those who have earned my gratitude for work on the preparation of earlier versions of the text are Kelly Mink, Kenneth Ferguson, Regina Mayhill, Mary McCleary, Mary Spurgin, Cathy Martin and, especially, Peggy Fogle. To the kind and patient workers in the Text Processing Center of the College of Arts and Sciences of the Louisiana State University who prepared countless "final" versions of this text I must extend my deepest appreciation. Thanks are due Louisiana State University for sabbatical leaves and to my host institutions. The study was begun at Edinburgh, Kemp Smith's University, during 1971–72 and, thanks to Peter Jones and John Llewelyn, brought into a resemblance of its present form through a fellowship at the Institute for Advanced Studies in the Humanities at the University of Edinburgh in 1987. French influences were cultivated at the University of Paris in the spring of 1980.

To my daughter Rachel Meredith, my stepdaughter Carole Marie Belleau, and my wife Anne who put up with me against all the odds I stacked against them I offer my very special thanks. Anne's editorial assistance was especially helpful.

ABBREVIATIONS FOR KANT'S WORKS

....

KANT IS CITED in the pagination of the *Gesammelte Schriften,*
1724–1804, hersg.von der Koniglich Prevssischen Akademie der Wis-
senshaften, Berlin, 1902 _____, as *AK* or under the following abbreviations. Other classical texts are cited in the standard format. All other
references within the text are of the author by initials, date of text,
and page number variety.

A or B   *Critique of Pure Reason,* Norman Kemp Smith, tr. (London:
         Macmillan, 1973).
Anth.   *Anthropology from a Practical Point of View,* Victor Dowell
         and Hans Runet, trs. (Carbondale: Southern Illinois Press,
         1978).
Beweis. *Der einzig m oglich Beweisground* (N.Y.: Arbis Books, 1979).
CAJ   *Critique of Aesthetic Judgement,* J. C. Meredith, tr. (Oxford:
         Clarendon, 1911).
CPR   *Critique of Practical Reason,* Thomas Abbott, tr. (London:
         Longmans, Green, 1948).
CTJ   *Critique of Teleological Judgement,* J. C. Meredith, tr. (Ox-
         ford: Clarendon, 1928).
Cor.   "Selections from Correspondence with Beck, Herz, Lambert,
         Sulzer, and Mendleson," in *Kant: Selected Pre-Critical Writ-*
         ings and Correspondence with Beck, G. B. Kerford and D. E.
         Walford, trs. (Manchester: Manchester University Press,
         1968).
Diss.   *The Inaugural Dissertation,* in *Kant: Selected Pre-Critical*
         Writings and Correspondence with Beck, G. B. Kerford and
         D. E. Walford, trs. (Manchester: Manchester University Press,
         1968).
Enq.   *Enquiry Concerning the Clarity of the Principles of Natural*
         Theology and Ethics, in *Kant: Selected Pre-Critical Writings*
         and Correspondence with Beck, G. B. Kerford and D. E.
         Walford, trs. (Manchester: Manchester University Press,
         1968).
Grund.   *The Moral Law: Kant's Groundwork of the Metaphysics of*
         Morals, H. J. Paton, tr. (London: Hutcherson, 1968).

LK   *Gedanken von der wharen Schätzung der lebendigen Kräfte,* HKI 1747, 1-81.

Logic   *Logic,* Robert Hartman and Wolfgang Schwartz, trs. (Indianapolis: Bobbs Merrill, 1974).

MF   *Metaphysical Foundations of Natural Science,* James Ellington, tr. (Indianapolis: Bobbs Merrill, 1970).

ND   *Nova Dilucidatio,* in F. H. England, *Kant's Conception of God* (London: Allen and Unwin, 1928).

NG   *Versuch den Begriff der negativen Grössen in der Weltweisheit einzuführen,* HK 1763, 165-203.

OH   "On the Idea of a Universal History," in *On History,* Lewis Beck, ed. (Indianapolis: Bobbs Merrill, 1974).

Op. Post. *Opus Postumum,* Eckert Foster and Michael Rosen, trs. (Cambridge: Cambridge University Press, 1993).

OP   "On the Proverb: What May be True in Theory, But Is of No Practical Use," in *Perpetual Peace and Other Essays,* T. Humphrey, tr. (Indianapolis: Hackett, 1983).

OQ   "An Old Question Raised Again: Is the Human Race Constantly Progressing?" in *On History,* Lewis Beck, ed. (Indianapolis: Bobbs Merrill, 1963).

Prol.   *Prolegomena to Any Future Metaphysics,* P. G. Lucas, tr. (Manchester: Manchester University Press, 1966).

INTRODUCTION

....

THE *CRITIQUE OF PURE REASON* is "an attempt to alter the procedure which has hitherto prevailed in metaphysics in accordance with the example set by geometers and physicists . . . it is a treatise on the method" (B xxii). Archeology is this new method in metaphysics. When his effort to reestablish his new way to truth in the sciences led Kant into the "blind and indispensable" imagination "without which we would have no knowledge whatsoever" (A 78/B 103) and when, after the critics' response to the first edition in which it seemed that he might be proposing imaginary, that is, fictional, foundations for these sciences, his "shrinking back" from this "abyss" (MH 1990, 110)— as Heidegger put it—seems quite justified. Even as he shrank back, he drew from its depths resources for phenomenology and, even as he drew the limits of knowledge, left traces that lead beyond. I propose to return to this "abyss" through his methods of analysis and synthesis and complete the task where he left off; greater treasures are to be found on this abandoned itinerary than remain to be discovered along understanding's well-travelled way (115).[1] These methods, the very soul of the *Critique,* lead into the depths of this *arché,* ambiguously translated by "origin" or "principle," to make manifest the mystery of the world's worlding. The use of Kant to map this journey invites destructive (Heidegger) and deconstructive (Derrida) violence against metaphysics, a task begun by Kant from within metaphysics which we may perhaps bring to completion by retrieving through him some unthought possibilities. To retrieve, *Wiederholung,* something from a text is to make manifest what it "did not say, could not say," in a "destruction" of metaphysics (WR 1965, 89–93). "Destruction" overcomes a tradition by returning to its historical *arché* in a search for undeveloped possibilities beyond the closure of metaphysics one can make productively one's own (MH 1962, 43). "Deconstruction" goes beyond the text to what was "bracketed out" as irrelevant to show that this continues to work in the text to produce unresolvable ambiguities. But "deconstruction" also invites a second, "deeper" reading, within which *différance,* a primary vehicle of deconstruction, is implicitly acknowledged and a way beyond the closure of metaphysics is opened or suggested, just as the Kantian spontaneity of thinking points to a deeper moral spontaneity beyond the wreckage of speculative metaphysics.

Today the textual metaphor offers a perspicacious interpretation of both ourselves and our world and yet, at the same time, this textual approach to the *arché*, traditionally translated as "principle" and understood as a truth grounded in a permanent presence, would seem to lead in an anarchical if not nihilistic world from which the gods seem to have fled. Could a text sustain a world? That would normally entail, as with Heidegger's "care" or Plato's "participation," the assimilation of a transcendent alterity for the sake of being a same. Even as deconstruction questions this possibility, it leaves open the further possibility that the *arché,* now construed as "originary source," may contain traces of the Good which transcends Being. Should we be able follow these traces and escape this closure, the Good would as if by grace deconstruct the egoistic, appropriative self and its participatory assimilation of the other so that it can be for the sake of the Other.[2] This too would be within Kant's orbit.

The way into the archeology of the first *Critique* begins in the *Logic* and passes through its second main division, the Transcendental Doctrine of Method, to the Aesthetic and Analytic. Whether the emphasis is on objects that appear through the "generally unknown" work of the transcendental imagination in the first edition or, as in the second edition, on the centrality of understanding, the "faculty of judgments," the Deduction must be approached through its methodological parameters. Kant's "Copernican Revolution" was occasioned by a crisis that threatened the possibility of gaining truth in analysis, "the method of discovery." The epistemic continuum, shared by Empiricists and Rationalists, in which understanding and sense were same in kind, differing only in degrees of clarity or force, could no longer be counted upon to relate the sensory and intelligible worlds. What third term could hold them together? After Hume there seemed to be no hope of an empirical grounding; more important from Kant's standpoint was the presumed invalidity of the ontological proof upon which had been founded the transcendent sovereignty of reason, its opening to the discarnate *Logos* by and through whom there is a world. With this loss of physico-theology's access to a constituting, active infinite, one also lost the standpoint of God, for whom alone there can be the infinite totalities and the possibility of understanding them required by mathematical analysis. Finite man must discover in transcendental synthesis an alternative *arché* for a world created through God's infinite intuition and a way to express it in a finitistic mathematical language. Kant's revolutionary application of the methods of analysis and synthesis effectively destroys epistemology and the older metaphysics of "grounding presences" and, if we follow aright its methodological threads, carries us through a philosophical archeology into the originary, a sort of Spinozistic *natura naturans,* from which worlds erupt.

Paul Ricoeur says that Husserl revealed the phenomenology implicit in Kant's epistemology (PR 1967), though Kant gives phenomenology an ontological determinate lacking in Husserl.[3] If phenomenology is to be more than another egology and is to disclose the possibility of a human world, an enduring structure of meaning and value, it must avoid the Cartesianism into which both Kant and Husserl fell. If one begins with Descartes' disengaged self and its desacralized, extentional world, one no longer lives through nature as it appears through the language of her book; the detached atomic self constructs itself and imposes its instrumental preferences, its "values," on an otherwise senseless world. Thus the self as *arché* seems to give only a solipsistic world of objects that express what has been projected on them, not things as inexhaustible epiphanies, offsprings of the Good encapsulating flame.[4] Nevertheless, Kant's methods restore sense to sense. Using what may be learned about analysis from him, I hope to replace the prevailing expressionistic view of mind and language with one which is open to the expression of Others and things.

The way back to Others and even things leads, rather counterintuitively, through Kant's institution of "transcendental philosophy" in his "Copernican Revolution" as the new way in metaphysics. Principles governing thought which physico-theologians believed to be grounded in a transcendent, constitutive *Logos* were no longer available; even if these are granted, the Empiricists' immanent critique left them without a field of applicability. Each approaches sense as if it were to be subsumed under a law; what would be a nomological law is a mere "truth of reason" whose empirical relevance is questionable or, conversely, there is no object (*Gegenstand*) to subsume under the law. Would it be possible to restore laws and things with the recognition that analysis, the way to truth, cannot be considered independently of the *arché,* "origin"? Understanding something entails knowing its causes and how it came to be or, since origins can be telic, that towards which it transcends. Aristotle, for example, understood *arché* as the process of manifestation through which what is hidden emerges into "visibility" (*arché* as "originary") to then take up its place within an intelligible order (*arché* as "principle"). At first glance, transcendental philosophy seems to turn away from this process towards the possibility of experience as a subjective genitive that lets us reach towards and, as an objective genitive, encounter meaningful objects. The Transcendental Dialectic, for example, questions first beginnings and final ends. Moreover, the classical analysis of change gives way to a phenomenological concern for meaning, for appearance as objectively significant, a focus which in turn eliminates essence or form in its classical sense. Nevertheless, unless analysis, the method of the exact sciences, is supplemented by an "originary" ontological synthesis, one cannot understand how it is possible to encounter objects having those modalities of significance that Kant proposes in the Principles. Kantian synthesis apportions the archaic sense of manifestation to the more modern sense of analysis by demonstrating how Principles objectively elaborate and are subjectively evidenced within original temporality. Thus, analysis is already disclosive, that is, hermeneutical, and not subsumptive; and since it harbors an ontological understanding, its imaginative and linguistic roots permit experimental procedures to unconceal the ontic necessities implicit in this understanding. Method shelters "an anticipated view of the sense of the being which one encounters" (EL, cited in JD 1978, 118). Thanks to Kant and Husserl, it is possible to show how appearances can emerge from the *arché* and, with Heidegger's assistance, be transformed from constituted or constructed objects into things which show themselves in *claritas*, the radiant splendor of form. This splendor is the Good's, not Being's, doing. This initiative by the Good which founds and stands beyond the limits of phenomenology is solicitous love, *agapé*. This central theme of God's initiative departs radically from Plato's Parmenidian intuitions; since he founds love on the need to fill a lack in order to secure or maintain self-completeness (*Sym.* 198E–199A), St. John's words, "God is love," would be incomprehensible (202C–E). The Good as infinite love that gives itself to us through the cross deconstructs Plato's unities, that is, justice as the community of the same, and empowers one to go out to accept responsibility and seek justice for those who are radically other, Alphonso Lingis's "community of those who have nothing in common" (AL 1994).

Granted this intuition, we can begin to see possibilities through Plato which we can claim only if we can first recover rights to the land surrendered to Aristotle and the judgmental or predicative interpretation of the categories which, if I may be pardoned a fashionable locution, fosters the interpretation of being as presence.[5] There is much in Plato that is unacceptable and must be radically modified if a retrieval is to be successful; beside the proto-fascism of most of his political writing, the separated forms of the middle dialogues are incoherent.[6] Above all, the Good which neo-Platonism understood as a fecund Parmenidian principle of emanation must, as beyond Being, deliver us from such encrustations of presence and open us to history. Aristotle was supposed to have delivered us from incoherence and the mysticism inherent in dialectic; however, he was so concerned to found change on presence that he made the possibility of history suggested through the Good all but inaccessible; his efforts to correct Plato's dialectic with logic were a disaster. Participation, and our human openness to one another in community, communication and communion with form became predication. Dialectic's dramatic unconcealment (*aletheia*, "truth"), which also conceals and thus warrants Socratic ignorance, was founded in a logistic intuition of essence and thus secured the conformity of our "mental affections" with things. Moreover, Aristotle assigned to the immanent working of the soul, as in concept formation, what analysis discloses in things. Admittedly, Plato has difficulties with a separationism between being and becoming analogous to that between concepts and percepts discovered by Kant; just as the latter's medial imagination overcomes this bifurcation and allows us to see form in sense, so Plato can find form in medial becoming through his reworking of the Gaea-Uranus myth of original creativity in *Timaeus*. The gap between earth and sky, being and becoming, spanned by soul and lighted by the Good "beyond being" (*Rep.* 509B) is the phenomenological open within which beings appear. Separationism is replaced by a relational ontology in which participation constitutes and spans the "open," the gap (*chaos*), within which creatures arise.[7] This gap lies between heaven, being as informing *peras*, and earth, the mother as a dynamical *apeiron*, a medial and formless becoming. Participation becomes not a precursor of predication but rather an account of how creatures dwelling in this ethical open, this free space, ecstatically and interpretatively constitute their being in responding to received alterity. What seems on its face to be a classical, objectivist version of the *arché* as the event of manifestation will become, when supplemented by Plato's account of soul, the form of hermeneutics and even experience as we have been taught by Kant to understand it.

The securities of self-certain subjectivity vanish with the recognition that the archaic English sense of "been" is "dwell." The myth of Gaea and Uranus is a more appropriate beginning than the *res cogitio*. The Cartesian "I am" would then be "I dwell" with others in the gap between earth and sky, the "chaos" from which worlds world, not with myself in the auto-affective and solipsistic closure of inner sense. How in this "inner" exile to which modern philosophy has sentenced us can the free man praise and rejoice in the glory of worlding? A clue is already present in our language. Many technical terms stress the priority of the "open" in their archaic, phenomenological-ontological formations. Among these are *doxa* (accepting a thing in the brightness of its phenomenal appearing vs. belief or opinion), *logos* (collecting and gathering vs. the expressive word, logic, science), *theoria* (one qualified to representatively participate in a sacred event vs. a theory), *aletheia* (unconcealment, the alpha-privative of *lethe*, hiddenness vs. truth), *einai* (durative, veridical, and vital presence vs. "to be" as the copula or even "existence"), and even at times *eidos* (the shining of that into which a being collects and limits itself vs. idea in the mind).

Heidegger was set upon his way towards this "free space" or "open" by Kant's discovery of an incongruity between the ad hoc formations of contingent sensibility and the synthetic necessities of thought or reason. Following the synthetic method as understood through the actual practice of mathematicians, which involved producing *a priori* by a rule the image through which the intentional object of the pure concept could be intended, he proposed to produce the *a priori* formality of empirical objects intended in sense that would, by virtue of their categorial constitution, serve as the ground for the sciences. This entailed constituting sensibility as *a priori* intelligible by making the transcendental object the ontic theme of the productive imagination. What had hitherto, as the "faculty" of phantasms, been the classical conceptualist's *deus ex machina* linking sense and the intellect became in Kant the origin of both understanding and sensibility. The Principles show how expressively generated temporality is the formal condition for the being of empirical objects. These objects in turn gather up sense into significance. The *arché,* "origin," of this extraordinary feat lies in transcendental apperception.[8]

Even if we abandon the judgmental approach to Kant and its predicative or subsumptive interpretation of empirical science, we must admit the abiding appeal of "pure" mathematics and logic. This is the main concern within which phenomenology surfaces. Though he did not share Kant's conceptualism, Husserl gave a more complete and rather Platonic expression to Kant's discovery. Even if we do not share his horizons, we must all be moved by Husserl's poignant appeal to "the absolute significance" of Plato's ideal of "genuine science" which set inquiry "on the path to the true idea": "The modern man of today, unlike the 'modern' man of the Enlightenment, does not behold in science, and in the new culture formed by means of science, the Self-objectification of human reason or the universal activity mankind has devised for itself in order to make possible a truly satisfying life, an individual and social life of practical reason" (EH 1969, 5). This appeal to genuine science is a reminder that eidetic phenomenology conceals the explanatory aspect of Plato's idea theory even as it unconceals ideas as meanings. The cosmological aspect, the theme of myth and "likely story," points to an *arché* "beyond being" that eludes phenomenology whose evident contingencies are incompatible with the Kant-Husserl ideal of "purity." Husserl sought to establish phenomenology as an exact science on the model of logic and mathematics. Can we preserve what is genuine in Enlightenment, the love of understanding (if not wisdom) and justice, which has always been our tradition's abiding goal? Only if we grant that the myths and mysteries marginalized by the Enlightenment are necessary to its lighting. Myth lets something of the unfathomable originary appear and likely stories, "romances of nature" rather than nomological laws, will make something of eidetic structure manifest. The epistemic disengagement must be abandoned, that is, the ideal of the disembodied and placeless knower-in-general whose object is a desacralized and transparent nature. We might know everything, as Plato says in *Charmides,* yet how can it profit us unless we know the Good? The Good, beyond being and knowing, is an impossibility which the analysis of the originary makes necessary.

Descartes disengages consciousness from the world and limits intuition to its immanent contents, ideas as objectively real, which then require some third thing, God, if they are to intend a world. The task for synthesis is to demonstrate that "the conditions for the possibility of experience in general are likewise conditions *for the possibility of the objects of experience* and for that reason have objective validity in synthetic *a priori* judgments" (A 158/B 197). In mathematics, construction supplies the third thing, the *x* in which subject and predicate are unified, that makes synthetic judgments possible; transcendental synthesis must supply this term by so constituting time that objects can be taken up and thought homogeneously in the categories. The usual reading of Kant offers no such insight into his problematic. We think of analysis, as in "philosophical analysis," as concerned with discovering the elements or arguments that justify our use of certain concepts, while synthesis is identified with deductively unifying things in a movement "from forms through forms to forms" (*Rep.* 511C); Heidegger says Kant remains within this "axiomatic tradition" (MH 1967, 184). None of these paradigms leads into Kant's generative matrix, the originary.

In order to arrive at this "originary," the methodological sense of analysis must be assumed to be primary. From his physico-theological beginnings, Kant was very interested in methodology, which he understood to be a part of logic, that is, inquiry.[9] Method is ontological, not epistemological, and determines "what becomes an object and how it becomes an object" (MH 1967, 102). Analytic and synthetic concepts are formed within the analytic and synthetic method. Unless we think about concepts within the methodological parameters in which they are produced, the way will not lead to what is of abiding appeal in Kant.

Plato thought inquiry was guided by a prior understanding, that is, *anamnesis,* that allows one to recognize what comes towards one from conditioned hypotheses and conjectures as their condition for being true. His analytic method was taken over by the classical mathematicians and scientists and became, as Paul Helmos says, the problem-solving orientation which is the heart of mathematics.[10] Kant's pure concepts of the understanding are also *anamnestic*. Analysis, Kant's "method of discovery," starts "with what is sought as if it were given" in order to "ascend to the only conditions under which it is possible" (*Prol.* 276). It puts its hypotheses to nature in the form of categorial questions in experimental projects and constrains it to answer "within [*anamnestic*] strings of reason's own devising" (B xiii).[11] One no longer had access to the *Logos* since analysis can no longer establish the truth of these categorial conditions; this becomes the responsibility of a logic of truth (A 62/B 67), the synthetic method of the Transcendental Analytic.

Platonic analysis is monstrative; it is a discourse which brings entities before us to let them be seen as exhibiting form or structure and proceeds by successively narrowing the matrix, e.g., the overlapping set of conceptual or sensitive fields, in which they are presumed to inhere in order to unconceal their *eidos*. One imaginatively regards the unifying unity, as Husserl was to say of its close relative, the eidetic reduction, "throughout all conceivable variation . . . so that it can be understood for all future time and all coming generations of men and is thus capable of being handed down and reproduced with the identical intersubjective meaning" (EH 1970b, 377). Though we are, thanks to deconstruction, attuned to dissemination, we must admit that such ideal identities may control, and even constitute the possibility of, these various representations. In order to be sure that the elicited *eidos* is not a feature of the monstrative set or matrix in which it is elicited, Plato would first have us map physical phenomena into and onto "eternal" mathematical form and then use hypotheses expressed in these forms as a monstrative or definitional matrix. Otherwise the elicited entity becomes a simple positivity which is a mere abstract from, rather than constitutive principle of, the matrix. Aristotle's abstractive methods, which are founded on sensible similitude, take this form. In the philosophy of science we are told that the terms in an explanation cannot be homogeneous with those being explained; heat is, for example, a kinetic and not a caloric property. Descartes, whose method is not inductive, nevertheless does not ask how thinking and its expression and communication are possible; instead he lets analysis prescind the "thinking thing" from the variant modes of cognition, from thought (*penser*) and sensibility (*sentir*), in which it inheres. Though such isolating acts are necessary in discovering sufficient conditions, there is a risk that the entity elicited and thus abstracted, in this case the *res cogito,* will become a "substance" requiring nothing save itself in order to exist. As another example, since propositions are expressed in a timeless present tense, analysis seems to yield an equally timeless truth. Like the externally related simples of physical or epistemological theory, as with Newton's particles or Hume's impressions, these posits of analysis are ahistorical inhabitants of the timeless present ruled by the copula, even if the "copula" still speaks of the creative copulation with a necessary alterity which Plato associated with participation. We thus mistake the finger for the moon. On the other hand, it is also vicious to ignore a concept's definitory, historical matrix and to assume that it exists quite independently of these conditions; these denatured concepts are cut loose from their origins (*arché*) in the life world to become as if terms in God's eternal lexicon. This is the tale usually told about Plato's idea theory from which he can, I think, be rescued. Kant said that "all knowledge is finally subject to time" (A 99). In Kant, for example, the concept "analytic" works within a complex set of historical parameters that have little relation to its contemporary usage. "Objects" purporting to ground knowledge are posits of historical, ontological projection and thus entail something like the hermeneutical circle.[12] Though things, unlike texts, have no explicit historical horizons to fuse with our own, as expressed in text analogues they bear interpretations which call us into question. This insight clears the way for an extension of hermeneutics to the physical sciences.

Approaching Kant, the founder of transcendental phenomenology, through his methods defines a path to the originary, the engendering *arché*, which leads to mathematics and the philosophy of science. If Kant was understandably wary of fictional foundations, his use of symbols to present the "supersensible" suggests to me that this may be the way to go. Some of deconstruction's resources will be used to establish these upon the single root of the soul's power, the imaginative and the creative resources in metaphor, and I will carry out some possibilities that will emerge in the light of the truth he "somehow made manifest" (MH 1962, 63). What is "somehow made manifest" becomes clearer when, in answer to his question, "What is truth?" Nietzsche answers, "A mobile army of metaphors, metonymies, anthropomorphisms" (FN 1965, 508). The "primal world of human fancy" is a chaotic *apeiron gignesthai* from which pours forth "a fiery liquid of similes and percepts" which congelate and coagulate into a "primitive world of metaphors" (510). But there is another concern, which sometimes clashes with the first, reflected in Kant's separation of the moral from the empirical. Though I have often, as a good Aristotelian, lamented this separation, I now see that this facilitates the retrieval of the Good and the receptacle which even Plato marginalized as beyond knowing and being, *epekeina tes ousias*. That Kant and Plato share the neighborhood of the *arché* suggests a chiasmus, a crossing of the *arché*, in which they might mingle and engender new meanings of Being. When Kant's "blind but indispensable imagination of which we are scarcely ever conscious" (A 78/B 103) is crossed by a schematized intention, it engenders the phenomenal world; and while the pure imagination is a creative matrix, it is constituted by a "principle," transcendental apperception and its schematized Principles of Pure Understanding. I suggest an alternative meaning of *arché,* the matrix as originary, which I find expressed by the equally mysterious Platonic receptacle, the "nurse and mother of all generation" (*Tim.* 49B), which constitutes, with an equally unknowable but ethically necessary Other, God (thought within the traditional onto-theology) or the Good (thought beyond Being), the possibility of a gap, *chaos* or *metaxu,* within which beings can appear. In Kant the gap is phenomenological and not cosmological, so that beings appear between the *schema*tizing understanding and sensibility as relational, extended magnitudes through quality to be thought modally within the Principles within a constituted spatial and temporal world. In due course I will show how the *arché* as "principle" generates space and time and how, on an alternative Platonic account, this spacing is the work of the originary receptacle.

Contextualization of form is a heresy that requires some defense. Let me begin with the inherent contextuality of a text and then see how something as non-contextual as a Platonic form can be contextualized. A philosophical treatise is always contextual, always a text within a text. However self-enclosed it may seem, it remains a part of this larger textuality being read and written by forms of domination, social, moral, and cultural, as strategies for mastering, distributing, or legitimating powers; this more general textuality is wittingly or wittingly re-presented in the philosophical text. The forces that play within a deconstructive criticism of a particular text reflect the polemos that transpire beyond it and from which it defends itself, perhaps by marginalization. Deconstruction is a microcosm of this age.

The contextualization of form can be approached through space, the condition for objectivity and its differentiating locations, in order to show how form can be non-reductively contextualized. We think space non-contextually when it is assumed to be indifferent to whatever may occupy it. Because form, *morphe,* is often modeled in sensible *schema,* it is read in these terms. Philosophy is then the ape of mathematics. Rather that beginning with the separation and placement of a face-to-face encounter that founds language and the possibility of reference, space is usually taken to be a sort of characterless container in which movable things can be encountered in separated or contiguous places. Granted some transportable and recognizably self-congruent spatial object taken as a unity, their extension and distance from one another can be measured. Kant's intuition of space, the form of outer sense, as a given, infinite magnitude of possible coexistences composed of spaces expresses the traditional position. Place, that from which we dwell and even gain identity, becomes either a container, as in Aristotle's' "innermost motionless boundary of that which contains" (*De Phys.* 212b 20) or a privileged locus, as in his *telos* of things naturally in motion (208b 10). From the example of something recognizable as self-congruent that can serve as a measure, we can show how it is often the case that the entity elicited in monstration is assumed to have the properties of the regions through which it is demonstrated. Since these will be mathematical and mathematics is the science of order (discrete magnitude) and topological form (continuous magnitude), any phenomena thus characterizable can be mapped into and described in this language. An eidetic reduction of geometry would show that a non-metrical projective geometry is primary and that the metrical kinds can be derived by the addition of alternative axioms of order. But we have a tendency to characterize what we "see" by the "geometry" of the monstrative conditions through which it is "seen." If we characterize the measure by our evident ability to recognize self-congruency, we can characterize it as a continuum of the order type η of the rational numbers. If however, it is to measure any interval, such as the diagonal of the unit square, it must contain an Archimedean, non-denumerable subset of real numbers which has the order type θ. Interpreting it as a rational interval can account for our ability to recognize it as same in various places and perspectives and thus pick it up, carry it about, and set it aside; if, however, we model it on the Archimedean subset, congruence will be stipulated as what the measure measures, rather than the equality we "see"; a dense, metrically amorphous set cannot support the natural recognition of congruence. The conditions we introduce in measuring, which is monstrative, could prevent us from seeing what is there to be seen. Only within Euclid's geometry are objects recognizably self-congruent in transport, rotation, and reflection. Kant's choice of Euclid, at least as an interpretation of the life-world, is justified. Sacred space, oriented to importances and sometimes expressed as if on the surface of a sphere, may be Riemannian.

If, as seems to be the case, space is the wherein of significance, we should begin where it is founded, on encounter, on dwelling together, and not with physical geometry. Dwelling presupposes *chaos*, the gap, between earth and sky in and from which we stand out with one another to world world. This *chaos* is the Platonic dynamical *apeiron gignesthai*, "formless becoming," which grants the emergent "living creature" a place, *chora*, in which to dwell. Prior to space is the possibility of having a home, a family, from and for which one goes forth to harness by labor the powers of the earth and to which one can return for renewal.

In the penultimate chapter of his *Phenomenology*, Hegel identifies revealed religion with "picture thinking" and proposes a movement that leads beyond it to the end of philosophy in the totalization
of Absolute Knowledge. Though Kant believed that things could be
thought, such as the actual infinite, that could not be understood, his
genius was to sensibilize concepts and to recognize that to go beyond
them is to abandon truth and falsity. Since, thanks to deMorgan and
Cantor, the infinite can be imaginatively schematized, this may not be
a limitation on mathematics and its methods. While mathematics
may be placeless, it does not give news from a nowhere beyond picture
thinking but rather, as we will come to see, makes such thinking possible. If something like picture thinking which will contextualize, and
even contaminate, forms with empirical content can be restored to
metaphysics, we may be able pass beyond its closure to the Good.

Plato was not oblivious to the possibility of forms being context-
dependent; the form "angler" (*Sop.* 221A) presupposes a historical
culture inseparable from specific environments. Perhaps a movement
towards a satisfactory account of the apportionment of form to context and context can be given with the aid of Husserl's distinction in
"The Origin of Geometry" between signs whose "two-leveled repetition" iterates a sign and re-presents for explication an "ideal object"
such as a triangle (EH 1970b, 357). Husserl believed (and I think he
was correct) that mathematical objects are historical and, therefore,
linguistic posits. Granted its linguistic institution and the preservation
of these texts, a mathematical object is otherwise context-free and
thus adaptable to any coexistent or successive context. Even if there
are alternative routes to the same object, for a point is the limit of
convergent sets of squares or circles, unlike the signs in a natural language, these instituting signifiers cannot be separated from their intentional objects. They carry their content with them. The correct use of
the sign presupposes that its content is always open to thematization,
to explication. Cultural formations are also linguistic, but saying
"The American Constitution" or the "Waste Land" does not institute
a political formation or a poem. Though other signs, such as the English "lion" or German "lowe," signify in the absence of their objects,
these objects would be inconceivable apart from the habitat and ecol-
ogy to which they are bound. Though "lion" is repeatable and lions
are recurrent, contrary to structuralist theory in which a sign is the
signifier/signified unity, the sign itself does not constitute or contain
an object which can be independently described and explicated through
the sign alone. Kant has shown that to know how to use "triangle" is
to have the *schema*tizing power to explicate it; this also applies, again
thanks to Kant, to the *schema*tic power of the concepts of scientific
objects for which mathematical language supplies the *logos*.

Forms do not clone their empirical instances. They come to be by representing themselves only if there is first a grant of *chora*, place, which orders form to her necessities and perspectival variations. Only then can there be things whose extensional ground, morphology and forms of order can be described mathematically. Plato is the first cartographer of and guide into this archaic condition which, Derrida says, "anachronizes being" (JD 1987, 270). His use of place qualifies his as a proto-perspectival geometry, but my non-conformist interpretation of his way requires some preliminaries. Edward Casey offers a point for departure with his observation that, in Plato, since dwelling precedes building, "there is in the beginning a dwelling place for all that becomes" (EdC 1993, 176). The Platonic receptacle (*hypoché*, "the capacity to accept and retain," [*Tim.* 49B]), the correlative of *metalambano* ("participation" in the sense of "grasping the beyond"), is the primal dwelling and condition for building. Building gathers (*logos*) the elemental powers from whose play—to anticipate Nietzsche— nothing definite becomes (28A). The receptacle provides the material conditions and, on responding to being "propositioned," the fecund perspectival focus, *chora*, from which the emerging creature gathers itself into its appropriate bodily form. This grant of life presupposes the diversified receptacle whose *dynamics qua* elemental becoming make possible this dwelling place (*chora*) and situation (*hedra* as "seat" or "residence") (52B). The receptacle as a potential for place, rather than place itself, is thus prior to the mathematical ordering entailed in the Demiurge's world-building (41D). This interpretation associates the gift of place from which the living creature can egress with the receptacle and presupposes that creation has two ontological levels; (1) diversification of the receptacle and (2) the place from which the emergent creature gathers this becoming into being something definite. (1) Becoming which grants life its body is to be understood as structured by the elements, the first fruits of the ordering of undifferentiated energy, *apeiron dynamis,* according to the mathematical forms (31B–32C). (2) This dynamical and medial becoming, assuming solicitation by the father's (50D) persuasive reason (48A), grants the place, *chora*, from which the creature gathers itself and stands out as an embodied and situated *here*. This distinction is intended to block a tendency to see Plato as a pan-psychist in the worthy company of Hegel, Leibniz, Peirce, and Whitehead. Like the Good, *chora*, a medial complex, is beyond Being. But doesn't this mean that ideas, though not reducible to images through which they are seen and perhaps precipitated, are also contextually *schema*tic? The receptacle is not a homogeneous and isotropic Euclidian space and the nodes from which its perspected are heterogeneous. Contextuality, this "errant cause" (48A) is beyond knowing (51A), through it can be apprehended in a "bastard reasoning" (52B). Only the Good is absolute, not as realized in the present in Absolute Knowledge but as *parousia*, the always outstanding hope for *aletheia* and justice.

The ideas elicited in monstrative acts are to be understood in relation to the place, *chora*, from which one is gathered into a world by language, where language is, by nature and like nature, (*physis*), "a root unfolding" that makes way for something to be seen (PE 1993, 330–32). The earliest gods are relative to the places in which a way-making liturgy discloses the sacred; we too must learn to contextualize what seems without a context. This is one aspect of *chora*, the chthonic contribution of singularity. In *Timaeus* the soul was created as same but, thanks to *chora* which effects embodiment, they become different (42D). Some sense of the manifold formations of this medial matrix, always same in her different expressions, can be gathered from James Joyce's variants on the Platonic receptacle in *Ulysses*. She undergoes a series of transformations ranging from Buck Mulligan's shaving bowl through Dublin Bay to the "bowl of bitter waters" Stephen's mother vomited as she lay dying, and then on to Molly Bloom, Dublin, and the Western World. Platonic ideas, in ideality invariant sames, must also undergo contextualization. This may be possible as a consequence of Hellenistic and Orthodox developments. Using a neo-Platonic idiom, how can ideas be "apportioned" to place? This is the gift of the "faceless, generous mother, matrix of particular beings, inexhaustible matter for things" which Levinas finds unsettling in Heidegger (EL 1985, 46) but which finds its human face in Mary, Mother of God.

Let me propose some Byzantine images in which the Platonic "reversal" can be thought. In mosaics which date from 1315–1320 in St. Savior in *Chora* (Kariye Djami) in Istanbul, Mary is represented as the place of the *Logos,* the place of the placeless (*chora tou achoretou*) (PU 1975). It is possible to achieve a deepening of Plato's insights in a "root unfolding way-making disclosure" through the icon *Zoodochos Pege,* a version of which was once in the Church of the *Chora.* In this variant of the great *Timaeus* image of original creativity, the Mother of God, the "life-giving source," brackets out the wilder, elemental waters associated with the earth mother, Tia'mat, Cybele, Gaea or Oceanus, which then become, as if by her *epoché,* the creative and healing waters of her receptacle that give God a place. In this little-known icon, the Virgin Mary is represented as sitting in a receptacle that gives off of itself healing waters and holding the infant Christ. *Chora* gives a place from which to gather and channel elemental nature into the life she nurtures and shelters as Mary gathered the dynamics of nature to nurture and shelter the infant Jesus. She is thus transformed into the originary *arché,* "the place of the placeless" (*Logos*).

"The Mother of God as the place of the placeless" from the Church of the Chora, Istanbul, c. 1420 A.D.

"Zoodochus Pege" (Life-Giving Source)

What does this image say to us? First that the creative power emerges, not from a masculine principle, a presence, but rather from beyond presence and absence through the creative originary. The mother through whose love we can love another makes possible being with others. Shared life, not the directed search of the ego, unconceals. In her for the first time we hear the voice of an other, "the voice of the friend whom every *Dasein* carries with it" which, Heidegger continues, "opens *Dasein* to its ownmost possibility" (MH 1962, 164). If this listening to the friend as an exemplar of *Mitsein* leads, on Heidegger's own account, to struggle, to the polemical model of community formed through Homer before the walls of Troy and cultivated by some mothers in the Third Reich, Mary speaks of another world, the world of compassionate and sheltering love.[13]

Moreover, the icon expresses an apportionment of the *Logos* to the "unintelligible" singularity of *chora*. With the exception of Aristotle's *phronesis*, Duns Scotus and Whitehead, this would be an abomination; recognition is always in a concept, a universal, and the datum a mere substitution instance thereof. The law-like typic in Kant's ethics perspects a placeless world: acting on a maxim you can will to be a universal law of nature models a rational will which is homogeneous and isotropic, as befits the space in which it is *in*. *Yet analysis is monstrative, a way of seeing through, from, and in a place.* Kant's methodological revolution will take us to things that express law-like behavior, not to laws that express things. The dynamics of this catachrestic *arché* are to be found in *différance*, Jacques Derrida's contribution to the archeology of this abyss. With some modifications it will, on being crossed, lead into the "proximity" of the Good, condition for any open explored by the saintly Emmanuel Levinas.[14] Could this particular methodological bias provide Levinas's "me-ontology" with an acceptable cosmology?[15]

In the Platonic image, the matrix is a medial becoming. The earliest strata of Indo-European language lacked a passive/active distinction and instead had active and medial forms. The "deconstructive" possibilities in the middle voice have been brought to our attention by Jacques Derrida. Though it is usually translated reflexively, as in the French "Je me pense," Jan Gonda, whose authority determines this discourse, says

> The 'original' or 'essential' function of the medial voice was
> not exactly to signify that the subject 'performs a process that
> is performed in himself,' but to denote a process that is taking
> place with regard to, or is affecting, happening to, a person or
> thing; this definition includes also those cases in which we are
> under the impression that in the eyes of those who once used

this category in its original formation some power or something powerful was at work in or through the subject, or
manifested itself in or by means of the subject on the one
hand and those cases in which the process, while properly performed by, or originating with, the subject, obviously was limited to the sphere of the subject. (JG 1960, 66–67)

This voice "gives a possibility that enables" (MH 1971b, 93) as, for
example, when the subject admits ownership of deeds even when they
seem, like grace, to be enabling expressions of a supernatural power.
John Llewelyn, my Virgil in matters of medial perplexity, explains
that "we need [is] a notion of power that does not just pass through
the subject, and the notion of a subject that is neither a conduit or
passage (the 'through' of pure passivity) nor the conductor who is entirely in charge of a performance (the 'by' of pure agency) but is performed by as much as he performs the process—or the procedure,
Verfahren, to employ the term Kant applies to the schematism of the
imagination . . ." (JL 1991, ix). He also notes that expressions of
extreme passivity, common to both the late Heidegger ("language remains the master of man" (1971a, 146) and Levinas ("substitution
beyond passivity" (1981, 138)), should not discourage this retrieval.

Gonda remarks that medial forms are not always found where we
might expect. The active voice does not necessarily denote a personal
agent, as in "gene action," and medial processes, though "limited to
the sphere of the subject," do not propose his intervention. Languages
lose the middle voice, replace it with the passive, and reinterpret the
active voice when "man comes to see himself as master of a desacralized environment" (JL 1986, 90).[16] Agents and their acts have correlatives in patients and potentialities; how to set the limits to the purposes
and freedom of the one and to discover causes and law-like necessities
working within the other becomes the task for thinking which follows
a misplaced ontology. We, children of Enlightenment, have long since
abandoned the voice of the sacred and its paradigms in myth and mystery to become self-defining and know that, for all the perplexities in
our position, there is no going back. If the middle voice is to be heard,
it will be in the problematics of self-interpretation and self-definition.
The activities and states once expressed in the middle voice, the over-
powering voice of the place-specific sacred, might present our condition in a new light were the phenomena once named by medial verbs
redescribed in the spirit of the effeminated middle voice. It will be
hear in Kant's imagination, a variant of the Platonic matrix.

Granted this linguistic insight into the "root" of sense and understanding (A 78/B 103), the imagination understood in its original,
medial form will be ambiguously spontaneous, like thought, and re-

ceptive, like sense. Like thinking or speaking, which were also medial, imagination comes upon us and gathers us into its free play, not as a cause, but as a process within which we spontaneously participate. Transcendental imagination receives only because it is already disposed to welcome uranian form and let things appear within its interpretative or context-forming matrix, where the context of all such contexts is an oriented, meaningful world. According to the "Copernican revolution" thesis, this matrix creates in its reflexive generation of time (B 68, B 155–56) the "look of an object which is possible" (MH 1990, 90), where "look" is a variant of *idea* signifying an ontological determinant, a category, of the phenomenal conditions of objectivity. The object (*Gegenstand*) encapsulating these expressed conditions is intended as "something-in-general = x" through sense (A 104). Heidegger says this x, the "something or other" of existential statements, is "nothing" (82).

Though often concealed by Kant's tendency to associate matter with sense and form with understanding, the doctrine of the schematism is a phenomenological thesis about imaginatively seeing form in fact. The form-matter distinction is redundant for, granted the "generally unknown" work of transcendental synthesis, sense is given as already significant. The empirical affinity thesis borrowed from Hume is a reductio, not a live option. Analysis discloses eidetic structure without benefit of these mediating psychic functions. Once we discern that the gap is not between sense and understanding, for experience in its active sense belies dualism, but between being and becoming, then the solution to the incongruity between what is given, as the physicist or the psychologist might consider it, and what is set up by man in the work of his spirit—the sciences, arts, laws, religions, and the like—lies in participation. The *arché* will no longer be the ego but, like Kant's imagination, the originary gap which now is seen as linking earth and sky, man and the gods in the creative worlding of world. This origin, to overwork a Cartesian metaphor, is the zero point from which radiate all axes, the eye's—and only then the "I's"—own "there" as the condition for determining determinables.

The discovery that makes it possible to advance participation, Plato's *metalambano* ("the beyond retained in the midst of"), the most powerful and neglected concept in all of Western thought, as the solution to our incongruities and the threat of incoherence, owes everything to Husserl. Correctly understanding himself as advancing philosophy within the possibilities of Kant's transcendental program, Husserl nevertheless freed us from talk of inspecting images and phantasms as if psychological contents were the beings known, as well as from confusing what is present with the psychical events through which they are meant. Moreover, and this too is Kantian, he showed that we already possess world as the correlative to transcendental subjectivity, thus putting to rest the search for epistemological criteria which has dominated philosophy since Descartes. For all of his talk, however, of returning "to the things themselves that show themselves in themselves and from themselves," we know that for Husserl sense receptivity, as a sort of *hyle,* is animated by intentionality, first as time and then by sense-giving intentionality. This latter, "active interpretation" is the metaphorical "seeing something as . . ." which is articulated in allegories or likely stories, scientific and moral.[17] Kant's subsumptive tendencies can be replaced by the "seeing as" to which analysis disposes us. Such seeing often falls within an imaginative and interpretative matrix, such as a myth or allegory. This imaginative synthesis which is founded on Kant's Schematism lets world appear. Kant construed constitution as world preserving, as sustaining natural inference through the metaphors of a microcosm-macrocosm (IP 1973, 65–104).[18] If Kant's position seems to demand a covering-law model of explanation, can we offer a phenomenological, model-theoretic alternative that does him greater justice?

Yes, if "ideas" and "concepts" are not understood as mental contents, dialectical or subsumptive, but as ways of noetic, interpretative, and projective "seeing as . . ." modes of Being-in-the-world. Heidegger observed that a Kantian concept gathers many particulars into a unity in reflective temporalization. In abandoning conceptualism we retain this insight; understanding bends back over and interprets sense through its matrix, mythical or otherwise. This Aristotelian insight (*De Gen. Anim.* 429b 15-8) modifies the force of Kant's Copernican Revolution: this is not a world of objects, the correlative of subjects, but of things that thing, that collect themselves and standout to us in a world. Just as we grasp the thing through the sensibilized concept, so too we grasp it as worldly—as a meaningful or significant entity within an extentionally indefinite, unified totality—through the poetics of reason. Life is self-limiting: "A boundary is not that at which something stops but, as the Greeks recognized, the boundary is that at which something begins its presencing" (MH 1971b, 174). In standing out from the *apeiron* receptacle by limiting itself through its active interpretations of receptivity—a general formula for "participation"— and collecting (the archaic sense of *logos*) itself into *eidos,* the radiant splendor of form, the living creature seems to replicate ontologically the epistemic functions Kant assigned to the senses, the forms of the understanding, and concepts. The ground that with the break-up of the epistemic continuum could never be gained from the analysis of sense, where "analysis" is the method of going from the conditioned to its conditions, is already available to Kant through transcendental synthesis, an original presencing by which meaningful (phenomenal) beings are present.

Retrieving Kant in a speculative hermeneutics leads, as Paton described the intent of Kant's first *Critique,* to a "metaphysics of experience." If experience depends on interpretations and self-interpretations, and not simply rules, in which our own Being is at issue, then it is cumulative and creative rather than rule governed, the Kantian constructivistic analogue to Plato's ideas. Our threat today is not so much from an Anglo-American infatuation with rules but from our continental allies. Nevertheless, Nietzsche revealed an interpretative dimension in participation I had previously missed. Is being understood as "directed power" (EB 1983, 7–14; *Sop.* 247E) the "will to power?" Will a doctrine acknowledging the ubiquity of participation offer an account of the "eternal return" as a creative retrieval of the *arché* be more respectful of his insights than the genealogies with which he, Foucault, or Deleuze replaced being, history, and truth? Yes, but only if we can learn the dynamics of the world, the general text, from Nietzsche and the dynamics of its microcosmic text from Derrida. Let us begin.

I

ANALYSIS AND SYNTHESIS: THE METHODOLOGICAL ROOTS OF KANT'S METAPHYSICS

....

1. Orientations and Destinations

BEING UNDERWAY—to the wars, on a pilgrimage, in a career, with a family, towards becoming who you are, on the way (*Weg*) of thinking and the like—is a pervasive and perhaps definitory image of the human condition. The way may be sacred, like Lao-tse's Tao, Hugh of St. Victor's *pereginatio in stabilitate* or the Buddha's path; it may be, like that of Fielding's Tom Jones, quite worldly. Since Heraclitus went in search of himself (DK 101) to the boundless boundaries of soul (DK 45) and Parmenides discovered that the way leads through every town to truth (DK 1), the journey has been a root metaphor for philosophy. It may now be threatened by the decentering, if not the loss, of the subject and its world. Do we wander, nobodies going nowhere with "them;" or do we find our identity in departing from, journeying towards, or returning to a place, *chora*, where we dwell, *oikos*? Even if the image of a journey is pervasive, is it a root metaphor, which it certainly is for "methodology," or does a journey, being underway, depend on something even more primordial? Emmanuel Levinas contends that arriving and departing pertain to the economics of dwelling primordially rooted in place, *chora*. The issue might be put as follows: is it of our essence to be underway, to attain something through seeking something, as Heidegger understands "care?" Kant will construe life in these terms and articulate in with Principles which will govern a dialectic of "faculties," reason, affectivity, and will. Or is the point of life its enjoyment, a medial image rooted in dwelling that "deconstructs" faculties?

To clarify this issue, let us focus on "experience." When Kant asks, "How is experience possible?" *Erfahrung,* his word for "experience," has the sense of setting out on a journey. Whither? What are the possible destinations? This question presupposes that we can think experience in terms of its *arché*, its limiting principles or its enabling powers. If experience does not just passively register but actively en-

1

gages what is received, the apparently ambiguous compresence of both active and passive aspects can be eliminated by following Plato's example in a similar context (*Rep.* 339E ff.) and assigning these to different faculties.[1] As in Descartes, this difference can be so exaggerated as to risk incoherence. Kant proposes to avoid bifurcation by offering the productive imagination as a middle term. This "blind but indispensable function of the soul . . . of which we are scarcely ever conscious" which gives and makes knowable appearances (A 78/B 103) is a rather close analogue of Plato's equally ambivalent receptacle. As a third thing which is "not this nor that" it is at the same time "this and that" (JD 1987, 266). Like the receptacle which, Derrida continues, withdraws "any opposition from any grammatical or ontological alternative of the active and passive" (267), the imagination is a third thing that partakes in receptive sense and spontaneous understanding without being either and, again like the receptacle, invites a medial interpretation. The imagination is the root or matrix which, like the *es gibt* (Heidegger) or *il y a* (Levinas), makes appearance possible. For Kant the imagination gives what appears within the horizon between (*metaxu*) those categorial activities by which we projectively interpret experience, the Schematism, and sensible receptivity informed by the Principles. Things that appear within this open as we travel "on the way" can be taken up into the understanding through judgment. Heidegger's hermeneutics reveals that meanings of being, our own and that of entities intended, determine the sense of the open.

"Method," "being on the way," has virtually the same meaning as "experience." The *logos* in methodology's suffix has been, at least since Heraclitus (DK 1), both a subjective and objective genitive. On the one hand, it pertains to *noein*, thinking and its formal or logical capacities, and on the other to *einai*, "being" and its structures, which Parmenides said were "same"; *to gar auto noein te kai einai* (DK 3). In a sense, at least as an ideal, *logos* is placeless, even though the knower and the known both presuppose a place or context from which and towards which they meet in this same. Moreover, its "meta" prefix ambiguously signifies the "within" of contextuality and the "beyond" of transcendence. Stressing the transcendent sets one on the way (*hodos*) to the ideal of context-free truth, *aletheia*, and concepts formed through it are universals or rules (A 126) governing *praxis*. Parmenides' remarkable image of Being as a well-rounded, and therefore perspectivally invariant, sphere discloses it as absolute or context free. To understand is to be empowered to act in countless particular situations. The singularities upon or towards which one acts will be particular substitution instances of universals; place would then be a location specified by a quadruple of real numbers in Euclid's isotropic and homogeneous space. This is Kant's story, but it immediately suggests another. Suppose place is the origin, the *arché*, that grants being and, not itself being a being, resists conceptual valorization?[2] This very resistance could mean that "being" must be thought, not only from within the ontological projections of *Being and Time*, but also in the Ontological Difference, from beyond Being, from a place which is both within and different from the trajectory of Heidegger's thinking. Levinas, for example, questions Heidegger's understanding of Being through the relation between existence and the existent in, for example, the hypostasis. He approaches "the idea of Being in its impersonality so as then to be able to analyze the notion of the present and of position, in which a being, a subject, arises in impersonal Being" (EL 1988, 19). I will have occasion to explore this impersonal Being, Levinas's *il y a*, which is almost an exact analogue of Plato's place-granting receptacle (*Tim.* 47E–52D), the chaotic *apeiron arché* which is "always becoming and never really is" (28A), from which creatures emerge.[3] Now I can only suggest that place is prior in consciousness and the latter's relation to the unconscious *il y a* that, as Plato said, "must be apprehended by a kind of bastard reason . . . [for it is] difficult of explanation and dimly seen" (49A). Though this seems remote from Kant, he too began in interiority and was able to find the originary in self-consciousness. Levinas, in some ways closer to Kant than Heidegger, provides terms for a more congenial approach than *Being and Time*. Heidegger shuns embodiment; but Kant, as in the glove problem, defines orientation through it.[4]

Unfortunately, the hard sciences have preempted "method" and "science" which, at least as seen within the philosophical mainstream, present a logistic or synthetic methodological ideal. Kant seems to facilitate this institution; when he proposes to revolutionize the methods of metaphysics (B xxii), he turns for his model to the mathematical and physical sciences (B x–xiv); and this subsumptive ideal seems to distance Kant from hermeneutics. Gadamer, for instance, models his hermeneutics on Platonic dialogue and thus offers a methodological ideal that is different from that of the exact sciences (HG 1975, 7–9), while Heidegger rejects "methodology" as synonymous with "calculating mind" (MH 1971b, 103). Perhaps these misgivings can be overcome and some basis for the non-reductive reconciliation of the human and natural sciences gained by returning to Kant. His method, understood within phenomenological parameters, derives from and preserves some of the possibilities of both the "upward" and "downward" way of Platonic dialectic (*Rep.* 511C–E) and, thanks to the imagination, traces of the Good "beyond Being" (509B) which is prior to and founds hermeneutics. Though Heidegger promises to renew Kant's theme of "sensibilizing our concepts" and the Husserlian theme of returning to the things themselves by invoking the phenomenological roots of language, e.g., *logos* as "gathering," we will still find ourselves in the metaphysics of logo-centric presence.[5] But if language, even the language of dialogue, begins and ends with the intentionally inassimilable other bearing the traces of the Good, then perhaps we can retain things and even the person "beyond any price" of Kant's ethics. The way leads, not as one might expect, via Kant's ethics but through his medial imagination and Levinas' discovery that individuating enjoyment and life lived along the way are also to be medially construed.

Not all journeys are spatial, if space is a condition for the interchange of perspectives in the interests of theoretical objectivity. NASA's space trips express our ideal of viewing the world as a totality; Heidegger says representing things in a world view "means to bring what is present at hand before oneself as something standing against, to relate it to oneself, the one representing it, and to force it back into this relationship to oneself as the normative realm" (MH 1977, 131). One can also take a journey to the center, the *axis mundi*, and the time before time, the *illude tempore*, in which we come to consciousness and gain an identity. Oliver Sacks says

> we live a singular narrative which is constructed, continually, unconsciously, by, through, and in us. . . . We must recollect ourselves, recollect the inner drama, the narrative, of ourselves. A man needs such a narrative, a continuous inner narrative to maintain his identity, his self. . . . Unable to maintain a genuine narrative of continuity, unable to maintain an inner world, he is driven to the proliferation of pseudo-narratives in a pseudo-continuity, a pseudo-world peopled by pseudo-people, phantoms" (OS 1986, 6).

The sense that the self is gained by leaving "the sweetness of one's soil" in order to discover who one is on "the loneliness of a journey" (II 1993, 23) has been our paradigm for the way since it was formulated by Hugh of St. Victor in the twelfth century. Journeys represent life in relation to a universal order symbolized in the more or less masculine Uranian or sky gods, the gods which are everywhere one and the same. Our tradition has been obsessed with the need for a universal, grounding *arché* ("principle"). For instance, identity is specified by a concatenation of universals, as when we define a person in terms of rights; but *arché* can also mean "origin" and identity or individuation would then be approached through chthonic imagery, as in St. Thomas's "relations of origin." This individuating relation to a place of origin, *arché*, is often retained in surnames, as in John Duns Scotus,

Thomas d'Aquino, or the border town Bigge(a)r. Philosophers are, as Derrida remarked, placeless and ignore place, *chora,* which—though beyond Being (*Tim.* 48E–49A) and the token reflexive "here's" and "there's" with which Hegel would sublimate it into a concept—makes encounter and significance, even life, possible. Though giving place to the *logos,* Derrida says *chora* "seems at times not to submit to the law of the very things she puts in place" (JD 1987, 266); beyond both being and becoming, sense and "the sense of being," she upsets the law of polarity and does "submit to any opposition" (267).

Chora, beyond Being, is also beyond discourse. As the giver of contexts she is beyond contexts and is the antithesis of the context forming intentions of Husserl's ego, which is also constantly escaping contexts, even that of time. Something similar could be said for Kant's Transcendental Apperception.

If *chora,* not being anything, is beyond *logos,* she is not beyond myth. We, as living creatures, have received her gift of time and place through which we are. It is to the experience of this giving, to the *arché* and its gift of time that we must look. She can be expressed in myths or images which point to giving in another kind of knowing, that of the woman by which she knows her lover, by which she knows that she is with child, and by which she knows her child, and thus to the kind of knowing all have who receive her gift of creativity.[6] This is the story of our kind and is as old as we are. In the chthonic images found at Çatal Hüyük (6000 B.C.) in Anatolia, the earliest evidence of human dwelling, the great mother is represented as giving birth between wild animals. In later sites she becomes quite place-specific and manifests herself, not always benignly, as Ishtar and Cybele, the Sumerian Ti'amat, Hesiod's Gaea or Artemis—who is transitional between the great Mother and Mary, the "Mother of God." Reflection on some of the forms taken by the mother is a reminder that dwelling, so closely associated with "place," has its darker side. The German *heimlich,* "home," already bears the sense of its contrary *unheimlich,* "uncomfortable," "repellent," and "uncanny" (Heidegger). Her context-specific character is apparent in Artemis whose forms are reflected in the physical features of her sites and the architecture of her shrines.[7] The Artemis of Mount Artemison is the virgin huntress, "calling up the powers of the wild"; at Aulis she demands human sacrifice, at Ephesus she is orgiastic, while at Brauton she presides over and protects young girls from the terrors of childbirth. She is also the goddess of openings and, with Hecate who guards crossings, of the moon and thus, with the Fates, gives time. This primordial matrix is, as we will see, insufficient to account for an individuated and individuating, sheltering and nurturing *chora,* place, which this "becoming that never really is" grants her creatures when she is solicited by the Uranian

Good.[8] I know of no better representation of this humanization of place in response to the Good than its incarnation in Mary as she appears in countless Renaissance Annunciations, as in Van Eyck. The Theotokos, "Mother of God," who through grace gives the placeless *Logos* place, represents a transformation of the elemental into the human, the singular and desirable Other.[9] Through the mother we have a body, a place, and through the beloved, a home and the possibility of new life. Working together, we make a home by transforming elemental being—which Levinas notes is, as elemental, the destructive fire or raging wind or violent flood—into possessions and property. This movement from the elemental to the human, the life which is my mother's gift I can never repay and the life I give with her to the child creates an economy without being an element in an economic circulation. Derrida notes that this circulation sets in motion "memory, present, anticipation, retention, protention, immanence of the future, "ecstasies," and so forth, always keeping in motion the process of the destruction of the gift" (JD 1992b, 14). In dwelling one receives the impossible gift of the *arché* which, even if erased in the waters of Lethe, makes a world possible. Dwelling, the priority of the feminine (EL 1990a, 33), expresses and articulates *chora*. Place is not something that results from building (MH 1971b, 125), but is expressed in dwelling and enjoyment over the projects we undertake to sustain it.

But our concern is with journeys, not egress and ingress, which often involve imaginative, even fateful, crossings between worlds or ontologically distinct regions. Since Parmenides said "there is a same for thinking and being" (DK, B 3), philosophers have been building bridges. Instead of granting easy commerce by a crossing that gathers earth and sky into a neighborhood in which "one side is set against the other" in the presence of the divinities (MH 1971b, 152), crossings end where they began, in the starry skies of idealism or a materialistic morass. Platonic participation, which defines soul as spanning the gap between earth and sky as the condition for any crossing, takes an optimistic view as to their possibility and presupposes that in some sense we have already been where we are going. Crossing from here to there is possible because we have always already been where we are going. Isn't this *a priori* orientation the methodological import of Descartes' innate ideas, Platonic *anamnesis* ("recollection") or Kant's Copernican Revolution? The way by which we reach something, Heidegger remarks, "lets us reach what reaches out for us by touching us, by being our concern" (MH 1971b, 91). Since Plato's *Timaeus* defined the reflexivity of soul as the intersection of the circles of the other and same "that bends back on itself" (36D) so that alterity can "reach out and touch us," the task for philosophical reflection has been understood as the reduction, as in Kantian construction, of random alterity to a significant same through an *a priori* hermeneutics. Dwelling is the condition for setting forth and returning, for the reflective lighting and empowering by some representative of the Good, our measure. We look to the sky (Being), as Mary looked to the angel, for an order which we then persuade the Other for whom we live to accept and make our own. In less personal Platonic language, we seek through the good to persuade the earth (the receptacle as becoming) to provide a dwelling. Having lived crossings that lead both to and beyond metaphysics, he may help us break away from the nihilism of subjective closure into which metaphysics leads and, with some help from Aristotle, into an open. Heidegger suggests that the passage from nihilism to a meaningful world requires that we find ways of dwelling with things that will "bring into them the presencing of the four-fold" (MH 1971b, 151), the presencing of the earth from which they arise, the sky that marks their periods and grants order, the gods who call us to rise above "all that is common and unsound" (153) to mortals who must spare and preserve. Kant thought the way was closed that leads from *metaphysica generalis* to *metaphysica specialis*. We must find another way into the possibility of dwelling, *oikos*, the Patristic term for this participatory four-fold. Yet one can move with his methodology, shared with Plato, over the gap between sensibility and understanding. In this crossing, which seems on the surface to be so Cartesian, we can go beyond this closure of metaphysics to the possibility of dwelling.

Assuming this priority of place, one can show that interiority is not substantial in Descartes' sense of substance, but is rather hypostatic, where "hypostasis," the Patristic term for "person," is medial and marks the emergence of a nominalized *ens*, consciousness as existent, from verbal, somatic processes.[10] These dynamics of the *apeiron*, Levinas's *il y a*, can be approached, though hardly described, through insomnia or even strong or decentering emotions in which one "holds on while losing one's base. All emotion is fundamentally vertigo, the vertigo one feels insinuating itself, that *finding oneself over a void*. The world of forms open like a bottomless abyss. The cosmos breaks up and chaos gapes open—the abyss, the absence of place, the *il y a* . . . [Place] is the irruption in anonymous being of localization itself" (EL 1988, 71) Is this the abyss from which Kant "shrank back" (MH 1990, 110)? If so, it is in a now that is not a part of time, the now of apperception, memory and recognition; moreover, this originary "there is" is not an existence (*exsistere*) cast over an abyss of non-Being.

2. Being Underway with Kant

FOR KANT THE PRIMARY CROSSING is between sense and understanding. Parmenides' "thinking and being" had become heterogeneous, but he could open the way by showing that both space, the outer world into which we egress, and time, the inner world in which we dwell, are transcendentally ideal and empirically real (A 37/B 53). This suggests that if one is to get the point of his transcendental philosophy, one must first take seriously the life-world's apparent empirical realism. Peirce's pragmatism was inspired by Kant's critique of spectator consciousness and polemic on behalf of thinking things experimentally. This suggests that the life-world is always already ordered and that the need for a transcendental methodology follows, not from common experience within which body participates in mind, but from difficulties encountered when empiricism fails to justify natural inferences, such as understanding the helpful effect of moderate rain on the crops, the warming sun that melts the winter snow, or the sound that signifies the neighbor's barking dog.

Hume raises grave doubts concerning the possibility of crossing over to science and justifying these inferences with explanatory theories. Shaken by his reading of Hume, Kant came to believe that *a priori* limits must be imposed upon sensory contingencies if experience is to be saved from the possibility of becoming a kaleidoscopic phantasmagoria. Realism grounds the self in or on things. Since without these, however suspect, consciousness is nothing, Kant founded the "I think . . ." on a relation to external things which, paradoxically, it also idealistically constitutes. His "Copernican Revolution" grounded the journey from thought to things in the imagination's sub rosa synthetic *a priori* constitution of objects, *Gegenstand* as a sensory representation of the "object in general = X," and their relations, as in the Principles. Structural features of "outer sense" enable the self to find and make sense of itself. Empirical objects that give themselves to common experience are "ejects" of an originary objectification. The import of this revolution in which objects are constructed according to the way they are thought is best seen through the apparent realism in which they are given.

The most perspicuous of Kant's questions, "how is experience [*Erfahrung*] possible?" would have led him to inquire concerning the possibility of meaning. That sense of "meaning" was not available to him even if he opened it by detaching meaning, the conceptual order, from the world, the sensible order. He sought to anchor meaning in things, unlike the British empiricists who thought of experience as something passively received; experience is already an understanding which develops as one does or puts something to phenomena that provokes their response. Though rooted in medial imagination, understanding is not something which, as Heidegger will say, makes an appeal to us, comes over and transforms us (MH 1971a, 73–74). We could, of course, begin with the *Prolegomena* by questioning the way experience is categorized in the sciences; but these sophisticated modes of knowing come late into human history and presuppose something more archaic. Aren't questions about the possibility of experience questions about the *a priori* conditions for any possible "journey" on which one crosses over to seek out and appropriate beings of all types, physical or intelligible, to enhance, enjoy, preserve, or give relief to being, one's own or another's? In such moments body and thought mutually participate in one another; the pianist's hand (in Aristotle's metaphor) becomes a second mind. In being underway, dualism seems to disappear. Kant's glove problem, the incongruence between the glove on the hand and its mirrored counterpart, reminds us that what is "seen" by the mind's eye is not how it is; there is an abyss (*chaos*) separating intention from fulfillment; crossing may be difficult and hazardous, even impossible. "Spaces" to be traversed are not necessarily homogeneous; the space of thinking may be incongruent with that of our hands. Self-orientation is required for understanding what we are about and may encounter. Hermes, guardian of boundaries, interprets the beyond so that it can be assimilated in ways appropriate to crossing, the crossing of a tradition, to another, into mystery.

The wayfarer's participatory ordering to a beyond that can never be present so as to make sense of the present is one of the forms of madness which Socrates describes in the *Phaedrus* (244A–45C) when he came to a halt before a crossing (242C). Our being is the open to what occurs in crossing boundaries, crossroads, thresholds from thought to being, from the phenomenal to the noumenal, from the inner to the outer, and so forth. In the language of participation, one crosses thresholds to assimilate the beyond, an alterity, as a same. Assimilating something presupposes a prior projective tropology that will allows differences to be grasped in a familiar same. Plato said that an other is seen through the projected image of the god with whom we were in heavenly converse (252B–53C); whatever the power of these other images to disclose or conceal, we must also follow Hermes, the god of crossings, to his tryst with *Chora*. If crossing is of our essence, then through his art, hermeneutics, we become what we are.

Can we interpret being in an image which overcomes the alienation inherent in the isolated Cartesian *inspectio?* Descartes' judicial model, to some extent shared by all, lets us appear to ourselves as infallible judges reading unintelligible briefs in sealed chambers. Are we not living creatures pursuing and enjoying goods through the mutual interplay and reciprocal translation of thought and action? Representing life as a journey avoids the Cartesian bifurcations now haunting both knowing and acting; the wayfarer's plans do sometimes succeed even as they sometimes go awry, but the outcome of mind in action, if not its plans or the good sought, is seldom problematic. Telling stories of these journeys is a natural way of sharing vicariously in worlding. Narratives tell of the gathering of actions, things, and happenings at diverse times and places; their coherent and significant unity are paradigms for self-interpretation. We create and make sense of ourselves and world through the reflective and hermeneutical dialectic between what befalls us and a paradigmatic *mythos* whose interpretative investitures promise identity and self-worth. We are in the world but are enjoined by saints and sages not to be of it.

This ontological duality will be more apparent if seen from within the world, the context of contexts. Husserl, who borrowed the concept of "horizon" from Kant, spoke of world as the "openly endless" horizon of all horizons. What Heidegger could then see in Kant's schematism was an ontological horizon within which one "prospects" and "investigates" that which must be "pro-posed in advance as identical" (MH 1990, 83) must, I think, be seen through the Good's lighting as a valuational nexus, something better or worse to be won or lost. Kant's world opens to the "what is . . . ?" question implicit in "how do we know?" But human experience, always growing, always changing, really begins when another, almost disjoint, world opens with "What am I to do?" This cannot be derived ectypally. Kant says that Plato's ideas are

> completely determined in the Supreme Understanding
> . . . and are the original causes of things. But only the total-
> ity of things, as forming the universe, is completely adequate
> to the idea. If we set aside the exaggeration in Plato's mode of
> expression, the philosopher's spiritual flight from the ectypal
> mode of reflecting upon the physical order to the architectonic
> ordering of it according to ends, that is, according to ideas, is
> an enterprise that calls for respect and even imitation. It is in
> regard, however, to the principles of morality, legislation and
> religion, where the experience, in this case, that of the good,
> is itself made possible only by the ideas . . . that Plato's
> teaching exhibits its quite peculiar merits. (A 318/B 375)

The world, if there is one, is not coextensive with the physical universe; though physical structures are presupposed, world is the inclusive referential or meaningful and valuational totality embracing a multiplicity of subworlds, art, finance, social life, and the like.[11] Worlds are where "the action is" and have a life of their own; we can doubt their possibility, or they may die. World as such appears, and with it our ambiguous status as spectators of world and as underway within its worlding, through sharing the gods' standpoint in cosmogonic myth, the standpoint of the Book of Genesis. Not until moral understanding directs one toward monotheism is the world thought as a cosmos, a beautiful, well-ordered, and unitary whole.

The warfare obtaining on Homer's fields of Troy, not a cosmos, opens to "what" questions if by "being" we mean power; power, *dynamis*, is an *apeiron* term with no intrinsic limit.[12] Nietzsche's forces posit counter forces and presuppose only such limits as may arise through opposition and struggle, *agon* and *polemos*. Plato's being, a transcendental, could mean power; it could also mean peras, limit, as seen in the Good. The Good, the fitting, appropriate, and due, apportions and empowers. World, as the condition for transcendence, is moral; and if fact and value are bifurcated, as in Kant, then its possibility must lie within a self presumed to transcend the merely empirical (B 155). We are in a world but, having something of a whole present to us, are not quite of it. If there is one rather than an archipelago of worlds, it is not an empirical datum.[13] One may be worldless. Nihilism is a fundamental doubt as to the possibility of a world. Nevertheless, thanks to Kant for whom it was the self's correlative, world as a moral contingency, a structure of meaning and value, is of our essence as seen in the Good.[14] Being, Aristotle says, has no opposite; world does.

Only a god can produce a cosmos in a creative intuition in which the "object [is given] in the idea" (A 670/B 696) by archetypal, not receptive (A 672/B 700) and ectypal (A 318/B 375) thought. Nevertheless, ectypal experience does not have Hume's atomistic form; it comes to us as significant, the crashing wave of a storm at sea, the moon's ring of rain. It is not possible, as Heidegger says, to define a single thing; we must think it through "the essence of nature in general" (MH 1967, 129). We are already oriented, as if anamnetically, towards world, first through myth and symbol and then, with the Enlightenment, through theoretical reflection which, as in Kant, finds in the self the unity otherwise given through the Creator. The formation of an order of concepts mapping sense is the work of reflection. This logical act, which follows on comparison ("the likening of presentations to one another in relation to the unity of consciousness") is gained by "going back over different presentations which enables them to be comprehended in one act of consciousness" (*Logic*, 100). Heidegger says "conceptual representation lets the many come into agreement in this *one*. In conceptual representation, therefore, the unity of this *one* must be anticipatively kept in view so that it can serve as a standard for all statements capable of determining the many. This anticipative keeping in view of the *one* in which the many can agree is the basic act of conceptualization. Kant calls it reflection" (MH 1990, 35). Even ordinary perception is significant only if a world is "anticipatively kept in view." Just as body participates in mind and things are never merely substantive but seem adjectives of larger wholes, so too mind participates in body and the sense of world lies in intuition. The presupposition of world in the phenomenological sense lets one see why our first itineraries are cosmogonic myths in which we share the standpoint of the worldmaking gods.

Kant began with prevailing physico-theology myths which, like cosmogonic myths, presupposed access to worlding deity. These myths, "anticipatively kept in view," are the itineraries for any possible journey. But by Kant's day nature had been denatured and posited *exsistere* had replaced self-positing *physis*. The God to whom one had access through speculative reason posited the world in an Augustinian creative and archetypal intuition (A 673/B 701) as an actual infinity in a *nunc standi*.

Induction is grounded in (proper) parts which bear traces through which an otherwise absent whole can be presenced for mind. This base of natural inference becomes a problem only when world becomes problematic. Kant's Critical Philosophy arises from the loss of an access to a beyond that grounds and deploys justified beliefs over the world. Analysis, besides its usual sense of dissecting a whole into its parts, is also and more importantly the method which leads from the unknown, treated hypothetically as if known, to a (anamnestic) known that grounds it. Receptive intuition must substitute for God's creative intuition; we must make do with the constituted world of possible experience. Since empiricism will not provide a ground for its own meaning conditions, for example, unity, we must turn to synthesis, not as the assemblage of a whole from parts, but rather as the method allowing a disclosive and unifying presence to come to be through our presencing, as drawing a line presences the line itself and unconceals its properties. This original presencing, Kant's "Copernican Revolution in philosophy," constructs objects which preserve the sense of a world to us, that is, the phenomenal world, and not that world as noumenally present to God. World is then the self's transcendental, not transcendent, correlative. Thanks to Heidegger, Kant's intuition can be seen as a clearing, not as contingent sensibility, in which being and Being are unconcealed. Plato's proposed itinerary led through the gap between Gaea and Uranus, demythologized as Becoming and Being in *Timaeus*, that world's world. The gap is spanned and even constituted by the possibility of soul by which one lives, moves, and knows. When Aristotle made these conditions immanent as the matter and form of *ousia*, "substance," he immanentized and finitized Plato's transcending conditions, the dynamics of the receptacle and the forms, and ordered these to soul. Psychology replaced cosmology. Since then the journey has been largely understood in theory, though hardly in practice, as interior and the Good as a proportioned, immanent end.

Though Aristotle's heir, Kant founds phenomenology and lays the ground for hermeneutics; he will also set us upon the way to Heidegger's "open" and a retrieval of Platonic insights.

That movement into the Open beyond metaphysics is a main theme of this inquiry. Its initial focus is on Kant's methodology. A method that leads to the securities of analytic judgments ("gold is yellow") that bind distinguished properties to things must give way as we move into the human world to dialectical distinctions which may be as unstable as the fabled statues of Socrates' ancestor, Daedalus.[15] Then the journey that begins among "objects" in apperception's cave-like "I think . . ." will lead through the labyrinth of psychical faculties to sunlit "things" in which, as Duns Scotus says, *esse manifestum sui.*

In the following section, I will continue these introductory remarks to situate the methodological crisis, and thus analysis and synthesis, in the Kantian text. With rare exception these terms have been taken to refer to judgments or propositions; since method admits to a phenomenological interpretations, a closer look at methodology will be taken in section 3 and at analysis and synthesis in section 4. In section 5 we will discuss the crisis in methodology that seems to have motivated the Critical Philosophy, while an examination of its experimental environment in section 6 is followed by a discussion of what analysis conceals. Synthesis presupposes an original presencing (*Darstellung*, "setting out," as in a mathematical proof) of the transcendental object which is, in turn, intended in any empirical representation (*Vorstellung*, something "set up before us" through which a being is intended or appears) as the condition for empirical meaning.[16] Intuition of significant quality is our access to nature.

3. Analysis as Phenomenology

SINCE PARMENIDES SPOKE OF A *hodos,* way, to *aletheia,* it has been presumed that it leads from ignorance to knowledge or, alternatively, to an inner way of justifying beliefs. Epistemology is thought to guard this route by the elucidation of meaning and truth conditions and offers guideposts and criteria that facilitate the journey. Criteria are of concern only in a crisis of belief, as in the Renaissance. Before that, one followed tradition, which has now become superstition. Though Kant may have written the first *Critique* as a treatise on the method in metaphysics in response to a crisis, it solved nothing and in fact precipitated a crisis that perhaps we are only now beginning to appreciate. Kant's methodology deconstructs epistemology and offers a way beyond the metaphysics it seeks to establish.

Methodology begins with Parmenides' claim that there is "same for being (*einai*) and thinking (*noein*)." Guideposts are needed for this crossing lest one fall into chaos.[17] The fear of the abyss leads one to seek certainty; but what is certainty? Is it to be found in Augustine's "inner man," a sense allowed by the Scholastic *certus*? Or does it refer to the behavior of a *theoros* underway towards world? "Certainty" would then have its roots in the Greek *keirein* or Latin *cernere*, "to cut," which we hear in "discriminate" and "discern." The latter, laden with valuations, entails intellectual virtues, such as singular judgments relevant to *phronesis*, appropriate to one underway. The methods of synthesis and analysis, which originated in Plato's dialectic, have to do with pointing things out, with looking or discriminating and seeing the point of what is shown.[18] The analytic dialectic, the original of Kant's analytic "method of discovery," tactfully approaches unknowns as "hypotheses, underpinnings, footings, and springboards enabling one to arise to that which is no assumption and is the starting point of all" (*Rep.* 511B).[19] Pappus attributes the methods of analysis and synthesis to Plato; "analysis is a method," he says, "of taking what is sought as if it were admitted and passing through its consequences in order to something which is the result of previous synthesis."[20] He distinguishes between the form used in the proof of theorems and constructions (problematical), for example, inscribing a triangle in a given circle (*Meno*, 86D-87C).

In a more modern vein, Kenneth Sayre says analysis discovers features necessary for something being a kind and sufficient to distinguish it from others (1969, 3-58). This logic of necessary and sufficient conditions gives an experimental bias to Pappus' interpretation. One assumes that some feature is common to things of a kind and then tests the instances collected to ascertain if it is present. If so, the feature would be necessary. One then adds to the definitory formula such additional features as are sufficient to distinguish the given kind from other kinds. One of these sufficient conditions, such as cinnabar red, can through its nomic, property times, that is, as an analytic concept, serve as a relatum in recognition (*anamnesis*) in which something is seen as something, just as a squarish schema is seen as the morphe square, which cannot be explained in terms of the sensory relata. This crossing to the "wholly other" (MH 1990, 79) also characterizes Kant. Recognition is intuitive and corrigible.

> Actual experience, which is constituted by apprehension, association (reproduction) and finally recognition of appearances, contains in recognition, the last and highest of these mere empirical elements of experience, certain concepts which render possible the formal unity of experience and therewith all objective validity (truth) of empirical knowledge. These grounds of the recognition of the manifold, as far as they concern

solely the form of an experience in general, are the categories. (A 125)

All recognition is categorial. Categories are ontological predicates of the object in general, the "monogram" of every empirical object; whatever is recognized has nomological ties in properties and causal conditions.

Heidegger's interpretations of Kant have the singular merit of focusing attention on intuition and metaphysics and, thus, prompt us to rethink him as a metaphysician and phenomenologist. Moreover, through his concern with early Greek language one becomes aware of how "Kantian" and phenomenological this language was insofar as it, quite unintentionally, "sensibilizes concepts" which are for us abstract and theoretical. For example, *logos* ("word," "science," "ratio," "structure," etc.) takes us into the fields with people who "gather" and lay out crops, where this sheltering is expressed by *legein,* "to say." Moreover, the *doxic* family of words characterizing the site of methodologies has both an abstract epistemic and concrete phenomenological sense. Since Kant can be made to speak on both sides of this doxic issue and since the epistemological aspects of his thought have received so much attention, is it not appropriate to bring out the beginnings of a phenomenological ontology and its hermeneutical roots in Kant? Let's "look and see" and then judge.

One would think that conceptualism, shared by Kant with Aristotle, Aquinas, and perhaps at times with Heidegger, would not make a good fit with phenomenology which, in spite of Husserl's protests, is rather more Platonic. It approaches universals from the standpoint of Aristotle's *techné* view of mind; one intends beings through the constructed concept, an *ens rationes,* which contributes universality and necessity to the mute singular recognized in it. Unlike the *eidos,* the concept cannot be intuited; it is a constituted *ens rationes,* a being of reason, in which the many are on reflection seen as one. Let us leave aside the evident difficulties in deciding whether this unity is founded on resemblance, as in nominalism, or on the realist's identity, neither of which does justice to Plato, and turn to Kant's rather impressive attempt to make it work. What is novel in Kant, though perhaps implicit in Aristotle, is the schematic imagery intermediary between sensed particular and the universal that lets us see this particular as if universally. Husserl's vocabulary may be useful here. I intend, direct my attention towards, an object, a noema, through the noesis. If I am angry at John, I intend him, the noema, through the anger, the noesis. Expressing Kant's conceptualism in these terms, we can say that the concept enables one to imaginatively form the noesis, the schematism, as homogeneous with the intended noema, the schematized category. Such "seeing" can be said to be active, constituting, and not merely passive. It may, for certain very abstract concepts, involve a series of formal models which finally are grounded in a phenomenological model. For example, showing the consistency of affine geometry may require first a metric and then a Euclidian model and a phenomenological modeling of the latter. We see through schemata, representing acts, which constitute significant things. The white something or other seen ahead on the road to Thebes is "seen as" Oedipus. A concept is a universal expressed in schematic or "signifying" iteration. Like Euclid's first postulate which lets us connect any two points by drawing a line, the "line itself" (Plato's idiom for the *eidos*) can be reflectively recognized through line being drawn, that is, set-out or represented. The "there it is," the "line itself" as the relatum in recognition, is a function of these repeatable, signifying acts and not a recurrent *ens*. Concepts are reflective, rule-like formalities expressed in representing or intentional acts in which something intended is recognized as intended; the line I am drawing, a schema, is recognized as the line itself, a *morphe*. These reflective acts generate, or contribute to the generation of, the categorial form of the sensory relatum recognized as _____. Unlike Husserl's categorial intuitions, Kant's categories cannot as such be intuited. Just as the line itself, the object of the universal concept, is intended in drawing, so we intend a quality as an intensive magnitude through an experimental set-up. The quality we intend is, *qua* property, nomically tied to its "metaphysical" object, the constituted object of the categorial concept. The categorial act is present only in a singular, particularizing doing, for example, as Stahl worked with oxides or Toricelli made air bear a weight (B xiii), that lets things be seen, as the line being drawn is seen, as particulars under or, as Kant says, *in* a universal. The term (*telos*) of analysis is recognition, a veritative synthesis of receptive sensibility and spontaneous understanding. Heidegger says that "through such a union thought refers mediately to the object which in the unity of a thinking intuition becomes manifest (true). In this way the synthesis of thought and intuition accomplishes the making-evident of the encountered being as object. . . . [This] true-(manifest-) making (veritative) synthesis . . . brings forth the relevant determinateness of the entity itself" (MH 1990, 19). Kant wishes to fix, as if in the amber of eternity, analytic distinctions by a methodologically warranted act of judgment. To anticipate, the nomic "is" that ties terms together in definitory "sames" is first a reflective allegorical or model theoretic mode of "seeing as." The reflective role Kant assigns to concepts is a function of the imagination and thus pertains to metaphor and hermeneutics, not immediately to logistics. As Descartes recognized in the fourth step of his method, fictions, "romances of nature," are required for the sense of a same. Later discussions of geometry will show how natural and conventional "sames" can be fused in physical theory.

In Plato's intuitive approach to analysis, one uses hypotheses to pass through "regions" (Wittgenstein's idiom for a concept) to "demonstrate" or point out defining features. A hypothesis is an unknown, an opinion (*doxa*) treated as if known. Thus the analytic method leads through regions of the unknown until something comes to be recognized and known, though we can end up with nothing except "wind-eggs." On this phenomenological reading of *doxa,* analysis is an experimental or discursive method of pointing which has its issue in *aletheia,* "unconcealment," and not just propositional truth. In Kant, synthesis is the work of the imagination which grounds the crossings of sense and understanding. What gives itself evidential is "imaginary" and derives from the imagination, a medial nothing that is "spontaneous receptivity and receptive spontaneity" (MH 1990, 134). In Plato, on the other hand, the situation is different; in the synthetic "way down" analytical results are ordered in the unity of a system, as in Euclid or Spinoza. On this journey from the known that reduces the encountered unknown to its terms, as a deductive proof reduces a statement to axioms and previous proofs, one nevertheless encounters undecidable statements, "surds," which reason generates. Catesby Taliaferro gives examples from *Timaeus:*

> Just as the downward dialectic must find the mean terms between one and many to reduce Necessity to order so arithmetic seeks to fill the octave with as many well-ordered terms as possible. For if strings are arranged in lengths approaching a continuous change from one to two as in the case of a siren, they give the impression of chaos, just a noise. But in the solution of the problems of the scale, Necessity shows itself again and again: in the Pythagorean chromatic by the comma and the approximations of the semi-tone; in the diatonic by the relatively smaller number of perfect fourths and fifths and the approximations of their semi-tones. Such is the ratio 2 : 1; whatever order is introduced, a disorder is also introduced. Necessity here manifests itself in the incompatibility of the orders; here the radical manyness of order seems to be its own undoing. Curiously enough the thresholds of the senses can be used to insinuate order; the imperfections of hearing allows a ratio between very large numbers to produce the sensible order rightly belonging to ratios between small numbers. (CRT 1944, 28)

Kantian synthesis reconciles the unknown to the known, inner sense to its world, and is not just deduction per se. Congruities are established by the phenomenal thesis in which necessity becomes *de dicto;* the imagination "insinuates" order.

Analysis begins with *doxa* which, since it may be correct or incorrect, requires a method if it is to gathered into *episteme*, "knowledge" or "science." How *doxa* is construed determines the sense of the journey. *Doxa* is usually taken to mean a subjective and epistemic "opinion," but it can also have, in Alexander Mourelatos' terms, the ontological and phenomenological sense of the "agreeable acceptance" of something in its appearing.[21] Though appearance initially has the form of *historia*, originally the visual knowledge gained from autopsy, this can lead through *akribeia*, "subtle interpretation" demonstrating the unseen in the seen, to a deeper unconcealment, *aletheia (Tim.* 52C). The "agreeable acceptance" of something as it shows itself in relation to a course of action is the root sense in *dok*-words which are often synonyms for words deriving from *phaino*, "to bring into the light" (AM 1970, 198–99). In *doxa*'s subject-oriented sense, opinions are true or false and require criterial justification. *Doxa* then means an (untrustworthy) "opinion" or "belief" as contrasted to *episteme*, "justified true *doxa*." *Doxa*'s earlier phenomenological sense, accepting something in its appearing, relates it to what appears (phenomenon), and the one to whom it appears *(theoria)*. Heidegger notes that *idea*, "that which in everything and in each particular thing endures as present," has a similar root in *id*, "to see," where what is seen "is the outward aspect that the visible things offers to the eye" (MH 1977, 20). When Plato makes this "non-sensuous aspect of what is physically present" the *telos* of the journey that begins with *doxa*, then *idea*, a catachresis, will also assemble *doxa*'s programmatic sense. The verbal root of phenomenon is *phaniesthia*, "to show itself," and is derived from *phaino*. What is "brought into the light" is accepted as it appears in this "objective" sense. If the subject "sense" leads to epistemology, the "object" sense points to phenomenology and fundamental ontology. These differences project two meanings of epistemic finality.

Though rich in phenomenological *dok*-terms, Plato's *Theaetetus* may also be the source of the thesis that knowledge is justified true belief. The dialectic's itinerary to *episteme* would begin with opinions and pass through these to theoretical science. Analysis provides criteria that relate what we believe to what is or what is otherwise warranted. Though it can confuse propositions with judgments and miss Kant's intentional thesis (MH 1967, 158–62), Popper's conjectures and refutations or the "covering law" theories of Carl Hempel and Ernst Nagel exemplify *doxa*'s epistemological interpretation. Since recognition is in universals, Popper's "conjectures" expresses how things are accepted in their appearing and is closer to the phenomenological sense than subsumptive theories. If we had only the second edition of the *Critique of Pure Reason,* these approaches would be fully justified.

If, however, intuition is primary and thought is in its service, *doxa* recovers its phenomenological and ontological import.[22] Then *doxa* is not something had, as we have beliefs and opinions or birds in a cage, but signifies the acceptance of things in their appearing. Though Kant speaks of sensibility as matter to be categorially informed, this is a procedural moment that terminates in the schematic "seeing as _____." Sense is almost always already interpreted to be enjoyed, acted upon, or further interpreted. "Seeing as" announces a phenomenological theme common to Wittgenstein, Hanson, and Heidegger and gives understanding an adverbial sense. "Ideas articulate practices," Charles Taylor observes, as "patterns of do's and don'ts" (CT 1989, 204). The surgeon, a *theoros* participating with beings in their struggle against dissolution and death, is his articulated understanding down to and in his fingertips. Dialectic is Plato's term for what transpires as one understandingly participates with _____ in occasioning unconcealment, *aletheia,* of beings. Whether dramatic, as Critias is unconcealed by Socrates in *Charmides,* or experimentally, as red is seen to be a property of mercuric sulfide, dialectic is phenomenological. If the goal of analysis is, in Plato's sense, to bring one to see, are we not justified in listening to what language can tell and show us? Whitehead said that all language is an appeal to intuition. Modern philosophers of science exhaustively explore "theory"; my interest is in a *theoria* who, though he may have few scientific beliefs, nevertheless understandingly sees. Duns Scotus said the drayman, though he had no concepts, knew more about horses than experts. "Theory" suggests a reflective detachment from things; a *theoria* has a reflexive and participatory relation to the world. As in Aristotle's *phronesis,* one sees form in the contingent and uniquely individualized fabric of the world and overcomes the gap that occurs when "theory" and its deductive intentions are primary. A *theoria* will not have to contend with a boundary between the theoretical and the practical, the philosopher and the king. Moreover, the priority of phenomenological *doxa* helps deconstruct from within Kant's own perspective the dichotomies between percept and concept, outer and inner, phenomenal and noumenal and, through the work of the medial imagination, the metaphysical distinction between potency and act and its Kantian correlate, act and receptivity. Each requires the other, as Kant knew in proposing that they are branches of a single root, the imagination.

Plato's *Meno* brings *doxa*'s phenomenological alternative into focus. Its epistemic sense is linked with Gorgias and sophistry (70A–

71B). The analytic method of dialectic begins when *doxa* is expressed in a "premise the person interrogated would be willing to admit" (75D). The *Meno* is critical of the opinion sense of *doxa* by showing that one can be brought to see form in the facts, as the slave was brought to see the form in the image Socrates drew in the sand. He had to be willing to open himself to the appearances as he was led by Socrates' questions to grasp in the seemings (*doxa*) the beingness (*ousia*) which terminated the quest. Meno, a Mr. Nobody, was a fabric of borrowed beliefs; habituated to questions by his teacher Gorgias, he expected Socrates to defend his reputation by sophistic argument (71B–C). Blinded by jargon, he could not even admit that he could see color (because he didn't "know" it) when figure was defined through it as its limit. Gorgias taught habits of questioning which were satisfied with meaningless verbal formulae in which, for example, what we know, color, is defined in terms of entities we can know nothing about: "color is an effluence of figures, commensurate with sight, and palpable to sense" made possible by "passages into which and through which the effluences pass" (76D). The C-fibers of contemporary mind-brain identity theorists is the latest eruption of this sophistry. When through the examination of hypotheses we are led "to look and see," "truth" retains its root in *aletheia,* "unconcealedness." Kant will return us to this archaic meaning.

Granted the priority of its appearing sense, to whom shall the being appear? A *theoros* qualified to represent the community at some sacred spectacle? The term can be extended to cover those qualified to participate in an event of *aletheia,* "unconcealment," as an astronomer is qualified to discriminate what appears in stellar phenomena. Only one who understandingly sees and thus knows, not as a child knows sums but lovingly, as the husband knows his wife, is qualified to be a *theoria.* That sense of "understanding," *Verstand,* has become common, especially in hermeneutics; but the classical tradition that continued through Hegel or even Cezanne understood that nature's text was written in mathematics. Here the phenomenological sense of *doxa* can be retained with the aid of *theoria* and "seeing as," where what appears is seen as intelligible in mathematically informed measurement. Nevertheless, the philosopher as "loving and striving to be wise" need not have a theory but, if he is to be true to the name he bears, must understandingly and questingly participate with others as a *theoros.*

This phenomenological approach to analysis leads through "knowing how" to reflexive "knowledge of." On reflection this latter comes to be entertained as "knowledge that." A doxic manner of seeing becomes a justified true belief expressed in a true proposition.[23] When a participatory involvement with beings in which they are understandingly "seen as _____" breaks down, one must reexamine beliefs, explain or justify what was done or believed, or to organize knowledge of diverse things into a comprehensive theory under the "ideal of reason," "knowledge that" is thematic. This reflective possibility always hovers as a penumbra on reflexion and, of course, the latter is the always latent in sense. Reflective knowledge is no longer what we are but what we have, no longer a form of life but a questioned possession. Dualism makes its appearance within this detached, spectator view. How are mental images related to C-fibers? How do beliefs and language attach to the world? Analysis and synthesis display the priority of intuition and how knowledge is gained and related to the world.

My use of *theoria* may seem cavalier. *Theoria* is often taken as the prototype, as in Heidegger's *Being and Time*, of the spectator view of knowing. A *theoria* is indeed a spectator. However, the epistemological tradition which treats knowing as onlooking begins with Descartes; consciousness cannot reach out beyond the "objective" reality of its ideas but must regard then in an *inspectio*. A *theoria*, however, is understandingly present at an event of Being by qualifications which empower him to see and judge things as they are. The spectacle (*doxa* as accepted in its appearing) will manifest or unconceal (*aletheia*) Being (ontophany, theophany, heirophany). I extend this notion of a spectacle to *physis*, "nature," which collects itself (*logos*) into presence (*einai* and its participial forms, *on* and *ousia*) so that what is visible (phenomenon) is seen in its *eidos* (its radiance) by one who understandingly participates *qua theoria* in this unconcealment (*aletheia*). The idea is the principle of gathering the gift of power from originary place and is the radiant form of becoming (*gignesthai*) and principle of being and being known. Thanks to Heidegger, this sacramental model of participatory *physis* enables one to marshal a host of terms, hitherto understood epistemologically, around a phenomenological and ontological theme.

4. The Methods

KANT WAS NOT A PLAYFUL *theoria*. Physico-theology had fallen apart: his immediate motive as a physicist, if not a theologian, was to ground what he had no real reason to doubt. Unhappily, his method of justification continues the tradition of denaturing and idealizing *physis* so that the phenomenon, its collection, showing, truth, and the like, is immanent in mind. Thanks to problems Hume raised, the spectacle now became *theoria*'s doing. Is there a self with its counterfactual baggage of shoulds and oughts that can orient itself to possibility? Can it have a worldly itinerary? How would one know the way, much less know that one is on the right way? Are there really things by which we can take our measure? To shore up what might on Hume's descriptions fall apart, the unitary relation of self and world expressed in moral life and physical theory, Kant proposed to investigate this from the Cartesian pole, Transcendental Apperception's everywhere one and the same "I think . . ." which accompanies all my representations (B 131). How do I know I am one and same? Descartes could imagine that he was just created with beliefs about an illusory past. Kant proposes to show, under the thesis of constituted objective unity (B 130–31), that by means of empirical objects we can sort out real from imagined whats and whens and order the private flux of inner sense by the public world it now becomes. Within possible experience there is no room for radical skepticism. The categories are ontological modalities of the beings we constitute through them; any questions about quantity, quality, relation, and modality can in principle be answered.

Peter Strawson suggested that the analytic unity of consciousness may be expressed in terms of the possibility of autobiography (PS 1966, 93–112). We make sense of and order our thoughts in relation to enduring, causal things in common experience. If one believes that he remembers so-and-so, that he did this and then saw that, their order and occurrence can be publicly verified and explained by citing things and causes that produced the original experiences, including our own attitudes and actions. The analytic method allows one to arrive at explanatory concepts which in principle permit the spatial and temporal well-ordering in one, identical consciousness of the events in one's life. My identical consciousness encompasses different events, the "I think" is same in its different thoughts, and its ability to unify this succession as mine is a transcendental condition analysis fills in empirically. "Only in so far, therefore, as I can unite a manifold of given representations in one consciousness, is it possible for me to represent to myself the identity of the consciousness in [or throughout] these representations. In other words, the analytic unity of apperception is possible only under the presupposition of a certain synthetic unity" (B 133). Being able to write one's chronology, if not autobiography, is the key to the possibility of meaningful experience itself.

Though a gifted historian, without a ground for analytic unity Hume could not account for the well-ordering of his own experience, much less that of his English history. Kant had also come to doubt that the classical method of analysis could ground itself through the "analytic" ontological proof in those structures of Being necessary for physical science. The physico-theology of Descartes, Newton, and Leibniz seemed to supply a basis for the former; but this belief was seriously challenged by Kant's "discovery" of the difference in kind between concepts and percepts and by his early doubts concerning the validity of the ontological argument. Kant cannot play the analytic game as philosophers such as Descartes, Leibniz, or Hume played it. Analysis cannot go from sense to the intelligible order. Sensation is not Leibniz's "confused conception"; space and time are not concepts. Whatever its use in collecting regularities, after Hume induction could not lead to an understanding of nature as determined by those universal nomological necessities characteristic of the physical sciences. The *Critique of Pure Reason* was Kant's response to this methodological crisis: "It is a treatise on the method " (B xxii; also A 14/B 28).

It would be tedious to sort out all the senses of "analytic" in Kant. Sometimes, as in "Transcendental Analytic," he means "transcendental logic of truth." Usually he means "dissection . . . into the elements" (A 64/B 89) or, as he said in the 1770 *Dissertation,* "a regression from a whole to its possible or mediate parts" (388). When in the same text he defines analysis as a regression from the grounded to the ground, or in the *Prolegomena* as "starting from what is looked for as if it were given and ascending to the conditions under which alone it is possible," the methodological issue is stated in terms that can accommodate both the *Prolegomena* and scientific methodology. By condition Kant means what is required, in Gerd Buchdahl's words, to get analysis "off the ground, to acquire some ontological significance or other." We have to prove or satisfy these "contextual conditions" if the discipline is to be taken seriously (GB 1991, 2). In the *Prolegomena* the analytic method (264) enabled Kant to move from the grounded (natural science and mathematics) to the ground (in the categories and space-time, respectively). The experimental method attempts to move from hypotheses, that is, something accepted as if true and reasonable, to a grounding recognition. The parallels with Plato and Pappus are clear. Unlike Plato, however, Kant is concerned with the law-like structure of things, with necessary and sufficient conditions inhering in the world and not with necessary and sufficient features in the definition of a kind. Because of Kant's conceptualism, the activity of the agent, the doing that lets things be seen, will be more prominent.

A simple example illustrates analysis' move from the unknown to the recognition which makes something known. If I want to know how many apples I can buy if I have a dollar and each costs a dime, then I can let x be the unknown number of apples, let $10x$ be the unknown number of apples equal to a dollar, and solve for x. "One starts," Kant says, "from what is being looked for as if it were given and ascends to the conditions under which it is possible" (*Prol.* 276 n.), for example, the given x as 10. Kant uses the analytic method, which leads to "perfection of cognition" (*Logic* 139), to arrive at analytic concepts formed through analytic judgments whose explication yields analytic propositions.

Though I can no longer make the ascent to the *arché* as principle and cause, the synthetic or constructivistic method of classical geometry provides an understanding of how space and time are generated that leads to a finitistic substitute. This synthetic method permitted the translation of statements about the actual infinite, required for Leibniz's mathematics, into the language of the Aristotelian potential infinite and, secondly, the justification of the thesis of intentionality through its a *priori* presencing of objects.[24] Once "concepts" are understood as having an *a priori* basis in ontologically determinate things that gather the empirical manifold into unity for thought, which is to reinstitute the archaic theme of the *logos* as prehensive unification, induction presents no problem.

In the Preface to the second edition of the *Critique of Pure Reason,* Kant proposes to discover the "path upon which we can securely travel" (B vii). There are echoes of Parmenides' *hodos* in those experimental and mathematical contexts reason "produces after a plan of its own" (B xiii) by means of synthesis, the active setting up of the reflective condition (apperception) as apt for sensuous solicitation.[25] Except in awareness, sense is never merely receptive but reaches out to receive within ontic horizons, that is, Kant's "leading strings," what understanding lets solicit it, as the line we draw solicits understanding to think the "line itself." This intention reflexively comes back as fulfilled in the drawing.

What is the essence of this experimental attitude that supplies experience and its general metaphysics with its paradigm (B ix)? Nothing more or less than the self-affective scheme just presented. Categories are not mere logical forms; in transcendental logic, the logic of truth, they are the determinate forms by which we question and through which we receive beings. When a categorial question is asked of something, it shows itself within these categorial horizons. Nature is made to disclose itself in the manner of Galileo or Stahl. What is unconcealed (*aletheia*, "truth") is a phenomenon brought to presence by placing it within understanding's "leading strings." Analysis arrives at the "perfection of cognition" (*Logic* 139) by constraining "nature to give answer to questions of reason's own determining" (B xiii). Through the give and take of imaginative, experimental questioning, something *p* may show itself as a necessary condition for the appearing of *s*. If *s* can be persuaded into showing itself only through *p*, then this sufficient condition will be its characteristic or mark.

One grasps (*begreiffen,* "conceive") something through a set-up ("representation," *Vorstellung*). This assemblage is set in place to categorially challenge forth (*katagoria,* "to bring a charge against") something, like a witness in the dock. Reason then must listen as "an appointed judge who compels the witness to answer questions he himself has formulated" (B xiii). The questions are directed towards categorial aspects of the object. Only as challenged forth will nature be brought into unconcealment (*aletheia,* "truth"). This is the essence of the experimental method (B xiii) whose synthetic grounds Professor Strawson dismissed as "questionable transcendental psychology." Kant tells us that "conceptual analysis" is irrelevant (A 716/B 744). The issue of Kant's methodology is technology and the modern world view (MH 1977, 115–54). A corrective lies in a deeper appreciation of analysis.

Experimental procedure is the methodological base for all but the most trivial analytic judgments. Categorial judgments arise as answers to categorial questioning. We are in the habit of thinking of analytic judgments as tautologies, but they are such because the concept expressed is constructed. Even sensible qualities can be analytic predicates. For example, if and and only if gold is always of a certain yellow color, there is a presumed nomic connection between them; the concept "gold" contains or entails the predicate concept "yellow" (*Prol.* 266). Analysis shows yellow is a mark of gold; "gold is yellow" is presumptively analytic. The possibility of establishing nomic ties is shown in Kant's novel application of the synthetic method to produce that catachresis, the synthetic concept of an "object in general," the only concept outside of mathematics which is constructed or synthetic (*Prol.* 272). To construct a concept is "to exhibit *a priori* to intuition an object which corresponds to the concept" (A 713/B 741). Since substance, quantity, quality, cause, and the like are forms of pure thought which are also, when schematized, transcendental predicates of this transcendental object (B 128), then the transcendental synthesis, a *logos* that imaginatively gathers and lays out a meaningful world for sense and mind, is categorical. What is discerned in analysis to pertain necessarily to an empirical object, which according to the empiricists could never be more than a post facto company formation of ideas, will have this as its ontic characteristics through the cointended transcendental object which the empirical object schematizes. The transcendental object grounds analysis and "cannot be separated from the sensible data . . . [and] can serve only for the unity of the manifold in sensible intuition" (A 250).

The transcendental object restores to sense what had been stolen from it by Descartes and Hume, its direct, non-inferential reference to empirical objects. What might otherwise be blind receptivity is through synthesis the perception of objects. Just as the mathematical thing itself, the line, is mediately present in mathematical synthesis through the drawn line, so too the physical object (phenomenal substance) is mediately present in its perceived marks. Transcendental synthesis, the soul's natural analogue to the synthetic method, grants intentionality to sense and makes it a proper ground for thought. Sense does not have meaning adjoined to it by judgment; even if "blind," synthesis gives sense as empirically meaningful. Kant lays the foundation for phenomenology. It has been proposed that "representation" is both private, my image, and public, a picture. Reading *Vorstellung* as a public "set-up" necessary for the unconcealment of being and not just as the power to imaginatively presence an object corresponding to the concept, sometimes called "representative thinking," stretches the German yet captures the sense of Kant's enterprise. How to produce the (synthetic) set-up (*Vorstellung*) which embodies the hypothesis which then provokes nature into showing herself in her idea, her "visible radiance," is a mystery "hidden in the depths of the soul." This imaginative and medial "play" dialectically produces even as it is produced by the Kantian empirical schema.

Had he not eliminated examples from the text, there would have been less confusion about the meaning of analysis and synthesis. To make up for this, the determination of water's boiling point can serve as an example of analysis. It must be brought to a boil in various conditions set up to presence and find out the constant's value (intensive quantity). A quantity of water is fitted with measures of temperature and atmospheric pressure, both being intensive quantities, and is caused to be heated; one awaits its boiling. Controlling rates of change and the length of time is very important. Things are set up that other things may come into play. In playing itself out, the questioned nexus may unconceal itself. As von Wright has said, we "repeatedly put the system into motion through acts of producing its initial state and then watching ("passively") the successive stages of its development."[26] The set-up either brings about the phenomenon, as heating brings water to boil, or allows something to happen, as in radioactive decay or cooling a room by opening a window. Given these necessary conditions, the system must be isolated in order to show that only these are operative or sufficient; this requires that the system must be acted upon to effect closure. This ideal of isolation provides us with the classical concept of the particle, a simple entity that is always and everywhere a Parmenidian same. We play with the apparatus to set the water molecules in play so that water can be present to us in its mark. "Present" is an aspectual sense of the Greek *einai*, "to be." Our play with the apparatus, if only to adjust the thermometer, and the play of the molecules are instances of verbal "presencing," *gignesthai* ("becoming," *einai*'s borrowed aorist). The processes set going by our actions unconceal (*aletheia*, "truth") the "beingness" (*ousia*, a participial form of *einai* usually translated as "substance" or "nature") of water. Analysis lets beings unconceal themselves under experimental restraints which enact the original question.

Standardization of procedure and other systematic constraints involved in putting into play let one see that 100°C marks water's transition from its liquid to its vapor state. "It boils at 100°C" is thus part of its "analytic concept" (*Logic* 141). If there are objects which give necessity and order to experience (A 104), and if certain qualities can serve as marks, analytic results are grounded. In putting things into play, our original questions are embodied in apparatus which imposes restraints (Kant's "leading strings") on presencing ("becoming"). Unconcealment, "truth," is a function of the original question. What one hopes to see is the nature (*physis* in the sense of *ousia*, "being-ness") of the entity, its natural necessities. What one sees, especially when other than intended, can interpret the experimental intention and lead one to revise the set-up (representation). It is as if we entered into dialogue with the being questioned, confronting it as if already understood; where we are not up to its measure, it can question us. The *logos*, understood as logic or theoretical science, is founded on a play of presence and presencing (being and becoming) through which nature collects itself and lays itself out (the archaic sense of *logos*) in "visible" presence. It seems that Plato's ontological understanding and method lingers in the laboratory.

5. The Pre-Critical Background

FROM HIS BEGINNINGS KANT WAS preoccupied with methodology. Since the crisis of 1772 and the following years of silence in which the Critical Philosophy was incubated resulted from a methodological breakdown that threatened the foundations of physico-theology, some historical background is imperative. "Physico-theology" designates the nexus of ideas out of which modern science originates. That the world is an infinite totality intelligible through God, its first cause, was a common presumption from Copernicus until d'Alembert. The cosmos either expressed God's idea or, more positivistically, his will. Knowledge of this totality was also the objective ideal towards which analysis aimed; something of this ontic logos in which things express ideas is retained in Critical Philosophy's "ideal of reason" and expressed as programmatic and calculative rationality. This prevailing aspect of Enlightenment was assumed to lead from idiosyncrasies of inductive prejudice and local history to a world in which laws express Leibniz's concept of progress and perfection, the greatest intelligible unity compatible with the greatest phenomenal diversity.

Newton thought of analysis as the division or resolution of a whole into its elements. One does not ground these results on reason but accepts them as simple positivities. This leads, as it led d'Alembert and Euler, away from physico-theology towards the positivism already implicit in Newton's theological voluntarism. Newton's physics was shaped to express God's sovereign will, not reason and its necessities. For example, he refused to form hypotheses, reason's "springboards," which would explain gravity; to restrain God's action by rational necessity would make miracles impossible. What falls by Galileo's law, a description entailing no nomic necessity, could equally rise. Moreover, space and time, "God's sensoria," were said to be absolute and infinite in order not to limit the arbitrariness of God's creative act; he could have created this world at any time or place. God's sovereign will was hardly sufficient reason:

> As in mathematics, so in natural philosophy, the investigation of difficult things by the method of analysis ought ever to precede the method of composition. This analysis consists in making general experiments and observations, and in drawing general conclusions from them by induction, and admitting no objections against the conclusions but such as are taken from experiments. For hypotheses [rational principles that would give reasons that would be a constraint on God's will] are not to be regarded in experimental philosophy. And although the argument from experiments and observations by induction be no general demonstration of general conclusions, yet it is the best way of arguing that the nature of things admits of, and may be looked on as so much the stronger, by how much the induction is more general. And if no exception occur from phenomena, the conclusion may be pronounced generally. . . . By this way of analysis we proceed from compounds to ingredients and from motions to the forces producing them, and in general from effects to their cause, and from particular causes to more general ones, if the argument ends in the most general ones. This is the method of analysis: a synthesis consists in assuming the causes discovered, and established as principles, and by them explaining the phenomena proceeding from them, and proving the explanations. (IN 1952, Query 31)

The conditions for the conditioned are transient, not transcendent, and the concern is with the division of wholes into its elements; but this does not prevent Newton from relating these in a hierarchy of laws expressing a theological unity.

Hume could not concede that contingent regularities in the inverse square law express the sovereign and arbitrary will of an all-powerful

God. Natural inference and induction which do not lead beyond "empirical affinities" will not justify belief in a world, the totality of what-is, which Hume takes for granted as an object in his *Dialogues on Natural Religion*. Apart from God(s), for whom there can be a given infinite totality, world is a meaningless concept. Kant was perplexed by the possibility of natural inference, that is, how one thing can be necessarily given through another, and attributed his awakening to the problem to Hume (*Prol.* 258), but he had already expressed his puzzlement in the 1763 *Negativen Grossen*. If Newtonian analysis cannot survive its positivistic demythologization, can the method as understood by the rationalists offer a justification?

Kant's two senses of analysis, "regression" from "grounded to the ground" and "regression from a whole to its possible or mediate parts" (*Diss.* 388), are found in Descartes. The *Discourse* sets out the method and records its successes, while the *Meditations* employs and justifies both senses of analysis by analysis. In spite of a tendency to accept appearances as veridical, sense can neither provide a ground for tknowing or for its own "formal," or in our sense "objective"—reality. By means of the procedural and hyperbolical doubts, Descartes moves from this conditioned totality to its condition in the "I think." Next, breaking the objects of consciousness into their proper parts, the idea classes, he finds that among these only innate ideas show themselves as unconditionally true. Among such ideas are those of mathematics; he can show with the eidetic reduction of the wax that the other classes presuppose the innate idea of extension. This double regression from totality to condition leads the "I" to discern in the non-deceiving God grounds for the formal reality of the ideas of mathematics and for all other things insofar as they are objects of this science. What is for thought only an objective, that is transmuted into our "subjective," totality is to God a formal totality, rather like the noumenal world in Kant's 1770 *Inaugural Dissertation*.

This analytic movement, especially in the light of the wax being seen as a "certain mode of extension," appears to justify Leibniz in calling sense "confused conception." This enabled him to find a sensible interpretation for his infinitesimal calculus. Thanks to Duns Scotus' legacy as transmitted through Suarez, Leibniz used univocal, disjunctive transcendentals, such as possible or actual and finite or infinite, and attributed the actual infinite to God. For example, instead of Newton's infinite space and time, he made these relative to the actual infinity of monads; only such a world could adequately express an actually infinite God. These transcendentals will play a major role in Kant's philosophy.

Even before Kant discovered difficulties in representing the actual infinite, which he expressed in a letter to Marcus Herz, 21 February

1772 (*Cor.* 111–18), he had earlier doubts about the validity of the ontological argument (*Beweis.* 1763). Were it invalid, all inference to the existence of an unconditioned condition for every condition would be cut off; he says "existence is not a predicative determination of anything at all" (72). Sense could hardly be "confused conception" if, as he argued in his first published paper, the "Thoughts on the True Estimate of Living Forces" (*LK*, 1747), it is not a concept. Analysis was unable to ground itself. The world is transformed from a realistic in itself into a phenomenal for us and will become the correlative of original apperception.

Most of Kant's Pre-critical writings were directed towards physicotheology, even if that movement was alive only in Königsberg. For example, he claimed that "the infinite perception of the whole universe is always internally present to mind, though extremely obscure. It already contains within itself whatever reality must be contained in the cognitions afterwards [by analysis] to be suffused by more light" (*ND*, 407). Similar thoughts are expressed in the *Negativen Grossen* (*NG*, 99). When access to a transcendent grounding is denied, synthesis must supply the sense of world threatened by the crisis of analysis. The method is that of giving a constructive, discursive analogue to the God-world relation in the I-world relation. Just as God's creative intuition was expressed as the noumenal world, so too the phenomenal world has its *arché* in the creative intuition of the transcendental "I." Our finite and successive intuitions condemn us to work out through this succession what is given to God in a single, eternal now. "The infinite perception of the whole universe" remains present to mind in its limiting, noumenal ideas. We can move toward the rational ideal of the completely determined if and only if space/time entities can be qualitatively discriminated as inferentially connectible in a world-preserving form, however incomplete, as thematized in the Principles. An *a priori* power to act, which is to question and schematize, in categorial forms discriminates quality (intensive magnitude) that intends quantity (like Descartes' wax) or extensive magnitude and its law-like constancy in the "permanent in intuition." Qualitative changes signify quantitative changes, in turn referable to other bodies as causes. In fact, these permanent substances are really Leibniz's reciprocally active and reactive forces whose story is told in the *a priori* dynamical physics of the critical *Metaphysical Foundations of Natural Science*. Though we cannot gain God's *nunc standi,* we bear the sense of the world *a priori*.

Only action can establish a causal relation which, in Kant's formulation, requires a completely ordered temporal succession (A 189/B 232), that is to say, one-way directionality. On Hume's "empirical affinity" thesis, successive moments are contingently ordered. Did *a* really occur before or after *b?* But if I am drawing a line, the second edition equivalent of the three-fold synthesis in the first edition (A 98–110), I know what has been done cannot follow what is being done nor occur as what is yet to be done (B 137–38, B 154–55). All meaning is founded on action, even physical meaning; if this does not resolve all problems of freedom and determinism, it points to the need for teleology in discerning physical significance.

Though we may begin with meaningful structures, *pace* Descartes' solitary ego, this "I think . . ." of Transcendental Apperception presupposes, or is founded on, the results of transcendental synthesis. Otherwise meaning vanishes into Humian nihilism, into contingent relations between contingent entities contingently related to minds by contingent signs. Significance, not Hume's infatuation with contingencies nor Descartes' God, is basic to a meaningful world. Ontology is prior to epistemology, as the existence of the known is prior to knowing; how otherwise could we say what knowledge is? One must demonstrate through the active synthesis underlying analysis that Being is thematized as "permanent presence." Let's look at some details of the realistic ontology assumed in experimentation.

6. Experimental Practice

HAVING ASSUMED A PROVISIONAL realism and having read analysis phenomenologically, the experimental context will give us a better feel for the region within which the Kantian problematic is most perspicuous. The method is paradigmatic for the dialectic of receptivity and activity in self-affective recognition (B 68). The analytic clarification of concepts makes them "distinct" by "making their marks successively clear" (*Logic* 141). A procedure, a narrative, sets one out on a succession of "experiences" that lead towards *aletheia*. Analysis yields nominal definitions "taken from an attribute" (*Logic* 144); something is water if and only if it boils at 100°C. Where boiling point is critical, water can be recognized through this mark; were there a doubt, we could let it appear as frozen at 0°C. Marks, criteria in verificatory judgments, pertain to (nominal) essence, the object of the analytic concept framed through analysis.

This phenomenology works counter to the more obvious (and untenable) alternative. The *Prolegomena,* written with the judgmental or subsumptive model in mind, held nature to be the existence of things as determined by laws; then the thing is their posited intersection. Is this how it is? If, for example, the experimental project embodies Newton's law, things are unconcealed as gravitational forces; other projects may unconceal these same bodies as electrical forces instancing Coulomb's law. Like Heraclitus' sea, which is "for fish drinkable and life sustaining and for men undrinkable and deadly" (DK, 61), a same appears as other in differing contexts. Does this perhaps mean that what allows the thing to express itself as gravitational and electrical is founded on Duns Scotus' formal objective distinctions *a parte rei?* Things and their inseparable formalities explain, not laws.

Analysis requires that something be done experimentally if something is to be present; this setting-up has its paradigm in the synthetic method of geometry. One can make the line itself present through the act of drawing according to an *a priori* rule given by the first postulate of Book I of Euclid's *Elements.* On Kant's account, a postulate is an *a priori* rule of action, "a practical, immediately certain proposition," and not an unprovable assumption required for a logical proof. According to the dominant logistic school, synthesis is deductive and postulates, unprovable assumptions, are counted among the "known" with which one begins. It is otherwise in classical geometry. Euclid's fifth or parallel postulate, usually taken as an unprovable assumption, is better thought of as defining the space of constructivity. The first three postulates authorize constructions through which something intuitively self-evidencing comes to be. What one can do can be expressed in a proposition, such as, a straight line is the shortest distance between two points. Euclid says one can (1) "draw a straight line from any point to any point," (2) "produce a straight line continuously in a straight line," and (3) "describe a circle with any center and distance." A "postulate" is a reiterable rule that sets something out. A "concept" is also an iterative rule (A 126); this blurs a concept's distinction from a postulate since both are forms of self-affective *praxis.* A concept has the reflexive form of an action that may be warranted by a postulate, "a fundamental proposition of which it is presupposed that the manner of executing it is immediately certain" (*Logic* 118). The first *Critique* is even more precise: "Now in mathematics a postulate means the practical proposition which contains nothing save the synthesis through which we first give ourselves an object and generate its concept" (A 234/B 287). This usage points to the context of setting up, *Vorstellung,* in which action and phenomenological *doxa* are primary.

One sets things up in order to put something into play. Play requires a certain looseness of fit, perhaps through an adjustable apparatus which perspects a range of options and thus some freedom of movement, as in a disengaged gear or steering wheel. Looseness opens possibilities; a response may then be terminated even as it begins. One acts to effect closure to let things play. Only in play, which as medial plays through us and makes us players, can one freely cope with contingencies. Thus this looseness, this free play, is possible through the *epoché* effected by action that is necessary if initial conditions are to be introduced into systems that let something play itself out. This free space allows one to initiate, regulate, and terminate nomological processes. Manipulation reveals law-like properties of things. Where one cannot act on a system, as in some aspects of the human and environmental sciences, the free play of the imagination replaces manipulative techniques. Closure interprets; in classical mechanics, for example, it posits a particle which is self-same in transport and manipulation. The bracketed play reveals meaning, lets truth happen.

Is it unfair to interpret the agent-oriented Kant in metaphors of medial play? Perhaps, but his dynamical physics requires that vector forces play out if they are to show themselves phenomenally. Play is a central theme in the finality of his aesthetics and, even in his rather stiff-necked ethics, he spoke of "playing the game of life." While we cannot attribute to him the full import of play, some features do fit. Phenomenologically, (1) play plays itself (2) in a give and take or to and fro (3) self-representing movement which is (4) relatively isolated or within boundaries. Finally, (5) in playing we model to learn dominating behavior. Kant's use of imagination was an important factor in the rise of Romanticism; the resulting imaginative freedom is as evident in the desacralizing technologies and entrepreneurial attitudes it has spawned as it is in the poetry of Wordsworth. The disengaged imagination widens the gap between self and things which has brought about our desacralized, manipulable and objectless world, the world of Descartes' wax. On the plus side, play is within the interface of chance, rule-governed action and nomic necessities, and the unity of this assemblage has been largely ignored in standard, covering-law interpretations of natural knowledge. Moreover, closure puts the focus on the thing that unconceals itself. Covering laws' explanations cannot cope with chance. There is a justified tendency to adapt a subsumptive, Hempel-Nagel explanation schema to Kant, but the method of analysis shows that stress should be fixed on the thing and the contingencies of its response unconcealed in "play."[27]

Kant's revolution begins with his recovery of the role questions play in analysis. Action is an *epoché*, a bracketing, within horizons already opened by the question to whose answer it addresses itself. Collingwood, more aware than most of the presuppositions in a question, could have credited Kant with this insight. Instead, he praised him for having corrected Descartes by "making a careful distinction between philosophical and mathematical thinking" (RGC 1932, 22). This is true only if both are thought to pursue synthesis in the logistic sense. That option of going from known to unknown was not open to Kant, since neither philosophy nor natural science is in possession of real definitions which are deductively "sufficient for a cognition of an object as to its inner determinations [real essence] by setting forth the possibility of an object out of these inner characteristics" (*Logic* 144). Kant, however, understood mathematics to be constructively synthetic, the paradigm case of a pure or *a priori* representation, which gave a unique interpretation of synthesis. Through drawing an image, we presence for mind the line itself. The image, a product of transcendental imagination, is the same that lets thought encounter being. Parmenides' *noein* no longer assumes a passive spectator that brings things to a stand (*Gegenstand*); as incarnate a *theoria* acts, iteratively represents, under an *a priori* rule; in such cases action and its motile expression are transcendental (B 154). The representing act constructs the conditions for meaningfully receiving sense as intending empirical objects. Just as one intends in the act of drawing the pure line itself, so categorial acts intend through sensibility the transcendental object as the noema in all perceptual synthesis. This gives sense its ontological weight. This experimental intention releases category-conforming objects to be and be known. The categorial forms which are implicit in questions will, when experimentally schematized, put nature in their "leading strings" and will, like drawing a line by the postulate, release objects for categorial judgment. Categories and postulates are both rule-governed acts which reflexively presence something that is then receptively given by sense for thought. Analogously, in line drawing we reflexively presence the seen line, a being, by presencing, for example, drawing, through a rule, a postulate. A representation is not a copy; it makes something present that would otherwise be absent, as the drawn line makes the 'line itself' present. We directly and non-inferentially see the intelligible line in its possibilities through the sensible image. Moreover, Cartesian self-certainty is also present in these active contexts; we know the form of what is given because we put it there. Just as in actively connecting points by a line segment I know that I am seeing a line with certain mathematical properties, so too acting within the parameters of a category allows the reception of an object as categorially determinate. As governed by *a priori* rules, acts reflexively given as motile, for instance, the motile hand drawing, will be well-ordered with respect to before and after and therefore not vulnerable to Humian skepticism. His understanding of mathematics is the real clue to an appreciation of Kant. Collingwood was mistaken.

A transcendental act schematizing the transcendental object is at the root of all phenomena of being. Since "presence" and "presencing" are fundamental interpretations of Being intended in interpretations of or judgments about any particular empirical being, Kant opens the way to a genuine phenomenological ontology. Wasn't his primary concern metaphysical? Apart from methodological contexts, can we make sense of Kant?

7. Rhetoric and Analysis

RHETORIC STOOD JUST BELOW LOGIC in the trivium. At its best, as in Augustine, it was supposed to make ostentatious or demonstrate what logic had to prove, roles Kant assigned to analysis and synthesis respectively. In his *Kant's Analytic,* Jonathan Bennett calls attention to Kant's denial of the epistemic continuum, the thesis common to empiricists and rationalists that percepts and concepts are same in kind (JB 1966, 53–56). The crisis for analysis produced by this failure was in part an artifact of the method of analysis. Since Plato (*Sop.* 253D) and Aristotle (*De Gen. Anim.* 431a 27–431b 6), thought has been understood as a union of separative analysis and unifying synthesis. When analysis is transformed from dialectic into a method and the "grounded" and "grounds" are understood as ontologically, axiologically, or epistemologically different, its separative aspects prevail and synthesis becomes a problem. The monstrative success of analysis in the middle dialogues landed Plato in separationism. For example, in pointing to something, the demonstrative gesture—an abstractive *epoché* formalized in the method of analysis—prescinds the thing pointed to from everything else, which is then left to lapse into relative non-being, as if the focal *it* alone is. Though it need not exist, for Socratic dialectic can produce "wind-eggs," the demonstrated it elicited through the "regions" (phrases, spaces, hypotheses, *doxa,* gestures, apparatus in a laboratory) through which it is pointed out is the *logos,* the principle, that orders and governs these same regions through which it is made ostentatious. The ordered demonstrative sets are representations, *Vorstellungen.* Can the ideal limit of a set, such as the point elicited by a nest of circles such that every circle covers another and there is no least circle, exist apart from its demonstrative conventions? Perhaps Kant began to face up to this in the Dialectic. This will be especially true of ideal objects belonging, like mathematics, to the schematizing or interpretative dimension of experience. Their demonstrative force, the truth that happens through them, saves these from being artifacts.

Pointing divides wholes into a collection of parts, this one or the one there; the disclosive sense of analysis leads to its other sense, the division of a whole into its parts. Pointing that lets us see form through doxic regions is a powerful incentive to think of "ideas" as separated. Prehensive and separative spatial and temporal relations give way to space and time as containers in which things are situated. The converse movement of synthesis "going from principles to consequents" collects these "simples" into "composites" (*Logic* 117). In applying the analytic method to experimental inquiry, a whole is resolved into proper parts and then, taking these as analogues of Aristotelian primary being, one proposes testable hypotheses to determine, by the second sense of analysis, their necessary and sufficient conditions. To determine sufficient conditions, the system must be closed or isolated, both senses of analysis conspire to bring one to a separationist reading of the spatial and temporal structure of the natural world. The results are seen in Gassendi, Dalton, Newton, and Galileo. The full import of separationism is evident in the phenomenalism of Berkeley and Hume, where minimal sensibilia are associated with temporal and spatial atomicity.

The influence of prescinding idealization is evident in Kant's use of "manifold" to characterize time and space; it suggests to a mathematical "synopsis" that something is given as combinable through an iterative rule. Underlying the concept is Aristotle's point that act, for Kant a rule, determines a correlative potentiality. The possibility of "manifolds" presupposes a rule generating a combinatorial potential. For example, the rules of grammar constitute the possibility of a sentential manifold. Kant held that both pure and empirical concepts entail schemata, iterative rules of synthesis: "Sensibility gives us forms of intuition, understanding gives us rules" (A 126). To think "number in general" is, for example, to think of "the representation of a method whereby a multiplicity [i.e., manifold] . . . may be represented in an image in conformity with a certain concept" (A 140/B 179). This double sense of analysis and synthesis, that is, parts/wholes and conditioned/condition, leads into one of the most important arguments for understanding the role of synthesis in the Deduction.

Analysis may divide a coexistent manifold into separable parts, as in the ideally isolated system of classical mechanics, to find sufficient conditions. Space and time understood as ultimately punctal sever and separate, rather than prehend and gather; it then may seem that anything associated with its punctal elements could exist apart from everything else. Kant's argument in the thesis of the second Antinomy denies on purely formal grounds the possibility of a physical monadology. This denial of atomicity will be a necessary, but not sufficient, condition for the objective unity required by analysis (B 133). To make a point that will be important in the sequel, the order type of continuua does not determine how continuua are to be empirically interpreted. The converse is more nearly true.

Hume made Kant aware of the need for a transcending sufficient condition for the unity of the manifold (which separative analysis concealed) which he came to see depends on Transcendental Apperception, the ground for significance and thus predication. Since by Galileo's time nature had become denatured of prehensive *physis*, if there is any gathering into unity, where this unity involves entities of every categorial type, its ground belongs to something transcending the sense manifold. Berkeley's notions and Hume's habits were, as subjective principles of combination, gestures in the direction of transcendental unity; but since empirically given "parts" of the sensory manifold are neither "coordinate" nor "complements," which must be the case if synthesis is to yield a whole (*Diss.* 388), no such whole is possible. Thus *a priori* apperception *qua* ground must warrant the movement through sense to the empirical object, in turn grounded in the object in general, apperception's transcendental correlate. The categories articulate or cut nature at the joints, into proper parts of a whole, and enable us to think what would otherwise be separated sensa as predicatively "coordinate" or as relational "complements," that is, synthetically. Categories are the possible ways of expressing the veridical sense of the copula in reflective judgments (B 142). They let us "tell it like it is" because the manifold has been unified in the metaphysical concept of an object that satisfies the universality and necessity noetically intended in the categorial predicates.

Hume pushed separative analysis to its limit; wholes are collections of separable parts. A being, Aristotle said, is not a heap. Since these additive wholes are only the logical sum of their parts, predication—lacking its synthetic ground—will be replaced by the set-theoretic relation of "element in." The "apple is red" becomes "red an element in the contiguously consentient set of 'apple' relata"; there is no logical subject, the apple, of which red can be asserted. Hume's impressions are, at the intensional level, constellations of impredicable predicates. There is no determinable for judgment to determine. Then, Kant says, "empirical consciousness, which accompanies various representations, is itself diverse and without any relation to the identity of the subject" (B 133). Instead of unifying space and time by prehensive things ("gathering"), Kant attributes synthesis to the imagination, an action "of the understanding on the sensibility" (B 152) that constructs the objective unity which must be thought if the forms of the understanding are to have any content (B 149). The content unified in judgment cannot be supplied by a manifold of separated sense objects. Analysis that grounds *doxa* in *episteme* cannot operate with separated sensa; and of course they aren't, for we see the tree rather than infer it from sense impressions contingently related and belonging together through encrusted habit. A particular red is to the chemist a mark of cinnabar and one could, on analysis, justify this as a necessary and sufficient condition for recognizing it. With separationism, there is no unitary ground for nomological (or real) relations of inherence or causation but only juxtaposition. Thought must supply the object as such to the manifold as the synthetic condition required for unity.

Husserl's descriptions of perception may be helpful. The thing perceptually intended, the noema, through the noetic flux of its aspects is the eject or constituted outcome of these successive intentions. This noema, as a profile of the cointended transcendental object, expresses a meaning of being that permits the empirical imputation of universality and necessity. In the second Analogy, Kant says: "What then am I to understand by the question; how the manifold may be connected in the appearance itself, which yet is nothing in itself? That which lies in the successive apprehension is here viewed as representation, while the appearance that is given to me, notwithstanding that it is nothing but the sum of these representations, is viewed as their object; while my concept, which I derive from the representations of apprehension, has to agree with it" (A 191/B 236). Each successive intention directed to the intentional object through the manifold instances a combinatorial rule or category and carries the predicative presumption of transcending objectivity. The thing is then the ontological unity underlying these manifold modes of appearing. Kant has said that "where the understanding has not previously combined, it cannot dissolve, since only as having been combined by the understanding can anything that allows of analysis be given to the faculty of representation" (B 130). Lest one be confused by this assignment of synthesis to the understanding, remember that the second edition account of synthesis plays down the role of the imagination: "all combination—be we conscious of it or not, be it a combination of the manifold of intuition, empirical or non-empirical, or of various concepts—is an act of the understanding" (B 130). This is a rhetorical claim which protects Kant against empiricism and its uninterpreted facts and preserves intellectualism's claim that all recognition is in concepts. However, it is misleading: "It is one and the same spontaneity, which in the one case, under the title imagination, and in the other case, under the title of understanding, brings combination into the manifold of intuition" (B 161n.). Understanding preserves the logical priority of intention and imputes objectivity in judgments, while the active gathering (another sense of *logos*) is itself left to the imagination. That these imaginative and conceptual spontaneities are same means that the rules in "judgments of experience" are the same as those by which we imaginatively constitute its sensed contents.

A "synthesis that is at once transcendental and also purely intellectual" determines receptivity (B 150); its object, considered formally, is nothing but the eject of this expression.[28] Though understanding cannot determine *a priori* the "matter" receptively given, the figurative imagination can invest this matter with the formal, categorial sense of an object being represented and, therefore, intended (B 151); the object as such is the grounds for a unitary consciousness (A 105). What is imaginatively intended through the schematized concept meets up with what has already been constituted as an object by that same imagination (A 142/B 181), as a plate is recognized as round through a circular schema (A 137/B 176).

One intends as actual, necessary, or even possible this or that empirical object in the schematized categories as an extensive magnitude through intensive quality in relation to other aspects of the possible or actual manifold of sensibility because the transcendental or metaphysical object is cointended. A focus on the intended noema, the expressivist outcome of imaginative synthesis, drowns out the presencing, the drawing by the drawn (A 103). Being aware of this presencing (B 153) while attending to the presenced is like self-consciously dancing; the springs of presencing run dry. The transcendental imagination "performs this [presencing] act upon the passive subject, whose faculty it is" (B 153). The object is received as if a gift from the one to whom it is given. Realism has its origin in the subject's medial imagination.

Kant's method of setting out and setting up answers the separative problems of analysis and eliminates its doubtful ground in either sense or reason. Its issue is the self-affective view of time, affecting oneself by rule-governed representing, an expressivist auto-eroticism (B 68). Listening to oneself talk is the example immediately at hand. Saying is a rule-governed, iterable activity that comes back to one self-affectively in the said. Iteration, the essential mark of transcendental idealism, is the basis for fulfilled presence in self-presence or self-consciousness. The iterative rules by which a subject domesticates the alterity of the world to subjectivity harbors a more radical approach to otherness than is apparent in a conceptualist reduction of universals to repeatable sames, to a virtual act, in the other and other of time.

Kant's concept of *Vorstellung*, "representation," is that of an expressivist rule-governed setting up by which the self is present to itself in self-certain doing. Through it one makes the passage from interiority to exteriority. Through the threshold of the imagination one crosses metaphysical distinctions, for example, Cartesian thought and extension or Parmenidian *noein* and *einai*. This threshold is the originary *arché* that gives being to thought and thought to being; but it is also the place of "trace" and *différance*, deconstructing distinctions it bridges. The imagination, though crossed by constraining sense and understanding, is a rather weak and unreliable bond between these "powers." Jacques Derrida makes the point that its spontaneous presencing in speaking or drawing requires "material" signifiers. The signifier/signified tie constituting the sign breaks apart because imagination is medial; like ourselves, products of Plato's errant cause, the signifier will be untrustworthy and more likely to disseminate than gather entities into a knower-in-general's presence (JD 1982, 1–28). There is a hiatus between intention and the locutionary and illocutionary forces of language. By situating his critique within the spontaneous imagination, Kant unintentionally opens novel possibilities for philosophy. Imagination is the *arché*, the origin, of the self and world, the threshold to an eventual philosophy of original creativity. This will seem less odd if it is recalled that the transcendental self stands away from the gap between the subject and object and generates this relation. Through imagination, humans are "betweenness" (A 138/B 177–A 142/B 181). In what might otherwise be the gap between the disengaged subject and the desacralized world, imagination lets the real, the thing, appear to the subject in an image (A 166/B 207–8) and lets the self through the schematized concept, pure and empirical, be that being to whom the image appears. Appearing results from "my generating time" (A 143/B 182). This new, creative role for the expressive imagination may be Kant's most important discovery (CT 1989, 198). In an early myth, beings arise and stand out in the gap between Gaea and Uranus. The *metaxu*, the "between" of Simone Weil and Plato's *Timaeus* or *Symposium*, or Heidegger's *das Zwischen*, express a crossed fecundity, the open between lovers.

II

TOWARDS PHENOMENOLOGY

·······················

1. Mental Acts

IN THE TRADITION WHICH HAS BEEN dominated by the predicative rather than participatory concept of being, mind has been understood as either patient to its intelligible object or, as in such conceptualists as Kant, Aquinas and Aristotle, its maker, its constituting reason and cause. Mind must make what realism supposedly finds and, granted some modicum of receptivity, construes itself as a mental act, usually in the form of a judgment or assertion, that makes present what the realist would leave to God or nature. Making or iterating a same for thinking and being replaces "seeing" a same. Theology was able to reconcile these alternatives in the *Logos,* as in St. Thomas, but with Kant conceptualism had to invoke what we call "mental acts" if it was to stand on its own. It is now fashionable to speak of mental activity, even Kant's theory thereof, but I do not think anything very intelligible is being said. Caught up among these "mental fictions," Duns Scotus' jibe at Scholasticism's labyrinth of second intensions, it is possible to overlook the fact that it is only through my body that I have a place (*chora*) in and from which to articulate power and act out intentions; the expression "mental act" is a sprung metaphor (EL 1988, 88). Action orients through the body's "hidden" proprioceptic sense, the "continuous but unconscious flow from the movable parts of our bodies" (OS 1986, 43).

There is much to be learned, however, from the unique thrust Kant gives to "construction" as "exhibiting *a priori* the intuition that corresponds to the concept" (A 713/B 741). Though this productive act is proper to mathematics in which, like creative gods, we exhibit the particular that expresses the universal (A 714/B 742), an analogous expressive act also lets something-in-general, already a latent mathematical schemata, "represent *a priori*" the "empirical contents" of experiences (A 720/B 748). When the object is intended in sensibility, it determines how sensory particulars are seen and understood. Kant understands "phenomenology" as concerned with the transformation of private, mental acts into knowledge of a public world of motile, material objects (*MF* 118–34).[1] The Transcendental Analytic,

the phenomenological center of the first *Critique,* establishes the crossing between sense *qua* perceptual judgment and understanding *qua*
judgments of experience in which motion will have an essential role.
This possibility of crossing lies in the imagination's *arché* synthesis
when its receptivity is solicited by Transcendental Apperception's intentions. "In as much as its synthesis is an expression of spontaneity
which is determinative and not, like sense, determinable merely and
which is therefore able to determine sense *a priori* in respect of its
form according to the unity of apperception, imagination is to that
extent a faculty which determines the sensibility *a priori;* and its synthesis of intuitions, conforming as it does to the *categories,* must be
the transcendental synthesis of the imagination. This synthesis is an
action of the understanding on the sensibility . . ." (B 152).

Perception thematizes imaginatively charged sensibility through
the categorially determinate "transcendental object $= x$." Imaginative
apprehension is already an interpretative opening between sense and
understanding that lets what is received appear within understanding's
parameters. Plato said appearances announcing objects are born in an
analogous "between" (*metaxu, Theaet.* 154A, 156E) through the
crossing and mingling of "passive and active motion" (156C–57C),
the opposition of earth and sky. But this opposition does not, like that
in Heraclitus, constitute things: the open in, for example, the form of
Kant's imagination, is possible only through their empathy. The Hebrews shared Plato's view that things appear when light from the eye
and from things meet and "copulate," the sense of "is" in a participatory ontology.[2] Appearances, first order representations, are primary
modes of significance and fall within the rubric of Peircian thirdness,
the complex relation between a sign, interpreter and interpretant,
rather than causal secondness. In recognition an appearing, seeing
"whitely" or "redly," is interpreted as a kind of object, "a white
stone" or "red mercuric compound."[3] This "same for thinking and
being" lets one cross over from apperception to world and, because
partaking in these opposites, is a "rift that carries the opponents into
the source of their unity by virtue of their common ground" (MH
1971b, 63). "Red" is, Merleau-Ponty said, "a sort of straits between
exterior and interior horizons ever gaping open" (MP 1969, 196, 131)
which is, Heidegger would say, a rift that allows the intimacy of their
belonging together. I approach crossing in the spirit, though hardly the
letter, of the progressive or objective deduction to show how understanding, "the faculty of judgment" (A 69/B 94), relates to objects *a
priori.*

How does one go from the empirical affinity of a post hoc Humian
manifold to a cosmos? Why does the rule of universal instantiation
work? Judgments arising from the necessary and sufficient conditions

imposed upon objects in analysis are presumptively universal and necessity. A concept is a predicate in a possible judgment whose logical
subject is the empirical object generated by "the synthesis of recognition in a concept" (A 103). Until it submits to empirical objects,
thought "has no meaning and is completely lacking in content" (A
239/B 298). Unless a concept is made sensible, it "would, as we say,
be without sense, that is, without meaning" (A 240/B 299). Objective reference through a sort of doxic "seeing as" within a context of
physical activity completely orders time and is the *a priori* condition
for meaningfulness.[4] In the spirit of Kant's Copernican Revolution,
the intended or meant, i.e., the noema, is constructed in an *a priori*
"combination of the manifold of sense" (A 250–51). Transcendental
synthesis grants the empirical object through objectifying acts that
unify this manifold. An object (*Gegenstand*) is, Heidegger remarks,
something we encounter which comes to meet and stand against us
(MH 1967, 137) and, as having been brought to a stand, "recognized
in a concept" in the verificatory judgment. Only by holding open the
Nothing, the object-in-general as the phenomenologically reduced
perceptual object,[5] can an act of representation let "something come
forward to be met" (MH 1990, 76). Because of this Nothing, the
sense manifold can never be construed as a succession of Humian impressions whose unity is *a posteriori*. In his concept of empirical affinity Kant assumes such a succession as a reductio, for on the grounds of
causality as succession he shared with Hume, it could never be well-
ordered with respect to before and after. Hume could not maintain the
analytic unity of consciousness, which rests on a prior synthetic or objective unity gained in judgment (B 133), an act—however diaphanous—
by which an entity is constituted and its experience made mine (B 134;
also B 145).[6] The combinatorial act, i.e., rule, that generates the Kantian succession "does not in its intelligible character stand under any
conditions of time" (A 539/B 567).

Something is a manifold, the correlate of a synopsis, only when
seen as combinable by a rule. "The representation of a universal condition," Kant says, "according to which a certain manifold can be posited
in uniform fashion is a rule" (A 113). Normally, a "synopsis" is an
overview, literally "viewing together," in which eventual structures,
accounts of activities or stories, are set out with a view as to their
possible relations, as in the synoptic Gospels. A pure synopsis presupposes knowing how to combine and order space (geometry) and time
(arithmetic).[7] Synoptically, space is a manifold of points relative to a
postulate, a rule, in which any two can be connected by a line. A category is to a sense manifold as a postulate is to a geometrical manifold.
Each is a synoptic form. Thus we are not given a succession of impressions to be somehow combined; the succession is experienced through

a prior combinatorial, i.e., categorial, act which constitutes the combinable succession. This Aristotelian point that (first) potency, in this instance a potency for combination, is always relative to a prior combinatorial (first) act is the moral of Kant's rather obscure first edition discussion of synopsis (A 94-95, A 97). What is synoptically given through a rule can serve as a relatum in various relations without being an actuality, a real being. Thus to a mathematical synopsis a point, which is nothing, that is, without parts, is meaningful only as a possible locus, the limit of a sequence or in relation to a line. Points constitute a manifold under Euclid's first postulate as "positions that limit [linear] space," not elements from which it is constructed (A 169/B 211). Just as space gives itself as receptive to acts of linear connection, so space and time give themselves as receptive of entities when they are schematized. The concept of synopsis, effected by the medial imagination, introduces (and threatens to deconstruct) the transcategorial (transcendental) concepts of action and receptivity.[8] The imagination is the supplementary 'between," *metaxu,* which as the *arché* is a No-thing that things through the crossing of sense and understanding.

Though seeds of this potentiating synoptic or reflective act are present in Aristotle's *De Physica,* there is a fundamental difference. Aristotle's account of *metabole,* the directed change from something to something, is a stage in his plan to eliminate Plato's separationism by combining determinate form and determining act on the *techné* model. A form-granting agent in second act, the doctor doctoring, does not change insofar as, *qua aitia* ("cause"), it lets *metabole* occur in another. Since the primary change is motion, *kinesis* (*De Phys.* 260a 22-261b 26), the reduction of a potential as potential through contact with a prior actuality, he is concerned to elaborate its conditions, such as place, time, chance and necessity, continuity, and the like. The parameters of mechanics, motion and rest, are fundamental to natural philosophy whose other parameters, for example, life and death or even knowledge or ignorance, are explained through, though not reducible to, those of mechanics. This prior act *qua* efficient cause is not a prior element in a succession but, at least in artifactual changes of place, simultaneous with that which it effects. Since time is the measure of motion with respect to before and after (219b 2), this prior act explaining change is (relatively) atemporal. The transcendent Platonic form is replaced by a transcendent act. This relative atemporal act (which moves only accidentally), whose formal expression orders time, is the clue to Kant's revolution. The fundamental difference, which Kant will use Aristotelian concepts to explicate, is that for Aristotle change is foundational and time is its measurable aspect; Kant must generate the very time in which change will occur.

One can best grasp the sense of Kant's project by thinking of the transcendental subject as noetic form in second act which, as such, is reducing a potential (*De Gen. Anim.* 412a 20–25). For example, consider how time is generated by counting, itself an act motivated by the question "how many?" The synopsis relative to an act expressing an intention discloses an "I can ____," such as draw, run, count, and the like. The intention to count has as its correlative potential a coexistent manifold of countable items, "fingers" or "points." "I can count" synoptically discloses a potential for sequential acts of counting, any of which divides the potential, for example, now or not yet. This intention *now* expresses itself in a counting rule. These rules, as reiterable, define ordinal nows which, as sites of counting acts, also generate the natural or counting numbers and, since something is counted, synthesize the manifold under the concept "numerable."[9] These time generating acts pre-structure intuition, provide a synopsis within which it is countable, and are implicit in all acts of the understanding or spatial intuitions, since recognizing something in a concept usually includes being able to use it to point out and count its instances. Whatever we receptively receive, if only to identify it, will be already something implicitly done; "time is nothing but the mode in which the mind is affected through its own activity (namely, through the positing of its representation)" (B 68). We return to ourselves in self-consciousness through our act-posits in the temporal series atemporally generated.

Aristotle knew of no such self-affective movement, an original temporality in which self and world are constituted, which Kant drops upon us like a bomb in the closing pages of the Transcendental Aesthetic. Though Aristotle and Kant say the now, since it is not a proper part, does not measure time, Aristotle says the now in which one temporally numbers motion "with respect to before and after" is the now of transition "in which something is moved to something" (*De Phys.* 219a 10). Time is the numerable dimension of change; for Kant "time is the formal condition for the possibility of changes and is objectively prior to them" (A 453/B 481). Kant does not define time by change but, on the contrary, defines the *in which* of change in terms of acts, potential or actual, such as counting. I count now and now and now . . . where the ennumerative act constitutes this formal succession and "forms its concepts of numbers by successive addition of units in time" (*Prol.* 284). The nows from which I count, fingers, points, or anything synoptically given as countable, are generated by successive acts of counting (A 143/B 182). The entities generated, such as the words "one," "two," . . . said in counting, succeed one another and divide time with respect to before and after; the time of this ordering is B-series "world-time." In A-series time, the real order of becoming which John McTaggart's *The Nature of Existence* distinguishes from this B-series, the future is being made in each now through the synthesis of possibility with received or reproduced actuality. Entities that appear in the process of becoming, like these words appearing on this screen, can then be ordered with respect to B-series time. Nevertheless, in Kant even the A-series now is the past present, the future present, the present present. A formal relation of succession replaces *metabole*, the achievement of being through becoming relative to some categorial determinate. Heidegger criticizes this traditional concept of time as a succession of unchanging nows, each a presence in a present; time is already being. This interpretation, while unjust to Aristotle, is Kantian. Time is the positing act par excellence, where positing has the sense of existence (*exsistere*).

Action is teleological. Modern science and philosophy began with the rejection of teleology by Galileo, Bacon, Hobbes, Descartes, and Spinoza. Leibniz, however, thought it was "dangerous to hand over everything to necessity and chance" (1945, 46). There are several formulae which can express non-colinear, continuous lines that connect a set of randomly posited points, an ad hoc ordering characteristic of mechanistic explanation. Explanation, however, must be "according to a certain formula" whose expression, which "would be uniform and constant," generates the points in the order in which they were first jotted down (10). Thus Leibniz practices the art of weaving together the twin strands of spontaneous freedom and rule-governed necessity. He then says that "in whatever order God may have created the world, it would be regular and in a certain order. . . . The results of necessity and chance" can be ordered, but their formulae would lack simplicity. The formula chosen by God in creating an actual infinity of beings is "the most perfect, that is to say, one which is simplest in hypotheses and richest in phenomena" (11). The true mechanistic law presupposes purposive institution. Leibniz believed "God's decree is always to carry out his decree by the easiest and most determinate way," which, in the case of light, would be satisfied by its rectilinear propagation (39). On this basis, Fermat and Snell established the law of refraction in which rays maintained "the same proportion of sines, which in turn corresponds to the resistance medium."

Though Leibniz mentioned the advantages of a minimalist concept of action in 1707, Maupertuis gave the "metaphysical principle" of "least action" quantitative form and from it deduced the laws governing the impact of both hard and elastic bodies. The principle of least action was one of the more important results of physico-theology: "if a change occurs in nature, the quantity of action necessary for this change is the least possible." God reintroduces "again and again into nature those forces which are always dispensed with the greatest economy" (PM 1746). Though maximal and minimal principles are teleological, any deterministic law can be expressed in these terms; Voltaire and D'Alambert quickly picked up the challenge.[10] For Kant the real issue was the role of teleology in the discovery of laws, not as an independent principle in explanation.

Kant held to this "metaphysical" concept of action in his Pre-Critical writings. Unlike Leibniz's *vis viva*, a sort of expressivist *conatus*, action is an "internal principle" which, in "Living Forces" was identified with intention (*LK*, sec. 28). Action was a ground of determinations, rather than an activity like *vis viva* explaining change of determinations; these changes could not result from an internal principle but would be a consequence of other changes, such as the different positions of another moving body (IP 1973, 90).[11] In the first *Critique* this metaphysical principle of God's action becomes the transcategorial act of transcendental apperception which, in working up the manifold of sense, constitutes physical objectivity. Teleology is then given a regulative or heuristic role through the idea of reason, thus reinstituting Leibniz's perfection as a scientific ideal. *The Critique of Teleological Judgment* proposes to discern the fitness of things in a "teleological estimate." Except as a derivative notion in the category of causality— where it is a sign of substance (A 204/B 249–A 206/B 251)—action is a disjunctive transcendental. Action is thus denied an immanent role and is treated as if transcendent. This could have been avoided had he been aware of the medial character of his Productive Imagination which deconstructs the passive/active dichotomy.

Why did Kant back up ordinary time-consuming activity, the mark of substance (A 204/B 250), with an originary atemporal, transcendental correlate? Isn't ordinary action the mechanism, as Dilthey later recognized, through which agents express themselves in making history happen? He made history. What happened and the acts that made it happen were incongruent. He acknowledged historical objects, as his name for his age, "enlightenment," testifies and, unlike Hempel and his covering-law theory of history, he thought that the study of man is founded on the laws of freedom, not on physics. However, these laws express the causality of an idea and are noumenal, not phenomenal, and are without historical, i.e., temporal, form. Though his interest in physical evolution was very deep, for his nebular hypothesis extended it to the cosmos, he remained basically an ahistorical thinker who found in his *a priori* basis for physics the certainty denied by theology. The truths of mechanics hold for all empirical beings everywhere and always. What would one expect from pure space and time and a bloodless "I think . . . ?" One must turn to Husserl's "The Origin of Geometry" to see what a tradition's *arché*, in its double sense of "origin" and "principle," could have meant to Kant. These quibbles should not detract attention from the *a priori* eidetic phenomenology of motion in the *Metaphysical Foundations* which this transcendental act makes possible. Otherwise motion, the condition for the possibility of experience (*MF* 13–14), would be contingent and its explanation mechanistic.

Kant's conception of act is transcendental analogue of a more mundane concept of action. In the analytic method something is acted upon and set into play through a repeatable set-up. This "causality [finality] of a concept" is an admissible teleology; according to the third *Critique*, it is "something we experience in ourselves" (*CTJ*, 361). The technical imperative, "whoever wills the end also wills the means necessary thereto," justifies experimental activity (*Grund*. 42). To bisect a line, for example, I must draw two intersecting arcs from the end-points. Kant's postulates warrant bodily activities. That repeatable and expressive act which sets things up by a necessary rule is his model for thinking action. If so, then the essence of Kant's critical idealism is the notion of a rule-governed, and thus reiterable, act. The virtuality of an act, the repeatable performance of a same as, for example, given in a category or a postulate gives mind its limited sovereignty. That I know that I can draw a line, and it is enough to imagine myself doing so (A 120), is evidence of that virtuality. But doesn't thinking understanding in terms of rules, that is, the iterability of a same, presupposes a placeless self in featureless world, such as that given in a synopsis, and overlook contextuality? Like the word whose meaning is sententially contextual, an act has meaning only within a concrete, historical context. Understanding is dialectical, not lexical, and invites hermeneutics, not proof. Kant's association of spontaneity with rules suggests that, like the rules in dance, they be understood in medial play.

What is the nature of the spontaneously expressed rule? Its most important application is that of positing a presence, the permanent, material substance of the first Analogy. This unchanging presence is the objective correlate of unchanging time. This is the evident consequence of an ontological interpretation which thematizes Being as sempiternal, if not eternal, presence. This affective or interpretative activity is more emmenological than causal or subsumptive; Kant's ground is the groundless text of an ontological hermeneutics. Hermeneutics is a way of interpretatively understanding, not a method. In Heidegger's terms, Kant proposes that we interpret through a prior ontological understanding in the disclosive method of analysis. What shows itself is already an interpretation, rather than something to be interpreted, and presupposes a certain, generally unthematic, understanding of Being.

Unless we think of a rule as the immanent *logos* of a medial activity, like playing or speaking, then it is a rather problematic concept. Language and even apparatus that discloses in its "root unfolding"

(*Wesen* or "nature") are instances of *Vorstellungen*, rule-like representations, through which an other is announced or made effectively present and constitute a "form of life" as they play out, as the play creates the actor or the dance the dancer. One cannot try or will to speak a language as if it were something set up by following a rule; one must let it speak. Grammatical rules, like their more explicit logical and mathematical analogues, are ideal fictions which articulate and make precise a competence speakers already possess. Like loving or breathing, these are voluntary activities, not acts of an agent. Games posit players, speech speakers or thought thinkers, "beings" who can play along with and even intentionally direct the process, e.g., the game, language or thought, from whose situational dynamics (*gignesthai*, "becoming") they arise. Following the Patristic usage that begins with Cyril of Alexandria and extends through Maximus the Confessor, we will call this "substantive" agent that arises from and plays along with medial becoming a hypostasis, a person. Rather than being a self-sufficient substance "requiring nothing save itself to exist," its being is through others in participatory relations as father, daughter, friend. On the other hand, while Kant says the understanding is the faculty of rules, these play a more significant role as categorical or hypothetical imperatives in the freedom or spontaneity of the will, which at the moral level is anything but medial.

Kant says the analytic method "begins with what is conditioned and grounded and goes on to principles" (*Logic* 148). The categorially saturated potency for receiving empirical objects, the nothing or object-in-general that things, is the principle (*arché*) grounding analysis. Regarded from the understanding rather than constitutively, this object is a "Buchdahl realization" of the transcendental object, the eidetic form of any possible object. If we start from sense, then this is the reduced empirical object, the object-in-general; in this heuristic context these objects may be treated as if equivalent.[12] This transcendental object $= x$ (A 109) is the correlate of the transcendental ego's categorial act, "I think x," just as "the line" is the correlate of the postulate. Simply put, the transcendental ego's intention to its noema is never intuitive; it is mediated by categorially schematized sense through which it is intended in empirical apperception which, *qua* intentional object, has those aspects known reflexively in the Principles. As Emmanuel Levinas said of a similar context in Husserl, this objectionable intellectualism with its focus on science at the expense of other dimensions of lived experience treats both perception and judgment under objectifying acts and has the important advantage of forcing one into an intuitive approach to truth (EL 1973, 63).

Sense is given synoptically as a combinable succession. Combinatorial acts release objects that self-affectively "return" (B 68) in the veritative synthesis. In this reflexive act, one recognizes in a concept the spatial/temporal object we generate in setting out its conditions, space and time. The transcendental act is time constituting: the succession—which in discussions of constitution always presupposes the spatial manifold that one generates, for example, in counting—has the form given by the transcendental schema.

Line drawing provides the story line for Kant's phenomenological paradigm. Its phenomenology straddles the transformation from motion's origin in a subject's intention to its objective expression. The hand that draws also straddles "these exterior and interior horizons," being to itself both subject (as feeling) and object (as felt). Moreover, the incongruence between them, for we are not simultaneously touch and touched, introduces—in however truncated a form—the body. This incongruence shows that these act instants, for example, counting, have a lag-like form and that self-presence is never immediate. Moreover, if at the transcendental level act is etherealized, its necessary empirical correlate, the motility of the hand, establishes its bodily, organic correlative which Heidegger ignored (JS 1987, 1–22). A Kantian project is an act of the subject enmeshed in sensibility and, like the fingers touching themselves, precipitates a presence lagging behind its presencing act. Kant, like Merleau-Ponty and Levinas, and unlike Heidegger, leaves room for the body. Kant says, "Motion as an act of the subject (not as a determination of the object), and therefore the synthesis of the manifold in space, first produces the concept of succession . . . if we abstract from this manifold and attend to the act through which we determine the inner sense according to its form" (B 154–55). This "inner" form is given in the three-fold synthesis of reproduction (memory), apprehension (presence here and now) and "recognition in a concept" through which, as Heidegger has suggested, the future object horizon is determined (A 99–110). In and through transcendental synthesis, as in drawing a line, I receive sense as meaningful. The categorial form of this prior act determines receptivity, just as the postulate lets the drawn line be seen as the line itself.

The analytic method makes concepts analytically clear by, for example, demonstrating some property by the line; the prior synthetic method gives analysis distinct concepts such as that of the line itself to clarify (*Logic* 63). In mathematics the synthetic method constructs an object arbitrarily or *a priori* which, in representing the mathematical object, establishes its possibility and meaningfulness (A 713/B 741). Experience, in the active sense of the French *experience* ("experiment"), is possible through a prior transcendental synthesis in which sensibility is combinable in significant nomological relations that sustain natural inference because it is grounded in the "metaphysical" transcendental object (A 720/B 748). Empirical experience, in the passive sense, is thus self-affectively presenced.

Since Descartes it has been hard to defend the belief that we could come face to face; yet objects, though alienated from consciousness, could hardly be denied existence (formal reality). Why? Because things, not laws, explain. Since the object is that in which the manifold is united or, in the language of synthetic judgments, that in which representations are related "in so far as they make up one concept" (*Logic* 101), and since without objects "our modes of knowledge would be haphazard or arbitrary" (A 101), objects must be and be accessible to impart necessity to our thought. Analysis presents a combination of representations as necessary while the synthetic method justifies this in principle as a "transcendental affinity" (A 122).

2. Kant's Ontological Hermeneutics

THE POSSIBILITY OF OBJECTS is founded on the self-reflexivity of praxis. To speak of the "constitution" of an object is to impute to receptive sensibility an *a priori* stratum of interpretative or informing spontaneity. "I see a book"; something announcing itself in passively received sensa is given as meaning the book, the empirical object meant by the colors and shapes, and so forth. The book is not Yeats's "ghostly spume" playing across the surface of a noumenal paradigm. "The distinction between the concept of the thing in itself and appearance "is not objective but merely subjective . . . it is not another object but another aspect of the representation with regard to the same object" as apt for our determination and as completely determined in Divine intuition (*Op. Post.* 653).[13] The transcendental object, like a transcendental, ranges over all objects, noumenal and phenomenal; it is the ultimately reduced ontological profile of any possible object. The "something announcing itself" which gives itself and stands over against me (*Gegenstand*) is, eidetically reduced, this minimal, non-categorially determinate *it* which is neither a cause or quantity, a shape or intensity, even if these predicates are its intrinsic determinates. In perceptual synthesis this object is realized, rendered more determinate; if the context is empirical, it functions as a "transcendental matter" (A 143/B 182) to be determined as the object-in-general.[14] In a verificatory judgment a sense (temporal) manifold comes to a stand as a categorial realization of the transcendental object. The empirical object is the determinate way in which this manifold is temporally united. In the now familiar terms of Husserl's passive, perceptual synthesis, successive sensa are received as adumbrations or perspectives *of* the intended noematic object, the identity pole that brings the flux of inner sense to a stand through recognition in a unifying object (*Gegenstand*). This constructed objectivity in turn affects the self which constituted it. This noematic or intentional object is nothing but the object intended by transcendental schema and is known as an object only through questions put to empirical receptivity. Analysis questions this structure. In language suggestive of Plato's schematically or stereometrically informed receptacle, Kant says that the pure schema, "in its application to appearances and their mere form, is an art concealed in the depths of the human soul, whose real modes of activity nature is hardly likely ever to allow us to discover" (A 141/B 180). Kant's transcendental schemata are "transcendental determinations of time" (A 138/B 177) which can reach out to beings "due to my generating time" (A 143/B 182) in a transcendental synthesis in order to let me receive them. This is "the pure synthesis, determined by a rule of unity, in accordance with concepts" (A 142/B 181), that releases objects as determinable, as drawing releases the determinable "line itself" to be determined in a proof. This formal, rule-governed activity determines how time is taken up and is, as formal, the prior structure of noetic adumbration. "Since this form does not represent anything save in so far as something is [respectively] posited in the mind, it [i.e., time] can be nothing but the mode in which the mind is affected by its own activity (namely, through the positing of its representation [i.e., the object in general]), and is so affected by itself" (B 67–68). The object that "gathers" is the synthetic, temporal form of the *logos,* the transcendental site of pure synthesis. Time is the ground of empirical reality. It is also the ground of meaning and truth.

Time is generated through an atemporal act that is not itself temporal as a flowing, rational continuum divided by the spectator's acts. This thesis requires that concepts be *reflective* in order that the many be compared and grasped as one. The Platonist, on the contrary, understands that participation articulates reflexive temporality; a *theoria* sees in acting on something by grasping sense understandingly in formal unities. The squarish schema, shape, the teacher draws on the board is recognized by her students as a square, a morphe or form. The form shows forth; things are epiphanies, not instances of universals. This practical reflexivity which spans ontological gaps, and not the causes in which Aristotle thinks craft, is a primary reason for Plato's choice of *techné* as a paradigm (*Char.* 162E–64E). Reflective apperception, which takes as its object the relation between the subject and the object, leads to the absurdity of either an infinite regress or a self-referential relation (166E–69C). In order to make something, intention must be directed to something in the world; one reaches out to a possibility as one sets oneself to be the occasion of its appearing. This intention reflexively returns as done. Just as the thing made is the maker's measure, so the deed measures the doer. My intention to write this comes back to me on the screen so that I can monitor and correct what appears according to my intention, in both senses of intention, that is, as meant and as the aim of projects. Looked at reflectively, as a spectator might regard it, time seems to flow from past to future. Thus the three-fold Kantian synthesis generates continuous time. Apperception, as in Husserl, thematizes the subject-object relation, just as the concept thematizes the many as one. Reflexive temporality is, as we know from Heidegger, ecstatic. It is what I am; unless I can return to myself, I am comatose or dead. The future comes back laggingly to the present as its retentive (Husserl) or reproduced (Kant) past.

The relation between the time of memory, apprehension, and recognition, the personal time of sensibility which McTaggart called the A-series, and world time, the McTaggart's B-series chronology ordering events with respect to before and after, brings into focus this ontological hermeneutic. The B-series is the "time" of the understanding that both satisfies variables in mechanics and is time as it might be known—but as a well-founded phenomenon probably isn't—to a Leibnizian God to whom beings would be transparently present and for whom all their predicates would be analytic. Kant's daily walks became legendary. As such, he is an episode in world history. He was also the embodied individual who traced the natural history of the solar system and saw space and time as "infinite given" magnitudes (A 25/ B40, A 32/ B 48). Time in the B-series does not change; it harbors the meaning of being, presence, and thus by treating time as a kind of being, Kant takes back the promise that our knowledge must be subject to time (A 99). Does his incarnate three-fold synthetic constitution of time and space under clearly subjective, A-series conditions of perception, memory, and anticipation generate time within an unchanging time (B 58)? Suppose one were to die? Wouldn't Being then be time? If analysis and synthesis are incarnate acts grounded in a transcendental ego and if this same ego *qua* "knower-in-general" which, qua transcendental apperception, lies behind the omnitemporal "is" grants a synopsis through which space and time are given as unlimited, then Kant must be man and God, mortal and everlasting, the constitutive ground of individuality and world. Isn't this odd?

3. Nominal Essence

T H O U G H   I D E A L I S M   A L W A Y S   R E C O G N I Z E S that "inner" and "outer" are distinctions within one "reflective" experience, they are not wholly same; one then must mark out such differences as thought/ being, spontaneous/receptive, form/matter, *a priori/ a posteriori,* private/public and fling the bridge of judgment across this gulf of one's own making. Bradley's definition of judgment as the "ascription of ideal content to reality" encounters only assimilable ideality (FB 1928, 622–30).[15] Rather than deconstruct differences, idealism reconciles them.

Aristotle's choice of predication, S is P, as a metaphysical and logical paradigm was supposed to solve all outstanding metaphysical problems and retain Parmenides' promise that thought and Being are same. When the subject term S is said of an "a this" (*todi ti*) or primary *ousia,* a presumptively unchanging being is captured for thought and expressed in such predicables as genus, species, differentia, and property. Unchanging S can take on accidentally contrary P's even if no P changes. The necessities of essence preserve S's self-identity, guarding its portals and holding at bay the disruptive flux of vagrant P's. Heraclitus has been domesticated to Parmenidian intuitions. Essence, though inseparable from S and expressed in its predicables, lends itself to logical formulae by which thought can monitor the necessities. In this exalted case of essential predication, the copula is the sign of identity with an ontological weight on the substance characterizing predicate. In asserting of something S that it is (same as) P, whatever it may be besides this is lost in the oblivion of non-Being. The predicative sense of *is* preserves the integrity of S and allows these ones to be members of a logical community characterized by P. The *Categories* assert a homology between the real "not predicable of" order and "predicable of" logical order (3a 1–5) and this possibility of a logic of truth may account for its attraction to Kant, who possessed both a Greek and Latin text. Nevertheless, the assertion of the homology between first and second *ousia* ("substance") denatures *ousia,* which originally had a sense close to *physis.* As "self-gathering emergence into unconcealment," *physis* was expressed in what counts as a medial doublet, "a doctor doctoring himself" (*De Phys.* 199b 30). As in the medial, Patristic *hypostasis,* a presence in the form of a nominal "person," arises from the presencing which it, to a point, controls. In Scholasticism, however, inseparable essence is separated and "existence" become a predicate. It was left to Descartes to discover the gulf between the logical order of consciousness and the real order of existing extensivity. The conscious subject now houses the wandering predicates and must somehow anchor them in a space and time which, Kant says, "are nothing but relations" (B 67). The condition for one's durative self-sameness lies in finding relata, usually understood as a material substances, on which it can anchor itself. These relata, according to the first of the Principles, are sempiternal, Parmenidian, material substances somehow endowed with dynamical properties. *Physis* has now become "physics" and nature "the existence of things, considered as existence determined according to universal laws" (*Prol.* 294). The immanent order of *physis* has been replaced by an impositional physics via the impositional man who replaces the impositional God whose creative intuition has given way to "representational thinking."

To make this work, Kant has to inject something like essence into things as the guardian of their necessities. Hume's empirical affinities threaten to lapse into a Heraclitian flux, for example, the sometimes red and sometimes black cinnabar (A 100): "Everything could be situated in such disorder that, e.g., in the succession of appearances nothing offered itself that suggested a rule of synthesis—and thus would correspond to the concept of cause and effect—so that the concept would be entirely empty, null and without meaning" (A 90/B 123). Something like "essence" must be injected from the side of the logical order by means of the forms of judgment which, *qua* logic can express the necessities and, *qua* apophantic judgment, reach out to existence. The nominal essence, the set of predicates characterizing the structure of something if it is to exist arrived at in analysis and synthesis will do the job Aristotle assigned to his essentialist realism and serves as a warrant for "as if" analytically necessary statements which, nevertheless, remain empirically corrigible in a non-corrigible second-order logic of truth. A material object is a shape, colored, weighs something or other, and so forth. Hume's skepticism is thus limited to predicates that are independent of the existence of something and will not extend to causality or substantiality.

Aristotle approaches synthesis in the *Posterior Analytics* through the demonstrative syllogism which, in Barbara, contains an essential definition as the minor premises. Given such a definition, Kant thought one could in principle arrive at a complete concept by a precise demonstration of all of its properties (A 241). Since we have real definitions only in mathematics, properties must be "grounded in a transcendental condition" (A 106), not in the explication of essence, "the first ground of possibility" (*Logic* 144). Natural knowledge depends upon this "transcendental condition," the ground form of empirical synthesis whose spatial-temporal structure, the manner in which things are experienced and recognized, is determined by a transcendental synthesis. "The pure receptive act of representation must give itself something capable of being represented" (MH 1990, 48). Though contingent on sensation and, therefore, lacking the arbitrariness of mathematical synthesis, an ontological understanding expressed in the transcendental object informs this creative synthesis which can "serve only for the [ontic] unity of the manifold [property ascription, causality, and the like] in sensible intuition" (A 251).[16] As a consequence, appearances will have the necessary "Aristotelian" homology with thought relative to syntactical form. Qualities adduced in analysis are marks of substance fixed through corrigible analytic judgments; gold *is* a yellow metal.

By a judgmental, predicative interpretation of Being as enduring presence in every associated present enacted through self-reflexive syn-

thesis, beings appear as interconnected, accessible, measurable, enduring objects. "The logical function of judgment," Kant says, is the
"possibility of things themselves" (A 242). This scientific realism is a
fundamental interpretation of Being founded on the paradigm of
judgment. Without concepts through which they are interpreted, percepts are blind. Kant constrains us to one particular interpretation
supported, on the one hand, by logic as a necessity of thought and, on
the other, by a respectable materialism. We can explain and predict,
given this mechanism, and, as the nineteenth centruy discovered, eliminate as evident nonsense its metaphysical foundation. Yet by showing
that this mechanistic ideology is an interpretation, like a Kuhnian paradigm, imaginatively projected as a world, Kant can also show that it
is inadequate. In the following pages I will sustain and support this
interpretation of Kant and its implications for the sciences of man.
Until now these sciences have been mostly inductive, thanks to the
empiricist's confusion that all science is inductive.

St. Thomas says "that which first falls under apprehension is Being, the understanding of which is included in all things whatsoever a
man apprehends" (*ST* II, I, q. 94, a. 2). That apprehension need not
be Parmenidian. Heidegger is perhaps the first to grasp the explicit ontological import of this formula; Being as apprehended determines
how things are ontically understood. Being understood by Kant as
permanent presence is made thematic in the relation between the categories and the constitution of continuous time through the ontology
implicit in the object-in-general.

For Kant self-consciousness is always through alien alterity, the
self-affection thesis whose import becomes evident in the Refutation
of Idealism. Self-knowledge requires material substance. Concern for
an ordered, coherent, enduring self of "fundamental ontology" lies
behind this interpretation. Did Kant really have such a concern, did he
really think the self about to collapse into an *apeiron,* kaleidoscopic
consciousness? Apparently he did. The invariant form he gave his life,
his childhood destitution, his obsession with regularities (made famous
by Euler's topological problem concerning the bridges crossed on his
daily walks) was not that of a man secure in his being. His moral rigor
is far from the contingencies of Aristotelian *phronesis.* We are told
that he kept his wealth in gold under his bed. Love, which as Augustine said, lets beings be is replaced by legalistic judgment and attendant laws, witnesses, rights, and the like. Logic had to certify what the
logos could no longer gather. Why? Because God, the rational grounds
of being, order, and truth, is no longer accessible; man must take over
God's role as the guardian of Being. Mind, "the faculty of rules,"
must do what physico-theology claimed to do, provide this ground.
The human mind is now "the law giver of nature" (A 126). Hume

had absented objects. One had to constitute them in a way that veri-fies judgments in a world from which God and real essence, the guardian of the integrity of beings, had fled.

Phenomenology, as understood by Kant, justifies the transforma-tion of private experience into knowledge of the objective, physical world and will find this in judgment which makes such linkages. The Transcendental Analytic, the heart of this enterprise, takes as its spe-cial problem our right (A 84/B 116–A 85/B 117) to the "representa-tion of the unity of consciousness of several representations, or the representation of their relation so far as they make up one concept" (*Logic* 101). Judgments link concepts ("representations of representa-tions") and join them to percepts ("representations"), unifying con-sciousness and enabling it to grasp a world. "All given concepts, be they given *a priori* or a posteriori, can be defined only through analy-sis. For given [a posteriori] concepts can be made distinct by making their marks successively clear. If all marks of a given concept are made clear [possible only through a knowledge of real essences], the concept becomes distinct. . . . Since one cannot be certain by a proof whether all marks of a given concept have been exhausted by a complete analy-sis, all analytic definitions must be held to be uncertain" (*Logic* 144). Only a synthetically grounded metaphysics gives certainty which is, in turn, contingent on sense already understood through the noumenally signified. The noumenal world is Kant's refuge.

Though space and time are intuitively given as determinable infin-ities, sensory intuition never confronts an object in the virtual infinity of its detail as it would be given through the creative intuition of (an Augustinian) God (B 71–72). In the 1770 *Dissertation* Kant thought we had access to this intelligible world in non-sensuous intuition that reappears in the first *Critique* as noumenal "in the negative sense" (B 307). As such it is the demonic limit governing the incompletable pre-dicative experience of empirical objects (A 255/B 311). We have to satisfy ourselves with something less than a total experience if we are to make these objects known. We must then intuit an object through its mark "which makes up part of its representation, or . . . a par-tial representation so far as it is considered a cognitive ground for the whole representation" (*Logic* 58). An archeologist sees gold in the glittering yellow, the mark of its presence, while a certain purple tells the chemist that he has successfully synthesized a manganese com-pound. Beings of a certain kind have been recognized through their marks, relata in sense recognition that enable the thing to be under-standingly seen by a *theoria*. Theory will get it wrong. Descartes, Locke, and subsequent neurophysiology assume that yellow and pur-ple are mental events contingently linked by the brain to physical events neither yellow nor purple. The monadic color predicate must be attached to mind. We no longer see what we see. Kant, who doesn't altogether surrender the sovereignty of *theoria* over beings to a theory about beings, can help get things straight. We need to understand why a manufacturer of the pigment vermillion would confidently set about to produce cinnabar.

Assume that "yellow" is not a vagrant predicate of "gold" and that the judgment, "Gold is yellow," is not synthetic *a posteriori;* then yellow is a mark of gold and pertains to its nominal or logical essence: "To the logical essence belongs nothing but the cognition of those predicates in respect to which an object is determined in its concept" (*Logic* 61). If yellow is a mark, and since its concept is a rule, an "I can," that allows me to display gold through it, then the secondary quality language Kant sometimes employs is misleading. Is there a way through these ambiguities to something that might be true?

"There is," Kant says, "a Transcendental synthesis [framed] from concepts alone, a synthesis with which the philosopher alone is competent to deal; it relates only to a thing in general as defining the conditions under which the perception of it can belong to possible experience" (A 719/B 747). Like mathematical knowledge, this synthesis lets the universal to be "seen in the particular." This is possible since we "construct the concept . . . by exhibiting *a priori* the object . . . without having borrowed the pattern from any experience . . . that corresponds to the concept." Philosophical knowledge "considers the particular only in the universal" and is therefore reflective (A 712–14/B 741–42). Transcendental synthesis makes possible the categorial formalities "seen in the particular" which is now the schema of the universal. This overlap of mathematical and philosophical synthesis insures that particular, contingent empirical laws instance universal laws which makes nature possible, and these laws are *a priori.* Empirical laws can exist and be discovered only through experience, and indeed in consequence of the original laws through which experience itself first becomes possible" (A 216/B 263). Do entities instance universal laws which explain even their existence? Or do things explain, as Aristotle, Whitehead, and Nancy Cartwright argue? Could Kant make room for a synthesis in which appearances are so constituted that, at the most fundamental level, they could express original laws. Wasn't this immanence the point of essence? Nominal essence relativizes this expression to changing, empirical and, therefore, contingent contexts which in turn have their condition in "original laws." Assuming for the sake of argument that Newton's inverse square law is original, changes in the gravitational field in non-local applications of Galileo's law of falling bodies would result in different, even falsifying, phenomena within an invariant Newtonian rubric. So too, to take a case closer to home, would be changes in Kepler's descriptions that express more basic

Newtonian laws. These laws are, however, not original; Kant's *Universal Natural History* suggests that these laws are evolving expressions of a more original dynamics. Things explain. As things change, so too do the laws which are statistical and model-theoretic descriptions of their behavior.

Continental philosophy has taken its lead from Plato, not Aristotle, though it has stressed the immanent rather than separated status of form or structure. Though Kant reads Plato in terms of the separationism of the middle dialogues and gives a noumenal interpretation to the Platonic *idea,* analysis will lead him, as it lead Plato, to "see form in the fact" (ANW 1978, 20). Understanding neither operates in a separated realm of entities or adds anything to empirical objects but "determines a new dimension of being" which, as Levinas remarks, is inconceivable without the sensible objects upon which it is founded. (EL 1973, 82). In a similar context, Husserl remarks that any categorial increments would result in "a new object in the primary real sense. Evidently the outcome of a categorial act, e.g., one of collecting or relation, consists in an objective "view" of what is primarily intuited, a view that can only be given in . . . a [perceptually] founded act, so that the thought of a straightforward percept of the founded [e.g., categorially determined] object, or its straightforward intuition, is a piece of nonsense" (EH 1970b, 820). Analysis, phenomenologically construed, lets beings appear in their properties. The distance between Plato and Kant begins to disappear. Of course Kant's transcendental imagination provides the conditions for presencing that Plato, at least in the later dialogues, assigns to *apeiron gignesthai,* whose original, eventual temporality grounds the temporalization of conceptuality which Kant proposes in the opening of the Deduction (A 99). Kant reassigns the creative role he attributed to Plato's ideas to the pure concepts of the understanding, the immanent formalities of the imagination are the logos of presencing. If we attend to the ontically determinate appearance, to the things themselves, there is no need to resort to conceptuality for the nomic glue favored by analytic philosophers.

Particular empirical laws have a categorial ground and are not inductive.[17] I feel the stone warm in the sun's light; using proper controls, I can act on the system, for example, shelter the stone from the sun, and adduce from the "perceptual judgment," the stone warms, the "judgment of experience," the sun is the cause of warming (*Prol.* sec. 17; also B 11–13). Concepts of law-like ties are formed by reflecting on the results of analysis, as if interpreting nature's text, presumably that of a wise and economical author who wrote it as if in the categorial language in which it is addressed. Hypotheses are formulated and tested in trying to make sense of what appears within what is taken to be an overarching and even hierarchical connectedness whose traces have been elicited in experimental inquiry. In the third *Critique's* "teleological estimate," it is assumed that even if nature cannot now be pieced together, as a text analogue nature has a coherent and connected sense. Hypotheses are stories that put it together, as I shall show, in mix of natural (essential) recognitions and conventional (nominal) assumptions. The movement is from nature as theoria's reflexive text to a theory developed in reflection. Texts invite interpretations, modes of seeing as, rather than subsumptive procedures, though these too play a role in the final theoretical outcome.[18] Transcendental synthesis supplies objective conditions which guide inquiry and make proof possible (MH 1967, 180) by ontologically grounding analysis; what is unconcealed (*aletheia*) has a metaphysical, not merely an epistemic, warrant. Beings disclose, and sometimes hide, themselves as they are categorially examined to make possible the analytic unity of consciousness (B 133).

The unification through which this unity is gained depends on judgment, "the unity of the act of bringing various representations under one common representation" (A 68/B 93). If by analysis "all marks are made successively clear" (*Logic* 142), the concept is said to be distinct and then the mark is a criterion for "recognition in a concept" (A 103). The haphazardness of sensuous receptivity, compared by Aristotle to an army in rout (*Post. Anal.* 100a 9–13), comes to a stand in the logical necessities of the concept through which the many are thought as one. The concept's schema makes objects present in their absence and grounds our transcendence from here and now into all times and places. Transcendental Logic turns *physis* upside down: we lawgivers gather nature into presence. The archaic Greek theme of *logos,* in which *physis* gathers and lays itself out, is now to be understood as a function of subjectivity.

The formation of the corrigible, analytic concepts necessary for analytic unity presupposes synthetic unity (B 133). Synthesis makes a distinct object whose concept is made distinct by analysis (*Logic* 64). This "distinct object" is the "eject" of transcendental synthesis, "the result of the power of the imagination, a blind but indispensable function of the soul, without which we would have no knowledge whatsoever but of which we are scarcely ever conscious" (A 78/B 103), lets sense represent (presence) by informing it with this transcendental object. We see the universal in the thing under the auspices of the transcendental object so that we can recognize something in its concept. Synthesis is the ground for both meaning and truth. Kant roots this act in creative intuition and its relation to concepts, ideas, and essences.

Kant's methodology develops around recognition, the veritative synthesis which is the term of his analytic method and, therefore, our "egress" into phenomenal nature understood as a casual nexus of world-preserving, material substances. Recognition carries in this constructive and ontological weight lacking in Plato's analytic dialectic where, through *anamnesis,* "right opinions" (*Meno* 85E) arise which then must be secured lest they walk away like Daedalus' statues (97Dff.). Transcendental synthesis supplies an *a priori* ontic horizon that makes recognition possible: "Actual experience, which is constituted by apprehension, association (reproduction), and finally recognition of appearances, contains in recognition, the last and highest of these merely empirical elements of experience, certain concepts which render possible the formal unity of experience, and therewith all objective validity (truth) of empirical knowledge" (A 125). Kant's central issues cluster around his intellectualistic overdetermination of intuition. The matter of sense must be given intelligible form.

4. *Creative Synthesis: Ideas and Concepts*

KANT'S BIAS TOWARDS INTUITION has its original in God's creative intuition, which is "such as can give us the existence of its object" (B 72). If God's intuition gives world, how does one go to such totalities when phenomenal "existence can never be presented in an *a priori* intuition" (*MF* 469)? "For were I to think of an intelligence which was itself intuitive (as, for example, a divine understanding which should not represent to itself given objects, but through whose representation [idea, the presencing power of pure intellection] the objects should be given or produced), the categories would have no meaning whatsoever in respect to such a mode of knowledge" (B 145). As patterned modes of spatial-temporal synthesis, the categories would have no application to a being who intuited all time in a single now. God would have "an understanding which through its self-consciousness could supply to itself the manifold of intuition . . . an intuition, that is to say, through whose representation [archetypal idea] the objects of the representation should at the same time exist" (B 138–39). Concepts are necessary conditions for phenomenal existence, the "beingness" of non-self-presencing *physis* to a knower. Though the "concept may be as imperfect or as obscure as it wants . . . its form is something universal and serves as a rule" (A 113). The ectypal aspect of a concept allows me to represent and recognize on the synthetic ground reflexively constructed by the pure archetypal of categorial concepts (*conceptus reflectentes*) which "have such ruling unities as their unique content (MH 1990, 50).

"Existence" is not one of the meanings of the Greek *einai,* "to be." The Latin *exsistere,* from whence "existence" derives its force, is almost the antithesis of *einai.* Charles Kahn says

The intrinsically stable and lasting character of Being in Greek . . . which makes it so appropriate as an object of knowing and a correlative of truth—distinguishes it in a radical way from our modern notion of existence, in so far as the latter has preserved . . . the semantic flavor of the Latin *exsistere* . . . Etymological, the latter suggests a stepping out or stepping forth, a coming into being, an emergence out of a dark background into the light of day . . . the sense of existence was originally acquired by the verb in the perfect: the existent was literally conceived as "what has emerged," *id quod exstitit*. Now what has emerged . . . is literally the contingent, what might not have emerged and what might easily have disappeared once more. Under the influence of the Biblical [sic] notion of creation, and the more radical distinction of essence and existence that follows from it in the medieval doctrine of created beings, these linguistic connotations of *exsistere* were preserved and developed at the theoretical level in the concept of a state of being which is inherently provisional and precarious, hovering on the verge of nothingness. (CK 1966, 255–56)

Having dismissed God from nature, the mind must sustain phenomenal being against the threat of its own nothingness. On Kant's rather neo-Platonic version of Plato, ideas contain or entail their instances and thus originate their objects in all their analytic detail. So too our originary intuition of space and time is strangely idea-like; it contains within it a "given . . . infinite" manifold of spaces and times (A 25/B 39, A 32/B 47).[19] Unlike ideas, concepts do not contain their instances. To this extent human intuition is creative. In the *Dissertation* Kant said that "time is a unique and unchangeable infinite in which all things are and endure which is the phenomenal eternity of the general cause, God" (410). As "substrates of the intellect" (405), space and time are created analogues of Newton's "God's sensoria."

    According to this pre-critical doctrine, there is in the intelligible world an actual infinity of substances and their states (*Diss.* 388) whose creative cause is a "singular divine intuition which, as the principle of objects, is an archetype" (387). This archetype must be the source of the noumenal world of things-in-themselves. Since Leibniz said that only an actual infinity of substances could express the reality of God as their cause and since Kant's problem was to reconcile this infinity with finite, temporal understanding, we can appreciate his remark that "the *Critique of Pure Reason* is, after all, the real apologia for Leibniz, even against his followers, who extol him with praise but who do him no honor" (*Ak.* viii, 250). There are traces of this creative intuition in Kant's philosophy of mathematics and ethics. Elsewhere ideas appear as regulative ideals or originate an objective and unconditioned unity too wide for understanding (A 407/B 433).

The moral ideas may ground both the phenomenal world and Kant's phenomenology. According to the ethics, the will is completely and unconditionally determined by reason *a priori,* an absolute ground which analysis can never make available to conditional, ectypal understanding (A 483/B 511, A 569/B 597). With an approving glance at Plato, Kant says "ideas are operative causes (of actions and their objects)" (A 317/B 374). "Sometimes we find, or believe that we find, that the ideas of reason have in actual fact proved their causality in respect to the actions of men" (A 550/B 587). The moral idea constitutes its object, that is, its freedom, in the law I give myself (B 427-28). These laws command an action as unconditionally, that is, as rationally, necessary out of no other motive than respect for the law. Everyone "must conceive of himself as giving in all the maxims of his will universal laws, so as to judge himself and his actions from this point of view—this conception leads to another which depends on it—the kingdom of ends. By kingdom I mean the union of every rational being in a system of common laws . . . in which one must treat himself and all others *never merely as means* but in every case *at the same time as ends in themselves*" (*Grund.* 51-52). One cannot determine the possibility of such an action by an imaginative schema. Action for duty's sake is possible only through participation ("causality of reason") in archetypal ideas by which we presence the will to itself in ideal form, a possibility which is made determinate by the Typic of Pure Practical Reason (*CPR* 159-63). Granted a world of empirical laws, can I also will the proposed moral maxim to be universally legislative? Clearly, the idea of freedom has a world-engendering form. This world, according to the doctrine of the Antinomies, is clearly too wide for the understanding. World is reason's ambivalent gift. Since this moral law is determined within as universal and necessary, the idea of a moral world is ontologically prior to sense constructions even though, in order to determine its possibility, we must turn to sense for an analogue in the typic to the schema of empirical concepts. "It is allowable to use the system of the world of sense as a type of a supersensible system of things, provided I do not transfer to the latter the intuitions and what depends on them, but merely apply it to the form of law in general, the notion of which occurs in even the commonest use of reason but cannot be known *a priori* for any other purpose than the practical use of reason. . . . Of all the supersensible nothing is known except freedom through the moral law" (*CPR* 162). Perhaps this supersensible, which is "too large for concepts" and of which—like the transcendental object—we know nothing, is the source of an ideal that gives sensibility the sense (*Sinn*) that it is within a physical totality, a cosmos. Is this kingdom of ends in the moral world, the legitimate domain of reason, the origin of the world-concept?[20] The *Dissertation* suggests that participation in the noumenal can be "symbolically cognized" (396). Through "an analagon of the schema of sensibility" (A 665/B 693), empirical intuition can be "provided with situations which could serve as models by which the ideas in question become comprehensible"(RW 1975, 70). The third *Critique* offers, together with the sublime, the symbol that, at the level of ideas, replaces concepts (HG 1975, 67–68)[21] and doubtless tells us more than we can say.

The gap between what we can think and what we can understand is perspicuously raised by Kant's moral philosophy. Understanding presupposes either abduction from inductions or the habitualities of "empirical affinity" which analysis seeks to render distinct. In this sense concepts are ectypal, derived from experience. A concept refers to but does not contain its object for the "reason that it is not original, that is, is not such as can itself give us the existence of its object—a mode of intuition which, so far as we can judge, can belong only to the primordial being" (B 72). In expressively presencing through a schema a particular representation of the concept, we share with God an originary power; intuition gives and limits this capacity. Human understanding is in the service of intuition. Since except in mathematics we do not have non-empirical intuitions, we can never understand non-empirical objects. Kant says that God (B 71), freedom and morality (B xxix) and things in themselves (B xxvi) allow of being thought though never understood in his rather positivistic sense of "understanding." The *Dissertation* says we can think the actual infinite (388 n.).

Reason or thought is prior to understanding: its theme, as we know from the Transcendental Dialectic, is knowledge of the world through God. Even if empirical objects cannot be exhibited corresponding to this knowledge in intuition, the noumenal realm seems to confer meaning on empirical objects in which, as a symbol, it is mediately presented. Sensible things can symbolically present the supersensible moral idea which only reason can think. "Since the symbolic is only a mode of the intuitive" (*CAJ* 351), the idea will be presented in a sensuous intuition. For instance, the shepherd caring for his sheep "presentifies" Christ as the good shepherd. It is as if the sensuous material were seized by the idea and transformed into a symbol as the vehicle for its own expression. Symbols express the constitutive idea. The idea is not inferred from things; having the idea enables us to see or constitute certain things as its symbolic presentations. Thought may lend an original power otherwise lacking to schematic understanding. Because the noumenal thing-in-itself is cointended in empirical synthesis it makes sense to speak of the Ideal of Reason which proposes a system of nature embodying Leibniz's idea of perfection. Since this ideal is embodied in the transcendental object which then sets to understanding the task of completeness, intending something through this object intends the noumenal without itself being noumenal (A 253). Mathematics also contains a residue of creative intuition. Without the lingering traces of Plato's ideas, the constructive concepts would never begin to produce a physical cosmology. There may be a gain. Plato can only make world thematic in myth. On Kant's understanding, however, ideas propose such an infinite horizon and enable us to thematize things as part of a world. Hegel returns to dialectic to articulate this sense of the whole without which inquiry will languish in trivia. Given the choice between myth, which is inherently cosmogonic, and dialectic, perhaps Kant's is the better way.

Construction winnows real from apparent possibility. Kant believed that while non-Euclidian geometry, like the actual infinite or God, could be thought, only Euclid's could be represented (GM 1961, 21–25). Mathematical knowledge is contingent on the possibility of pure presencing: "the object that it thinks it exhibits *a priori* in an intuition" (A 729/B757; also *Prol.* 269, 281). By means of what is seen or intended concerning mathematical objects through this schematic image, one can form new *a priori* synthetic concepts. Synthetic concepts arise from this originary presencing through which something is present to understanding which could never be present to sense per se. The line is present in its drawn schema, the universal in the particular in a disclosive and participatory (*metalambano,* literally "the beyond possessed in the midst of") rather than subsumptive relation. The possibility of synthesis is the basis for representation.

In projects the imagination provides "circumspective" sensibility with its latent schematic imaging, "a support for becoming intent on something, picturing to oneself possible actuality" (MH 1962, 262). Without this forehaving that lets us envisage possibility as if actual, sense would be blind and understanding empty. "That which so determines the manifold of appearance that allows of being ordered in certain relations, I term the form of appearance" (A 20/B 34). This expressed form, that of the archetypal idea of the *Gegenstand* as such, otherwise known as "the transcendental object = *x,*" is a Nothing that lets beings appear. Though the concept of existence cannot be constructed (A 720/B 748), given the receptivity of this or that series of sensations, "we can determine our concepts in an *a priori* intuition, in as much as we can create for ourselves, in space and time, through a homogeneous synthesis, these objects themselves—these objects being viewed simply as quanta" (A 723/B 751). The pure concepts are the self-reflexive forms of action whose ejects are brought to judgment as past, present, and future moments of the object in general. The thesis that time "can be nothing but the mode in which the mind is affected by its own activity"(B 68) is the empirical analogue of the pure act of line-drawing. In drawing a line, we see what we have done, know what we are doing, and because of this recognition, know that our intention is being carried out. The pure "I think . . ." has, like the intention to draw, an originary mode *a priori* in the constitution of time, while the empirical "I think . . ." receives sensibility through this originary temporality as meaningful. For the Platonist, concepts mediate and constitute a same with the idea's ineluctable alterity and fecundity and, as noetic, let aspects of the thing be seen. The idea retains its radical alterity and, thought, because it cannot encompass its object, will be subjected to an inherent "Socratic" critique. Kant lacks a transcending ground for empirical alterity and its conceptual correlate; what had mediated to the Platonist must now have a creative function, constructing what Plato could not accommodate. Concepts are rooted in the fecundity of the productive imagination and, as iterable "I can's," are rules for experimental presencing. Because an empirical object is *qua* presence an expression of a transcendental or ontological understanding, the horizon within which it arises neutralizes it, deprives it of a site, and lets it be anamnestically reduced to a same (EL 1985, 43–44.). The Critique will have to come from excluded reason.

5. Qualities

THE STATUS OF SECONDARY QUALITIES in Kant poses, Ingrid Stadler confesses, many "vexing questions."[22] The phenomenology Kant founds is likely to flounder in a psychology of inner sense unless it can be set free from a Lockean bias towards primary qualities which would render much of the natural world inaccessible. In this section I shall attempt to free him with a minimum of sophistry. Cartesian indubitability is not an issue for Kant.[23] He restores confidence through a scientific methodology that, as Hegel said of experience, is its own criterion. Qualities are often marks in analytic judgments; "Gold is a yellow metal" (*Prol.* 267). The discovery of black gold, like Cook's discovery of black swans, would change its nominal definition. We are contingently tied to a nomological nature often accessible only through secondary qualities. Unless the phenomenological experience of these is accepted as primary, constructions will not reach out towards world.

Though yellow is a mark and, therefore, an access condition to gold, it is seems to be a secondary quality which the Transcendental Aesthetic attributes to inner sense: "Colors are not properties of bodies to the intuition of which they are attached, but only modifications of the sense of sight, which is affected in a certain manner by light" (A 28). One sees, not gold, but rather a yellow, private datum, a dream, contingently linked with its conjectured bearer. Theoretical dualism questions *theoria*'s doxic disclosures. Gorgias, who taught Meno to explain seen colors by unseen and unknown "effluences," reemerges from the ashes of time.

While sight is the threshold of outer sense, the blind and deaf can still have the possibility of a significant relation to the world. From what we know about those who have regained sight, it is hard to say just what this comes to. Through a free, motile access to extension, a succession of tactile and kinesthetic data "in inner sense" is schematized as a coexistent manifold and recognized as a spatial object (in tactile, temporal rather than visual, coexistent space). This would be a quantitative access required by some applications of the Axioms of Intuition. "All bodies are extended" is analytic only because it is founded on synthetic *a priori* conditions for a coexistent multiplicity, as in the Principle of Extensive Magnitude. Like the line drawing postulate, which determines the *a priori* possibility of a punctal manifold, action expressing a category determines *a priori* loci for motility: "We cannot think a line without *drawing* it or a circle without *describing* it. . . . Motion, as an act of the subject (not a determination of an object), and therefore the synthesis of the manifold in space first produces the concept of succession—if we abstract from this manifold and attend solely to the act through which we determine the inner sense according to its form" (B 155). Motile acts, not sense data, determine the possibility of extension. Just as presencing a line does not depend on the color of the line being drawn, neither does the spatial "figurative synthesis" depend on colored figures: "Taste and colors are not necessary conditions under which alone objects can be for us objects of the senses" (A 29).

Granted action and its motile expression as this non-contingent link between inner and outer, a qualitative science is possible. Color is such a link. Though Helen Keller schematized a tactile succession as a world of coexistent objects, it is doubtful that she could transmute this succession into concepts of spatial objects. John Hull, speaking as one who lost his sight late in life, says that "the sense of being in a place is less pronounced. . . . Space is reduced to one's own body, and the position of the body is known not by the objects which have been passed, but by how long it has been in motion. Position is thus measured by time . . . for the blind, people are not known unless they speak. . . . People are in motion, they are temporal, they come and they go. They come out of nothing; they disappear" (OS 1993, 65). Ms Keller's concept of a person must have arisen from touch and suggests a more primitive space of encounter within which meaning is given, in this case by another's hands. Since she had words for, but no images or concepts of, color, she could not have been an analytical chemist.[24] Before the days of pH meters, chemists employed a wide range of color indicators; color is within the public world.[25] Moreover, without motile experience of color, our hold in space is tenuous. Assuming normality and allowing for illusion and vagrant sense objects, it is false or misleading to say that "colors cannot rightly be regarded as properties of things, but only as changes in the subject, changes which may, indeed, be different for different men" (B 45). Color is not an "empirical affinity"; analysis is justified in assuming that it has a nomic tie to an object (A 114). Cinnabar is red (A 100). The pigment manufacturer can go on producing mercuric sulfide.

The worst is yet to come. Kant appears to say that we cannot have a concept of red or yellow; were that the case, we could not have the concepts we do in fact have of gold or mercuric sulphide. I do not think Kant, the phenomenalist, was making Aristotle's point that only substance has an essence (*Meta.* 1029b 13–1030b 2). This confusing issue needs a closer look if Kant is to be saved for phenomenology. Contrary to the evidence in the Seventh Letter and the account of perception in *Theaetetus* in which Plato counted colors among the ideas, Kant says that one "must find it intolerable to hear the representation of the color, red, called an idea" (A 320/B 377). "Idea" should be reserved for that which is archetypal, not ectypal, if justice is to be done to a neo-Platonic idea (originary kind) theory (A 318/B 375). Moreover, "the representation of the color, red . . . ought never to be called a concept of the understanding, a notion" (A 321/B 377). Is this really intended to deny cognitive status to qualities described in the Principles as "intensive magnitudes?"

While Kant thought figure can be known *a priori* in a pure intuition, he would not deny Plato's point that it can also be known through color. Consider a person standing close to a white wall which cannot be seen all at once. Kant says that sensation is not itself "a successive synthesis proceeding from the part to the whole representation" but "occupies only an instant" (A 167/B 209). The wall *qua* white is present all at once and involves no succession, but the perception of the wall as such requires a succession of white sensations. The "absence of all reality in the field of experience" is "empty space" (A 172/B 214) which is impossible (A 212/B 259). Among these realities are colored things without which there would be no spatial intuition. The doctrine of the Analytic requires that color is among a thing's properties appearing in the outer world. In the Anticipations "the real . . . is an object of sensation" (B 207) or, alternatively, "sensation, and the real which corresponds to it in the object" (A 166). The real, *res,* is a transcendental marking determinable quiddity and not the existence of something (MH 1967, 213).

The solution to this "vexing problem" occasioned by Kant's various remarks lies, in part, in their context of utterance. In criticizing Hume and Berkeley in the Dialectic, Kant says that color is neither an idea nor "concept of the understanding or notion." In their tradition concepts were mental pictures, not the schematic power to represent through an image. Nor are sensa products of mentality, such as in Berkeley's account of imagined color in which its image is displaced and generated. Though to have the concept red is to be able to image red, red itself is, as he says in the Aesthetic, a "modification of the sense of sight . . . in a certain manner by light." Moreover, since the distinction between "inner sense" and "outer sense" is made within experience and is thus phenomenal, we are not committed to primary qualities. The transcendental object, a Nothing, is not a proxy for Locke's "generally unknown" material substance, the bearer of those powers that are expressed in us as primary qualities. Color belongs to the "matter" (*Sachheit*) of experience, its hyle, and only derivatively to its act or form. This may not be adequate to a genuine phenomenology of perception, in which color is structural and formal, but it avoids the bifurcations suggested by an initial reading of Kant.

In the context of the Transcendental Aesthetic sensory detail is loaded into "inner sense" to show a prior non-empirical access to pure spatiality and temporality which both exhibits their transcendental ideality and will be useful in schematizing quantity and quality, the "mathematical" categories. Once this is established, qualities can be returned to the world. In their empirical reality, space and time are only experienced through objects and events. Seen in context, Kant's remarks support the "empirical realism" of some qualities.

Restoring quality to nature does not mean, however, that its discussion in the Anticipations of Perceptions is adequate. It appears that Kant's intensive magnitude was intended to bridge the gap between secondary and primary qualities which *qua* secondary could be sensed and *qua* primary could be extensively quantified. Force is such a bridge, not as the kinematic quantity appearing in Newton's $F=MA$ formula, but as the attractive and repellent field of forces Leibniz introduced to overcome the simple positivity of Newtonian impenetrability. "Wherever there is action—and therefore activity and force—there is substance, and it is in substance alone that this fruitful seat of appearances must be sought" (A 205/B 250). Indeed, "action is a sufficient empirical criterion to establish the substantiality of the subject" (A 205/B 251) which stands with other such subjects in a "dynamical community" (A 213/B 259). Repulsion, not impenetrability, is a mark of matter. The third chapter of Hegel's *Phenomenology* correctly identifies and describes the movement of the Analogies from substance through causality to reciprocity in terms of forces and their play, a set of images I will borrow from Kant in interpreting the receptacle in Plato's *Timaeus* as a play of forces. To return to Kant, let the absence of a force $=0$; we can then imagine "force" increasing to a "given measure" (A 166/B 259) on a scale of intensive magnitudes "corresponding to this intensity of sensation." One might wish for a similar linkage between hot/cold and temperature. But it is just not true that every quality, force for example, can be assigned a continuous measure; few are continuua. Moreover, the quality through which we have access to an entity is only equivocally that quantified quality figuring in physical laws. Kant's effort to retain a qualitative physics does not seem promising. Hegel learned from Kant that force does not take us into the "fruitful seat of appearances."

The Anticipations are intended to give a scalar magnitude to any qualities, if Kant should have looked more closely at them. He would have recognized that all too often we imagine ourselves possessing a range of quality concepts correlated with private images which we then predicate over things as if they were pigments that could be arbitrarily spread over their surfaces. This overlooks the manner in which things are recognized through their specific color. The "yellow" of a lemon and of gold is not a variously instanced same. We might try to well-order our concepts by an intensive scale; black is the absence and white the presence of all colors. However, the seen white is without color while the black is its superabundance. The absence of sensation would be, not black, but rather a dark room to which we might admit white light in varying degrees to determine the threshold for any color. This tells us something about the physiology of vision in relation to surface absorption, but it would not give us much information about what we see. Our concern would be with the phenomena of color awareness, not with things as colored and singled out by their color.

Separating quality from the empirical object trivializes sensation. Kant says "the real of sensation" that fills up space and time is "merely subjective representation, which gives us only consciousness that the subject is affected, and which we relate to an object in general" (B 207). Once we think of colors as possible predicates of objects, then we totally ignore the differences between surface color (absorption), film color (refraction) and iridescence (interference). In the latter two we really see the color of light. Sticking to surface color, there is no way that the yellow of gold can be separated from the gold and presented on a color chart. One must use gold if Justinian's mosaics at Ravenna are to be represented in the same golden color. The only way that we can get apple red, as Plato remarked in *Cratylus,* is by making an apple. This red is the apple's inseparable red, the yellow the gold's inseparable yellow. This is the color as having an intrinsic essence. The painter might use a pigment to tell us how he sees the apple or the gold, revealing through differences aspects of the color we did not notice. What something is not may tell us more about it than what it is.

Kant thought intensive magnitude could be represented by an ordinal continuum "ranging from 0, the absence of sensation, to any assigned magnitude. Every color has a degree which, however small it may be, is never the smallest; and so with heat, the moment of gravity, etc." (A 1611/B 211). Of what order type is this continuum? Is it rational, possessing gaps, or is it a dense continuua? Would it be of the same type for color as for heat? The mingling of primary colors can create dense continuua; inter se these constitute a differential field combinable in ways that elide differences, but these differences are prior to the continuities. Spreading one color, such as a red water color pigment, on white paper with an electrostatically charged brush, forms a gradient field whose intensity ranges from red to white, its absence, without a least red. Other gradient fields, analogous to the red, may be continuua in Kant's sense.

Until I can reintroduce a weak version of the metaphor of the book of nature that will do justice to the phenomenological strand in Kantian science, please indulge this reflection on the role of sensa in significance. The bacterium E. coli has a single sense (receptor or binding site) for each nutritional substrate and recognition functions over a gradient, like Kant's intensive magnitude, that enables it to zigzag to the source. It makes judgments as it zigs and zags over this continuum, correcting its zig by a zag on comparing the present concentration with the previous discrete concentration.[26] When, however, sense is not so specialized, thanks to Merleau-Ponty and de Saussure we know that it functions differentially in signifying contexts, a formal and not a material characteristic. The gold's own yellow is given as field invariant, rather than identical per se, in the relatively unfactored, though structured, sense field under a restricted range of light changes. White paper is white all day long, even if grey when examined apart in early morning or yellow when isolated and examined through a slit in candle light. Just as Segovia's transcription of a Bach cello suite is still the same (intentional) object as that played by Casals, so the sense field is an identity in otherness, each being what it is in relation to others. *Qua* field, relational essence is phenomenologically prior to intrinsic essence. Of course Latour will represent "essential" aspects of a white surface lit by a candle that will not be present in Matisse's representations of such surfaces at mid-day on the Cote d'Azure. The relational color field is different. Color is subject to interpretation, both at the level of sense, feeling tones, and at the level of the painter's intentions, but a whole field comes into play. The play of difference, rather than intrinsic quality, is essential to color. Differences can be set out in a chart, which is not a continuum, even if the differences are elided, as a siren might elide the differences in discrete notes. A missing and previously unseen shade of blue, Hume remarked, would be recognized.

Color is, as A. S. Byatt says, the "natural language of light and earth" and is born of their mingling.[27] So too, with Plato's myth, is philosophy, a discourse born of the mingling of *logos* and *the earth, the receptacle.* Perhaps we should look to the sun's child, to color. Color speaks to us of the incarnation of form—not, as Van Gogh said in a letter to Bernard, "in some imaginary Gethsemane," and is rescued from originary chaos in "a horse, a portrait, your grandmother, apples, a landscape." New life emerges from the "marriage of two complementary colors, their mingling and their opposition, the mysterious vibration of kindred tones." Each term, earth and light, is custodian of its own disorder. Euripides' maenads or Artemis' rites at Sparta and Ephesus, perhaps the "blood and earth" of which Hitler spoke, spring from an obsession with the earth. So too, I fear, do Foucault's alternatives to *Geist.* On the other hand, the sun not looked at is Apollo's symbol of music, serenity and order, but looked at spawns a nihilistic "will to truth." Bataille notes that van Gogh's sun became a "flaming, exploding, light source" which, on being looked upon, is the cause of "madness, the experience of combustion and subsquent waste."

The two senses of sense, something noetic or occurrent, suggests that none may be altogether subjective or objective; what is registered is the mark of *how* a certain structure having both physical and physiological conditions is entertained or "seen," which also marks this duality and is expressed in the hermeneutical "seeing something as. . . ." Consider the statement, "this is a red apple." Roderick Chisholm, noting that the red is ambiguous, proposes locutions which express two occurrent senses. In "The apple appears red," we refer not to its manner of appearing ("redly"), but to the appearances's comparative sense, as if one were trying to decide what to call it ("it seems red, but I am not sure") (1957). In the non-comparative case, "redly" marks the eventual reception of the apple's own red which may then be patient for other interpretative formalities. Philosophers usually begin with the comparative case, as if one did not know how to describe its difference-structure or how to represent it. One then ignores it adverbial qualifications and takes a color as one among a standard set of differences, rather too crudely represented for the painter, as if they were predicates contingently attached to the world or private objects contingently related to public objects. Kant's own ontology offers him a way out, and one is sorry that he did not see its phenomenological import. One has to look and see, where the seeing may carry with it the interpretative structure of an apparatus. Nietzsche's thesis that everything is an interpretation is supposed to spell Plato's doom. Did nothing ever shine for him? A color is an eidetic same recognizable in differing interpretative contexts. The situation is hopelessly confused if we begin with names and assume a one-one relation to color patches.

There are evident limitations to Kant's transcendental approach to quality. Some qualities are formal, not material, in that they form systematic, structured fields characterized by contrast and difference. Kant's monadic predicate logic is also faulty; for this requires that quality belong to some one thing, mind or matter, and color is not happy in either camp. Idealism neglects the thing as experienced, the gold seen in its own yellow, for the privacy of incorrigible sensa. Materialism fails to give weight to the spontaneous, interpretative element and the priority of quality to any quantificational account. Many qualities are given as phenomenological aspects of things and, at the same time, they are also subject to various "subjective" conditions because quality, lying in the between, is the adverbial form of participation. Kant deserves credit for restoring quality to nature and for recognizing the spontaneous or interpretative character of perception.

While Aristotle thought each sense may be in a sort of ratio to its proper objects, sensuous receptivity as such is ontological, what we are as Open, a Nothing, within which beings can appear. As such we are not limited to this or that formal mode of appearing. Even E. coli can develop new receptors when raised on a different nutritional substrate. Helen Keller constructed a world out of tactility, taste, and smell. Analogous phenomena accompany certain forms of brain damage. The spontaneity of life, not just mind, encourages the ancient belief that soul is the act determining the potentiality of the body and not always conversely. That life reaches out to a world in sense, a fabric of meanings, is common to Kant and Husserl.

6. Kant and Phenomenology

ONE MUST TAKE SERIOUSLY THE title, "Phenomenology," Kant gave to the first part of his projected "The Limits of Sensibility and Reason" in his letter to Marcus Herz, 21 Feb. 1772 (*Cor.* 111–18). Interpreting *doxa* as "how something is seen and accepted as ["endorsed," "accredited"] in [the flux of] its appearing" gives it a phenomenological and ontological import that "encroaches on the territory of *phainomai*" ["to appear," "phenomena"](PR 1967, 196). *Theoria* understandingly shows and discriminates phenomena in apophantic judgments of recognition and verification (MH 1982, 102).[28] This contrasts with the usual reading of Aristotelian *episteme* as the possession of theory one can prove and teach.

Paul Ricoeur says the "merit of phenomenology is to have elevated investigation of the appearing to the dignity of a science by the reduction" (PR 1967, 201). Naturalism assumes that I am an episode in a transcending world and thus "loses me into the world, sticks me with the world as seen, sensed, and acted upon, [but] its being in itself is a false in-itself of a being without me. . . . In putting an end to the omission of the subject, in uncovering the for-me-ness of the world the [phenomenological] reduction opens rather than closes the true problem-set of being. These problems assume the conquest made by a subjectivity, and they imply the reconquest of the subject, the being to whom being opens itself" (PR 1967, 177–78). Phenomenology is a check on explaining away appearances in sedimented habitualities; it lets sense encounter meaningful structures. The results, if not the rhetoric, of phenomenology are implicit in Kant. If, by releasing the world from bondage to a transcendent metaphysics, he seemed to deliver it over to naturalism and positivism, he also let it be seen in an interpretation of Being and opened a way, beyond his own prejudices, which leads through phenomenology to ontology.

Though Husserl proposes a route "back to the things themselves," we never get there; one comes to see that there is no partition between what gives itself in itself and from itself and what we contribute. This is a conclusion implicit in Kant's schematism. Intuition is the place of corrigibility, not incorrigibility, since it is the place of action not contemplation. Sense has in its transcendental object a program for determining significance. Things are meaningful, but this meaning is conferred, not self-given. Kant founded phenomenology and went on to develop such phenomenological themes as the construction of thinghood and its linkage to the structure of temporality and, in the Refutation, a definition of intentionality (PR 1967, 184). Ricoeur also notes that the priority of transcendental subjectivity to the phenomenal-noumenal distinction is an original contribution of Kant's philosophy.

The Kantian ego cogito claims for itself a manner of being that cannot be reductively described by its immanent phenomenal experiences nor its participation in the transcendent noumenal order: ". . . in the original synthetic unity of apperception, I am conscious of myself, not as I appear to myself, nor as I am in myself, but only that I am" (B 157). The being of the self, the nothing or clearing lighted by understanding, is prior to any interpretation. Nevertheless, there is a strong tendency to identify its essential openness with that kind of being one takes most seriously. Medieval interest in angels was occasioned by the belief that in these allegories man should take his measure and self-knowledge from what was presumed to be higher. We are more likely to see ourselves in the allegories depicting the animadversions of matter or energy. "Just as for the knowledge of an object distinct from me I require, besides the thought of an object in general (in the category), an intuition by which I determine the general concept, so for knowledge of myself I require, besides the consciousness, that is, besides the thought of myself, an intuition of the manifold in me, by which I determine this thought (B 158). . . . Thought determines this manifold, which *qua* inner sense is successive, by reference to material objects. Time will thus be thematized as continuous" (A 208/B 254–A 209). The self is tempted to interpret itself through this mechanism. This Parmenidian interpretation of the object in general yields the concept of durative (nominal) rather than epochal self be-ing, the latter alone being compatible with genuine teleology. Kant, if he can offer no alternative to mechanism, does not stick us with it. Since most of us are in the same fix, he can show us its meaning and the possibility of moving beyond.

Apperception is original, transcending manifolds of sense and the prompting of desire. Its being is transcendent and cannot be identified with either; "original consciousness is already given thereby [by the "I think" of original apperception], but the mode in which I am to de-termine this existence, that is, the manifold belonging to it, is not thereby given" (B 158 n.). The mind's atemporal spontaneity deter-mines "my existence" which *qua* finite constructs succession and those categorial manners of appearing through which something, always temporally other and other, is a same, a unity, and as such can be taken into thought through identifying and identity-intending recog-nition. Its correlative is the transcendental object. Since its intention to this object depends for its fulfillment on a contingent manifold, prior to the gift of this manifold this is an intention without an intuition.

We can attribute many of Husserl's themes to Kant or, more questionably, extend Kant's thought in Husserl's direction. The possi-bility of a transcendental phenomenology begins in the Transcendental Aesthetic which establishes the phenomenality of space and time and thereby the "for-me-ness" of the world. This, like Husserl's *epoché*, dismisses naturalism's "in-itselfness" in which human experience is a mere episode in a lifeless cosmos whose mechanistic realities drink up the springs of human meaning. But we have begun to exploit, in the context of the three-fold synthesis, Husserl's account of perception which, had Kant been more aware of possibilities opened by his phe-nomenology, he might have introduced himself.[29] In apprehension inner sense flows along with its sensa until recognition introduces the noematic object and sensa become its noetic perspectives. But the difference between a Platonist and a conceptualist, reflected in the dis-tinction I do not always respect, is between "constitution" and "con-struction." Platonists constitute, project *a priori* interpretative overlays on something which, in its formal objective distinctions *a parti rei* allows them to be entertained, but never construct concepts, that is, presence an object to an intuition *a priori*. There is also the difference, which Kant does not always observe, between two senses of "object." Construction is an original spatial and temporal presencing of an object (*Gegenstand*) under the constraints of a self-imposed ontological condition, the transcendental object. *Objekt*, which originates from the Scholastic "objection" that invites a reply, reflects its subjective generation and is usually employed to *ens rationis*. Sometimes, especially in the second edition where the imagination goes into hiatus and the understanding is paramount, *objekt* has an extended usage. For example, *objekt* is that to which determinate representations are related (B 137) or even that which we are conscious as a determinate space (B 138). When the perceptual surplus that the imagination expresses is central, then *Gegenstand* is appropriate. I construct the perceptual noema, the empirical *Gegenstand* (A 372), through a synthesis intending in successive sensibility a transcendental *Gegenstand* (A 305) that is not constructed. Husserl, a closet-Platonist, will come to a stand before intuited *eidos*, and constitution "unfolds the intendings of consciousness merged together in the natural, unreflective, grasp of a thing" (PR 1967, 9).

There are other obvious connections. Husserl's phenomenology establishes a correlation between meaning intention and its object. Kant's transcendental synthesis also correlates what is intended in thought with its reidentifiable appearances. For Husserl no object completely fulfills these intentions and thus establishes a ground for certainty. The object always contains a surplus of meanings, nor can we forever be sure that what it is meant as will always stand. Nevertheless, Husserl does not seem to realize that things are given under ontic interpretations, a thesis that we have been at pains to establish for Kant. The pure synthesis of the understanding is a sort of eidetic reduction giving intuition the form of the *eidos* "object-in-general," while the analytic method establishes criteria for the kinds of objects making up "regional ontologies." Kant's intuition never confronts things themselves that show themselves in and from themselves; intuition is corrigible. Nevertheless, from Husserl one learns to desediment appearances; applied to Kant, this revealed the meaning of Being that animates his ontic interpretations. Given its imaginative grounding and its roots in Plato's fanciful dialogues, analysis invites imaginative variations through which eidetic structure is intuited; the eidos is a unifying unity intended in manifold noetic and noematic modes of possible and actual appearing. Synthesis gives analysis a metaphysical ground, the eidetic object-in-general, so that sense already has an ontological weight.

This ontological weight, lacking in Husserl, will yield, thanks to Heidegger, the concept of an ontological "horizon" within which beings can be seen as _____. These ontological disclosures invite corresponding "ontic" interpretations. If "time is Being," then beings will manifest themselves through this ontological understanding as durative presences. Eidetically reduced ontic interpretations give object horizons. Applying this to Kant, one can see that the pure schema understood within the scope of the subjective deduction yields the noetic horizon in virtue of which the unity of consciousness is possible. The three-fold synthesis unifies these temporal modes around the theme of the intended object in general. On the other hand, the object or noematic horizon is constituted by the categories as forms of temporal synthesis. Transcendental synthesis gives horizons and, like a filter, permits things to appear as knowable presences through its form.[30] Can it, by any stretch of the imagination, give place and its geohistorical horizons? Maybe not, but still Kant's usage is wider than Husserl's.

The phenomenological concept of "horizon" originates in Kant's *Logic*. He refers to three sorts of horizons, not in terms of the *a priori* structure through which beings interpretatively appear, but rather as forms of human interest: (1) logical or cognitive, (2) aesthetic or feeling, and (3) practical. While he does not exploit the descriptive possibilities of phenomenology, he does suggest that beings appear through these forms of interest. For example, were a person to determine a horizon aesthetically, he would seek "to arrange science according to the taste of the public" (*Logic* 45). The logical horizon determined by the faculty of judgment lets us encounter objects as either historical or rational, and "the former is wider than the latter, for our historical horizon has no boundaries." The horizon determined by reason "can be fixed: we can determine . . . to what kind of objects mathematical cognition can not be extended." Kant's horizons are best seen as limiting structure rather than openings to immanent possibilities; what there can be "judgment on, and determination of, what man can know, what he needs to know, and what he should know" are the horizons determining modes of significance. Kant thinks "horizon" within the parameters of the initial title of the first *Critique*, The Limits of Sensibility and Reason. We can combine Husserl and Kant if we recall that for Husserl "world" is the "horizon of all [openly endless object] horizons." This has its Kantian analogue: "The sum of all the possible objects of our knowledge appears to us to be a plane, with an apparent horizon—namely, that which in its sweep comprehends it all, and which has been entitled by us the idea of unconditioned totality . . . all the questions raised by our pure reason are as to what may be outside the horizon, or, it may be, on its boundary line" (A 759/B

787-A 760/B 788). Kant then praises Hume as a geographer of human reason who unsuccessfully tries to determine the logical shape of this horizon. "Our reason is not like a plane indefinitely far extended, the limits of which we know in a general way only; but must rather be compared to a sphere, the radius of which can be determined from the curvature of the arc of its surface—that is to say, from the nature of synthetic *a priori* propositions—and thereby we can specify with certainty its volume and limits" (A 762/B 890).

In introducing world as the oriented, already familiar correlative of the "I think . . . ," Kant moves well beyond Hume and the empiricists for whom, given their method of constructing wholes from parts, the concept of the world as an *a priori* totality would have been nonsense. Of course the world with which we are familiar *a priori* in Kant is essentially that of an oriented space and time understood through objects and the conservative structures of physical law, not the orientedness of Heidegger's moods, understanding and language characterizing *Dasein's* "facticity." Nor is it necessary that the meaning of historical objects be understood in terms of the laws of freedom or that progress be seen through Kant's moral philosophy and his writing on history. Nor is it clear how we can move from the immanent temporality of the three-fold synthesis, McTaggart's A-series time, to the world-time in which events are ordered with respect to before and after, McTaggart's B-series time. Nor would we wish to say that the fundamental structure of man's project towards world, understood as the completed totality of the idea of reason, is the fundamental motive of human understanding, setting for it an openly endless constructive task. But the world as such is cointended in all experience of this or that.

The horizon concept anticipates the movement from phenomenology to hermeneutics in Dilthey, Heidegger, and Gadamer. Kant's concept of a "historical object" was particularly important to Dilthey. He sought to do for significant actions, the objects of history, what Kant had done for empirical objects by means of categories that would make possible the historical sciences of spirit. Our access to action is not by some quality, a cry, related to something independently describable, a drowning child; sharing life, we can ask, "look, and see," as would be evident in a narrative recounting what happened. Nature is not a collection of laws: it is a meaningful text (analogue). Would it be better to say with Dilthey that the object of historical understanding is life, the immanent striving for meaningful being as expressed reflexively in traditions sustained by autobiography, biography, art, literature, and the like, even if the expression is strange and alien? Reflexivity is already textual, as Plato proposes in *Philebus* (38E–39E), and life is a Derridian "writing" constantly editing itself, as E. coli reads and repairs its DNA in replication, as it constitutes its own biological and spiritual closure, as if a unitary book, from its interpretations of the general text of culture and nature. The unity of life is not that of the expressive, bloodless "I" but is achieved through experience as *Bildung*, spiritual formation. The expressive self, as Kant could tell us, that sets out and returns to itself phenomenally is not self-transparent. The problem of understanding is hermeneutical. Dilthey's categories are historically conditioned; there are no *a priori* determinates for grasping historical being in its "objectivity." As Gadamer has taught us, the goal of unprejudiced access to objectivity is unattainable and objectivity is at best an intuited eidetic same in a historical horizon of interpretations. We do not always understand what we are doing, and the reasons are often concealed by, if not artifacts of, language, the unconscious, our immersion in everydayness, culture, and the like. Autobiography is in part fictional self-interpretation, not a record of a monadic self that objectively grounds what is said. The human sciences with their texts and text analogues are more evidently hermeneutical than the natural sciences, even if these have hermeneutical or interpretative characteristics as Kant and, more recently, Kuhn, Feyerabend, and Hansen could testify. The phenomenalization of the analytic method, which since Plato has been restricted to the sciences, gives it a scope wider than it enjoys in Heidegger or Gadamer. Perhaps this study will narrow the gap between the humanistic, teleological disciplines and those given over to mechanism.

Kant sets out to derive the conditions for understanding from temporality and anticipates Heidegger's derivation of intentionality and the hermeneutical structure of *Dasein* from the between of understanding and sense. The foundations for hermeneutical ontology in the ontological difference between Being and beings have been laid in Kant's transcendental synthesis. The horizon of the human world is Being. What gives Being? How are horizons possible? Plato saw the answer in the crossing of the Good and the receptacle, the mother, in place.

7. Questionable Questioners

A REMARKABLE FEATURE OF Socratic dialogue is the way the original question opens an horizon. Socrates asks, "What is Gorgias? What is the power (*dynamis*) of his art?" from which everything follows, as if fated.[31] With Aristotle, dialectic surrendered to logic and rhetoric and "giving an account" became a speech or a logical demonstration. Such questions as were asked, for example, by Peter Lombard, Abelard, or Aquinas, were invitations to an argument. Was Kant the first philosopher since Plato to recognize the fundamental importance of questions? Answers must follow the setting-out procedures proposed by Galileo's questions or the constructive method of Euclid. Therein lies the clue to establishing metaphysics as a science after what has "hitherto been a merely random, and what is worst of all, groping among mere concepts" (B xv). This groping began with Aristotle's "what is Being?" (*Meta.* 1028 2–4).

Kant never directly answered Aristotle's question. It might seem difficult to say much, since "Being is not a real predicate, that is, it is not the concept of something that could be added to the concept of that thing" (A 598/B 626). But this is true of any of Aquinas' or Aristotle's transcendental predicates convertible with Being, for example, one, *aliquid, res.* Kant adds that "the small word 'is' adds no new predicate, but serves only to posit the predicate in relation to the subject . . . or posit the subject in itself as an object that stands in relation to my concept" (A 598/B 626).[32] The many senses in which Aristotle said something may be said to be have been reduced to that which posits and preserves the identity of the logical subject. Should nominalizing *einai* blind us to the possibilities of Being? If it did not blind Aristotle, it certainly blinded Kant. "The subject in itself with all its predicates . . . [is posited] as an object in relation to my concept" would be like a monad as known to God. Who else could claim this concept as mine? Behind this vestige of Leibniz lurks Augustine, Aristotle, Spinoza and Parmenides. If, as Kant says, all our concepts are subject to time (A 99–100), then this time must be a continuous quantum (A 169/B 211) reaching out from the past to the present, so that there is a continuity of becoming rather than Whitehead's becoming of continuity, in order "that appearances of past time must determine all existences in the succeeding time" (A 209/B 244). Since time is only experienced through objects, its correlative will be unchanging substance. The conservative structure of mechanistic explanation, its fascination with continuous functions, results from an ontological hermeneutics of original temporality. The succession of the same which is always same (material substance) in the same (continuous time) is the discursive analogue of the complete subject creatively intuited by God.

Kant's philosophy opens with our question, "What is a thing?" Not this or that sort of thing, but rather "something in general $= x$ distinct from all our representations" (A 104–5). The transcendental predicates of this logical subject represent modes of temporal access to things as understanding's predetermined determinable object and the manner in which it can be taken up and considered in "my concept." The "thing-in-itself" as known to God is the *telos* of the openly endless, predicative task set for the transcendental "I think. . . ."[33] This uncompletability resembles Sartre's endless striving to be *pour soi-en soi.* We creatures of a day should beware of this Romantic nonsense. The proper limits are found in Plato's questions which dispose us to regard idea as the *peras* ("limit") within which the creature, a *mikton* ("mixture"), arises and stands forth through the power of the *apeiron* (Anaximander's "boundless" power). The *mikton* is a *koinon* ("participation," "communion," "community") of nominal presence and verbal presencing. Kant, distrusting change, finds solace from Dionysian threats in Parmenides.[34] The thematization of beings through an understanding of Being as enduring presence is given in the original question, "What is a thing?" "In all change of appearances, substance is permanent" (B 224). This is the same that underlies all otherness, the rest for every motion, the one for every many. Being is reidentifiable (contingent) sameness that positions us. Contingent on what? The ineluctable modality of receptive givenness, *praesens.*

Since Parmenides began his *hodos* to *aletheia*, methodology has been determined by *hos estin* ("what is something really?").[35] A search for atemporal beingness (*ousia*) is the horizon opened by Parmenides' question. Of special interest is the statement form in which the question about being is answered. Both Plato and Aristotle thought the standard form of a statement was noun-verb. An answer stressing the priority of the verbal would run counter to the 'signposts' by which Parmenides marked the route to truth. Being must be "ungenerable and imperishable" (DK B 8.3).

From the Whiteheadian question, "What is going on?" one presumes that an occasion awaits definition in the manner in which a plot determines a drama. The ontological primacy of becoming suggests statements about events and processes, actions and happenings, living and dying, of narrative rather than logic. Parmenides dismisses this as a way of "seeming" since what something is is then what it is not, its possibilities that may lie before and its historic route that lies beyond its presence in a present. The unchanging individual variable, x, which is same in change of predicates, memorializes Parmenides. "Coming to be" and "arising" are ways of non-Being. To ask of x what it is is to get an answer of the form, "x is. . . ." On Parmenides' understanding of this particular sentence frame, the copula cannot be identified with the is of accidental predications, "is. . . ." Kant reflects Parmenides' strong identity sense that the copula "is nothing but the manner in which given modes of knowledge are brought to the objective unity of apperception . . . in virtue of the necessary unity of apperception in the synthesis of intuitions, that is, according to the objective unity of all representations" (B 141–42). This unity is possible through the analytic method, which sorts out identity-preserving categorial predicates. The *is* of categorial ascription is not contingent, as if something could be otherwise than what analysis says it is. The self-sameness of the ahistoric self (its analytic unity) is a function of our capacity to order experience as a unity gained in the methodological analysis of objects which are the conditon for its objective unity, which could in principle be shared by all, since they are secured through recognition in a concept whose form, "is P," entails reidentification and thus identity.

III

Objects

. . . .

1. World-Making

IT SHOULD HAVE BEEN evident that Kant's Copernican Revolution in which "objects must conform to our faculty of intuition" (B xvii) was metaphysical, if not cosmological. In the second edition preface to the first *Critique* he announced that his intention to place metaphysics "on the sure path to science" (B xix) with the claim that "we can know *a priori* of things only what we ourselves have put into them" (B xviii). It is not to our credit that most thought of him as an Anglo-American analytic epistemologist before discovering this metaphysical bent through Martin Heidegger, Heinz Heimsoeth, and Gottfried Martin.[1] "To categorize" is "to question a witness," "to compel an answer" in a legal context calling for judgment; since judgment is a rather outmoded logical concept, his revolutionary methods in metaphysics which were founded on phenomenological disclosure, *aletheia,* through categorial questions, were overlooked.

Appearances reveal the conditions for a world only if one is already persuaded there is one, which of course none doubt. Even if these conditions will not take analysis to the world as an unconditioned totality, which is far too wide for understanding, can we use these to articulate one that satisfies the requirements of scientific realism? The way leads, not through induction or postulating or conjecturing covering laws, but rather through part-whole isomorphisms; what is read in the part must tell the whole story. If this journey is to be a success, these "parts" must satisfy three necessary—if not sufficient—conditions: access, discriminability, and connectedness. Like a good butcher, one must discriminate (Gk. *keirein,* Lt. *cernere,* "cut," "judge" or "choose"), select and articulate things at their world-preserving joints. In place of the recollection that governs division in Plato's account (*Phaed.* 265D–66D), Heidegger proposes a prior ontological understanding which in turn articulates the ontic horizons by which one gains access to a world. This prior understanding in terms of which beings are discriminated as . . . is known as the hermeneutical circle. Access lets one encounter entities schematized as quality and quantity in the "mathematical" categories and lets us infer how changes in these, reverberating throughout a connected nature, can be understood within the "dynamical categories."

Justifying these conditions would demonstrate how one enters into and understands world in its vastness and historical complexity without ever leaving home, Kant's situation in provincial Königsberg. Through our cuts or discriminations, which as extensive are rather Cartesian, we enter a common, physical world through the mathematical categories which is devoid of local idiosyncrasies. Traces within extensive magnitudes and their intensive, qualitative variations led the young Kant to the origin of the solar system and into the secrets of Saturn's rings. Understanding can bring anything anywhere within this totality into focus by its dynamical connections with this here and now. Infinite given totalities, space and time, underlie these conditions; since these are open to various descriptions, space and time must be founded on the primordial possibility of encounter and, since this is significant, reference.[2] The space and time of this proximity is different, however, from that Kant would have us discriminate.

The appearance of Deaden's impressive French edition of Leibniz's *Theodicy* (1768) with its summaries of the controversies by Voltaire and others caused Kant quite a stir. Leibniz had spoken of "understanding" as a "simple vision to which truth offers itself like a landscape to an eye." In this "simple vision" one 'sees' things *a priori* through "causes" (GL 1945, 148–49), which entails knowing that God in his goodness makes something X and makes it to be an F, where the latter is a Platonic idea to which we have contemplative access (GL 1945, 242). Leibniz transforms the "hypothetical" method of explaining by "causes" which Socrates recommends in *Phaedo* (100 C ff.) into an account of God's acts and intentions. With the failure of this shared physico-theology, one could no longer found the results of analysis in a Being; this "simple vision" was empty. Its possibility would have given access from any time or place to the physical cosmos: "For it must be known that all things are connected in each one of the possible worlds: the universe, whatever it may be, is all of a piece, like an ocean: the least movement extends its effect there to any distance whatsoever, even though this effect becomes less perceptible in proportion to the distance" (GL 1945, 9). For Leibniz the connectedness articulated in natural inference rests in a divine knower; for Kant accessibility and connectedness are constructs, not ontic articulations, by the human mind. There must be a discursive analogue to God's intuitive and creative *nunc standi*. One constitutes the conditions for phenomenal being in a finite succession of intuitions. Presence, "being," is grounded in human temporality—ontologically interpreted as a line! Accessibility depends, as the Deduction proves, on how a succession in inner sense can present an object that grounds the truth relation. The categories establish connectedness through the experience of objects in the Principles. God's creative intuition of presence becomes for us the meaning of Being ontically thematized in the Principles; permanent phenomenal substance is to us as the sempiternal presence of the world is to God.

Discrimination presupposes the imaginative Open which Being needs for unconcealment *(aletheia)*. My bodily "here" is Being's *Da,* "there," where entities may be disclosed in a world-preserving manner. Since Parmenides asserted that there is a same for thinking and being, nothing is closed to mind; nevertheless, the question remains; how is Being to be understood that lets beings be same for thinking? Or, starting from thought, in showing themselves to us in the privacy of sense, how can things be thought as significant of a world, supporting inferences to an unperceived past and future, sustaining the referential totalities expressed in quantification theory and the necessities of physical law? Socrates would follow the dialectician who can preserve "this one and many in nature . . . as if he were a god" *(Phaed.* 265E–66B). Proper parts must be as if microcosmic, signifying the macrocosm, and form coherent wholes. Descartes is incoherent and Hume failed to preserve induction. The Kantian categories articulate experience so as to preserve this sense of a world. In the context of the now vanished physico-theology, the analytic method led from conditions to their condition *(Prol.* 276) in a deistic God. Unless regulative ideas can point us towards a hoped for uniformity within the scattered results of conscious synthetic acts—of which we are scarcely conscious— this unity will be problematic indeed. The consciousness of the formal, unifying act may be so faint that unity will be attributed to the generated representation; in drawing a line one focuses on the drawn, not the drawing (A 104). Identical acts engender only aggregates of identical objects, even if these are intended as world-preserving. How can a transcendental philosophy preserve this sense of a world, a referential totality that makes sense? If this sense is *a priori,* for am I not always out in the world if not worldly, and if, as Kant said in the posthumous work, the thing-in-itself is the empirical object as completely determined and if this sense is retained by the transcendental object, the eidetic identity common to objects of all types, then the analytic method can make things show themselves as naturally significant within the interlocking referential horizons of a world. Only when Hume, as Kant understood him, proposed that the thing is a contingent psychic product, rather than justifying the transcendence of mind towards its non-present causes and conditions, is this faith seriously challenged. I summarize this referential possibility in a phrase, "the sense of world." As far as I know, nothing has been made of this point; at the risk of repetition, bear with me as I linger over it.

A theologically grounded micro-macrocosm or part-whole iso-morphism was explicit in the early Kant (1755): "If you take away God, not only all existence of things, but even the internal possibility of them is completely abolished" (ND, Ak. I, 395, prop. 7). This whole whose existence and possibility lies in the mind of God is also present to the human mind: "The infinite perception of the whole universe is always internally present to mind, although extremely ob-scure; it already contains within whatever reality must be in the cogni-tions afterwards to be suffused with more light" (240). How can we ground and constitute in successive, finite and contingent intuitions what God did and sustained in an intuitive act (B 135)? Categorial self-expression enables us to intend and then constitute objects, which formally are nothing but ejects of these schematized categories, whose necessary and universal features permitting, in principle, complete ac-cess to the phenomenal world.

Since access in sensuous receptivity presents apodictic, though not fulfilling, evidence of something or other, everything hinges on the significance, not mere givenness, of sense. Writing to Jacob Beck on 20 January 1792, about a proposed system of metaphysics: "I now prove that no experience of the objects of the senses is possible, except in so far as I presuppose a priori that they have altogether to be thought of as magnitudes, and so of all other objects. . . . Perhaps you can avoid initially defining sensibility by receptivity, that is, defining the kind of representations, as they are in the subject, insofar as it is affected by objects . . . [receptivity] is merely a determination of the subject. . . . I begin by defining experience through empirical knowledge." We are openly oriented to what is formal and mathemat-ically determinable, the imaginatively rooted condition for empirical significance, if not encounter and reference (MH 1967, 31). Access, underlying all other conditions, is not to be identified with determin-able space and time but is, rather, what lets distinguishable and iden-tifiable things be encountered as significant. Heidegger's understand-ing of space as the disseverance that lets beings come near, where "near" is contextual perspicuousness (EB 1983, 66–86), is close to the mark. The loved one, though in the next room, may be more distant than the furthermost star. Nevertheless, Kantian receptivity is an on-tological interpretation of this more primordial receptivity that grants position, not place, to a synopsis that already understands things as mathematically determinable presences. Whatever appears will be rec-ognizable and determinable as a magnitude whose changes point to causes and substances, to an interconnected world.

"The receptivity of the subject" (A 26/B 42) is, apart from any ontological interpretation, already a soliciting receptivity, imagina-tively and spontaneously reaching out to receive determinations; it is also creative, giving its dynamics to what is received. But in analysis one is receptive because an imaginatively attuned apparatus intends the Open, letting appears what otherwise is beyond conception. The imagination's profoundly playful dynamics, apparent when deprived of a conceptual focus in the perception of beauty (*CAJ* 217), match those of medial becoming. The imagination institutes distinctions, such as receptive and spontaneous, or understanding and intuition, in which each bears the trace of the other. Is it a stand-in for the receptacle? "As finite," Heidegger notes, "the act of pure intuition is an act of representation that is receptive. But that which is to be received, if its cognition is ontological and not just ontic, cannot be something already at hand [i.e., reproductive imagination] that presents itself. On the contrary, the pure receptive act of representation must give itself something that is capable of being represented. Pure intuition must be in a certain sense creative" (1990, 29–30). Heidegger is indispensable for showing how the imagination offers the prospect of a "model-theoretic" approach to creative presencing; one can travel with him beyond Uranian formalism through set-ups to a maternal *arché*, origin—and ultimately beyond synoptic Uranian space to chthonic place.

Aristotle said that in induction, which has the sense of Kant's recognition in a concept (A 103), vagrant sense, like an army in flight, comes to a stand in the "company formation" of a concept (*Post. Anal.*, 100a1–15). It comes to a stand, Kant might add, in and over against (*Gegenstand*) understanding because sense gives back what understanding gives it, a Principle (*princeps*), a rule.[3] Thus sovereign understanding has a limited rule. Traces of receptivity will appear in understanding which make the schema possible, but sensibility is also active, soliciting understanding. Intuition and understanding arise from the imagination, the medial gap or "free space" that gives/receives as they cross over one another in a chiasmus: spontaneous understanding becomes receptive and sensibility becomes creative. Recognition is recollection's (*anamnesis*) heir; empirical recognition is within a category and, as a proto-eidetic reduction, institutes object horizons. Discrimination preserves connexity through the imagination's categorial gathering. Though one may be wary of Kant's own categorial restraints, recognition in experimental context is an analogue of Kant's imaginative and playful crossing of sense and understanding; appearances solicit recognition, but only when propositioned by a *theoria* attuned to imagination's necessities and what she, an analogue of Plato's "errant cause" (*Tim.* 52D), might let arise. Truth (unconcealment, *aletheia*), which Nietzsche says is a woman, sometimes happens in this play. Hypotheses, which are likely stories or images, are phenomenological model theoretic modes of seeing as. These allegories, stories, metaphors, or descriptions within the model nevertheless point beyond to what these posit.[4] Once an appearance is recognized in theoretical matrices, the essentially abductive and metaphorical 'mother' of invention, then these enabling myths or paradigms can be forgotten and scientific tasks can be handed over to theoretical understanding. Before it is a faculty of rules and judgments, a principle imposing form, understanding must elucidate appearance, participate with it in experimental *praxis*. Thus the imagination, of whose function we are scarcely ever conscious, is the medial root, the nothing that things, the between of sense and understanding that makes possible their chiasmas. Kant replays the theme of the receptacle which, as Plato says in a similar context, cannot be understood (*Tim.* 49A) and—as the Good's supplement—though not a being partakes of Being in a mysterious way (50C).[5] Except that in Kant's world everything is dead and placeless.

Having looked, if all too briefly, at the intuitive conditions that give access to a world, some attention must be directed towards apperception as the transcendental ground of experience. Paul Ricoeur says that with Kant's transcendental turn, "the for-me of the world has the sense of Husserl's *epoché*" and founds phenomenology, whose "explicit sense was then revealed by Husserl" (PR 1967, 180). Nevertheless, nothing resembling Husserl's self-experience is available to Kant. He believed that self-consciousness is empirically mediated, but transcendental apperception is a formal principle transcending empirical apperception in the direction of noumenal being which generates objects and the conditions for their experience. These constructs are the empirical conditions for its mediated self-presence. This self-consciousness is not, as in Hegel, shown to be necessary by an examination of naturalistic or objectivistic theories. For Kant, consciousness (mistakenly) recognizes itself in what it sets up (*Vorstellung*) before itself as an object. On the other hand, Hegel's phenomenological consciousness, reflecting on ordinary consciousness, discovers how the latter comes to see itself in the extrinsic standards or criteria that objectivistic thinking keeps proposing but cannot consistently establish. Building on Kant's discovery of the untenability of the "natural attitude" of naive realism in which the object is both known and the criterion of knowledge, Hegel shows that sense certainty and perceptual consciousness must justify themselves by a higher form and avoids Kant's narrow categorial theme by substituting for their "deduction" the subject's dialectical experience of the world. Hegel never doubts the basic truth of realism, however, for his forms of self-consciousness are forms of critical and self-critical intelligence that lead it towards adequate knowledge; "experience is for itself its own Criteria."[6] Kant does not have the luxury of a dialectical supersession of categories, for his categories construct possible experience, in the context of experimental or scientific understanding. Unless he is read from his philosophy of science, we will confuse him with the larger possibilities opened by Hegel. Since the epistemic self exists in generating and self-affectively thinking its objects, there is no room for a dialectical development of self-consciousness, as in Hegel's movement from the master-slave to the citizen in civil society. Kant's active sense of experience shuts off Hegel's dialectical development, which assumes a greater passivity.

2. Expressive Acts

THE CONDITIONS FOR THINKING, the categories, are also horizons for appearances. "Every category," Kant says, "makes possible and capable of representation only a determination of time" (A 140/B 179). The tie between things and categories lies in the original temporality in which they are formed and the categories in which they are formed and the categories in which they are thought. The link lies in "schemata"; imaginative images through which something is intended are homogeneous with the image in which it is received through the work of the "pure productive" or "figurative" imagination, and so forth.

The synthesis of apprehension, which is empirical, necessarily conforms with the synthesis of apperception, which is intellectual and contained in the category completely *a priori*. "It is one and the same spontaneity, which in the one case, under the title of imagination, and in the other case, under the title of understanding, brings combination into the manifold" (B 162 n.). If form is seen in the facts, it is because facts are constructed to be epiphanies, as we might make a linear mark to let the line itself be seen.

One usually approaches Kant's constructive thesis in the philosophy of reflection where, Hegel said, "*pure* self-recognition in absolute otherness, the other *as such*, is the ground and soil of Science or *knowledge in general*" (GH 1977, 14); but perhaps Charles Taylor's use of "expressivism" may render self-affection, its prototype, more intelligible. "Expressivism" is Isaiah Berlin's term for the movement that began in Germany in the 1790s and which later came to be known as Expressionism. In the face of alienation from a world that denied teleology and within which one could no longer define oneself, one turned inward and became expressively self-defining.[7] Taylor says

> this self-defining subject brought along with it an objectifying of things; that is, it debarred notions like "meaning," "expression," "purpose" as inappropriate descriptions of objective reality and confined them to the mental life of subjects . . . meaning is now an external relation which

certain marks, sounds, things or ideas (representations) have
for us. . . . that some things can be described in meaning
categories is not an objective fact about them . . . it rigorously segregates meaning from being . . . in an uncom-
promising extension of medieval nominalism" (CT 1978, 14).

Most important, it rendered unintelligible the medieval and renaissance idea of nature as a text.

Expressivism is concerned with the "realization of a form when
we see it as the unfolding of self . . . [by striving] against obstacles
[which] make clear what the form is" (15–16). Expressivism, born of
Kant's "autonomy," sought to restore a personal teleology in a world
increasingly surrendered to mechanism. Like its self-affective relative,
expressivism fuses ejective and objective components; one expresses or
objectifies oneself, perhaps alienating oneself in the process, and returns from self-alienation in the constructed object. Something vital
though concealed, like freedom to Hegel's slave or the creative potential of Marx's laborer, must be projected and become an object if one
is come to self-knowledge through its mediation. Kant's friend Herder
found a role for Spinoza's *natura naturans* in a world that took mechanism for granted; transcendental synthesis is not without affinities to
Spinoza's *natura naturans* or, as Gadamer noted, *emantio intellectualis*
(HG 1975, 370–91). Expressive theories originate in the logocentricism
of Aristotle's *De Interpretatione,* where the spoken word is said to be
a sign of a "mental affection" (16a 4) or, as Aquinas says in his
Commentary on this text, a "mental conception." In these instances
we seldom hear ourselves, but in Kant's line drawing the presenced
object affects us and, were it to tell us something about ourselves we
did not know, then the circle is complete. However, once we focus on
the object and not the presencing, the conceptualism position will be
undermined. This will be especially evident in cases where our presencing is limited to representing, not constructing, which lets things show
themselves as if epiphanies within schematizing projects in which the
schema must submit to the things that are. I will be attempting to
restore the text metaphor, in opposition to these expressive accounts,
in a disclosive model of language. In Helen Keller the virtuality of the
world lies in this single name, "water," that Miss Sullivan's marks
called into being. Nevertheless, this Romantic model is important in
facilitating an understanding of constitution theory as expressively
ejective and objectively receptive.

A "category" is most often understood as an irreducible predicate
in a judgment. Every assertion has a quantity, quality, expresses a relation, and has a modality; as quantity it is either universal, particular,
or singular, and each may instance a relational category, substance and

accident, cause and effect, and reciprocity, *et cetera*. Kant says that "apart from the formal conditions of sensibility, [categories] have only transcendental meaning . . . they may not be employed transcendentally . . . in as much as all conditions of any employment in judgment are lacking to them" (A 248/B 305). It might be meaningful to speak of God as first cause, for example or as manifest in a symbol, "a mode of the intuitive" (*CAJ*, sec. 59), but no "determinate object being given" (A 248/B 304), these assertions lack truth value. Intuited "conditions" let representations be seen under the determinations posited by the judgment. I am not concerned, however, with the meaning of "category" (A 247/B 304), which "signifies nothing [determinable] at all" (B 306), but rather with its limiting, "schematized" usage. The schema of an empirical or pure concept gathers alterities, empirical or pure, thought or extension, into a unitary same. One imaginatively sees ahead of oneself, in something like a spatial/ temporal profile, the shape (Gk. *schema*) of the intended future. That future will be present in the empirical object that verifies our progress towards its comprehension. Kant's example is that of self-reflectively drawing a line (A 102; B 138; B 154–55). But how can one express a world?

In Aristotelian Scholasticism, the transcendental "truth" is convertible with "being" and is the only such term signifying a relation, in this case to a knower. The epistemic bias of the tradition is apparent, for all that metaphysics would say about "being" signifies a relation to the intellect, divine or human. This carries over into Kant; categories signify *a priori* the ways in which a phenomenal object can be encountered as empirically meaningful, which is then a condition for the unity of one's own self-being. Kant speaks of this unity as the analytic unity of apperception, a well-ordering of events in a (possible) autobiography with respect to their befores and afters. This ordering comes about by applying the analytic method to things ("objective unity") which function in explanation as causes, permanencies, distinguished by characteristics and the like (B 133).

The transcendental object is cointended in schematizing beings through the categorial questions governing this or that experimental project; but unless sense is disclosed through this projection, the categories "would have in themselves no objective meaning" since they do not "rest on an intuition" (A 349; also A 246) and, as such, express only "the thought of an object in general, according to different [categorial?] modes" (A 247/B 304). Even if this is the form in which the empirical object is constituted, how would it carry a worldly significance? How indeed would the categories differ from the logical forms of judgment? If these are clues to the sense of the categories, as the "metaphysical deduction" suggests, how in heaven's name could they determine any object of possible experience *a priori?* Kant has a rather more robust sense of the *a priori* than our logical formalisms might allow us to imagine. One has only to look at the scope of his *a priori* physics in the *Metaphysical Foundations* to be convinced that something more than a logical formalism is operative in shaping the transcendental object. If, as Kant requires, we expressively determine these conditions that bear the sense of the world *a priori,* does that mean that, aside from formal principles which would apply indifferently to anything, this sense of the world is also present *a priori?* It seems to determine how a logical table of judgments will be transformed into a table of categories; for instance, a hypothetical statement in logic has the form of a causal sequence. The noema empirically meant through categories is described *a priori* in the Analogies. Transcendental apperception and its correlative transcendental object constitute, as Husserl will put it, a "ruling apperception which determines in advance what is a natural-scientific object" (EH 1989, 4). The "material" aspect, *Sachheit* (A 143/B 182), of the transcendental object exercises this rule on apperception's original construction of *Sachen,* "states of affairs." *Sachen,* to borrow from a similar theme in Husserl's *Logical Investigations,* is the ground of eidetic necessity, the structures necessary to a thing if it is to exist. It is "a content constant in idea despite endless variation—variation that is free—that is not excluded by a law in the content's essence—of the content associated with it and, in general, given with it. This means that it is unaffected by the elimination of any arrangement of compresent contents whatsoever" (EH 1970b, 443). Though details of this "expression" have to be worked out, transcendental matter lies in the "between" and gives the *logos,* the spontaneity of thinking, to receptive sensibility and a world to apperception so that they "can go out beyond themselves" and gain "what dignity they thereby acquire [through] relation to an object" (A 197/B 242). In this phenomenologically reduced form, the transcendental object cointended in every intention to a being prevents Kant from falling, like Husserl, into a transcendental egology. Let me spell this out in what threatens to become tiresome detail.

If I ask, "what is the shortest distance between two points?" space is synoptically intended as a manifold of points, any two of which can be connected by a right line. Line drawing, expressing the postulate that enables one to represent the "line itself," is a clear case of "constraining nature to answer questions of reason's own determining" (B xiii). Intending the line itself, a universal, expresses itself by the act of (schematically) drawing a line segment through a postulate, a repeatable rule which is "the identity of an act" (A 108), the power to generate a reproducible representation (A 106), and as iterable plays the role of the realist's recurrent sameness or the nominalist's reduction of this sameness to resemblances. The understanding is the faculty of rules (A 126); it is also "the source of principles according to which everything that can be presented to us as an object must conform to rules" (A 159/B 158). Concepts, reflectively grasping the many as one, express the synthetic form of apperception. Some are derived by reflection and others, the pure concepts, express the reflective form of the understanding (MH 1990, 59–60). This presents to reflection (self-affection as temporalization) the impossible task of being simultaneously aware of both the constituting act and its expression in the triune synthesis, reproductive, apprehensive and recognitional. Nevertheless, it is at the heart of the constructivistic program: "To construct a concept means to exhibit *a priori* the intuition that corresponds to the concept. . . . The single figure that we draw is empirical, yet it serves to express the concept, without impairing its universality. For in this empirical intuition we consider only the act whereby we construct the concept" (A 713/B 741–A 714/B 742). The rule of construction, characteristic of the synthetic method, makes the act of drawing, though empirical, a (Aristotelian) formal act (B 137–38) of doxic presencing whose possibility is given *a priori* by a postulate: "in mathematics . . . [a postulate is] the practical proposition that contains nothing save the synthesis through which we first give ourselves an object and generate its concept" (A 234/B 287). But Kant says that "motion, as an act of the subject (not as the determination of an object), and therefore the synthesis of the manifold in space, first produces the concept of succession" (B 154–55). Since the concept of succession, the pure form of time "to which all our knowledge is . . . subject" (A 99), is given through this motility, the motile, bodily expression of a categorial act entailed in pure synthesis is also warranted. It then follows that any synthesis requiring oriented motility which instances an *a priori* rule, that is, a concept, has a transcendental, not causal, justification. I do geometry under a non-empirical authority; surely this has implications for Kant's ethics. If my hand can represent the postulate, can it not express the Categorial Imperative when it is extended to aid the stranger? This action is the "eject" given *in* the idea of freedom. Since the schematized categories, like postulates, are rules governing acts, cannot they also be means whereby "we give ourselves an object and generate its concept?" A mathematical postulate is, as Kant says, a practical rule of action; granted the methodological context, could this also be true of the schematized categories? All representations are referred by the understanding to some object. We intend the object (noema) through this noetic "set-up" (*Vorstellung*, "representation"). Temporal unity of consciousness necessitated by this (intentional) object, which "is nothing to us—being as it is distinct from all our representations" (A 105), is achieved first at the perceptual level, where it is intended through sensory manifolds which are, secondly, thought as instances of a concept, where sense or concepts are differing modes of intending the same entity. But sense alone intends nothing; sense is hyleic and must be "animated" and informed by iterative acts. Since empirical intentions instance categories, as one might intend substance through intensive magnitude, one may speak of a categorial intention.

Every empirical object categorially intuited is a something or other, *res*. This reduced "empirical object $= x$" to which pure categorial intentions expresing transcendental concepts intending x as cause, substance, and the like are referred would be further reducible to "the transcendental object" (A 250). Even Kant's casual reader might imagine that this object, being intended through an arbitrary sense manifold whose very possibility as spatial/temporal lies in this intentional act, would assume that its rule-governed synthesis, the Schematism, produces the required empirical objectivity. The noema is found in the Principles.

Our present task is to make the best case for Kant's critical program as it appears under a proto-expressivist interpretation: everything depends on being able to generate *a priori* the manifold of space and time as the necessary condition for worldly access by an atemporal act expressing itself in recursive arithmetical rules that generate nows. The "matter" of this manifold is arbitrary, for it makes no difference what one counts (*Prol.* sec. 10); arbitrariness marks a synthetic concept (*Logic* sec. 102). We can number a heterogeneous array as long as we treat it as if it were a homogeneous collection of points: "Number is simply the unity of the synthesis of the manifold of a homogeneous intuition in general, a unity due to my generating time itself in the apprehension of the intuition" (A 143/B 182). From this it follows that if one could establish the order type of this ordinal series of nows (the logical form of Kant's diachronic series) and the geometrical ordering of the correlative coexistent and thus countable punctal manifold (whose synthesis is synchronic), then their possible forms of diachronic and synchronic synthesis would yield objectivity's noematic structures as expressed in the Principles that are schematically intended in categorial, experimental projects. In the transcendental analogue of mathematical synthesis, the intention to the always and everywhere one and the same transcendental object (A 109), the synthetic condition for empirical objectivity, is through the arbitrary representations of sense (in the above mathematical sense).[8]

Kant thought the homology between what we categorially think and the object's response to the questions put to it in a set-up ("representation") is "as if" a pre-established harmony. This congruence is possible if the object is constructed. "If the object (as object of the senses) must conform to the constitution of our faculty of intuition"

(B xvii), then as given in space and time, these subjectively generated forms of intuition must nevertheless bear as Objekts the sense of objectivity ("transcendental matter," *Sachheit*) (A 143/B 182)). We are able to ejectively ("throw out") constitute through these forms what is then experienced as a given empirical object (*Gegenstand*). Objects expressively generated and experienced must also, as appearances, conform to our mode of representation" (B xx). Representations are perceptions (A 320/B 377) "immediately related to an object" (A 68/B 93) which are then thought in "representations of representations," that is, in concepts.

And so the hermeneutical circle is drawn. The *Prolegomena,* if not the Transcendental Aesthetic, makes it quite clear that space and time are synthetic conditions for mathematics, the paradigm of objective knowledge. The subjective succession of time has the form and order type of the constructive, rational numbers; space, its associated and generated coexistent manifold, is totally transparent in geometrical construction and the locus of the indefinitely variable shapes (schemata), like Descartes' extended wax, of objective reality. Whatever else they may be, "things" are spatial and temporal. If we could work out how pure time and space are generated by us *a priori* so as to be mathematically determinable and empirically real, this, and not the injection of objectivity through the logical features of judgment, would be the clue to understanding the apparent "empirical reality" of these synthetically constituted "ejects." Kant says that the metaphysical deduction is the clue to the transcendental deduction; the former establishes the priority of the logical order so that—though this is fatal to Kant's project—discursive ideality gives temporality its form.

Moreover, if through that constituting act an analogue to the necessities of thought could somehow be injected *a priori* into the empirical objects by something like a transcendental object that would express the categorially intended sense of "being" that, Aquinas says, is "first in the apprehension absolutely and is included in whatsoever else one apprehends," then these objects would manifest the law-like necessities discerned in empirically objective states of affairs by the sciences (*ST* I, II, q. 94, a. 2).

3. Transcendental Apperception

TRANSCENDENTAL APPERCEPTION is original, the principle of principles, and it rules sense through its intentional object, the transcendental object. But since its relation to this object, and indeed to its own consciousness of itself, is mediated by contingent sensibility, that which grounds everything else is strangely groundless. Idealism is as if turned upside-down and we must begin thinking about it bottom-up.

Even if one had not read Kant, one might surmise the sense of a "transcendental object." In characterizing an "a this" (*todi ti*) by "is P," one determines a determinable and enduring presence, a being. This object cointended in empirical synthesis gives experience the objective necessities that the mathematical object intended in the schema gives to what is being constructed arbitrarily. We ejectively express through its form that which comes back to us as an object bearing the world-preserving sense of the transcendentals, the universal *in qual* determinates and in quid determinables that can be said of any *x a priori*. This classical usage survives in Kant's denial that space and time have "transcendental reality" (A 36/B 53), that is, they cannot be said of things as such but only of phenomena. That sense of "being" implicit in transcendental predication derives from the sense of the Greek verb, *einai*, "to be," which is then expressed in the omnipresent tenseless *esti*, "is," in judgments. At this point, Kant can pull off a neat trick. The traditional transcendentals, *ens, res, aliquid, unum, bonum, veritas*, the most universal things sayable about being in any category, dispose being to mind, to a noetic order, rather than to one another. The transcendentals do not determine an immanent order in which entities participate inter se but something transcendent, namely apperception, to which they are noetically directed. Only indirectly, as God's ideas, would they refer to a totality. If the categories are forms of judgment, the standard interpretation given to Aristotle's *Categories* since Porphyry's *Isagoge*, and dispose things for mind *a priori*, could it also be that as ontological determinates they determine the relations between "appearances" inter se as, for example, cause or substance?[9] These categories would temporally order beings, not in or for themselves, but phenomenally, as manifest to us.

If this is the story told by the first *Critique*, why has it been so difficult to discern? It is a palimpsest, not because it arose by patchwork, *pace* Jonathan Bennett or Kemp Smith, but because Kant let Teten's psychology distract him from his phenomenological concerns.[10] This led him into the epistemological trap of Locke's inner and Newton's outer world. One then begins with the perception of images, constructs out of memory, sense, logic, thought, projective tendencies, and the like by the "blind but indispensable imagination . . . without which we would have no knowledge whatsoever" (A 78/B 103). No wonder the constitution thesis got lost. The necessities of thinking things in a transcendental logic seemed to submit to the contingencies of empirical psychology for which it was necessary to find a transcendental analogue. Kant had to bridge the abyss between given, receptive sensibility and spontaneous thought by means of the imagination, which has often been called upon to bridge such ontological gaps; but in his enlightened age, what more solipsistic and idiosyncratic faculty could have been chosen? The logical necessities of judgment, borrowed by the second edition from the *Prolegomena*'s "judgments of experience," are injected in order to shore up a potentially wayward imagination. Attention became increasingly focused on the objectivity-making role of judgments, and so on concepts, rather than on what openly shows itself. Kant's solution to securing stability in *a posteriori* representations lay in an *a priori* transcendental analogue for the psychological functions in his empirical model. In one fell swoop, the contingencies could now play across the surface of the transcendental necessities, their synthetic ground.

The transcendental substructure entails that Hume's empirical "I think . . . ," a mere theater in which vagrant impressions and ideas severally showed themselves, is really grounded in a transcendental "I think . . ." whose intentions give these a form appropriate to analysis. This original unity, expressed as "I think *x*," is always categorial and surpasses the flux of empirical consciousness (B 157–58) which activates it and through which, when worked over categorially, "I am conscious of my own existence as determined in time . . . through the existence of actual things I perceive outside of me" (B 275–76). Just as the empirical experience of a self has its correlative empirical object, so transcendental experience has its "correlate" in a "transcendental object" (A 250), where the "transcendental" is presupposed both for the existence of, and as the *a priori* intelligible ground for, empirical receptivity—yet is nothing without it. The empirical is, therefore, not redundant; without it, the intending subject would be God. The entire transcendental machinery depends on intuition. These transcendental apperceptive acts stand Kant in good stead even in the immediate judgements of aesthetics, where the manifold of feeling that can't be worked up into a concept, and in the reflective teleological estimates, but come to a blind end in the Other who cannot be constituted or even thought.

However, these nominalized faculties reduce knowing to a flow chart, lending Kant to the distortions of artificial intelligence theorists or non-empirical linkages between unknown entities. There are imaginary objects and events and there are objects or projects which we may imaginatively entertain; but when Kant suggests—as Collingwood noticed—that the object of apperceptive synthesis is imaginary, doesn't it confuse the issue? Musical sounds are private, meaningless and successive, but the music to which one listens is public, durative, structured—and imaginary? This suggests dualism has been implicit in the tradition since Aristotle for whom "the imagination" produced the image (*phantasm*) intended to bridge the gap between the singularity of sense and the practical generality of experience. Sense in act, as in seeing something white, is its object, but since an 'affective quality' is subjective (*Cat.*, 9a 26-b 9), the things we perceive and intend through sense objects (the seen white as Callias) are also images. One may speak of the imaginary intention or object, since we do know the difference between imaginary music and the music to which we listen or between imaginative and prosaic thought. Were they the same, would it explain anything to say that objects, the explanans of the explandum, are really imaginary? Since imagination, though "indispensable," is "blind," a "function of the soul" of which "we are scarcely ever conscious" (A 78/B 103), why not follow Gilbert Ryle and translate nominal "imagination" by the behavioral adverb "imaginatively" and open synthesis to phenomenal description? Should one not abandon, if only for the time being, phenomena which like the medial imagination defy phenomenological description? Kant says schemata are "means of demonstration" (*CAJ* 252 n). Subsumptive judgments falsifying Popper's conjectures or verifying Hempel's covering laws would make way for apophantic judgments through and in which form is seen in the fact.[11]

Nevertheless, we must be cautious in replacing the soul's powers with intentional operators. The formal necessities of the transcendental superstructure do not just replicate and shore up the contingent structures of empirical consciousness. There are two positive consequences. If we translate judgment as statement and replace faculties with intentional prefixes, such as "I feel *p*," "I know *p*," then the *arché* whose mechanism, transcendental synthesis, ejects the empirical object will be overlooked or arrogantly dismissed. So too for the phenomenological turn in which things appear as meaningful or meant within the rubric of intentional, not physical, objectivity. What shows itself may be causal, but the phenomenal showing is not causal. Kant's "spontaneous" or "affective" pertains to intentionality and meaning, even as in aesthetics to interpretative moods, and not to causal relations between "facts," physical or psychical. For example, Kant speaks of the affection of sensibility by an object. Since objects are themselves meant and ejectively constituted, they cannot be phenomenal causes of their own hyleic experience. I can experience causes, but experience is not produced by causes. Sensibility, though passive or receptive, spontaneously interprets objects which, as meant, give the experience its appropriate variety and unity. A phenomenal theory has causal conditions; mind requires, without being reducible to, a brain; sensibility links us with things and has causal roots, but "red," a form, isn't caused by anything. The "affective" formula tells us perceptual experience comes as already interpreted, where what is expressed or instantiated in this affect is "redly" effective.

"What-it-is-to-be-an-object," the sense of the transcendental *ens*, is the interpretative program given through sensibility to the understanding by the transcendental object. Perception is self-affection by an empirical object formed through "those *a priori* representations constituting the condition under which objects are given to us" (A 15/B 29–30). Affection by self-constituted objects, like seeing a line one is drawing and intending through this a mathematical object, is the form given experience by the creative or interpretative activity of the understanding on sensibility (B 155). The transcendental object is the correlative of transcendental apperception (A 250). In a very obscure passage, Kant says that this object has "transcendental matter" (*Sachheit*) and thus its expression would make possible something like complex states of affairs and their logical formalization; for all its nothingness, it retains something of its source in the noumenal thing-in-itself which defies representation and so understanding and yet can still be thought (A 143/B 182).

To see the point of this, let us follow up Kant's late interest in Spinoza and play at being his God. The realization of *Sachheit* in *Sachen* or affair complexes presumes that there are formal and eidetic necessities that must be given in any eidetic expression. Suppose that this shadowy *Sachheit* is a rather pared down *idea Dei* as expressed in the mediate infinite mode, the "total face of the universe." Expressing yourself through this complex would be "nature naturing" [*natura naturan*], which you would reflexively receive as *Sachen* in nominal "nature natured" [*natura naturata*]. The formal intention of transcendental apperception to this correlative generates and supplies to the forms of intuition, space and time, the possibility of interpretation in a formal or categorial intuition (B 160 n.).

This transcendental grounding may offer a deeper understanding of transcendental synthesis. The presencing of ejects, that is, *natura naturata*, proposes itself as a solution to the loss of a world in Hume's inductive generalizations and his failure to rise above associationist psychology to explain natural significance. Rationalism, and the pre-Critical Kant, never confronted this problem; didn't they have a methodological access to the intelligible world that made them as if privy to God's sufficient reasons? The eject theory is founded on an analogy between God's creative intuition (B 72) and its finite human analogue, our expressivist constitution of objects through a "formal intuition" (B 160 n.). Time, the primary "form of intuition," is "generated" and self-affectively experienced through the reception of self-constructed empirical objects (B 68). By generating successive and coexistent manifolds in intending mathematical objects we experience the origin of well-ordered time and its associated synchronic or coexistent manifold. When we categorially intend empirical objects through hypotheses and instruments, sense is appropriately ordered and disposed to represent objects that will ground empirical meaning and its law-like necessities. Mathematical constructivity is therefore the clue to the secret workings of transcendental synthesis. We must now create the conditions for our own phenomenal world, the world of transcending and interrelated things in space and time as given to a knower. The key to this possibility lurks in Kant's self-affection thesis concerning the generation of temporality:

> Now that which, as representation, can be antecedent to any and every act of thinking anything, is intuition; and if it contains nothing but relations [e.g., before and after, during, together with, etc.], it is the form of intuition. Since this form does not represent anything save in so far as something is posited in the mind, it can be nothing but the mode in which the mind is affected by its own activity (namely, through this positing of its representation [as eject]), and so is affected [expressed eject as object] through its own activity. (B 67–68)

Self-consciousness, transcendental or empirical, is never intuitive, never immediate. The constitution thesis entails empirical mediation, as mentioned above, between transcendental apperception and its object. The form of mediation will, however, give experience the mechanical form of repetition rather that the quest suggested in *Erfahrung*.

This, I think, is the game plan: the transcendental object is intended by atemporal apperception. An empirical object can be intended through sense because, thanks to the productive imagination, these representations are materially sensuous and formally representative of the transcendental object. Sense can satisfy or fulfill categorial intentions, since it was meaningfully formed through them. Each act of empirical consciousness intending this or that within the unity of an experimental project expresses the formal intention of transcendental apperception in its categorial directedness (noesis) toward its empirical object (noema). Since sense is interpreted around the theme of the transcendental object, this intention will be (categorially) fulfilled. Intentional projects and their satisfactions take time. We know that consciousness experiences its own eject, the empirical object intended in the succession of its received contents, and it intends it as satisfying the categorial necessities. The chemist hardly notices the color property "red" through which he perceives the mercuric sulfide. We see the formal object in the appearances.

4. Creative Intuition

NOW THAT THE TERRAIN is sufficiently complex, some precision and simplification is in order. Kant's methodological revolution requires that objects be constructed to conform to the conditions of receptive sense and spontaneous thought. Sensibility is given in a "form of intuition" to spontaneous thought's "formal intuition" (B 160 n.). The possibility of these intuitions has something to do with the transcendental constitution of time and space as empirically real, and thus as having *a priori* the shape (schema) and form of things. The Principles present sensibility to empirical inquiry in this intelligible formality. The novel steps in this demonstration of Kant's constructionist theory lead one to see how intending to count, which Kant describes as a "formal intuition" or synopsis (A 97), constitutes an ordinal series of nows reflexively experienced through the generated manifold of coexistent, countable points in the forms of intuition.[12]

W. H. Walsh doubted that Kant employed the same sense of synthetic *a priori* in pure physics and pure mathematics; he "contrives to bring the two groups of judgments together in a formal respect only" (RW 1975, 257). They agree in "a formal respect" because the manifold of countable points has as its empirical content entities that express themselves according to the Principles. The schematized categories express an openness to beings whose formal being is given in temporal (diachronic) and spatial (synchronic) synthesis. The imagination's rule, the categories as a transcendental *logos* (archaic Greek, "to gather"), synthesizes sensibility so as it can schematically express the transcendental object in its eject. Since a formal act presupposes a correlative potential, and space and time as continuua are such potentials, we can turn directly to their generation. Just as the first postulate of Euclid I authorizes *a priori* drawing "a straight line from any point to any point" and determines its correlative manifold of connectable points, the schematized category also determines an empirically connectable manifold and permits me to connect it synthetically as expressed in the Principles. In drawing or representing the line through an *a priori* rule of synthesis, I also represent time (B 154) self-affectively (B 68) and well-order points with respect to before and after, just as experience is well-ordered by a categorial act, an *a priori* rule of synthesis. This well-ordering by *a priori* act gives time that necessary form lacking in Hume's account. For example, his account of causality entails a contingent succession; the series of moments A, B, C has no necessary order. Irrespective of any propensity to believe, A could in principle come before or after either B or C. But if causality is an *a priori* rule, just as a postulate is such a rule, then these moments, each expressing an intentional act, will have a necessary order known through the constituted objective correlate of these acts. I know that I am well-ordering time in drawing a line by watching myself continue to draw it.

The synthetic method in mathematics is pure and "has the peculiar character that it makes possible the experience that is its own ground of truth" (A 737/B 765): "Philosophy confines itself to universal concepts; mathematics can achieve nothing by concepts alone but hastens at once to intuition, in which it constructs the concept in concreto, though not empirically, but only in an intuition which it presents *a priori,* that is, which it has constructed, and in which whatever follows from the universal conditions of the construction must be universally valid of the object of the concept thus constructed" (A 716/B 744). In order to prove something about "the line," one draws a segment to "exhibit *a priori* the intuition which corresponds to the concept" (A 713/B 741). But this means that space and time, which in the Aesthetic seem finished and inert, are constructed forms of intuition in which objects are receptively given as empirically real. Clearly time is prior; it is both wider than space and, as Ricoeur has noticed, it must be "traversed" "retained," and "recognized" in temporal moments as an identical sense in the three-fold perceptual synthesis (A 98–110); we can account for it through (atemporal) acts of temporal generation.

Looked at as if from the standpoint of *natura naturans* or, if you like, of a formal intuition, space/time will, as expressing the transcendental object, be extentional potentials for division or motility, where motility is dynamic and not merely kinematic. This receptive potential, not absolute space and time, is the human sensorium. Pure intuitions of space and time are activated by the geometer when, for example, he intends to draw a line. Experience is a more dynamic analogue of this synthetic method. We "see" empirical objects by intending this transcendental formality through Hume's impressions, as if the categories were its *logos.* These categorial acts well-order a temporal succession, nomologically disposing what would otherwise be vagrant data, black cinnabar and frosty summer (A 100), into experiences of categorially determined objects (A 104–5). Kant's only example is line-drawing: "The single figure that we draw is empirical, yet it serves to express the concept, without impairing its universality. For in this empirical intuition we consider only the act [whose form lies in an *a priori* postulate] whereby we construct the concept. (A 714/B 742). The act of a transcendental agent, who is not subject to any condition of time, in expressing a rule is not an element in, and so not a Humian cause of, a succession (DH, IV, pt. 2); acts give successions through rules which order empirical apperception. These acts are atemporal and formal, generating a correlative potentiality *a priori.* An expression always reduces a potential. Since an agent in act does not change in so far as it changes another, just as the doctor does not cure himself in curing another, and time is the measure of a potential being reduced with respect to before and after, the act may be said to be (relatively) atemporal. Kant says the "acting subject would not, in its intelligible character, stand under any condition of sensibility: time is only the condition for appearances, not of things in themselves" (A 539/B 568). Of course this differs from Aristotle, for whom these "conditions" are given as determinably potential through the prior act but, as first actualities, antedate this act. Not so for the potentially combinable manifold given by the intention of original apperception through sense to its transcendental object. It can have no prior phenomenal actuality of its own, and yet for all that is not nothing. The potentiality of receptive sensibility for the representation of empirical objects, as expressed in the interpretative formula, "seeing sense impressions as" objectively significant, is the necessary condition for this act's directedness towards its transcendental object. Why? A "realization" of the pure intentional tie requires empirical receptivity. Is there a gift, a present to each signifying present, of a prior hyleic sense to be imaginatively worked up into a form? Or better, is the object itself hyleic, to be seen as this or that? Can we make any sense of a non-temporal or non-spatial sensibility?

5. The Transcendental Object

AT THE RISK OF REDUNDANCY, I will address and try to make sense of everything Kant says on the uncommonly difficult subject of the transcendental object. He says the "transcendental object [Gegenstand] . . . is the "subject of thoughts" (A 358).[13] This isn't too helpful. Following what we have learned about analysis, could we assemble thoughts in a monstrative set, or metaphor, disposing these towards the disclosure, if appropriately modeled, of the transcendental object? We will meet up with it on every road we travel within Gerd Buchdahl's reduction-expression scheme as the eidetic identity common to all possible objects of whatever type unconcealed through an eidetic-phenomenological reduction of its various realizations, cultural, logical, theological, scientific, linguistic and the like. These realizations are to be taken as if imaginative variations (Husserl) or a K-set of regions associated with K-sets of De Pater-Ramsey descriptions which converge on an eidos—if there is an eidos to converge on. Thus no ontological claims are possible short of some sort of synthetic methodology, in this case the fusion of analysis with speculative demonstration within the context of an eidetic reduction. Can we exploit Buchdahl's insight by assembling Kant's remarks into a catachresis leading beyond this object to the arché—if there is one?

World is the horizon of all intentionalities and their correlative object horizons. If world is to be constructed and characterized through a priori intentional and generative acts, these must be oriented by the sense of the world that lies in and is realized through them, not in some extrinsically given hyle to be shaped by categorial form. We must learn to deny the separationist form/matter distinction and, like

Meno's slave, "see the forms in the facts." Husserl's eidetic reduction shows how this can be done. Applied to Kant, this reduction would let us see that even the phenomenal is, if not its epiphany, a symbol of the noumenal. The transcendental object is their between, their *metaxu*.

If the "I think" is its Archimedean point, then world as such must be already understood before it is expressed in this or that *Sach*, "state of affairs." Kant raises the difficult problem of *Sachheit*, "expressing a state of affairs," in the Schematism of quality:

> Reality, in the pure concept of the understanding, is that which corresponds to a sensation in general; it is that, therefore, the concept of which in itself points in itself to being (in time). Negation is that the concept of which represents non-being (in time). The opposition of these two thus rests upon the distinction of one and the same time as filled and as empty. Since time is merely the form of intuition, and so of objects [*Gegenstände*] as appearances, that in the objects which corresponds to sensation is not the transcendental matter of all objects as things in themselves [*die Sachheit, Realität*]. (A 143/B 182)

In its nothingness the transcendental object must also be the meaning of Being, in its full realization the noumenal thing-in-itself as known to God and in its reduced form cointended by us in all expressions of empirical synthesis which give experience its world-preserving form. *Sachheit* is the potential for *Sachen*, the ideal relational structures, logical and mathematical, of all possible states of affairs. "Reality" is used intensionally, as the transcendental *res* and, like *ens*, pertains to what makes so and so "a what" whether it exists or not and means "thinghood" (MH 1967, 213). This prior sense of the world has evident affinities with Plato's anamnesis.[14]

The transcendental object is outrageously complex; and though I think it a monstrous fiction, its difficulty and importance to Kant justifies an exhaustive treatment which will be, I fear, repetitious and exhausting. Since this interpretation may seem to do unwonted violence to Kant, my reading will touch base with texts important to any interpretation. The convergence towards Gerd Buchdahl's "reduction-realization" scheme is not altogether fortuitous; his generous responses and challenges to earlier versions have shaped my understanding. Buchdahl approaches the reduction through the life-world of Husserl's *Crisis;* I come by way of the archaic gift of phenomenological *doxa* within the parameters of analysis. I therefore assume the centrality of intuition and the phenomenology of perceptual consciousness in which, first, the object-in-general and then the transcendental object appear as the eidetically reduced being sense of empirical objects as such.

On a non-intentional reading, Kant attempts to refute Hume as a transcendental Locke. Like the "generally unknown" substance whose powers cause ideas of its primary and secondary qualities, Kant admits that the "something that underlies the outer appearances and so affects our sense that it obtains" empirical representation in space, time, shape, and the like "may yet, when viewed as noumenon (or better, the transcendental object), be at the same time the subject of thoughts" (A 358). But surely no transcendental object, a nothing, "underlies" and "causes" in Locke's sense. The spontaneity by which things are constituted and thought would fall under a causal rubric. What obtains representation in space and time is phenomenally oriented; an underlying nexus of Lockean causes would never yield an oriented world. We may of course speak of noumenal causes, but we must then honor this in the distinction between schematic and non-schematic causes, where the latter has a sense close to Plato's *aitia*, that is, to participation. Speaking in the latter vein, Kant says that since appearances are "not things in themselves, they must rest on a transcendental object that determines them as mere representations; and consequently there is nothing to prevent us from ascribing to this transcendental object, besides the quality in terms of which it appears, a *causality* which is not appearance, although its *effect* is to be met with in experience" (A 539/B 568). The sense of the Greek *aitia*, "occasion," and not the Latin *causa*, "to fall out from," seems to be operative in a "causality which is not appearance." The transcendental object is the "occasion" for something being represented (as the unschematized effect of the transcendental object) in sensibility. Kant says that "the effect of an object upon the faculty of representation, in so far as we are affected by it, is sensation" (A 20/B 34). As I have argued, to be "affected" by an object is to experience it as meaningful and act on it interpretatively; as a meaning, we are conscious of "something as something." To experience something, such as an explosion, as schematizable "cause" is to register it and look for its subsequent effects which may then perhaps be affectively interpreted. An "intelligible cause of appearances" accounts for the meaningfulness of sense as immanently characterizable by "cause," "substance," and the like. A schematic "effect" invites explanation of an already interpreted given; a non-schematic "effect" posits and interprets the given. Questions concerning the affection of sense by an object of reason's own determining are to be explained by the possibility of perceiving self-constituted things through sense data. "Is an affection of" is interpretative, not schematically causal.

How can an *it* be meant in its sensory aspects? How can these private sensa take on public meaning through an object? Let's translate these results into Kant's phenomenal context, invoking Chisholm's adverbial locution for non-comparative "appearing" terms (RC 1957) and taking "affection" to have the hermeneutical sense of understanding something through its occasion, *aitia*. If one sees a green tree, then Kant could say that sensibility (receptively given sense contents) is greenly affected (where affection is the transcendental object as *aitia*) by a tree (as its empirical reason). The transcendental object "makes" the sensed green mean a tree. What "causes" one to see trees greenly (receptive sensibility as affected by objects) requires explanation by reason of the transcendental object, which lets sense impressions mean the empirical object, that is, "which makes the greenly appearing to be the appearance of a tree." As indicative signs drop out of explicit attention when they are animated as meanings, so sense contents drop out in perception; we usually say, "I see a tree." More simply, intention through sense to the transcendental object is the reason why empirical things appear through these sense contents. Since perception is an ontic interpretation of oriented sensibility, this may be expressed in the generalized interpretative formula, "*n*-ing *x* as *y*," where *n* is some noetic act or intentional prefix, *x* the noesis or meaning (*Sinn*), and *y* the noema or reference (*Bedeutung*). The perceptual formula, "seeing the tree greenly," would then read, "seeing green as (an aspect of) a tree."

What does it mean to say perception is an "affection of sensibility" through its interpretation under the formality of the transcendental object? First, perception is a synthetic, interpretative act that gives its form to space and time, that in which the transcendental object "obtains" representation. When I say that sense is "affected by empirical objects," I mean that the thing directively gives itself to me as near or far in a system of phenomenal spaces and times. Second, the object must have an ontological loading which will sustain counterfactual law-like explanations and universal generalizations. "Affection by an empirical object" is an oriented and ontologically meaningful experience of things that explain, where the "for me" of oriented, sensory meanings are given from "there" to my unique *locus standi*. "Affection" is an intentional phenomenon and entails interpretation and self-interpretation, not some species of phenomenal causality. If intentionality is ignored and the transcendental object determined in the causal category, then it would be empirically intuitable. That by which something is an empirical object is not an empirical object.

But then Kant says that this object may be considered as an "intelligible cause of appearances . . . in order to have something corresponding to sensibility viewed as receptivity" (A 494/B 522); this invites explanation by Platonic reasons. The transcendental object makes perceptual, and so knowable, objects present in sensibility and also justifies counterfactual references. Historical inquiry or projections into the future will encounter the phenomenal intelligibility of the world; "to this transcendental object we can ascribe the whole extent and connections of our possible perceptions, and can say that it is given in itself prior to all experience" (*ibid.*). Even though sensibility is an inexplicable gift, a presencing of a presence to us in a present, it is most often received in perceptual interpretations or schema characterized by the Principles.

Is there more to the sense of an "intelligible" cause than that which lets x be and be an F? These causes can be traced to Leibniz and, through him, to Augustine and Plato; in fact, this is Kantian interpretation of the *Phaedo* formula for the causality of ideas (100B–102E). Consider the distinction between the intelligible and phenomenal worlds of the *Inaugural Dissertation* where, in a modification of Leibniz, the world of sense shows itself in its "noumenal perfection" to God in his creative, intellectual intuition as complete and wholly determined. This creative intuition reappears, in contrast to "derivative" and successive human intuition, as an *intuitus originarius* (B 72) that gives its object through the archetypal idea (A 313/B 370). Augustine thought the world was given to God as infinite totality in a creative intuition *semper standi*, a now without past or future. In 1763, Kant said while "the succession of things to each other in the world is in his [God's] power, he does not thereby determine even one point of time in this series, and, consequently, with respect to himself, nothing is past or future. . . . From thus it can be apprehended that there is no difference at all between knowledge of the future, past or present, with respect to the activity of the divine understanding" (*Enq.* II, 297). Something like this power to presence objects *a priori* is found in mathematics. While we may imaginatively presence objects by schematically sensibilizing concepts, if we are to make conceptual judgments which require verification by objects, we have to search out instances. Thought, as Descartes reminds us, can impose no necessity on things. Not so for the idea which expresses its instances, not just as fictions, but as intelligible, the "object which it thinks it exhibits *a priori* in intuition" (A 729/B 757). In mathematics we produce in a pure intuition a sensible object *a priori*; this sensible expression of a concept, together with subordinate constructions and background knowledge, enables one to intend the intelligible object through the constructed object, as its image or schema, as if the expressed object were the figuration or image of the intelligible object. There is thus the appearance of realism. What seems to be given as real is transcendentally ideal; for intelligible objects are nothing but expressions of the concepts through the mediation of *a priori* constructive sensibility. This *a priori* sensible mediation enables me to synthetically enlarge the concept, as if with the assistance of auxiliary constructions I were reporting on what I saw in the image. Though the image is my own doing and expresses only a concept, a rule, what *seems* to be given in the image is an idea. Plato has been turned upside down: "The single object we produce must in its representation express universal validity for all intuitions that fall under the same concept. Thus I construct a triangle by representing the object that corresponds to this concept either by imagination alone, in pure intuition, or in accordance therewith on paper, in empirical intuition—in both cases completely *a priori*, without having borrowed the pattern from any experience" (A 714/B 742). This is the mathematical paradigm of transcendental synthesis. Unless something like an intelligible object could be intended in sense, thought would lose itself among Hume's phantasmagoric contingencies. Just as an intention to the mathematical object produces a sensuous affection, so too the intention to the transcendental object is an "affection of sensibility." The transcendental object, the condition for intentional objectivity, is always intended as same (A 109) through all the differences of contingent sense. Though it is the most empty of all concepts, Dr. Buchdahl suggests that every other type of object in Kant will be either its reduction or expression. Being interpreted as *Gegenstand* entails that it is an *in quid* or "simple" determinable presence which may be taken up repeatably in various projects from a variety of perspectives and which, even when thought in intuitive absence, can be present in manifold modes and circumstances as this self-identical presence. This object can have this ontological role only because it is the bearer of a fundamental hermeneutical interpretation. This is where we are going even if the way will not always be clear.

We can begin again with this red, this crystalline shape, and the like which are aspects of cinnabar, sensible contents that are meanings of their meant, noematic object. Sense instances the category, becomes meaningful when affected or interpreted through the transcendental object, so that its empirical noema may be experimentally addressed as cause, substance, extensive or intensive magnitude, and the like. This is not to be confused with thinking it "through any category, for a category is valid only for empirical intuition, as bringing it under the concept of an object in general. A pure use is indeed possible, that is, without contradiction, but it has no objective validity" (A 252). In this pure use, thought, though perhaps busy, is busy spinning wheels and "has no objective validity." Yet this transcendental object is also said to be a "subject of thoughts" (A 358). In the *Dissertation* whose sense often governs the *Critique*, Kant says that "abstract ideas which the mind entertains when they have been received from the intellect often cannot be followed up in the concrete and converted into intuitions" (I, 1). We can think and presence symbolically what we cannot represent and understand: "To think an object and to know an object are by no means the same thing: Knowledge involves two factors: first, the concept through which the object in general is thought (the category); and secondly, the intuition through which it is given" (B 156). To identify this transcendental object, which partakes in the noumenal, with the intelligible object does not take one very far. Perhaps there is nothing to understand. The transcendental object, though "it has no objective validity, confers objective reality on all our concepts" (A 252), that is, the synthetic truth condition required by analysis and not the wholly determined eidetic correlate of this or that empirical object. A Kantian idea is regulative, admitting of more or less, when "the issue depends on freedom, and it is the power of freedom to pass beyond any and every specified limit" (A 317/B 354), and not archetypal. Any vestigial trace of a divine idea in Kant probably has a regulative role; the transcendental object does not prescribe limits and may retain something of the infinity associated with its noumenal realization. This object, bearing traces of an infinite totality given through God's creative intuition, gives understanding its goal of completely determining the determinable, even if this leads "to that notable characteristic of our nature, never to be capable of being satisfied with what is temporal" (B xxxii). In showing itself as sequentially receptive and so determinable, sense presupposes an ideal completeness to us through its world-preserving transcendental object. The Analogies must preserve the part-whole relations as an analogue of Leibniz's monads, which conservatively reflect all things. For example, reciprocity among phenomenal substances replaces the egress and ingress of forces among Kant's own pre-Critical monads. Besides this expression of the infinite, which sets the task of constituting and determining the determinable for finite constructivity, this object also gives us the meaning of Being (ontological) that enables us to have meaningful beings (ontic) in a world. How so? Because what is a fulfilled presence for God is for us, like Hegel's "bad infinite," endlessly determinable. To cite again his marginal note, Kant said that "the distinction between the concept of the thing in itself and that of appearance is not objective, but merely subjective. The thing in itself is not another object, but another respect of the representation with regard to the same object" (*Op. Post.* 625). If the "thing-in-itself" in the positive sense is the completely determined "eject" of Divine intuition which discursive understanding seeks to replicate in its sequential determinations, and if the transcendental object is entailed in objects of all types, might it not be that it is the middle term between these extremes, preserving through the categories (for which God has no use, B 145) the sense of the world conferred by God and the contingent determinability of phenomena? The transcendental object would be "an aspect of the representation with regard to the same object" were it taken as a sort of eidetic reduction that orders the noumenal "in itself" to the phenomenal "for us." In this reduction we would respect both the given necessities of the *Sachheit* and the contingent givenness of sensibility, the condition for meaningfully intending any object. The object is an identifiable and reidentifiable, openly endless, horizon signifying other such object horizons which in overlap, fusion, and even bifurcation make a world. The transcendental object would then be an eidetic identity, which is the possibility of any intelligible, object horizon. Now consider this reduced object as the transcendental object, the "subject of thoughts" (A 358). We cannot think it through a category, that is, schematize it, for as purely determinable there is nothing determinate to think. Though the transcendental object has no content by which it could be distinguished or individuated, this lack is its virtue; every object of every type is *qua* object its expression. The transcendental object, a something that isn't anything determinate nor determinable, is the condition for determination and thus intelligibility. "This something, thus conceived, is only the transcendental object; and by that is meant a something $= x$, of which we know, and with the present constitution of our understanding can know nothing whatsoever, but which, as a correlate of the unity of apperception, can serve only for the unity of the manifold in sensible intuition" (A 250). Aren't we looking at a medial phenomenon that is, like Plato's receptacle, a nothing that things? If so, doesn't this suggest that we have been looking in the wrong direction, to transcendental apperception rather than to some analogue of the imagination? Attention should be fixed, not on objects, but on the *arché* which gives them. On an active, generative nothing? Really?

    This is what I want to say, but is it true? There are vast philosophical complexities and innumerable textual hurdles along the way that must be leaped. To begin with the latter, suppose we ask Kant directly, what is the transcendental object? Kant's answer is not encouraging: "No answer can be given stating what it is. . . . The question itself is nothing, because there is no given object [in the context of this question]. . . . A question as to the composition of that something which cannot be thought through any determinate predicate . . . is entirely null and void" (A 479/B 507). So we end with nothing. But why would one expect this question to make sense? Like Jacques Derrida's *différance* which confers textuality, whatever confers objective reality is not a being but rather a medial, non-present *arché* which can be thought only in a catachrestic assemblage. What determines sensibility *a priori* as a determinable manifold cannot be more than the purely *in quid* determinable and otherwise undetermined *it*. Gerd Buchdahl says that, in some realizations, it is the logical object, the logician's x which, while open to quantification and other logical operations and relations, is completely empty. Among its realizations are noumena in the positive, for example, the self as a moral entity, and negative senses. It is also the transcendental logician's *x*, an open possibility for various real relations to other beings in the phenomenal context of truth relations to a knower. This is all very true, but what gives *x*? Is this between the abyss from which, as Heidegger said, Kant drew back? Before we become archaeologists, we must learn all we can from Kant about desedimentation and construction.

The "thing" as a Humian set of contiguous impressions is not determinable. In the absence of any determinable object in which the manifold was nomologically united things could end up as *ad hoc* company formations of impressions. If related only by the resemblances and contiguities of "empirical affinity," impressions could neither characterize nor make up the objects which explain. There is nothing there, neither determinates nor determinables. Let us accept Hume's challenge. The transcendental object is a no-thing which is, however, apt for *in quid* and *in qual* assertions of "being." It is, minimally, the same Parmenides sought for being and thinking, the possibility of encountering an *it* that can unify a spatial and temporal region and grant some sort of qualitative access through it to world. The Principles, noematic forms constituted through *a priori* diachronic and synchronic synthesis, make this possible. In having been constituted by the very synthetic forms that enable us to take it up into thought through questions reflecting the dynamical and mathematical Principles, the *it* is the pure possibility of determinability which, assuming empirical content, answers to categorial questions.

The object-in-general is the realized transcendental object as apportioned to the transcendental schema (A 251). It gives its form to the empirical object so that it can answer categorial questions, even though it is never itself determined and, as a quiddity, is "null and void." The "object in general $= x$" is this something or other which is the synthetic truth condition intended in any empirical concept, and the empirical content would then verify a hypothetical or conjectural response to the experimental question. The *it* is the object, the *x*, of synthetic judgment *a priori* as such: "The categories represent no special object, given to the understanding alone, but only serve to determine the transcendental object, which is the concept of something in general, through that which is given in sensibility, in order thereby to know appearances empirically under concepts of objects" (A 250). Ontology begins with what the Scholastics called *res*, "thing," a transcendental convertible with *ens* which is sayable of Aristotle's first (*tode ti*, "a this") and second substance in the *Categories*. A "transcendental object" would then have at least this ontological loading; it is that about which being may be said in some primary sense and which is, thus, patient for articulation in the logical order. We have suggested that it expresses the meaning of being by which other beings are interpreted. But unless an object is determined, and this is merely the determinable as such, it is the same as nothing: "The supreme concept with which it is customary to begin a transcendental philosophy is the division into the possible and impossible . . . [but since division presupposes a still higher concept to be divided, this comes to] the concept of an object in general [an alternative tag for the transcendental object], taken problematically, without its having been decided whether it is something or nothing" (A 290/B 346). According to Gerd Buchdahl, the transcendental object results from the eidetic reduction of any intentional object "that represents a state where no ontological account is (or is yet) provided, or where such an account is only implicit, or unacknowledged" (GB 1982, 45). One needs to say something stronger: no such account can be provided. The transcendental object, which makes possible ontological accounts, is not open to explanation. That which occasions, the "*F*" in "what lets *x* be *F*," does not require reasons of the same type, if it requires any at all. The transcendental object is just this sort of *F* that limits regressive explanation. "Does the form of cat have long claws?" that is, is it a "cat?" invites a regress. There can be no ontological account, implicit or provided, of the expressively intended being of transcendental apperception, the condition for its own being (in analytic unity) and for that of all other beings that can be anything to or for thought. Being is not itself a being. But how is it, given this object which is nothing, that in referring to any object I can intend its worldhood and justify this intention through the transcendental object? I shall explore the role of the transcendental object in synthesis from this perspective.

A "'transcendental'" object conforms "with the mode of our knowledge of objects in so far as a mode of knowledge is to be possible *a priori* (A 12/B 25). Playing on the received sense of "transcendental," this object in its role as the "*x*" unifying the manifold of sense is determined *a priori* as omnipresent by omnipredicable transcendentals or, which comes to the same thing, the transcendentals as "concepts of an object in general" (B 128) of the traditional *metaphysica generalis*. I assume that this object, being intended in the transcendental synthesis by which empirical objects are given as ejects, gives to that synthesis its intelligible form. The transcendental object is a unity intended prior to experience and, like a mathematical object, given as present in its schematic realizations and not like objects of empirical concepts to be searched out and subsumed under them. This is the everywhere one and the same object of every intentional act, though it is significantly intended only in the experimental employment of the categories and derivative forms of consciousness.

Realization of the transcendental object in the "object-in-general" is, Buchdahl says, the "formal expression of what goes on in the context of experience when we call upon sensibility and understanding . . . to generate or derive the empirical object from the transcendental object" (GB 1982, 45). I understand this object-in-general, which supports categorial ascription, to mediate between the transcendental object, which does not offer that support, and the empirical object. Both precede the empirical object, the *Sachheit* of the world (A 143), which through the intervention of sensibility is converted into the existence of affair complexes, *Sachen*. Kant seems to suggest that concrete sensuousness is to the phenomenal object as *Sachheit* is to the transcendental object, where each is a sort of *hyle* to be formed. If it is like *hyle*, it would be determinable; but I do not think this can be his meaning. *Sachheit* must be construed expressively, as *natura naturans*, and not objectively, as *Sachen* or *natura naturata*.

The transcendental object gives sense its objective reference, supplying the condition under which it gives itself to be experienced as meaningful and not as something to be worked up in an objective form. These determinable objectivities are given in the Principles as further determinable as, for example, a specific cause, a determinate substantial magnitude, and the like. The object, and not its determinable matter, is the "matter" for determination. What then would be its form? Since Kant thinks objects are knowable only if the formality in which they are intended is transcendental, *a priori*, and homologous with what we understandingly meet up with in them, couldn't we say that here too the form of this object is as if an imaginative "ejection" of the formal intention of transcendental apperception, which is categorial? But this object is not knowable; categories are significant only when schematized, that is, temporalized. This employment is really no employment at all, for there is no determinate object, not even a determinate form (A 247/B 304). We are then told that categories "are the pure forms of understanding in respect of objects in general" (A 238/B 305). That pure form meaningfully disposes sense when the object in general is intended, while at the noumenal level Kant says that "the whole meaning of the categories entirely vanishes" (B 308). The "object-in-general [*Objekts Überhaupf*] . . . thought in the category" required for "knowledge of an object distinct from me" (B 158) is an expression within the *Sachheit*-like nexus of the transcendental object, or, conversely, the phenomenological reduction of the empirical object in which the transcendental object is realized. Would a mere "*x*" at the transcendental level have more determinable content? But there may be another interpretation.

Why do categories vanish at the noumenal level? Because nothing stands over against God as a determinable or as determinate object. As eject the creature is totally transparent to God. To an understanding "which is itself intuitive (as for instance a divine understanding which should not represent to itself given objects, but through whose representation the objects should themselves be given or produced), the categories would have no meaning whatsoever. . . . They are merely rules for an understanding whose whole power consists in thought . . . in the act whereby it brings the synthesis of a manifold, given to it elsewhere in intuition, to the unity of apperception" (B 145). We ejectively express and generate through iterative rules the spatial and temporal forms which configure the self-affectively experienced object as a discriminable access to a connected world. In this synthesis of the sense manifold (by the imagination) which thematizes this object in general, it too is transparent, a mere "*x*." But this is a rather loaded "*x*," for it expresses a Parmenidian interpretation in which the transcendental object is archetypal. This understanding is ontically thematized in transcendental synthesis that lets beings appear as worldly, durative and determinable. If this is getting a bit thick, remember that being is not in but divided by categories and, though said *in quid* of determinables and *in qual* of their determinates, is neither determinate nor determinable. I suggest that this is not lost to Kant. The Axioms express determinable being and the Anticipations its determinates, and from these we are to infer substances, causal nexus, and the like. All of these "divide up" the sense of being, at least as it functions in *metaphysica generalis*. Because it is transcategorial, "being" is said to be a transcendental. An object that expressed that sense would be properly "transcendental." From the formal side, this tells us little. Aside from the syntactical possibilities appropriate to such an X, a mere something or other, what is the point of these possible categorial determinations? These are meaningless without sensibility.

What about the "material" aspect of the transcendental object, the *Sachheit* expressed in *Sachen*, states of affairs? Will the expressive act intending the *Sachheit* of this object carry the meaning of Being that is constitutive for any world of possible experience in any realization, where the sense given to this constituting and sense-making empirical synthesis is that of the Principles of Empirical Thought? Approaching this with a slightly different perspective, one may ask. What sense must this *Sachheit* bear to ground the transcendental sense of the world? Since the sense is that of possible experience, it must lie in the "material conditions" of thought, which would be nothing less then the significance of sensibility. Isn't that the work of the imagination? Isn't the object intended and the category schematized a function of this blind and indispensable faculty? But doesn't it come to be through language which expresses rather than constructs things?

The significance carried by one discriminable thing gathers us into significant others. An empirical object must be discriminable in ways that justify natural inferences, as the high tide tells us about the moon or a storm at sea. This possibility lies largely in the connectedness of space and time, which make any past object accessible from the conditions of intuition, where what is intuited is either a variable intensive magnitude or manipulable extensive magnitude, such as might be accessible only to the blind. These intensive and extensive "quantities" should permit inferences to substance, which is sempiternal, or through their variations by means of the causal categories to something else posing as substance (JB 1966, 197–201). This is the theme imagination, productive or figurative and reproductive, plays in the Principles.

6. Kant's Hermeneutical Circle

IF WE LET ST. THOMAS AQUINAS speak in Kantian terms, then being (as expressively thought in the transcendental object) is first in the apprehension absolutely and (its expressed ontic sense) is included in whatever else one apprehends. This categorially predelineated possibility would be the determinable "non-empirical x" of synthetic *a priori* judgments which unify sense. The constituted object x in the expression "object $= x$" is "some third thing" which grounds synthetic judgments (A 9/B 13–A 10/B 14) because it is first the ejectively constituted "object in general $= x$" of synthetic *a priori* judgments (A 104–5). This "non-empirical" object that makes empirical objects possible is the pure possibility for the generation of the forms of intuition and the formal determination of the resulting spatial and temporal manifold in a categorial nexus so as to convey meaning and unity to the received sensory manifold through which it is meant and to the apperception discerning it as meaningful (A 109). An interpretation of the transcendental object has been offered that does Kant justice.

When a transcendental intention, a formal act expressing the pure forms of the understanding or transcendentals, is directed to its correlative transcendental object (A 250), the intended "subject of thoughts" (A 358), the mind disposes mediating sensibility affectively, where "affects" are ontic interpretations. In being conscious of such empirical objects, we are self-consciously or self-affectively present. Kant's bold extension of the *logos* of the constructive mathematical method to experience in general reveals "a transcendental synthesis [framed] from concepts alone, a synthesis with which the philosopher is alone competent to deal . . . [that] relates only to a thing in general, as defining the conditions under which the perception of it can belong to possible experience" (A 719/B 747). The categories, transcendental predicates of this object in general (B 128), "contain a pure intuition" and so express the possibility of a constructable thing as such (A 719/B 747). Kant's thesis cuts deeper; the spatial/temporal form within which any constituted object, empirical or pure, appears is also a construction. Time, the form of succession, is the primary "form of intuition." A successive or diachronic temporal manifold of factual and counterfactual acts of empirical consciousness, now and now and . . . , and their possible synchronic or coexistent contents "presupposes a synthesis," which Kant describes as occurring through a "formal intuition . . . which does not belong to the senses but through which all concepts of space and time become possible" (B 160 n.). But the concepts are founded on the generation of these pure forms by a pure act, as paradigmatically given in mathematical construction, which will intend its object, not through empirical sensibility, but through the manifold of pure sensibility. Such manifolds are schematically given when things being counted are taken as units and represented punctally (*Prol.* sec. 2).

I have shown that pure apperception, "a formal intuition" that does not stand under any condition of time, gives to sense through its correlative transcendental object the objective conditions for the "autobiographical" unity of the understanding (empirical apperception). Now I must show how the pure successive and coexistent manifolds are given by "my generating time" (A 142/B 182). How are we to think of time as determinably given by a formal intuition? As is usual with Kant, a formal intuition of a line expressively being drawn is "the figurative representation of time" (B 154), a self-affective continuous doing in which each act in the series acquires its "determinate position in this relation of time only in so far as something is presupposed in the preceding state upon which it follows invariably . . . in accordance with a rule" (A 198/B 243). The postulate that authorizes this act *a priori* is analogous to the causal rule Kant has in mind.

There can't be the diachronic time of dread or insomnia nor will it allow doubts about the being of past or future. We experience ourselves in time we atemporally generate. Death cannot be an abyss but is simply one among many events to transcendental apperception. Though Kant denied it, Herder said Kant was an Averroist; isn't the knower-in-general rather like an impersonal world-soul? The atemporality of apperception's "formal intuition" shores up the self against the abyss, not by its creative grasp of real possibility, but by clinging to the substantial being of the past that, through the ontological interpretation of Being, manifests itself as continuous presence. The past unrolls, like a carpet before a bride, in the physics of continuous functions so that she, the present, will remain as she was, chaste and pure, in any possible future. By identifying oneself with the mechanism of nature as a condition for well-ordered inner sense through the atemporal analytic unity of apperception, and by determining this time of inner sense through sempiternal material substance, as in the Refutation of Idealism, Kant has a guarantee that what passes in the logical order as self-ascription will, in the existential order secure the self against the abyss, the "impossibility of possibility." In Heidegger's phrase, this "ownmost possibility," death, is concealed. The first of the Postulates assures us that future experience will be conformal with the past. Remember Kant's walks and the wealth he converted into gold and slept on? Methodological doubts are also put to rest. All that is certain is of our doing as reflectively apprehended in the done. Our categorial acts are apprehended through their presenced object (*Objekt*) (B 137–39), even when we are not immediately conscious of them (A 103–4).[15] In constructing the object through the categories, what is certain is the feedback from the analytic method of questioning the unknown by and through the categories as embedded in experimental set-ups. "Judgment" is legal and not logistic, as one will see from a careful reading of the second edition Preface; *theoria*'s "certainty" (*cernere*) that it can carry on is "discriminatory" and prudential rather than a theoretical indubitability. We can be certain (*certus*) of being able to make sense (*cernere*) of what shows itself in analytic representations. Isn't this epistemological optimism founded on a hermeneutical circle? The "I think . . ." replaces God as the noetic ground for beings and manages to block out thought of its own radical contingency by thematizing these beings it constitutes as durative presences, substances in the phenomenal sense. Reading knowledge of itself back off of these condemns itself-understanding to mechanism. The "regressive synthesis" cannot capture teleology (A 411/B 438), while the image of time as a flowing river (A 170/B 211) and his line-drawing examples (A 33/B 50, A 102, B 137–38, B 154) preclude William James's time that grows by leaps and buds; instead, it continuously unrolls itself from the past through the present and into an already settled future.

IV

TIME AND NUMBER

....

1. Continuity in Aristotle and Kant

ARISTOTLE SAYS that drama is a durative or eventual unity of action that is expressed in the plot, the complete ordering of a sequence of episodes. Unless one wishes to convey the meaningless of life, an episode in a play is determined by what happens before and what will happen; we cannot divide and rearrange it arbitrarily. Even medial activity has the unity of a game or a play; things happen because other things happened and it could not have been otherwise. We must understand the relation of act to time in this light. Just as a life is the expression of gene activity or Spinoza's *natura naturata* is an expression of *natura naturans,* so the time in which things endure is an expression of possible and actual time constituting acts. This was not appreciated by Hume and other more recent act theorists, for example, Danto.

Augustine was attracted to a text from the Book of Wisdom in which God was said to have created the world "in measure, weight, and number." When Kant handed world-making over to us by transmuting his pre-Critical thesis that act is the ground of determinations into transcendental apperception, he too made the methodology and schematic power of pure and applied mathematics central, though this position is almost always overlooked (IP 1973, 90). His relation to Augustine's triune and subjective view of temporality is evident in auto-affective self-constitution; time is a form of presence in which I, as transcendental spectator, empirically experience myself. In the second edition he ceases thinking of himself as a participatory *theoria, and then* the phenomenology he founded tends to get lost in a maze of mental fictions. Some of that phenomenology can be restored at the expense of his theory of time and, in the final chapters, in the expressivist foundations of mathematics.

The basis for the transition from the phenomenological A-series to the successive linear time of the B-series lies in Kant's use of mental acts to generate a potential infinite. The actual infinite could not be represented.[1] A finitistic approach in which numbers were set out through iterative schemata solved his problem with representing the infinite. "I can (did, could have or will) act" grants synoptic time as a divisible by acts now and . . . and so forth.

Aristotle defines the infinite as potential, not as actual; his point is that something is infinite if recursive division or addition is incompletable (*De Phys.* 251b 10–252a 4); more or less can always be taken in the same ratio, for example, ½, ¼, ⅛, and so forth. The line or time is continuous if the point (or now) that cuts it is alternatively the least upper or greatest lower bound (or before or after), but not both together. Though he says that the now is both the reason for the continuity of time and what divides it with respect to before and after, there is an acknowledged difference between a point on a line and a now in time. A point on a line is not defined by the linear stretches on either side of it; but the countable now, which is to time what the moving thing is to motion, always refers to past or future, to what lies on either side. In this sense, Aristotle says that a now is like the end points of, not a point on, a line because it has an intrinsic reference to what it begins or terminates (220a 10–20). An instant or now, having no magnitude, cannot be a part of time for it cannot serve as its integral measure. Every now is always same (establishing continuity) and other (the contextual difference). Time is divided and made continuous by the now (200a 4).

Kant and Aristotle associate time with subjectivity.[2] Aristotle wonders, "whether if soul did not exist time would exist or not . . . for if there cannot be someone to count, there cannot be anything to be counted, so evidently there cannot be number" (222a 21–23). Though time is just this countable aspect of real motion, yet we are aware of time "in the dark and are not being affected through the body, [for] if any movement takes place in the mind [e.g., a succession of thoughts], we at once suppose that time has elapsed" (219 4–5). However it does not follow that time is a transcendentally ideal construction within inner sense. God's existence secures continuous and sempiternal motility; but the form of this motility depends on the proper place of the moving thing. The unity and continuity of time is a function of the motion it measures. Motion (*kinesis* or *metabole*) is not just spatial (*chora*) but is durative, always stretching out. Heidegger translates *suneches,* "stretching," as "being-held-together-within-itself (MH 1982, 242). Stretching is "away from something towards something" (224b 35). Telic directedness pertains to the unity of motion; but for Galileo's heirs, the "towards" is descriptive of a determined route and not telic; there are no proper places; direction is a parameter of motion, not a gift of that towards which something is stretched or stretches out. Aristotelian time belongs neither to the motile thing nor the spectator, but rather to the between, the *metaxu;* so too for Kant, except this between is the imagination.

For Kant, however, we generate time; its unity and continuity lies in the generative act, not in a transition held together as one time. The implicit "I can" of a possible iterative act generates the numbered now and its numbering. The point manifold is an "away from here towards there" (MH 1982, 245). For example, I begin generating the ordinals, now first, now second, and so on. I retain the origin and, in its successor now, name it "first"; retaining that first, I now name it "second," etc.[3] The natural numbers are generated as I stand out "away from here towards there" from each now, in order to count something in the associated synchronic manifold of outer sense, the form of coexistence. We assume a synopsis under the intention "to count" yields an order-indifferent or synchronic manifold of countable entities in each diachronic, ordinal now. This "synchronic" manifold is more or less equivalent to the timeless space associated with instants in a four-dimensional spatial/temporal continuum. The archetype for time constitution lies in a recursive rule that generates these natural numbers by counting these order-indifferent manifolds in ordinal temporality. From these counting numbers, Kronecker said, all the other denumerable classes can be derived. Since *qua* series, these associated nows are "earlier" or "later than," Kant can exhibit the Aristotelian continuity of time in a pure intuition by drawing a line in an *a priori* motion. That time is nothing but relations (A 33/B 50, A 49/B 67) whose relata are nows, in the sense that they are given in a synopsis as real relata under an appropriate synthetic intention, means that each marks a division of an endless (A 32/B 48) time line (A 33/B 50). Time is the *a priori* condition for motion (B48–49), not its "number" or metrical aspect.

Is the "greater than" and "less than" relation between the numbers generated in counting the same relation as the "before" and "after" of motility and time? If each now represents nature at an instant, and it refers to the point locus of a moving object, then there could be no motion; a set of constructively generated points does not constitute a line nor can generated nows make up a duration. Aristotle would assume that something seen as motile is seen as in transition "from something to something" (*De Phys.* 229a 10) and would occupy the points of a track but would not be at rest in any. Kant, however, refers the recognition of motion to the subject who holds together *now* the three dimensions of time, the retentive past, the apprehended present, and the anticipated future. My experience *now* is the function of a three-fold synthesis in which I am a spectator of a succession I generate. The now is a synthesis of three B-series moments, "then at *x*, now at y, and going to be at z," where x, y, and z are actual and possible moments on a time line brought back together in an objectifying three-fold synthesis. But Aristotle could reply: I remember, apprehend and, anticipate the motile thing as in transition from something to something. Each before and after is the now of transition, each point having the meaning of having been passed through in a route from "there through here to yonder." Motility cannot be understood unless the nows in which I address it, what I am in this address, also express their transitional contents. We remember something moving; its motility cannot be the function of a reproductive synthesis. I will try to make a strong case for Kant; but Aristotle is surely correct.

Representing time as the form of succession in general and then discerning its synthetic character through the number series which knows nothing of transitional nows, leads Kant to confuse the logical with the real order, discursive inference with time. Time is like a flowing river (A 170/B 212) and is represented by a line whose parts are not simultaneous (B 154); Kant, not Aristotle, spatializes time. He identifies our finitude with intuited nows and the need to put these together in discursive understanding which will secure for thought what was intuitively given for Augustine's God in an eternal now. Kant, like Spinoza, labored under the belief that all determination is negation, that the intuition of finitude presupposes the infinite. Need we go beyond our "ownmost possibility," death, to secure that recognition?

Kant shares Aristotle's view that act presupposes a correlative potentiality.[4] To see a being as motile, as actualizing a "potential *qua* potential," presupposes it can be moved by a prior act that is the occasion for, if not the efficient and formal cause, of its motility. Change is between contraries in the same genus. But what generic potential can we associate with a non-contextual, transcendental act? A potential would be pure only if it does not of itself present limiting conditions on that prior act. An untalented non-musical person is a serious limit on anything the best of teachers might accomplish. Transcendental synopsis posits pure potentials which, under a formal intention, become possible forms of experience. A synopsis is a purview correlative to a constituting act and unconceals a pure manifold whose potential for synthesis is determined by the form of the act. The Kantian synopsis determined by the rule generating numbers unconceals or interprets time as a potential succession of now-sites for acts of counting; "now 1," "now 2," et cetera. The apperceptive synopsis under a project unconceals these nows as appropriate or timely beginnings or terms of actions; nows lying within its scope give access to the means-end structure of beings released in categorial aspects by the project's in-order-to.

Each such now entails a three-fold synthesis which through apperception, memory and, above all, recognition binds me into durative being
—whose inner form is the objective unity of consciousness—in a public world. Consciousness reflexively unifies itself by intending these
beings as Parmenidian identities, continuously present in every present
(A 97; A 99-110). This is the hermeneutical ground of Kant's subjective Deduction.

In the light of this synopsis, finite, human act is the demiurgos of
an ordered, empirically accessible world. The secret source of this
power is the copula (B 140-42). Time is made into a substantive by
the omnitemporal "is" of predication, the architect of our illusions of
pure presence, which first gathers the world into the objective unity
for consciousness and then, as being itself, sublimes all this into an
"intelligible world" of completely determined noumena which, like
the monad as known to God, always haunted Kant.

This labyrinthine onto-epistemology has a musty smell, as if
spun out in a basement. Can this theory have any roots in *theoria?*
What could have led Kant into this spidery, expressionist sense of act,
so fashionable today among those who confuse computation with
understanding? Is all this really required to demonstrate that cinnabar
is not "sometimes red, sometimes black, sometimes heavy, sometimes
light," that a man will not be "sometimes changed into this or that
animal form," that the "longest day" is not "sometimes covered with
fruit, sometimes with ice and snow" (A 100-1). As *theoria,* we know
ourselves to be active in more mundane matters. Is this understanding
that we already have a condition for meaningful order and the significance of worldly beings? Kant deduced significance through act and
time. However, his model for action will not support the teleological
structure of interpretative or schematic projection.

Kant joined issue with the relation of empirical meaning and action through Hume, whose spectator view of mind yields only contingently associated "empirical affinities." These synthetic *a posteriori*
aggregates could become transcendental affinities when ordered by appropriate temporalizing acts. Consider a now succession such that of
any two nows, then necessarily one is earlier or later than the other
and there is a third which is later than one and earlier than another.
Without well-ordered time, Humian causality could not be stated—
the conjunction of a lively idea with a present impression—since there
could be, assuming the requisite resemblance, a chiasmus in which one
would be both before and after the other. Line-drawing will make his
case for this complete ordering: one can't begin after ending or reach
the end before arriving in the middle—nor boil water before one turns
on the heat. A ship going downstream cannot be below a certain mark
before it is above it (A 192/ B 237): "Only in relation to something

which precedes does the appearance acquire its time relation, namely, that of existing after a preceding time in which it itself was not. But it can acquire this determinate position in this relation of time only in so far as something in the preceding state upon which it follows invariably. . . . I cannot reverse the series" (A 198/B 234). The pre-Critical Kant had already taken over Leibniz's thesis that only action produces events in a meaningful order. I understood what I saw as I drew a line segment only because it was done through an intentional project. Without that intention, the mark would be virtually meaningless. Action is always story-relative, certain things being done in order that overarching intentions can be realized. I step to walk to get to class in order to tell the students what I had decided they should hear. Most natural, non-entropic processes are reversible; mechanism presupposes a time order analogous to the series of natural numbers; I can subtract as well as add. Our time, short, directional and irreversible, will not permit a return to the past; there is nothing to return to. Living systems, on the other hand, are irreversible, that is, completely-ordered, in matters of growth, development, and action; though stories can be told about the dead, they are gone, and gone too are the unique opportunities and challenges through which they, like us, worked out their lives. The corn eaten will not, in J. R. Lucas's example, reissue from my mouth, like a film run backwards, and reassemble on the cob (JRL 1973, 48–49)[5] If only mechanical causes are admissible in explanation, our stories could only reflect moral frustrations or reduce all that is loved and valued in life to an epiphenomenon of matter's linear, conservative movement. The for-the-sake-of-ness of action frees beings for meaningfulness, puts entities together in significant structure so that the agent may unconceal the meaning of beings, including the use of analysis to discover nomological laws. Purposive acts are prior to discerned purposelessness. How in the name of this mechanism unconcealed by action can we possibly deny the action of the interpreter?

2. Expressivist Mathematics

NUMBER AND THINGS NUMBERED have the same root in "my generating time" (A 142/B 183). Because the empirical or *a posteriori* presupposes the *a priori* as its ground, and since pure space and time and the synthetic mathematical knowledge these make possible are implicit in empirical space and time, the familiar distinction between pure and applied mathematics breaks down. We are familiar with mathematical synthesis in which space and time are self-affectively generated and then experienced in the three-fold synthesis of reproduction, apprehension, and recognition. This synthesis is the paradigm for a pure transcendental synthesis (of the figurative imagination) in which, given an empirical manifold of sensibility, mind can express and be affected by the formality of its own ejects. If time is generated as an ordinal series of nows in each of which there is a (possible) act reproductively apprehending and recognizing an associated countable, coexistent manifold, then these forms of intuition could be configured through the transcendental object's expressive *Sachheit* to yield empirical objects.

The *morphe* of this configuration, the product of noematic rather than the noetic synthesis, gives a unique insight into the extraordinary unity and coherence of Kant's thinking. His theories about mathematics and its foundations are not just clues to transcendental synthesis; his discursive view of temporality embeds every *in quid* determinable and *in qual* determination in a mathematical matrix. Since this matrix from which objects arise is written in *mathesis universalis*, empirical generalization will have the form of universal generalization, even if sense is arbitrary and contingent. Logic may be a clue to transcendental logic, the logic of truth, but one will never have anything to think truly unless it is first intuitively shown, *aletheia*, as homogeneous with the forms in which it is thought. The generation of number and shape is the *logos* of this synthesis, for acts generating the elements of mathematics are implicit in acts generating things of possible experience.

The specificity of a formal (categorial) intention determines the form of sensibility. Anything experimentally intended through sensibility will synoptically release the sense field as possible relata for mathematical synthesis according to the Principles. Why? Because substance, the constant quantity of matter in the first Analogy, is intentionally prior to the other Principles; except for the Postulates, these are implicitly quantitative, synthetic judgments *a priori*. The noematic schematism of the categories is quantitative and what it shows through the apophantic judgments of recognition will be expressed in terms of mathematical functions. Since things explain, we address them in hypotheses that presuppose access to them in the mathematical categories of quantity and quality. The presumption of a direct quantitative access is an answer to Berkeley for whom "primary" qualities were derivative, while the Anticipations uphold qualitative physics against reductive materialism. These noetic schema and noematic principles give access to things and their states and, through these, to the dynamical categories which express their significance. Things are not mere presences to be stared at but, like any signifiers, gather us into the presence of other things.

The manner in which the significant things and their states are intended determines the relational form of the signified. Thus, if a certain qualitative synthesis is temporally uniform, that is, an iterated

same in a succession of nows, it may be significant of a state of a substance, while heterogeneity in syntheses suggests that this variation has
an identifiable cause. These Analogies determine the necessary time
order one may discover in taking up coexistent manifolds. As with any
(implicitly) mathematical intention, empirical schemata intending
things through quantity, the Axioms, and quality, the Anticipations,
generate relational manifolds, respectively homogeneous and heterogeneous, which are prior conditions for the intuition of empirical
forms. If we can show how these intuitions are generated in arithmetic
and geometry, then given the need to measure and assign numerical
values, we can show how the syntheses proposed in the Principles are
possible. The unity of the Critique follows from this *arché* (principle,
origin, originary), "my generating time. . . ." Kant proposed to find
through an expressivist construction of time, the pure form of the succession of inner sense, the synthetic *a priori* basis for the truths of
arithmetic (B 15–16; *Prol.* 283) and, according to the Preface to the
second edition, the basis for physical knowledge of the phenomenal
world. Space and time would be "without objective validity, senseless
and meaningless, if their necessary application to the objects of experience were not established" (A 156/B 195). Apart from these objects,
inner sense would be "a rhapsody of perceptions" (*ibid*). Understanding may "posit" objects of its representations, but apperception must
first "posit" the manifold that is apprehended as countable. The possibility of this self-affective succession lies in the expressivist schema
of number, the successive addition of homogeneous units. Number is
"simply the unity of this synthesis of the manifold of a homogeneous
intuition in general, a unity due to *my generating time* in the apprehension of the intuition" (A 142/B 182–83; italics mine). Being able
to count from the successively generated ordinal series of nows the
coexistent manifold as "one," "two," and so forth, is original temporality, the "formal condition of inner sense . . . [to which] all our
knowledge is thus finally subject" (A 99).

God's original or creative intuition, which has no use for categories (B 145), gives the existence of its object (B 72). On the other
hand, transcendental apperception, which "does not stand under any
condition of time" (A 539/B 581), is condemned by the Spinozistic
definition of the finite as determinable to discursive receptivity within
phenomenal limits. It thus generates successively, given empirical receptivity, what is present all at once for God. Even so, we participate
in the infinite in intending the transcendental object cointended in
empirical synthesis. Through this prior intention to the transcendental
object, an atemporal, non-empirical, spontaneous categorial act synoptically determines a correlative potentiality experienced in the (A-
series) three-fold synthesis of reproduction, apprehension, and reflective

recognition. This potentiality, through its associated countable manifold, is spatial. What I would want to call "reflexive" is, in Kant's usage, reflective. In reflection, Heidegger says, a "pure synopsis and pure synthesis meet and fit with one another" (MH 1990, 67) in the pure concept. Through its cointended transcendental object, the empirical object becomes, as in Husserl, an "openly endless" object horizon. Every such potentiality is determined by a rule.

When attention is focused through a categorially structured project, the diachronic form of consciousness is brought into relief by three-fold synthesis. The "grounds for the recognition of the manifold, so far as they concern solely the form of an experience in general, are the categories. Upon them is based not only all formal unity in the [transcendental] synthesis of the imagination, but also thanks to that synthesis, all its empirical employment (in recognition, reproduction, association, apprehension) in connection with the appearances" (A 125). The categories represent ["set up before us," "intend"] "no special object given to the understanding alone, but serve only to determine the transcendental object, which is the concept of something in general, through that is given in sensibility, in order to know appearances empirically under concepts of objects" (A 251). What the analytic method could no longer attain, a permanent and intelligible condition for every conditioned, had to be supplied by object intending synthesis (A 719/B 747). The formal identity of synthetic act authorizes the reference to something as same in spatial and temporal schemata. "The schema of substance is the permanence of the real [i.e., pertaining to thinghood and thus essential and not existential] in time, that is, the representation of the real as a substrate of empirical determination of time in general, and so as abiding while all else changes" (A 143/B 183). Kant thought we fulfilled real intentions in the synthetic method of mathematics, the very paradigm of objectivity. It follows from this metaphysical need for synthetic grounding under the rubric provided by the transcendental object (A 538/B 506) that the extentional or noematic relatum in recognition and its synthetic possibilities is the basis of our synthetic knowledge of the world: "Actual experience, which is constituted by apprehension, association (reproduction), and finally recognition of appearances, contains in recognition, the last and highest of these merely empirical elements of experience, certain concepts that render possible the formal unity of experience, and therewith all objective validity (truth) of empirical knowledge" (A124-25).

How is the relatum generated that will be self-affectively experienced? Counting is an example of expressive constitution reflectively recognized "in a concept." The previously established ordinal series of nows can be used to generate the natural or counting numbers. From each ordinal now one addresses the coexistent synoptic manifold (A 94–95) and releases its arbitrary elements to be recognized as "one," "two," and so forth. The integers are generated in this spatialization of time by successively collecting elements in the coexistent manifold which is associated with each ordinal now. From the first now I collect 1, from the second 2, . . . in a three-fold synthesis, where this movement from . . . towards . . . is ecstatic, transcending towards. Notice, however, that transcendence is towards the having been, the past, which presumably is the ground of possibility; can this mechanist ground sustain the teleology of projects, such as counting? The temporal succession of nows is recursively generated by a rule, the now of "1," the now of "2," . . . This recursive rule sets out integers which, on being expressed, set up the possibility for self-affective recognition in number concepts.

The synopsis implicit in counting posits the pure or arbitrary, synchronic manifold of points, fingers, or anything whatsoever. But I could have begun earlier, and these counterfactual acts could be represented in negative ordinals, -1, -2, and so forth. Anything can be counted and is released as an element in an arbitrary manifold by the formal intention to count. In the acts intending synchronic manifolds through combinatorial rules, content, which could be imaginary, is irrelevant and the purity of space is preserved. One could connect the counted as if points by lines. The recursive rule expressed in these acts entails that "all combination—be we conscious of it or not, be it a combination of the manifold of intuition, empirical or non-empirical, or of various concepts—is an act of the understanding" (A 130).

One must also see this as temporal synthesis. In reflexively counting this manifold, now "1," now "2," and so forth, in the second now, "1" would be reproductively present in the set 2 under which a novel something or other is gathered under the concept "+1," therefore, from this now I would recognize and address the manifold as "2." In general, given "pure" and so inexhaustible diachronic and synchronic manifolds that fall within the scope of an intention to count, if from any now the associated "timeless" synchronic manifold is addressed as n, then it will be reproductively present to its successor now when something else in the associated manifold is now discriminated as different from this n by "+1"; this manifold may be addressed as "$n+1$." Kant says that "the concept of number is nothing but this unity of synthesis" (A 103). Temporal genesis spatializes; what as now and now is always other is, as coexistent, same.

The temporality correlative to counting will be continuous; any empirical act begins and so divides this potential *now,* the lower bound of the later segment or the upper bound of the earlier. The ordinal now series of possible loci for empirical acts is given through this transcendental, intentional act as possible sites from which one may address world. The prior acts positing coexistent manifolds may also be directed, not just numeratively, through the transcendental object's *Sachheit*, an ideal formality that is "the possibility of states of affairs," towards categorial recognitions. Differing categorial intentions cause the world to be seen in differing lightings. For example, the intention to something as a substance will, by the Axioms of Intuition, release this coexistent manifold as patient to a diachronically indifferent and so as if timeless, synchronic synthesis.

Granted the Refutation of Idealism, all efforts to assign representations a place in personal history, that is, the analytic unity of consciousness, entail a ground in an unchanging, material substance; this is rooted in the expressive act that generates a spatial or synchronic synthesis which is indifferent to the place in the diachronic series in which it is set out and taken up. If such-and-such synthetic conditions are satisfied, then necessarily certain others will also be satisfied. Space and time are nothing but relations (A 49/B 56), whose combinatorial possibilities are given in a "synopsis" or "formal intuition."

Leibniz remarked in a letter to DeVolder that "a continuous quantity is something ideal that only pertains to possibles and to actualities only so far as they are possible" (GL 1890, v.2, 282).[6] Extension is a potential for division, configuration, and motility. Kant said in his late *Reflexionen* that "the quantum alone wherein all quantity can be determined is, with regard to the number of parts, indeterminate and continuous; such are spaces and time" (*Ak.* v.23, 1038). Intentional acts cut reality and atomize ideal continuity. These are made with an understanding of Being as a continuous and unchanging presence ontically expresses a continuous time. If the original intention towards Being projected in the Schematism determines the ontic horizon within which beings may show themselves categorially, then the temporal and spatial configuration that allows them to appear to and in the synthesis of "recognition in a concept" is given in the continuity affecting, noematic synthesis.

Temporal continuity permits the definition of several classes of numbers within the constructive limits of possible or actual cuts. The ordinal now terminates an earlier (last moment) or a later (first moment) series, but not both simultaneously. Were it both, the series would admit of Dedekind cuts and would have the non-denumerable, and therefore non-constructive, order type of the real numbers. All of Kant's syntheses are regressive and explanatory. This regressive and conservative cast of mind wreaks its own kind of havoc with his morals, since any act aiming at an end must submit to explanation by pathological causes.

The concepts of *Sachen* and *Sachheit* may be of use in showing that Kant's realm of understanding is not disjoined from sense but rather "sees" it as if in a new dimension. One ejectively expresses *Sachheit* in constituting *Sachen*, relative to any empirical content. *Sachheit*, Kant's "thinghood" (A 143/B 182), determines how something must be seen if it is to enter into formal, eidetic structure, for instance, parts and wholes, genera and species, classes, disjunctive and conjunctive orderings and, in the best of all possible worlds, would be restricted in its usage to *Objekt*. We never see the parts of a sense field except through certain merelogical predicates which then allow it to the thought in these terms. *Sachheit* is the "transcendental matter" of a transcendental object, its formal determinability that lets it be thought, and is analogous, Kant says, to sensation that lets one intuit an empirical object, a *Gegenstand*. Its noema or *Sachen* is the corresponding entity's eidetic core, the necessary and sufficient set of predicates describing the invariant structure it must have if it is to exist.

Kant's finitistic time may be thought of as an asymmetric diachronic synthesis over the spaces, that is, coexistent manifolds, associated with each now. Any moment effecting a cut in this time line defines a three dimensional, spatial frame, that is, a synchronic or coexistent slice; these "pure," isomorphic frames together make up the timeless space associated with the given diachronic series. Such a frame would be a *Sachen*, an eidetic structure expressing dynamical necessities in the *Sachheit*. Assuming orientation, rest in any dimension would be expressed as a parallel to, and motion by a line intersecting, the relevant axis.[7]

In any empirical intuition in a connected world, there is some reason why things appear as they do. Just as qualitiative variation suggests causality, coexistence suggests reciprocal causality, fields and not aggregates: "Simultaneous things ["the most important consequence of time"] are not so because they do not succeed one another. For when succession is removed there is abolished some conjunction which there was because of the series of time, but there does not immediately arise therefrom another true relationship such as in the conjunction of all of them in the same moment" (*Diss.* 401 n.). In a connected world, aside from being locative and separative, space will also be prehensive. As a reminder note that there is a prior potential, a between, for encounter and significance; "space" is more primordial than anything posited by a synopsis.

One successively addresses the spatial manifold which is "nothing but relations" (B 66; also A 284/B 340) in constituting acts as a potential for relatedness. The now's associated manifold of coexistent loci, its frame of timeless three-dimensional space, is originally constituted in a synopsis as patient for synchronic order (by the figurative imagination) as the formal condition for apperception's correlative objective unity (A 94). Any point taken up in a synchronic order, like those on the surface of Parmenides' "well-rounded sphere," will have the same relations to the others on a possible circumference. The points in a frame, each having the same sense, permit a homogeneous synthesis. Drawing is also the image through which time, a diachronic series, is to be understood: "We cannot obtain for ourselves a representation of time, which is not an object of outer sense, except under the image of a line, which we draw, and by this mode of depicting it alone would we know the singleness of its dimension; and similarly by the fact that for all inner perceptions we must derive the lengths of time or the points of time from the changes that are exhibited for us in outer things" (B 156). Just as the intention to draw synoptically constitutes this manifold of possible end points which the act of drawing connects and well-orders by lines, so too original apperception well-orders in one dimension all possible and actual nows from which an act can address beings in "an arbitrary synthesis that admits of an *a priori* construction" (A 729/B 758). We assume only that the construction could be carried out recursively by a Turing machine, rather than in an actual series of synthetic acts.[8] These two forms enable us to construct a world.

The pure manifold as mathematically generated and categorially connectable is the schema (shape) of the object in general. Intending a being constitutes a now series as pregnant for empirical meaning and significance. The schematized categories are ways of taking up sense in ordinal, diachronic (and so arithmetizable) and synchronic (and so geometrizable) syntheses that preserve and respect congruence in generating significant appearances. This secure ground is given through the transcendental object intended in any manifold; the empirical content being arbitrary, sense has a nomological bond.

3. Kant's Pythagoreanism

EVEN THOUGH KANT'S REMARKS on mathematics are mostly directed to geometry, the schematized categories are founded on the modes of time, duration (substance), succession (causality) and coexistence (reciprocity), and the extentional and intensive numerability of what therein shows itself (B 219–20). Appearances are received as variable intensities (Anticipations) of determinable extended things (Axioms) in relations of inherence or causality (Analogies) and thought in the way these stand to time (Postulates). These Principles are rooted in counting and its numerable correlate. Is everything really made of number? Perhaps these self-affective experiences will give us some basis for extending and developing Kant's views on mathematics and its relation to the categories.

"Transcendental synthesis framed from [*a priori*] concepts alone"

(A 719/B 747) must supply empirical knowledge with its truth conditions. This arbitrary synthesis, that is, one applying to anything whatsoever, is like those that provide objects to mathematical intuition and is carried out by the immanent *logos* of the productive imagination whose "eject," an empirical object, is given "in an intuition that corresponds to the concept" (A 713/B 741). This object will be determined by the predicates and thought in the concepts of "the object in general" (B 128), Through this *a priori* epiphany there is a basis for the synthetic assignment of nomological ties (A 9/B 13), such as the ascription of the property yellow to gold.

Since what is counted is arbitrary (*Prol.* 269), number will collect anything. A "frame" is the instantaneous possibility of such collections in a now's associated synchronic manifold. These elements, given receptivity, could be elements in the same noema if taken up in any order: "The apprehension of the manifold in the appearance of the house that stands before me is successive. The question then arises, whether the manifold of the house is also in itself successive. This, however, is what no one will grant" (A 190/B 235). If these arbitrary entities schematize points, then given Euclid's postulates and axioms, one could generate his geometry. Any empirical object will have a geometrical schema and will be measurable.

The generation of a diachronic series of possible and actual nows and their series of frames which present possible forms of synthesis (diachronic, synchronic, and mixed) provides a temporal and spatial basis that allows things to appear as noema instancing the schematized categories. Recursive acts in this diachronic, ordinal series of nows generate and order the arbitrary (A 729/B 757) manifold being counted. A ship moving downstream relative to a fixed bank illustrates the mixed synthesis; "my perception of its lower position follows upon the perception of its position higher up the stream" (A 192/B 237). Each frame in the asymmetric, diachronic series will yield at least two possible synchronic syntheses, the ship's and bank's "object horizon." If we orient the ship series of frames to those in the bank, the latter series "here," that is, the "here" of the "from here to there," entails a synthesis that is isomorphic inter se but the ship series towards which I look from here on the bank (an analogue of the "permanent in intuition") will not yield a synthesis isomorphic and symmetric with the bank's. Indeed, it will intersect the vertical axis of the bank's homogeneous, timeless space, which in itself admits of isomorphic synthesis over its associated frames. Descriptions of its relative position are dependent on the now it occupies in the diachronic series. Mixed syntheses, of which there will be a least one in any empirical apprehension, signify causal and substance phenomena. The ship as such, like the house, admits of a homogeneous synthesis in each frame and is a substance candidate. However, it is also heterogeneous compared with the place of the bank in the frames and so is time dependent.

> It is impossible that in the apprehension of this appearance the ship should first be perceived lower down in the stream and then higher up. The order in which the perceptions succeed one another in apprehension is in this instance determined, and to this order apprehension is bound down. In the previous example of the house my perceptions could begin with the apprehension of the roof and end with the basement, or could begin from below and end above. . . . In the series of these perceptions there was thus no determinate order specifying at what point [or now, for that matter] I must begin in order to connect the manifold empirically. (*ibid.*)

Though these descriptions are tedious, they disclose how the diachronic and synchronic syntheses generate phenomena evidencing the Principles. For instance, assuming an appropriate synthetic definition of contiguity, which is not possible in the rational continuum, a deformed or non-isomorphic synthesis occurring within the presumption of a constant object horizon, such as a ball falling upon and depressing a pillow (A 203/B 248), could be seen as the ball's (causal) intersection with the pillow's horizon. The series is causal which synthesizes the (diachronic) horizon of the ball's approach to the (synchronic) horizon of the pillow, their intersection, and the subsquent depression in the pillow. The whole fabric of the world could be constructed in this analogue of the synthetic method in mathematics.

Next, assume that something is intended, correctly or incorrectly, in a sortal concept as substance. According to the Axioms of Intuition, when something is intended and recognized as a determinable quantity, each frame presents the possibility of a synchronic synthesis which, over the series, will be corrigible, invariant, and quantitative. On the other hand, if burning wood were intended as substance, the resulting synthetic syntheses would be heterogeneous and we might assume a misguided purpose. Thanks to Lavoisier, we now know that it is invariant; the transformation from a piece of wood to ashes and smoke schematizes mass, a discrete quantity which is invariant over the series (A 185/B 228–A 186/B 229). By the Refutation of Idealism there is at least one such "timeless" homogeneous synthesis in the timeless space of any family of frames (B 274, 276). Though the elements may be arbitrary, this schema must present an *a priori* invariance (B 152). Kant says the "[dynamical] mode of combination (nexus) is the synthesis of the manifold so far as its constituents necessarily belong to one another, as, for example, the accident to some substance or the effect to the cause. It is therefore synthesis of that which, though heterogeneous, is yet represented as combined *a priori*" (B 202). Constructively stated, the condition for something being accessible to us as an object *qua* enduring and recognizable synchronic content, lies in certain relations to our original apperception as expressed in a diachronic sequence for qualitative content and its associated synchronic manifold for extensive quantity. Thus, Kant achieves non-dualistically and constructively what Descartes in Meditation II can say about the formal reality of his bar of wax only with God's help.

Still, isn't Kant something of a "spirit seer?" He makes time the expression of an atemporal agent who stands beyond the temporal and incarnate facticities of action in and by which time is kept. How we sort out and schedule affairs in the world through the complex tense references of action verbs in ordinary language entails an understanding of time that is the foundation for any theoretical understanding. Prior to clocks, upon whose uniform markers and equal intervals a theory of time is usually founded, we already understand it, as Heidegger says, as spanning (which includes duration as well as the overarching structure of intention), datable, and public. We could recognize congruences prior to accurate clocks. Here in this public arena, not in inner sense, one begins experimental practice. Our approach takes us through phenomenological descriptions in which language, not the categories, unconceals beings, the being to whom these are disclosed and the beings unconcealed.

4. The Measurement of Time

WE LEFT KANT WITH HIS possible synchronic synthesis in a generated, ordinal now succession. The sequence stretched indefinitely backwards and forwards from the arbitrary origin of the generating act, . . . −2, −1, 0, 1, 2. . . . While these ordinals might name dates, given their subjective origin, how do these and their intervals relate to objective, or intersubjective, time? A rational theory of clocks is required if phenomenology is to link A-series, psychological "time in the making" to featureless B-series time in which entities are situated in cosmic history (PS 1963, 208–33).[9]

A rational theory of clocks entails date and place indifferent clocks. However, it is circular to require clocks as a condition for date and place indifferent physical laws if the clock depends on a repeatable, date and place indifferent law established with its aid. The circle can be broken if by nature we can recognize congruent intervals. Augustine describes the measurement of temporal intervals in *De Musica* long before clocks were invented to tell the hours in monasteries. Since the laws of mechanics are time-dependent, we must find a non-circular way of approaching its mensuration. Since time is of our making, perhaps Kant will give a way out of this circularity.

Let me begin by saying that I must reject Kant's finitism even if I retain, in principle, his synthetic approach. Kant finitism (constructivism) yields continuua of order type η, the constructable rational line, but not the featureless or metrically amorphous time necessary to measure and accommodate all events. In certain key respects, constructivism must be abandoned for the fictions of a non-finitistic mathematics and physics and yet we can retain its intuitive appeal by insisting that recognition of congruence is prior to, though extended by, clocks. Secondly, the thesis that time is generated by unchanging, expressivist acts must give way to a mundane perspective on human action in which the time that we are is anything but featureless. Assuming the ontological priority of the threefold A-series synthesis, it is possible to develop a weak synthetic *a priori* account of this transition from private to public time as an example of hermeneutics in the philosophy of science.

Temporal constitution becomes explicit in generating numerical series, ordinal or counting, paradigms for the three-fold A-series synthesis. What I apprehend and recognize as one is joined to its reproduced predecessor. Through analogues of this active, temporal synthesis, such as heart beats, a completely ordered, or asymmetric, succession is possible. I must first count one before two, have drawn this then before having drawn that. The intelligibility of the phenomenal world is grounded in egocentric action. These A-series events that generate time are transmuted into events in changeless B-series world-time. Physical phenomena suited to tell time to wayfarers instance directionless and reversible laws in which time appears to be atemporal. When such laws explain our incarnate existence, the teleological, experimental directedness required for their discovery becomes unintelligible.

If Kant had used pendulum motion rather than line drawing as his example of temporal synthesis, he could have ordered its periods only through memory and anticipation. The irony of interpreting ourselves through B-series phenomena, characteristic of Grünbaum, Reichenbach, and Einstein, is that it denies us the knowledge required for these interpretations. I shall show how to construct a transcendental theory of clocks that preserves freedom and gives action its deservedly central role; my example of talking or writing reflects the phenomenology of some non-conservative processes; their ego-logical synthesis verifies time's asymmetry. If dialogue is possible, then contrary to Einstein we do live in a completely ordered world within which Kantian causality is possible. I will also defend an analogue of the absolute time proposed by Newton and Kant.

The concept of B-series time depends on periodic or reversible

mechanisms which mark off ordinal (and thus datable) isochronic intervals by law-like regularities that are invariant with respect to dates
and places. When God's sensoria become the transcendental forms of
human intuition, how my time is related to any other is a problem
whose solution is necessary for physics, where a B-series seems to relate
all events inter se. How does one go from private and spanning A-
series time to this unitary, completely ordered time, if indeed it can be
said to be so ordered? These transcendental grounds are only the prior
conditions for empirical determination; we must find their empirical,
objective analogues. How do we have access to beings in a way that
relates them to a common time and world?

The only world to which we could have access is one that responds to us; we must be reciprocally connected. I act upon it causally,
as on a modem, and causally receive its reply. Any interpretation of
the world must preserve Kantian causality: what is identified as a
cause always precedes its effects. Since B-series time is determinable by
reversible processes, its physics is often said to be accusal, as in some
accounts of relativity. A convenient way of identifying causes and
effects is through a discursive model. Identification of causes and
effects in separated relativistic observation events takes Platonic dialogue as its model. While I can never achieve God's view, I can construct objective time if and only if hermeneutics and its associated
participatory community of discourse is possible. The B-series is the
derivative result.

Unlike the time of festivals, sowing and reaping, and the like, the
time by which we measure events and processes must be relatively featureless and homogeneous; these are *a priori* synthetic requirements for
a rational theory or schema of a clock (JRL 1973, 85–91). The schema
is regulative in the sense of the second Analogy; given the possibility of
natural knowledge, something or other will satisfy criteria for a clock
and, moreover, the choice of any one form of a clock can be superseded by another in progressively approximating an ideal. If congruity
is to be recognized in different kinds of events, time must be featureless; otherwise each sort of event would determine its appropriate
measure.

Knowledge is grounded in intuition, not because sense is self-
evidential but because only in or, less restrictedly, from intuition can
evidence, such as measurement, be gained and tested. If the criteria are
themselves theoretical, the results are regressive or circular. Some, such
as the intuitive recognition of congruence in qualities (Kant's Anticipations) and magnitudes (the Axioms) are innate. Recognition links
these criteria with sense which in turn gives itself under these interpretations as congruent. Unless one recognizes the same thing or kind of

spatial or temporal thing at various times and places, the "same cause-same effect" rule and the use of temporal variables in physical formulae would be without instances. Plato was correct in thinking that we have an innate capacity for recognizing congruence or equality (*Phaedo* 73C–75A); does it not follow from Kant's claim that space and time are transcendently ideal that their continuua have an inherent metric and that we possess an innate congruence standard? Recognition of equal spatial/temporal intervals in something less than a Protean world is therefore not to be defined operationally nor, as in the Riemannian space of general relativity, by a stipulated self-congruence. Since we are temporal, do we need something transcendentally atemporal or ideal to mark out, or add and subtract, congruent intervals? I do not think that we need a theory of such measures to tell time nor a theory of measurement to tell us what the measure of time is. A measure tells us something and does not create what it is supposed to tell. It must let the recognized congruences speak for themselves, telling us something we already understand, "how long," even if it extends and makes public a precision beyond anything the unaided senses can grasp.

We must provide a schema of temporal measurement that respects natural recognitions and presupposes that the time measuring other times be without features of its own; otherwise the measured time would be an artifact of the measure. Time moves slowly in boredom, rapidly when interest is high. Featurelessness must be an *a priori* possibility if we are to avoid idiosyncracies, yet we must not explain away their possibility by stipulating that time be featureless and defined by place and time indifferent laws. We can surrender our innate congruence sense to clocks only if they tell time more accurately than we can and do not define or constitute it. There is, however, a conflict between our ability to recognize congruence and the date and place indifference required by the laws upon which clocks are based. Recognition is egocentric, while clocks assume a non-egocentric and law-like manner of constituting equal, date-indifferent intervals. Featureless time is the equitable flow of before and after in the B-series and requires, contrary to Kant's constructivism, the stipulation of an order type θ of the real numbers in which it is modeled as dense, denumerable and amorphous; recognizing congruence will be relative to what we naturally are in the A-series as modeled by a rational and denumerable interval of order type η. We can found the B-series on these conceptual desiderata and recognitions in a dialectic of custom and nature, *nomos* and *physis,* remaining within extended Kantian parameters, roughly those inspired by the subjective and objective "deductions" respectively, which will make congruence and its metric possible.

The speed with which we iterate and generate the ordinal series has nothing to do with the metric properties of the continuum. Probably something on the magnitude of the interval provided by the heart beat is most natural, since otherwise we would have either no duration long enough in which to notice anything simultaneous to be measured or the durations would be too long to retain. The theory of ordinals, which gives isochronic intervals, is also the basis of calendars. Even though we could use linear clocks based on non-recurrent processes, candles or Galileo's ratios between time and the weight of water collected, these give no basis for dates and cyclical intervals.

The original temporality we are in inner sense must be represented by a linear change in outer sense; this line always being drawn represents the continuous time in which phenomena appear and in which they are related to their states and one another by public dates. Since Kant takes time to be an *a priori* form of intuition which applies to everything intuited, it must be empirically featureless though egocentric and denumerable. Thus we can recognize congruent intervals between them even if we have to make each non-denumerable. Clocks must tell time, answering such questions as how much time and when, the former as these clocks mark off equal intervals and tell how long and then, as ordinals, say when. Recognition of temporal congruences in music or poetry (to cite Augustine's examples) or in the heart's beats (MH 1982, 43–62) is quite accurate, extending down to intervals of one-fortieth of a second.

Understanding of featureless continuua is greatly advanced through the theory of order types. An iterated and iterable ordinal now series stretching endlessly backwards and forwards from an origin is of the type $*\omega + \omega$. Besides the usual axioms for a discrete, transitive series, (1) any now divides the series into nows earlier than and later than the given now, and (2) every element has a successor and predecessor (EVH 1917, 22). While Kant seems to have thought of this series as "infinite," as when he spoke of space and time being given as "infinite magnitudes," this series is numerable. The intervals between these ordinal markers must be additive and equal if they are to be used to measure changes, and this creates some problems. We would normally require that intervals in a linear continuum used to measure other processes be of the non-denumerable order type θ. Cuts defining the real numbers could not be effected by successive rule-governed acts. Kant's infinite, like Aristotle's, is only potential. A constructive theory requires that we have, not a relation describing an order, but rather a "can do" rule for successively dividing the continuum and generating equal intervals between points or instants: "Points or instants are only limits, that is, positions that limit space and time. But positions always presuppose the intuitions which they limit or are intended to limit; and out of mere positions, viewed as constituents capable of being given prior to space and time, neither space nor time can be constructed" (A 169–70/B 211). A dense or actually infinite set of points will, however, constitute an interval, but there is no corresponding intuition of space or time and no metric property to provide a recognizable congruence standard. Amorphousness, without a basis in stipulation or recognition, could not satisfy the schema of "extensive magnitude," the Axiom of Intuition. The magnitude of intervals could be based on a stipulation, such as the vibration of a crystal or wavelength of a particle of cesium. Would our ability to measure be axiomatic? Would not the "law" be founded on a prior ability to recognize congruence in more simple states? Is a continuum potentially divisible into a non-denumerable set of points or instants, even if not divided into them (which would be of the order type of the real numbers required in physical theory)? Kant might have been satisfied with the results of the great nineteenth-century mathematicians, for example, the Dedekind-Cantor definition of the irrationals as the limit of sequences of rationals or Weierstrass's finitistic methods (which allow one to "see" the term of an infinite, convergent series through the series, as in extensive abstraction), if understanding can be restricted, in principle, to "I can." This tastes like unacceptable psychologism. Yes, but isn't it transcendental and not psychological?

On these grounds, Kant could assume that the continuum between equal intervals is of the order type η of the rationals and, since this series will not be metrically amorphous, stipulate featurelessness and use approximation techniques to obtain the desired results. According to Huntington, this rational continuum (interpreted temporally) satisfies ordinal and three additional axioms: (1) between any two instants there is another which is later than one and earlier than the other (density), and (2) any now divides the series into two segments such that it is alternatively the last moment in the first or the first moment in the second, but not both. If Aristotelian finitism is unacceptable, then it can be replaced by denumerability; (2a) the elements of the series can be put into one-one correspondence with, for example, the elements of an ordinal progression. Finally (3), complete order: given any two moments one is earlier than or later than the other but not both, where the relation R is accessible and permits comparison. The order type will be η (EVH 1917, 34–39).

There are conceptual advantages in assuming that time is of the order type θ of the real numbers which, though non-denumerable, will contain the class of ordinal markers $^*\omega + \omega$. This "can be" order η may be extended by restating the second condition for a rational series in the Dedekind form: (2b) given two intervals such that every instant in a duration belongs to either the earlier or later interval, then there is at least one instant such that every earlier instant belongs to one interval and every later instant belongs to the other. Because it is stipulated

to be Archimedean or linear, it will contain the non-denumerable sub-
class of the irrationals and make possible a theory of clocks of order
type θ which both marks off and measures intervals and orders events
therein.[10] By Galileo's formula, for example, it is impossible to assign
a rational number to the time at which an earthly body has fallen 32.2
feet, but surely there is such a time. Because its order type is that of the
non-denumerable real numbers, it will have no inherent congruence
standard, no natural measure. Platonic recognitions would be empty.
Nevertheless, if the ordinal markers measure isochronic intervals within
the scope of recognized congruence, there is a phenomenological warrant, in Kant's sense of phenomenology, for making the intervals featureless. Lucas gives the example of a drowning man. During the
rational interval from 0 to 1, he floundered, cried for help, and was
seen and saved by another, say at 1. Within this spanning there were
public events which could be assigned rational intervals, such as what
went on during the first quarter, and so forth. But it is more appropriate to make this interval metrically amorphous. To the drowning man
and his rescuer a virtual eternity may transpire, while for the onlooker
it may have happened in the blink of an eye. In the same way we want
all sorts of natural processes to take place at various rates during the
same time. Though the desired featurelessness may have been pur-
chased at a price not to Kant's liking, it does enable us to coordinate
entities by interpreting time as as container and, thanks to Lucas, has
an intuitive, even phenomenological, warrant.

Discussing space and time or geometry and the notion of a numerical series in terms of mental acts seems to confuse an *a priori* with
a contingent science, mathematics with psychology. Kant cannot be
faulted for defining continua by the "can do" of a cut; all concepts are
subject to time (A 99) and *only by our actions* can complete order and
congruence be justified. Kant's generation of a dimensional manifold
entails that an oriented agent knows what he is about, the famous
self-reflexion thesis, while from a formalist perspective mathematics
was said by Russell to be the science where we do not know what we
are talking about or that what we are saying is true; and all this in
spite of the fact that most of the major developments in mathematics
are the consequence of non-formalistic analysis and interaction with
the physical sciences. We speak of classes or sets, operators and relations, rather than of Kantian schematic, interpretative acts; and while
the results of this formulation have been successful beyond the dreams
of its founders, Dedekind, Hilbert, Cantor, Piano, Frege, Russell,
Whitehead, and the like, we can also learn from Kant. He is far better
on the interface between pure mathematics and the world than he is
said to have been.

5. Complete Order

COMPLETE ORDER, THE STRONG disjunction between aRb or bRa, where R tells us which and by how much one event is earlier or later than another in a non-egocentric manner, is determined by reference to a common calendar. Since, however, calendars are constructed with reference to systems not completely ordered, the possibility of this ordering depends on human activity and dialogue. Complete order is a crucial link between the causal and phenomenological aspects of a human world.

Calendars may be cyclical or linear, ordinally ordered by token or real recurrences, like the Jewish Passover or the Babylonian New Year. A linear calendar imposes non-recurrent events on a recurrent or cyclical grid. Thus Jeremiah speaks of "the ninth year of the reign of Zedekiah, in the tenth month . . ." or Luke of "the days of Herod" or of a decree issued by Caesar Augustus "when Cyrenius was governor of Syria." Unless years are assigned ordinal names, there is no good integral measure of the separation of Zedekiah from Caesar; and without any dates, just how long from anything was or would have been the stipulated birthday of Christ? Cyclical temporality, common in ancient Egypt or Babylon, can find heavenly configurations that, when named, completely order intervals, but how are intervals ordered among themselves? In spite of ritual reconstruction, a variant of the "eternal return of the same," not even the king of Babylon could ignore linear orderings; each year he promulgated the same code and was recognized as the same king, even if reborn. The linear ordinal series ω is the basis of calendars.

The self discovers its temporality in recognizing that its future is not its relived past. The egocentric I interprets and perhaps even constructs time as linear; when I must myself found my own life, where else can I turn except to my roots in my own past linear time? History, phenomenology, and Kant's account of time generation conspire to persuade us that only in and through action is the past irrevocably past. Only within a culture that has discovered that freedom lies in self-responsible acts which, though founded on the past, are open to the branching possibilities of the future is complete ordering possible. Nietzsche's eternal return was a chance throw of dice that fell back into linear, determinate order.

Reversible views of time aim, G. J. Whitrow says, at its "elimination and the other [egocentric view] is based on the belief that time is ultimate and irreducible" (GW 1961, 310). If the human sense of time is to be primary, if not axiomatic, the now is the present of an act terminating the inalterable past or, alternatively, the node from which the possible futures branch out like limbs from the past's trunk. Projective action, bringing to be, translates possibility into actuality in a Kantian well-ordering of time. But mechanism says that action and its results are epiphenomenal. If so, then nothing like B-series time could be known.

It is reported that during a boring sermon in the Cathedral at Pisa, Galileo noticed, by counting his pulse, that the period of the swinging chandelier seemed to have nothing to do with the amplitude of its arc. Returning home, he discovered through varying the length and the mass of its bob that a pendulum's period is a constant function of its length and that the mass of the bob is irrelevant relative to the mass and distance from the earth so that its own mass and change in gravity could be ignored. He could determine intervals by assigning length. Though familiar with linear measures of time, having used a water clock in experiments with inclined planes, he could not be sure of the constant flow of water or rate of the candle's burning. In discovering the non-egocentric time invariance of intervals marked out by a process that might be presumed to hold always and everywhere through a phenomenological recognition that each to and fro interval was congruent with so many isochronic heart beats, Galileo founded the rational theory of clocks. Once he established the regularity of the pendulum, he could abandon the egocentric clock, the place and time variant heart beats and the issue of being and non-being that makes it speed up and slow down or even stop. The swinging pendulum, though not quite context independent, could mark equal Archimedean intervals. This marks the shift from McTaggart's A-series to B-series time (JM 1927, v.2; 10–13).

Kant's description of the continuity-securing synthesis of reproduction, apprehension and apperception (or recognition) insures the endurance of the same thing or recurrence of the same event (*qua* token). Even if designed to capture the continuity of line drawing, his account fits periodic processes whose "future" is their past. The demiurge of complete order is memory and anticipation, even if what is remembered and anticipated is, like the drawing of a line, always same. We act to place ordinal markers that determine an asymmetric time in which even B-series type events will be non-repeatable. How could we verify asymmetry? If a theory of clocks is tacitly prior action contexts, then action is problematic; and if Kant's original ordinal series takes its intervals from clocks founded on periodic and thus reversible processes, he will have grave trouble with freedom.

Featureless, date and place indifferent time is no time at all. Though the conceptual importance of featureless homogeneity was not fully realized by Newton, his fluxions prepared the way for eliminating temporal variables from physical theories. Though we express his second law as F=ma, in his formulation it says that "change of motion is proportional to the impressed motive force." By motion he meant momentum, the quantity of motion expressed as mv. The change in momentum depends on how long the force acts and is known as impulse, Ft. As restated by Maxwell, the law says that "the change in momentum of a body is understood as proportional to the impulse that produces it and is in the same direction." Mass being constant, the change in velocity $(v_2 - v_1)$ is determined by their difference relative to the time in question, then $F=m(v_2 - v_1)/t$. If acceleration, $a=(v_2 - v_1)/t$, then $F=ma$, where v is additive. Leibniz's differential calculus expresses a as the second derivative of distance with respect to time, where v is the first derivative, and in this sense time is eliminated from physical equations. Like Euclidean space, where the size and shape of an object has nothing to do with where it is or its orientation, we arrive at a direction indifferent, non-egocentric time we are in, as against the time we are. Except for the disputed second law of thermodynamics and the phenomena of radioactive degeneration, most other laws are reversible. Professor Whitrow convincingly argues that it is impossible to derive complete order from any other non-directional or probabilistic law (GW 1961, 266–307).

In at least some presents we are aware that we can do something we have not done, that novel possibilities can be grafted onto and made continuous with the settled past. From this now of writing I perspect, within the limits of grammar and settled style and limited understanding, the future to be written as a branching set of possibilities, best represented in C. I. Lewis's S 4 *de re* modal logic. Not even God can alter the linear past, though He can relieve its burden of guilt; and if action is to mean anything, some of these novelties can be grafted onto the past as a S 4.3. linearity (JRL 1973, 268). Otherwise action is a joke. Apart from our activity, if only a Kantian attending to, we cannot completely order time (nor experimentally discover a mechanism). Surely time is continuity in the making. If it is continuous and can be uniquely characterized by linear or periodic functions, however, then its directionality is eliminated. B-series time is a timelsss way of talking about time. Let us summarize a "deduction" of complete order.

We can imagine Kant iterating an ordinal now series, perhaps separating the "now 1," "now 2," and so forth, by his heart beats. If he is to find a time suitable for physics, he might consult a pendulum and let it publicly tick out isochronus intervals between nows. Each ordinal now in the series perspects a denumerable past and future, that is, $^*\omega + \omega$, which can serve as markers on isochronic intervals of the order type η; he could use algorithmic techniques for approximating the irrationals. But when he surrenders the autonomy of recognition to the clock's mechanism, he has by *nomos*, convention, created a rational order of time such that separated intervals are always and everywhere equal. Since the pendulum is not invariant with respect to mass or length, he can make a Platonic appeal to this idea of congruence to justify looking for a time indifferent law. Even the rotation of the earth will not do; for though angular momentum is conserved, the tidal effect breaks it. A search ensues for an ideal isolated system, perhaps in Popper's waves causally propagated from a single center, perhaps to be detected in the vibrations of a quartz crystal or behavior of a cesium atom. Such periodicities combine the advantages of both discrete and continuous measures and are basic. Periodic processes are reversible, even if this is not true of the waves they propagate.[11]

Kant is probably correct to define (some modes of) time on the morphology of intentional action, but if he is to communicate his time thoughts in the mechanisms of natural laws, he will have to have a public measure. This possibility of a public time, which can hardly depend on the fiction of a continuous material substance in outer sense, is the basis for the objective order of thinking. But Kant is on target when he represents time as a B-series by the featurelessness of substance, a continuant, even if this reflects its "elimination" in favor of space. The self which egocentrically completely orders nows submits of a mechanistic order in which complete order can not be established! However, causality requires complete order. "If my perception is to contain knowledge of an event, . . . it presupposes another appearance in time upon which it follows according to a rule. Were it not so, were I to posit the antecedent and were the event not to follow necessarily therefrom, I should have to regard the succession as a merely subjective play of my fancy; and if I still represented it to myself as something objective, I should have to call it a mere dream" (A 201/B 247). Complete ordering establishes a unique succession, and the odd thing is that in the resulting physics it is difficult to make any sense of complete order. Herman Weyl has mistaken the finger for the moon: "The objective world simply is, it does not happen. Only to the gaze of my consciousness, crawling up the life-line of my body [and it would be only a contingent fact that it could not crawl down], does a section of the world come to life as a fleeting image in space which continuously changes in time" (1963, 116). F. H. Bradley's image is perhaps better: the present moment of consciousness is like a lighted cavern through which, from past to future, passes the river of time; what we see was already there, having always been (1928, 1:54–55). Kant's saving merit is to have ordered things by action, even if by a bizarre act of transcendental constitution. He represents time in a line and expresses the laws of nature in terms of the permanent in

intuition and a substantial past from which in turn possibility is derived, rather than ecstatically from future possibility which the past
renders relevant and appropriate. We then tend to identify this timeless time with time. Lucas summarizes this misplaced concreteness:

> The homogeneity of time is not simply a fact forced upon us
> by experience [and Leibniz, no fool, denied it], but, like con-
> tinuity and date indifference, also a fiat, is something we im-
> pose upon our schemata for organizing experience. We view
> things in a certain way in order to accord with the topology
> required of it as the concomitant of consciousness, and to se-
> cure the sameness we require for a rational theory of clocks;
> and then discover the same uniformity and sameness in things,
> and then announce it as a conservation law or rename it te-
> dium, and either boast that we have revealed the underlying
> uniformities behind the flux of phenomena or complain that
> time is indifferent to our affairs, not realizing that in both
> cases we are discerning in our experience of time only what
> we have constructed into it [*pace* Kant] for our own special
> purposes, and that we should neither be surprised if we detect
> it to be regular nor think we have anyone to blame but our-
> selves for an indifference we insisted on. (JRL 1973, 86–87)

Luckily, Whitrow says, Newton's laws provided the universe with a
clock. Kant discovered that this is our interpretation. The point of
time's featurelessness is that processes can be relatively isolated and
controlled from any here or there. Leibniz, who may have been right,
thought the universe was a clock; any change in a monad entails
changes in every other, since each mirrors all. This is a featureless
clock that expresses every local feature. Though the theory of general
relativity supports Leibniz, it must accept our natural congruence recognitions and agency, which institutes the original laws. If being free
entails setting things up in order to let other things happen by necessity, the general theory of relativity must respect the Euclidian group
of transformations and the complete order of human time.

So far we have been concerned with an egocentric Kant and the
objective conditions for objective knowledge, the tense indifferent
knower-in-general required for completely ordered, absolute time. This
time and place indifference enables Kant to have an analogue of Newton's absolute space and time, God's sensoria. But this standpoint can
be nothing to us. Not being such a knower and no resources except
those given in acting, how can we establish complete order which,
J. R. Lucas can show, leads to a derivation of the Lorentz transformations of special relativity theory. I will stop at the dialogical preliminaries.

Consider the events a and b as completely ordered aRb for an observer at O_1 in the inertial frame t_α and the events c and d as completely ordered cRd for O_2 in the similar time system t_β. Consider now the case where two series intersect so that c and d are present along with a and b for O_1 in the sequence a, c, b, d while for O_2 they are sequenced as c, a, d, b. Then the relation between d and b would be both bRd and dRb and, lacking complete order, Humian causes and effects of one another. Some way of determining the complete order of these events, a prerequisite for recalibrating the clock at O_1 with that at O_2 and conversely, would give a basis for causality. It must be shown that the sequence, if not its metric, is invariant.

Consider the completely ordered series of events in time t_α with respect to the observer O_1 who proposes questions a and b. There is similar, separated time system t_β in which the observer O_2 answers these in the communication events c and d. Assume, furthermore, that there is some sort of causal communication link between them. We can order these events absolutely. Since language is a necessary condition for objectivity and since it is causally transmitted, then communication events that completely order the sequences will also enable observers in different systems to communicate with one another or calibrate their clocks inter se. Platonic dialogue is, as a sequence of questions and answers, completely ordered. If a is a question asked by O_1 and c is the received answer from O_2 which could not have been sent before the question was received, then these events are completely ordered with respect to both t_α and t_β. An answer cannot be transmitted until a question is received. If b is a question raised by O_2's answer c and d its answer, then complete ordering relative to both systems is a, c, b, d. We presume answers must follow, not precede, questions and that one answer can elicit another question in such a way as to order the sequence. This entails the two senses of "communication," causality and meaningful discourse that discloses. Since one cannot hear a question until it is asked nor hear the answer until it is said, we accept only the completely ordered sequence a, c, b, d which is one and the same with respect to O_1 and O_2. This is the sketch of a transcendental argument for a meaningful world on the basis of transmitted questions and answers. It must not involve "virtual communication," as in Weizenbaum's Lisa program (JW 1976, 1–16).

V

FROM TRANSCENDENTAL
IDEALISM TO PARTICIPATION

....

1. Intention and Temporality

THIS AND THE FOLLOWING TWO CHAPTERS mark the transition from Kant's transcendental philosophy to a philosophy founded on the transcendentals, the ubiquitous, all-pervading terms, such as being, or disjunctions, such as finite and infinite or inner and outer, which define the way of metaphysics and its deconstruction. That turn will take us from the *arché* as principle to its original, creative role. By means of the classical methods of analysis and synthesis, we have seen how the *arché* as "principle" through its original temporality gives its rule and constituted objects to understanding. The methods have brought us to see the profound truth in Heidegger's remark that understanding is always in the service of intuition and will now let us discern through intuition original creativity itself. If now the elaborate sense-making structure of synthesis which let us see sense in sense can be set aside, we can turn with Husserl to sense itself for an even more original giving of the "primal datum" and, with this, self and world. The categories that gave us meaningful sense will now be superseded by language, thanks to which Kant's world of scientific realism can be superseded by one founded on the more fundamental relation of personal encounter. The Kantian approach to method that bifurcated knowing and acting (*praxis*) will thus undergo a correction that places an analogue of his ethical intuitions, which he thematized as freedom, dignity, and infinite worth, at the very center of what has been the epistemic enterprise. The *arché* will be the between of this encounter which, as the matrix of language, facilitates a different, but not altogether unKantian, view of the self and, in the final three chapters, the fundamental meaning of physical science and those conditions of its possibility Kant discusses in the *Prolegomena*.

Why abandon transcendental idealism for a philosophy of transcendentals? The best reason is that it will not explicate common experience, such as Husserl's "life-world," upon which all other structures seem to depend. To show why, we must again take up the theme of apperception.

Kant opens a way to the originary, the *arché* as imagination, which, when crossed by sense and understanding, grants a world. Platonism, a philosophy of creativity, thus has much in common with Kant. A word of caution, however, before I go onward: though my way to the originary lies through Plato and Kant, it is not their way; I follow my contemporaries to language in and from which world erupts. We must begin where Kant should have begun, with a phenomenological analytic of temporal, communicative acts, not with drawing lines and counting. My alternative descriptions owe much to Heidegger's 1927 lectures, *The Basic Problem of Phenomenology*, even if I am unable to accept his meaning of temporality as fundamental. These lectures make it evident that *Dasein's* clearing and even the later Open has its inspiration in Plato's image of the sun and the idea of the Good, even if he identifies the Good with the demiurgos of *Timaeus,* "the producer pure and simple" (MH 1982, 286). Old habits persist. Aristotelians define Good in terms of the second act of being or the universal object of desire; in each case it is defined in terms of being rather than as that lighting that makes Being possible. Its identification with the will, rather than with the generosity of the Good, is consistent with Heidegger's thesis that Plato set Western philosophy on its way to the nihilistic *Ge-stell* and the technological appropriation of nature as a source of energy; but as Gadamer remarked, Heidegger read Plato as an Aristotelian.

Clocks define time as a countable now succession. Unless time is already understood, clocks tell us nothing. They tell us such things as "how long since . . . ?" or "how long do I have to . . . ?" in order to begin, consider, examine, continue, wait out, discontinue, suspend, or terminate an action. Time is, on this interpretation, what it takes in-order-to or for-the-sake-of an action, and action harbors (as Kant saw) intentionality in the sense of both meaning and directedness. A clock guides me in what I already understand; just as biological clocks regulate bodily processes, our clocks regulate action in a world with others. "Hurry up, please, its time. . . ." Would Kant, a clock to Königsberg housewives, have understood that? Crabs do. They even keep the time of their Amazon tides in a Chicago laboratory.

The time I am in addressing anything is always shareable now. Now, the only possible locus of an act, is that from which explicitly or implicitly I address; "now I have waited . . . ," "now we should . . . ," "now I have enough time to . . . ," and so "address the being that we ourselves are" (MH 1982, 259). We look at clocks, not to well-order our thoughts to their intended objects, but to order our lives in a public world of things always present in each of the modes of time that we are. Schedules are useful if one is to live effectively and meaningfully with others in the time we do not have which other things take. "The being that we ourselves are" is temporality insofar as it stands out as an embodied and irreplaceable here-to-there in the world in each of the modes of time. This is the *here* of my life, my dwelling, my enjoyment and never Hegel's recurrent, token-reflexive "here." In action, a primary state of being, what is at issue is the being that each is together with that of things that depend on our being. By first being temporal we can then be in time. Though my immediate concern is with "care," temporality can entail different meanings of and relations to being.

Kant seems to have a fundamental understanding of self-being that ill-accords with the way he shows, in the three-fold synthesis, that our knowledge is subject to time (A 99). One might imagine that in the A-series the "world is in the making and being made"; from this it does not follow that we are abandoned to the now and must shore up that being by thematizing it around the "permanent in intuition." Beings are always present to thought as it ecstatically reaches from now to the past or future. When I remember, for example, I do not look within at an image; I confront the thing itself re-present in the image, if there is an image, in its mode of having been. Analogous descriptions hold for the possible beings of the future, as in Kant's schematism.

Concrete examples are in order. Consider the following non-repeatable synopsis:

> Tomorrow I shall have to grade tests, since during the last lecture on Nietzsche I promised the students that I would return them on Monday—when, by the way, we shall have to leave home early if I am to record the grades before class—but now I shall have to sit down and write about Kant if I am ever going to finish it.

The scenario I just wrote concludes with this writing, a self-reflexive action that will measure itself, not against the "line itself," but rather by its own historical consciousness, which gives the act transcendence without being transcendent. The self-consciousness seeking self-certainty in line drawing and in counting gives way before a self that promises and, therefore, whose auto-affective return is contingent.

I expressed my intention to write and to return papers on the next class meeting through grammatical variants on expressed or implied verbs, such as "to promise," "to return," "to record," "to leave," "to write," whose tense structure makes temporal reference possible. Thus the sentence opens and addresses a temporal horizon from the now of writing in which possibility is ordered by performative proposals, that is, class meetings, promises, writing this. These came to be, not like mentally constituted numbers, through physical actions in time. The projects of grading and writing are tied to a public world of schedules and commitments ordered by the tense and syntax of verbs within a structure of acts and performatives ("I promise . . .") which projects in an ordered succession modes of my own being whose issue is my being as trustworthy, as a teacher, and so forth. The Aristotelian plot has a beginning, middle, and end. My project is sustained in playing itself out by what I do, like a play whose being is in the playing; there is nothing transcendent, not even the substantial ego, that supports and secures its transcending temporality. The phrases open and, on being carried out, sustain a world in which I can come back from a future understandingly projected to a now in which that future is being made only if I can now see myself as having done what I said I would do. The past is neither retained (Husserl) nor reproduced (Kant); it depends on what is being represented, how I understand what I am about in terms of the larger picture I have of myself. I choose and sustain this past by a promise that I let work in this "slot," this now, as the project works out. My failure to return to these nows as the scenario proposes marks the death of the project. I can come back to what I am only if I am first outside of myself towards the future. The nows are not sustained because I transcend time; in being temporal I am transcendent.

The above synopsis shows how intentionality is founded on temporality. In Husserl, primordial intentionality is temporality: the flux that constitutes objective time is "absolute subjectivity . . . the primal source point of the now" (EH 1991,100), where primal intentionality is the unitary retentive past, protentive future and apprehended present. As in Kant, intentionality constitutes time. However, in transcendence towards futurity, *now* is just that possibility of possibility, of the possibility of being outside of the present present towards a possibility from which I can return and, in that return, be outside present in the retentive past in which this possibility appears as more or less actual. This retentive past is the result of archaic synthesis of the traces of the immediate past with this possibility. For example, these present acts of writing hopefully instantiate my decision to open certain possibilities for understanding in which you can, in reading, share in this now as you ecstatically stand out from it into new possibilities for understanding. Participation is shareable transcendence towards beings and is not merely inner, found lurking in mentalistic constructs, attitudes, beliefs, and the like. This comportment towards beings is mine, founded on "my own particular ability to be" (MH 1982, 265) ahead of myself from which I can return to discover what "I myself am in my having-been-ness" (266).

Kant had a point in speaking of time as self-affection. Unhappily, he thought of time as a continuous appearing which is reflectively known (self-consciously) as universal. Even so, one holds open the horizons of a project so that from out of the projected future I can encounter and measure my progress against my having-been-ness.

Before we take up some problems in Kant's view of action, we might note that there is in him a different and more familiar strata of sensibility, that of his blind percepts without concepts, I have largely ignored but which, when divested of its blindness, will play an important role in the sequel. Prior to intentional acts that temporalize protentively or retentively, there is a more primordial level of becoming which, though not without a sort of reflexivity, is prior to the knower/known form which the subject/object relation usually takes. Perhaps we too hastily intentionalize Kant's sensibility; an earlier generation, including Bradley, Santayana, James, Bergson and Whitehead, took it seriously and described it in terms of non-judgmental or non-objectifying apprehension as, for example, "sense awareness." One hoped to begin with this verbal or process aspect of the participle *ousia*, "being," and to define its nominal aspects, for example, objects or substances, in its terms. With an eye towards Husserl's treatment of the sensible flux as *hyle* "lived in time in the form of *psychic* life" (EL 1981, 31), Levinas reappropriates these insights by returning to and, within limits, accepting as primordial the solipsistic closure of the British empiricists. "Sensation is the ambiguous unity of the temporal flow ["Common act of the feeling and the felt"] of the lived element and the identity of beings and events, designated by words" (*ibid*). In Berkeley, for example, "the sensorial qualities are not only the sensed; as affective states they are the sensing" (32); an idea is neither subjective nor objective but is something lived rather than had by a self. Instead of taking this closure as epistemic, he sees it as pertaining to a world enjoyed within the self-reference individuating *me*. In other words, the phenomenality of the world is affective, as even Hume tried to say, rather than datal and reflective. "Enjoyment" is Levinas's term for this elementary stratum of life. Its self-referring closure can be broken by its need to sustain itself by labor, which can reintroduce *Sorge*, or by a desire for the other who can be encountered, even in its most erotic depths, as an unassimilable alterity. While the proto-reflexivity applies to all sentient life, Levinas says that man himself, as "a rational animal, is posited in being . . . by labor and will" (EL 1987, 27) from the more medial state of "enjoyment."[1] Even these more object-oriented states, though deriving from an original experience of the other as an absolute alterity, will continue to be dominated by *Dasein*'s appropriative structure.

But now let us return to Heideggerian projects that thematize Kant's schematism under the rubric of "will and labor." Given its Aristotelian perspective, there is a continuity of act amid all sorts of interruptions, the need to mow the lawn, care for the children, eat, and the like, only if certain nows in which the projected future is enacted are contextually "animated" as same in their otherness. Continuity is that of action and is measured by time; something like a unity of activity must define its epochs. Could it be that Kant and Hume got their temporal directions wrong? What counts is the progressive, not the regressive, synthesis.

On Kant's view of act there can be no meaning or significance. Any who struggle to keep going know that temporal synthesis is not homogeneous. The shareable now in which each is addressing others is hardly a relatum in the manifold of inner sense, a private possibility founded on an atemporal act. Kant says the lines we draw in successive acts in inner sense can appear in outer sense (B 154), but these products of figurative synthesis can appear in the imagination without the assistance of an actual drawing. I then understand the interior now as a member of an endless sequence of befores and afters of possible (mental) acts, transcendentally constituted. An activity being played out need not return to its origin; one can do something else or die. Time can also be represented, not in a line, but by a story; only the Ulysses Dante meets in hell, having lost all substance, could tell an unending tale. The endless series of nows, assuring for Aristotle everlasting motility and therefore life for the universe and for Kant the security of abiding presence in a self-constituted other, begins to look like death's time. Time measures our finitude because for each there is a last now, not because we are condemned to discursive inference.

When time is said to be transcendentally ideal and empirically real (A 35–36/B 52–53), something quite important, if misleading, is being said. First, though, what is this empirically real time? The time shared by judgments determined by clocks that yield the same substitution values in formulae? Otherwise we might self-indulgently warm in the sun of mere perceptual judgments (*Prol.* 297–300). When we stop enjoying and start measuring, "experience" is gained in categorial judgment and dissipates "seeming." Common time is physical time in which the ego as such is not contained. Because the acting subject in its intelligible character is not subject to time (A 539/B 560), we are in time only in a derivative, phenomenal sense (B 157–58 n.). If time is what each is and each is different then, contrary to the old song, my time cannot be your time unless I give it to you. I can give you my time, be with you or do for you. But I can also give you time by giving you an organ or dying for you. This gift of my time to you is the gift of being. Time is life, the differing and deferring by which something lives. In my scenario I could sort out my time only by representing others who in one way or another call me forth into a common world. My actions, such as my promise to be on time, are public and are known to others quite as well as I could know them. We share a common time, not by preestablished harmony, but through the windows of language. But can we go from this sort of world to that of physics?

What we think of as world time is the gift of sacred time. Until the late seventeenth and early eighteenth centuries, no one had a clear conception of time as ordering the histories of various peoples within a common chronology. In principle, given Newton's absolute time (with space God's "sensoria"), there is no problem. But what was actually known were bits and pieces of local histories, for example, the Bible and writings of Greek and Roman historians, and some overlaps, more like different stories by different authors in the same book than accounts of coordinatable events. World time, McTaggart's B-series, was worked out by Jesuits involved in missionary work with all sorts and conditions of people all over the globe who needed to relate the events of each people's past to our history, B.C. and A.D., in order to share with them a common story of God's redemptive acts. Past nows, differently dated and described, lie on a single time line.

I promised my students to return their papers in a shared now of common expectation, analogous to the meaning of A.D. of the Christian calendar. Each could now give this a different description, if only by the student's "he said . . ." and my "I said . . .". They can expect to wait and I to work; and though the issue for each will be different, these cluster around a now to be shared and dated when the papers are returned. In representing action we must represent ourselves as in one another's now, i.e., "now you do as I . . . ," "now let us. . . ." This entails communicating as rooms opening onto one another and not as forces. Communication, Plato's *koinonia*, is the basis for a common world.

Aristotle said that as its number, no now could be identified with any particular motion; it could number every motile sort of thing (*De Phys.* 220b 20). This entails that time is common, something everything changeable is in, even if the now would be differently dated. This also means that a world is meaningful through a transcendent being who is the common intentional object of its striving (119a 22–24). Aristotle was right to describe world through the Good, wrong to ground it in the sempiternal act of God rather than in human transcendence and to take the common *in* as primary. We should question Kant's view that common time does not change but is that in which changes occur (A 183/B 226). If time changed, there had to be an absolute time in which to measure these changes. But surely the only absolute time is that of a community, defined in terms of communication's two senses, causal and phenomenological.[2] Such a family constitutes a world on the possibility of discourse, an odd justification of Kant's discursive view of time. Communication is not the expression of an ego, the line being drawn and the numbers iterated, but is rather the transcendental condition for the possibility of world. Beings are in common time only if they can be "bound to one another," and thus rendered meaningfully accessible. Like that sought by the Jesuits, community so understood is perhaps endlessly open. The time we are in through shared nows, as in the scenario above, belongs neither to the subject nor the object but is that through which each can mutually become in participatory projects. Time is what we are as transcendent towards beings, not something we have because we are transcendent.

Though much that has been said could claim Kant's authority, his view of act will not sustain these horizons. We need to look more closely at the empirical counterpart of the transcendental ego in "the representation of myself as object" (A 37/B 54). The self I represent to myself is objectively understood through the nomological necessities of mechanics. I must explain and order inner sense through external objects since "it is bound up with the existence of objects outside of me" (B 276). While the constitutive intention to the object in general can never be an object, any schematizing intention must have a place in objective time prior to what it brings about. If this empirical act is to explain behavior, such as what is now being written under an intention announced in the scenario, then this act will have to be a continuously acting phenomenal cause or related to some such physiological cause that explains it (A 205/B 250). There are at least three problems in this account. I will deal with two briefly; but I will be self-indulgent with the third, since the argument has been with me for thirty years and it is time to let it stand or fall in public scrutiny.

First, action is not something in consciousness which gets externalized in behavior; the surgeon or pianist thinks with his hands and fingers, a point with which even Descartes or Aristotle would concur. In "narrative" actions we know ourselves as in a common world, not as beings publicly expressing the results of hidden causality. An act or intention takes time; in many cases, if we treated it as a cause, we should have to use causal parameters or their equivalents to describe it, such as intensity or force or effecting a rate of change, and the like. In many cases of action, as Aristotle notes, there is no independent result. In music, for instance, the intention is just the temporal structure sounded, danced, or played. Intention is a structural, publicly accessible, unifying, and directive feature of an action, its meaning and its *logos*, not something resulting from a cause.

Second, according to the Refutation, the well-ordering of inner states of consciousness by an objective unity requires reference to the permanent. Don't we tell time by recurrent events, the vibrations of a quartz watch, festivals, and schedules? The topological properties of events, part and whole or overlapping, do a better job of explaining and ordering than anything permanent whose existence is extremely doubtful anyhow.

Third, an act understood in a causal sequence may be durative, but it cannot transcend. Kant's transcendental argument makes action inexplicable. To see how this is so, let us return to Hume who treats an intention as an antecedent causal component having contingent effects (DH 1894, sec. 7, pt. I). Intending or willing to move my hand does not always result in the hand's movement, while those without a leg can "wiggle" their toes. On this description of intention, the future springs (contingently) out of the past, the movement from the earlier act. For a wide class of phenomena, this is true: the car I see coming that I cannot avoid does meet up with me through the past. There is also the sense that I can intend to grade papers and then do it later. Putting it off brings on the pangs of guilt, but this occasions, rather than causes, my action. The act of grading papers for the sake of a commitment to return them aims at a future state. The action arises in, not because of, intending an end, a formality, while the reason for acting lies in the promise brought up in consciousness by occasioning guilt. The act expresses the promise, not the guilt, and becomes a parameter on possibility. If the hand did not move or the toes wiggle, intention would be short-circuited; these conditions are necessary, but not sufficient, for an action to transpire. One intends to bring something about which *is not*. The Zen archer hits the target only if it is left to reach out to him; if we shove things back into the past to explain an action and thus treat intention as a Humian cause, wouldn't it be as if aiming at something future by looking back over our shoulders?

In the Analogies Kant improves on Hume's story by showing how a durative act temporally orders events falling under its scope. Kant still persists, however, in treating intention, not as meaningful directedness, but as an element in a temporal succession. Though an action may be simultaneous with its cause, "I still distinguish the two [the act and its effect] through the time relation of their dynamical connection" (A 203/B 248). "Causality leads to the concept of action, and this in turn to the concept of force, and thereby to the concept of substance" (A 204/B 249). Unless action expresses a rule governing a succession, like counting, we are condemned to empirical affinities, to being Humian causes. Time would flow from the remembered past, present in the form of contingent, lively ideas to this presentationally immediate moment. Granted empirical affinity, the joint result of contiguity and resemblance, then a contiguous lively idea, the past impression, when associated with a present impression, will motivate a belief that in a resembling context there would be a similar succession. This is, in brief, Hume's causal formula. If one could accept this, then one might think that impressions were causal consequences of associated ideas. One lives the present from within the past. The temporal structure of this Humian paraphrase is reproduced in Kant's flowing time and time line. Look at Kant. Doesn't memory, the reproductive synthesis, have an ontological priority in the three fold synthesis? The future is lived out within the parameters of memory (A 170/B 211–12). Kant closes explanation under mechanism in the last *Critique.*

Why is Kant stuck with a Humian account of action? Assume that an intention is an antecedent condition. In the first edition the second Analogy reads: "Everything that happens, that is, begins to be, presupposes something which it follows according to a rule" (A 189). Suppose the rule were teleological; the antecedent is defined in terms of the consequent and Kant's rule is trivially true; one eats healthy foods for the same of health. The act is done for the sake of the consequences. Moliere's soporific agents cause sleep. The effect can "acquire this determinate position in this relation of time only as far as something is presupposed in the preceding state upon which it follows invariably, that is, in accordance with a rule" (A 198/B 243). If we take the now seriously, then contrary to the Thesis of the first Antinomy, an infinite regress of conditions is impossible. In this thesis one situates each antecedent in a now; and since each now marks a before and after, there can be no first now. This problem, which so perplexed Christian theologians, assumes that God had a clock and that nows tell his time. But surely this now completes the series up to the present and adds another moment. A time that grows is not infinite. All nows within an act's expressive scope are completely ordered; a cut, its "decision," brackets the action from the past and establishes an epoch in which each moment is either before or after another but not both gives us time to act. Since Hume's nows are externally related, any could be first. Let the now be the site of an effect which, given initial conditions, such as a need to sleep that induces me to take this pill, would be deducible on the covering-law model. "Sleeping pills induce sleep" cannot be the law, for though I take them with this end in view, by naming the end by the cause, I have a tautology, not a law. What are we expected to deduce? What I have done? I was sleepless and, motivated by this need, I searched for a pill. Since actions can fail or be mistakenly carried out and since intending can never entail doing, the only laws we have are inductive and prudential; these never assign anything a determinate place in time according to a rule. Action may well-order, but its psychological context is Humian, the result of certain habitualities, beliefs that doing this or that enables us to bring to pass a result in conformity to our pro or con attitudes. The agent is loaded with just the past he needs to do what he did. This is true enough, but it never gets to the project one acts upon and for-the-sake of. Projection is never deduction, induction, habituality, or what have you. One stands forth for the sake of the being to be within horizons determined by ontological understanding; this is an ontological truth about man and not an epistemic-psychological complex accounting for his behavior which would be only an *a posteriori* generalization; taking powders or trying to move does not always produce the intended result. The connection is definitionally necessary *qua* intention and contingent *qua* causal result.

In the standard covering law theory, the law explaining the phenomenal effect has to be expressed in terms non-homologous with what is observed. The observed sleeplessness, the tossing and turning, the getting up and going back to bed, the war with the covers, and the like are to be correlated with variables ranging over brain states, pulse rates, and other fashionable fictions which are then treated as instances of biochemical laws. Given the administration of a certain compound, the observed behavior will cease and dormant symptoms will prevail. This latter state is predictable from the law and these initial conditions. Only if the behavior were predictable could we read backwards ("retrodict") to the action, the "presupposed something" upon which the effect "follows according to a rule." Then we could be said to understand the behavior. Could it be that the sleeplessness was ontological, Levinas's *ennui* or Kierkegaard's *angst?*

Before we let scientific realism talk us out of our intuitions, we thought of decision in terms of what it says; a choice or decision is a cut that frees us from the necessity of living out time in terms of what has been and opens us to a choice among possibilities, where that opening may be the result of reflecting on that past, i.e., facticity, as the matrix of the novel possibilities. The dogma of continuity says that what can be depends on what has been; the future is like the prolongation of the line or the continuation of the flow. If the only possible explanation is, as Kant contends, mechanistic, then possibility understood "as that which agrees with the formal conditions of experience, that is, with the conditions of intuitions and concepts" (A 218/B 265) can hardly accommodate action. The regress of causes never anywhere admits of decision, an initiating now. This requires that the past, rather than being retained in the "living present," be next to and, within evident limits, instituted by the cut and intended in that present.

Retrodiction can never come upon closed series; according to this mechanist ideology, whatever I do follows from already settled facticity, from some meaning of permanent presence that makes apparent change or novelty epiphenomenal. The story we told about paper grading could never have gotten written, since no act closes the past and begins futurity. Only when comportment towards the past is under a future intention (ecstasis) is it possible to speak of a beginning: I graded papers because I made a promise. Doubtless there are all sorts of reasons for promising, ethical, prudential, utilitarian, or aesthetic. In treating action as a cause, I lose its decisive hallmark. A promise to grade papers was sustained in my acts; so too for its *arché* in a decision retained as I begin grading. Otherwise a promise would be unintelligible. Induction tells us that few are kept. Decisiveness is the self-limitation of being through which an act is specific and completable.

In order to grasp transcendence towards possibility, suppose I am called upon to join two boards. For a change I set about it ungrudgingly. I have been taught to use hammer and nails. With this occasioning motive, I go to its usual place and look for the hammer. I see that it is not there. I then find a substitute and join the boards. If one looks with Hume and Kant, one finds no impression corresponding to a lively idea nor percept to be recognized in a concept; a prudential induction or technical imperative that would have led one to a hammer was disconfirmed; lively ideas and concepts were left dangling. Kant might have listened to himself and heard what pragmatists heard him say: "When we speak of water and its properties, we do not stop short at what is thought in the word, water, but proceed to experiments" (A 728/B 756; cf. also A 716/B 744). If we cannot experiment, we can sensibilize our concepts. What do we see when we "return to the things themselves"? The friends of impressions never look; otherwise, to paraphrase Galileo's Cardinal, their eyes might cause them to believe that which by their philosophy they know to be false.

If we look closely at the phenomenon of the missing hammer, we notice that only in its absence is the hammer present as an object. Its nullity makes it conspicuous for the first time. After letting my gaze linger over all the things that are there, the projected intentional object is clearly seen: "I see that it is not there." Had it been in its accustomed place, I would have picked it up without thinking about it. Heidegger speaks of this "circumspection" as the sight that action has, the sight which already interprets things in their referential structure without ever looking directly at them. You cannot directly hear certain sequences of notes in a Bach fugue unless other notes are sounded, dominating the field. Sight is like that!

This place rejects my interpreting it as the hammer's abode; though I try to force my interpretation upon them, things will not submit. I transcend towards the task and then come back empty-handed. I then look around for something else that will do the job. This task of joining is the projected meaning of these beings that releases them from concealment in familiarity. Had the hammer been there, I would have picked it up without noticing it. Because of the breakdown of functionality, "the possibility of commerce with and orientation within the intra-worldly" (MH 1982, 311), the hammer is an (missing) object. I set about looking for something else that will do on the basis not of resemblance but functional equivalence. There is no relevant *empirical affinity* in the lively idea of a hammer. I know what I wish to bring about and then see beings in this light. If I become frustrated, it is not because I can't behaviorally respond to the ideational stimulus: it is because I can't do as I intended. I keep coming back empty-handed to the decisive now. Possibilities in the present will not allow me to be the being I need to be. My desire to be is the ontic correlative of the ontological structure of time, its incompleteness.

On the presumption of functional equivalence, I try other procedures within the project's orientation. No substitute sense impression resembles a hammer nor does anything follow from this concept as a rule, for I do try to see things as functional substitutes. I can look about in this manner only because I understand what needs to be done, not because I have impressions resembling a hammer. Beings are significant for this or that, not in terms of the causal past, but spontaneously in the orientation determined by the project. The "transcendental affinity" thematized through imaginative variation is interpretative, not causal. Kant might even approve of that. The future opens up alternative routes, the past only a uniquely structured one.

Obviously I could not hammer without a ready familiarity with hammering, but this familiarity does not, with a causally active motive, reach out from the past into the future. Familiarity with significant action within a world, not with objects, frees me to possibilities, this rod, this rock, this wedge, with which to do the job, rather than binding me to the necessities of frustration. Knowing what has to be done, I might find another way to connect the boards. When I come back from the future, I do not return to a self transcendent of process and its ground, but "to a self I have already chosen to be" (MH 1982, 287), which I maintain in action from out of the future. By resolutely holding to this future, world comes into view and maintains itself (268). The time of human community arises from an actively structured futurity that Kant cannot accommodate.

2. A Philosophy of Transcendentals

KANT'S PHILOSOPHY IS A "transcendental idealism" and this is usually understood as advancing claims about the mind's *a priori* knowledge of objects which, moreover, it constructs after a plan of its own devising. But why "transcendental?" In the Scholastic tradition, a term such as *unum* (one), *bonum* (good), *verum* (true), *ens* (being), *res* (thing), and *aliquid* (something) are "predicable of" every category and are thus transcategorial or transcendental. Each can function as a determinable subject (*in quid*) and thus substantially, if not as substance, or as a predicate or determinate (*in qual*) in one of the other categories. In "red is a quality," red is the *in quid* subject even though it is a quality and not a substance.

Duns Scotus said that transcendentals, such as "being," or "unity," cannot be contained in any genus (of being).[3] Transcendentals were originally employed by Aristotle, Aquinas, Duns Scotus, and Thomas of Erfurt to solve the problem of how to talk about the nature of and relations between a transcendent being who is Being itself and incommensurable, finite beings. This incomparability may rest on the absence of a ratio between the finite and infinite, on the belief that one is the non-univocal cause and exemplary ground of the existence and perfections of the others, or on the thesis that one cannot be cognized and the others can. Following Bonaventura and Scotus, Leibniz and Kant treated some as disjunctive, finite/infinite and act/potency. One of each pair, such as finite or infinite, ontically characterizes any entity or sets up and distinguishes the transcendental domain to which it belongs, such as inner/outer or receptive/active. These differences are usually hierarchal, as in Hegel, and thus invite deconstruction. The "higher" opposing term, such as male, interior, reason and the like, dominates as a "principle." In *différance,* the "inferior" is shown to govern and determine the superior. The result is that though one may be allowed to rule as a quasi-transcendental, as coordinate they should be allowed to play in a generative crossing. Metaphor is our paradigm for this chiasmus. Kant often uses disjunctive transcendentals and these may be the root of difference in post-Kantian philosophy. If the strong disjunction between Being and Becoming can be deconstructed in the way the difference between receptive and active was deconstructed by the transcendental imagination, one might wonder if all disjunctive transcendentals which seem to invite deconstruction have a similar, medial root.

Kant's most explicit use of "transcendental" is restricted to the conditions for an *a priori* knowledge of objects (A 12/B 25). This follows from the claim that "synthetic representations" (the categories) of the transcendental object are sensibilized by the productive imagination to constitute the conditions for intuitive receptivity (A 92/B 125). Plato noticed in *Theaetetus* (185A–187B) that these *a priori* or non-empirical terms—and one of each of the disjunctive transcendentals is probably non-empirical—posit a transcending, if not transcendent realm. Though they originate the intelligible order, transcendentals and the knowledge they make possible are curiously dependent on that which is to them secondary. Plato seems to recognize this; the one is many, being is not, and the many one; the same to be same partakes in the other just as the other to be other participates in same. Yet something rather bizarre seems afoot when a disjunct is predicated of its opposite. What can it mean to say that the finite is infinite or that the inner is the outer? Nevertheless, something like this must be said. For example, time can order inner sense only if it is already spatialized. What purports to be an *a priori* or transcendental science seems ripe for deconstruction.

Since transcendental terms are said of everything, this justifies Kant's calling his categories transcendental predicates of something-in-general. Thus, apperception can be said to be transcendental because it transcends the categories which are the conditions of its own possibility. Since the only relational term, *verum*, orders being, *ens*, to a knower, founding the categories on the logical forms of judgment continued and deepened "the transcendental philosophy of the ancients" (B 113) without quite admitting it. As acts of the always one and the same "I think . . . ," it auto-affectively thinks through them about everything. But Kant is suspicious of the traditional usage; to the Schoolmen's *quod libet ens est unum, verum, bonum,* he replies that they were concerned with the logical use of the category of quantity, with unity, plurality, and totality, and not "with the possibility of things themselves" (B 114). In some sense he was correct, for Aquinas (or whoever wrote *De Natura Generis*) derives the remaining convertible terms from *ens* as its conceptual distinctions. In the *Summa Theologica* One and Good are said to be same in reality with Being but to differ in idea, that is, in aspect, the former referring being to its unity and the latter to its intrinsic end (*ST* I, q.5, a.1 and q.9, a.1). Nevertheless, by restricting "transcendental" to the conditions for givenness and thinking, Kant deprives himself of the language that can go beyond and connect these. Recognition of these terms as such would have enabled him to articulate the relation between transcendent act, object, and unity in relation to the possibility of a categorially articulated knowledge of beings. He will employ "unity," "act," "many," "finite-infinite" and the like as categories or categorial derivatives and render their real role as transcendentals obscure. The "transcendental philosophy of the ancients" faced Kant's problem of synthesis by establishing the possibility of discourse over Being and beings; this relation, however understood, marks a shared interest.

These predicative terms are to be contrasted with Plato's "greatest kinds" in, for example, the *Parmenides* and *Sophist,* which constitute his as a relational ontology. To return to Plato is to seek the root of these "all pervading connecting terms that enable the other kinds [the some that "copulate" with some] to mingle; and conversely, in divisions . . . cause whole classes to separate" (*Sop.* 253C). These terms also refer beyond Being to the Good and the receptacle, supplements to the text of nature from whose participatory dynamics creatures come to be. Thus, in *Philebus* being and the other "all connecting terms" could be said of the *apeiron* and the *aitia,* perhaps referring to the Good as cause, as well as the more common attributions to "mixture" and *peras* (*Phil.* 23C ff.). While the traditional terms order being to a knower and, as analogical, permit discourse to range over beings of every ontological type, the Platonic terms—joined by good, truth, beauty—determine how otherwise opposites or separated classes, such as Being and Becoming, creatively interact, blend or mingle. These are "the some that mingle with all . . . the all connecting terms of discourse" (*Sop.* 253C), such as same, other, one, many, being and, perhaps, motion and rest, which explicate participation, transcenent ecstasis or immanent life (which the *Timaeus* characterizes in these transcendental terms), as it emerges within the gap (CB 1968, 115-56).[4] These Platonic transcendentals, together with certain supplements from beyond being, deconstruct transcendental idealism. Once we grant that a same is only through others, then for example the *a priori* identity and constituting pole of Kantian philosophy, transcendental apperception, will be only through marginalized *a posteriori* alterity.[5]

Though "transcendental" is not Aristotle's term, it reflects his use of being (*Meta.* 1003a 21 ff.) and terms convertible with it, such as "one" (1003a 32-1004a 9), "true" (993b 30), and "good" (*E.N.* 1096a 12-1096b 1), as omnipredicable and transcategorial, that is, transcendental. Since his ontology is not relational, then if Porphyry is right, these terms are the determinables and determinates of a predicative and judgmental ontology that defines a universe of discourse within which beings of all types can be related to a knower and continually instate Parmenides' *on* rather than, with Plato, participate in his patricide (*Sop.* 241D).

What is, however, common to and at issue in the use of "transcendental" by Kant, Aristotle, Plato, and the Scholastics is crossing what would otherwise be an incoherence or gap between differences, such as that between past and future, symbol and symbolized, or God and creatures, which I suspect is associated or carried by *mimesis,* whether this is heard as imitation, representation, *Vorstellung,* likeness (ikonic or fantastic), expression, reproduction, and so forth. In Plato, the relation of the living creature to the everlasting, to other beings, and the real to the illusory and sophistical is generally expressed mimetically (*Rep.* 509–11E, 595B–600A; *Par.* 132D–33A, *Tim.* 28C–31A, 37D). Both the *Sophist* and *Parmenides* introduce transcendental terms in a mimetic context; nothing less is at stake than participation and philosophy itself. *Mimesis* is the context through which something can be known about a "beyond present in" (*metalambano*, "participation") the represented and is thus the basis for a community, communion, and communication within a connected universe, one accessible in some unitary manner in its being and truth from here. Transcendentals, however understood, allow us to use or let something present within experience "re-present" something that is not and/or cannot be present which explains or is explained by, justifies or is justified by, or—to shorten what promises to be a long list—exists through or by the represented. Representations represent and are represented; the relation is contextually asymmetrical.[6] Is this an icon showing us something in the proportions of the original or is it a phantasma through we project and/or are trapped by illusion (*Sop.* 235D)? *Mimesis* harbors a fundamental ambiguity; something both is and is not, but to talk about what is not invokes non-Being. We know things above, St. Paul says, from things below, while Plato finds an image of cognition in a line and of the Good in the sun. Are these distinctions illusory? If representation is eliminated, does this also eliminate language? Kant identifies representation with transcendence whose condition is the imagination; is this medial playfulness a clue to "representation"?

If something represents another, then it exists *qua* representation through an other it makes present. In sensible representation it is the sensible design, the form woven into its fabric, and not the matter as such that represents. Moreover, as we will learn from de Saussure, even the formal design is what it is through alterity. However different, this fabric presences an otherwise absent same. At this point, in arguments familiar since Plato, we might be tempted to say that though the represented and representation are other, there is a same that is the being common to expression and expressed. Then this same, different from either, would require a further same to gather these differences in the unity of a representation; but already an infinite regress threatens, as in the "third man." Being, same and other, the very form of the soul, are the transcendentals facilitating this participatory relation; through them the idea is supposed to participate in the dynamics of incarnate life or its cultural expressions. As long as these realms are disjunctively—in the sense of the Latin *aut*—and predicatively defined, the gap between the sensible and intelligible will never be bridged. In Kant the imagination bridges this gap.

A Kantian "concept" is a representation of a representation . . . of a representation. The term of this movement is sensible sense, the work of the imagination, and the root of transcendence and transcendental alike. If approached as if from on high, from the transcendence of transcendental apperception, representation will have the context-free sense familiar in mathematics and the world, insofar as it is mimetic, will be a mere clone of the forms. Part, though perhaps not all, of the difficulty lies in failing to recognize the procreativity inherent in becoming's medial matrix. Plato came to acknowledge this when he extended the *arché* to cover the chthonic complement of the Uranian Good, the receptacle. The receptacle isn't anything prior to the receipt of form, but the schemata received, like signifiers, have their identity in the play of others she holds (contextually). The context of all contexts cannot be addressed apart from or "out of context." The receptacle is nothing apart from its communicative potential. On the other hand, the m-other who is the condition for this play gives the form a dwelling, makes place for the placeless and, through her *mythos*, contextualizes *logos*.

Perhaps the issue will be clearer if approached through neo-Platonic apportionment. Prodicus, for example, understood form as apportioned to a species.[7] This may be more familiar as "the analogy of inequality" in Cajetan's *Analogy of Names* which, along with attribution and proper proportionality, were taken to be the main types of Thomistic analogy. As an example of inequality, men are said to be to their animality as rats are to theirs, yet men and rats are not equally animals. Recent Thomistic scholarship has maintained that participation plays a greater role than analogy in Aquinas and that the fundamental apportionment is not of forms but of *esse* in which, in a reversal of Platonic intuitions, forms participate. Let us assume that the form in question is "simply simplex" (Duns Scotus). Moreover, let us also assume that, as the form of a process, it is verbal, like the plot is to a play or the game to the player or language to its native user. Its durative presence requires constant adverbial interpretation and reinterpretation, where every interpretation is a representation of the text, the way an actor represents his role or the player represents the game, and this of course requires adjustment and readjustment to alterity. This adverbial instantiating of a verbal form which interpretatively expresses or represents that form and which we, in turn, express in such medial doublets as "worlding of the world," "nature is the doctor doctoring himself," or *natura naturans,* is Duns Scotus' *haecceity.*[8] Self-instantiating beings live by contextually apportioning form to *esse,* the process of individuation, where *esse* is a medial becoming. The apportionment is hermeneutical and is effected in adverbial interpretations of its verbal text, even as E. coli self-reflexively interprets the text of its DNA as it unfolds and replicates. What Heidegger said about the *wesen,* "essencing," of language is also true of the "essence" (or Levinas's medial "essance") of nature: life is a "root unfolding" that gathers and discloses what is there from an embodied here for the sake of its being and well-being. Like the genotype read and interpretatively expressed in ecologically contextual phenotypes, form is always a same only because in species and even individual life it is also always other. Like a sign, sameness of form is through contextual alterity. The hypostasis is a sort of reflexive fold in the matrix (or general text) which, like an enzyme whose jig-like configuration controls a vital process, is the product of the contextual processes it suasively regulates. What was as a medial process a sequence is now through deferral and difference "the animation of a neutral and homogeneous time" (JD 1992a, 40). It raises processes up to life, which Aristotle says is the being of a living creature, by enclosing them within its limits.

The *Prolegomena* is often cited as of paradigm for transcendental argument. Analysis uncovers the presuppositions for an established domain, such as natural science; taking these as given under conditions, it moves to their condition, ground or principle. We may argue from the possibility of arithmetic to its transcendental ground; this is a transcendental, not categorial, use of "possibility." For instance, the possibility of number is grounded in time apperceptively constituted as the form of succession, in turn the condition for empirical possibility that is also grounded in the transcendental ego. For reasons given in the Paralogism, the self or soul is not categorially determinable. Presuppositions do not entail their truth (*Prol.* 388) and, therefore, analysis must be underpinned by the synthetic method in an original intuition that produces significant objects *a priori* (A 713/B 741). This object, the extrinsic ground for the synthetic judgment that goes beyond concepts to the posited or positioned thing, is the truth condition for analysis. In giving Kant's transcendental argument for time, number, and the categories, we first "laid out" (*legein*) and "gathered" (*logos*) beings under a certain ontic interpretation, number as a counted succession; and then ascended to its ground in original temporality. An ontological interpretation shows this ground of Being in self-presencing (self-consciousness) or, ultimately, groundless self-affection. We showed, from the perspective of atemporal apperception, how this act was present to itself *a priori* only through an original presencing in self-generated temporality. This argument concerning the *arché* of self-consciousness is properly "transcendental" because it bridges a gap between a transcendent being (the transcendental ego in act) and other beings (*ens*); it is the necessary condition for their beingness, in the sense of posited *exsistere*, and being understood; it articulates these beings in a logical discourse rooted in this transcendent being so that a science of beings is possible; and it argues and elaborates structure by means of "transcendental" terms.

In our theistic tradition the participatory relation that founds a community of beings sharing the task of sustaining meaningfulness was replaced by the cosmological relation in which beings are through God, the being who is His essence and thus Being itself. The creature is neither same with God (pantheism) or other than God (deism) but is ex nihilo. As in neo-Platonism, the relation between God and creatures is noetic, the *logos* theme common to Philo, St. John, and Plotinus. We are through his *logos,* even as through the *logos* we return to him, now in dialectic or ecstasy or sacrament and in the end in intuition, "face to face." Kant stands firmly within this tradition, even if the way back to the divine *arché* is blocked by the inescapable temporality of our noetic acts. Left only with temporal transcendence, Kant grounds our access to world in the atemporal apperceptive act. In knowing beings in concepts formed through judgments, I know a being under the formality of nominalized objectivity. Nevertheless, world is now a meaningful human horizon, not a divinely instituted totality of settled fact. Kant's approach promises the security of the durative presence of the self to itself as against the open possibilities of becoming. If Kant's philosophy results in the fetishism of matter, which was indeed the positivistic result of his "demytholization," we cannot but admire his rigorous spiritual quest.

Let us return to the double affection thesis in the light of these hurried remarks. Why does Kant look to number for an understanding of time? Generating number in iterative acts will, through spacing, let appear the openly endless number series, a horizon of possible experience, of deeds and affections, and secure the possibility of durative self-presence. Should I say "necessity of?" Could the knower-in-general be anything less than Averroes' world-soul? Can this constructive possibility really promise anything? Numbers are iterated and successively experienced in spacing, Derrida's "becoming space of time." But Kant says time is the *form* of, not a formal, succession. To experience a succession as an object is to transcend it. The promise number makes to us is that we are not stuck in a now bounded on each side by—nothing, nothing at all. Each now, like Aristotle's end points, has its meaning in the past it terminates or the future it begins. But the fact that time is generated by the atemporal acts of transcendental apperception points to an *arché* of temporality and thus of empirical experience; if not a plenitude of being, than neither is it Heideggerian nihilation. If the self that generates time, characteristic of Husserl and Kant, can be transformed into a hypostatic self, the way beyond Being will begin to open.

3. Platonic Archeology

IN RETURNING THROUGH KANT to the transcendentals which make a phenomenal world possible, we also return to Plato. Though more common on the Continent, most English-speaking philosophers find Kant's connection with Plato tenuous. Nevertheless, Kant's is a transcendental philosophy and therefore is, as has been shown, a philosophy of transcendentals. That the self is same for itself through alterity is in fact a formula for participation. Plato has no single word for what we call "participation." It is either an artifact or disclosed through metaphors. The *meta* prefix, which can mean either beyond or amidst, should be heard in both in *metaskesis* (*Phaedo* 101C; *Phaedrus* 252E), "change to a beyond state" or "show of the beyond amid"; *metalambano,* "take from beyond" or "receiving amid" (*Par.* 129A, 131A, 131B; *Sop.* 248D, 251D; *Tim.* 51A; *Phaedo* 248E); and *methexis,* "sustaining or holding the beyond amid" (*Phaedo* 100C; *Tim.* 44D). "Participation" presences a presence by drawing something transcending into immanent conditions, usually in terms signifying copulation and birth (*Theaet.* 160A). *Koinos* words signifying the "common," as in communication, community, and communion, are also used. "Communicate" has the dual sense of opening into and power; Plato's assertion that "Being is Power" (*Sop.* 247E) suggests that, granted its effective mechanisms and affective interpretations, we should think "experience," *Erfahrung,* in terms of "directed power."

The Platonic transcendentals that survive, even in Derrida, are being, same, and other. In his account of the living creature, Plato describes this creaturely directedness in terms of its soul, formed by crossings of the same and other. These are said to move in circles, an image of the assimilation of time, which is always other, to a circle, always same. One assimilates alterity, "the circle of the other," by a reflective crossing of the "circle of the same." Plato says that "time [the living creature] imitates eternity [*aiona*] and circles around according to number" (*Tim.* 38B); what is true of the whole obtains for the parts (30A–C) and, therefore, each creature images "by circling round according to number." This, the circle of the same, articulates the hermeneutical basis of creaturely being and expresses the reflective power of the soul which, through number and measure, assimilates the other to itself. As the same crosses the circle of the other, and each is other to the other as with terms in a metaphor, a same maybe engendered. But crossing also lets language world: when Miss Sullivan's fingers crossed Helen's hand, two intersecting circles of the same, i.e., reflective consciousness, crossed their other—the flowing water and the hand's wetness—world and word were born. The being and well-being of creatures lies in the power to represent; the motile, embodied self *represents* possibility to itself (reflexively "circling round according to number") just as this computer screen represents possibility to me as I write. Even as I write my cells are writing and reading a text, the text of DNA and the communications from other cells concerning this or that product they need or supply. This embodied self, a matrix, represents and is also a representation. The body is not a mere means of representing something to understanding but is the *chora*, the here, of any access to being there.

Representing and self-representation effected by the "circle of the same" are the grounds of error and illusion. Like Aesop's dog and the bone, we can get it wrong. The image we have of the body is the matrix of possibility, of possible acts, possible appearings. I contingently return to myself from the future in imagery. The reduction of possible meanings of alterity elicited from representative sense in acting resolves the mind-body problem, just as Kant's analogue for participation, transcendental constitution, resolved it for Kant. Participation, whether relating being and becoming or each of these inter se, expresses how the beyond is grasped and retained in the present through the power to represent and embody possibility (EB 1983, 127–31) thus making the other same.

Intending an intelligible object to which we can phenomenally return as embodied—or discover to be noteworthy in its absence—is a unitary structure embraced in the one time which is the life of the intending self and the "object" intended (CB 1968, 90). Participation is the relation between two or more entities such that each is through the other(s); each may be said to be, the participated as being *in quid* and the participant as being *in qual*. I follow Duns Scotus in using the transcendental "being" as an *in quid* predicate of a determinable subject and *in qual* of its determinates, where "subject" is defined—as I will explain in a moment—by the Ontological Principle. Though differing in ontological type, the participating subject is and is knowable or explicable through the transcending other(s).[9] If we disregard the case for the formation of form, these others could be (a) *forms* in virtue of which something is and is a determinate event of being or (b) the past (or future) in which this event of being effectively and affectively participates in self-formation (*Sop.* 253B-C). Normally form is a same for the participated, which is as temporal always other and other. But the converse relation holds, that is, by the Principle of Relativity, in which case form would be an *in quid* determinable.

Let me reintroduce notions I once had the temerity to call Principles, Ontological, Mingling, and Relativity, which were useful in explicating participation (1968). In *Theaetetus*, as we will see in the following chapter, Plato sketches a relational and, therefore, field-theoretic ontology of appearing that is a participatory analogue of Kant's phenomenalism. In the more familiar substance ontologies, "truth" is the only relational transcendental and tends to relativize being to a knower. According to the Ontological Principle, to be is to be in relation to and for another, where this other may or may not be the epistemological subject. The ontological subject is same for itself through these others; as effectively expressing its power it also makes its unique interpretative contribution to what is received from them. The clarity of crystal is its own. That which appears within such a relation can be neither objective (*Theaet.* 155 A-C) nor subjective (154A-D). According to this Principle, there is no "single thing that is in and by itself" (153E). Relativity expresses the ubiquity, context relativity, and unrestricted application of "being" and the other transcendentals. "Being" may refer to determinate or determinable, to becoming and eidetic being, and each can be determinate and determinable. This Principle of Relativity obtains in relations of the present to the past (interpretation) and its converse (causality), the present to the future (eros), the past to the future (founding), etc. or between being (form, *peras*) and becoming (*apeiron, gignesthai*) and conversely (248B-E). Relativity expresses this omnipredicability of the transcendentals same, other, motion, rest, one, many, and being, the some's that mingle with all (*Sop.* 253A) which are therefore the all-connecting terms of discourse (253C). According to the *Phaedo* (100C ff.), any thing (*res*) explicable through others as reasons by which it both is and is as it is and not otherwise is said to participate in those others (CB 1968, 128–35).[10] In deference to Heraclitus, the Principle of Mingling expresses the fact that transcendentals are the "all which mingle with all." Unfortunately, mingling can replace the Ontological Principle, as in the countervailing forces in Nietzsche or Foucault, so that the subject is defined as the dominent force in a quasi-Hegelian master-slave dialectic. The rather erotic Principle of Mingling lets entities which are other to one another cross one another and engender. In this chiasmus through "intercourse with one another all arise in all their variety as a result of their motion" (*Theaet.* 157E). Creaturely coming to be is through the mingling of form, whose logic is that of the transcendentals, in accord with the Ontological Principle. These Principles range over forms, determined and determining, and mark the limit beyond which "being" cannot be said. But to say that there is something of which "being" cannot be said is not to solicit nothing, but rather that which, beyond being, gives determinate being, the Good, as well as that which, beyond proper knowing, gives it place (*chora*), shelter, nurture, and the power to arise and stand out for itself. This self-assemblage, which Aristotle identified with a thing's *physis*, entails the coming to be of an other that cannot be defined as the same of others, as white is the same for the stone and what is seen.

   Plato's accounts of the generation of the perceptual or sense object, taken as a paradigm for participation, seems to differ from the account of generation he gives in *Timaeus* which, besides these "works of reason," introduces in the matrix the "works of necessity." One perceptually participates in something as white, according to *Republic* VI, when the sun's light "channeled into the eye" crosses "other things lit by the sun" (508B). In the *Theaetetus,* this account is given an erotic modification. Socrates invokes Artemis, the "childless patroness of childbirth" (149B), and proposes that the placeless sense object, which is neither in the object nor subject, that "arises only in becoming" (153E) is born of the mingling or intercourse of the receptor and the sensed object (156D). This object, the stone seen as white, gives the form *whiteness* place. This reintroduces the matrix but, as is appropriate to the virginal Artemis, in the form of a "virtual" birth. White cannot engender fecund whitings. Note, however, that in this birth the active motion of this physical object gives the sovereign eye a rule against which it must measure itself (105B); the sensum given to the eye by place is as a birth the gift of the maternal object, an other, to the eye as emergent in the crossing of their between (*metaxu*). As a universal or recurrent it signifies within contexts of concern something from and about the place of its situation. Sense is a condition for orientation, not just meaning.

His account of genesis is contrary to Aristotle's belief that, except for monstrosities, the material principle contributes only identity and neither activity nor process (*gignesthai*), nor a formal increment. In the *Timaeus* the "material" or maternal origin of life, which is open to the persuasion of but is not the subject of a principle, continues to have a determinate dynamism lacking in Aristotle. The male "principle," the spermatic idea, never subordinates the originary matrix. In Aristotle the father is efficient, formal and, relative to the eternity of the species, the final cause of genesis; his sperm overcomes the chaotic motion of the matrix and though its "imparted movement makes the embryo in the likeness of itself" (*De Gen. Anim.* 767b 15–17). The fact that the mother as such is left behind, never gathered into the circle of form, is especially apparent in *Metaphysics Z* (1032b 20–33a 2): matter prior to information is other than matter after being informed. The gold as *a that,* the *hyle* or matter in the scholastics' material partitive mode, on being formed into a ring becomes golden, *thaten,* and is now *hyle* as understood in the inseparable substantial mode. Though his examples are from art, Aristotle attributes vitalism to masculine increments so that, for example, the chemistry of living systems would differ from its non-living analogue. In Plato's original version we are to say, if asked, that the ring is "gold" (50B) or, even better, "such as golding" (49E). There is, in other words, no *it* which was "gold" and then, *qua* ring, is now "golden." That which receives form, even if its appears different (*Tim.* 50C), is as a natural occurrent or as informed a same (50B). Embodied life carries with it a representation of its life-giving mother. Matter is the maternal dynamical matrix from which the creature makes its ecstasis and whose representation, as embodied in the child, continues to nourish and sustain life. When solicited by form, *it gives* place (*chora*) and shelter, a dwelling (*Heim*), to its creature and then lets itself be other (*unheimlich*) to this potential determinable; thus the Platonic receptacle partakes in being in a mysterious way (49A-B).This effeminated *arché*, like its complement the Good, is elicited in a disclosive catachresis—and I push analysis beyond its phenomenological limits—as the no-thing which presences or gives being to a being and, like its close relative, the transcendental object, is not any kind of being. Rather than being an act, like apperception, it is indeterminate activity, a medial and, therefore, subjectless and objectless *mouvance* or "spacing" that generates events whose abstractive features are space and time and is, I believe, the prototype of Derrida's *différance* (JD 1982, 9). Change is prior to form. This will have grave implications for Kant who, like Aristotle, tries to subsume change under the impositional formality of act.

Yet there is a serious limitation in this picture; when the father crosses the mother and solicits emergence, it is not apparent that she also gives, apart from the forces bound by her chemistry, any other formal principle. The patri-archy has been weakened, though hardly destroyed. The insight into the fusion and mingling of form, gained in the perceptual model, should have been carried over into the genesis of the ecstatic other that is never a same to either parent which is, as Derrida says, a gift in excess of any return.[11]

4. Phenomenological Archeology

EDWARD BALLARD'S PHENOMENOLOGICAL perspective on perception brings Plato into the neighborhood of Kant and Husserl. Perception has both physical or causal ("the active motion" in the perception model in *Theaetetus* (156C-C) and passive, interpretive dimensions (the "passive motion" in the same model). This is analogous to Kant's crossing of sense and understanding. Plato says of the subject and object that "there is a law that binds us one to the other, but not to any other existence, nor each of us to himself; so therefore we can only be bound to one another . . . (*Theaet.* 160B). Ballard says of this mingling, a sacred marriage whose offspring is *eidos*, that:

> These mythological and Platonic accounts of perceiving may be brought up to date by briefly referring them to the phenomenological doctrine of intentionality. According to [Husserl's] version, the stream from the object, which I called presentations, is present as hyle, the matter of perception. The stream from (or in) the eye, the intentional stream, is analyzed by Husserl into two factors. One is the noetic activity

which originates in consciousness. This is the activity forming
hyle into meanings. The second factor is the issue from this
activity, the noemata or meanings as such. [In] the Platonic
marriage of the two streams, the presentations and the noemata, . . . the object becomes experienced as the specific
object which appears. (EB 1983, 129)

In a form/matter context reminiscent of Kant, Husserl understands
that *hyle* to be the undetermined object of an intuition which, on being crossed by "recognition in a concept," comes to a stand as deter-
minately this or that. In perception, Plato says, the "helios-like eye"
crosses the physically given to engender and animate the sense object
by which it is seen or known in the Good's lighting. Husserl says that
this hyletic data is "animated by construings within the concrete unity
of perception and in the animation, exercise the "presentative function," or as united with the construings which animate them, they
make up what we call appearings of shape, color, and so forth" (EH
1982, 88).[12] These "construings" animate such hyletic data as "pains
and tickle sensations" (172) and other "stuffs for intentive formings,"
as meaning something transcendent (238).[13] The noematic component
emerges when

> we discover in this [transcendental] reduction an absolute
> sphere of stuffs and noetic forms whose determinately struc-
> tured combinations possess, according to immanent eidetic
> necessity, the marvelous consciousness of something determi-
> nate and determinable, given thus and so, which is something
> over against consciousness itself, something fundamentally
> other, non-really inherent, transcendent; the characterization
> of mental process as transcendental rests on the fact that this
> is the primal source in which is found the only conceivable so-
> lution of those deepest problems of cognition concerning the
> essence and possibility of an objectively valid knowledge of
> something transcendent. (239)

This reduced, phenomenological consciousness admits to a further reduction in which the originary passes from a positing apperception to
an original giving, the appearing of the appearance. In his analysis of
internal time consciousness, Husserl makes a series of approaches to
this creative moment, the *arché,* in which something appears. Since
our phenomenological approach to participation entails an appearing
of analogous hyletic material, we must look from within temporality
to origins. Approaching the originary within the ambiance of *Being
and Time* or the Ontological Difference seems out of the question. To

find being within a version of Hegel's first triad through an experience of nothing flies in the face of logic and ignores the hypostatic self that emerges from "nothing," a more pregnant nothing that gives being rather than nihilates it. Kant founds time on presence. Husserl founds it on an originary presencing, a more fruitful way into the originary.

If we look with Husserl at the intentional acts by which Kant describes time formation in the three-fold synthesis, we converge at the lowest level of analysis to primal, non-intentional givenness. This possibility of non-reflective presence and thus, I suppose, of givenness apart from context-forming intentionality immediately becomes an awareness of being appeared to, not of myself in relation to an appearance, "in the growth of the primally generated," the appearing noetic profiles, the protentions and retentions pertaining to inner sense (EH 1991, 100). These profiles, retentions and pretensions, and not acts per se, are the temporal modalities of context forming intentionality that "animate" the "primally generated." It is upon this original experiencing in which I am being appeared to in a temporal flow that all further formations of consciousness are founded (JH 1992). The "primal datum" that appears is not intentional, but the temporal profiles, retention and protention, with which it is endowed constitutes original intentionality. The movement from this appearing, from the silence in John Cage's "Silent Concerto," to the appearance, the recognition that the silence is intentional, is usually precipitated by a name, though Husserl approvingly cites Kant's "recognition in a concept."

Even though Kantian recognition is always reflective, our approach to the origin must follow Husserl's lead and, to this end, a few pointers may prove useful. Husserl distinguishes three levels of reflection, none of which sets out and self-affectively receives (B 68). He begins with the natural attitude in which consciousness is taken up in the object which (1) I am reflectively aware of seeing; (2) with the reduction the emphasis is explicitly reflective and the domain of self-experience in which phenomenological descriptions of intentive modalities, such as perceiving, are now possible; and (3) this reflection is founded on inner sense, being appeared to in the stream of consciousness. At level two I am aware of the intended entity as past, passing, present, or to come. The last level founds the second and discloses the primal datum that, on being made the object of intentional analysis, shows itself in retentive and intentive profiles. The retention does not presence in the mode of passing away the just past; it also contains the past successive presents, these making up the living present that, like Kant's apperception, is not temporal but constitutes phenomenological temporality. Husserl speaks of this as internal time consciousness.

In neither Husserl not Kant is the self substantial; it is self-

constituting temporality, where this temporality is the origin of consciousness. Kant says that we are present to ourselves "only as we
appear to ourselves, not as we are in ourselves. For as we intuit ourselves only as we are inwardly affected, and this seems to be contradic-
tory, since then we should have to be in a relation of [active affection]
to ourselves (B 152–53). . . . How the "I" that thinks can be distinct from the "I" that intuits itself . . . and yet, as being the same
subject, can be identical with the latter; and how, therefore, I can say:
"I, as intelligence and thinking subject, know myself as an object that
is thought, in so far as I am given to myself [as something other, or]
beyond that [I] which is [given to myself] in intuition, and yet know
myself, like other phenomena, only as I appear to myself, not as I am
to the understanding" (B 155). Thanks to Kemp Smith's brackets, a
kind of sense can be made of the last sentence. Insofar as I, the open
for whom there are objects, am an object to myself, I am only an appearance. Transcendental apperception must express itself empirically
if it is to be self-present. Is the apprehensive act an appearance and
thus phenomenal? Then would it not be a cause? If it is not empirical,
but rather originative, then how does it know itself? By another act?

   In expressing a concept, such as instantiating the postulate by
drawing a line, are we aware of the expressive act rather than the expression? Apperception constitutes inner sense as a condition for being
appeared to, i.e., self-consciousness or self-presence. Not in the natural objectivist attitude, perhaps, for while Kant maintains there is no
unmediated self-consciousness, intentionality is virtually, if not explicitly, reflexive; otherwise one would not know what one was about.
I know that *I* see in seeing, but can the "seeing," the being appeared
to, through which there is the "seen," the appearance, be thematic?
Are we not then threatened with a regress, an awareness of an awareness? Aristotle, for instance, says that sense perceives itself; "if there is
a separate sense perceiving sight, the process will go on *ad infinitum*"
(*De Gen. Anim.* 425b 10–12). Reflection may not be apparent within
the natural standpoint of unreduced experience, yet for Husserl every
turning back from this standpoint, whether noematic or noetic, entails
reflection (EH 1989, tr. note 7). Kant proposes a similar movement
from the objective standpoint of ordinary consciousness to a reduced
self-consciousness:

   We cannot think a line without drawing it in thought or a
   circle without describing it. . . . Even time we cannot represent, save in so far as we attend, in the drawing of a straight
   line (which has to serve as the outer figurative representation
   of time), merely to the act of the synthesis of the manifold
   whereby we successively determine inner sense, and in so do-

ing attend to the succession of this determination in inner sense. Motion, as an act of the subject (not a determination of an object), and therefore the synthesis of the manifold in space, first produces the concept of succession—if we abstract from this manifold and attend solely to the act through which we determine the inner sense according to its form. The understanding does not, therefore, find in inner sense such a combination of the manifold, but produces it, in that it affects that sense. (B 154–55)

In the reduction we intend the acts which determine inner sense. Kant says that presencing can become thematic. Granted that intentional acts of drawing, not the line, can be intended in the phenomenological reduction, is this procedure really adequate to consciousness in the natural attitude which it is supposed to found? For instance, is this how the act of moving something appears to self-reflection? One might want to say that motion, not "motion . . . [expressed through] an act of the subject," is what one attends to. This is not what Kant says. According to his doctrine, I attend to the act, not the motion or the moved, in "the synthesis of the manifold." By parity of reasoning, in ordinary apperception I can self-consciously determine inner sense as empirical receptivity, its enabling condition, rather than allow myself to be caught up in consciousness of presencing or the object presenced. Granted that phenomenology is a method within which phenomena in the natural attitude are reduced to their eidetic necessities and grounded, isn't there something circular in this appeal? Its problems are those of any descriptive metaphysics which unconsciously entertained presuppositions that color the natural attitude are carried over into the reduction.

Is one thematically aware of one's self-presence in intuitive receptivity? Kant almost resists the strong tendency to assume that since receptive sensibility is meaningless, its sense is to be sought in a transcendental analogue of sense, a second self-affective seeing that bestows sense by making it representative. Husserl faces the same problem, since *morphe* is conferred by animating act on *hyle* that would otherwise be without sense. But if sense is nature's book, sense makes sense. Considered at the level of Husserl's life-world or Levinas's enjoyment, the book of nature and its reader are rather closed off from the larger world of the polemical text, its opposing and shifting forces, it forms of domination. Sometimes, being polyvalent or obscure, this book requires further interpretation. While there is a place for both representation and self-representation, those set out by apperception's expressive apparatus will surely become extinct unless they enable the creature to cope with the larger text of nature it is always reading and rewriting. I express the line, not myself. In fairness, one should admit that the idealistic focus on noesis brings us closer to things than has been the case since Aristotle. We set things up so they can express themselves: *Esse manifestum sui.* In intending to represent the line I come back from the intended future to perceive my hand expressing the line, as if the hand as ready-at-hand were the circumspective focus of an "equipmental totality." Intention must return to itself in given actuality if there are to be options, if I can correct or modify what I am doing. Perception is not the present's vantage on the present, but on the past. This is not the past continuously present in a B-series, as if it were being unrolled from some remoter past, but is the present's vantage on the past of the intended future. Receptively seeing myself as an object discloses its causal conditions, not as binding behavior to the past, but as necessary parameter on future expression. The drawing or print on this screen my hand makes are original and representative; when intentionally animated, these are mimetic means by which meanings are present in a public, shareable world. Sense as meaningful, as it always already is to the Platonist, represents or images form, the line or, in general, a communicable proposition. The solicitation of medial receptivity by possibility is the generalized form of reflexive self-experience.

Self-identity, the capacity to return to myself even in partial self-fulfillment, is contingent. Death or neurological failure can prevent an intending to say from returning as said. Moreover, I am always catching myself doing otherwise than as intended. I usually spell "hermeneutics" as "hermaneutics." That sensibility presences the just past in fusing possibility means that the presencing present is never self present; what is presenced is the past as an act of completed synthesis, as Kant recognized when he spoke of the difference between the "I" to whom the "I" appears and the appearing "I." If in intending to write, I saw that my hand was not moving, I would consult a physician. Since, however, the "I" is fully present to itself only through contingent signifiers, can it construct for itself a permanently present, univocal "I" or its material correlative? Though Kant seems not to have acknowledged the force of a radically contingent transcendental ego, its very groundlessness tells us that timeless identity is questionable. Yes, there is a same, but it is partly the gift of and partly the overcoming of others. Being "the same for itself" (*Sop.* 254D) is only through difference and issues from an (erotic) project. "As the identical subject," Hegel's "I = I . . . the emptiest of tautologies," never.

Husserl's *On the Phenomenology of Internal Time Consciousness* is the most direct route into the originary's offering. His approach is egological, not participatory, and though we can begin with his analysis, it is necessary to look beyond his concern with the hither side of appearing if one discerns in the *arché* the possibility of communication, community, and communion. His concern is with the impression received now upon which, on being recognized, apperception supervenes. Apprehension of the "primal impression [which] is the absolute beginning of this generation—the primal source from which all other are continuously generated . . . it is the primally generated, the 'new,' that which comes into existence foreign to consciousness, that which is received as opposed to that which is generated [i.e., the retentive and protentive aspect of the primal datum] through the spontaneity proper to consciousness origination of the primal datum" (EH 1991, 101). This is in no sense "an apprehending act" (119), but rather the spontaneous generation, a "primal creation," of the impression (100) prior to its objectification as an appearance. Levinas finds the root of creativity in this temporal flow "behind the exhibiting of being" (EL 1981, 34). Husserl asks,

> Is not the flux a succession? Does it not therefore have a now, and actual phase, and a continuity of pasts we are conscious of in retentions? We can only say this flux is something which we name in conformity with what is constituted, but it is nothing temporally Objective. It is absolute subjectivity and has the absolute properties of something to be denoted metaphorically as "flux," as the point of actuality, primal source point from which springs the now . . . a continuity of moments of reverberation. For this all names are lacking. (EH 1990, 100)

because, as Levinas suggests, "the thing itself is beyond the nameable" (EL 1981, 188).[14] The primal impression, though non-intentional, is immediately given to consciousness in an intention which, Levinas says, is time itself (EL 1981, 32). Husserl asks of the "now" in which the primal impression gives itself:

> Is it inherently absurd to regard this flow of time as an *objective movement?* *Certainly!* On the other hand, memory is surely something that has its *now,* and the same now as a tone for example. *No.* There lurks the fundamental mistake. *The flow of the modes of consciousness is not a process; the consciousness of the now is not itself now.* The retention that exists with the consciousness of the now is not "now," is not *simultaneous* with the now. . . . These are important things, perhaps the most important in all of phenomenology. (EH 1990, 333–34)

The inner objects, such as sounds, are earlier or later, but "the parts of the time flow cannot be said to be now earlier or later in the same way" because, Robert Sokolowski continues, it is not in time (RSo 1974, 134). Analogously, Plato says the receptacle is always same (*Tim.* 50E) even if its most primordial determinations, the elements earth, air, fire and water, are features, only "such," never "this" or "that" (49E). Like the references of the symbols of highs and fronts which move across vast areas of the nation on the nightly TV weather reports, "features," Peter Strawson's term of art, are non-particular, spatially-temporally individuated instancings of universals. Insofar as the receptacle is prior to its features, that which gives time and space is not in space and time. Like the Good, it lies in the margin of Being whose text it helps to write.

Husserl's "primal impression" is a non-intentional hyle, a "feature" of consciousness, given temporal form—the intentional form of Kantian inner sense—by its retentive, comet's tail past; the result is identity in difference, "sameness and otherness in its most primitive form" (RSo 1974, 160), in the anonymous constitution of consciousness and its object. Perception is the fusion of this present and non-present, the impression's identity in difference with its retentional trail; but what of the protended, the horizon of the future? Protention is fundamentally different from retention; in the Platonic account, it would be defined by suasive alterity, by possibility, while settled actuality is retained as a trace, not a retentive positivity. Protention entails a self with an object horizon; in enjoyment, however, a medial matrix is persuasively and erotically "propositioned," where a proposition is a formal solicitation which may or may not be expressed and retained through the matrix. This translation of possibility into actuality is participation's temporalizing. On the other hand, in Husserl this primal impression, Levinas says, "is retained, remembered or reconstructed; accumulating according to the admirable Kantian formulas, through the "synthesis of apprehension in intuition" (that is, in the sensible becoming cognition) and by the synthesis of "recognition in imagination," the impression is temporalized and opens upon itself . . . [this] temporal modification is not an event, nor an action, nor the effect of a cause. It is the verb to be" (EL 1981, 34). The "living present" is the matrix, the phenomenological origin of phenomenology. Being is the gift of this medial spontaneity in which "activity and passivity are completely one" (33). Husserl's words take one as close as it is possible to come to Kant's intuitive receptivity and the phenomenology of original creativity. To go further is to court the resources of metaphor and myth; perhaps Plato will provide both.

With the discovery of this matrix, why not bypass the "faculty of imagination," that "generally unknown" and "blind but indispensable faculty" that presences for Kant, and turn directly to the original myth of presencing, to Gaea, the Greek version of the Ti'amat? What is given by this matrix to presencing, aside from shelter and nourishment, but power to be channelized and directed by form (*Sop.* 247E). Instead of defining these conditions of possible experience phenomenally, Plato demythologizes Hesiod's Gaea/Uranus. Gaea, the dynamical earth mother, self-generates and separates off Uranus (and Chronos and Zeus), the masculine as principle of limit, who in turn fertilizes her so other creatures, gods, animals, and mortals, can arise and come forth from within the gap (*chaos*) between them. The sky god(s) and the earth mother define active and receptive conditions cosmologically. That which appears is the eventual creature that gathers its powers from becoming that in itself never really is, as symbolized in the mother's *apeiron* and determinable powers, into form that never becomes, the father's determinate *peras,* to dwell for a while from the gap. Creatures draw their conditions for being from the field-like potentials on each side of the gap, the formal potentials of Being and the dynamical *apeiron* potentials of Becoming (*Tim.* 27E). As with Kant, soul is the agent of synthesis. In Kant this is noetically defined in terms of apperception that transcends the conditions of sensibility and even reason. Plato defines the soul, the embodied Ontological Principle, in terms of the creature's participatory life through the Principle of Relativity as the vital and noetic microcosm of the creative demiurgos; its primary role is to effect a same through crossing or mingling (an analogue of Kantian synthesis). Life, spanning the gap and circling back on itself "according to number," is that by which "there is a same for Being and Thinking" (Parmenides, DK B 3). Having the formality of measure and music (*Tim.* 44B), soul spans the gap by persuasively mingling indivisible Being, Same, and Other with their divisible, extentional counterparts (34C–36D). I think of this mingling as supplying gradients, the opposites of the earlier cosmologies or the contraries of Aristotle, to the receptacle for the channelization of her powers. What would have been a Jackson Pollock "action" painting can now partake of Cezanne's natural geometry.

Suppose that the context is really participatory and suppose with Luce Irigaray that the gap is a chiasmus between a man and a woman in "which each can move out to the other and back to itself" (LI 1991, 16). The gap, the neglected "third term between lovers" (33), is the creative matrix, *chora,* the originary *arché.* In this archeology, it appears in a variety of maternal forms; its avatars would form a progression from subjectivity through language to a participatory open. It first appears in this text as the medial Kantian imagination and reappears in a somewhat similar form in Husserl's time constitution. The gap (*chaos*) originated in variants of Gaea and Uranus whose polemics posit Foucault's discursive or enunciative formation, Nietzsche's will to power, and Derrida's *différance.* An alternative and rather more creative route, whose patron is Mary, "the place of the placeless" and "well of life," will lead through Plato's receptacle, *chora,* and *metaxu* into the open, a way prepared by Heidegger's ontological difference and the between, Eugene Gendlin's slot and Levinas's proximity. Though often expressed subjectively, as imagination or the condition for assimilating the other, even as a play of forces, the gap is the primordial *arché,* the place of desire, dwelling (LI 1991, 15).

Participation has, however, never been altogether participatory. The other is likely to be an idea, not the beloved. Transcendent conditions take precedence over their immanent origin. Plato, for instance, begins with the masculine "Being is power." "Being" *qua* the participle *ousia* "participates" in substantive presence (*einai,* "to be") and presencing (*gignesthai,* "becoming"). From a logical point of view, form is instanced, in some cases as a feature and in others by hypostatic individuation in medial emergence. *Hypostasis* (from the medial *hypostamai*) is uniquely fitted to express emerging apperception in a medial ontology. It was first used by the neo-Platonists to designates the various levels of expression by the One and then by the Fathers to mean person. In the active voice it meant "to stiffen," while its medial root designated a precipitate or sediment, like land in a delta, and referred to the transformation of a verbal process into a substantive. Though Jerome said it was "the poison of faith," Athanasius used hypostasis as synonymous with *ousia.* Cyril of Alexandria distinguished it from *ousia* and used it to mean "person" in Trinitarian formulae; the Council of Constantinople (381 A.D.) spoke of one substance (*ousia*) and three hypostases and Chalcedon (451 A.D.) said Christ was "made known to us in two natures" and one hypostasis. St. Maximus the Confessor said an hypostasis was "what is according to itself in a distinct and constituted manner" (*Ep.* 15). Hypostasis is more concretely individuated, more dynamically "according to [or "for"] itself," than what is said more abstractly by *on* and, especially, *ousia,* with which it was more or less equivalent.[15] However, unlike *ousia* or the Latin *substantia,* it has being only through personal, e.g., the word of another, or familial relations, for instance, daughter. The person, the *hypostasis,* is also medial and decentered; it too is lived, in Auden's words, "by powers we scarcely understand." As reflexive, the *hypostasis,* a presence haunted by these powers, arises from becoming (*arché* as originary presencing) which it in turn controls (as principle) in order that it endure, i.e., durative self-presence.[16] The term was introduced by Emmanuel Levinas in *Existence and Existents* to account for the emergence of the self from medial becoming; it does not reappear in the analogous development of "separation" and its sentient root in his later writings. Its being is realized by persuasively soliciting the dynamics of *chora* into ecstasis through the lure of possibility, an alterity not necessarily founded on creaturely actuality, so that it can return to and be for itself a same.[17] Its personhood is the gift of others, an artifact of history, language and society. Identity lies in an "eternal return" to self, not by contingent sense, but through the loving mediation of an other; David Wood says that, in such cases, presence is not foundational but is appropriated (DW 1989, 34).[18] Participation appropriates presence.

Plato understood that the necessary condition for the emergence of a *hypostasis,* as I shall designate his "living creature," lies in the stereometric symmetries of earth, air, fire and water (*stoichieia, Tim.* 48B) which formally differentiate the *apeiron,* channelizing and storing its power to be released in entropic processes, for example, in metabolism. These forms, becoming's initial precipitates, are the dynamical conditions for eventual things. Like the molecules of ATP in the Krebs cycle, these are sources of the energy which the living being requires if it is to "stiffen" and ecstatically stand out. In living systems enzymes are the bridges erected to cross this dynamism, "guiding and tending the stream . . . gathering it up [so that life can stand out in the between] before the divinities" (MH 1971b, 153). Putting these medial and active senses together, *hypostasis* refers to something that comes to be and stands out through process, as life stands out from medial becoming. Moreover, its face, *prosopon,* is not like the Latin *persona,* a mask, but openly interprets personal life, e.g., manifesting love or anger. The phenomenalization of this movement from process to *hypostasis* began with our discussion of Kant's synthesis of recognition and was effected by Levinas's descriptions of the temporal modification of the original flow of time into reflexive awareness which "is the verb to be" (EL 1981, 34).

Life is a hypostatic and appropriative same for itself only through relating itself projectively as interpretative noesis towards transcending physical or ideal alterity which, on synthesis, appears through the interpreted noema—as I read off this screen what I intended to say. Something desiring to be same for itself crosses otherness, either to assimilate it, as in nutrition or knowing or, as in beauty, to procreate novel alterity.[19] The form is engendered in the crossed "between," the *metaxu* (*Theaet.* 154A, 156E). The *hypostasis* emerges from the dynamics of becoming through the gift of an alterity in which it participates; but unlike an epiphenomenon, its reflexive interpretation of this alterity is a control on its becoming. Phenomenally transcribed, this means that reflexive consciousness emerges when the temporal flow comes to a stand in recognition's crossing, where what appears on being recognized is something to be preserved in discourse, the dwelling place of being. The naturalism that Husserl so carefully avoided provides the physical basis, interpreted for us by sensa in "passive genesis," for the supplementary intentionalities through which it is meant.

The *hypostasis,* unlike pure apperception, has a personal life that lets it participate in historical, cultural, and spiritual worlds—which also invite medial characterization.

Finally, we must note that by constructing *psyche* as a St. Andrew's crossing, X, of same and other on the analogue of the world soul, Plato describes this demiurge of participation in a metaphor about metaphor. After blending the same, other and being drawn from and therefore expressing soul's participation in both being and becoming (*Tim.* 35A-B), then articulating it in arithmetical and harmonic proportions that express discrete (dance) and undulatory (music) motion (35B-36B), the demiurge divided *psyche* lengthwise, joined the ends of each together as the circle of the same and the other. The circle of the same, understanding, and the circle of the other, sense, were then crossed like the zodiac and sidereal heavenly circles (36B).

Kant's engendering chiasmus between sensibility and understanding has been understood, following upon Heidegger's revealing interpretation, as the productive imagination. Through Husserl and Levinas, we have penetrated the gap as far as catachresis allows to seek out the conditions for emergent apperception in the gift of the primal impression; we then associated this impression with Gaea's gift of being and, more philosophically, with the similar gift of the Platonic matrix. With the emergent word, with names, literally engendered for Helen Keller in a similar crossing, a world is born. The metaphor of engendering crossing is a metaphor for participation and, as such, Plato's metaphor for the demiurgos of participation, the soul of the world and the form of individual life. Plato gives soul a musical form; dancing most perfectly images life. Since crossing, like the Kant's Schematism, is schemata and language, Derrida says, is a proto-writing, then writing that calls something into being is choreographic.

We are a crossing of the circles of the same and other. What is the sense of the crossing, their constitutive "passing by . . . their nearness"? Plato says:

> The soul, interfused everywhere from the center to the circumference of heaven, of which she is also the external embodiment, itself turning in herself, began a divine beginning of never-ending and rational life enduring throughout all time. . . . And because she is composed of the same and being and the different and is divided and united in due proportion and in her revolutions *returns upon herself,* the soul, when touching anything that has being, whether dispersed in parts or undivided, is stirred through all her powers to declare the sameness and difference of that thing and some other, and to what individuals are related, and by what affected, and in what way and how and when, both in the world of genera-

tion and the world of immutable being. And when reason, which works with equal truth whether she be in the circle of the diverse or the same . . . is hovering around the sensible world and the circle of the diverse also movingly imparts the intimations of sense to the whole soul, then arise opinions and beliefs sure and certain. But when reason is concerned with the circle of the rational and the same moving smoothly declares it, then intelligence and knowledge are necessarily achieved. (Italics mine, 36E–37C)

The soul, in the presence of the other, turns back upon itself as an *hypostasis* and so becomes an open. Plato tells only part of that story. He fails to notice that soul cannot turn back on itself except it discover an other in a double or mutual crossing, a chiasmus. The open will appear when the circle of the same goes out to an "unknowable other that differs sexually from me" (LI 1991, 171) and returns, not as same, but as for the other. Then, and only then, begins the creative and procreative movement of love that bears the mark of Diotema, "gift of god." Instead of being the place of the "polemical master-slave relationship" (174), the gap can become an engendering place, a dwelling; "If a pair of lovers cannot care for the place of love like a third term between them, then they cannot remain lovers nor give birth to lovers. Something gets solidified in space-time with the loss of a vital intermediary milieu and of an accessible, loving transcendental (33). . . . The mystery of the divine is present at the heart of the copula . . . and turns us from mortals into immortals" (25).

The *Timaeus*, not quite a set of opinions or an eternal truth, is an irreducible myth about what arises in the crossing of these circles of same and other. To borrow Max Black's metaphor for metaphor, when the same, the focus, crosses the frame, then perhaps word and thing are born (1962, 28). In "living metaphor's" reflexive crossing, the "is," explicit or implied, is hermeneutical; the semantic space of the predicate term crosses over and interprets the space of the subject— and even conversely—thus unconcealing a same, a horizon within which beings show themselves in new ways. This same may be, in contexts to be explored in due measure, a model theoretic "seeing something as ____." Moreover, language is the gift of another through crossing by which, in turn, the other can be a same—or a face. Language and world are unconcealed in the light generated when thing and signifier cross each other, like the graphemes written by Miss Sullivan on Helen's hand, like the soul's great circles of same (reason) and other (sense) (*Tim.* 37B). Measurement is also a metaphor; two objects, the measure and measured, are to one another as unity is to x; "all things are made of number." Metaphor contextually unconceals structure, as if the predicate were a meaning intention animating the subject's *hyle*, and not necessarily as if the structure is *a priori*. These structures are articulated in likely stories, in scientific models or allegories.[20]

Whitehead's generalized description of the mapping relation applies to all sorts of crossings, to interpretation, truth, metaphor, and participation:

> Two objects may be such that (1) neither may be a component in the other, and (2) their composite natures may contain a common factor, although in the full sense of the term their "essences" are different. The two objects may then be said to have a truth-relation to each other. The examination of one of them can disclose some factor belonging to the essence of the other. In other words, an abstraction can be made and some of the elements can be omitted. The partial pattern thus obtained can be abstracted from the original. A truth-relation will be said to connect the objective contents of the two prehensions [Whitehead's non-egological genevalization of intention] when one and the same partial pattern may be abstracted from both of them. . . . Plato used the word "participation" to express the relation of a composite fact to some partial pattern which it illustrates. Only he limits the notion of the partial pattern to some abstract pattern of qualitative elements, to the exclusion of concrete particulars among its patterned elements [*sic*]. With this enlargement of meaning . . . two objective contents are related in a truth-relation when they severally participate in the same pattern. Each illustrates what the other is. Thus they interpret each other. (ANW 1931, 310)

This group theoretic approach may obscure the creative and inassimilable aspects of crossing. Nevertheless, in those hermeneutical crossings in which "truth happens," the horizons of the present cross those of an "unknown" past in a partial mapping of the unknown onto the presumably known. Since each is a situational complex having within its historical "substance," embedded understandings and ways of life, only a dialectical hermeneutics can find a rite of passage between them and disclose a novel, assimilable, and understandable same. Whitehead treats metaphor as an ontological disclosure, the form of the truth relation, and avoids its usual restriction to a sentential paradigm. Lexical, even linguistic, meanings are not primary.

VI

SIGNIFICANCE

....

1. Referentiality

ST. THOMAS SET THE STAGE for ontological hermeneutics with the proposal that "being is first in the apprehension absolutely and is included in whatsoever else a man understands" (*ST* q. 94, a. 2), but it remained for Heidegger to see that being is "the lighting process by which beings are lighted up" (WR 1965, 6) even as it is concealed by the beings it lightens. Presumably the *Umwort* "being" assures "the possibility of "being-word" to all other words" and is "as such pre-comprehended in all languages" whose sense is, Derrida continues, "neither the word 'being' nor the concept of being" (JD 1976, 20–21). Since it is tied "to the possibility of the word in general," the task set for the destruction of metaphysics and taken over by deconstruction is formidable indeed. Without underestimating the difficulty of the problem of significance this sets, perhaps we should begin with the Good and not Being and grasp signification in its light. Significance, like signification, is a phenomenon of reference in which one thing is a "substitute" for another, but in signification proper I address, go out to, the other and presuppose the ethical originality of the face-to-face.

Boethius says in *The Consolation of Philosophy* (3) that the Good is "of all things sought the first and reason why all other things are pursued." The Good which philosophers love is also, for the Christian, a person, the "word made flesh," a face. The Good's lighting is the condition for Being's unconcealment and it must, therefore, have a basis in the singular individual, not the universal. Ethics is "first philosophy." Does the Good provide a standpoint beyond the "history of being" that has led to nihilism and the closure of metaphysics? Is a dialectical hermeneutics possible which can propose, disclose, and criticize ontologies, as we have criticized Kant's identification of Being with the subject who posits substance, an enduring presence, as the condition for self-presence? Can we, claiming the Good's vantage, open a critique of ontological interpretations as such?

Until now, interpretations have been ontological; but if we begin with some meaning of Being, however covert, can we—having committed ourselves to the metaphor of a route or journey—hope to cross

184

and pass beyond it? Crossing thresholds, transcending through intention to world, would be difficult on Kant's ontological interpretation.
In Heidegger's more promising venture, the wayfarer is already in a
world released to him through his prior understanding of Being as referential or meaningful within projects undertaken "in-order-to" bring
about such and such "for-the-sake-of" this or that. Transcendence
towards the life-world is possible through that ontological understanding which lets beings be seen instrumentally, as significantly
placed for this and that. Significance is a structural feature of the
world in which *Dasein* is always already in.

Yet as actively underway, don't we usually experience nature as
something to be read within an equipmental totality? As they started
up to the pass, one member of the ill-fated Donner party noted that
the moon has a ring around it and warned, "If we start now, we will
be caught in the snow." When, however, nature becomes a book, it
becomes something to be described.[1] After Hugh of St. Victor and St.
Anselm, who may have instituted the book metaphor, descriptions
and the problem of universals emerges and meaning gets detached
from things. Exegesis and hermeneutics operate on a book, not a
world (II 1993, 117), in which things no longer come to signify grace
but number, the language in which, as Galileo said, it is written.
However, as late as the seventeenth century, as Foucault noted, the
separation of language from the world is not complete and continues to

> combine here and there with the things of the world and be-
> comes interwoven with them; so much so that these elements,
> taken together, form a network of marks in which each of
> them can play . . . in relation to all the others the role of
> content or of sign . . . language is not an arbitrary system.
> It has been set down in the world and forms a part of it, both
> because things hide themselves and manifest their own enigma
> like a language and because words offer themselves to me as
> things to be deciphered. The great metaphor of the book one
> opens, that one pours over and reads in order to know nature,
> is merely the reverse and visible side of another transference,
> and a deeper one, that forces language to reside in the world.
> (MF 1970, 34–35)

Today the text metaphor has replaced that of the book; the latter has
come to signify a logocentric closure (JD 1976, 18) while the more
open "text" and its traces may in some enigmatic manner point
beyond. However that may be, both book and Derridian text are far
from the minds of those for whom reference is determined by sense, an
expression of thought; so that beginning with Frege and Russell, de-

tachment from things is completed and the text is a writing that is independent, like Internet or the "Information Superhighway," of reader or writer, speaker or hearer, and becomes a totalizing experience without the unifying unities of the *logos,* apperception, reason, or spirit. Information is conveyed and the book as it was lived and digested by Hugh of St. Victor's "munchers and mumblers" recedes. Perhaps departures, arrivals, and homecomings open and close experience in which reader and nature are as one; is this medial process sustained by and sustaining enjoyment more primary? Though all sentient life reads nature's language, it becomes a book through the *epoché* of language and, when enjoyment replaces comprehension, a release from logocentric closure. To take a further step beyond this closure is to hear the other, Levinas says, and thus to accept an "obligation to the one speaking . . . which is not an eternal return to one's self" (EL 1990b, 48), while to speak "is to assume a responsibility towards someone on behalf of someone else" (21). "The solipsist disquietude of consciousness, seeing itself in all its adventures a captive of itself, comes to an end . . . before the face . . . with the total uncoveredness and nakedness of his defenseless eyes, the straightforwardness and frankness of his gaze" (EL 1987, 55).

To some extent the book's meaning depends on who is underway.[2] Whether with Hugh of St. Victor the book reveals homologies with the divine or with Descartes the secrets of nature, all must accommodate "behavioral" significances. Apperception must be embodied; granted that Kantian embodiment is as ghostly as the space wherein we find it, putting hypotheses into experimentally testable form, setting things up, consulting texts, and the like are things to be done with the body if other things are to happen. "Motion, as an act of the subject (not a categorial determination of an object)" (B 154) is *a priori.* The equipmental is set up, *Vorstellung,* "in-order-to" accomplish something "for-the-sake-of" *Dasein* within a referential totality *(Vorweisungsganzheit)* which schematizes an "I can _____." In a phenomenology of action, which may overlap the "looking at" of a method, the intention being worked out factors its field in terms of how it lets entities be seen, usually within a story, a *mythos,* we tell ourselves about who we are and what we are up to. This gathering and laying out, archaic senses of *logos* and *legein* respectively, is a function of the *mythos* which opens and lightens a horizon. The meaning of Being would be appropriate to *cosmos,* in the dual sense of an ordered totality and something beautiful within which one may meaningfully dwell.

Kant thought that the only permissible explanations are mechanistic (*CTJ* 394). Humans would be schematized within the mechanism implicit in the Principles. On Heidegger's account of what technology

as the heir to *techné* discloses, we see ourselves as set upon and challenged forth by the *Ge-stell* to become "human resources" and freely
join other faceless "standing reserves" in the objectless world of cal-
culable, orderable energy (MH 1977, 27). In categorizing things, we
categorize ourselves. In the third Critique, Kant says that "the possibility of living matter is quite inconceivable. Its very concept involves
self-contradiction, since life-lessness, inertia, constitutes the essential
characteristic of matter" (*CTJ* 394). Does this not mean that the
agent is an aggregate, one of whose causal strands is a caused intention
to set things up?

Nevertheless, if not fundamental, the approach to nature's text
within an equipmental totality is of fundamental importance. We are
as a clearing a nexus patient for disclosedness by interpretative projections and it is quite possible that alternative meanings of Being would
appear in founding roles. The hunter's world is probably totemic and
animistic, and hylozoism is at least as fundamental to his intention as
mechanism is to the chemist's. Once it is accepted that we are hermeneutical, the being required by Being to be its *there*, analysis can
undertake the larger task of inquiry into Being itself. Some meanings
of Being will have lost their primordial appeal. Kant's thesis that
nature is "the existence of things as determined by universal law" will
not survive the dialectic which must account for the place of the
experimenter.

To bring about something, we construe entities through the
schematized project in a hermeneutical "seeing as" within which they
fall into a particular referential assignment within a totality of possible assignments. "In interpreting, we do not, so to speak, throw a
'signification' over some naked thing which is present-at-hand, we do
not stick a value on it; but when something within the world is encountered as such, the thing in question already has an involvement
which is disclosed in our understanding of the world, and this involvement is one which gets laid out by the interpretation" (MH 1962,
190–91). In *Being and Time* the present-at-hand shows itself when
the referential structure breaks down. The hammer laid aside because
it was too heavy for the job would, as a pure presence, become something questioned as to its weight and categorized as a quantum.

Through projects entities are "freed" for referential relations.
When the tool is circumspectively seen as handy and appropriate and
"things are manipulated and put to use . . . this has its own kind of
knowledge" (MH 1962, 93) which is in our fingertips, under our skin
and in our joints, a "knowing how" that is to *Zeug* as the surgeon is
to his knife, the pianist his keys, the dancer his body, the potter his
clay. The Kantian empirical schema, a model-theoretic mode of seeing
as, anticipates Heidegger. To know an object is to grasp its horizon of

possibilities and thus envisage its significance ahead of itself. Things are like signifiers; they gather one into meanings. We glance at the sun, not as an inductive datum, but to let it tell us the time of day. On the other hand, "theoretic behavior is just looking, without circumspection. But the fact that looking is non-circumspective does not mean that it follows no rules: it constructs a cannon for itself in the form of method" (MH 1962, 69). Understood circumspectively, the pure schema of the understanding determines a formal intuition of world as a totality of referential structures before anything comes into view. Kant's analytic method assumes this referential structure in *Vorstellung* through which something is it disclosed as present-at-hand. To be a *theoria* is to participate in an event in which being is unconcealed, *aletheia*. What shows itself as present-at-hand is possible only through the ready-at-hand. Kant has shown that only through equipment as set up, such as pen and ink, is the presencing of the *Critique* itself, possible. A Kantian object, like a word recognized through graphemes, is the eject of interpretation. "The [analytic] cannon" understanding constructs "for itself in the form of method" is disclosive; its projects are hermeneutical.

Concepts, rooted in imagination, ought to free entities from their de facto, sedimented involvements. Was not Galileo's *Dialogues on the Two New Sciences* among the greatest feats of Renaissance imagination? By Romantic standards, Kant may have been too severe in his restrictions on imagination, but by his own admission the first *Critique* is a treatise on the scientific imagination (A 78/B 103). Power is also a Renaissance theme. Granted synthesis and the transcendental object, analysis shows an entity's worldly significance is grounded in a physics of forces, not merely extended quanta. Substance, the permanent in intuition, is best understood as a sempiternal vector force (A 204/B 244), a far cry from Newton's kinematics. As we can see in Hegel's "play of forces," the analogue of Kantian reciprocity, this understanding of Being in (medial) play in which rules must sometimes be made up as one plays, already bears within it the death of Parmenides. A force lends itself to chance and teleology as well as to nomological necessity.[3] If the energy we release does not destroy us, perhaps we are on the way to a genuine Platonic understanding: Being is power (*Sop.* 247E).

Just as Kant uses the relational categories to ground the worldly significance of present-at-hand entities, so Heidegger founds signification on our involvement within significant "referential" nexūs. Signs as such are constructed as elements within the equipmental (*Zeug*) context which open some region of the world to circumspection. An item constituted as a sign, given or assigned a reference, is conspicuous as "this definite equipment" and as "something indicative of the ontological structure of readiness-at-hand, of referential totalities, and of worldhood" (MH 1962, 114). Signs effect an *epoché* which lets us "achieve an orientation in our environment" and raise "a totality of equipment into our circumspection so that with it the worldly character of the ready-at-hand announces itself" (110). "That wherein *Dasein* understands itself beforehand [i.e., the world] in the mode of assigning itself is that for which it has let entities be encountered beforehand" (118). Assignments are possible through signs which hold *Dasein*'s familiar involvements before it in which "it gives itself its Being and its potentiality-for-Being as something to be understood with regard to Being-within-the-world" (120). Though sensibility as a language is a part of the ready-at hand equipmental totality, it may be that the meaning of Being unconcealed by the ready-at-hand is too restrictive for a lived world; the resulting language would be similar to the language games of rules and instructions which Wittgenstein cites and criticizes in the opening sections of his *Philosophical Investigations* (1968).

2. Significance and Signification

HEIDEGGER FOUNDS SIGNIFICATION on significance, which in turn reflects the referentiality of ready-at-hand formations characteristic of *Dasein*'s spatiality. The latter's "disseverence" is in many cases effected by reference, that is, *Verweisung* as "something turning or pointing away towards another" (MH 1962, 97). Insofar as this is a signification, something is elicited for another and presupposes the possibility of encounter. This has the advantage of making language a structural feature of a world, but does it let us see sense in sense in a way open to animals, who also read nature's book to their weal or woe? Kant's conceptualism gets sensibilized, but do animals have concepts to sensibilize? Has Heidegger been blinded by Scholasticism and Kant—for whom recognition is in a concept—to the reality of shared sensate life? In the phenomenology of *An Enquiry Concerning the Principles of Natural Knowledge* and *The Concept of Nature*, A. N. Whitehead makes a strong case that recognition—the identification of qualities or congruence which "takes place in the present without intervention of pure memory" (ANW 1921, 124)[4]—and significance— "the disclosure of an entity as a relatum without further discrimination of quality . . . a relatedness with the emphasis on one end only of the relation" (51)[5]—are the basis of all natural inferences. In a philosophy with medial roots, these should replace Hume's "relations," resemblance, contiguity, and cause and effect. Like *anamnesis,* neither recognition—which elicits a feature that does not change—nor significance—which pertains to the morphology of events in which the feature is situated—require concepts and judgments; as in E. coli, these are co-extensive with motile life. Though we begin our lives in such a world, it is difficult to construe experience in these terms. Nevertheless, it must be medial, as in Husserl's "primal impression" or Levinas's *il y a,* and proto-reflexive, since E. coli knows what it is about as it moves along its nutritional gradient.

Signification, however, is for another and thus originates in face-to-face encounter with one's mother in a sacred place of mutual crossing and not in significance per se. Since signification is a substitution, one thing being in place of another, Emmanuel Levinas proposes that this chiasmus is an ethical substitution in which I take over responsibility for the other. If Levinas is correct, one begins reading nature's book in medial sensibility, if only in Freud's primal narcissism, rather than in appropriative projects. We move from this world in which we are immersed in the enjoyment of significant processes into a world of signified things, objects having names that can be characterized and recalled through ostensive signifying acts. This world of sense and reference, of noesis and noema, originates not in signs founded on referentiality but on the Other through whom "the world of my enjoyment becomes a theme having a signification" (EL 1985, 209).

In linguistics a sign is a signifier-signified unity; in phonetic languages, and thus unlike symbols, icons, natural signs or—may we add—apparatus and its printouts, signifiers are "unmotivated and arbitrary" (FdS 1959, 69) and their identity lies in their differential structure; "whatever differentiates one sign from another constitutes it" (121). Since they are significant for all animal life, the sensible aspects of appearances which are often elements in differential fields may function in natural signs like arbitrary signifiers. If one is to reinstate the book metaphor or approach language in the European style, one must begin with de Saussure. Plato's dream in *Theaetetus* of the letters will bring de Saussure into focus.

In Socrates' dream, things are reduced to collections of simple objects, as in the letters in the alphabet or Russell's logical atomism (*Theaet.* 201E–204A). These "atoms" of "which all other things consist" are such that "no account can be given of them." They can only be named; all else said of them, such as "just," "it," "each," and the like, "run loose about the place and are attached to everything." Complex things may be ostensively defined in "combinations of names" (202A). Plato wants to say that these elements, like the letters, are without sense apart from real world-like, intelligible wholes. Though unknowable, letters are distinguished intuitively, but nothing can be asserted of them; anything said would be neither true nor false. The elements are "objects of perception and cannot be known" (202B); to know something is to be able to pick out its instances. Elements are not discriminated by their intrinsic essence or quality, but by difference.

Socrates then objects that the whole alone is knowable and not the parts. He shows that absurd consequences follow however these wholes be understood, whether as "emergent" unities or "heaps" (Aristotle), or whatever interpretation be placed on these (intrinsically distinguishable) simples, such as epistemic or metaphysical atoms or Wittgenstein's objects. Wittgenstein cites Plato's myth in his *Philosophical Investigations* (1968, 46) as a reason for abandoning the *Tractatus'* logical atomism. Nevertheless, I think the abandonment of combinatorial simples would be a mistake. The argument hinges on "present-at-hand" intrinsic quality as the unintelligible basis of intelligibility. Here again Wittgenstein (45–64) is helpful; language users do not, in general, have paradigmatic samples against which entities are matched to see if they are properly named. Suppose, however, we were to take these elements, whatever else logically, epistemologically, or metaphysically they may be, as signifiers, not because they are integrally such and such but, on the contrary, because each is defined by what it is not; its being is through non-being, its difference from others, the generically same but formally other elementary kinds. Each combinatorial element works through the absent others in its formal, differential field. These simples work in virtue of their relational, not intrinsic, essences and make up an ordinal field of formal differences, such as phonetic sounds or graphic shapes. Each element is what it is because it is the trace of the absent others. Plato wanted his elements to be combinatorial, but he also wanted each element to be intrinsically distinguishable. Something must have an intrinsic essence to have a relational essence, for otherwise there would be a relation with nothing to relate; and there is no reason why this intrinsic essence cannot be complex. The intrinsic nature of signifiers is more evident in a language we do not understand in which its signifiers leap out to us; when we encounter a familiar graphic or phonic element, we pass over it to its function. Their relational essence, its difference from the others, allows us to talk about their intrinsic nature, so that one can know and not only name them. Given some rule in virtue of which certain combinations are possible, then these formal differences are potentials for structure. Perhaps we can now begin to see that the "Rube Goldberg" apparatus for constitution and judgment is redundant. In matters of signification, the nature of a signifier, its identity, follows from the others which it is not in a double sense, namely, its otherness from what is signified and its otherness from other signifiers. The seen grapheme offers itself through the occasioning computer as an interpretation of a circuit and then as signifier for interpretation. Signifiers are not characterized "by their positive quality . . . [but] simply by the fact that they are distinct. Phonemes are above all else opposing, relative, and negative entities" (FdS 1959, 119).[6]

To whom is meaning to be expressed? The wayfarer underway

among meanings or the proto-positivist searching for verifications? Whatever the answer, this is the burden these arbitrary graphemes and phonemes will carry. What resources does Kant offer? Not many; but some of his accomplishments are worth preserving. To question beings is already to be involved in language (B xiii), but language was never a focal issue for the Critical Philosophy. It should have been, at least if we are to judge the importance now attached to language by all schools of philosophy. Can we arrive at an account of language that will do him justice?

The obvious approach to language would be through the logistic paradigm, long recognized as important for understanding Kant. The Metaphysical Deduction which is founded on logical forms would appear to be the place to begin; however, the categorial claim of Kant's table of judgments is suspect. Our list of logical forms would differ, since negation and either disjunction, conjunction, or implication are functionally complete. That, however, Kant gives priority to second over first intentions and impositions and thus to the logical over the ontological order has not gone unnoticed. Sir Peter Strawson, for example, understands the *Critique* to be the descriptive metaphysics of our conceptual scheme. Russell's logical constructions and Wittgenstein's *Tractatus* are among many testimonials of analytic philosophy to Kant's logocentric approach.

Language is not possible, according to Kant's *Anthropology*, without sight and hearing. Though its indefinite field of coexistent objects makes vision the primary epistemic sense, the transformation of what is seen into knowledge is the work of the mediating auditory sign. The deaf man "will never attain real concepts, since the signs necessary to him will never attain real universality" (*Anth.* sec. 22). What about Helen Keller? And why is the auditory sign alone capable of true universality? What happened to Kant's line-drawing? Though both speech and gesture are auto-affective, it is easier for us, if not for a Helen Keller, to animate a sound and to experience its apparent "dispensability," its disappearance behind its meaning, its signified: "The inner sense is not pure apperception, a consciousness of what man does . . . [it also contains] what man feels, to the extent that he is affected by his own play of thoughts" (sec. 24). Is thought, playing without benefit of "material" phonemes, Plato's silent conversation with one's self? Are the players the ghosts of sounds remaining after animation? Though it is difficult to imagine this silent soliloquy taking place without even the memory of verbal or visual marks, Helen Keller could think.

Jacques Derrida has sought to show that Husserl's failure to consider the necessary role of sensibly embodied signifiers, which Kant also ignored, led him into his idealism, and this critique will shed light on Kant.[7] The importance of sensible bearers of sense becomes evident on examining Husserl's distinction between indicative and expressive signs. Kant's line being drawn is an example of a sign being animated by an act of the mind. The drawing is invested with a meaning, the line itself, signified by the drawn segment.[8] When the signifier "disappears" before the signified, it is said to be "animated" and becomes an expressive sign and is filled with a surplus of meaning, noetic and noematic. An indicative sign is said to signify, as an unknown word might be said to signify, but to be meaningless, without sense, unless it is intentionally animated and becomes expressive. The disappearance of the signifier leads to the illusion that reflective self-consciousness is a primordial introspective datum. The resulting "private language" would be a consequence of overlooking physical signifiers in the unmotivated play of thinking; it is then assumed that significance is secured by thought at the level of meanings rather than at the level of sense through de Saussure's fields. Linguistic signifiers are usually arbitrary, where a natural signification is not, yet each has formal relata and operates within empirical structures rather than within the mind—to which Kant will subordinate all significance. Mind is then the basis of form and sense is formless. We do not "see" structure; we think it in its rule-governed generation. Husserl remarks that "motivation occurs when an object or state of affairs of whose reality someone has knowledge indicates to him the reality of certain other objects or states of affairs, in the sense that his belief in the being of the one is expressed (though not at all evidently) as motivating a belief or surmise of the being of the other" (EH 1970b, 270). The motivating context retires as one grasps intensional ties. One spontaneously or unmotivatedly *sees* real meanings when indicative become expressive signs. The "reality" of which "someone has knowledge" becomes a "formal sign" or concept whose significance lies in its entailments. Note that one finds a basis for significance, not in extensional features of events, which analysis as monstrative abstraction preserves, but in meanings. This way of looking at things gives, in germ, the Kantian motive for replacing "empirical" with "transcendental affinities." In the expressive intention, a creature of the phenomenological reduction, what was never fully present through the indicative sign is raised to the level of a fully present, logical, objective essence. If, however, the emphasis is placed on the expressive sign, it is to be presumed that there is something to express, a meaning intention or, as in Frege, a "thought which is expressed in a sentence."[9] In other words, the conceptual order is prior to the order of signification. Frege was persuaded that *Sinn* (sense) determines *Bedeutung* (reference). Prior to both is the mystery of pointing that sometimes connects with and discloses the thing which one points out for another that I have been celebrating

in this story of analysis. The participatory, not the expressive, community is that from which one should begin. The thing, not the expression (or representation) gathers. Husserl's indicative sign that is
allowed to indicate something for another and, in recognition, delivers
the thing over to a signified-signifier diad marks the phenomenon
whose origin we seek. Husserl never thought to take the way of indication: "Immediate 'seeing,' not mere sensuous, experimental seeing,
but seeing in the universal sense of an originally preventative consciousness, is the ultimate legitimatizing source of all rational assertions" (EH 1982, 36). Contingent indicative signs disappear in the
ideality. Derrida notes in *Speech and Phenomena,* however, that this
presentative experience must be reported in language, as in the text
just cited from *Ideas.* Clearly the sense of the assertion functions in the
absence of "originally presentative consciousness," but this reporting
is not just about ideal objects; it also concerns the moment of truth
when presentification occurs. This cannot be the "I" of a logically
proper name. In an ideally reduced and shareable experience, what is
reported is addressed to any "I." "I am ill," when said by anyone, is
sometimes true and sometimes false. Like Descartes's "I am," it must
be token-reflective and function as a sign only if it is possible to make
sense of the expression after the death of whoever first expressively
used it. The sense of the sign thus depends on absence. The expressive
intention which is supposedly an *a priori* act is contingent on the indicative *a posteriori* sign. Husserl remarks that "If we read this word
"I" without knowing who wrote it, it is perhaps not meaningless, but
it is estranged from its normal meaning." On his own premises, Husserl should have declared the opposite to be true. The theory depends
on contingent fact, that someone read it, for instance, and used the
token-reflexive, indicative "I." As John Llewelyn says, "What Derrida hopes this discussion of Husserl's theory of token-reflexivity will
bring to our notice is something that escapes the notice of Husserl
himself; that the supposedly immaculate interiority . . . of allegedly
pure meaning is hymeneally conjugated with the exteriority of indication. This exteriority is not simply appended to expressive meaning.
. . . Its supplementation is not an additive and adulterative ingression; it is a complementation in the sense that there is no expressive
meaning without indication" (JL 1986, 26). The Kantian echo with
which this concludes should remind us that a private world of expressive signification, the world of drawing imaginary lines as an image of
empirical synthesis and as a condition for meaning, is hardly a foundation for the referential structure of the public world. Nevertheless, an
analogue of Kant's synthetic method may be the best guide to this
referential structure. That should perhaps begin with the body's "here"
which is beyond being and, therefore, Hegel's critique of immediacy;

nor is it token-reflexive, though as origin, the "here" of a 'there is" orients and individuates the "I."

Kant begins the Deduction by promising to think and express concepts temporally (A 99). Through recognition in a concept, being appeared to in an intuition in inner sense is translated into the apperception of an appearance in objective time. Alternatively, recognition establishes sense as representative, as indicating, announcing, presenting or giving notice of an object (MH 1990, 28), and at the same time the concept as representing, as one that gathers and orders many representations. In commenting on Husserl's usage of *Vorstellung*, Derrida appears to ignore the conceptual bias, shared with Frege and Kant, that sense determines reference and extends "representation" to include "reproduction or repetition of presentation" or the "modification that neutralizes a presentation" (JD 1973, 49). Though "representation" invites deconstruction, mere iteration can be mindless, as in a Turing recursion. If monstration is prior and the thing allowed to disclose and express itself, "reproduction of presentation" is in the service of the presented and, however this "representation of a representation" may modify an original representation, one presumes that it will continue to express its sense. This suggested inversion of Kant leads beyond expressive signs, concepts and separated ideas. Before we seriously contemplate this turn, let us go as far as possible with Kant.

Though Kant says a "concept" is a rule (A 127), his emphasis is on the iterative act, on "I can (self-affectively) presence," rather than on the iterated presence. These acts are teleological; we act on systems, whether of traces or forces, to direct them to representative ends. This would mean that on some occasions signifying must be understood in terms of representation and not conversely. In these cases, an iterable sign has its cause in the idea (*Phaedo* 100C ff.) which it would make reproductively present and which gives a rule to acts which express it. I hope to find a way to explore the *arché* of language, and thus of a world, through these parameters. I will approach this originary, first discerned through Kant's iterative acts that crossed imagination and let number appear, in a series of scattered reflections, not in one swoop, and latch a Kantian philosophy onto some of their results. The immediate task is correcting a bias against any form of representation. Kant's approach to representation relative to the "veritative" or recognitional synthesis shows why it would be impossible for Husserl to restrict phenomenological description of meaningful "primal data" to inner sense. This already presupposes an exteriority which Husserl took some pains to avoid.[10]

Meaningful inner sense requires an objective reference; its time can be represented and well-ordered only "in the *drawing* of a straight line (which serves as the outer figurative representation of time)"

(B 154). Line drawing, indifferently real or imaginary (A 102), is Kant's most obvious example of signification and becomes his self-affection paradigm. He might have been better advised to attend to what was involved in the possibility of writing the first *Critique* and language's role in the "possibility of experience"; both speech and lines would be temporal forms of self-affection, but one would have involved assembling arbitrary physical marks into syntactical ordered, non-continuous, linear expressions and the other the (imaginary) playing out a continuous function. Language involves iterable signs; iterated acts, as in counting, constitute a present. Intending to say or express something seems to involve representing what is to be said, not what has been done, and gives a telic focus lacking in the three-fold synthesis. Speech reaches out from here to the other yonder lighted by the Good and is participatory, where "here" and "yonder" are, as Heidegger says, neither adverbs nor pronouns but rather "*Dasein* designations" (MH 1962, 156). They designate *Dasein*, not as token-reflexive, but as the articulation of a primal proximity which is, Plato might add, the gift of the receptacle beyond Being.

Iteration, the repeatable, rule-governed act that posits the same in the other and other of time, marks conceptuality only if the universal is expressed.[11] Derrida's nominalism emphasizes the structure of iteration and not—as far as I can see—the represented structure. While the linguistic bond with community, whether that of Heidegger's *Mitsein* or Levinas's *l'Autre*, is threatened, Derrida provides a unique insight through the appearing of the signifier into the dynamics of the originary. But this approach, unlike Levinas's, is within Heidegger's ontological parameters; perhaps the fact that early study of Levinas, "Violence and Metaphysics," was written before Derrida's explicit recognition of the medial play of presence and absence in "*Différance*," explains why the medial aspect of founding phenomena in enjoyment or "The Phenomenology of Eros" went unrecognized.[12]

Like Husserl and most others before Wittgenstein, Kant probably thought that concepts are independent of their expression in language and that when there is a need to communicate, words can be fitted to meanings. What are we about when we fit a word to a concept? After our immersion in de Saussure or Wittgenstein, this apparent priority of thought to language seems bizarre; nevertheless, something important may be at stake. To recognize something in a concept is to schematize it. What is recognized, that is, apprehended as appearing and apperceived as an appearance, announces itself as a possible future, not as something to be synthesized with a reproduced past it empresences. Kant seems to have thought that one receives the line announced by the drawing, real or imaginary, as a reproduction of what was being done through whose necessities the future unfolds as a continuous presence. If like Husserl I could become the spectator of my "internal time consciousness," I might now perceive the past act of drawing retained, not imaginatively reproduced, in this present and fading as it drops down into the past like a sounding note (EH 1991, 311–12). I do not recognize this primal impression in a present but rather through what is "reproduced" or "retained," the other by which it can be a same. In this sense Kant is right to suggest the primacy of the reproductive synthesis, even if locating what is retained in "memory" is inappropriate. I am aware of the line being drawn, the tune being heard, and not the "primal impressions." Does not talking about this line presuppose that I also represent myself as intending the line in a veritative judgment through which I recognize what I make appear? Instead of writing about lines, think about writing on a word processor. The written word is not a reproduced past; it is a matrix bearing traces of a past from which one can envisage a possible future, for its identity lies in traces of iterable others. From the point of the view of the teleology of consciousness which intends beings, the object horizon or schema entailed in recognition is prior to the closure that would otherwise be effected by the continuity making reproductive synthesis; I cross from sensibility to understanding, from the immanent privacy of inner sense to the transcending public world.

Saying what I am doing is said to entail reflective "recognition in a concept" (A 103–4). The future schematically represented in this present has the non-being, the otherness, of possibility, which allows this "primal impression" to be apprehended as significant. Recognition of an object is conditioned by the dynamics of signification and, at some primal stratum, the signifier is recognized only through retentive alterity; but the sense of its now is not a consequence of its spontaneous graft onto a reproduced or retained past. The present is the future's return as more or less fulfilled. David Wood says in a similar context that "time theoretically embraces the necessary intrusion of representation" (1989, 122). Representation differs from and yet is similar to retention, and both differ from the primal impression, even though perception covers both the retained and the impression. Representation, which presupposes iterability, is evidently an exteriority that transcends the immanent and supposedly internal necessities or medial propensities in the originary. If so, the originary now of the spontaneous appearing is already contaminated with this alterity, this non-being. Originary presencing, the time constituting "flow" or flux "for which all names are lacking" which Husserl identifies with "absolute subjectivity" (EH 1991, 79), is really a medial matrix or "spacing"—an analogue to Kant's productive imagination—through which the impression is given to the hypostasis. The flux as medial "source point," a spacing which is the "becoming space of time" and the never-present source of being, would be neither subjective nor objective and alike foreign to realism and idealism. Are we to take this in relation to the said or the hypostasis? In the one case our movement is towards constituted signification (Derrida) and in the other towards the receptacle (Levinas). Since the receptacle is the place of the trace, Plato's choreography accommodates both. Let the flux be the *Timaeus'* "becoming that never really is" (27D), and interpret this as the *Philebus'* entropic *apeiron* (24D) which, as in Plato's example of a continuum of sound, could be differentiated by notes or letters. Phonemes and graphemes, differentiating forms of *peras* (18B-D), define gradients and, as novel to the immanent flux, introduce counter entropic possibilities. Granted the difficulty in this position, and it is still the case that Becoming requires its participation in Being if the hypostatic creature is to endure. Something beyond the flux is the "cause" of the flux. Without this relative transcendence, any context inviting interpretation as medial would have its paradigm in the completely ordered world of Endymion (*Phaedo* 72B); differences would be elided ("if everything was combined and nothing separated"), the "processes between them" (71D) would cease, and all would "sleep." Signification retains dynamism and the novelty of iteration alone can not sustain it.

The "primal source point" lies in the flux, not in the act of transcendental apperception. Until now our way has been with Kant, but we have to part company. He situates the synthesis of recognition within the continuity of an imaginatively reproduced past; while this might hold for a continuous process, like sounding the same tone or drawing a line, recognition must be open to novelty, to chance, and take advantage of these in weaving the fabric of action. One must see what is coming up in what has come up. Moreover, Kant failed to recognize the interdependence of representation and signification: "where the word is not no thing may be." His rather "operationalist" understanding of a concept as a rule for gathering and ordering has no necessary connection with language. Representation, which should be understood as a rule for collecting possibility into actuality, is intentional and presupposes schemata. Speech intentions are not merely expressive; they are also monstrative and, as propositional, can be expressed by different signifiers using different rules. The going will be rough when iteration fails to accommodate representation. Representation, not re-presentation, marks the transition from inner sense to the objective order, from immanence to transcendence; when Husserl limits his descriptions to inner time and fails to construe protention within the rubric of recognition, the relation of signification to original temporality becomes obscure. In the phenomenological reduction, the transcendent is an acceptance phenomenon, not the phenomenon of its acceptance; but this may not have been clear to him at the time of his 1905 lectures, published with later supplements as *On the Phenomenology of the Consciousness of Internal Time*. At least in principle, he restricted his descriptions to consciousness of inner time to the primal impression and its retentional modification and excluded "every assumption, stipulation, or conviction concerning objective time" (EH 1991, 4); though he discussed reproductive or "secondary" memory, he was apparently unconcerned with how this might be translated into objective time. If one describes a simple, immanent appearing, a sounding tone, without placing upon it a representational value, then the spontaneously appearing impression will be perceived as if it were same as the retentive past that is always slipping back. When we hear it as musical, it becomes representative. But if retention is a primal intentionality, isn't it already representation? The lectures never develop this protentive aspect, "the future course of the stream" (89). The object horizons of the later work, such as the *Cartesian Meditations*, in which the future, unlike the past, is riddled with contingency, suggests that protention is an (unsuccessful) editorial addition to immanent temporality from what is known through recognition about objective time.

The way to a beyond sufficient for creativity, for which iterability is only a necessary condition, can be seen in the transition from a bookish to a textual metaphorics. Books appealed to vision, to the light of truth. The word had a "revelatory force" so that matters discussed could be seen in the "clarity of truth" (GS 1994, 20). The text transformed "the spoken tongue into an artifact, thereby separating it from speaking and making it a language" which could supply the conceptual foundation for philosophy and science (EAH 1963, 6–7). Nature was a book, a closure, before it was a text; and as readers underway, we should begin it in a ways closer to the "munchers and mumblers," the monks of the Dark Ages, than the way we usually read a philosophical text. A bookish approach, not an exclusive reliance on the text metaphor that has been dominant since Hugh of St. Victor and St. Anselm, is characteristic of Levinas's "enjoyment." The medieval book was unique, carefully illuminated and decorated, and thus hardly a token of a type. Can a book lead the way beyond being? Immanuel Levinas may have written the book, *Otherwise than Being, or Beyond Essence*. The relative closure of a book now makes sense only within a general text-context; this is a microcosm of the dynamics of effective history.

To see why, we must ask Levinas's question. Are we "duped by morality? . . . Does not lucidity, the mind's openness upon the true, consist in catching sight of the permanent possibility of war? . . . We do not need obscure fragments of Heraclitus to prove that being reveals itself as war to philosophical thought. . . . The visage of Being that shows itself in war is fixed in the concept of totality [unified by a principle that reduces alterity to sameness] . . . individuals are reduced to being bearers of forces [of domination and control] that command them unbeknown to themselves" (EL 1985, 21). The play of forces in the textual model developed by Nietzsche, Foucault, and Derrida reflects the polemical context of political and social life today. Is it the whole story? So we try to write a book, relatively closed to context, to try to show a way beyond being that may reveal the possibility of messianic peace (22).

We now must look closely to what lies yonder from totalizing intention to the dynamics of signifers, whether of a book or a text, to discover how "reason [can] persuades necessity" (*Tim.* 48A). The *arché* is a dynamical abyss diversified by schemata, whether by Derrida's graphemes and phonemes which empower the languaging they give or Plato's stereometric shapes that empower emerging life. The notion of iteration is that of a cut that may or may not be discriminatory. In any case, it introduces *qua* iteration a relative novelty into becoming by the ingression of a new gradiant for vectoring forces. Even the reiteration of a same is *now,* a now always new, never young or old. Thus the present is not continuous with the past; ithe immediate past is related through the trace, by what it excludes, and is never the fulfillment of presence; there is a "becoming of continuity, not a continuity of becoming." For example, "being" excludes time yet bears through its roots in *einai* the trace of time, that is, the aspectual sense of presenting itself in a present; then what I say when I say "being" is other than the intention governing speaking. If discrimination is invoked, then there will be a possible *polemos* between what is seen or heard (and the traces that haunt recognition) and the intention (and its traces) to speak or hear that crosses it.

Derrida speaks of textuality and the medial *mouvance* of signifiers, along with such related terms as *différance, pharmakon,* supplement, and the like, to express the "temporalization of a *lived experience* which is neither in the world or in "another world," which is not more sonorous than luminous, not more in time than in space, that differences among the elements or rather produces them, make them emerge as such and constitute the texts, the chains, the system of traces . . . the unheard difference between the appearing and appearance [*l'apparaissant et l'apparaître*]" (JD 1976, 65). The trace retains "the structure of delay" (JD 1982, 21) which he assembles from texts by Levinas ("a past that has never been present") (21), Freud and Nietzsche ("who put consciousness into question in its assured certainty of itself") (17) and de Saussure's difference. His stress on iteration retains the standpoint of immanent time and weakens the role of representation, e.g., the power of the concept to represent. Perhaps thinking texts within books will eliminate reductive tendencies in the textual approach. Be that as it may, the focus is on the trace, on signifying graphemes and phonemes (B 154);[13] how indeed would representation, conceptual or imagistic, be possible prior to sensible signifiers? Without them, there can be no Cartesian *cogito,* nor is there any denying that what they say or the style in which they are set out (*Vorstellung*) imposes limits on how or what we think. Except in iconographic languages, such as mathematics, iteration is within de Saussure's field of formal differences and entails the instantiation of "differential" concepts which, if shorn of representation, determine what is expressed. The autonomous ego choosing its words in its chosen language seems to have given way to an iterative play of traces "languaging" us, but these dynamics are sometimes in the service of one addressing from here a yonder in the appropriative reduction of alterity to sameness, vital, intellectual, or emotive. In paradigmatic instances of knowing and communicating the intention (*vouloir dire,* "willing to say") or schematized "fore-conception" crosses this medial field to let signifiers appear in demonstrating or expressing something which is the Platonic cause for the appearing of the signifiers, even if these as traces are (marginalized) supplements to the apparent text. With the "intrusion of representation" indicative signs are animated and open a horizon of possible iterations to the signifying "I can. . . ." The threat of reductionism lingers unless signification is understood as interpretative expression of the thing, not the speaker. What sense would Kant's regression to sensibility in the subjective deduction have without the guidance of the objective deduction? The Deduction bears traces of constitutive reason which still rules in practical reason which constitutes its object, the moral will. Sense is threatened if the concept or *eidos* that breaks into and reorders the *polemos* of forces is dismissed as a transcendent signified. Does Derrida disagree? No. A phoneme or grapheme "can function as a sign, and in general, as language, only if a formal identity enables it to be issued again and be recognized. This identity is necessarily ideal. It thus necessarily implies representation . . ." (JD 1973, 50). Of course Derrida recognizes intentionality, but it is mediated by public language that disseminates meaning.

The trace, anything but a presence, is iterated. Its status as a trace results, first, from its being sign-like, significant only in the absence of the signified; and second, as defined by differences it has no positive content of its own. Its iteration, whether or not intentional, constitutes a present which, paradoxically, is present only in relation to what is retained, and thus is neither evidential or fulfilling, for it is as much a non-presence as a presence. Didn't Husserl acknowledge that a present is never instantaneous? Through retention and protention it is what it is not, a becoming rather than a being. Time generated by these iterated differences is unlikely to reveal a meaning of being as presence. Kant's emphasis on representation, set-ups that are never merely mental, promises a way beyond some traps guarding the threshold of the Open.[14]

Derrida takes the relation of the living present to its retained and falling away past, perceptually given as an identity in difference, as paradigmatic for signification. Insofar as we posit the signifier as a presenced being, this is appropriate; for its identity and continuity depends on its relation to the retained trace, an alterity, so that what Husserl saw as unified, Derrida sees as different (DW 1989, 125). The trace, not the sign, does the work of the signifier with, however, this difference; a signifier, understood within the unity of a sign, is a presence referring to a presence; the trace which does not bind to anything and is not a presence (or absence) though it dwells, like Husserl's primal impression, in the "living present" as the prior condition for presence. As David Wood says, "we are dealing with a movement that precedes and conditions presence, and hence identity, the possibility of identifying, and hence naming, and even the intelligibility that would go with this" (127). Does Derrida assume from this immanent (and medial) standpoint that this "signifying" relation to an other obtains if it is a "recollection" or, for that matter, any other form of "representation?" Yes, for he never rejects intentionality and admits that his practice ignores, not denies, other and more evident aspects of literature. Perhaps we cannot ignore them for, when marginalized, they nevertheless continue to do their work.

Like internal time, signifying can represence without a Kantian mental detour through memory, and while it is an admirable move to let sense be retained by sense, suppose its other is the Other from whom the Good addresses and in whom it commands? Husserl, having eschewed all such objectivities, focuses on the relation of the impressional present to its retentively modified other, but this is not the relation of this same present to a representation, also other. Wood says that lumping retention and representation together as alterities meant by a trace obscures their differences (1989, 125); retention and recollection are concerned with actuality's closed horizons, while protention and recognition schematize "openly endless" possibility. It will not do to mark off this signified idea as if it were a Kantian transcendent. Were creatures clones, their separated ideas would be presences transcendently signified; but ideas have to be evoked and responded to if they are to linger for a while as part of a rift design, a "conflict of measure and unmeasure" (MH 1971b, 90), in the gap between Plato's being and becoming. All explanation devolves upon things and ideas determine how they express themselves; things are meant (*Bedeutung*] eidetically and, as their measure, *eidos* is also explanatory of their expressive horizons. If structure is disclosed and not just instanced, and if it is recurrent and invites iterable signifiers, it does not follow that eidetic structure is context-free and thus a posited same in each occurrence nor that it is a resultant of "linguistic" forces like those at play in the *apeiron dynamis* of *différance*. Recognizing something in a concept neutralizes contextuality. Therefore, if monstration, the primary entree into objectivity, is construed nominally, as naming, things will be fixed forever within the amber of Parmenides. Animals recognize, like Aesop's dog, sometimes mistakenly, without iterating signifiers. Reification of relata in conceptual recognition seems unavoidable until we recall that even Duns Scotus' drayman hand knew more about horses than the philosopher who wove them into a concept, a web of mental fictions. Just now, however, we need to be on our guard when it is proposed that iteration of the trace within the deferring and deferring dynamics of *différance*, like Kantian iterative acts of counting, generates time and virtually everything else. We will end up, in his name, with those standardized concepts against which Derrida has so vigorously protested. Wood observes that Derrida's "pure self-affection, with which he associates différance (with an *a*), is credited with a whole range of constitutive capacities . . . space, the outside, the world, the body and so forth. . . . It does . . . not belong to the subject of which it is true; rather it produces that subject " (DW 1989, 127).

With this inversion of Kantian representation, *différance* is a more or less molar account of deconstructive forces operating in generating and reading epochal texts expressing the dynamics of the receptacle, "the place of the trace." Plato's creative demiurgos was a lion-like beast who wandered across the desert eradicating his tracks, traces, with his tail. Can we assemble a world from traces of the Good? If our journey is made within nature's book, then isn't life a *lectio*? Do we represent as we read, as if in a phantasmagoria, or do we enter into nature through the text to nourish ourselves, to enjoy its delights? Both are intentional, yet the text is reflective and the book, which can make truth claims, yields medial, reflexive satisfaction. Can this be among things and not as if enclosed like chambermaids in its significations?

Echoing Boehme, Joyce's Stephen Daedelus says that the flotsam strewn about on the bay's shore is "the signatures of all things I am here to read," but this requires that there be things to read, empty bottles, a dead dog, sea weed. . . . Our methodological parameters demonstrate aspects of *things* which are then expressed in language and, in the last analysis, serve as reasons in explanation, an insight easily lost among the structuralist's signs. This insight does not sit well with Charles Peirce's semiotics. A devoted student of Kant, he believed with Duns Scotus and Ockham that a theory of categories and concepts is dependent on a theory of signs. He mounts a counter-movement against hermeneutics through the ancient book/text meta-phor at the expense of disclosive reference and the things that explain. A sign is "anything that determines something else (its interpretant) to refer to an object to which it itself refers (its *object*) in the same way, the interpretant in turn becoming a sign, and so *ad infinitum* (2. 300). His contention that anything can be a sign, natural, iconic, or conven-tional, reinstates the book of nature. According to Hugh of St. Victor, "The entire sensible world is, so to speak, a book written by the hand of God. All visible things, visibly presented to us by a symbolic in-struction, that is, figured, are proposed for the declaring and signifying of things invisible" (*Didascalicon*, PL CLXXVI, col. 814). We may now read sense as Berkeley's "universal language of nature," not as a language based on resemblances and signatures that "folds back upon itself, duplicates itself, reflects itself or forms a chain with itself so that things can resemble one another" (MF 1970, 27), but rather as if it were signifiers in a guide book to be read rightly for weal or woe. Nevertheless, the regress of signs must stop at the thing, though in other contexts it too could signify. Only things, not ideas, laws, prin-ciples, and the like, explain.[15]

Peirce says that "a sign stands for something *to* its idea which it produces or modifies . . . that to which it stands is called its *object*, that which it conveys its *meaning*, and the idea to which it gives rise its interpretant" (1. 339). But when the thing become a sign, explana-tion is terminated in a beyond that is never reached. For both de Saus-sure and Peirce, signs are unities of signified/signifier, but this unity of this binary pair is challenged by the iterative character of the signifier and the various contexts, each of which may be a determinate in meaning, in which it may be understood and misunderstood. Con-cepts, Kant's representation of representations, interpret representa-tions but, since concepts are formal signs, objects get eliminated. "The object of a representation is nothing but a representation of which the first representation is the interpretant. . . . But an endless series of representations, each representing the one behind it, may be conceived to have an absolute object as its limit" (*ibid.*). This absolute object must be the transcendent invisible—the Good?—of which Hugh spoke:

"The sign and its explanation make up another sign; and since the explanation will be a sign, it will probably require an additional explanation, which when taken together with the already enlarged sign will make up a still larger sign; and proceeding in this way, we shall, or should, ultimately reach a sign of itself, containing its own explanation and those of its significant parts, and according to this explanation, each part will have some other part as its object" (2. 230). As Umberto Eco remarks, this biogenetic image of signs generating signs is useful but, unless stopped, results in a "global field of unlimited semiosis."[16] Something perceived may represent something else; but unless something can be perceived and then re-presented in memory, imagination, or as anticipated and not simply represented in these diverse modes, signifying activity would never terminate: "We therefore demand that a bare concept be made sensible, that is, that an object corresponding it be presented in intuition. Otherwise the concept would, as we say, be without sense, that is, without meaning" (A 240/B 299).

Needless to say, there are no concepts and thus nothing to be made sensible; we have to think in accordance with the sensate beings that we are; but if we, together with the sense world, are epiphenomena of the flux, the order, stability, and judgments, moral and rational, secured for us by concepts is threatened. With the loss of language as a means of expression, are we to lose a self-responsible ego and world? Suppose we effect a Kantian synopsis under a "speech intention." In this potentiated pure intuition, the *arché* to be crossed by a dialogic intention (*vouloir dire*) manifests itself as combinatorial relata, graphemes and phonemes playing as if a field of forces, rather than Kant's nows and points. This is the differential field of graphemes and phonemes which, in this communication context, could be taken as Nietzsche's flux of countervailing forces. J. L. Austin extends this reductive theme by interpreting language within the parameters of force, illocutionary and locutionary; this has the advantage, however, of bringing the other into the matrix. How is this other to be thought?

In the sciences of man the face is too often a mask, a *persona* behind which is a play of sociological, ethnological, biological, economic, political, legal, and psychological forces but nothing uniquely personal. Michael Foucault sought to purge teleology and the "metahistorical deployment of ideal significance" from history and the historical sciences by denying the ontic gifts of an *Ursprung, arché,* "origin," by means of Nietzsche's dynamical genealogies (MF 1984, 77). Doubtless, as he remarked, the cure for historicism is history itself and that what we mostly hear, as we listen to history, is "something altogether different behind things than a timeless and essential secret."

The secret is "that they have no essence or that their essence was fabricated in piecemeal fashion from alien forms" (77). The workings of Hegelian Spirit which distributed and monitored power in different social contexts was assigned to his play of forces. No two forces being equal, differential forces play back and forth, checking and countering each other and precipitating different strategies, such as the classification and punishment of criminals or diagnosis and treatment of mental disorder.

> Foucault's most impressive results lie in his analysis of the
> role of sexuality in our lives today. "Sex" has come to func-
> tion as a "unique signifier and universal signified" by group-
> ing together "in an artificial unity anatomical elements,
> biological functions, conducts, sensations and pleasures." This
> "fictitious unity" is then treated as a "causal principle, an
> omnipresent meaning, a secret to be discovered everywhere
> . . . [which] appears to dominate us and to be that secret
> which seems to underlie all that we are, the point that
> enthralls us through the power it manifests and the meaning
> which it conceals and which we ask to reveal what we are and
> to free us . . ." (MF 1990, 124-125)

His analogue of the receptacle, the enunciative function, serves as the proto-*arché* which gives the placeless *logos* a place. Levinas has shown that "there is" is a similar field—at times even less benign—that provides a "here" from which hypostatic structure can egress. This may extend to larger fields of discourse. While I think that the "token reflexive I" must answer to another and say, like young Samuel in the household of Eli, "Here am I," these forces should remind us that archeology is not eschatology. Didn't Kant show us, however, that a teleological estimate may be appropriate to cases in which justice calls us into activity? This is the moral teleology found in quite limited events, such as the French revolution, as sacred history has always recognized, but it cannot be applied to a whole.

Sentences emerging as discursive formations from enunciative functions, the contextual text matrix underlying the human sciences, are strategies within an economy of forces and, on Foucault's estimate, express neither the self nor refer to things. Platonists must agree that though ideas may transcend any pattern and be its creative determinates, all too often what is taken to be an idea is a precipitate of institutionally sanctioned do's and don'ts (CT 1989, 204). This is not to be overlooked, for we in Louisiana survived for a while thanks to the "do's" and "don'ts" of the Army Corps of Engineers that channel-

ized the Mississippi. Moreover, since being also participates in historical becoming, there is no reason why a practice should not generate
constitutive and even "regulative" eidetic structure. Christmas, which
wasn't celebrated by Protestants before this century, is now celebrated
by Moslems in Turkey. There is even a certain veneration of our St.
Nicholas, a native of its southern coast. I have seen Moslem women
come into a church and pray to the Virgin. Doubtless various powers
are at work, but then again the incarnation says something about ourselves that cannot but raise respect for the Other and thus all others
who come naked and vulnerable among us. Bosnia suggests that some
Christians have yet to get the message.

Enunciative formations are potentiated fields determining and
determined by discursive formations, reductive variants of Hegel's
forms of spirit, and are not, Foucault has said, "made up of things,
facts, realities or beings, but of laws of possibility, rules of existence
for the objects that are named, designated, or described within it and
for the relations affirmed or denied in it. The referential of the statement forms the place, the condition, the field of emergence, the authority to differentiate between individuals or objects, states of things
and relations that are brought into play by the statement itself" (MF
1972, 60). In the same vein, Nietzsche says that the "I," the expressive
or disclosed to subject that once had an ontological or transcendental
weight, has become a grammatical fiction "adapted on perspective
grounds of practicality and utility" whose reality lies in dominant
"treaty drafts of will" (FN 1966, #715). Foucault adds that this
token reflexive I "should not be regarded as identical with the author
of the formulation—either in substance or function." I become "a
vacant place that may be filled by different individuals which, instead
of being defined once and for all and maintaining itself as such
throughout a text . . . this place varies—or rather is variable enough
to be able to persevere, unchanging through several sentences, to alter
with each one" (MF 1972, 95). "Continuous history," like Kant's
continuous time, "is the indispensable correlative of the founding
function of the subject" (12). In a world without subjects or things,
there are only discontinuous documents and no book of nature. History is not, on this Nietzschian genealogical and "annals" model,

> the interpretation of the document, not the attempt to decide
> whether it is telling the truth or what is its expressive value,
> but to work on it from within and develop it: history ["the
> documentary mass with which we are inextricably linked"]
> now organizes the document, divides it up, distributes it,
> orders it, arranges its levels. . . . The document is no longer

for history an inert material through which it tries to reconstitute what men have said or done, the events of which only the trace remains . . . [in order to] refurbish memory. History is now trying to define within the documentary material ["books, texts, accounts, registers, acts, buildings, institutions, laws, techniques, objects, customs, etc."] unities, totalities, series, relations. (6–7)

The self, however decentered, and world, however fragile, must emerge from discontinuities, from the play of signifiers in differential force fields. As Kant said, a Deduction is "a question of right," and after these centuries we do have a right to the self. Remember how the inquisitor broke the old general, hero of the revolution, in Koestler's account of Stalin's purges in *Darkness at Noon?* He was told that the "I" is the garbage can of Western history, that one must speak the collective "we." As Socrates said of Anaxagoras (*Phaedo* 100A ff.), conditions which make an act possible have been confused with its causes, the idea by which something is and is definite. Granted that the self is now decentered, it has not been replaced.

Genealogy denies that practice is under the rule of ideas that we, as responsible to a world, give ourselves. *Eidé* are determinates which through the Good have an accusative and deconstructive potential, and only these—and not sentences that rationalize determinations— deserve the status of "proposition." One establishes a genealogy by taking as the origin something we would recognize as more or less pathological, such as a particularly revolting public execution, as if a microcosm of a historical hypostasis, a personal whole, and then generalizes it in order thus to show it to be an enunciative formation that collects and distributes the locutionary forces underlying an epoch. Genealogies are more or less causal and not hermeneutical, since nothing transcendent solicits and there is nothing reflective to interpret solicitations. The elimination of the agent self, at least as foundational, is praiseworthy; this does extend to assigning it a passive status in which it is a mere conduit of forces. In denying the self and letting both it and its ideas be posits of practice, ideas become determinables, not determinates, and behavior is the expression of a drive. There is enough truth in this to make one pause; but not for long, for the point of Platonism's realistic aspect is that ideas can be possibles, determinates of and relatively independent of *praxis* and, as propositional, can solicit novel behavior. Equally important is the need to acknowledge that contextuality, even genealogical contexts the Nietzsche/Foucault sense, can constitute ideality. Historical strands do come together in the nominal unity of a genealogy, but this woof can through metaphor's warp be transformed into something noble

and beautiful. Thanks to Byzantine iconographers and the popular beliefs to which they gave expression, we can trace various strands of the
earth mother from Cybele to Artemis which precipitate as Mary, the
place of the placeless. This genealogy precipitates an eidetic intuition,
that of the incarnation, where effeminated matter, the receptacle of
life, is itself brought into the Godhead in ways still to be understood.
The immediate and forgotten fruit of this is the Patristic movement,
effected by Basil of Caesarea and the two Gregories, Nazianzus and
Nyssa, in thinking the person through the Trinity, not as the mask
(*persona*) of substance (*nominal ousia*) but as the relational and medial
hypostasis whose face, *prosopon*, reveals the mystery of the Good.

Thus Foucault's particularistic and historical method shows, as if
in spite of himself, how a principle can be apportioned to a particular,
originative place. His places are, however, sites of "struggles, strategies
and tactics," which grant only fields for perturbations, the Jackson
Pollock-like world in which we live. But this masculine will to power
that runs off into entropic decline must be effeminated, seen through
the receptacle as the supplement of and not the alternative to the
Good, and thus in relation to Heidegger's *es gibt* or Levinas's *il y a*
which, not being a being, nevertheless receives a gift of form and
grants being.[17] Foucault lacks a tropology which can justify the selec-
tion of a paradigm event that makes possible truth claims in its discursive strategies. Nothing comes to be, to stand out in its integrity; there
is no "sky" and no gap from which it can egress. Dynamical and individuating originary places, *chora*, must be comprehended in relation
to the "divinities" in a glance that "remains on the earth" even as it
"spans the between of sky and earth." In words recalling his reflections on such medial phenomena as Kant's imagination and the medial
"ring-dance," which resonate with images from the *Laws* (dance) and
Republic, and *Timaeus* (soul as spanning the gap between earth (Gaea)
and heaven (Uranus) and measuring itself by the Good) Heidegger says
the between "is measured out for the dwelling of man. We call this
span thus meted out the dimension. . . . The nature of the dimension
is the meting out—which is lightened and so can be spanned—of the
between; the upward of the sky as well as the downward to earth. We
leave the nature of the dimension without a name . . . man spans
the dimension by measuring himself against the heavenly . . . man is
at all only in such spanning. This is why he cannot block this spanning, trim it, disfigure it, but he can never evade it" (MH 1971b,
230). Though the words "poetically man dwells" are Hölderlin's,
isn't the "upward of the sky" the "dimension" of the Good which is
beyond being and as such never present or named? Isn't he echoing,
if not resounding, a Platonic note he usually avoids? The Good is
the condition for any measure; man "measures himself against the

godhead" (MH 1971a, 221). Doubtless measures can be idols, the phantasma Plato warned against in the *Sophist* (234D ff.), that "do not preserve the proportions of the original." The measure, Heidegger goes on to say, "consists in the way in which the god who is unknown is revealed as such by the sky" (1971b, 223). The Good is separated and known only in lighting and lightening. It is present as the day is present, as a young Socrates tells Parmenides (*Par.* 131B), that lets me see the other. The formality of this vision is justice. Only what appears in the between can have a dimension, have its measure taken by infinite "regulative ideas," Beauty or Goodness (130B).

Kant's three-fold synthesis makes explicit the translation of form from its "real" locus to its status as a permanent presence in or to mind for thought and logic. Once language is understood as the vocal means of expressing thought, and once the signifiers themselves have disappeared in self-affectively hearing oneself speak, it seems natural to secure significance within the order of second intensions, meanings and their implications and family resemblances, rather than through the signification of things meant and made manifest by signifiers. Having stripped the world of its real affinities, the remarkable achievement of so-called empiricism, one must work up the material of sense by formal logic and the imagination, the ad hoc bridge invoked by philosophers which links orders that analysis has left behind as ontologically other. Significance in denatured nature requires a "transcendental affinity." However, animals recognize and appropriate all sorts of natural significancies without benefit of concepts. Recognition is coextensive with animal life. If recognition is assumed to take place only in concepts, then what is disclosed by the word is transformed into the use of the word to express the formal sign and then world is lost in their play. "Expression" is too valuable to be left to the logicians (statement as expression), conceptualism (express a concept), artists ("express yourself").

In Kant, understanding and sensibility cross their common root in imagination and engender knowledge and its intentional object. This root is the medial nothing that things. Is there anything besides Foucault's archeological fields analogous to this in language? Yes, but it is hard to say what it is, except ostensively. The story of Helen Keller gives the analytic perspective necessary if we are to escape from differential fields which, like waves, play across this matrix. She had been blind and deaf since early infancy. Miss Sullivan, her teacher, had taught her certain behavioral responses to marks (Gadamer's "preschematism") she made on Helen's hand. One day, after spilling food during a temperamental dinner, Miss Sullivan took her into the yard to wash her off at the pump:

Someone was drawing water and my teacher placed my hand
under the spout. As the cool stream gushed over my hand, she
spelled into the other the word water, first slowly and then
rapidly. I stood still, my whole attention focused on the
movement of her fingers. Suddenly I felt a misty consciousness
as of something forgotten—a thrill of returning thought; and
somehow the mystery of language was revealed to me. I knew
that "w-a-t-e-r" meant the wonderful, cool something that
was flowing over my hand. The living word awakened my
soul, gave it light, hope, joy, set it free! There were barriers
still, it is true, but barriers that could in time be swept
away. . . . Everything had a name, and each name gave
birth to a new thought. As we returned to the house, each object that I touched seemed to quiver with life. That was because I saw everything with the strange new sight that had
come to me. (1965, 23)[18]

The "light" through which she saw the world as a totality is the virtuality of the single word. We become the clearing which, through the
play of language, is the place of Being. Dialogue and dialectic will
take us beyond Helen Keller's to all worlds. But first we must know
what gives *It,* whatever it was that gave the deaf and blind Helen
Keller a word and place for things when Miss Sullivan's fingers crossed
her wet hands with w-a-t-e-r. From *da,* there, a being is disclosed.
Significance discloses, even to the decentered self. Something is present
which would otherwise be absent, as the marks Miss Sullivan made on
Helen Keller's hand suddenly became signifiers disclosing the intentional object water, not just something wet. In the *epoché* marking her
discovery that everything has a name, world was born. In this focused
and demonstrative act graphemes ceased to play, at least quite so
freely, with the emergence of being, the self to Helen and thinghood to
world. Language can also create: electricity was not a current until
water became its interpretant. Both Levinas and Heidegger describe
this gap or slot in terms appropriate to a medial matrix.

Some ground has been gained by the proposed synopsis in which
a context potentiates linguistic forces. What gives an entity a there
from which to show itself for the monstrative *"there is ____," il y a*
or *es gibt?* Things are disclosed and expressed by words arising from a
differential matrix within something like Foucault's "ennunciative
functions." A way through, and perhaps beyond, this play of forces
may lie in what Heidegger's catachrestic *Ge-stell* unconceals, Being as
"standing reserves." The poet sees that the *Ge-stell* is "where the
danger is" and with his word "Holy" raises hope of salvation. The
"truth" of Being disclosed by technology, the *Ge-stell,* is that we have

become resources in the *Bestand;* the "Holy" points beyond to an analogue of physis, that is, self-gathering into the radiant splendor of
form and standing out for a while. This perspective is ours if one
understands the medial *hypostasis* as Plato's living creature, the
demiurgos of its own life. In Plato's *Timaeus* the emergent creature
gathers itself into *peras* through, and only then to stand out from, the
apeiron receptacle, the middle voiced "becoming that never really is."
This creature engendering-context, the energized *chaos,* is not unlike
what shows itself to a linguistic synopsis. Words too emerge. But suppose that synopsis is in turn a further reduction to the originary in
which the monstrative function is primary. The medial matrix will
not then be the placeless flux of forces that grants being power and
place; it is rather the nothing which, like Kant's imagination when
crossed by sensibility and understanding, generates and grants the
word and thing. This generative crossing of receptive forces and form,
that is, participation, is possible only through a shared *pathos* (*Gor.*
481C–482D), the matrix that makes communion, community, and
communication possible. On Socrates's example, the strategy of philosophical discourse generates this enunciative possibility from its potentiated fields. This synopsis is Kantian in spirit; it aims at understanding something giving itself in relation to an end, not as a primal
or pre-predicative datum for a purely receptive registration.

Derrida makes this chiasmus of language and being more perspicuous, if not more hazardous. Life speaks in the medial *différance*
"which is neither simply active nor simply passive . . . of an operation that is not an operation, which cannot be thought of as an action
or a passion or as the action of an agent upon an object, as starting
from an agent or a patient, or on the basis of or in the view of, any of
these terms. . . . The active and passive voice has been constituted in
this repression" (JD 1973, 137). If for example we assume a synopsis
over such a field in which we might catch emergent consciousness, i.e.,
intentionality, it is going to be virtually impossible to determine
whether what gives itself belongs to the intentional act or to the receptive, datal stratum.[19]

3. Participation as Significance

THE LOGIC OF "to express" is ambiguous. Since the beginning
of Romanticism in Germany in the 1790s it has been given a subjecti-
vistic meaning. One expresses one's thoughts, concepts, and feelings or
oneself in going out from oneself to constitute objects in which one
then discovers oneself and so overcomes alienation. This tradition is
rooted in Kantian self-affection. In expressing a "proposition," one
says how it is with things, not how it is with the self. In the sequel we

propose to cut through this constituting, self-affective confusion by a participatory analysis which is neither subjective nor objective, to a theory of meaning sensitive to the evident truth of realism and the interpretative strictures of idealism. A clue to this confusion, first noticed by Whitehead, is the dominance of the subject-predicate analysis of propositions and, in its subject-object variant, the assignment of an ontological priority to one or the other. But the primordial expression is what the face says, the joy, fear, furtiveness, courage, openness, the unfathomable uniqueness of each Other that shows through this nakedness and addresses me, as if an *a priori* from a past that has never been present; "This is my beloved son/daughter in whom I am well-pleased." Significance begins and ends in relation to an other to whom I am hostage, a "substitution" which Levinas says marks the origin of signification.

My interpretative remarks are biased towards place-bound participation at the expense of placeless predication. Participation is to our real world, mental and physical, what Kant's ideality is to knowing. The difference is evident in, for example, the context of the *Symposium,* in which the appropriation of the alterity that makes us whole begins in our need for goods such as food, status, sex, and children and is transformed through the beauty of an Other into responsibility for all Others in "just institutions and laws" and leads through a love of order to an ecstatic rebirth in "the science of Beauty everywhere." Desire that motivates this transformation is beyond need, a gift of the Good beyond being. Our separationist and bifurcated philosophies may yet be overcome as one stands out towards, even crosses over into,[20] an alterity empowered by the Good.[21]

In *Theaetetus* Plato speaks of the "passive" and "active motions" of the perceived and perceiver whose crossing engenders the sense object (sensible idea) (156C-E). In a theory of perception still retained in Orthodoxy's experience of an icon, this copula(tion) marks the birth or ingression of an idea in and through the mingling of the subject's passive motion, "slow with respect to its motion without change of place and with respect to what comes within range of it," and the object's active motion. Sensibility is now the matrix to be crossed by the movement that comes out from sense-making, the eye's interpretative, "helios-like" beam (*Rep.* 508B). In "I see a white stone," *white* is the meaning or form (*idea*) of becoming engendered in this crossing (*Theaet.* 156D-E) which illustrates an extensive region ("active motion"), such as a play of signifiers or forces. This medial movement, which Derrida expresses with *mouvance,* also generates the perceiver-perceived or subject-object relation (*ibid.*) and the identity over time of the object and subject. A sensum is also a parameter presiding over a variable range of eventual, occasioning conditions through which something, the stone, is interpretatively "seen as" white.[22] These events are gathered into a unity by the white, a parameter signifying the existence of a relatively constant physical state within a series of causally linked physiological, transmissional, and physical events whitely apprehended under received geometrical conditions as interpreted through the sense object's mediation. Because it is a same for seeing, for being appeared to, as in "I see white," as well as same in the appearance, for "it is white," sense objects are constants of externality defining the manner in which sets of variable conditions are satisfied. Sense is interpretative in illustrating and giving meaning to a causal route. Illusions (the white entity seen behind the mirror) and delusions (the perception of the white entity induced by neural stimulation or drugs) raise questions as to the necessity and sufficiency of these conditions. Normally, white signifies and illustrates a spatial, physical nexus. The white is a logical constant whose arguments are the ingredient events, each of which may admit to a range of variation under the parameter white. Expressed in terms of parameters and subparameters, the formula is Ψ (Σ, Ω), where Ψ is the parameter "whitely," Σ is the subparameter ranging over "subjective" conditions and Ω has a similar range over objective variations. Realism, for example, would be "actively" defined by the conditions $\Omega(y_1, y_2, \ldots, y_n)$, where the constant of externality is the sense object and the subparametric y's range over a variety of physical and geometrical conditions, including the neural events in the brain, which occasion the occurrence of the object. Even physical events, the neural reception of a color, may be interpretative, as in Land's color theory of vision. In this formulation, the *eidos* white belongs neither to the perceiver, as in "I see white," nor to the perceived, "It is white," but is rather a constitutive, relational form, as in "It is perceived by me as white." To this analysis of participation ("ingression" or "pre-hension"), which defies definition in an ordinary monadic predicate logic and so plays havoc with the concept of category, we add Plato's contribution of the interpretative aspects of the perceiver's "passive motion," where perhaps Plato meant by "passive" the subject's *locus standi*. Only interpretations can be the bearers of truth and falsity. Through the mediation of white, behavior interprets the stone as weapon, specimen, and so forth.

Sense is always given under an interpretation. In Nelson Goodman's phrase, the eye comes ancient to its task, while John Dewey spoke of perception as funded knowledge. The subject's passive motion adds the interpretative dimension, for example, Husserl's context-forming intentionality, to the actively conditioning place which may or may not, if seen in a mirror, be the perceived situation of the stone. In practice it is difficult to sort out passive from active conditions, some of which are also interpretative. The interpretion *white* is how the entity is seen within books or texts of need or desire, such as Platonic Eros, whose condition is a lack, need, or felt incompleteness reaching towards a possible futurity through "for-the-sake-of" projections. *Theoria* is out there among others, but it could be just enjoying what it is seeing, a sufficient condition for just onlooking. To grasp the import of this participatory account of perception and spatiality which passes over and unifies mechanism and teleology, realism and idealism, and the like, we need to look at Aristotle's account.[23]

Plato's relational ontology, "P is Ψ-ly to S," is translated by Aristotle into a monadic predicate logic, "S is P." Though he gives a formal account of sense in *De Anima*, be loses the ubiquity of form by abandoning events for substances in which form is inseparable. He also translated participatory relations between events into causal linkages in which one, the patient, comes to be informed through contact by another, the agent, though he never assumed that sensible species are epiphenomena or causal ejects of physical changes as we may do when we imagine that consciousness of white is caused by neural events. Aristotle, and Aquinas after him, confused Plato's "passive" motion with (first and second) potency and active motion with (first and second) act. In informing sense by contact through a medium, the physical object seen is the efficient cause which is, in causing, reduced from first to second act (alternatively, from second potency to second act); where white is its formal cause, the eidetic same linking perceiver and perceived is the immanent telos of this mutual becoming. Sensibility, the material cause, is reduced from first potency to first actuality, seeing whitely. Alas, such qualities are affective predicates of the percipient subject (*Cat.* 9a 27–34) from which the existence of the qualified thing has to be inferred. As informed by the sensible species, the eye *qua* second act can be (with the objects common to other senses and those singular to some, together with memory, pleasure-pain, and the like) a causal component in the synthesis of the phantasm by the imagination. The phantasm is the perceptual object, that is, the seen white shape judged to be Callias. What we see is thus imaginary. On the illumination of these images, the *hyle* of thought and, I think, the first potential of the intellect per se by the agent intellect, the concept is produced in an act not referable to lower faculties as its necessary and sufficient conditions. Is this the source of Kant's spontaneity? Otherwise the analysis is realistic. To say that it is realistic is, however, to be lost among the either/or's of realism and idealism sanctioned by the syntax of monadic predication. Aristotle, it will be recalled, has no place for real relations, only for relative terms (*Cat.* 6a 36–8b 24.). White, a quality term, is clearly a monadic predicate. Descartes and Locke let this predicate logic guide their ontology and, forgetting their role as "meanings," asserted that sense objects were predicates of consciousness. These objects then qualify mental events contingently linked to extended, causal nature. The place within a K' set of monstrative regions from which the thing presents itself to sensory interpretation threatens to become the imagined correlation of a private datum. Sensation is no longer the original for our participatory encounter with beings: sense objects are now "ideas," predicates of non-extended inner sense. By idealizing outer sense, Kant restores referentiality to sense objects; but this outer sense is an opening to the contingencies of receptivity, such as self-affectively continuing to speak or to write. There is no possibility of submitting sense to things, which are imaginary, and thus no possibility of submitting interpretations to things or to Being either. Admittedly the "I" in its passive motion is freedom to see things in a variety of ways, but only in madness and disorder do we have the freedom to posit objects as such.

Can we get at this by a figure? When I use my pen as gear, to employ Lacan's strategy, I can imagine that I see it and that it sees me. I am looked at from the pen's perspective, seen as one who uses and misplaces, lets ink dry up, and drops and bends a point. The pen calls into question my autonomous ego. In questioning my looking, it accuses me of its neglect and reinserts itself into my life as valuable. Cezanne, even van Gogh, never subordinate the Being of a being to subjectivity. Their painting is kinaesthetic, tactile. Light is not a presence but is "the form of corporeality and the perfection of all bodies" and is filled with mystery. Monet, like Robert Grosseteste, treats it as a presencing, a process, never itself present which congeals in radiant materiality. It does not lighten; like a Byzantine ikon, it shines forth as if each thing were a source of light. Since then the theme of subjectivity and its sovereignty over the space of perceptual encounter has dominated art.

4. The Book of Nature

BEFORE WE FOLLOW Descartes and try to read the book of nature in mathematics, we must first restore Berkeley's thesis that sense is its universal language. Like the illumination in a medieval manuscript, this lighting that things encapsulate reaches out to touch the eye to let be seen what is there, while the eye's beam, which we have understood as linguistic, brings this before the mind in order to know and experience their glow. Though there is no "natural" book free from interpretative posits, it is possible to found the human and natural sciences on nature's book and its reflective, textual interpretations. These express the *nomos* as "law" and "convention" in myth, mappings or conceptual models which signify and disclose things (*physis*, "nature") in their powers. The use of "book" rather than "text" pre-supposes that the text, its traces, meanings and universals, is the con-dition for, not the efficient or formal cause of, the book. We interpret things as they appear in the "book" through their signs. In the past this metaphor was founded on the Patristic and Augustinian "ontic logos" in which ideas are the "basis of reality" (CT 1989, 188); in this more radical reading of Plato, (constitutive) ideas mark the be-tween, the place of the matrix, and are the posits of nature and inter-pretation, that is, the creative imagination.²⁴ Books have a certain closure, whether that of enjoyment or being and well-being, which does not characterize the general text; I will speak in these broader terms in accord with current usage.

Modernism's self-defining subject was a wholesome protest against the medieval use of this book metaphor; things were signs of their purpose, for example, the color of liverwort marked its pharmaceuti-cal applications, and their homologies, for example, the seven aper-tures of the head and the seven planets, expressed a meaningful order among the ideas against which the self defines itself (CT 1978, 4); yet if we look back from our objectless world from which self and God have absconded, the book/text metaphor calls for a partial restora-tion. By allowing analysis to be seen as a hermeneutical chiasmus or crossing, Kant opened the way to a retrieval that retains interpretative or active and causal or passive, that is, medial and linguisticized, as-pects of experience. Things from which we live are not, Levinas pro-tests, mere equipmental items and in their inseparable formalities, as in Duns Scotus' formal-objective distinction *a parte rei,* these and these alone, not laws, explain within a more constitutive view of rea-son. Reason as shared is lost as things recede from view when language itself becomes a communication medium and the text is replaced by the computer, as in Heidegger's objectless *Ge-stell.* Things must, however, be thought within metaphor and its mythic and allegorical extensions if experience is to bear the trace of the Good.²⁵

Self-representations are also necessary for creatures underway towards world. The homology Kant sought between concepts and per-cepts is founded upon metaphors, allegorical or model-theoretic modes of "seeing as _____," that keep these attuned. The self's way is mimetic; if seeing ourselves as characters in our allegories is often escapist, as Walter Mitty, Scrooge, or as pathologically narcissistic, *mimesis* is necessary for a meaningful journey. We interpret ourselves by reflexively representing ourselves in roles being played out, either as lived by these mimetic formulae, or more sanely in a dialectic with the world that leads through comedy and tragedy to self-knowledge, to *Bildung.* Playful self-representations link the child and the tragic hero; each is involved in *mimesis.* "I am Oedipus whom all call great" is playing at being kingly; children play at mothering with dolls. Mimetic paradigms bring together in personal or symbolic unity an ensemble of worldly relata and forms of behavior usually separated and concealed in everydayness. Scott Buchanan's neglected masterpiece, *Poetry and Mathematics* (1975), suggests ways to bring together the natural and human sciences in an allegorical and metaphorical extension of the analytic method. Allegories, if they fit, give a defensible if partial perspective on things; but when taken as theories, their usual fate, we are apt to mistake them, the finger that points, for the moon pointed to. Plato's repudiation of representation was always in the interest of a world that is only insofar as it represents or interprets the ideas and is as such mimetic.

If nature is a text, sense contents must signify, which is what they do in all sentient life. Graphemes and phonemes are sense objects and form, with other such objects, differential fields. Their role is to illustrate regions, as in the tree's Autumn colors; but since regions have various topological qualities, such as overlap and part-whole, like the clouds in the sky or the heat we suddenly feel, these combinatory structures reveal features of these regions, the coming rain or a fire. Sensa are parameters, constants on externality, which are relatively invariant, like any other signifier, within sense fields. The white is a same in signifying an x taken as a stone, weapon, or doorstop. Sense signifies; how? What characteristics let it work?[26] In this version of the ancient text metaphor, we are not concerned with homologies between the parts of nature, but rather with sense as a language. Each sense appears to have its own language; though color differences seem innate, we must learn its language, the language of shaped things in space, which is a task beyond that of any computer, in playfully interacting with parents in the first few months of life. Unless like a natural language it is learned early, then it is likely to remain beyond our powers.

Textual nature leaves no place for what Heidegger dismisses as "representational thinking," the schematic tertium quid linking concepts with empirical alterity, but at the same time it passes beyond any fullness of presence sense may have to meanings, which if not a linkage nevertheless has a sort of virtual reality all of its own. We must do justice to sense as such; even in the text metaphor, sense is not always a text; sometimes it is good to the taste, shines like "shook foil," or "gashes rose vermillion." Kant approaches things instrumentally, but there is no reason why they cannot be enjoyed for their own sake. As John Sallis reads Heidegger, this does not seem possible. To see why, and to appreciate the virtue of this textual metaphor, we begin with transcendence, which is always towards the Good.

The Kantian "I," whose rational or transcendent nature is never in doubt, thus transcends sensibility which it can then rework according to a plan of its devising. It may form time by the affective circuit, but its primary ecstasis is towards the actual past, to the line being drawn, and not to possibility. Its existence is stuck to its being through contingent sense. Thus sense, which allows us "to take a stance at a site" (EL 1988, 80), has an ontological status. On the other hand, *Dasein*'s "transcendence [which] projects into Nothing [not from a place, but] on the basis of hidden dread" will hardly allow it to enjoy something finitely perfect or even beguiling; it is on the way to overcome "what-is in totality" (MH 1975b, 254). This Nothing allows the strangeness of the what-is to dawn (256), though not in the Open between the Good and the receptacle. One is thus condemned to find the meaning of Being in ecstatic temporality whose circuit under the rubric "care" is self-relatedness. Nature's text, as interpreted in projects, gets assimilated to Being. When, however, assimilation is proposed as a remedy for the bifurcation between sensibility and understanding, it becomes a pharmakon, curing and poisoning. All creatures find meaning in situations; Heidegger finds that meaning "belongs to that which an understanding interpretation Articulates. . . . [It is not] a property attaching to entities, lying behind them, or floating somewhere as an intermediate domain. *Dasein* only has meaning" (MH 1962, 151). How about bats and E. coli?

Does Nietzsche's sensible "shining"—as David Krell translates *Schein* (MH 1981, 215)—eliminate the subordination of the sensible to the intelligible? (JS 1987, 2) Not immediately, for the neo-Platonic sense of epiphany also overcomes separation. In its more Platonic version, epiphany is the radiant presence of the form into which becoming selectively gathers herself. Granted participatory mutuality, neither side of the rift is subordinate to the other. Becoming collects itself into the radiance of form, measures itself by its rule; beauty marks its presence in its form which is, in turn, apportioned to place. Heidegger, seeking to avoid Plato's notorious separationism, may have been attracted by the possibilities for reconciliation he saw in Kant's imagination; the result would be an adverbial and positional understanding and a sensibility tuned to circumspection. However, when sense is disclosed in projects, doesn't it get displaced by meaning? One sees the actual text one reads only if the font or language is unfamiliar or beautiful, as in a work of Celtic or Islamic art. Since the sign relation is arbitrary, meaning attaches to signifiers only if "an interpretative understanding articulates it." Isn't reading nature's text circumspective, a reduction of sense to referentiality and thus to "equipment" in which nature never appears in its "shining?" John Sallis, commenting on Heidegger's attempt in *Being and Time* to avoid "presence," be it sensible, intelligible, or self-reflective, notes that this subordination to meaning

> serves to effect the transgressive move beyond Being as presence. Recall the configuration: a turn towards disclosiveness is a move beyond the mere apprehension of the sensibly present-at-hand that is guided by the referential context that is utterly irreducible to intuition of presence . . . [a move which] cancels what would otherwise be taken as the specifically sensible character of things? . . . Is it not precisely with respect to the intelligible, in view of the eidos, that the sensible shining of things is brought back under the grid of presence? Is it not from the intelligible that one turns back to interpret the sensible as presence? (JS 1987, 15–16).

If we read a text, even one in which signifiers are arbitrary, we do not project meaning on it. Reading is medial, not a projection, and sense, like a hypostasis, appears in the process. Nature appears in its disclosive language. What does E. coli project when it meaningfully relates to its substrates? Heidegger is still caught up in Aristotle who would confer meaning and his Plato is still a separationist. Insofar as sense refers, it is not a present; insofar as it is enjoyed, it testifies in its presence to the bodily bond the hypostasis bears with being-here.

Though the signified can also be a sign (of a sign of . . .), decisiveness closes this circle of reflection and, within its project, treats the signified as its absolute object. As Hegel said in a similar context, the hungry animal does not contemplate; he falls to without more ado and eats. This reduction of alterity to being (a condition for being a) same, the movement of Platonic or Hegelian or even Heideggerian thinking, leads to certain moral problems, such as utilitarian manipulation. However, transcendent alterity is preserved by the unassimilable Thou, the being beyond price, that makes a moral demand upon me to transcend towards him for his sake.

5. Hermeneutical Ontology

WHILE IT CANNOT take us into the originary, hermeneutics can articulate the between. This entails an intuition of the Good in the other and not just an ontological understanding. Articulating beings through an understanding of Being is a central theme of *Being and Time:* "That which can be Articulated in a disclosure by which we understand, we call "meaning" . . . Meaning is the "upon-which" of a projection in terms of which something becomes intelligible as something; it gets it structure from a fore-sight, a fore-having, and a fore-conception" (MH 1962, 151). Meaning, the "upon which" of projection, is determined by an "articulation which takes the first cut" (150). The possibility of articulation, of discerning the joints and expressing these meaningfully, is at the heart of Plato's dialectic. The dialectician, like the butcher, cuts up beings at their natural joints (*Phaedrus* 255E). Plato's own articulations range from the separationist ontology of the middle dialogues to something which, on Whitehead's account, anticipates his event ontology.

I take the first (Parmenidian) cut when I ask: What is *x* really? As we learned from Kant's schematism, this determines ontic interpretations. Only in terms of one's power to release entities in a set-up as ready-at-hand does it make sense to ask the initial question. Through the fore-sight, the horizon, opened up by the first cut, I fore-conceive the object. I fore-have it in a ready familiarity with procedures, experimental ingenuity, and the like. I put my fore-concepts to the test, stand back and await the challenge of what is put into play. Through this give-and-take of analytic dialectic, science is woven into a fabric. Does the fabric, the descriptive patterned matrix, determine what we see?

In the great *Cratylus* image of language as weaving (387A–390E), Plato shows that the pattern being expressed determines how things are discriminated. The hidden ontological and paradigm-relative presuppositions in analysis, for example, determine what it points to, just as the pattern being articulated governs the way the shuttle separates the warp. But this same pattern, the design being woven, is itself articulated through these cuts. This design, the descriptive, apophanic, sense-making component, both determines and is determined by the fundamental cuts. What is other, being, can be assimilated as same, but in the appropriation the same is also transformed and reinterpreted. The same is never a positivity; it is "same for" itself only in or through others. We weave together by taking apart, but we equally take apart only because of possible synthetic wholes.

By founding "meaning" and "intention" on the fore-structure of *Dasein* and making world its correlative, Heidegger hoped to eliminate subjectivity as the ground of beings. Projection is often spoken of as a conferral of meaning by the subject, but this is not to be understood as an eruption of subjectivity, as in the objectifications of Feuerbach or pathological projections studied by Jung or Freud. In a projection, ontologically understood, a being ecstatically grasps possibilities and comes back to itself from this future to synthesize these as perceptually actual; the movement is like Kant's self-affection, except that I affect myself as my future returns to me through the necessities of my perceived just past. Projection is always within a project where our being is in some sense at issue, a movement not unlike that of Plato's eros towards the creative and self-creative fulfillment of some lack. Yet the referentiality, and even world, entailed in projects is subordinate to encounter. I must begin from dwelling in which the other is encountered.

Though procreative Eros harbors deconstructive possibilities, Emmanuel Levinas is rightly suspicious of the claims of love, which seeks something common as its focus rather than alterity as such and thus must deconstruct the self through the address of another who cannot be assimilated or brought into the ambiance of a same. The Good beyond Being is expressed or reflected in my neighbor who thus can never be appropriated as a same. Aristotle says self-knowledge is his gift (E.N. 1170a 28–1170b 7), and while this true enough, it contines to effect an egological closure. Since we "can contemplate our neighbors better than ourselves and their actions better than our own, and if the virtuous actions of friends are pleasant to good men" (E.N. 1169b 34–1197a 1), then consciousness of that other is the condition for consciousness of my own worth. But justice requires that this closure be broken, that I respond to the worth of the outsider with whom I have nothing in common. The demand for justice imposed upon me in this encounter is the basis for a common world, even in physics. As a matter of historical fact, the sense of the moral order sounded by Aeschylus in *The Persians,* a sympathetic tribute to his former enemies, was prior to the discovery of physical order, a Stoic and equally moral undertaking.

Interpretation of self or anything else is mediated and called into question by otherness. The dialogical structure is moral and only thereafter ontologically disclosive—and is, as such, an essential condition for being what we are. The neo-Kantians and Husserl believed that the spirit of Kant was preserved in a philosophy based on reflection, the unmediated presence of itself to itself, in the form of its thoughts, meanings, and the like, which are open to true description. Reflection enables *doxa,* in the opinion sense, to be transformed into *episteme* ("knowledge"). If beliefs could be expressed in empirically significant sentences, they could be justified by determining their truth value. Equivalent sets of these sentences can be ordered into a theory about something if certain conditions, mostly logical, can be satisfied. Like the birds in Plato's cage (*Theaet.* 188C–89B), knowledge is something possessed. If I distrust my thought, a natural consequence of the metaphor of possession, I must be skeptical and distrustful. Knowledge is like the gold Kant was said to have hoarded beneath his bed, an insecure possession rather than what we essentially are. The question then arises: is what we primordially articulate, "the first cut," an artifactual function of an ontological understanding sedimented in a linguistic culture and thus language-relative, as Worff or

Sapir thought? Let us return to Kant for an understanding of what is involved.

On Kant's nominalized view of language, isn't it natural that his "first cut" should yield a world of objects? Given objects, how can they form a world-preserving structure, since each is an instance of material substance? One has to attach quality to this being by synthesis and then show that variation in its intensive magnitude takes us over and into (natural significance) other substances as its causes,and so forth. The point is just this: synthesis overcomes externality by constituting combinatorial potential, assuming that as mere matter sense needs mind to impose upon it significant form. The ontological project of the "I think _____," means entities are determined by the predicative "is ϕ." The copula converts entities into enduring, predicatively determined presences. Traces of *einai* structure Kant's first cut founded on his project to secure his being and his knowledge of beings against the threat of Hume's "empirical affinity." Being as understood determines how beings are articulated. Does it not follow that language is that through which significance is discerned, if not constituted? Isn't this very close to sophistic rhetoric? Or do we have in language a way beyond relativities, Protagorian, Kuhnian, or Worffian, to the things that are? Yes.

But what sort of language, written or spoken, conventional or iconic? Spoken language, for example, represents becoming and the flux and not an inscribed permanence. Dialogue, with its attendant possibility of raising questions, as well as the counter-thrust of dissemination and locutionary and illocutionary forces, is a better paradigm than writing. Speaking, a medial phenomenon in earlier strata of our Indo-European family of languages, is a paradigm for a hypostatic ontology that derives a being and its ontological distinctions, such as active and passive, essence and existence, subject and object, and the like, from medial becoming. In Aristotle's image of nature as the doctor doctoring himself (*De Phys.* 199b 30), being (the life of the doctor) arises from becoming, *metabole,* and (*qua* doctor) orders and controls it. So too the said, or at a higher level, the proposition, arises from the saying or sentence addressed to the other who sometimes orders and controls it. What would be a virtual rout of de Saussure's signifiers comes to a stand as if in company formation in speaking with the other. Speaking and the spoken provide us with an important ontological model for the alterity and objectivity of outer sense. Compare this with Kant's line-drawing.

How can we go from the evident relativity of articulation to a language, its "first cuts," to the *Critique* of this relativity? Here again Plato is worthy of attention. In *Cratylus,* the dialectician, "the first giver of names," is not bound by the "first cut," the ontological

understanding implicit in a language. The "first nouns" that phoneti-
cally found *physis* designate Heraclitean *gignesthai* (459C). Dialectic
can reform this hermeneutical circle; for if "being" is understood as
this flux, it cannot be articulated; "all would mingle with all" and, as
the *Euthydemus* makes evident, no sense could be made of world.
Having disposed of Heraclitus, he argues in the *Sophist* that "father
Parmenides'" thesis cannot be articulated (241D–245E). Evidently we
are not stuck in any language; dialectic can gain the power of language
itself. What is this power? Hans-Georg Gadamer gives a beautiful
answer: "Language is the single word whose virtuality opens up the
infinity of discourse, of discourse with others, and of the freedom of
'speaking oneself' and of 'allowing oneself to be spoken.' Language is
not its elaborate conventionalism nor the burden of pre-schematism
["an existing whole composed of words and phrases, concepts, points
of view, and opinions"] with which it loads us, but the generative and
creative power to make this whole fluid" (HG 1975, 498).

VII

"POETICALLY MAN DWELLS . . ."

....

1. Enjoyment

ERFAHRUNG, "EXPERIENCE," SPEAKS of a journey homologous with "methodology," being on the way. Appearances make sense because sense is Berkeley's "universal language of nature"; however, nature's text is a corrupt palimpsest and must be supplemented with fictions, romances, theories, myths. . . . Our problem is even more acute; how can one make sense when intentionality breaks down, as it must, on the way "beyond being?" Is one really going anywhere when "beyond" reinstitutes a metaphysical distinction? Yet through such a journey we, poetically dwelling on the earth, hope to found even the natural sciences and mathematics. Is there a way through images within experience rooted in *différance* rather than in the destruction of presence?

Having been underway with Kant encourages the construal of significance as a chiasmus over the imagination by sensibility and an intention to the transcendent, where both the imagination and reason elude the understanding; even as this seems to close metaphysics, traces of a beyond appear in, for instance, the transcendental object or the moral law. The infinite horizons of the former—for the object constituted within its parameters has its prototype in God's idea—suggests that even mundane experience can serve as a model for the moral order, as in the Topic of Practical Reason. These ways, spiritual and linguistic, come together on Heidegger's "way to language" which, like the Tao, is "the run-off of a great hidden stream which moves all things along and makes way for everything" (MH 1971a, 92). Our experience with language as a medial, creative matrix may be a springboard for a leap beyond being. Like the soul whose "erotic" life it is, language is a poetic "between"—one root is the face to face relation with another, inexplicable within the assimilative parameters of participation, phenomenology or fundamental ontology and the other is the procreative originary, the heir to Kant's imagination—in which these ways unite.

In the next two sections I will make rather extensive use of Levinas's *Existence and Existents* (1947) and *Totality and Infinity* (1965) to point our a way through phenomenology to that which transcends it both in the direction of the dynamical *apeiron* and the Good beyond Being. The later *Otherwise than Being or Beyond Essence* (1974), though more sensitive to the problematic of the "beyond," will prove to be useful for what it can tell us about this gap. Levinas uses the face, not as a surface but as that which appeals to and contests my will, as a between, and thus as a way of defining the limits of phenomenology. Hitherto faces have founded Hegelian phenomenology, the face of the Greek god who assumed a human form and of Jesus, the other who was the infinite Other, initiated and perhaps even controlled the dialectic in which Spirit resolves the mystery of incarnation. But Levinas uses the face, as Heidegger uses death, to mark the limit of phenomenology and, indeed, to deny the possibility of any such proportion "between things below and things beyond" by which we rather hubristically attain God's standpoint. To counter Hegel's intellectualism, Heidegger proposes an experience of Being in dread and Levinas offers the existential appeal of a destitute face.

Our interest is, however, in Levinas's use of the face to mark the limit of phenomenology. The face makes an erotic appeal and, with the other, I can pass beyond consciousness into primal becoming; at the same time, the other is Other and addresses me from beyond Being. In sensibility I am "susceptibility and vulnerability" to the face of the Other who manifests the Good beyond Being. In "Violence and Metaphysics," Derrida notes that the face, the visible manifestation of the Other (*Auturi*), "is not in the world, since it opens and exceeds the totality . . . , [it] marks the limits of all power, of all violence, and the origin of the ethical" (JD 1973, 104). Just as the Good is beyond Truth and Being, so the face can never be unconcealed, described, or known as an intentional object, nor can it be constituted after the fashion of Husserl's passive genesis. In order to make this point, Levinas must first reinstate the classical distinction between sense and perception so sense can have a perceptual or a linguistic weight, can both mean and say or even be enjoyed in itself. Though Heidegger neglects sensibility, with this distinction Levinas can show that the Other can "express itself in the sensible" even as its epiphany rips it apart (JD 1973, 104). In returning with Husserl to sense, he opens the possibility of founding language, including the text of nature, in Husserl's originary rather than, as with Heidegger, on referentiality and care. The self-reflexivity of care cannot destroy metaphysics since it celebrates Being's coming to itself in self-presence. An alternative to time as Being's self-reflexion, which must be found if we are to escape closure, is in the experience of the face and its "saying" which point to a world I cannot unify under a concept, spiritual formation, or idea but from which I must take my measure. That I take my measure within a face-to-face encounter reinstates the classical and dialogical sense of rationality, familiar as Plato's alternative to Protagoras' eristic. I can either destroy or submit, for I cannot oppose the Other. Not because she is a force that limits me, but because she looks and speaks, "Thou shalt not murder," my one remaining intentional act whose alternative, "Love thy neighbor," must come from "an *other* origin of the world which no finite power can restrict."[1] The 'between' separating me from the Other is a procreative matrix, the *arché* of life and language.

Suppose "experience" is regarded under the formality of the Good, not under being and its acts or conatus. Its being as conscious, as hypostatic, will be happiness which arises from and motivates responses to vital and appropriative processes. Since sensible enjoyment is, in Heideggerian terms, an attuning mood whose intentionality does not seem to fall under the formality of care, it may to serve as a key to how one can be underway to the Open. Enjoyment is the "existential formality" of the hypostasis; it originates, individuates, and maintains itself through diversifying and controlling becoming and is indeed our "essence," "the process or event of Being."[2] For Aristotle, happiness, human good, is the second act of being (as computing is the second act of the mathematician) or being in its highest sense (God being completely active, it is our god-like condition). Enjoyment, being medial, cannot be defined in terms of act or passion. Moreover, enjoyment, always mine, individuates. It is not a matter for ontology. Heidegger individuates *Dasein* by death, its non-being as its ownmost, non-relational possibility; but aside from problems raised by non-Being, it is not fundamental. Enjoyment is, as we saw in the last chapter, caught up in a process founded on more primary levels of sensitive awareness in which sense and sensed are as one. Another age discerned this medial and non-intentional state in such variants as Bergson's "duration" or Bradley's "immediate experience;" but perhaps it speaks most clearly to us as vertigo in Levinas's *il y a* or in the voluptuousness of Rimbaud's "I is another." We visited another form of primordial becoming which founds sensibility in Husserl's "continuity of moments of reverberation" (EH 1991, 79), the "fluxions" (303) which, given the primal datum, constitute "time consciousness" as original intentionality. The intentionality in sensing, acknowledged by Plato and Aristotle, is the initial reflexivity whose non-representative or non-reflective form is enjoyment or satisfaction. Emmanuel Levinas describes this as the *primordial gnosis;* the "I" is its hypostatic crystallization (EL 1985, 146). We live, and sometimes die, for the sake of satisfaction, where the satisfaction is itself the primary reflexive relation to things, to food, shelter, companionship and the like, disclosed by sensate needs. Adriaan Peperzak notes that "the motivation of enjoyment must not be sought in some reasonable thought, such as the one that tells me, 'If you do not eat, you will die'; the tendency towards pleasure and enjoyment is completely spontaneous, it is the upsurge of life itself [life is for Aristotle the creature's being]; but it is also true that the *experience* of enjoyment includes phenomenologically a movement of *restoration* (of our force, energy, vitality, mood, etc.)" (AP 1993, 150). The things we live from are not Heidegger's *Zeug;* we cook to eat and eat to live, but in so doing we are not conscious of these as activities that constitute our being but, rather, in the enjoyment of doing we are conscious of these contents. The world, Heidegger says, fascinates; if, however, it is first a text, then as in reading a novel, enjoyment separates us from what would otherwise call us into world. To live in enjoyment is to be beyond being (EL 1985, 120).

The hypostasis is medial life bent back on and enjoying itself. Levinas will use the hypostasis to contest his closure in metaphysics by founding intentionality in this enjoyment. Existence, whose base is the vulnerable, naked body, requires a protective place, a dwelling, that separates one from the world so that one can gather oneself into oneself. Interiority is not Cartesian but rather the Augustinian "inner man" in which I discover myself. Only then can "consciousness come out of rest, out of a position, out of a unique relation to a place" (EL 1988, 70) to sustain happiness by transmuting the threatening wind, earth, fire, and the waters, the elemental "there is" (*il y a*), through labor into possessions and property. The here of consciousness is radically different, Levinas says, from the *Da* of *Dasein,* which presupposes a world. The ready-at-hand, the phenomena whose reduction discloses world, also unconceals *Dasein*'s being as coming towards itself in authentic care, that is, the "between" of a throwness towards death (MH 1962, 427). Prior to ecstasy that projects itself over nothing is my *place here* that grants being; its absence is not "nothing" but rather the abyss, the *il y a.* With an eye to Plato, Levinas says that place, *chora,* "precedes every act of understanding, every horizon and all time. It is the very fact that consciousness is an origin, that it starts from itself, that it is an *existent.* In its very life as consciousness, it always proceeds from its position, from its preexisting 'relationship' with a base, a place . . . in positioning itself on a base the subject encumbered with being gathers itself together, stands up and masters all that encumbers it; its *here* gives it a point of departure" (EL 1988, 71). Levinas's Platonic *arché beyond Being* is on behalf of life which, within its limits, can productively transform the elemental and, at least for a while, enjoy it. This ambiguousness of the *il y a,* which gives and destroys, is retained when it is transformed into Eros. Sensuality is Levinas's alternative to the Heideggerian anxiety, while the originary is the fecund "nothingness of the future buried in the secrecy of the less than nothing" (EL 1985, 266).[3] We live, Levinas says, from and not by means of needs as forms of nourishment:

> Nourishment, as a means of invigoration, is a transmutation of the other into the same, which is of the essence of enjoyment; an energy that is other, recognized as other, recognizes . . . as sustaining the very act that is directed upon it becomes, in enjoyment, my own energy, my strength, me. . . . These contents are lived: they feed life. To live is a sort of transitive verb, and the contents of life are its direct objects. . . . The relation with the direct object of the verb to *exist* . . . in fact resembles the relation with nourishment, where there is a relation with an object and at the same time with this relation that nourishes and fills life. Enjoyment is precisely the way life nourishes itself with its own activity. (111)

Dwelling is the place from which I egress and to which I return. Indeed, if the seclusion of dwelling is to be neither infantile or psychotic, it is because the Good "beyond Being" is within the totality as the very condition for its significance and even objectivity. Though totalities originate in dwelling and may even, as in Aristotle or Hegel, be a model for the polis in which "I is we and we is I" (GH 1977, 113), this form of presence is inadequate to my responsibility towards Others with whom I dwell. The call of the Other is to "me," never to "I." Separation is laced with responsibilities to others; only for analytical purposes can enjoyment can be treated as separated, as atheistic. My body, the primordial relation I have to needs, is both dependent and, in its sovereign motility and freedom, independent of them until in age, sickness, or disaster, it is their slave. "The ambiguity of the body is *consciousness,*" an ambiguity suspended in the postponement of death, that is, temporality, by acquisition and labor (165). These ambiguities point to a medial root.

Though Plato let the living creature egress from *chora,* he failed to notice that this is possible for us only if, like Odysseus, one can return home to renew life in recollection and, above all, in the gentle face of the other. The self-separation and return of expressivism has its analogue in dwelling. It differs in that, though my goal is to return home as a same, meeting the other face to face may so transform me that, like Paul on the Damascus road, I am never same again. Rendering alterity as same is a common theme of Plato, Heidegger, Husserl and, with more subtlety, Hegel. Levinas speaks of these unities, conceptual, vital, or social, as totalities. The medial and separated self, though appropriative and totalizing, is individuated by place. Together with the infinite Good beyond Being which cannot be reduced to a same, these are the poles within whose play life finds itself. This play is founded in dwelling. Dwelling articulates and elaborates the nurturing power of *chora* and facilitates the separations required to sustain satisfaction, preserving and sheltering us from the elemental *il y a*. Happiness arises in a movement "radically different from thought when the constitution by thought finds its condition in what it has freely welcomed or refused" (EL 1985, 130) and is the meaning of our being that, so to speak, stands out and preserves itself against the more elemental flux. Pleasure is a reflexive relation to a need, good soup, my glasses, an appealing woman, *et cetera*, which I appropriate or in which I take an interest; such objects, Levinas says, are that *from* which I live. "Qua object the object seen occupies life, but the vision of the object is the 'joy' of life" (112). This affective life we consciously live as happiness through attending to need, where the attending can precipitate projects, is a medial condition founded neither on acts nor receptivity, and thus defies the intentional analysis of projects it motivates which are presumed to cultivate or enhance it. In my wife's welcome and in her caress I experience the transformation of another with whom I share happiness into the Other who speaks as if from above. If so, then *Dasein* is founded on a hypostatic, not a substantive, "who," and its "nothing" will be the affective and medial clearing lighted by the Good. But this medial clearing points to the instability of happiness. The self is not *ex nihilo*, founded on nothing and determining itself by its being towards death; its dread derives from its own source in becoming, "the horror, trembling and vertigo" of the *il y a*. The separation of the I, its egoistic satisfaction, is its refuge, its dwelling, its "being-at-home with itself" (143). Levinas's rejection of metaphysical unities begins with the autonomous ends presented by sensibility and culminates in justice. The relation with the unique and infinite Other obligates me to act justly towards and seek justice for all others. Justice defies totalization and unity and the community it found is, in Alphonso Lingus's happy phrase, that of those who have nothing in common.

2. Archaic Poetics

DOES "TRUTH" APPEAR IN THE working of a trope and belong to rhetoric, not to logic? Is rhetoric, not that of Gorgias but that of Socrates, the true heir of analysis? Rhetoric, like analysis a way of pointing that makes beings ostentatious, provides us with a theme or mythos for making sense of them, playing on enjoyment in order to lure us through the mystery of the word into perspectives in which they can be perspicaciously seen. Miss Sullivan rubbed together two physical objects, her fingers over Helen's hand; then "Everything has a name." This original (*arché*) metaphor that lets us *see* the signified in the signifier establishes the "truth relation" through the sign so that thereafter words may interpret things and things interpret words. The cool something running over my hand is now "the water is cold." When one set of entities exhibits a partial identity of form with another, either may be said to interpret and be the truth of the other. The neighborhood generated by a fortuitous crossing is the "between," the engendering *metaxu,* in which truth can happen. We can begin now to explore its anarchic depths which are beyond being. First, what is meant by being?

Let us return to the assimilative structure which maintains itself by the reduction of alterity in order to cross and deepen it with Plato's more general account of participation. He describes the architecture of the *Timaeus* gap between Being and Becoming in a myth about the soul participating in both. The homology between these others to one another was not as with Aristotle logical (the analogy between primary and secondary *ousia,* (*Cat.* 3a 1–4) but was generated or created from or within this between in terms of the transcendentals being, same, and other. These terms define recurrent and reflexive crossings— the circle of the same and the other—which engender structure when lighted by the regulatives, Good, Truth and Beauty. These "regulative ideas" are, like transcendentals, sayable of all things and, as reflexive, propose the possibility of the Being of beings and the Goodness or Beauty of Being and Truth.[4] Hitherto one has spoken of the Being of Goodness which construes the Good as a kind of Being. For example, Aquinas says that it is not as if Being and Good were two different things but that this is a distinction of reason concerning a single reality (*ST* q.5, a. 1, 2). So read, being (in its primary sense an individual) is granted a proper perfection. If the Good is prior and this single reality thesis is retained, then I suppose we refer to ecstatic transcendence and being is then interpreted as "operation." Something like this is appropriate within the "between." If the Good is beyond Being, however, we may acknowledge that it could dwell in Being without falling prey to the scruples of a Parmenidian mystique. With this recognition of transcendental "being" seen through the possible beyond which is thus gained with no appreciable violence, the images we make of Being, which like the Good will now defy proper knowing, will have a sacred aura, the sacredness of the fragile, the vulnerable, the naked. Thus, as a participial, "being" denotes that both power (*apeiron*) and its possible vectors (*peras*), determinable becoming and determinate ideas, and their mixture. *Apeiron gignesthai,* dynamical becoming is the immediate source of Levinas' *il y a* (EL 1985, 140–42). The Demiurgos' blend of these "unsociable opposites" founds "deconstruction" in a strategy in which we grasp through its trace the "impossible-unstatableunthinkable" or "incoherent incoherence," the Good. Levinas avoids the use of "becoming"; but in its elemental form, the "there is" is Plato's *apeiron gignesthai* which, when domesticated or, perhaps better, reflected in the hypostasis, the mixture, is designated as *l'existence* or even "to be" and its participatory life is expressed in terms of "same" and "other" (*l'autre*). The Demiurgos, with which all life is homologous, forms life by this mixture. In a more originary account, one would begin with *il y a* as divisible same, other and (the transcendental) being *que apeiron* or *il y a* and show that as blended in soul and ordered by number and measure it becomes the body, its needs and their objects, the verbal "existence" from which we live.

The order of enjoyment is, as primary consciousness, a modality of being in which the ego is more or less for itself or, as Levinas says, atheistic; but its attendant satisfactions are never really satisfying and point beyond themselves. Bearing the trace of the Good, they become Desire. The Other who commands the movement beyond Being and into proximity with others and the Good can thus break into and destruct this egological structure of enjoyment. But the task is not simple; such metaphysical topics as experience, logocentricism, phonocentricism, principles, unity, and the like, reassert themselves and, moreover, the "beyond" threatens to either reinstitute inside/outside distinctions or to constitute the Good within an ontological totality. Being perpetuates itself.

Life for a totalizing ego expresses itself in and through appropriative, participatory relations. It crosses the circle of the other, a counter movement to the same, and reflexively reduces alterity to sameness. Though not constructive or self-affective, life is a "circle of the same . . . that bends back on itself." The reflexive reduction of alterity is participation's controlling image; the soul's morphology shows how the same is through what is other, the "beyond held in the midst of." As life's bond, soul stretches between the heavens and the earth, its parents, and has the rational form of the diatonic scale (*Tim.* 40C) so that living has the differings and deferrals of music, generating and articulating time and space as it dances. The crossings in Plato's construction are hermeneutical, participatory, and embody the metaphorics of weight and measure; the sciences are poetry and *poiesis*. The formal homology between interpretation, metaphor, and participation is founded on crossings, their differing as other to one another in a chiasmus that generates or posits a same. Being is the gift of dwelling in a face-to-face chiasmus over chaos. In participation something comes to be when the gap is fecund; in interpretation a same appears in the gap within or for language when horizons cross or, in metaphor, an (ontic) horizon is constituted when the semantical space of the predicate, or an analogue of *Dasein*'s fore-structure, crosses and interprets, rather than subsumes, the subject in a dwelling thinking. This *metaxu,* open, is by the Good's lighting the place of dancing.[5] True to her medial roots (divisible being as *apeiron*), she is *différance,* generating and deferring, giving and withholding, retaining and disseminating presence and absence, the metaphysical differences and their cognates. Thanks to Mary, this impersonal and mythical "she," the *Magna Mater,* becomes the personal "mother" whose face founds signification and the resulting world of "objects."

Robert Bernasconi notes that Heidegger's usual deconstructive strategy is to "attempt an exit . . . without changing terrain" through a play of opposites which, I think, reflects the soul's root in the receptacle, the medial (and deconstructive) here from which one dwells. Levinas's alternative, Bernasconi continues, is "to change terrain in a discontinuous and irruptive manner by affirming an absolute break and difference" (RBr 1993, 191–92). Of course, opposites may form a chiasmus rather than stand fixed. These reflections suggest that combining both ways under the rubric "play" (JD 1976, 81) may lead beyond being. Derrida's profound insight that play does not negate a difference shows, with St. Augustine (1953, *De lib. arb.* 20:54), though contrary to Hegel, that the power of the negative eludes reason.

Significance, as characterized in Levinas's early writings, is to be understood in terms of a meaningful or happy life; it is an "understanding," a *gnosis,* without a concept and lacks a referential or even circumspective core. Rather than being founded on referentiality and thus *Dasein*'s spatiality, significance begins in satisfactions concretized in those things from which one dwells. Satisfaction is prior to the elevation of sense into the conceptual order of projects and presupposes dwelling and the other. It is founded on sociality, beginning and ending in face-to-face encounter. Since the latter is not a form of presence and assumes a separation rather than a possible Aristophanic union, the other as my other half, then this "exteriority" or "proximity" is prior to and founds spatiality, the possibility of nighness. One begins, as Winnicott saw, with the obvious, the mother's expressions as she plays with the child which lead from possible autism or narcissist interiority into the meanings of things. This face which founds signification is not, however, significant; it resists appropriation and manipulation and, in a manifestation foreign to "truth and untruth" (EL 1985, 202); but in a signification to which it attests, it makes its appeal and solicitation (200). Can dwelling, which shelters the face of the other so that solitude becomes solicitude, be a threshold to a world because it is first an opening to the empowering Good? Does not the Good solicit place and require justice of all that therein dwell? As Nathan said to David, God does not require a house but will "appoint a place for my people Israel and will plant them that they may dwell in their own place" (2 Sam. 10). In Christianity, God through Mary has a place.

The face-to-face that founds dialogue and the possibility of hermeneutics is also its limit. As John Caputo remarks, the Other may not be up to being a dialogue partner "if only because she has been deprived of speech or an idiom, may have been silenced or rendered unable to register a complaint or state her case . . . , not quite up to the speed of Rorty's conversation of mankind and may even be a little illiterate. She may be done in by being drawn in to such a conversation . . . [she] comes to us, not as a conversational counterpart, but as a claim" (JC 1993, 211).

Suppose then that the world, a referential totality, does not derive, as Heidegger supposes in *Being and Time,* from in-order-to and for-the-sake of but rather from the Other, first present in the mother's face, who cannot be intentionally assimilated, brought within a totality? This anarchical *arché,* experienced in diachronic sensibility, is vulnerable to the Other it cannot thematize, remember, retain, or historically reconstruct: "Not out of weakness; to what could not be contained there corresponds no capacity. The non-present is in-comprehensible by reason of its immensity or its superlative 'humility' or, for example, its goodness, which is the superlative itself. . . . The Good cannot become present nor enter into a representation. The present is the beginning of my freedom whereas the Good is not presented to freedom; it has chosen me before I have chosen it" (EL 1981, 11). Like Mary, one is a prisoner of Grace, enslaved by the Good, and the first signification is her response; "Be it done to me according to Thy word." Signification is founded in "despite-me, for-another." The constituting freedom one enjoys among totalities is put into question; "Meaning is the face of the other" (EL 1985, 206). The face is not is a Scotistic or Peircian formal sign; it terminates participation and signification.

We referred to Heidegger's way of founding significance on circumspective referentiality within the context of the ready-at-hand; linguistic signs, primarily monstrative, are instituted to promote circumspection, as in his example of an automobile's mechanical turn signal. This, however, makes language a representational activity, a form of presencing Heidegger later rejected. Levinas tries to pass beyond the metaphysics implicit in these intentional acts by founding language on the transformation of hypostatic satisfaction, dwelling or interiority, into desire, the significant relation "assisted by language" to the inassimilable Other. "Language," Levinas says, 'takes place across a void . . . in the dimension of absolute Desire by which the same is in relation with an Other . . . in which absolute exteriority presents itself by expressing itself" (EL 1985, 172). Opening to the

Other is not, however, to be explained in psychological mechanisms. She is present as an Other who casts a responsibility upon me that empowers, as if by grace, my response. In other words, being Open to receive this expression requires that I first be responsible for and to her; receptivity to this expression from which the self and world is born is, as Levinas is later to say, "a passivity more passive than the passivity of matter, that is prior to the virtual [intentional] coincidence of a term with itself" (EL 1981, 113). This receptivity which I, if not Levinas, understand as medial is expressed in an infant's first speech, her smile, as she is empowered by the mother's concern to receive and respond to love.

Even the closure of primitive satisfaction requiring "being with" another is founded on the Other's gift of language, on a crossing that lets being appear, as in the crossing of Miss Sullivan's and Helen's hands. The elemental *il y a* becomes a thing with the coming of the word. In order to show how the word can arise, as if *ex nihilo*, and found a world, it must be approached through the crossings, participatory, metaphorical and hermeneutical, which it founds. Saying that crosses an abyss and opens us to one another in a world is itself a disclosive metaphor. We must establish the consequences of disclosive metaphor for understanding nature as a text for the human and natural sciences.

The metaphor is disclosive has been evident since Plato said the "state is the individual written in large letters." The state is not an individual, and yet "by examining them side by side and rubbing them against one another, as if they were fire sticks, we may cause the spark of justice to flash forth, and when it is thus revealed, confirm it to our own minds" (*Rep.* 435A). Metaphor is an *epoché;* its terms, when crossed like fire sticks, light and open a horizon. This is the converse of the Kantian *schema;* instead of sensibilizing concepts, it conceptualizes sensibility. Thus the transcendence of sense (sensibility) by sense (form or meaning) set up by the Platonic myth of the sun and the Good can be overcome. Does the separation deconstruct itself in this double sense of sense? The soul's medial root in sensibility in which, as I will argue, form is "seen," makes metaphor an appropriate instrument in a strategy that will avoid some of the pitfalls of logocentricism. But there is an additional advantage. Metaphor will institute science through its models or, as I prefer, allegorical mappings of the domain of medial and ultimately undecidable sense into a formal model. But like Kantian imagination metaphor is a two-way street; the predicate and subject, or their analogue, sensibility and understanding, can play back and forth and thus interpret one another. The two strategies of deconstruction, Bernasconi says, "of withdrawing within and forcing outside are inseparable . . . [and] belong together in an ambiguity for which Derrida prefers the title 'play' " (RBr 1993, 192). Perhaps we can show that metaphor, though rejected by Heidegger, is a living, not a stone, heliotrope within whose play there is a trace of the Good, a way beyond the closure of metaphysics. The need to restore sense to sense motivates a restoration of the book metaphor. Isn't sense written in the language of sense, the language of satisfaction, whose medial roots give an opening to the Other and thus the Good?

Metaphor is usually thought to be assimilative, attributing or appropriating an other to a same. The eye becomes a window through which we can peer into the soul. In a more complex example, Aristotle's *pros hen* metaphor allows the attribution of *on* to entities which are not predicables (genus, species, difference, essence, etc.), just as we say health of man predicatively and of others as its sign, cause, and the like. (*Meta.* 1003a 33-b 10). On this account, said by Cajetan to be "attributive" (1953), metaphor assimilates differences to a same. Suppose on the contrary that a crossing constitutes its disclosive same which cannot be and often cannot be said otherwise. Faraday's discovery of a same between certain galvanic and electrostatic phenomena and the flow of water created the possibility of a science of electricity, for galvanic piles were not seen as involved in "flowing" prior to the constituting metaphor. This allegory of "flowing" lets us see phenomena through a constituted same; this "flowing" as a way of seeing, the same that links them, is constituted by the metaphor. In allegories the mapping is supposed to be one way. Any interpretations offered by the interpreted domain, usually the subject, result in new allegories, new theories. Of course we can try to institute a play. In Hobbes' "man is a machine," mechanics interprets our behavior and its enabling psychology and physiology, but does it really make sense to say that thereafter machines are humanized? Any survey of exhibition catalogues or visit to industrial museums, such as the steam displays associated with Watts and his successors in Birmingham, will show that the opposite has been happening. In Plato's account, an horizon is opened in which for the first time the state is humanized, concerned with justice, and man is seen in relation to woman, as social and loving, rather than as in an *agon* before Troy. What is the discerned identity in Plato's image? Crossing, the form of metaphor that creates even as it assimilates the state and individual in an horizon of an unsayable same, also characterizes interpretation.

Another of Plato's examples shows how the trace from beyond the phenomenal operates as a certain surplus in the interpretations the perceiver casts over (*aitiaomenio*) something as the "reason" (*aitia*) through which it receptively appears as _____. In the *Phaedrus* he speaks of meeting up with the other as if he were a mirror of oneself;

. . . and when he is nearer to him and embraces him, in
gymnastic exercise and other times of meeting, then the foun-
tain of that stream, which Zeus when he was in love with
Ganymede called Desire, overflows the lover, and some enters
into his own soul, and some when he is filled flows back
again; and as a breeze or echo rebounds from the smooth
rocks and return whence it came, so does the stream of
beauty, passing through the eyes, which are the windows of
the soul, come back to the beautiful one . . . the lover is his
mirror in whom he is beholding himself. (*Phaedrus* 255C-D).

How one sees something depends on "the trace within themselves of
the nature of their own god . . . they are possessed by him, and from
him they take their ways and manners of life, in so far as a man can
partake of god" (253A). The trace that remains of our choice of the
god determines how we perceive states of affairs and is the reason why
this or that cause is operative. Being a reason for entails the interpretative selectivity of participating through the projection of the paradigm
with which one returns from visiting the gods. In *theoria*'s allegorical
paradigms, gods are archetypal: "The followers of Zeus desire that
their beloved should have a soul like him; and therefore they seek out
someone of a philosophical and imperial nature, and when they have
found and loved him, they do all they can to confirm such a nature in
him . . ." (252E). Each must return home from his projects to confirm his own nature, hopefully through a gracious empowering presence, recollected or with the Other. Interiority is the possibility of
self-return, the reflective moment of reflexion, necessary if one is to
sort out false and even delusive projections. In his charming essay on
the *Lysis*, Gadamer describes this *philia* as a movement to the self by
dwelling or belonging together (1980, 8–20). *Bildung*, "spiritual formation," begins when "those who have no experience of a disposition" turn "to anyone who can teach them . . ." (*Phaedrus* 252E).
Dasein's fore-structure has its roots in these allegorical projections.
Plato says these are "recollections of those things which our souls once
saw when following God" (249C). This is a between, a *metaxu*, of
encounter and significance, a holy place.

3. Arché: *Origin and Principle*

ARCHÉ, TEMPORAL "ORIGIN" OR atemporal "principle,"
marks a site that can only be described in an oxymoron. Classically, as
one can see from its sense as "principle," *arché* has been linked with
reasons and causes providing necessary, if not always sufficient, conditions for intelligibility. Principles establish Parmenides' "same for
thought and being" [*to gar auto noein estin te kai einai* (B3)], as in

Kant's "System of the Principles of the Understanding." Perhaps, however, principles are the vapor trails of "being." Nietzsche's observation that "nothing possesses a more naive persuasion than 'being'" unless, I add, it is the "nothing" through which Heidegger proposes that it is experienced. Any attempt to think or experience Being, the "emptiest concept," will lose itself in "the last smoke of evaporating reality" (FN 1954, 483, 481). On the other hand, origins fare no better than "principles." *Arché*, understood medially, names beginnings that continue to govern historical or developmental processes as a style or trait, not a rule. We can return to such origins in an event, a rite or festival, that is no less original than what is memorialized. This return is said to empower one to stand out, to be effective, and commemorates "a presence that was never present."⁶ Though commemorated for granting unity and being to a tradition, these origins, bereft of their complementary principle, the Good, are fit topics for deconstruction. For this reason they have been replaced by discursive formations within genealogies in which, like those of a family, vagrant strands from nowhere intertwine. These entropic genealogical strands harbor the metaphysics of death, not life. Nothing integral is engendered from "family resemblances" that can stand out of the riff and set truth to work, as Heidegger said of origins, nor do these have the unity granted by a universal, for example, "man" or "renaissance," and are nominalized, given determinate form, on pragmatic grounds (FN 1966, sec. 715). The origin of standing out, since nothing really began or stands out, is a fiction.

The originary, which is "otherwise than being," seems to offer itself only in a catachresis; among its various avatars is the Platonic receptacle, Gaea, Cybele, Mary, Artemis, Foucault's enunciative formations, the Tao, Levinas's *il y a,* and Heidegger's *Ereignis.* The mythical variants harbor the opposites, as in Heraclitus or Zen. Each lets some aspect be seen, and some, like the orgastic Artemis of Ephesus, point to a demonic primitivism, such as in the "fetish of native land and mother tongue" in Nazi Germany. The route to the *arché,* to being's supplements, the Good and receptacle that, though beyond Being, nevertheless give beings, begins with the homeless, the dispossessed, the marginalized lost sheep and, unlike its analogue in Kant's transcendental synthesis, will be conditional. Metaphor can retrieve what Kant attained by the imagination, the origin of synthesis. The abyss and its linguistic crossings must play the role of Kant's categories in worlding worlds. The recovery of the *arché* begins with Kant's constructive analogue to his pre-critical onto-theology. He made invaluable contributions to an understanding of the originary even if he identified it with atemporal transcendental apperception's self-positing expressivist act of generating numbers. These are then taken up in concepts in reflective consciousness through forms of judgment through which anything must be thought. In taking as primary the possibility of discourse, an epochal event from which space and time may be relativistically construed, and language rather than logic as the transcendental condition for experiencing and knowing a world, we hope to reinterpret Kant in ways that, though leading beyond metaphysics, respect his insights. He anticipated hermeneutics by showing how durative being is constituted by the *arché* in an "interpretative" synthesis to provide an objective ground for the self's unity. This ontological interpretation of being as permanent presence yields the questionable presumption that intuition is ontically grounded in phenomenal substance. Rather than begin with apperception and its grant of being, we propose a return to the *arché*, origin and principle, neither of which is a being, to discover the possibility of the hermeneutical dialogue that founds a world. This final phenomenological reduction has focused, not on the primal impression which founds sensibility and sense, but— with the assistance of such unlikely partners as Foucault's analogue of the receptacle and Levinas—on unconcealing the medial "between" that, on being crossed, lets dialogue happen. Kant's construction can be inverted so that subjects and objects will be interpretative ejects; then perhaps we may understand Heidegger's *Ereignis*, "event of appropriation," as the "earliest beginning that grants," for "only what is granted endures" (MH 1977, 31). That the Kantian *arché* grants the possibility of beings through an interpretation of Being is a major, though overlooked, contribution.

In its early usage *arché* is a close relative to Anaximander's dynamical *apeiron* or, in Plato's example, the "becoming that never really is" anything definite *(Tim.* 28A), or the place of the as yet undifferentiated Gaea in Hesiod's myth. *Gignesthai*, "becoming," usually marks the arrival of something at its *telos,* for instance, the foetus at birth. For Plato, presencing is a suasive solicitation of the mother by the father that may lead to the receptacle's welcome of the idea as cause, *aitia.* This medial gap or slot, *chaos,* isn't a presence, a being. Reiner Schürmann says that, in overcoming metaphysics, one must "forestall a relapse from the understanding of origin as an *event* into its *principal* comprehension . . . a transmutation through which presencing institutionalizes itself into principles ruling and justifying action" (1987, 147).[7] The *arché*, like Kant's medial imagination, constitutes the gap which it is then supposed to bridge as a Principle ruling mind (anti-realism) or being (realism). By the mediation of the *arché*, a nothing, and solicitation by the *eidos,* a same which gathers and orders in defiance of the always other and other of time, this dynamical flux is gathered into form so that the creature can for a while stand out against diremption. As "origin," the *arché* effects an appropriate unity, on the one hand, between an atemporal conceptual order, usually represented in logical or moral rules, or real being that grounds thought in God or matter, and on the other hand, in contingent and localizable individuals; through it events, things that "take time" and have a place, are somehow same with that from which they most radically differ, the logically tenseless and the eternally present. However that "eternal" present, whether it be species life or an institutional form, does not found but, as *wesen,* "essencing," endures only through the dynamics it is instituted by and institutes.

We noted that Husserl describes the presencing originary as beyond presence or absence, like the dead time from which speech arises; this is the primal flux, "a flow of continuous change . . . of something that originates in a point of actuality, a primal source-point" (EH 1991, 79). Levinas says, commenting on this passage, that "to speak of time in terms of flowing is to speak of time in terms of time and not in terms of temporal events" (EL 1981, 34). In this way "presence" is banished. He suggests the itinerary I have followed as he asks, "do we not in fact find the unthematizable flow of time from reduction of the said?" This is the medial essencing of Being which Husserl describes as "absolute subjectivity, " the originary within which, at the "primal source point . . . the now," the primal impression is presented in a "continuity of moments of reverberation . . . for all this we lack names" (EH 1991, 79). But the verbal "saying" becomes the "said" as the reverberating appearings becomes the nominalized (intentional) appearance, as if hypostatically. A process is substantialized and submits to distinctions such as universalization, phenomenalization, representation, and the like, which saying's unsayable medial root will deconstruct. The infinitive "to be" is to exist, the gift of the presencing originary, a "pre-phenomenal, pre-immanent . . . quasi-temporal disposition of the phases of the flux" (86). "Absolute flux" constitutes temporality without being temporally objective; though we "name it in conformity with what is constituted," it makes no sense to say that temporally "constitutive phenomena" are "individual processes" or that they are objects which "succeed one another temporally" (76). "We can no longer speak of a time that belongs to the ultimate constituting consciousness" (78). The hermeneutics of temporality leads beyond hermeneutics to an unconcealment that defies ontic thematization. Absolute consciousness, the living present, is the *arché* presumably disclosed in the apodictic or final reduction which Fr. Robert Sokolowski calls the "phenomenology of phenomenology" (RSo 1974, 158–62). If phenomenology is founded on intentional presence, this foundation is in question.[8]

Nicholas Poussin's *Dance to the Music of Time* illustrates our problem. The now, where the dance is, is unknown to the stone, double-faced Janus who sees only past and future. The dance, the *arché,* cannot be present as retained or protended in original temporality, the primal form of apperception. The Janus-like phenomenologist has reduced the world to stone. Doubtless words elude us as we turn to original presencing, but to attribute an "absolute subjectivity" to a flux that gives an intentional form to the contents of inner sense is surely a mistake. Yet we begin with words and on this hither side of the flux, with the primal appearing.

Husserl's atemporal flux plays the time-constituting role of Kant's atemporal apperception (EH 1991, 189). Without being temporal, it gives experience its temporal form, initially that of the present-and-retained-presentified. It is, Sokolowski could add, "perpetually energetic . . . [as] inner time presencing . . . separates and gathers itself" (RSo 1974, 167). If we look at the "primal impression," it is indifferently said to be sense or sensation. Separating itself, drawing itself out, is to be out of phase and thus not fully present with itself: "The temporalization of time—the openness by which sensation manifests itself, is felt, modifies itself without altering its identity, doubling itself up by a sort of diastasis of the punctal, putting itself out of phase with itself—is neither an attribute or predicate expressing causality "sensed" as a sensation. The temporal modification is not an event, nor an action, nor the effect of a cause. It is the verb to be" (EL 1981, 34). "The primal impression, the gift or originary absolute subjectivity, turns out to be "only ideal, something abstract that can be nothing for itself" (EH 1991, 30), whose identity lies in difference, that is, in what is reproductively retained. The "heart of interiority must be opened to the other, to "exteriority in general" whose trace it bears" (JP 1994, 24). What is the *logos* of this gathering? Suppose we follow Levinas's suggestion that this primal flux be construed as "the unthematizable flow of time [given] by reduction from the said." That reduction points beyond the hither of the flux to the yonder of *différance,* to the possibility of appearing prior to *logos* or a trace of *telos,* to the primal matrix which can respond to a solicitation by the Good. Thought at this level can find a guide on the hither side, though not of reason's own devising, "in the continuous accommodation of the now to the not-now." Some relative transcendent intention may be at work, as David Wood has proposed, which "can choose its retention" and slip it in under the rubric of protention (DW 1989, 94, 96).[9] This is possible if the "absolute beginning of this generation—the [unmodified and individuating] primal source point from which all others are generated" (EH 1991, 70) is, as Levinas notes, "without a today or tomorrow" and must, he continues, precede its own protention and thus its own possibility (EL 1981, 33). Taken as a paradigm of creation, the creation of the self answers a call to be that "could not have reached it since, brought out of nothingness, it obeyed before hearing the order" (113). "Through the notion of the living present, the notion of origin and creation, a spontaneity in which activity and passivity are completely one, tend to become intelligible. When it turns out that this consciousness in the living present, originally non-objectifying and not objectified, is thematized and thematizing in retention, without thereby losing the "temporal place" that gives individuation, then we see the non-intentionality of the primal impression fitted back into the normal order . . ." (33).

Could the call or injunction of the Other determine this impression?[10] Then that original consciousness is not, according to Levinas, self-coincident and thus not substantial; the norm is not self-presence but rather "the significance of the responsibility for another . . . and the impossibility of coming back from things concerning oneself with oneself" (114).

The energetic "infinitive of presence" makes sense only within the between determined by the Good and the maternal receptacle which, as in Mary, gives place to the placeless. The "inner time-flow," a "permanent flowing" in which "consciousness of the now is not now" (EH 1991, 333), gives the primal impression as a "separation and reconciliation," an identity in difference (RSo 1974, 161); medial becoming begins to look like the threshold to the Open, the originary we seek. If that primal impression is something posited, like a grapheme or phoneme, the problem in distinguishing an original from an intentional component, retention from primal presence, becomes more manageable. Sensibility is then something self-given. Nevertheless, there are deconstructive possibilities and, yes, threats in the *arché*.

Perhaps Kant's quite different approach, from an egological rule and not an enfeminated origin, can show how *différance* defers and differences. The intentional fulfillment of transcendental self-presence, i.e., apperception, in its *a priori* transcendental object is mediated by temporal deferrals. Doesn't significance require the absence of the signified, not its presence? Sense is meaningful only through deferred presence, that is, the absence of rather than unity with the signified. The synthetic condition for mediated self-presence intended or signified in every empirical intuition is its objective correlative, sempiternal material substance. Stories about my autobiographical unity, the "analytic unity" of my conscious thoughts, require a prior objective unity. I must refer to relations with substances, their qualities and relations, which make up my world, if I am to temporally order these thoughts inter se.[11] This is why the spontaneous self has ethical problems with its objectified self and so seeks to give itself a more spiritual form, as in the Paralogisms.

Kant already had a way beyond this dilemma. When he discovered that dynamical categories are forms of time determination to which the mathematical categories give access, he might have taken another look at his understanding of time. He would have discerned a granular succession of reflexive epochs, the time it takes to mean and to receive this embodied meaning back from the world. When Kant says that space and time are transcendentally ideal he suggests that the self is, like Spinoza's substance, *natura naturans;* what is given as the eject of this act, empirically real things in space and time, is *natura naturata.* The clue to the phenomenal being of the world lies in my generating time, the form of succession and so of number, and its correlative manifold which, as coexistent, might be taken up in any order, counted and numbered. As Kant might say, granted the resources of Derrida's *différance,* this *mouvance* generates the (cardinal) becoming-time of space and the (ordinal) becoming-space of time (JD 1982, 8). Rather than facing up to the eruption of being as if it were *natura naturans* in the *arché,* he turns to the *natura naturata* and "spatializes time."

One must deconstruct the *arché* as a principle of presence to arrive at an *arché* which is undecidably present or absent and beyond both. In writing or speaking, the signifier seems to give itself in a process that is neither active nor passive and, nevertheless, partakes in both. We normally avow passivity, "it happened to me," or activity, "I make it appear." But even as I willingly speak, what speaks through me is not something I will to do or must let happen. If "I try" or "strive" to speak in, for example, French, I speak self-consciously and unintelligibly; but if I am the speaking that runs through my head, the result is verbal spinach. In Sanskrit and archaic Greek, most verbs of speaking and imagining are in the middle voice. This too is the voice of creativity, of building and poetry, *poiesis,* which, Heidegger says, "first brings man onto the earth, making him belong to it and thus brings him into dwelling" (MH 1971b, 218). Heidegger recalls that "by the most ancient tradition of thinking, the word gives Being. Our thinking would have to seek the word, the giver that is never given, in this 'there is that which gives'. . . . By virtue of the gift of the word there is [*es gibt, il y a*], the word gives" (MH 1971a, 88). Miss Sullivan's monstrative "there is ____" gave "w-a-t-e-r" and *water* and a world.

In commenting on a line in Stefan George's poem, "The Word," Heidegger remarks that it could be rewritten as, "No thing is where the word is lacking": What gives the word? "But if the word is, it must be a thing, because 'thing' means whatever is in some way. . . . Or could it be that when the word speaks, *qua* word it is not a thing—in no way like what is: Is the word a nothing: Whatever bestows itself, must it not 'be' itself, all the more and before all else, be most in being, more so than the things that are: . . . if the word is to endow the thing with being (sufficient reason tells us) it too must be before anything is—thus it too must be inescapably a thing" (1971a, 86). Contrary to "sufficient reason" and with the spontaneity Kant attributed to thought, the word, a thing that emerges from the abyss, is *qua* word a no-thing, a transparency, through which the nothing-ing, the fecund abyss that separates us, things. Language, the gift of the Other, calls us into a common world.

It is now appropriate to attend to the "yonder" side of appearing, to *chora*, a nothing that grants place to the placeless and who, in the dynamical images provided in Foucault's enunciative formation, makes discourse possible. Moreover, to now follow Heidegger, this play of forces grants the "possibility of face-to-face" (MH 1971a, 104).[12] This yonder side, the back side of being, is to be gained only in the between of the fecundity of silence and the appearing of the word. The place, the slot or gap, from which we await the word is not a being; the word, if it arrives, is that by which a thing "may be" and is "what holds, relates, keeps the thing as thing" (83). The gap is not an anonymous *il y a;* to cross it is to erotically solicit the word; that which gives the word has the density of "mater" (matter) and vulnerability, traits Levinas identifies with *femininity*. Like Mary in a Renaissance Annunciation, this slot ecstatically awaits the possibility of the word as if in a state of Grace. When crossed by a speech intention, like the dove whose rays go out to Mary, this medial and fecund gap welcomes in a "passivity beyond the passivity of matter" a trace "down from above" that may engender the right word. The dynamical forces which condition appearing play through the slot; these may unify in a *logos*, drawn from paratypical linguistic fields of formal differences, by giving it a place of its own, a dwelling. *Place,* a nothing, welcomes, as "Being" welcomes "Time," because it harbors its trace.

Derrida invites us to rethink the originary in terms deriving from Husserl, Kant, and Heidegger as an anarchical archaic presencing. Like Kant, he begins with space and time, though not by drawing lines, but in the non-egological appearing of signifiers in a general textuality. In its coming to be, the signifier generates medial space-time as if from a chiasmus; in *différance* temporalizing deference crosses spatializing difference "to annul or temper their effects" in "space's becoming temporal" and "time's becoming spatial . . . as metaphysics or transcendental phenomenology would call it in the language that is here being criticized and crossed out" (JD 1982, 8). The generative *arché,* having lost its claim to being, is "behind the exhibiting of Being," as Levinas says of Husserl's originary, and grants the appearing of, for example, phonemes or graphemes, in the differing and deferring in

Husserl's granular "continuity of change," without which signification is impossible. How can any being, even a word, arise and stand
out against this dynamical *apeiron*?

An answer may be found in the "trace . . . that no longer belongs to the horizon of being" (22), and *différance* which, "according
to classical strictures," designates "a constitutive, productive, originary causality, the process of scission and division that would produce
or constitute different things or differences . . . a playing that produces by something that is not an activity these differences, these effects
of difference" (9–11). Unlike soul in Plato and its moving harmonies,
though like the "divisible being, same and other" from which life
issues, this Nietzschian "moving discord of different forces" (19) is
a medial and polemical play (8) which in playing us lets differences
appear which may respond to the Good's trace, a possibility Plato
ascribed to the receptacle "which partakes of being in a mysterious
way" (*Tim.* 51B). "Language," de Saussure says, "is only differences
. . . phonic and conceptual . . . that have issued from the system"
(1959, 120). For example, can one conceive "of a presence, a presence
to itself of the subject before speech or signs, a presence to itself of the
subject in a silent and intuitive consciousness?" (JD 1982, 16). In my
dogs? Of course. But no matter. Just as the wave is inscribed in the sea
by a polemical play of molecular *mouvances,* so language, rather than
being a "function of the speaking subject," constitutes the "subject
(in its identity with itself or, eventually, in its consciousness of its
identity with itself, its self-consciousness) is inscribed in language, is a
'function' of language, is a *speaking* subject only by making its speech
conform . . . to the system of the rules of language as a system of
differences" (JD 1982, 15; see, however EL 1985, 177–83). This linguistic *epoché* disclosing the anarchical *arché* demands a deeper question; how is signification possible? Kant's analytic posits the for me of
transcendental apperception as the *arché* of possible experience; Derrida's quasi-analytic, now taking the form of a phenomenological reduction of the appearing of signs, leads to "trace" and *différance,* as if
these were quasi-autonomous processes rather than the *metaxu,* a between. The trace, playing a role both antithetical and analogous to the
continuity effecting role of retention in Husserl and reproduction in
Kant, occasions the unmotivated sign, and the system of oppositions
within which it occurs

> requires a synthesis in which the completely other is announced
> as such—without any simplicity, without any identity, any re-
> semblance or continuity—within what it is not. Is announced
> as such: there we have all history, from what metaphysics has

defined as non-living up to consciousness, passing through all levels of organization. This trace, where the relation with the other [as a field of differences] is marked, articulates its possibility in the entire field of being, which metaphysics has defined as the being-present starting from the occulted movement of the trace. . . . When the other announces itself as such, it presents itself in the dissimulation of itself. (JD 1976, 46)

The trace is one of Derrida's images for expressing the medial *mouvance* which produces these differences even as it deconstructs them. "The pure trace is *différance*. It does not depend on any sensible plentitude, audible or visible, phonic or graphic. It is, on the contrary, the condition for such a plentitude. Although it does not exist, although it is never a being-present outside all plenitude, its possibility is by rights anterior to all that one calls sign (signified/signifier, content/expression, etc.), concept or operation, motor or sensory" (JD 1982, 62).

In the "speculative" proposition, "The pure trace is *différance*," the copula is hermeneutical and proposes a reflection on the subject through the predicate matrix, as we see Kant's *Sachen* through *Sachheit*.[13] In "the *arché* is *différance*," the subject is seen as the originary of signification. Doubtless I exceed my rights by assuming that the Good can gather otherwise entropic traces into *aletheia*. That gathering will occur when some perspicuous moment, perhaps by what has been shown in the matrix of myth, allegory, or even theory, something beautiful and holy appears as, for example, it appeared to Mary. Under these very special conditions, the trace perspects formal possibilities, differences, irreducible to forces, their necessary condition, under the suasive sovereignty of what, with an eye to Kant, I have called the regulative ideas, the contextual absolutes, such as Beauty, Goodness, and Truth, under which these possibilities are potentiated. What is the alternative?

Derrida's trace is an ambivalent assemblage. Is it causal, like Freud's "primary processes," or as the Good's trace, teleological? That "trace" assembles a text from Levinas which suggests that it may be from beyond Being. Moreover, like a Freudian "drive," it is a quasi-causal component in behavior and, like Leibnizian appetition, it may have a telic bearing. It may speak of a supplement from beyond Being announcing "the completely other as such" (JD 1976, 46) that makes possible the metaphysical text. "No concept is by itself, and consequently in and of itself metaphysical, outside the textual work in which it is inscribed" (JD 1981, 57). What is true of concepts is also true of Derrida's medial assemblage, trace, *différance* and the like that pertain to the medial *mouvance* of forces, which thus is and is not mechanistic or purposive. How can Being be understood from "otherwise than Being?"

What is involved may become clearer through Heidegger's reading of the "Anaximander Fragment" (MH 1984, 13–58). According to Anaximander, "the source (*arché*) of existing things is that in which destruction too happens 'according to necessity; for they must pay penalty and restitution to each other for their injustice according to the assessment of time'" (DK 12 a9). Heidegger offers the following translation of the segment within scare-quotes: "Enjoining order and reck, usage delivers to each present being the while into which it is released." Along the way to this gift of time that lets things be he interprets "according to necessity," *kata to chreon*, in terms of something being handed down (*kata*, "something from which something lower comes to presence") "from up there" or "from over there" (MH 1984, 49) which determines *chreon*, "usage." If the *arché* is, as most commentators have assumed, a dynamical *apeiron*, then is a trace of the Good from beyond Being, "an other as such," offering itself—to speak in dynamical terms—as a gradient soliciting primordial becoming, which is neither Husserl's "absolute subjectivity" nor its realistic opposite, as an unsayable and unthinkable *apeiron* on behalf of order and justice? Plato says of his version that it partakes in reason in a mysterious way. Heidegger, accepting only the part with scare quotes as authentic and, ignoring the *arché*, the dynamical *apeiron* (*il y a*) as the origin and end of things, refers instead to *eon*, "being," understood medially—or at least with an emphasis on verbal aspects most find lacking in the Greek—as "the presencing of what is present" (33–37). Thus this uraboric Being hands down to time, *chronon*, the durative presence—implicit in all formations of "to be"—of order (cosmological) and justice (ethical). However, being as the archaic and entropic *apeiron* possesses no natural limit and thus, unless unopposed will, like a militant dictator, infinitize itself. Being alone can hardly hand down "order and reck" (57). On the other hand, the *apeiron* as Plato's becoming or Levinas's *il y a* is anything but a sufficient condition for beings. The Good alone can transform a polemical and archaic origin when "from up there" it calls us to justice. But the call is not direct, for there is a deconstructive strategy to be observed.

"*Différance* announces, or rather recalls, something like the middle voice," a "play of forms without a determined and invariable substance" (JD 1982, 9, 15). In such play, Heidegger crosses from German to Greek and Anaximander's *to chreon*, "necessity," and *Brauch*, "usage" or "observance," appears within the "ringing silence" of the slot. Commenting on this passage, Derrida notes that "being has left its trace in time or, more accurately; time is the trace of being. The destiny of Being unfolds in world-history" (25). Derrida suggests that this language of Being "in which the word *Brauch* is dictated to thinking in the experience of Being's oblivion" calls for a "necessarily violent transformation" that refers us to "something beyond the history of Being" (25). In the next section we will see how crossings, evident in the appearing of the awaited word or in the working of metaphor, can revector the "moving, active discord of different forces" and the "energetics and economics" (18) of their playful *mouvance*. Have we forgotten Hegel's telling demonstration that forces are anthropomorphic and thus already reflexive (1977, 221–26)? Interpreted medially, this reflexivity is the active or interpretative "circle of the same" that crosses receptivity, "the circle of the other," in Plato's definition of being as active and passive power. It doesn't do to explain away, as seems to be the case with Nietzsche and Deleuze, the reflexive subject and his purposes by differential forces which presuppose it (HG 1975, 181). Yet doesn't the reflexivity of temporal being entrap us within the closure of metaphysics? Perhaps ecstatic temporality is founded on medial becoming, i.e., satisfaction. Then we can "speak of time in terms of flowing" and not as present present, past present, and future present, and therefore "speak of time in terms of time" (EL 1981, 34).

Plato could have said of need-driven Eros, deriving from its parentage in poverty, that he/she can through solicitation by the Other can be transformed into the desire for "something beyond the history of Being." Heidegger translates the relevant passage from the *Symposium* (205B): "Every occasion for whatever passes over and goes forward into presencing from that which is not presencing is *poiesis*, is bringing-forth" (MH 1977, 10). Like Kant's imagination, the *arché* through which forces are redirected is undecidably a presence or absence, active or passive. This reflection, to which we will constantly return, appropriates Derrida's *différance* as *arché*, and may take us beyond the closure of metaphysics. This differing and deferring originary "where the relation with the other is marked" lets a same arise and be through "the displaced and equivocal passage from one term to another, from one opposition to another" (JD 1976, 62). These "rites" lead beyond metaphysics to "dwelling thinking" (EG 1983).

4. Dwelling Thinking

Too often language is treated as an autonomous formation to which we may, as in Heidegger's *Mitsein*, or may not, as in structuralism, belong. Heidegger is aware that though what is "spoken in various ways appears cut off from speakers and speaking and did not belong to them, it alone offers to speaking and speakers whatever it is they attend to" (MH 1971a, 120). In his later work he was perhaps more concerned for the being of language as it befalls the solitary poet or thinker than with the neighborhood, "the dwelling in nearness" (93), with "being face to face within the world's fourfold" (106), it makes possible. Even were he successful, more primordial encounter is required. Heidegger's encounter in the generative matrix of the four-fold is at best a Kantian face-to-face with an equal, not a face-to-face with the inassimilable Other.

Dwelling in nearness presupposes the possibility of proximity which, in turn, rests of a debt contracted before any present and any consciousness. This paradoxical debt is the origin of signification which, as for the other, requires that substitution, to be for the other, "is the very subjectivity of the subject" (EL 1981, 12). Prior to the self-congruence of the phenomenological ego, there is a fundamental diastasis, an open to the other rather than "an equality with itself" (115). In the emergence of consciousness, Levinas says, the "thought that names creation differs from ontological thought . . . this passivity undergone in proximity by the force of an alterity in me is the passivity of a recurrence to oneself which is not the alienation of an identity betrayed . . . a substitution of me for the others" (113). The other is thus in the same and can never be wholly effaced. Language, always for another, is the vehicle of alterity. Even language as truthful is, Levinas says, founded on the face, an "exceptional presentation of the self by self and incommensurable with the presentation of realities simply given. . . . To seek truth I have already established a relation with a face that can guarantee itself, whose epiphany is somehow a word of honor. Every language as an exchange of verbal signs refers already to this primary word of honor. The verbal sign is placed where someone signifies something to someone else. It already presupposes the authentication of the signifier" (EL 1985, 202). Only a *hypostasis* has a face. Basil of Caesarea (279–330 A.D.) was the first to use the medial "hypostasis" and not "substance" (*ousia*), to designate our being. The *prosopon*, "face," expresses rather than hides the person as, for example, angry. In the Latin, the person is designated by *persona*, a mask, which would be an accident of substance (*ousia*) hiding the face and dissembling who we really are. While the unity of God is essential (*homoiousia*), to be God is to be a *hypostasis*; a person is always in relation to others as a mother, brother, aunt, and the like, whose being is social. Thus the real unity of the Godhead, as it was developed by the Capadocians, lay not in the common nature, the *ousia,* but rather in the mutual participation of the persons. They are not functions, as in St. Augustine, nor subsisting relations, as in

St. Thomas Aquinas, but are to be thought as persons in communion. Since the social role is accidental to substance, freedom is possible only behind the mask; in the Patristic or Greek tradition, freedom lies in community.[14] This community, founded by Christ who took upon himself the form and face of a man, is not founded on something in common as understood both in classical philosophy and in German idealism, but is one of difference, as if through a kind of grace the Good participates in us rather than we in Him. The infinity of the Good, which is in itself limitative, is not a Plotinic fecundity; it is a pluralizing infinity rather than a unity, spiritual or existential, in which individuality is subsumed. "Being is exteriority," not an Aristophanic unity; the exteriority of one to another is prior to the more autonomous formations of language to which Dasein is subjected.[15] In everyday contexts, the original experience which we are is not with the ready-or present-at-hand, but with familiar things from which we live and in which intention is concretized, which "naturally belong together" (physai oikeion), like the things in a household. Through the "distantiation" of these things, the objectivity gained as the mother points out and names things in the sacred place of play to the child as she moves them about, puts them in her mouth, or gives them a toss, the movement from a pre-human seclusion, from something like Freud's primal narcissism, to objectification, language, and apperception occurs. Language contains "the thought of others" (EL 1985, 210) and play, not categories, makes objects possible and is already a proto-substitution of the other for me.

Given a shift of emphasis to forms of the English "to be" which have their root in "been" ("to dwell"), then to be is to "belong together" within the semantic space of oikos, the "household", as paradigmatic for shared life, where "shared," koinoneo, which links participation with what is "common," as in community, communion, and communicate. "Economy," pertaining to the oikos, was also the Patristic term for God's providential care in creation, salvation and the like. How things are placed or set up, conveniently or inconveniently, appropriately or inappropriately, rightly or improperly, is a necessary condition for things showing themselves meaningfully, that is, as significant, useful, beautiful, sacred, and the like. When something "within hearing" or "on call" is set up, it may explain and unconceal Being, even issue in a new epoch, as Apollo's smile on the kouros became the Buddha's. But speech makes dwelling possible and thus even the ready or present-at-hand. Apollo's face in which we first meet the God as human, even humane, was also the origin of the first representations of Christ. This ethical face-to-face relation, which "brings the first signification . . . tears [separating] consciousness up from its center, submitting it to an Other" and thus founds language (EL 1985, 207). If this infinity and universality which "reigns in the eyes that look at me" defines reason, the *Logos,* "then it is not the impersonal in me that Reason would establish, but an I myself capable of society, an I that has arisen in enjoyment as separated, but whose separation would itself be necessary for infinity *to be*—for its infinitude is accomplished as the 'facing'" (208–9).

By the time of his "On the Way to Language" (MH 1971a), Heidegger had abandoned the attempt to think the originary in terms of Being and, approaching language as language through language, thought to find it in the speaking to which we belong. The originary is now a "ringing stillness," the *Ereignis* and the way, like the Tao, "an empty vessel, undepleted by use; bottomless, it is the source of everything." Languaging is through a medial "between" that we cross when face to face, a possibility that survives even in the poet's separation. Heidegger's many medial doublets and oxymorons suggest he was aware of this root. But speech is always addressed to another who, even as absent, makes a world possible. Belonging is granted by the Other's speaking that crosses the abyss separating us. We can actively speak, express ourselves and address another, only as language speaks us. Heidegger, however, has something rather darker and more mysterious to convey that involves, in Robert Bernasconi's words, "a transformation of our relation to language . . . [in which] what enters the sounded word is the silent speaking of language itself" (RBr 1993, 202). Language must be entered through language, for we cannot say what language is and must, "through the lack of something common," renounce the effort to think it metaphysically. Through this lack, Bernasconi says, we enter into "dwelling in *Ereignis.* What looked like a task we set ourselves becomes a way-making (*Be-wegung*) which is *Ereignis* itself. The transformation of the formula about bringing language as language to language is the passage from Being to *Ereignis*" (203). For example, recall the crossing of Heidegger's German with Anaximander's Greek in which there is an originary unconcealment. This retrieval is a "way-making" in our historical epoch for a "root unfolding" of language which, listening and responding within the horizon of Being, unconceals. This root unfolding allows "the initiatory character of words to emerge and vibrate" (PE 1993, 337). *Ereignis,* the event that gives the word, cannot be said or discussed. There is no universal binding us and saying; but Heidegger describes this lack as "the most binding relation;" thanks to *Ereignis'* "delivering bond" that binds us by saying (MH 1971b, 131, 134), where saying "is to offer and extend what we call world" (93).[16] One must assume that this is possible, at least on our itinerary, because of a prior proximity with an Other with whom language opens and discloses as it crosses the abyss, the between, as "the most binding relation" that grants. Robert Bernasconi says this is "to enter into the grant whereby the silence transforms speaking" (RBr 1993, 205). Doesn't this suggest the receptacle, a "ringing silence," and the Good, whose trace it bears?

We shall not comprehend the dynamics of this grant until we know how and what is granted. Since the grant of sense is the grant of self, we can pass over to the appearing of language that makes sense of sense. Eugene Gendlin's "dwelling thinking" focuses, not without risks, on the appearing of language and the prospect of being "bound over to the *Erleibnis,* into his own as he who belongs to language" (RBr 1993, 203). Let us begin, not with the "event of appropriation," the *Erleibnis,* but with the appearing of the word in a play of differences. Rather than looking behind the primal impression to the *arché,* Gendlin focuses on the conditions for the appearance of the word on its hither side which are never quite so conspicuous as when no word appears. I intend to say something, but a saying does not let a new said appear in the slot potentiated by the just said and I come to a stop. I cross this slot with this or that solicitation, that is, a "proposition"; yet nothing happens as I await the appearing of the word in the "ringing stillness." Though no word come, silence speaks; something is said and understood, as we might understand a dance that cannot be put into a saying.

Eugene Gendlin invites us to listen to this empty slot calling for the poet's word.[17] May we not think the silent *a* of *différance,* the "dead time," as the *arché* receptacle potentiated by a proposition and therefore as *chora?* May we cross and dwell in rather than displace or supersede this difference with a difference? This medial and fecund slot, the "saying not-saying," where language happens is the gap between the said and the sayable. Gendlin says of this "not" that

> Some phenomenologists wanted to say that we explicate into language what we have lived pre-verbally. Heidegger denies anything pre-verbal as if before language. That would leave language in a secondary role and miss its always having already been there in building the symbolic situations in which we live. Nothing human is pre-verbal. Others would like to say that everything is discourse. Heidegger would deny that as well . . . [Opening, the clearing for the appearing of things, equally comes by other modes, as in art and poetry] though never before and without the context that involves language. What we ordinarily call pre-verbal may well be a living that has no words to say it. Language forms are implicit in it never-

theless. That is how we know that the ordinary words cannot express it, that we have no words at this moment.

In this slot we may await the appearing of the word (phrase, sentence, and so forth).[18]

It is all well and good to speak, as we did in previous chapters, "from below" of how intention or representation was sneaked into the originary in the name of protention, but now we must show as if "from above" how something new is achieved, something other than an iterated same. Can we experience the creativity of the *arché*? In an appropriately named essay, "Thinking After Distinctions," Gendlin evokes the silence in which the poet searches for the word and, when it appears as a living metaphor, extends the semantic space of its "subject term" by gathering this "subject" of its reflection into a new configuration.[19] Heidegger says that only when the poet is compelled to put into language that for which there is no language, "language speaks itself as language" (MH 1971a, 59). In this "ringing of stillness" (108), the play binds each over "to *Ereignis,* into his own, as he who belongs to language." Then, Bernasconi says, language "touches us in its mystery, unconcealed as concealed in the sounded word" (RBr 1993, 203). Gendlin continues:

> The already written line wants something more. . . . Many
> lines come. Some of them seem good. The poet listens—and
> reads the written lines again—and again. Suddenly, or perhaps
> all along, the poet hears (senses, knows, reads, . . .) what
> these words need, want, demand, imply. . . . Now the
> poet's hand rotates in the air. The gesture says that. Now the
> lines that come try to say—but do not say—that. The blank
> seems to lack words, but no. The blank is very verbal. It
> knows the language well enough to understand—and reject all
> the words that come. The blank is not a bit pre-verbal; it
> knows what must be said and that the lines which come don't
> say that. The blank is vague but it is also more precise than
> what was ever said before—in the history of the world. My
> words, "more vague and more precise," when said in that
> blank—how did they work? Do you not already follow what
> this vague word says here? Need we go back and cross it out?
> . . . Its new workings could not be helped by a crossing out.
> It works newly as it brings its old ways into the slot, so that
> we cannot cross its old ways out. (1987)

While the use of "is" is unavoidable, the deconstructive solution that places it under erasure is too radical; we want to preserve "being" as the absolute flux and so retain old ways in its sentential slot because, you see, we have a perspective from beyond, the Other, to whom we belong before anything is spoken. The medial "between" which is neither a presence nor an absence allows this disclosive, rather than nominal, usage. Utilizing the play of opposites which Bernasconi describes as characteristic of Heidegger's "deconstruction," Gendlin proposes that we think in them. This play will, as Bernasconi remarks, "seem to force out of metaphysics what seems to stand within it" and thus to transgress it (RBr 1993, 192).

Gendlin reads Heidegger's "dwelling" as thinking in the distinctions which Derrida displaces. For example, on Bernasconi's deconstructive reading of Heidegger, the place of *logos*, this "oldest word in the rule of the word" (MH 1971a, 155) and the name for being and saying (163), in Heidegger's thinking on language comes into question and is displaced (RBr 1993, 203). *Logos* cannot assert itself as it once did but slips away into the abyss to "return to where it came from, the silence of speaking language" (204). This "way-making," Derrida's "transgression" and "displacement," makes what was called "metaphysics" unsayable (ibid.). Rather than being displaced, perhaps even its old ways can dwell within new ways to thinking when thought from beyond Being.

The "slot" is not the uroboric Gaea but is the Mother, the ripe receptacle bearing vectors of alterity, the unsaid, distinguished from, and the like, which Derrida suggests have been relegated to the margins yet leave their trace. Words, like the *schema* that vector primal becoming, have a kind of being and thus encapsulate and release forces, do something, if only like Heraclitus' bow, express countervailences. Forces presuppose a receptacle, the possibility on a grant from above of a home, an *oikos*—however *unheimlich* it may be. The differences do not stand to this receptacle, that is, slot, as determinates to the determinable but leave traces, like motes in the sunlight or marks on the screen of a Wilson chamber. Any term appearing in this gap (*chaos*), born of its womb, works through the traces of its others within; it occurs with a comet's tail, not unlike Hegel's historical substance, that brings an excess into the *chora*-like slot that grants it being.[20] But to dwell on these dynamics and disseminations at the expense of what appears is like dwelling on the role of Socrates' bones and nerves in sitting, rather than on the real cause that brought him to prison. Causes are not conditions. And if, as presumably the *Philebus* maintains, the Good, *agathon,* is the cause, *aitia,* of mixtures of *peras* and *apeiron,* then this "ringing silence" is not altogether autochthonic but can respond to a solicitation from beyond being. What is solicited, as place-granting *gignesthai,* gives back to us Being, not mere *Ereignis,* to work in new ways in new slots.

Crossing a metaphysical distinction with its difference does not necessarily cancel it out or even cause its displacement; the chiasmus lets the displacing term (word, phase, line, etc.) dwell in what would otherwise be displaced. Distinctions can of course be displaced, that is, marginalized, and as such modify one another in the enunciative field according to social and institutional ways of generating protocols for saying and ordering. This displacement posits a deconstructive polemos that preserves differences that, like waves in a sea, can destroy and even guide thought, yet the resulting entity is epiphenomenal, without ontological weight. Some Nietzsche commentators suggest that the will to power posits the self as an epiphenomenon of this countervalent play. Thinking about the text as a matrix rather than polemos, about the word (or institution) as engendered rather than precipitated fits, I think, with Gendlin's proposes that we think in, rather than make judgments with, distinctions.

In Heidegger's *Andenken* ("commemorative thinking"), as Robert Bernasconi tells it, "we are witnessing a transformation of language that, because language always stands in a relation to previous language, cannot simply turn its back on what has gone before. The transformation of language is a 'saying not-saying.' This does not mean only a passage away from the priority accorded to the assertion. The 'not' of 'not-saying' is the lack of a word of Being in the way it permeates all language. *Aletheia* says "unconcealment" and at the same time says this pervasive concealment" (RBr 1985, 87).[21] Though the process in which a distinction appears is "a process that always disappears, exhausted and absorbed in what it makes" through its nominalization, the world arises from becoming and never exhausts its resources. Is much ado made of being in this oblivion of becoming? Wasn't *Lethe* a river "into which other and other waters flow?" In the apparent oxymoron "being is time," "time" crosses over and makes a place for itself in "being," commemorating it in the emergent event. But time defined as crossing is already reflexive and presupposes a meaning of (self) presence. Can time be thought as time?

We can also think in a distinction through its difference that "comes down from above." The hypostatic self preserves a meaning of being from such a play, as in the polemical *il y a*. We think being in becoming. As another example, "time" and "being" draw nigh and cross in Heidegger's titles. In *Being and Time*, "and" marks the between which "time" crosses to dwell within and interpret "being;" "being and time" is not the same crossing as expressed in the *Kehre*, "time and being." "Being," through its nearness, brings new ways into the slot, conditioning this matrix and "time," as in the time of its life, is thought.[22] Though "being' is never sublated in absolute knowing, is it necessary to think of this "alongside" as denoting whatever is concealed in unconcealment? Let's look at this problem through dwelling.

Consider the chiasmus "being and time." Exactly which of the meanings of being is at play in "being?" Is it some variant noticed in its history, substance or subject? Or is it *einai* as durative or even vitalistic presence, the Latin *esse, ens,* or *exsistere, bin* as dwelling, or Heidegger's verbal interpretation of *eon?* How about "and" or "time?" Is "and" a conjunction, or does it suggest a bonded between, a matrix, that generates a vast array of sentences given various assignments at play in these meanings? Seeing "and" in the Good suggests the latter. On the usual understanding of deconstruction, these differences displace one another and deconstruct whatever is said even if, perhaps, their play reveals in the free space a trace of the byond. What is required is a "way-making" that can dwell in the distinction as disclosive "root unfolding." Thinking through the disclosive formality of dwelling, Gendlin continues, "does not ignore, round-off, or merge precise distinctions and forms . . . we get beyond the forms by thinking precisely in them [as the physician thinks the disease in the symptoms in order to go beyond these to the ill person]. The thinking is inseparable from the distinctions, but it is not the distinctions. . . . Coming after all the others each also say the languaging the others do. Each says how words work after each other: They make a spot, they play each other, they march further. Their differences still work, but do-not cancel, because after all each does its saying" (1987). Something about something is said to an other in the actual workings of language—or thinking undoes itself. This is possible only if the medial and effeminated subject nexus is retained. Thus, in "being and time," being would be understood medially, as a sort of *il y a,* an elemental becoming. Since this gap, the fecund "being" in which we await time's gift of durative presence is lighted by the Good, not Being, whatever is disclosed will be through the Good's light.

Dwelling thinking is the converse of the speculative proposition by which Hegel's philosophy of identity reconciles differences.[23] Thus, for example, differences are. Each is an identity; thus the whole, difference, is constituted by identity and difference. But being *qua* identity is only through difference; thus identity is also a whole that is and, together with difference, a part. Each moment is itself only as excluding its opposite, which is thus to exclude also itself; the result is a contradiction in which opposition is destroyed. John Protevi notes that "the introduction of identity into difference (or the recognition that identity is necessary to meaningfully think difference) is only possible at the level of thought or meaning [i.e., Reflection] . . . which thinks the essence as the unity of positive and negative. We must note the total self-reflection [in which a whole is constituted by reflecting its other into itself] of both sides; there can be no remainder as both sides are reflected as part and as whole" (JP 1993a, 61). "Being" is as existence a dynamical process. The opposites are, as Derrida remarked, forces and these, rather than cancelling one another, as oppositional have the resolution of a wave in the sea. If, as Leibniz thought, forces have an analogue of appetition, then we cannot pass beyond them to a level of pure or absolute thought in which these are effaced. This play in "Being" continues for, as Gendlin remarked, it retains some of its old meanings, even if other Parmenidian possibilities are bracketed out by the Good. A further determination is made by whatever appears in the slot as if to make its home there.

Making a home overcomes alienation from self, nature and the god and, said in this way, is the telos of Hegel's philosophy. In Heidegger's formulation, this means participating in the "ring dance" with earth, sky, and the gods. These are alternative ways of expressing the task to which hermeneutics sets itself. What is at stake is the apportionment of one thing, a difference, to its opposite that one may either dwell in or take its measure from the other. Apportioning one difference to another is not a reconciliation in some higher synthesis, Hegel's *Aufhebung,* or even a play between them. "Apportionment" is hermeneutics or, for that matter, translation. We must now let time dwell in "apportioned" being. In itself, for example, time may be thought as time or as being, as presence. Isn't it to be thought as presence in dwelling with, not just alongside and in the neighborhood of Being? If time is to dwell with being, then time will be the time of being, its apportioned periodicities and epochal presencings, its destinings and renewals. Since this remains within ontological horizons, perhaps the chiasmus "time and being" lets time be thought as time, as a flow rather than a succession of presents which must make a dwelling for being. When thought as dwelling, it is apportioned or interpreted by "being." If time interprets being as becoming, then being interprets time as the more primitive receptacle, the *arché* beyond being that, as *chora* "spaces" being. There is more to be said, but this should show that even after deconstruction, dwelling thinking has a place for "Being" and beings, for the "it" that doesn't cancel itself in the objectlessness of the *Ge-stell* and the "is" that refuses to be placed under erasure.

The *said* preserves the *logos* and proposes a meaning of presence lacking in the slot or even the saying. Whatever we claim as an exception of Being, e.g., the Good, becomes on being said an event in Being. Diachronic saying serves the synchronic said; in language, Levinas says, "everything is conveyed before us, at the price of a betrayal"

(EL 1981, 6). Levinas's *Otherwise than Being, Or Beyond Essence* avoids the predicative use of the verb "to be." Perhaps dwelling thinking, in which "is" is metaphoric, hermeneutic, and participatory, will apportion language to the between and be less of a betrayal. One must do justice to the *arché logos* in its classical, constitutive sense and its more recent transcendental meaning.

5. Metaphor

THOUGH ALLEGORY IS DISTINGUISHED from metaphor by structural features, I will follow the advice of the Venerable Bede and, except where noted, treat all tropes as metaphors. On this account, though it may be limited in scope, the interpretative reflexivity of participation, the circle of the same that crosses its other to engender a same, is the form of metaphor and hermeneutics. Metaphor is often a mode of dwelling and, as perhaps always hermeneutical, a way of introducing allegorical interpretations of common experience which extend hermeneutics to the non-human sciences. Heidegger's recognition of the reflective structure of Kant's "veritative" judgment shows how metaphor and its "shock of recognition" have a similar root. Recognition takes place in "the representation of unity that lets something [apperceived] stand against it" (MH 1990, 53) "as *a power*" (A 117; Kant's italics) through a reflexive act that activates the self as a self (129). This reflexivity in which something bends over to interpret or dwell in another collects various modalities of significance, such as recognition, participation, and interpretation. The dynamics of the metaphorical synthesis effected by the *arché* is "unconcealed" when Heidegger's interpretation of apperception's "I can ____" is transferred to the affectivity of the medial imagination. Thus we move upward, as it were, through that which comes "down from above" (Heidegger's rendition of Anaximander's *kata*) into Husserl's flux and the dynamics of Derrida's traces to the hypostatic self awaiting with Gendlin the appearing of the word that gathers us into the world.

Metaphysical statements must first be understood as speculative propositions (which as I employ the term are the converse of Hegel's), and these in turn related to "speculative demonstration," the interpretation already given to the method of analysis. This speculative import has been present since Parmenides denied change and novelty with his "there is a same for thinking and being," *to gar auto noein te kai einai* (DK, B 3). This cause is advanced if "being" is given its archaic Germanic root, "to dwell," the sense of the English "was" or German *Wesen.* It should also collect the Greek *oikos*, "household," which the Patristic tradition used to express "providence," the belonging together (*zugehören*) of God and man. The name of this belonging is *aletheia*, "truth." What exactly is unconcealed (*aletheia*) when one "sees" Being in beings? The usual translation of his answer, "Being is and it is not possible for Being not to be," *eon opos estin te kai hos ouk me einai* (DK B2, 1.3), is like a glance at Medusa; a quest becomes frozen as doctrine. Even when as *eon*, "Being," first became thematic, there was no talk of an intuition of Being, as if it were some signified transcendent. This existential use of the copula "to be," which we wish to retain as the medial existence (becoming) is not available in ancient Greek. Something quite different from "Being is" or "exists" is being said.

In his *The Way of Truth*, Parmenides proposes a syntax for inquiry into the unconcealment of *eon*, an archaic participial form of *einai* ("being," "what-is") which is the grammatical subject of the deductions in B8, the main body of his argument. As with all inquiry, this too begins with a question which, like an *epoché*, opens ontic horizons. Asking his question, "what is *x* really?" opens the horizon of permanent presence and invites an answer of the form, "＿＿ is. . . ." Parmenides gave the sentential form of any possible answer; "＿＿ is . . . and it is not possible for ＿＿ not to be . . ." (AM 1970, 55).[24] The hermeneutical circle is drawn by the homology given the answer by the question. His "signposts" to *aletheia*, to the "unconcealment" of *eon*, such as "one," "ungenerable," "imperishable," should eliminate the fear that hermeneutics has been surrendered to the ordinary use of the copula. Borrowing a term from Hegel and denying, perhaps on insufficient grounds, its Hegelian implications, Mourelatos says that in a "speculative predication," the verb *einai* does not collect facts, assert identities, classify or describe the sorts of things usually gathered by "is" in sentence frames; it is used hermeneutically, as a way of explanation and interpretation (56). Mourelatos says that in these propositions, whose sense was available through earlier pre-Socratics, the copula, like "the 'is' of identity, expresses a removal of distinctions, a simplification. But unlike it, and more like the 'is' of predication, it expresses an asymmetrical relation. . . . This use resembles the 'is' of classification in suggesting that the predicate, the term on the right, belongs essentially to or is a necessary condition for the subject, the term on the left. But unlike it, and more like the adjectival "is," it makes a claim of novel description and discovery" (57). This hermeneutical interpretation, with its "seeing something as ＿＿" overtones, lets us see the predicate reflexively bend back, like the soul's circle of the same in Plato's myth, to make a dwelling in its other, the subject. In analysis understood as "speculative demonstrative," overlapping "regions," perhaps as myths or concepts, within which monstration occurs make manifest that which is thought to lie in them; in the same way metaphor lets the "predicate" cross over the subject which is then "seen" within its interpretative matrix. Heidegger noted that this "hermeneutical as" in which something has been circumspectively discriminated, that is, "taken apart" (*diaeresis*) with "respect to its in-order-to, and taken apart as such . . . has the structure of *something as something*" (MH 1962, 189). The "as" of "pre-predicative seeing as" in "circumspective interpretation" through a set up ("ready-at hand," *Vorstellung*] is then leveled down and as something present-at-hand is given a definite [univocal] character . . . the existential-*hermeneutical* "*as*" has become the "apophantical as of assertion" (201). "Predication [*synthesis*] is what it is only as a pointing out" so that what "is already [pre-predicatively] manifest can be made explicitly manifest in its definite character" (197). Heidegger's language, which sensibilizes concepts by reducing them to modes of being-in-the-world, reflects his early religious training; language is essentially sacramental, bringing us to see things as incarnating and manifesting form. Thus, though he denies metaphor, his work seems to me to be essential to understanding how it operates.

I have noted that and must now explain how the movement of disclosive metaphor is the converse of that expressed in Hegel's "speculative proposition."[25] I propose it as an extension of Kant's discovery that thought should always be in the service of intuition. The "intuited" subject, rather than being taken up into the predicate matrix as if that were its truth, is a chorographic matrix that engenders a same (to the subject and predicate as other) when reflexively "seen" through the predicate's semantic space. A horizon belonging to neither, a same, is posited in these other; while the subject, rather than being sublated, is left open to further interpretation.

In Hegel's speculative proposition, the subject is superseded or sublated, *Aufhebung,* by the predicates' semantic field so that further interpretation is blocked. Hegel say that "the Subject suffers, as we might put it, a counter-thrust. Starting from the Subject as though it were a permanent ground, it finds that, since the Predicate is really the Substance, the Subject has passed over into the Predicate, and by this very fact has been sublated; since, in this way, what seems to be the Predicate has become the whole and independent mass, thinking cannot roam at will, but is impeded by its weight. (GH 1977, 36). On the contrary, the reflexive predicate dwells in the subject and perhaps conversely; their belonging together in proximity is a *metaxu,* a birthing place. The movement reflects back onto sense to discern incarnate sense, and only then is an epiphany, and not away from it in the direction of the Absolute. Thus metaphor need never efface itself in the text of philosophy.

Interpreting metaphysical statements as sentence frames in which the copula hermeneutically deploys the predicate over the subject and lets them creatively mingle is the threshold we cross in order to dwell in the open beyond metaphysics. The alternative lexical interpretation of metaphor in which terms are literal or metaphorical has enshrined it in the metaphysics of presence and hidden its sentential or semantic nature. Rather than being concerned with the transfer of lexical meaning, the metaphoric sentence frame is semantic, truth-showing. In this phenomenology of metaphors, one sees its point through the clearing opened by its terms under the constraint of form, as one sees quite unwittingly in gestalts, as in Wittgenstein's duck-rabbit. But the Wittgenstein example reminds us that, though metaphor is disclosive, it is also mimetic, "representational," in ways that, as Ricoeur says, propose " a suspension of reference in the sense defined by the norms of discourse [which] is the negative condition for a more fundamental mode of reference, whose expression is the task of interpretation. At stake in this explication is nothing less than the meaning of the words reality and truth, which must themselves vacillate and become problematical" (PR 1987, 229). At its best, the mimetic content has a visual constraint, a "shock of recognition," yet at the same time we are aware of the words and the "semantic impertinence" in their usage. Though, as Ricoeur says, the "place of metaphor, its most intimate and ultimate abode, is neither the name, the sentence, nor even discourse itself, but the copula, 'to be.' The metaphorical 'is' at once signifies 'is not' and 'is like' " (7). Is "like"? The "is not" suggests the impertence of the usage, while the "is like" suggests the mimetic aspect which mediates and perhaps discloses reality. Mourelatos says the hermeneutical "is" tends towards identity. Ricoeur notes that in hermeneutics the referential claims of a scientific or literary text that give it a truth value are of the form, "This is how it is with the world." *Einai* already has this fact-showing sense. The *epoché* effected by the "semantic impertinence" of the hermeneutical "is" permits a chiasmus of horizons which lets something be seen and said as if for the first time.

The old substitution thesis which held that a figurative term may be replaced by a literal or proper term without change of truth value presupposes that the "is like" being expressed is known independently of the term in which it is being expressed. "To produce a good metaphor," Aristotle says, "is to see a likeness" (*De Poetics* 1459a 7–8). The substitution interpretation also taught that a term becomes metaphorical by being transported from genus to genus, from genus to species, from species to species and by analogy (1457b 10–25). For all its faults, it calls attention to the apparent violations in standard usage without which one would never discover the presence of metaphor. Moreover, naming is often metaphorical and carries with it all the re-

262 Kant's Methodology

sources of what Derrida calls the "general text." Words bring with them, Foucault says, "their substantiality [in Hegel's sense], like a fragment of silent knowledge, the immobile properties of living beings."

In *Nausea*, Sartre uses words, under the fiction of their loss, to let us see their disclosive power. For example, his Roquintin is puzzled by the way "black" is ascribed to things: "the root was not black . . . it was not black that was there on that piece of wood . . . black, like the circle, did not exist. . . . I thought without words, on things, with things. Absurdity was not an idea in my head, not a murmuring voice, but that long dead snake at my feet, that snake of wood. A snake or a claw or a root or a vulture's talon." There is, A. S. Byatt remarked, "a moment in all of this when we see the tree vividly . . . , the metaphors in this passage of deliquescence and flux have their fat, precise, informative life" (AB 1993, 12).

Since the "resemblance" expressed in a metaphor is, on the semiotic interpretation, often generated by the metaphor and since the hermeneutical *is* is still assertive and makes a statement, the only bearer of meaning, reference, and truth, there are no figurative or literal terms and no prior resemblances to be redescribed. According to Jacques Derrida, the distinction between the "proper" and "figurative" has its origin in the metaphor of the sun in *Republic* VI. By separating the visible, changing order from the intelligible order of eternal presences characterizable only within the univocal requirements of mathematical statement and proof, he creates the proper and literal as paradigmatic (JD 1982, 170–71). There is no non-metaphorical way for defining metaphor. For example, Aristotle's *epiphora* means to "transfer" or "carry over" and so refers to "motion." There can be no theory of metaphor or, for that matter, "theory of theory"; the very concept of theory rests on a metaphor. The moral? There is no going beyond *theoria*'s understanding of how to use language.

In classical semiotics, a sign is the unity of signifier and signified. Therefore its value, according to Emile Benveniste, "is only generic and conceptual and has nothing to do with any particular or contingent signified, and everything individual is excluded . . . [so that] circumstantial factors are to be regarded as irrelevant" (cited in PR 1987, 72). "The apparatus works only if the wires are connected so that current flows from a higher to a lower potential" is true or false only if such contingencies do admit of reference. Something must be unconcealed if meaning is to mean. Having made semantic claims about metaphor, how is truth value established when the "facts" which support it may themselves be metaphorical posits?

But there is a problem. If worldly reference is mediated by the metaphor of nature as a book, are we not condemned to a semiotic interpretation after all? According to Emil Beneveniste, "one is never confronted with a relation between the signs and the things denoted [noema, *Bedeutung*] nor a relationship between language and world, which now becomes a closed system of signs (cited in PR 1987, 229). Of course not, since linguistic signs are sentence relative, and only sentences are true or false. Even nature's signifiers, since they have to be read and interpreted, are contingently linked to what they signify. Living beings, like Aesop's dog and the bone, are error prone. The structuralist's bond between signifier and signified is broken and a new intentionality instituted.

Since the only proper parts of sentences are sentences, meaning is sentential; there are no literal and metaphorical meanings as such, but usages can be fixed within a determinate context or tradition by monstrative convention or stipulation, usually within an allegory. Prior to Faraday, for example "electricity" collected a variety of phenomena, rubbed amber, galvanic piles, Sir Thomas Browne's "converts the needle freely placed," and Franklin's kite experiment. Faraday saw these expressions within the focus of "flow." This in turn is common to all "frames" in which "electricity" is the subject. Electricity is then interpreted and explained in hydraulic allegories. On standardization, "current" loses its "focus," its "way-making-root-unfolding-disclosive-power," and becomes standardized in reflection as a theoretical predicate; prior to standardization, these models are suspect. Its interpretation within the semantic field of "flow" opens an "electrical" horizon in which phenomena are seen as flowing. Allegories do not, however, bring news from the transcendent; they map what we do not understand into things already understood.

Undoubtedly it is necessary to distinguish, as in the formal sciences and even in dialectic, between the literal and the metaphorical use of language upon which the literal is in fact founded. For example, polyvalence must be eliminated in the formal and information sciences. If this erasure is pressed to its logistic conclusion, words lose their power to create worlds, to enliven and extend thought. Faraday shocked us into seeing electricity as a liquid. Given such a formal model instituted through metaphor, as "ampere" was introduced by a coil and a moving pointer to measure the flow of electricity within the model, then by mapping sets of entities into and onto one another by measurement, itself a metaphor, terms can be univocally "fixed," like an image is fixed on a film. To distinguish the metaphorical, reflexive "is" from its more familiar forms is sometimes difficult; the context, if not semantic impertinence of the usage, usually lets us see the distinction.

In developing this hermeneutical interpretation of metaphor, I have followed several promising suggestions about how to retain the bit of truth in the metaphorical/literal distinction and avoid its apparent lexical thrust. One hears that a term must have a literal sense before its can be given an extended, metaphorical meaning. Max Black's distinction between "frame" and "focus" avoids this dichotomy by pointing to a structural feature of metaphorical statements. Terms in a frame are "seen" through the focus of another term, as the semantic space framed by "man" in "man is a wolf" is seen and interpreted through the focus of "wolf" and conversely (MB 1962, 28). In allegory, there is no such chiasmus. I. A. Richards offers the more logocentric distinction in which the metaphorical meaning appears within the tension between "tenor" and "vehicle." The vehicle is the expression as written or said, while "tenor" is used as Berkeley used it to say he "once and for all desires . . . that whoever shall think it worth his while to understand . . . that he would not stick to this or that phrase or manner of expression [the vehicle], but candidly collect my meaning from the whole tenor of my discourse" (IR 1954, 4). The dynamical tension between tenor and vehicle opens the horizon also opened when a frame is focused.

Derrida's doubts raise problems for a non-metaphorical account of metaphor. In "The White Mythology," he cites Marsias' definition of metaphor as "a species of Trope; the word which one uses in the metaphor is taken in another than the literal, proper sense; it is, so to speak, in a borrowed dwelling, as one of the ancients says, which is common and essential to all Tropes." The figure, "borrowed dwelling," is there, Derrida says, "in order to signify metaphor itself; it is a metaphor of metaphor; an expropriation, a being-outside-one's own residence, but still in a dwelling . . . still a residence in which one comes back to oneself, recognizes oneself, reassembles oneself or assembles oneself, outside oneself in oneself . . . the metaphysical trajectory of the Platonic eidos to the Hegelian Idea" (JD 1982, 253). Yes, but if to dwell, *oikos,* is to belong together with, not merely borrow, and metaphor is not a carrying over but a crossing, where does this trajectory take us? Beyond the subject? No. Towards the things that are. In metaphor, we transcend towards world. It will be in a saying, Ricoeur remarks, "more appropriate than ordinary speech, a saying that would be a showing and a letting be, a mode of thought that would never leave discourse behind" (PR 1987, 312).

The *arché,* dwelling's threshold, must be crossed in transcending towards world. If, however, the *mouvance* of *différance* presences, the prospect is not promising. A "prospect" is a standpoint, a "status"; as John Llewelyn remarks, it is "a place where one stays. If his work has any status it is that of a working over of this assumption of which Heidegger refers to in one of his titles as dwelling, *Wohnen,* and thinking, *Denken,* and *Bauen,* construction. It is an investigation of the familiarity of family resemblance, a reconnaissance, re-con-naissance [note the medial 'ance'], of the threshold between semantic home and abroad, a querying of *Heimlichkeit*, the own-most (*eigenst*), authenticity, propriety, property, enclosure and the close" (JL 1986, 122–23). But a place is also that from which one goes forth by identifying entities, where identifying is already a reconnaissance "exploring in advance" and "watching out for" (126) that must be "held before us . . . as a same" (MH 1990, 127). If "dwelling" is not merely borrowed but has the sense of participation's *oikos*, then the procreative and nurturing household as archaically experienced is the natural place that grants which, with its choreographies, also deconstructs genealogies—and perhaps through metaphor gives them the unity of a spiritual formation. We sometimes talk things out and even understand one another. This common experience, which Dilthey suggested as a paradigm for the human sciences, is a more fertile *arché* than high German poetry.

Llewelyn suggests that archaic difference is an "indefinite dyad" which "engenders gender, genus, genre, and generality, the very life of language, of philosophy, the poem . . . [and] is at one and the same time their degeneration and death." How can the dyad function as the slot? When dwelling is granted its place by the *apeiron*, the engendering *chaos*, then how can language cross and engender? A threshold is the heir to apperception's generated now; though absent from itself and never a presence, like constituted time it marks emergence. Crossing a threshold, a medial *chaos*, is hazardous. Like the *chaos* between Gaea and Uranus, it could be unpredictably generative and creative—and destructive. In participation's terms, this gap between being and becoming is the place from which a creature becomes same for itself by selecting and assimilating alterity. Or fails. And dies.

Plato's "indefinite dyad" was also deconstructive: any form of order or *logos* generated by a cut, such as the rational numbers, in the receptacle as *apeiron plethos* posits relative disorder, as these numbers posit surds.[26] This "infinite dyad" of the great and small, which Aristotle attributed to Plato in *Metaphysics N*, seems to derive from *peras* and *apeiron*, two of the four kinds of being in *Philebus*. Dedekind's cuts in the *apeiron* line provide an image of what may be involved. Both C. S. Peirce and Charles Hartshorne suggest the generation of ideas on the model of Dedekind cuts; Plato seems to present this alternative in the second and third hypotheses of *Parmenides*. Just as number classes are formed by cuts articulating various senses of unity, ordinal, rational, real, etc., so ideas, forms of *peras*, are generated when this eidetic continuum is cut by unity whose sense is given by the Good. Aside from certain quality classes, can all *eidé* be generated in this manner? They are always decisive, telic enactments of limits from beyond for the sake of being. Given some articulation of unity, cuts first generate formal fields of differences as real possibilities, like de Saussure's graphematic field posited by the decision to write.

How shall being be articulated? Is the understanding that lightens ontological or does it emanate from the Good beyond Being? In a Platonic variant of the Ontological Difference, the Good and the receptacle beyond Being must supplement Being, being as *peras* and as *apeiron*, determinate and determinable. On Heidegger's reading of the Anaximander fragment, the gift of Being (*eon*) is "order and reck," justice (MH 1984, 44–57). But this will not happen until the Good, not Being, lightens and being is replaced by medial *gignesthai*. I propose to substitute for Being in Aquinas' "hermeneutical" formula an understanding of the Good that is thematized in the other. This proximity is prior to the Ontological Difference. Being is said either *in quid* of a substantival determinable, *in qual* of a predicative determinate, or, if we are to express the participle, of their unity. The former is dynamical. Thus, unless determinate being is drawn elsewhere than from *chaos*, the unity of "being," its participial enactment, will be epiphenomenal, like a wave in the sea. Is this the appropriate sense of "order and reck"? Being seen in the Good, a limiting term, will take limits, e.g., *peras*, but otherwise it is a dynamical *apeiron plethos* that overpowers as it overcomes.

The possibility of an ontological hermeneutics originates in Plato's *Phaedrus* with the search for a meaning of Being that will articulate beings. Socrates says that he would follow in the footsteps of anyone, as if he were a god, who finds a one and many "following the natural articulation; we are not to attempt to hack off parts, like a clumsy butcher" (*Phaed.* 266A). The idea is, as Heidegger said of the *nomos*, the "unifying unity of what would otherwise fall apart." To choose is to decide or cut (Lt. *caedere*, Gk. *keirein*) and thus to introduce new differential conditions, possibilities, or novel forms of definiteness, as gradients for becoming. Decisiveness aiming at some form of unity through the Good is, as we now know, required for freedom. The cut that generates an idea also defines a (*apeiron*) potential and as a gap or slot, which as chaos can be crossed and originate. In a metaphorical crossing there is a double cut, a cut establishing pure possibility as potential alterity, and a cut away from a determining sameness which, in giving epochal time, provides a dwelling for the former. Whether made in interpretation or in metaphor's crossing, the cut as an *epoché* eliminates bonds to, if not traces of, determining (existential) and definitory (eidetic) alterity and grants a place for dwelling. Freed possibility, alterity as *peras*, now has a place, *chora*, in that which has been set free as dwelling, the epochal *epoché*. In other words, the epoch set up by this existential cut is an engendering *arché*, that from which the word or creature arises and gathers itself into unity as if for the first time. The cut of metaphor, like the cut of a reflexive return from possibility to receptivity, allows being to work in new ways. The cut sets being free to let alterity dwell for a while within its "semantic space." This is possible if the predicate, "is . . . ," that cuts and gives a determinate difference is metaphorical or copulative. Metaphor effects its cut as the (interpretative or hermeneutical) predicate reflects back onto and dwells within the framed (received) subject.

Metaphor must be defended against our friends who have said it is the *exergue*, effacement, of the sensuous; its elimination would be desirable were philosophy exclusively concerned with principles and epistemic *doxa*; as phenomenological, metaphor is uneliminable.[27] We will not understand *idea*, for example, apart from its visual root; this is effaced when, after Descartes or Locke, it is allowed to refer to mental events or contents. Were philosophy not a historical science, this might be acceptable. Metaphor is the creative interface between man and world, facilitating a break from and movement beyond such bonds. Metaphors depend on the use, not erasure, of the "is"; the vital and disclosive senses of *einai* are prior to its predicative or existential use. This movement towards effacing sensuous imagery from language begins with Plato's Seventh Letter. The point is perhaps best made by Husserl, whose *Logical Investigations* detaches intentional acts from "pertinent mental pictures" (EH 1970b, 299) and from psychological explanations which "seek empirical bonds tying the thought contents in question to other facts in the flux of real happenings," that is, to their empirical origin to satisfy "the sense of [intentional] fulfillment" (348). He proposes that we should, when in doubt, "take well-understood algebraical signs or complete formulae, such as 'Every algebraic equation of uneven grade has at least one real root' and carry out the needful observations. . . . To report on my own findings in the last case: I see an open book which I recognize as Serrat's Algebra, I see the sensory pattern of an algebraic equation in Teubnerian type . . . the familiar . . . without experiencing the slightest trace of accompanying images" (300). This is not to deny the necessity of the "Teubnerian type" or some sort of inscription or the "intuitive presentation as its very foundation" in which "the experience becomes constituted as a physical object" (310). The mathematical reality intuitively presenced through the sign is presented and held fast through the hermeneutical is. "Every so-and-so is so-and-so" has an origin that binds us, not to an empirical fact, but to "the thing there and relates it and, so to speak, provides its maintenance with which to be a thing" and as keeper, Heidegger goes on to say, is the "relation itself" (MH 1971a, 82). While it is clear that the word preserves and maintains being, it does so only because the effeminated slot lets nearness or significance be and is, therefore, co-creative.

Have I salvaged metaphor from the effacement and literalization of Hegel's *Aufhebung* which purges a term of the metaphorically sensuous and frees it for "spiritual usage,"[28] and from Heidegger's claim that "the metaphorical exists only within the bounds of the metaphysical?" (MH 1957, 88). At stake is my thesis that we participate in world by the active, projective interpretation of what is passively received, which is in turn the reflexive structure of original temporality. The possible homology between what is 'expressed' and received, which Kant establishes by a theory of categories, lies in this same which language calls to presence that is then actively interpreted, not through ideas as eternal archetypes, but in (allegorical) paradigms. Plato says that the paradigmatic method "operates, does it not, when a factor identical with a factor in a less-known object is rightly believed to exist in some other better-known object in another sphere of life. This common factor in each object, when it has been made the basis of a parallel examination of them both, makes it possible for us to achieve a true judgment about each of them as forming one pair. . . . Would we be surprised then to find our mind reacting in the same way to the letters with which the universe is spelled out?" (*Politicus* 278C-D). Though this overlooks the creative dimension of language, isn't this also a definition of metaphor? Hölderlin's "flower of the mouth" interprets "language" in "Language is the flower of the mouth" in a metaphor about metaphor and its participatory and hermeneutical extensions, in which "flower" is focused on language which is then seen as living, as blooming (cited by MH 1971a, 99).[29] Aristotle's *epiphora*, as Ricoeur remarked, "becomes a conceptual migration . . . [of] an entire realm from alien territory . . . guided by the use of the conceptual network in the country of origin." (PR 1987, 236).[30]

Luce Irigaray says lovers must care for the place (*chora*) of love between them (LI 1984, 33); but the poetry which is born of this place, this slot, must tell them how to say it and philosophy how it is to be thought. Poetry, the creativity that speaks itself, and thought dwell in the neighborhood of the word. The dead time in which through the trace "friendship" words appeared "like flowers" to Hölderlin is also, Llewelyn says "the between-time in which the poet, who mediates between mortals and immortals, awaits a second coming with a presentiment of a presence that will inaugurate another epoch of the history of being that is discontinuously continuous with an earlier."[31]

Understanding Hölderlin's assertion, "Language is the flower of the mouth," as speculative captures what is active (*De Rhetorica* 1411b 34–35) or alive in metaphor. Metaphor lets beings, not just *apeiron* selves, express themselves. Metaphor as hermeneutical never alienates us (MH 1974, 37). The "bloom of the mouth" is nature's.

In this vital understanding of "Being" the hermeneutical "is" interprets beings through eventual paradigms in which life and death are parameters. Do metaphors really commit us to a metaphysics of sempiternal presence?[32]

VIII

ARCHAIC EPISTEMOLOGY

....

1. Philosophical Archeology

HITHERTO METAPHYSICS has been first philosophy and in its greatest master, Aristotle, came fully into itself came to itself by securing its first principles in theology's *analogia entis*. Since Kant that route has been closed to most; but even if his constructivistic project in which the self replaces God as the principle of principles is counterintuitive, his methodology led into, back out of, and then around the *arché*, and thus to first philosophy. Though philosophy has always begun in archeology, uncovering and gathering itself around *its arché*, its justifying principle or origin, it seems that the way is now said to lead beyond being and philosophy is itself in crisis. Aristotle, in a similar quandary, resorted to metaphor. Could we resort to its close relative, myth, whose marginalization may have created our problem? Levinas says, and I think correctly, that all myth is a myth of Being (EL 1981, 180).[1]

We once turned to origins for evidence and for principles; but before we turn our back on these vestiges of onto-theology, perhaps we should listen to what is being said when such concerns are first expressed. Interest in an *arché* is implicit in the child's earliest questions, "why does . . . ?" or "what is . . . ?" I recall being told that the snow fell because these were feathers Mother Goose was plucking and being satisfied with the explanation. Could a child really be requesting reasons or explanations in, for example, covering law? His questions, and most of ours, reflect a desire that would be satisfied with a coherent and interesting story which, as with most stories, answered what's and why's. Story-relative understanding, which reaches profound depth among Zen masters, is existential and sense-making. Such stories may be dismissed as infantile and the question taken as a request for a ground in a formal *logos,* a proof, or in some modality of self-certainty. "Understanding" then names a nominal power (*dynamis*) perfected in an act (*energeia*) of theoretical thought in which the thing thought (*ens rationis*) is of and for thought. In spite of the high principles we can marshal to defend this view, isn't this formalistic latency derivative from participatory dwelling with?

Kant's metaphysics of experience, did we not know otherwise, seems to propose a story-relative form of understanding through which one receives the gift of a world. Experience, however, rests on metaphysics, something beyond *physis*, the *marginalized Other*. Perhaps we can see her trace in the regulative ideas which become, in the second *Critique*, the postulates of practical reason which found and express freedom, with its implications of justice and dignity. Perhaps this also glimmers in the finality of those aesthetic feelings which never achieve the status of a concept which, thanks to Santayana's *Sense of Beauty*, we know to be erotic. Eros and ethics "unconceal" the supplements, the receptacle and the Good, that make experience possible. Having glimpsed the Good, as dwellers in the cave we must return and now map our habitation.

Analysis points to both senses of *arché*. One might take as a guide "origin," or one could look to the royal rule of an instituting and explanatory "principle." In the first case, an *arché*, an origin, grants being to an eventual and genetic sequence. Each event gathers itself into being as if eucharistically commemorating the originative manifestation of Being which, though perhaps never present in face-to-face encounter, founds and continues to destine a tradition. But this manifestation to Moses, Abraham, Jesus, or Paul is place-and-story-relative and the tradition has less to do with a myth about a primordial and certain manifestation than with man's efforts to establish a proximity with one another and God. To this, thanks to Philo and Justin, is joined a Greek genealogy within which we have been seeking principles that can guide and direct this more historical journey. The alternative to commemorating an advent that grants a tradition or epoch is an always present "principle" or element, *archei*, that causes existence, governs changes, establishes the possibility of a *logos* and intelligibility, and provides a measure of action. One moves from the temporal to the logical order where succession is modeled on the relation of theorems to an axiom set. Principles determine metaphysical unity, leaving nothing for a being's initiative, while origins set the task of getting it together within the parameters of a genesis. If principles are, however, derived in dwelling thinking, then they will have systematic entailments. We must know that if certain more or less ideal conditions are satisfied, then so and so necessarily; but their sway will be limited, hypothetical, and provisional.

Error can be as historically effective as truth. That Constantine never donated his Roman empire to the Church did not mitigate against the efficacy of papal claims to supremacy nor did the erroneous belief that St. Paul's convert, Dionysus, was buried at St. Denis in Paris or that he wrote the *Celestial Hierarchy* effect Suger's creation of the Gothic. In the first case, a fiction was a disaster, in the second it was the occasion of an upsurge of Being, an event of *aletheia*. Kant, sharing Cartesian horizons, thought he could understand Plato better than Plato could understand himself. In Kant's sense of a world as a constructive, phenomenal totality, "idea" functions to regulate or guide discursive understanding in the direction of the completely determined; but for Plato idea was, in most cases, constitutive *peras*. Since all things are both *peras* and *apeiron*, the Kantian ideal adds to our grasp of contexts, such as truth or goodness which partake of the infinite and which, thus, cannot be completely determined and so admit to more or less. Something being more or less true? Yes, for then truth respects the Socratic principle of ignorance. Kant is entitled to claim his to be a true interpretation. Thanks to Kant, we know that through the medial imagination which sustains neither realism nor idealism and which is the prototype of the between, language has become a transcendental *a priori*. As idealists, there can be an intuitive return to the things which show themselves within its more or less "constituting" parameters, while as realists we insist that things must be able to question these interpretations. Kant teaches us that an intuition does not provide an uninterpreted and fulfilling presence but rather an evidential basis, a ground for questioning. Thanks to the way he has shaped our vision, we can read Plato's texts phenomenologically which, as transcendental, has given us a greater sense of rigor. If "participation" is to be salvaged from scholarly archeology, it must have its transcendental warrant in an analogue of Kantian "construction." Since Descartes, it has become almost axiomatic with vast segments of the learned community that the language of universal mathematics, the unambiguous language of simple foundations and deductive consequences, in which everything is leveled down into being a substitution instance of a variable, is the language of truth.

Since the trivium was abandoned and rhetoric lost its central place in the curriculum, the conflict between the sciences and humanities has ignored the single root of the soul's powers, the *logos* or *ratio* and its expansion in the poet's analogy or physicist's proportion:

> Since falsity is deception and deception is immoral, one must eschew poetry. The reasoning here is bad enough, but the poetry is good, at least, in its expression of human moral intent. The actual point made is a vigorous preference for one as against another kind of poetry, namely that which has a literal interpretative reference to personally collected fact. In this light, science becomes the modern and authentic technique of poetry. The scientist is the contemporary monk copyist, writing over old literature on the palimpsest of experience, triumphantly announcing his faithfulness and accuracy in

transferring the copy, *Hypotheses non fingo.* He only selects according to the canons of his school. (SB 1975, 12)[2]

Science is an allegorical formation whose interpretative framework, deductive and procedurally narrative, solicits a movement towards truth and univocity. By the analogy of measurement, phenomena are mapped into some mathematical domain, a paradigm form of order and transformation, and through its operations one discerns the truth of beings. These reflective maps or models, the contexts within which theories are generated and tested, are essentially hermeneutical, reflective forms that open for us what is otherwise inaccessible because it harbors a depth of meaning foreign to common experience.

Allegories are model-theoretic ways of "seeing-as" instituted by metaphor. When nature's book doesn't quite make sense, we reinscribe it in an allegorical text to preserve its "spiritual" meaning against its own decay, as Walter Benjamin has shown, or to rescue its "real" meaning from the threat of ambiguity.[3] Allegory presumes to adduce concealed levels of meaning from what is already (partially) meaningful. Thus allegory never brings news from the gods, even if they are among its characters, or from supersensible reality, even if it posits such a realm, but it must make sense by reflecting what is to be known through a construction in terms of what is already familiar. Though it lacks the immediacy of metaphor's "inspectio" and has an entre into its subject only through the mediation of an interpretant text, allegory can support a spiritual or anagogic understanding, for example, Dante. Kant overlooks the possibility of such a reflective structure in the Analytic, though there is a sense in which it is implicit in the Ideal of Reason.

Scott Buchanan says the storyteller's "Once upon a time _____" and the mathematician's "Let us assume that _____" announce imaginative allegories that promise high adventure. Allegory articulates a paradigm transcending the apparent meaning of something or other in a likeness within which more can be seen or known than would be available in its original. Ideally, the variant reading given in the allegory preserves that structure in bringing us to see it in a different way. Allegory confers universal meaning on an agent who, in seeing himself as Zeus, Pangloss, or a hen-pecked husband, therein discerns the worldly sense of his action. We learn, especially from its pathological applications and forms, that allegorical interpretations remake the apprehended world so that it will explain acts. Don Quixote is a constant reminder of what happens when interpretations become truth-bearers and do not submit to the things that are. Scientific allegory is explicitly paradigmatic. Unless we are careful, we will insist that the laws it adumbrates really do determine the behavior of beings in any and all contexts. The humanist tradition, with its memory of Oedipus, Lear, and Don Quixote, has been a constant critic of this tendency to take allegories as literal.

An allegory is an analogy, $a/b = c/d$, such that the expansion of the predicate, "seeing as" ratio explains the subject. In Hobbes's "man is a machine," human behavior is interpreted by the science of mechanics. The story told by the predicate expression is, by its asserted likeness, the image or mirror in which we come to understand the subject. Thus the allegory, the systematically extended predicate complex, expresses an interpretative likeness, not a predicative tie or identity. In narrative allegory, as in the trickster tales studied by structuralist folklorists and anthropologists, the interpreting self experiences no difficulty in finding its likeness in the paradigm, even if it takes an animal form, as does Brer Rabbit; the allegory offers an interpretation of what it is to be an agent in slavish, plantation culture. In a scientific allegory this identity claim is usually discussed in the context of theoretical models, which are either maps of one formal domain into and onto another or assign empirical sense to a theoretical term, as when straight lines in geometry are first identified with Galileo's "uniform right line" transcribed by particles and then with geodesics in the propagation of light in Einstein's theory of general relativity. Since theories are usually taken to be deductive systems, model theoretical interpretations usually borrow their interpretative structures from the vocabulary of formal systems; thus a model is said to be "a set of elements, together with relations between these elements, such that operations on these elements are also members of the set." When science is understood in a deductive, synthetic methodology, then the system's undefined predicates, such as "force," "mass," "resistance," and the like, or a Kuhnian, experimental paradigm, determines the model. Given an empirical interpretation, the model represents how the world is "seen as" through the theory. Even if we recognize that the model is only a model, theoretical entities will seem more real than the appearing facts; it really determines only how we are supposed to see them.

Bas van Fraassen, lamenting the tyranny of theory over fact that dominates post-positivistic philosophy of science, argues that while theory does not have the truth value and explanatory power claimed for it, it does give rise to "empirical substructures." These are aspects of the model which are "direct representatives of the observable phenomena." These are "structures which can be described in experimental reports we call appearances: the theory is empirically adequate if it has some model such that all appearances are isomorphic to empirical substructures of the model" (1980, 64). But the appearances are themselves interpretations, and if they are to be determined by the theoretical terms, we have a vicious, not a hermeneutical, circle. The analytic method, to which phenomenology offers a powerful extension, can establish these empirical ratios. Understood without its idealist loading, phenomenology is concerned to articulate what we already know as active, oriented beings towards world. Science is unimaginably rich and can tell us about everything except—and this is Kant's move—the presupposed archaic experience at its root wherein things are uncovered as meaningful. Science must assume this orientation. To presume that understanding's orientation is learned from theory is to disvalue and ignore the priority of already oriented *theoria* who understandingly sees things, selves, space, and time under further allegorical interpretations.

There is probably a plausible theory that establishes one's incompetence to pass judgment on anything over which one might be expected to exercise a sovereign vision. For example, some logics are not predicative and support semantic theories that deny the existence of particulars. Hume, Nietzsche, Watson, and Skinner have given the self a bad press. The reports on space or time that issue from physical theory have nothing much to do with lived space and time. All of these doctrines are convincing and powerful and have their uses, but it would be fallacious to take them as original, foundational interpretations. Doubtless the self, at least its ineliminable phenomenological perspective, has had a sufficient defense. Time has had its day, and so too will space; but what do we hear from things?

Kant saw that things must be questioned by us. We go beyond him in allowing the things to question us also. If a *thing* is only "that in which the concept of the manifold is united," is this really different from nineteenth-century positivism, Duhem or Oswald, in which things, especially unobservable things required by theory (such as electrons), were said to be mere formulae of calculation? Reading the book of nature with Kant's aid lets it appear as a punctal manifold with, on one reading, masses assigned point loci as centers of gravity by Newton's inverse square law or, on another, as analogous point charges by Coulomb's law. Using formally similar laws, the gravitational attraction and the electrical force can both be calculated. What will the thing do when acted on by both? Each of these "modes of knowledge" of an object "must agree with one another, that is, possess the unity that constitutes the concept of an object" (A 105). Since Kant's object is transcendentally constituted, one can determine the resultant force using vector algebra. This begins to look as if nature were "nothing but sensible representations incapable of existing apart from our power of representation" (A 104). Alas, the calculations don't work, exhibiting again nature's contrariness. Kant based his paradigm on experimental rather than logical procedures; in making things disclose themselves, they exhibit causal powers in which, Cartwright notes, "the Coulomb effect swamps the gravitational one, and the force that actually occurs is very different from that described by the law of gravity" (NC 1983, 5). It would be swamped in something of the same manner that reality might swamp the shopgirl's illusions of being a *Playboy* centerfold. Gravitation and electrical "natures" coexist in the thing; perhaps the laws are really founded on Duns Scotus' inseparable formal distinctions *a parte rei*. Finitude, fashioning its "own perspectives . . . imposes itself on its environment" (ANW 1938, 28–29). If the thing is to keep modes of knowledge from being "haphazard and arbitrary" (A 104), it must act from "its own perspective" in determining the outcome.[4]

Truth will not suffer if beings are let be and allegories are offered as the condition for their being understood. Allegories uncover meanings, disclosing those of the self and unconcealing those of other beings. In this day when realism seems everywhere in retreat and we are confronted with a host of conflicting theories, it begins to seem that Nietzsche's condemnation of the nihilistic "will to truth" is justified. Confronted in the human and natural sciences with conflicting promises that seem to close down, rather than open, the power and effectiveness of man, except where they lead to demonic technologies, we need to recover the reality of the thing. The surplus of meaning lies not in this mass of theory but in the thing, the inexhaustible *it*, an eruption of being into world. Truth is *aletheia*, not correspondence or coherence, though these too have their proper role. Like the gods, *it* is the source of endless myth and imagery, guardian of its mystery. Allegory may be the best shepherds of this mystery. It claims to find in one relational complex which we more or less construct from familiar materials a map for the more complex set of relata under scrutiny. Unlike symbols that direct one to the transcendent or "living metaphor" which can entrap one in language, allegory is rather off-putting; it is always stilted, always reflective, and therefore somewhat dead. Isn't this the advantage of bringing interpretations, the wayfarer's narratives and the scientist's laws, under its rubric?

I do not fully understand how narrative is transmuted into allegory and that in turn into its first-person autobiographical form, but since Peter Strawson's useful suggestion that the possibility of autobiography ("self-ascription") is the key to an understanding of what Kant means by the objective unity of consciousness, some reflections on the historical conditions for this phenomena and its possibility are in order.[5] As Hegel says, narrative is a work of reason where "the understanding runs quickly to symbol or allegory" (1975, I: 312). One's allegorical resources first become explicit when experience becomes textual and ambiguous rather than the mimetic recapitulation of a mytho-poetic formula projecting fixed possibilities, rules and roles, for interpretation and self-interpretation.

Literacy frees memory and thus self-interpretation from the burden of the remembered past characteristic of an oral culture (EAH 1963, 6–7); allegory seems to begin with self-distantiation and the reflection on meaning. Mythical memory is recollective while that of a literate culture memorializes or commemorates. Eugene Vance describes commemoration as a ritualized gesture to recover through narrative configurations in the name of a collectivity "some being or event either anterior to time or outside of time to fecundate, animate, or make meaningful a moment in the present" (1979, 377). One identifies with aspects of this memorialized past in the common struggle to preserve world against non-Being. When memory of a sacred past is preserved in a text, however, the new experiences of the more or less alienated individual who would seek his *arché* in this past require that it be allegorized to remain meaningful. For example, Hellenistic culture allegorized itself in the astral religion of Plato's *Laws*.

Suppose that, though alienated from one's tradition by cosmopolitanism and philosophical or even religious maturity, one still desires to maintain a place within in it through connection with its *arché*. Philo, cut off in Hellenistic Egypt from Palestine, transformed sacred history into a metaphysical allegory to discern and appropriate its deeper truth. The godding *YHWH*, becomes a Platonic one; history gets left out of the gnosis. Having lost *YHWH*, the living God of Abraham, Isaac, and Jacob, the God of sacred places, the possibility of mutuality (God's initiative and man's response) was also lost. The gain was the promise of a God with us, even in exile. But even this hermeneutics requires a stable culture; and when that breaks down, one must search for this metaphysical order within. Memory closes around traces of an abiding presence, the God Augustine memorialized in his *Confessions*. Later writers, such as St. Anselm, spoke of texts as food to be digested, internalized and then ruminated upon so as to release their spiritual sense. Memory as prayer and plainchant is lost to those of us who must gather a past from archeological debris, appropriately allegorized in the image of the museum or library. Memory, rather than guiding participation, becomes an onto-theological grounded system of knowledge. This image of a centered and completed system has been expressed by Umberto Eco in the *Name of the Rose*, by Flaubert in *Bouvard and Pecuchet*, and Borges in "Library of Babel." For example, the baptismal font Bouvard and Pecuchet discover in a museum has to have been a Celtic sacrificial stone which, as *arché*, provides a master pattern for history:

whence it must be concluded that the religion of the Gauls
had the same principle as that of the Jews. Their society was
well-organized . . . Some uttered prophesies, others chanted,
others taught botany, medicine, history, and literature: in
short, "all the arts of that epoch." Pythagoras and Plato were
their pupils. They instructed the Greeks in metaphysics, the
Persians in sorcery, the Etruscans in augury, and the Romans
in plating copper and trading in ham. But of this people who
dominated the world there remain only a few stones. (Cited
in ED 1979)

Meaning now belongs to a nominalizing, ahistorical understanding that
remembers principles, not its journeys nor its adverbial, participatory
arché. In returning to intuition where we are always already underway,
Kant stumbled upon the *arché* and explicated it proto-commemora-
tively in his continuity-affecting three-fold synthesis.

The autobiographical "I" which became Kant's expressive transcendentally apperceptive "I think _____" was born in the conflict
between the "I" of memory, where Monica prayed and scripture kept
repeating itself, and Augustine's own worldly desires, ambitions, and
talents that seemed to lead elsewhere; from this conflict and crossing a
new possibility of life emerges which is non-heroic and still memorial-
izable as meaningfully lived. What led him astray was not the text of
scripture by which he interpreted himself, but the ontological interpretation it was given. Augustine's Stoic and neo-Platonic tendencies led
him into memory which, as its "belly," was virtually coextensive with
mind and away from the hermeneutics of lived experience. His spiritual descendants forgot that Christ had freed us from the mimetic text,
a form of bondage; and experiencing alienation (sin), they sought pur-
ification in mystical union with the memorialized *arché*. Perhaps the
Orthodox had a better idea: they memorialized the risen, not the cru-
cified, Christ. Plato first thought this centering was cosmic (*Gor.*
503D–504E); by the time of the *Laws* he came to think it was to be
found in a strange mixture of rigid orthodoxy and playing and dancing. Play is not something a subject does; it hypostatically precipitates
the subject as it plays. The freedom of which St. Paul spoke in *Gala-
tians* is that of faith playing us.

The reappearance of the philosopheme "inner man" through
Luther, who abhorred self-absorption at the expense of a world, has
been the occasion for Cartesian excess. However, the price of its elimination must not be at the expense of its truth; if the ego must be decentered and life thought of as a unifying unity, this does not entail its
elimination. Kant thought that personal center was to be founded on
the objectified moral ideal that, in personifying virtue, serves as our

archetype. Such a disproportionate ideal cannot center. The possibilities in play had been abandoned for the will, ironically the "source" of sin: "We have no other standard for our actions than the conduct of this divine man within us [whose origin is the wise man of the Stoics], with which we compare and judge ourselves, and so reform ourselves, though we can never attain to the perfection thereby prescribed" (A 569/B 597). Products of the imagination "have an entirely different nature . . . fictional, . . . representations," which must respect "natural limitations," constantly "do violence to the completeness of the idea . . . and so cast suspicions on the good itself . . . that has its source in the idea . . . giving it the air of being a mere fiction" (A 57/B 598). Eliot epitomizes our post-Baudelairian urban landscape:

> Under the brown fog of a winter dawn,
> A crowd flowed over London Bridge, so many,
> I had not thought death had undone so many.

With rare exception, literature leaves the good to the averted faces.

A narrative structure being played out is a concrete universal; the agent appears, not as a transcendental ego, but like a dancer dancing a dance. It is not by willing or trying to dance that we dance; one dances well only by cultivating the gift of dancing and willingly and responsively letting dance happen. Oddly enough, one can't dance an allegory, though the dance may be allegorical, because it is never quite the person we are. This conflict, which goes on behind the "mask," is the condition for being a persona. Lost to the play that plays out, it becomes banal or ugly. The locus of struggle is now "between" the self and its masks. Life is rather like an allegory, something we must let play, even if we feel estranged in the playing. Augustine, for example, saw that though his life and its options were not his to own, he had to answer for it. Thus he was not something played by Manichean externalities nor was he self-defining, the illusion of Pelagianism. Though life plays through one by God's general grace, one may still experience integral personhood while being underway. One is not the always one and the same "I think _____"; this would be like the sign over a pub in the image of a tombstone from which Kant drew the title, "Perpetual Peace," but is rather the hypostasis that arises from and strives to stay abreast of, if not control, these strange powers that live us.

Concrete universals of character arise from the fusion of regulative and persuasive ideas expressed in these quasi-symbols and what is "receptively" given as our generative matrix. Narrative is to action and its immanent and transcendent ends, causes, chance, unintended consequences, and the like what logic is to the analytic method in the sciences, a way of making sense and trying to understand. We reflectively tell the story after the action, presupposing immanent and transcending ends. Analysis sets out its procedures in scientific papers as if in the give and take of dialogue, and demonstrates that action, like the *epoché*, effects the closure that lets things happen; what is unconcealed (*aletheia*), the identity of Oedipus or the red shift observed in the star's light as it passes near the eclipsed sun, is the point of narrative, if it has one, that gives it the paradigmatic form of allegory. "All concepts in general, no matter whence comes their material, are reflective; i.e. representations raised to the logical level of general applicability" (*Ak*. 23, *Reflexionen*, 2: 554). Allegory, an heir to Kantian imagination, *schema*tizes behavior to the level of general applicability and sensibilizes our concept. Kant finds his allegories in the ideal of reason that disposes us to the encyclopedic unity of science.

The point of narrative is seldom exhausted by the information it conveys or the amusement it occasions; the pattern raised to general applicability is an archetype. Though the naive Platonism of the "collective unconscious" is suspect, Carl Jung brings its interpretative theme into a useful focus:

> "archetype" is an explanatory paraphrase of the Platonic
> eidos. . . . It tells us that so far as the collective-unconscious
> contents are concerned we are dealing with archaic or—as I
> would say—primordial types, that is, with universal images
> that have existed since the remotest times. The term "collective
> representations," used by Levy-Bruhl to denote the symbolic
> figures in the primitive view of the world, could be easily ap-
> plied to the unconscious contents as well. . . . Primitive tri-
> bal lore is concerned with archetypes that have been modified
> in a certain way. . . . The archetype is essentially the uncon-
> scious content that is altered by becoming conscious and by
> being perceived, and takes its color from the individual con-
> sciousness to which it happens to appear. (1977 9:1, 4–5).

Archetypes and our relations to them, either identificatory or projective, plot possible forms of life. For all their somewhat woozy quality, archetypes are more appropriate unities for action theory than Danto's "basic acts," which are never stated within a rubric of meaning. Archetypes can be concatenated like those children's mysteries that are "written" by the reader: for example, at the bottom of page 41 you are told that if you think A did it, turn to page 45; if you think B did it, turn to page 31; and with each of these choices, new alternatives are presented. So-called basic acts do not concatenate to give a unity of action. If Oedipus were to go to Thebes, he had to walk, to lean forward and put his foot out to prevent himself from falling, and to put his foot out he had to twitch, et cetera. Within the narrative the twitch is a basic action if and only if it involves some projective and thus interpretative rubric. Events qualifying as actions or as its proper parts must fall under a narrative description of wider scope; under some other description they may not qualify. We can tell different stories or different forms of the same story, as in the synoptic gospels, of the same event and, in telling them, invoke alternative paradigms.

2. Participatory Poetics

EPISTEMOLOGY BECOMES A REFLECTIVE DISCIPLINE when Plato (unsuccessfully) defines knowledge in *Theaetetus* as right or correct opinion that can give an account of itself. In the *Gorgias* he says having *episteme,* knowledge, entails that one is certain of what is claimed to be known, knows how one knows it, and why it cannot be otherwise (454D-E). Secondly, one must be able to give a *logos,* an account, of what one knows (465A). Finally, knowing is one's mode of being (460B).[6] These criteria are usually frozen into covering laws based on certain principles under which instances are subsumed. The existential aspect is all but ignored; but if one begins here, things take on a different cast.

"Certainty" does not entail an a *priori* ground and, therefore, does not have the sense of the late Scholastic *certus.* If there are "certain things you should know," these are important truths empowering discrimination and decision. This sense of "certain" derives from the Greek *keirein* and the Latin *cernere,* "to cut," and like Aristotle's *phronesis* appeals to contextual sensitivity rather than a knowledge of principles.[7] In thinking as "dwelling" the physician understandingly participates "down to his finger tips" with the patient for the sake of his being. His account is his praxis, a "harmony of words and deeds arranged in the Dorian mode" (*Laches* 188D). He knows the standard articulations of being, what has been already cut out, and appeals to what lies beyond our words or theories, even to forms of language and procedures which, by disclosing and dealing with pathological conditions, will gather us into a participatory struggle for health. Thus, when Dr. Gendlin appeals to language to "thrust beyond what is already formed, the already cut," he is appealing to a creative usage that takes us beyond lexicons and structuralism's binary pairs.

Oliver Sacks, the neurologist, says his shift to understandingly participating with others was occasioned by reading Leibniz and talking with W. H. Auden, the poet. He was working with encephalitic patients "awakened" after years of "sleep" through the administration of L-DOPA and was deeply moved by the response of the patients to their sickness . . . what one studied was not just disease or pathology, but people strug- gling to adapt and survive. This too was realized by . . . Ivy McKenzie: 'The physician is concerned (unlike the naturalist) . . . with a single organism, the human subject, striving to preserve its identity in adverse circumstances.' In perceiving this, I became something more than a naturalist (without, however, ceasing to be one). There evolved a new concern, a new bond: that of commitment to the patients, the individu- als under my care. Through them I would explore what it was like to be human, to stay human, in the face of unimaginable adversities and threats . . . my central study and concern became identity—their struggle to maintain identity—to ob- serve this, to help that, and, finally, to write this. All this was at the junction of biology and biography. (OS 1987, xxi)

"Thinking" is less a matter of judging, asserting, and so determining the determinable as "dwelling" with beings in sensibility. This sense of participatory understanding leads away from *arché* as a timeless, if not eternal, founding presence or principle towards its temporal form, the originary event of Being in which the effeminated between gives and lets develop epochal beings or unconceals Being and so founds a tradition within which this meaning may be commemorated.

We perceive ourselves among these actualities as an always novel object (B 68), even if it is the hand that just drew or the voice that just spoke (B 131, 135).[8] The token event that "just happened," even if it is same (type), is a novel accretion and is never merely same. In any case, the experience is always new, never a settled facticity nor a mere instance from a stock of possibilities. Life is creative. But this power is lost to nominal understanding. Since first person expressions and avowals are temporally, epistemically, and ontologically prior to re- ports about them, then the claims of phenomenology, especially those in the philosophical and human sciences, which make an evidential appeal to a human intuition, are clearly prior to mythical Parmenidian ideals of subjectless objectivity. Though as a regulative and even moral ideal objectivity is indispensable, when this image of the perspectivally invariant "well-rounded sphere" is assigned a legislative role and its derivative, phenomenological roots are ignored, then it generates most of the serious problems we have with minds and bodies, faith and rea- son, freedom and determinism, and the like. Isn't it time to look other- wise than with sightless eyes?[9] Why not look and see?

But the eye that comes ancient to its task will look and see more if has learned the secrets of Kant's schematism. In his *Dialogues on the Two New Sciences,* Galileo turned away from Aristotelian descriptions, which lead only to classifications based on observed properties, with the suggestion that we follow Plato's advice and begin with mathematics, "measuring the measurable and seeking to render measurable what is immeasurable." Plato assumes that there is a congruence between the second (actual objects) and third (understanding and its hypotheses) levels of the divided line, thereafter the paradigm for what it is to know and how this is related to powers or faculties. On the third level (*dianoia*), the Being (*idea*) of the actual objects of the second level is intended hypothetically through mathematics (*Rep.* 510C–511A). This intention yields the standard form of scientific allegory, mapping things onto number by measurement, and has its roots in the Pythagorean discovery of the nature of harmony.

We can imagine Pythagoras in his garden, picking up his instrument, and breaking off bits of the end of a twig until it could be laid along each string an integral number of times; the twig : string :: unity : *x*. The solutions generated for *x* form an harmonic proportion, 6 : 8 :: 9 : 12. The heard sounds and their musical modes, Lydian, Ionic, Dorian, or Phrygian, are lost forever; yet what he disclosed at a particular time in a particular place was true within Pythagorean harmonics for all times and places. All times and places? Though the full import was not clear until Galileo's denial of the diversity of lunar and sublunar laws, the numbers presence a homogeneous world in mensurational acts. When the metaphors propose a harmonic proportion, the hermeneutical "is" becomes definitional and number is the truth of being. A metaphor of measurement engenders a proportional literalism, a "theory," that seems to give itself out as the truth about the actual object.

While *techné* is both an activity and a means of production, it is also an intellectual virtue and prototype for understandingly dwelling-with. In both Plato and Aristotle it is a paradigm for knowing, through its causes for Aristotle and for Plato in its manner of disclosure. A god or a worker who intends to make something first has it in mind as a "sighted presence" (*Rep.* 596B; MH 1982, 106–12). Undoubtedly Plato gave us the ocular metaphysics that entails the spectator view of knowing. "The soul is like the eye . . ." (*Rep.* 508D). Thus it was relatively easy to subject *theoria*'s object to the requirements of theory, especially after dialectic and its models were replaced by logic and the open became subjectivity. In *Charmides,* as was shown in an earlier discussion, Plato argues against associating knowing with theory in the epistemic sense; participation in the later dialogues is a non-foundational account that should be of interest to a "postmodern" era.[10]

That the senses are already doxic modes seems evident from the status given them in the later myths of the sun and line in *Republic* VI.

Plato and Aristotle assume their reflexivity. We have seen how Levinas opens us to enjoyment as their mode of being. The senses are not sufficient for knowledge proper, since such terms of reflective judgment as being, same, other, and the like are never perceived (*Theaet.* 186B–187A); but as soon as it is said that the senses do not reflect, as is the case with St. Thomas, then we are on the way to a disjunction among faculties; Kant's blind percepts and empty concepts are "two powers or capacities [which] cannot exchange their function" (A 51/B 75). Of course Kant restores these doxic modalities by means of transcendental synthesis, but that is a high price to pay and ignores what is already apparent, that beings are meaningful without being thought. Aesop's dog with the bone reflected, even if mistakenly. Unless we are already always oriented in sense so that we know here and there, now and then, and can discriminate sames and others, no conceptual map will give us our bearings in a common world. Maps overcome distance rather than create its possibility. Isn't it the business of the sophist to disorient us so as to make us easy prey to this or that ideology, so often founded on a reflection that gathers all into its scope? When *doxa* is taken as mere opinion, rather than that which appears, we are rootless and manipulable. Even if the difficulties in an unmediated self-relation can be overcome, which is doubtful, there is a greater difficulty. If knowing is directedness to what is unconcealed to that knowing, then a man who knew "only knowledge without any knowledge of health or justice" would never know whether one who claimed this knowledge had it or not (*Char.* 170B). Criteria lie in *theoria*'s praxis, not in what one has in one's head. Rhetoric can implant an opinion in one's soul, but its rightness (*ortho*) is shown in its manner of directing acts, in the identity of words and deeds and the power and orientation it gives to practice. Even if this ruling science, not the practitioner of the art, is the judge, of what use would it be without knowledge of the good? (171D–174C). Rhetoric, especially the rhetoric of origins, and narrative descriptions of actions have made ostentatious the priority of the phenomenological and ontological sense of *doxa*. Now the question is, can one legitimate these intuitive claims to scientific objectivity and exhibit its ontological possibility? Phenomenology's answer to the first question is yes, while the second finds its answer within analysis, the way of pointing something out to others.

Kant retained an inflexible and nominalized faculty concept of mind; "the senses," "the understanding," "the imagination." What it means to have an understanding of a rainbow is, for example, to be able to explain how it occurred through climatic conditions and the quantifiable laws of optical refraction that explain the mechanism of the display of colored light. Though accounting for its occurrence (A 45/B 63), they can not tell us what color really is. Kant (who by his own qualitative physics was in a position to know better) will say that color "does not belong to the objective determinations" of the colored entity but is only "a modification of the sense of sight" (A 28). Objective determinations are, minimally, spatial and, according to the Axioms of Intuition, are accessible independently of primary qualities. Plato's thesis about the relation of color to shape has been experimentally confirmed, however, for without color, moving shapes would not be perceived.[11]

Husserl allows us to restore sense to sense. According to his "Principle of All Principles," "every presentive intuition is a legitimizing source of cognition, that everything originarily (so to speak, in its 'personal' actuality) offered to us in 'intuition' is to be accepted simply as what it is presented as being, but also only within the limits in which it is presented there" (EH 1982, 44). Phenomena present themselves meaningfully, even if at too dear a price. Phenomenology claims intuitive access to the things themselves, but too often these things seem to her critics to be psychic objectifications to be explained by genetic psychology. In replying to the charge that an imagined flute playing centaur is a psychical product, Husserl says that

> Obviously the centaur itself is nothing psychical; it exists
> neither in the soul nor in consciousness, nor does it exist any-
> where else; the centaur is indeed "nothing," it is wholly
> "imagination"; stated more precisely, the mental process of
> "imagining" is the imagining of a centaur. To that extent the
> "supposed-centaur," the centaur phantasied, certainly belongs
> to the mental process itself. But one also should not confuse
> just this mental process of imagining with what is imagined
> by it as imagined. As a consequence, in spontaneous abstract-
> ing it is also not the essence that is generated but instead the
> consciousness of the essence, and the situation for this is that
> . . . an obviously originary representative consciousness of
> an essence (ideation) is in itself and necessarily spontaneous,
> whereas spontaneity is extra essential to the sensuously presen-
> tive . . ." (*ibid.* 43)

Even if sense comes always already interpreted and the concept of intuition is cloudy, do we not sometimes know the difference between consciousness as originarily presentive of, for example, a flute-playing centaur, and as spontaneously presentive, as when a musical man and a horse seen to be moving as one? The difference lies in the monstrative route one required to arrive at each; one should appreciate Husserl's non-psychological approach. Presentation is "closed to mind"; an intentional object can be thought without thinking about its status in thought. By seeming to take the idealist route, Husserl frees us from some of its snares and traps; and by denying mental status to form, allows us to grasp it in self-showing meaningful things. Is the intention of thought to Being satisfied with this result? Kant did not think that it was. He understood his task to be that of raising metaphysics to the status of a certain, complete, and discursively clear science; and though he founded phenomenology, his real interest lay in ontology. This overriding concern is expressed in the very beginnings of the *Critique* and *Prolegomena*. Thought transcended its own immanent contents since, as we have tried to show, its intention to the transcendental object is incapable of empirical fulfillment and is structurally prior to experience (JS 1980, 1). That beings can be understood is dependent on the fact that Being can be thought. Moreover the intention to the transcendental object was the condition for transient, worldly significance.

In Kant's noetic understanding of Being, which may be roughly identified with *nous*, the fourth and highest level of Plato's divided line, it does not follow that the meanings or senses of Being are ever fulfilled. Thought provides the transcendental architecture for understanding, but understanding depends on contingent sensibility; and except in morals or symbolic presentation, one can never rise above this same sensibility to reason. "The determination of my existence in time is possible only through the existence of actual things which I perceive outside me" (B 275), for the "I think . . ." passes into act only on reception of a manifold. Because I am finite I am temporal, not conversely, and my finitude rests on this intention to an actually infinite God. Thus with Spinoza we can say that all determination is negation, resting on a positive, infinite ground. The time I generate is the constructivistic analogue of the time which appeared in the physico-theological *Dissertation:* time is "a unique and unchangeable infinite in which all things are and endure which is the phenomenal eternity of the general cause" (*Diss.* 410). When he discovered that one could only think, not represent, the actual infinite, then what had been, with space, "the substrates of the intellect" (405) became that to which all our concepts are subject (A 99). With this last point we must agree.[12]

3. Romances of Nature

THE TEXT METAPHOR can illuminate some issues in the philosophy of science; for example, the "externality" of meaning. The Romantic imposed meaning and then faced the crisis which occurs when one's allegories are mistaken for reality and reality no longer seems to work. Something similar occurs in science. The competing allegories overdetermine the natural text, and the result is that the drive to unity and order threatens to flounder on relativities, "mere interpretation" or the abandonment of reason for pragmatic success.

In its hypothetical-deductive form, the analytic method is frequently criticized for the corrigibility of confirmation sentences and the threat of an infinite regress this seems to entail. Popper's method of refuting conjectures suffers from a similar defect. The inductive and idealistic alternatives are even less attractive. Natural science has a place for induction; but it has no place for induction's martyr, Bacon, who weighed this empiricist thesis towards nominalism and thus contingency so that it cannot capture the necessities in its concept formations. Kant thought that only if one posited being as nominal essence by synthesis, could one meet these stronger analytic requirements. The thesis that observation is theory-laden, as in the versions of Kuhn and Quine, is Kantian; but in its paradigm or pragmatic form it lacks an ontological ground and invites Whitehead's quip that "nature is the conjecture and science the dream." Those who founded science never had to face these problems. Observation within mathematical parameters invited the treatment of all phenomena as universal instantiations; universal quantifiers can be reapplied since nature is written in the language of universal mathematics that, in turn, makes manifest the *eidos* instantiated by its Author. Aside from the fact that rationalism could not accommodate statistical inference, it totters and falls before Kant's thesis that percepts and concepts differ in kind. We seem left with subsumptive theories. However, these suffer from the view that meaning is externally assigned to sense. This issue is nicely put by Goethe in one of his *Reflexion:*

> It is a great difference whether the poet searches for the particular to go with the universal or whether he sees the universal in the particular. From the former there arises only allegory, where the particular is only an example, an instance of the universal; the latter is actually the true nature of poetry; it utters the particular without thinking the universal or indicating it. Whoever now vitally grasps this particular acquires the universal at the same time, although not then aware of it, or only later. (No. 279)

Goethe thought this "vital grasp" was the origin of the symbol which, in this romantic formulation, derives from Kant's discussion in the last section of the *Critique of Aesthetic Judgment* (351–54). Like the symbol, the *schema* and its allegorical extension allows us to see "the universal in the particular."

Subsumptive judgments see the "particular only in the universal" (A 714/B 742). Allegory avoids subsumption by the reflective methods of theoretical science and gives the formal structure of a large class of interpretations. But the immediate issue before us is Kant's own rejection of the externality of subsumptive judgment. How can the universal in thought and the universal in things be one and the same without recourse to rationalism? The subsumptive view finds powerful support in the analytic method of the *Prolegomena*. On the other hand, the *schema*tic sensibilization of concepts in the first *Critique* enables one to meet up with a meaningful individual through the imagined particular. Wittgenstein's authority, great as it is, should not lead us to bifurcate imagination and understanding: "It is no more necessary to the understanding of a proposition that one should imagine anything in connection with it, than that one should make a sketch from it" (LW 1968, 396). Allegory is embedded in certain propositions, solicitations to see things in a map that extends imaginative *schema*. What is for judgment the "particular in the universal" is through the scheme of a concept the "universal in the particular" (A 714/B 742). The individual is intended through the image, the roundness "thought in the pure geometrical concept of the circle" can be intuited in a "plate" (A 139/B 177). Conversely, transcendental synthesis of the figurative or productive imagination assures us that the intuited individual will have a categorial form. The universal, the predicate in apophanic judgements of recognition, is not attached to the data by external reflection. A meaningful object is brought under a determination for which it is patient. All observation is therefore an interpretative "seeing something as something." Even if the resulting judgments are corrigible, Kant is able to avoid a regress. How? The "seen as something" is the interpreted empirical object, while the "something seen" is the ontological basis of this interpretation, the transcendental object always and everywhere one and the same. Any empirical datum will already be understood as a categorial aspect of this object. Kant could say that nature is a text that articulates the transcendental object. Who could be satisfied with this today? Who can buy this ontology? But at least we can assume the meaningfulness of sense and, except perhaps in the higher reaches of quantum physics, the irrelevance of subsumption. Once we grant this, the theory of concepts and percepts can yield to a theory of allegory and its related tropes.

Kant recognized that orientation towards the world is an *a priori* truth. Though his *a priori* account is unsatisfactory, for it is contingent on neurological function, orientation is necessary. E. coli knows which way to move and the appropriate way to get there. Each creature bodies forth its projects in environmental situations pregnant with meaning that still have to be articulated, worked out. *Theoria* orients to a world, not merely an environment, by understanding. The concept is never itself an object; *one* is out to make sense of beings, not express propositions. That a concept can be itself an object in, say, a formal calculus was possible only after its isolation by the Stoics and the continuing interest in Lull-like *ars combinatoria.* This dimension is usually called reflection. Kant says that in reflection we are "conscious of the relation of given representations to the different sources of knowledge" (A 260/B 316); and though he says that it is necessary to distinguish the cognitive faculty to which concepts belong, he denies that it is a source of knowledge and criticizes Leibniz for failing to observe this restriction. Theoretical knowledge is reflective.

When theory gets the upper hand and proliferates alternatives, then we reflect ourselves out of existence in the resulting overdetermination of empirical meaning. Analysis is the asceticism of the intellect, succeeding by the elimination, not addition, of significance. But analysis is said to be circular. The book of nature appears to be a page of a medieval manuscript, a tissue of many texts and glosses, that must be purged of excess if any one meaning is to be established. This fixity is first given in allegory, the most common form of reflection. We reflect in the proper sense when we critically examine allegories recognized as such.

Scott Buchanan, who has inspired my thinking on allegory, says: "The Cinderella story is in the most primitive folklore, is exploited in the cult of mariology and is now in the current American magazine story, just as it is a pattern running in a phrase of music in the head of the tired stenographer or shop girl. Is it a story, or is it a metaphysic of morals?" (1975, 69). Of course our allegories lack truth value even if they are conditions for *aletheia.* They may inhibit the course of life. Numbers, like characters in a plot, have a life of their own. Plato spoke of these offspring of our rhetorical arts as our children who, in living their own lives beyond us, grant us a kind of immortality.

What conclusions we can draw from this discussion? First, insofar as nature is a book, the initial level of signification is found in non-conceptual, sense recognition of significance (ANW 1921, 86–90).[13] E. coli, having no linguistic skills and no self-consciousness, nevertheless recognizes and zig-zags up a nutritional gradient or swims straight away from a poison. Aesop's dog recognized a bone in the water. The pacific islander navigates by recognizing through a waves' form its source in a particular groundswell hundreds of miles away. Do they read nature's book? Are these "recognitions in a concept?" No. They think in distinctions, as Gendlin says.

Unlike these natural signs, language is mostly made up of arbitrary signs making up formal fields of combinatorial differences, whose perceptual form, reference, and meaning are, unlike symbols, radically other. There is a third class of signs, which we may think of as quasi-symbols, where the sign presents its meaning and leaves its reference dangling. Personifications are an example. We know what *Zeus* means, but its reference is indeterminate; many could bear his trace. Mathematical signs are such quasi-symbols. Use roman numerals to determine the square root of MDCLXVI and you will know what I mean. What does number number? A character within a certain linguistic game?

Allegory uses quasi-symbols, universals of character, as speculative predicates. Allegory is already rooted in the interpretative structure of those projections which release beings to meaning. For the most part, however, differential fields of arbitrary signifiers are conditions of disclosure and their free play opens up an infinite power of signification. As Paul De Man says, "to the extent the sign is independent with regard to the objective, natural properties towards which it points and instead posits properties by means of its own power, the sign illustrates the power of the intellect to 'use' the perceived world for its own purposes, to efface its properties and to put others in its place" (1982, 767). This effacement is often at the expense of natural signs. Analogies (to keep things simple) implicit in speculative predication establish a possible mapping and thus an allegorical interpretation that determines a more or less univocal range of predicates; participatory *theoria* has a theory to project. It can claim truth insofar as this projection submits to the beings released for meaning.

Walter Benjamin recognized that allegory, unlike the symbol, is essentially a historical form of understanding. The Baroque painters often represented the nativity within the ruins of an old world; the past is dead. It is alive only in its form if form can be saved from time. The setting focuses the nativity through which even stones take on a new life, as the Roman stones took on a new life in Justinian's St. Sophia. The Platonic tradition tends to place a supersensible world beyond this as the place of form. We bear the traces of the God because we followed him in the world beyond this. Mathematics, that symbol of our pilgrim status, has been thought to give us proof of our true home among eternal forms. But of course allegory is not just history; it is the "spiritual sense" of history, a manner of recovering and appropriating from the texts left by the past an everlasting possibility. Because the interpretative language of nature is mathematics, scientific allegories pass for eternal truths. The timeless, impersonal "is" is the artificer of eternity. Can we give a theory of mathematical quasi-symbols that retain the "spiritual sense" of the intelligible world?

4. Making Sense

CHARLES TAYLOR SAYS THE CRITERION of a good interpretation is that it makes sense; but too often the sense made comes from a gnostic supplement beyond the text, the Platonic idea realm, the naturalism against which Husserl rebelled, the Kantian ego, or a theory of mentalistic concepts contingently expressed and communicated. The only way to make sense of anything is to begin with the assumption that it is already meaningful and, if it is a philosophical theory, generates meaning and the possibility of its truth conditions.

When he was younger, Socrates says, he "sought the causes of things: Is the growth of animals the result of the putrefaction which the hot and cold principles suffer. . . . Is blood the element with which we think, or the air or the fire—or perhaps nothing of the kind—but the brain may be the originating power of the perceptions of hearing and sight, and memory and opinion may come from them?" (*Phaedo* 96B). To seek out causes experimentally would be to explain the phenomena of life and mind through nomological necessities. Socrates admitted that he got nowhere with his search. He could not explain why he was in prison facing death by showing "that I sit here because my body is made up of bones and muscles; and the ones are hard . . . and have joints that divide them, and the muscles are elastic . . . so that through the contraction or relaxation of the muscles I have been able to bend my limbs, and that is why I am sitting here" (98C-D). Knowing far more about Socrates' physiology than he did, we should recognize that it would be silly to pursue this mechanistic theology. These idols are always changing, but the point remains the same. Walking as a happening, though much that happens could be explained, is a meaningless sequence of law-like changes of scientific objects occupying successive loci in space and time; and from them no one could ever understand what happened, what Socrates as a new Theseus was intending to do and why his projects led him to die in the god's service. We know why he left Euthyphro and walked to the Assembly without knowing anything about how he did it. Whatever causes were operative —the gravity by which he continuously fell and the way he, by outstretching his feet, checked his falling—were enabling conditions bodied forth in his acts; otherwise he could not have walked. Even if its meaning is endlessly debatable, we know he acted as he understood things to be.

Where is one to draw the line between reasons and causes?: wherever recognition and thus interpretation is seen as relevant to behavior. Interpretation orients one's self. Behavior expresses this understanding. Action is contingent on recognition, on being able to make sense. When, however we understand a phenomenon causally, with von Wright in the logic of necessary and sufficient conditions or with Hempel and Nagel in covering laws, intentionality, making sense of _____, seems irrelevant.

What is involved in "making sense of something," seeing it as meaningful? Perhaps we can see this through an imaginative variation, essential to Husserl's eidetic reduction, that has recently been advanced by Harvard philosophers. If a severed brain were kept alive in a nutritional vat and its severed nerve stumps could be appropriately stimulated by an operator, could that brain have normal experiences of embodiment and never know it did not have a body? In this clever retelling of Descartes' fable of the malign genius, understanding is not an ontological feature of man and that his orientation towards world is a contingent result of stimuli.

Unless that brain were wired through the experimenter's eyes and body, how could it ever judge how it stood to its itinerary, express and change its orientation to other beings, and interpret and question its interpretations in a background dialectic between acquired skill and chance that is always going on whether we are aware of it or not? The only meaning the brain's sensations could have would be to the operator, an "I see a red apple" display or printout when he turned a certain dial. Unless the vatted brain could show a variety of responses or no response at all to a given stimulus, there is no reason to believe that it has the faintest glimmer of consciousness; but if one got all these responses, wouldn't the normal interpretation be that the apparatus was defective? Orientations depend on all sorts of medial processes, each making its own circumspective interpretation. In walking I shift my balance to go uphill; I never know this as such. The interpretations we make in walking depend on countless sub-systems, some molecular. We interpret in our hands when we play the piano, in our feet when we walk. The body, Whitehead said, has its wisdom. The context of interpretation is always narrative, something like walking towards taking place in a world. Motility, as Kant saw, is a transcendental condition for interpretation, for putting things meaningfully together and questioning both ourselves and what we encounter, even if the testing is unconscious.

IX

Space

....

1. A Place in Which to Dwell

KANT'S FIRST CRITIQUE appropriately begins with space and time as the necessary conditions for shared things, the most general conditions for being underway. Except for the starry heavens, the moral law within, and wallpaper designs he found beautiful, his horizons were those of scientific naturalism. Duns Scotus' wayfarer had a different destiny, yet he too believed that the way, the *hodos*, led among things and their powers. Though his itinerary was formed by liturgy and Kant's by laboratory procedures, these divergent ways presuppose a familiarity with world and number; if either is to be understood and justified, we must begin where each began, in a common world of time, space, persons, and things. Exploring the common places where children play with one another and their parents founds other interpretations, however remote from the commonplace they may be.

Kant began with space and time, not with the thing and its formalities, as the necessary conditions for the presence of anything; in beginning with these inseparable formalities of any intuited *ens,* the thing (*res*) became a homogeneous object instancing a law by which it was constituted. In his originary spatial synopsis, Kant offers the image of a punctal manifold, a potential for combination, through a transcendental motility given in a postulate, an *a priori* rule of *praxis.* Space is then an oriented potential for motion and rest defined, relative to the *a priori,* knower-in-general, as a set of homogeneous and isotropic loci describable by triplets of real numbers, the locii of mass points characterizing a gravitational field. Nor is this far from urban space in our decaying cities which has, no doubt, induced the nostalgia for another and more maternal sense of space. As Henri Lefebvre says of Bachelard's dreams, which "he distinguishes from the representations of space as developed by science . . . the dwelling passes everywhere for a special, sacred, quasi-religious and, in fact, almost absolute space. . . . The contents of the House have an almost ontological dignity . . . drawers, chests and cabinets are not far removed from their natural analogues . . . namely the basic figures of nest, shell, corner, roundness and so on. In the background stands [almost uter-

293

ine] nature. . . . The relationship between Home and Ego . . . borders on identity" (1991, 121). We have already explored the identity of home and thinking in Heidegger's "dwelling-thinking" (MH 1971b, 160) and, more to the point, experienced through Levinas this maternal sense of home. Home is the place of encounter and significance in which we meet and work together in making or passing time and from which we egress to school or workshop. Home is the nest cherished by lovers, the creative originary.

The possibility of this encounter, rather than being in space, makes possible near and far, that is, space. However we define this condition, with Heidegger as the "between" (MH 1982, 220) or Levinas as "proximity," it is the relation to an Other through whom desire for this or that is poetically transformed into Desire to do justice to the other and Others. This is not space lighted by calculative understanding, but rather the region within which "poetically we dwell" lightened by the desire for the Good. We have now moved full circle from the expressively constituted space and time of a private synopsis to the time and space of dwelling and encounter. In the one case we were concerned to constitute and assimilate alterity; in certain primordial encounters almost the opposite happens. No longer is the dwelling in space; it constitutes this possibility because it is the life-giving between, an orienting here, *chora*. In Patristic theology, the "economic" nature of God which pertains to the household, covers the theme of Spirit in the world. God who is everywhere nevertheless needs a dwelling, a "place for the placeless," which introduces a feminine component into divinity. The child is in communion with divinity and the vulva is the paradigmatic place of entry and egress, life and death. A familiar version of this theme begins with El's temple-building in Canaan's indigenous Ugaritic mythology which the Hebrews take up in the Jerusalem temple of David and Solomon; even the sky-god *YHWH* needs a dwelling. In sections of Tibet, religious practice centers around providing the god a house and then taking him about in it from village to village with which he has kinship relations. Our fundamental modes of experience center on dwelling with others among goods, instrumental and intrinsic. Heidegger notes that when *Bauen*, "building," speaks in its original sense, "to dwell,"

> it also says how far the nature of dwelling reaches. That is, *bauen, buan, bhu, beo* are our word *bin* in the versions *ich bin*, 'I am,' *du bist*, 'you are.' . . . What then does *ich bin* mean? The old word *bauen*, to which *bin* [and so too for the English 'been'] belongs, answers . . . I dwell, you dwell. The way in which you and I am, the manner in which we humans are on the earth, is dwelling. . . . It also means at the same

time to cherish and protect, to preserve and care for . . . both
modes of building [as cultivating and erecting] is dwelling.
(MH 1971b, 147)

Plato associates nurture and care with the place granting receptacle.[1]
    If the Good, as Plato said, is beyond Being and being known
(*Rep.* 509A-B), then possibilities for being as seen in the Good are,
though concrete possibilities entailed in dwelling, indefinable in terms
of, and therefore transcendent to, its immanent necessities. The place
of return and renewal that empowers us to enter public space is moral,
not merely physical. Charles Wesley asks the Holy Spirit "to fix his
dwelling in our hearts," but the dwelling is granted, not by the Spirit
or even the Good, but by some medial and feminine variant of the
receptacle, the Good's supplement, which is also beyond being.[2] In
two of the fourteenth-century mosaics in the Church of the Chora in
Istanbul, Mary, the Mother of God, is called "the place of the placeless." She was also represented—though now only fragments remain—
as the Zoodochos Pege. In this icon, which seems to have originated in
the monastery of the same name just outside the walls of Istanbul during the reign of Justinian, the Virgin giving the placeless place is the
Platonic receptacle generating of itself "living waters."[3] She is the paradigm enunciative function that makes possible community, communion, and communication, that is, participation. She brings us near
things as they are intrinsically and as significant. Near or far depend
on how meaning is conferred, how beings are intended in this or that
context-making intentionality (EB 1983, 33–36). Our capacity to encounter one another in playful, and therefore medial, relations is the
gift of our parents, especially our mothers; this is the context forming
intentionality at the root of all spatial meanings. The threshold of
each place, which is as egocentric as its temporal A-series analogue,
seems to determine its appropriate conditions of egress, and yet that
into which we transcend seems common.
    We are thrown, as Heidegger would say, into interpretative con-
texts. The familiar place where Socrates cut stone would confuse us;
but imagine a Socrates who had to teach Meno's slave by computer
graphics! Space is culturally constant, same irrespective of the sorts of
instrumental interpretations and the kinds of activity it supports.
These have less to do with measurement than with seeing things as in
place or missing, clearly or obscurely, in intimacy or as remote. This
common space must sustain a vast variety of interpretations, but none
would have much to do with the space you might read about in the
article on "geometry" in the *Encyclopedia of Philosophy*. With the
multitude of geometrical interpretations available, to say nothing of

the n-dimensional vector spaces of algebra, non-metrical geometry, and the eleven dimensions of Paul Davis's super-force, it is difficult to say what space is and which geometry describes it. According to Ernst Cassirer, even sacred space supports an indefinite set of interpretations (1972, 212-93). Somewhere between these mythical and scientific projections lies common space or place where one learned to play.

Possibilities that inseminate receptivity and constitute a new actuality are specific to times and places, the perspective of dwelling when seen in the Good's light. Home is where the mother gives us a self, talks us into being and saying through play. In the oral erotic phase in Freud's myth concerning ego maturation, the primally narcissistic infant interjects the world, assimilates its alterities by projectively investing them with his fantasies. At this point the mother, lovingly interacting and playing with the child, begins the long process of leading him or her out of the appropriative, egocentric self into an objective world. D. W. Winnicott, with Melanie Klein a founder of the English school of object-oriented psychoanalysis, proposes that the "transitional objects" to which the mother opens the infant in the "transitional space" of play mediate between private fantasy and concrete worldly relations. This "between" is granted by the proximity through which the infant transcends towards a world and is created in play by personal address, in this case by "shifter" words such as "you," "I," "here," and "there." Through the playful, teasing motility and address of the mother, primary process fantasies are projected onto real inassimilable objects, pacifiers, beads, or the mother's hands, whose movements the infant can neither anticipate nor control; expressivist projections are replaced by intentions that become concretized and oriented in real relations (DWW 1986).[4] Kant said that in the concept of the object the field of sense in united. Doesn't this begin when the mother's "isn't this nice" or "isn't this pretty" introduces a proto-contemplative attitude in which the object becomes significant in its own right? Euclid's is the only geometry that interprets the object-oriented play world of very young children in which the object is self-congruent, and thus recognizable, in reflection, rotation, and transport. Through the mother, child, and toy we learn how things express themselves and gather on into a world. The meaning of our turning away from expressive selves and the apparatus of representational thinking to expressive things that gather us into a world beyond Being lighted by the Good should now be becoming clarified. As in most cases, one begins at home.

Home is where things are set up in ways that facilitate interiority, nourishment, healing, reflection, succor, and, above all, the presence of the other. Dwelling, the place and the verb, refers to shelter, nurture, welcoming and returning to oneself through the presence of the feminine. Dwelling is *chora,* the identificatory place of origin, the *arché.* Dwelling creates the space into which we egress as meaningful, the space of projects and the world towards which, through these, we transcend. If we are fortunate, home is where we learn with Dante that love and justice are the axes of the world. Through the grace of others, transactional space becomes, in Emmanuel Levinas's term, "proximity," or moral space.

Empowered by home, we go out to the other, not as Kant's autonomous law-giver beyond price, but rather as to the beloved, to the child, orphan, and the widow through whose need I am addressed by the Other, the Good beyond Being. In proximity possibility will also be feminized, apportioned to growth and nurture rather than to the masculine will's technical domination. The *arché* receptacle that gives beings dwelling, a place for emergence and nurture, is medial. Though perhaps soliciting and accepting the gift of her supplement, the *logos,* and thereby letting the creature emerge and be, she is also beyond Being.[5]

"Dwelling" stands expressivism or so-called representational thinking on its head. Doubtless the thinker makes himself (*Bildung*) by objectifying himself. For example, in Marx's account of labor, one objectifies oneself in making an object that calls upon all the resources of creative imagination, thought, and motor skill, and then through this objectified self-experience he returns to himself. In representational thinking one *schema*tizes the world through the expressive power of a concept, as in Frege or Kant, and intends the objects thereby posited, a gesture familiar in Fichte or Quine, through the existential "is." By so constituting the object, one has power over it—and conversely. Doubtless there is a proper role for appropriation, but dwelling gives us self and deconstructs its care structure, thus placing me in the accusative case for the other's sake.

Dwelling is the place of the empowering Good that surrounds me from which I am and am underway through participation in activities and relations towards a concrete, human world. A dwelling, according to Emmanuel Levinas, is among the ready-at-hand features which, beyond its use, makes possible the intimacy and reflective interiority that is the "from which" of transcendence towards world (EL 1985, 152–54). Interiority is, as we could say with Kant, the "mineness" of the world; but this mineness is not *a priori* but is rather a gift of language and history; it is the access condition on world. Radical reflection, the power to give or withhold assent to the Good which is mine alone (CT 1989, 137), is also, thanks to gift of the other's intimacy (EL 1985, 157), the "latent birth of a world." Connexity lies in Platonic world-engendering eros when—though Plato almost forgot to mention it (*Sym.* 210A)—lovers cross and mingle in the between, the place of lovers (LI 1984, 33), just as love constitutes the capacity to discriminate and respond to the intense and fragile beauty in all things. Home welcomes, and its welcome, the theme of a quest and not inner sense, is the condition for transcendence and return.

A dwelling "is not situated in the objective world, but the objective world is situated in relation to my dwelling." Though I can shut myself up in a house, it is a home only when it lets the other be near. Here I can meet the other face to face and situate myself with respect to the non-I, the furnishings and possessions we enjoy and from which we live. This began when, face to face with my mother and through her loving expression and her words, I discovered a world in playing with her. Thus dwelling, a private, intimate, nurturing place to which one may return in rest is also that from which I enter a world, not in subjective representation, but through "the intentionality of concretization." Levinas goes on to say that "consciousness of the world is always consciousness through the world. Something of that world seen is an organ or an essential means of vision; the eye, the eyeglass, the light, the lamps, the book, the school. . . . Civilization refers to the incarnation of consciousness and habitation, to existence proceeding from the intimacy of a home, the first concretization" (EL 1985, 153). Concretion is the antithesis of expressivist objectification: "Interiority concretely accomplished by the home, the passage to act—the *energy*—of recollection in the dwelling, opens up new possibilities which the possibility of recollection did not contain analytically but which, being essential to its *energy*, are manifest only when it unfolds" (154). Contrary to Plato, recollection does not, Levinas says, entail a "perilous landing" after having been cast forth from "intersiderial space" (152). With perhaps a glance towards Heidegger, he says that "to dwell is not the simple fact of the anonymous reality of being cast into existence as a stone one casts behind oneself; it is a recollection, a coming to oneself, a retreat home with oneself as a land of refuge, which answers to a [medial] hospitality, an expectancy, a human welcome" (156). We are incarnate participants in world through dwelling, through the intimacy and feminine gentleness to which we can retire for the sake of recollecting on ourselves, our possibilities and the situation (154). "Recollection" as radical reflexion should replace "reflection." "Welcome in itself—the feminine being" (157).[6]

2. A Phenomenology of Space

SPATIAL INTERPRETATIONS ARE ORIENTED with respect to bodily *schemata*. There is a straight-awayness from here, where "here" is the congruence between a plane between the eyes and one

running through the body from the shoulders to the legs, thereby
aligning our motility with what we see and, as Descartes noticed in his
Dioptrics, the place of our members. Studies of brain damage indicate
that this is a complex process of automatic interpretation. Kant understood orientation through the *schema* of the body and thought that
this was *a priori;* but since even chicks are born oriented towards their
environment and this can be lost or impaired by disease or injury,
orientation is an original interpretation contingent on the functioning
of the automatic nervous system. This was Descartes' approach.

Granted orientation, next in importance is "context-forming"
intentionality. The relatively disembodied epistemic spectator must be
dismissed and "near" and its conditions understood within the phenomenological context of participation. The quality by which a chalk-
board is perceived as green, slate, or a molecular lattice is itself an
interpretation of a physical process involving the physical event, biological events in nerve, eye, and brain, transmissional conditions, and
the like, as well as theoretical projections. The quality is primary
within a context; when I want to know the board's color, the context
of common experience determines a near from which it is green. The
desire to know its shape or its microscopic structure lets it be seen as a
rectangular shape or a lattice. Theory brings us "near" to the latter, as
it enabled Duns Scotus to be certain that the board far away was the
same board he had seen close at hand. According to Edward Ballard;
"It may be imagined to be something like the initial orientation or
primary direction of movement which a person journeying through a
countryside gives himself. This direction determines what comes into
view, how it appears, and what is concealed. It is the initial determination of a kind of object to which one will respond and the way one
will respond to it" (1983, 36). Common experience, mythological investiture, and scientific inquiry are such primary orientations. Let us
begin with some articulations of liturgical space.

Many early Latin church arches, which had their origin in the tri-
umphal arches of the Caesars, separated the public space of the nave
from the liturgical space of the apse. These liturgical settings are
*schema*ta which elicit the inseparable formalities *a parti rei* of common experience, scientific inquiry, and mythic projection. Ballard's
phenomenological description of an arch shows that closeness and object identification are functions of ambiguity-eliminating contexts,
ideas to which we will return in discussing distance and shape. Prominent liturgical arches may be found in St. Paul's Outside the Walls in
Rome (late fourth century); St. Apollinare in Classe; St. Front in Peri-
geux (eleventh century); and the Norman cathedral at Cefalu (twelfth
century). Arches separate and support, divide space and provide thresholds, openings. Hermes, no stranger to thresholds, will go with us. In

this framing the arch must be relatively unobtrusive, not like the *Arc de Triomphe* which, in serving as a monumental center, attracts attention to itself. On the other hand, it also makes the *Champs Elysées* a sacred way, as all must feel as they walk along it. In St. Apollinare's the arch frames an apse within which there is an altar—in form, if not in fact, a Roman sarcophagus. The framed apse is a cave or tomb and its vault expresses the heavens. The arch sets up for a *theoria* a place of sacred action, of victory over death. One is being prepared for ontophanies even if one doubts or does not share their reality. To pass through the arch, which may involve remaining where I am, is to participate in the originary experience of birth. The arch functions as an *epoché,* setting aside a place whose very nature is to focus events and point towards things that really matter. Of course one can notice its decorations. Those, for example, at St. Apollinare show no marks of a Caesar and his mighty deeds: above the arch there is the image of a stern man, the Pantocrator, and the sides are embellished with strange animals and sheep. Even if I do not know what is being communicated, in the sense that communication is properly a common focus on an Open through a framing, I know it to have been an important triumph. Here Being dwells in the Good and is commemorated. How?

The landscape represented is Mt. Tabor, the place of the Transfiguration. The arch gathers us into this place, the "between" of heaven and earth, life and death, through this great vaulted apse. The *Logos,* the word that shows and gathers, is thematized against the background of a green, fecund earth against the golden dome of the sky. An image of the Christ presides over the gathering and focusing arch. He collects us into his blessing with one hand and holds a book with the other. He is flanked by images of the Evangelists and sheep that emerge from cities on each side of arch's outer face. Are these "vehicles" Jerusalem and Bethlehem, the tenor of the old and new Covenants, or are they—as Justin Martyr would have said—Jerusalem and Athens, the law and the *logos* gathered in the Christ and expressed through his book? At the bottom and still on the outside of the arch two angels bear banners saying *Hagios, Hagios, Hagios. Hagios* is the name Hölderlin gave to Being even in the danger of this destitute age. The poet and the angels call us into "an inaugural naming of being and the essence of all things" in this showing that, as John Llewelyn has remarked, is "for all who have eyes to see" the proclamation of the second coming, the *parousia* (MH 1982, 87).[7] The *salvatus mundi,* "the salvation of the world," is framed in this focus. The import is cosmological, in the sense of Clement or Origin, and not personalistic. All nature participates in the promise into which we are gathered, even as it gathers us into the unconcealment of St. Apollinare.

St. Apollinare is the occasion for this hypostatic gathering within the apse. He stands in the lower center reaching prayerfully upward to a medallion enclosing a cross and outward to us. He is flanked on each side by sheep, one for each of the apostles present with Jesus on Tabor. Around his feet more sheep are gathering. He was, St. Peter Cristologos said, "like a good shepherd standing amid his flock." The earth, even the rocks, are alive; there are birds, roses and lilies, trees of every description, bushes and shrubs. Above this scene and surrounding the medallion is a golden sky in which God appears as a hand reaching down from above and from which emerges, among reddish clouds, the figures of Moses and Elijah, one on each side of the medallion. It is framed with gems and contains a jeweled cross within a blue sky filled with golden stars. Here is Christ in glory; he is portrayed, as if a jewel, in the crossing. Guiseppe Bovini says of this surface that "light does not fall in a beam as in a mirror; but is cut up in as many parts as there are tesserae which . . . create a multitude of chromatic effects . . . shimmering continuously and creating the impression of something changing, vital, alive" (1957, 55). The language of frame and crossing is being used to let this be seen as a metaphor about metaphor and about the *arché* itself. The thing stands in the gap through the regioning of earth, sky, men, and gods as a vehicle of ontological truth, as if in fulfillment of Heidegger's "On the Origin of the Work of Art"; as originative discourse the arch tells us something of what it means to dwell near, face to face, from an *arché* in which "earth and sky, the god and the man reach one another" (MH 1971b, 98).

Theoria's intended noema may or may not be real; that is not the immediate issue. In dramatic time a *theoria*'s being is at stake and the arch functions prehensively, like the receptacle empowering her through its ontophany, the plenary experience of the *arché Logos* as creator, redeemer, and judge. Its presence unobtrusively opens us to being, animating intention with its symbolic power. When we are closest to the arch, we are most distant from it. The arch, in being unobtrusive, lets the landscape incarnate the obtrusive *logos*, lets it gather. Mythic projection in part determines and is in part determined by the possible shape of objects. Obviously these *arches* depended on the discoveries of Roman engineers; many early churches retained the basilica form of Roman public buildings. But as one moves away from the imperial projections towards the Gothic, something else is being said. Perhaps only the discovery of the groin vault make the developments after St. Denis in Paris possible, but the abbot, Suger, thought the quasi-apostolic author of the Celestial Hierarchy was buried there; and this, together with Eurigena, Grosseteste, the neo-Platonic metaphysics of light and geometry, and the new import of Mary, entailed the elimination of the framing arch and the development of the church as microcosm. Note also that a new liturgical motility required the ambulatory and side chapels, as well as those behind the main altar. The mythical investiture is cosmological and supersedes origins. All that remains of the *arch* is a dedication to Mary. Things themselves symbolize. Today the projections of theory determine common space, whether public or the space we would share in a laboratory.

But the arch also occupies scientific space, and then being close is a condition for answering certain questions, such as pertain to its structural function or composition. I have seen plastic models subjected to stress and observed in polarized light to see how the arch and its vaults function. Within the context of these interpretations, the arch is near. Plato's *chora,* place, gives Being dwelling and is also Holy. Both the mythological and common contexts are concerned with places, a structure of relations orienting us towards a meaningful participation with beings. The scientist would invoke space and represent it geometrically, in a diagram exhibiting a strain, marking a module like those proportions of the "golden section" used at Chartres, or as a layout.

3. Euclid Revisited

WHY IS EUCLID CARVED in half-relief at Chartres? His geometry interprets the world as a non-oriented, homogeneous, punctal manifold, every point having analogous relations to every other. I have often invoked Euclid as a paradigm of ennui; nevertheless, his is the space of common experience. This is the only "space" in which most objects are invariant and self-congruent in transformation, an intuition suiting the manipulative (if not sacred) orientation. Ordinary place lets things be handy, close or far depending on need. Thus the supply of wood may be over there, the tools here. There are private and public places, each having its appropriate geometry; but homogeneous, isotropic, and continuous space has no locative power, no meaning, unless we confer it. If we can begin with this geometry of the ready-at-hand as most appropriate to archaic experience of the thing as a spatial relatum in circumspective sense recognition, other geometrical interpretations can be fitted through investitures and context bestowing intentionality. As Poincare showed, Euclid can even serve as their *schema.* We can show that Euclidian geometry is synthetic *a priori* in the spirit, if not the letter, of Kant. Isn't that desirable?

Participation is the clue to the place of meaning in the spatial web of necessity. Meaningful place is oriented to the agent whose interpretative context determines the horizon from which each stands forth as center. The potentialities for discriminating, dissevering and severing, near and far, clarity and ambiguity, encounter and significance are relative to intentional, meaning-giving contexts. Place gathers the necessities into unitary meaning, as if in a sphere; the force vectors of entities in this assemblage would otherwise lead them, as by some entropic dispersal, in every direction. The "action paintings" of Jackson Pollock or representations in a cloud chamber show this aimless, essentially meaningless play of force in a world that has been leveled down, stripped of the Good. The mythological investiture offers another world. The world that presents itself to disinterested sense is without a center, a unification or synthesis, without an *arché*, while when interpreted in myth or even common experience its sense presentation is invested and disclosed as meaningful. Such is the self-centering, counterentropic character of life that it stands over against the catabolic forces of dispersal and death; but the myth invests this same life with a higher meaning, say that of arches and openings and renewals. These three formalities of a thing, three possible modes of interpretative envisagement, define its participatory structure; (1) presentation disclosing the necessities of the *apeiron* world of energy first brought into the light in sensa and then interpreted as meaningful in common experience (2) through its oriented power to transform and assimilate alterity for this or that and, (3) in its higher mythic formations, unconcealing Being as bearing traces of the Good and so disclosing what and who we are.

The utility of the common strata of interpretation can lead in a dialectic of means and ends to the Good, the light in which both being and truth are to be understood. But as science probes the strata beneath presentation in the name of truth and, with positivism, comes to understand being by the nomological necessities, then the Good will be transformed into something that can be experienced by everyone in all contexts. Meaningful being, happiness, reduces to Hobbes' hedonistic attractions and repulsions. Then even common place will be victimized by the space of the modern, alienating city epitomized by Baudelaire in "Spleen (I)" and "In Passing."

Merleau-Ponty does not overstate the case when he says that "Husserl's thought is as much attracted by the haecceity of Nature as by the vortex of absolute consciousness" (1964, 165). It is true, however, that for Husserl, as for Kant, the *telos* of experience is absolute knowledge; even experience is "prepredicatively" understood as apt for judgment and thus already within the cultural formations of western metaphysics. The appropriate space is Euclidian; we hope to retain it as fundamental to an egress from dwelling even as it is being deconstructed. Beginning with something like ready-at-handness and its referential structures has the advantage of taking us among the haecceities and their formalities and allowing one to see how it founds the other interpretative modes. Surely this experience is common, if not primitive. Even more archaic play space is our access to a common world.

Once experience is approached through judgment and its theoretic formations, common experience and mythic projection are both suspect.

Of all possible geometries, Euclid's alone does justice to perceptual recognitions of something as _____ into which size, length, and shape enter. Invariant shapedness (Gk. *schema*) is essential to something being a ruler. Since some objects are *seen to be self-identical* and suitable for rulers, it can be shown in a transcendental argument that only Euclid offers an appropriate *schema* for this archaic spatial experience. Can it be shown that Euclid's story is privileged and is founded on a formal, objective distinction *a parti rei?* Since I believe pure mathematics is founded on the shapes (*schema*ta) of things, this weak synthetic *a priori* argument should establish many of Kant's basic Euclidian insights and prepare a way into the foundations of mathematics. Greek number theory was geometrical.

When Euclid's geometry is assumed to express metaphysical rather than transcendental necessities, physical interpretations tend towards classical atomism. Shape invariance leads to unchanging atoms; Leibniz's protest against the positivity of Newton's defining particles as impenetrable was quite in order. As a convention, however, it has advantages; it is the space of particulars. Individual instantiation is, as Sir Peter Strawson shows in his classical *Individuals,* a requirement of our usual conceptual scheme (1963, 136–219). The singular subject term identifies basic particulars, such as Kant's material objects, to a linguistic community and by the sortal or property ascribing predicate universal ϕ makes an assertion. These particulars must be otherwise identifiable, in the sense that this community can know something else about them, such as being able to reidentify something in various times and places. Recognition, which entails possible reidentification by others, presupposes shape invariance in transport, rotation, and reflection, the latter being the point of Kant's glove example: these operations uniquely determine the Euclidian group. J. R. Lucas shows that if shape enters into their recognition as objects are moved about, used to measure other things and determine areas and volumes, and if scale models and graphs are to be made of these measured things, then space, including the space of special relativity, must be Euclidian (1973, 193–94). Whitehead was also a proponent of Euclid; if we can recognize self-congruence, then the resulting space must be Euclidian (ANW 1921, 20–42). We need to look as closely as possible at the issues that raise and support these claims. A point of terminology: schema refers to concrete shape, *morphe* to mathematical form.

Not every recognition proposed by language is of a basic particular. We recognize tokens of types and instances of mass terms in what

Strawson calls "feature placing" languages; these are not, in the appropriate sense, particulars. Nor is every basic particular suited to measure congruence. In selecting a measure of distance, we want a rigid body or string that will not stretch and paper ruled in parallel grids which allow the shape of the entity to be represented as same. This possibility is uniquely Euclidian.

Understanding nature in Euclidian allegories respects certain fundamental intuitions, such as the natural ability to recognize congruence. The space of our archaic experience of manipulable and motile things should be as featureless as possible so that the "thing" is itself in any place. In effect, this is the point of Euclid's misunderstood congruence theorem (I, 4) in which a triangle is translated and superimposed upon another. Only his geometry permits shape invariant transport and rotation. Requiring Euclidian interpretations, a convention based on congruence recognition, imposes nothing upon the being of things but allows them to be the same in any space. This featurelessness, as Lucas calls it, is to be contrasted with a modified Leibnizian view that allows monads windows, as in Kant's *Dissertation;* change of perspectival standpoint entails a change in the internal essence of the monad. Its phenomenal analogue would be a spatial-temporal nexus like Duchamps' "Nude Descending the Stairs," and thus monads would be changing adjectives (non-uniform object) of unchanging space-time. Something true is being said, but when this relativity is made foundational rather than derived from local Euclidian descriptions, geometry is allowed to determine the features of things.

Euclid's is not the only way to interpret physical fields. For instance, the curvature of Riemann's geometry determines how shape is characterized in transport, rotation, and possible reflections. As employed by Einstein, this geometry nominalizes time, reduces it to a presence. Instead of having both force and spatial tensors, which preserve the directionality of time, force and its deformations can be identified (as in least action) with a spatial geodesic and time reduced to a spatial tensor. But if forces are to be retained and things, not geometry, are to be allowed to count as causes, there are good reasons for retaining Euclidian intuitions. Among these is the belief that objects, not events, are continuents. G. E. Moore says that "it certainly can't be, as language suggests, that the same event is at all times and possesses at one time what it doesn't at others. This would assimilate an event to a thing that persists and has at one time a quality which it hasn't got at others. The time at which an event is present means the time it is. How can an event have a time it isn't?" (1962, 92). Objects, the subject's constituted correlative, retain *einai*'s sense of enduring presence. Becoming is the condition of their being present and taking on or losing this or that quality. The *arché* is the eventual now, an epochal gathering into denominated definiteness through regions or fields expressed in its dynamical potential.

Was Kant right to give Euclid's geometry priority? Gottfried Martin reports that though Kant recognized other geometrical possibilities, he chose Euclid's because only it was representable (1962, 29).[8] In a sense he was mistaken; Poincare showed that other geometries could have a Euclidian model. Yet Plato held that equality recognition is innate; Euclid's geometry allows us to recognize congruence and self-congruence (*Phaedo* 74A–76A). Perhaps this led Duns Scotus to say that though a stick seems to bend when placed in water, it is "not broken as the sense of sight judges . . . the intellect judges by something more certain than any testimony of the senses . . . [and] knows that the measure used to measure remains equal to itself. Now the sense of sight as well as that of touch judges that the identical measure can be applied to a nearby object as well as a distant one" (1962, 123). Though we do not "see" inequality, nevertheless we do understandingly see things as unequal. Duns Scotus' distinction between sense and intellect is appropriate, but for *theoria,* who understandingly sees, the ensuing judgment is aesthetic, not subsumptive, as when things are seen as appropriate, well-arranged, harmonious, or in place. These arguments persuade me that rather than build strains and orientations into geometry, it is better to make them expressive features of things in space. So too for physics. We want to retain the finite things that variously express themselves rather than surrender them and their powers to an abstraction. Except for science fiction and the greater simplicity non-Euclidian *schema*ta offer some scientific allegories, the geometry learned in school fits in with the gods and theories we also learned.

The space of Gothic painting is hierarchical; rank determines the size and order of things in their spherical space. A featureless geometry, as in Giorgio de Chirico's "The Mystery and Melancholy of a Street," may menace or, as in Andy Warhol's "100 Cans," express alienating banality. In Cezanne's tactile space, we experience the epiphany of thingliness; through these sorts of *schema*ta, Euclidian geometry lets one see that dwelling depends, at least in some measure, on how things are set up. Indeed, it reflects the featureless of the *apeiron* receptacle which in turn grants *chora,* place, for dwelling.[9]

4. Congruence and Recognition

WE NEED UNDERSTAND neither geometry nor physics to know what space is or even to justify simple measurements. We recognize congruence. How is this possible? When Pythagoras broke off bits of a twig until it could be laid along each of the strings of his tetrachord an integral number of times, creating the first physical theory by mapping the lengths of these into and onto 6, 8, 9, and 12, a harmonic proportion, it was essential that he select a measure having nothing to do with a natural, spatial metric, which is not the case in the geometries of Riemann and Bolyai-Lobachevsky, the only geometries which, together with Euclid's, are metric and have axioms of congruence. These spaces are not direction and orientation indifferent.

Most logical accounts of identifying reference neglect, except as the condition for numerical distinctness, the spatiality involved; but unless we begin here, it is all too easy to follow Quine into a canonical notation in which singular terms are replaced by quantifiers and the robustness of Duns Scotus' contracted and self-manifesting *ens* is lost to instantiation. Contextual distance determines phenomenologically what counts as a particular. One must be near to something to share what a speaker is identifying, where nearness is a function of what is being made ostentatious. I can see the blackboard from any place in the room, but the triangle inscribed on it or the microscopic features of its surface are perceivable only from a particular place under certain orientations. When I speak of Plato to my students, he is nearer than they are. Here the predicate term does some of the work: "the board is green," "the board is slate," "the board has a complex molecular structure," and the like entail a standpoint appropriate to the kind. Predicates express an appropriate distantiation lost to logic. Every proposition has its implicit demonstrative phrase that points out what is then predicatively qualified (ANW 1921, 6–12). "Near" is *Dasein's* ambiguity eliminating *da* which permits things to be recognized and apophantically asserted under relevant sortals.[10] We are unable to tell what something is, as it flips back and forth in gestalt shifts, until we get to an appropriate near. That we can orient ourselves to what is being demonstrated, dissever it from its field or ground, and bring it meaningfully near are the spatial conditions we already understand prior to any geometry and are necessary conditions on the possibility of discourse. These conditions are functions of motility and orientation, the context of Kant's synthetic method. Dissevering, orienting, and bringing near are phenomenological conditions requiring connected, continuous, and multi-dimensional space.

It might be objected that neither nearness nor congruence have anything to do with phenomenological recognition. The fact that something transported and rotated is seen in various ways depends on the space itself, while distance is purely a metrical convention determined by a ruler. Adolf Grünbaum can demonstrate that synthetic *a priori* congruence recognition will not obtain in Riemann's geometry; he is convinced that Einstein expresses a metaphysical reality to which appearances must conform. Recognition will then be theory dependent.

Riemann's geometry will not support "natural" congruence recognitions. In his "Inaugural Lecture" he proposed that "the measure must come from elsewhere" in the form of a rigid rod stipulated to be self-congruent and satisfying his non-Euclidian axioms. Dr. Grünbaum says that a congruence convention for Riemannian space is now imperative since it represents the real number line (an actual infinite, dense point set) required for physics. Though it constitutes an interval, a dense set is metrically amorphous. By a Zeno argument, any interval would then have the same number, an actual infinity, of points. Therefore one measures by imposing a rigid rod representing the stipulated congruence standard. Near is a matter of measured distance and its conventions and has nothing to do with the elimination of ambiguity or the sense recognition of congruence (AGr 1963, 3-65).

We chose our rulers from self-congruent things. Should it dissolve, stretch, or melt, we look about for something more suitable. Even if Kant's finitism is ignored, one is still reluctant to use a geometry to explain away recognized congruences. Recognition is a parameter on "spatial" interpretation; the rest can be handed over to enabling conventions. For instance, it can be stipulated that a spatial interval taken up by a recognizable, self-congruent thing have the properties of the real numbers. Even though there will then be ordinal intervals, each with a rational mesh, there will be no natural criterion of congruence, the king's foot, the standard meter, or length of a wave.

The issue joined by Grünbaum goes back to a famous dispute between Henri Poincare and Bertrand Russell in the 1890s. Poincare said that the choice of a geometry and, thus, of a definition of congruence was arbitrary. Russell bristled. Insisting that this was like trying to determine the direction a ship's movement from the color of the crew's eyes (doubtless ignoring Nordic or Mediterranean features), he argued that we understood the meaning of equality "without measurement. . . . Whatever one can discover by means of an operation must exist independently of that operation. Any method of measurement is good or bad according as it yields a result that is true of false" (1899, 687-88). On the other hand, he seems to have opted for a space with an intrinsic metric. Whitehead, approaching this through his intuitions on special relativity, noted that the choice of a metric and its geometry involved both nature (*physis*) and convention (*nomos*). Given recognized congruence, we can follow the procedure employed for time and stipulate arbitrary ordinal markers, feet or meters, and let each have an appropriate Archimedean or non-denumerable sub-set.

Language enables us to have community and entails, as Aristotle recognized, something more than communication. Most animals communicate, mostly about their individual needs and feelings; but we can speak together and explore what is good and useful, just or unjust, what must objectively be the case and thus for the common good (*Pol.* 1253a 10–14). Our need for "things" is not just a requirement of our conceptual system. If by things we mean any limit on thinking to which we must submit that can be (perspectivally) shared, then language is the condition through which things address us. To speak of a community is already to speak of agreement, of what is common. Being already in agreement on some matters, it can be enlarged by conventions and stipulations, as in a technical or scientific community. Agreement about shapes (*schemata*) can be extended by scientific agreement to form (*morphe*), as in pure mathematics. The transition (or hermeneutical translation) can be abrupt. As Husserl remarked, we can fantasize about shapes and translate them into others "more or less straight, circular, flat, etc.," but the pure form is without gradation and fluctuation. But even if what we say of the pure form (*morphe*) can never be said of the concrete shapedness (*schema*), the recognition of the latter is the *schema* for recognizing mathematically significant form, a *schema* for technical agreement already present in our language.

For the sake of rigor, not sense, one could choose a measure under the topological formality of perspectival invariance and add to projective geometry such axioms as would give all observers a common metric. The simplest resulting geometry, whose order would be cyclic, would be Riemann's elliptical geometry. Granted serial order, one might then define absolute geometry, though like projective geometry it would be without a concept of distance, congruence, and angle. The addition of axioms for many parallels gives hyperbolic geometry, while those for a unique parallel yields Euclid (JRL 1973, 156–58). The order of discovery, however, has its ontological claims. Then one will settle for recognition of quality; among these would be the characteristic self-same shape of our ruler. This sets the stage for Whitehead's solution.

It is difficult to imagine that we do not recognize quality. Even Quine permits recognition of the identity of certain "retinal stimulations." Granted this, Whitehead says that "measurement presupposes the matching of quality . . . What is the quality that matches?" (1922, 57). Anything that we can recognize, the recurrent object that characterizes a particular event and, under the operative contextual intention, makes it to be the kind that it is. Wittgenstein suggests we may disregard Riemann's requirement that we look outside the language game, the intentional context, for a criterion or standard unless that move is part of the game. We recognize green as characterizing the board without having to check it out with a set of color samples. Differential sense fields make these recognitions possible. Qualitative identity is a special case of congruence. If this holds for green or any other sense relatum in recognition, it follows that "our physical space must already have a structure and the matching must refer to some qualifying class inherent in that structure" (51). A shape or length recognized as self-congruent is an inherent quality in the physical structure of space, not something brought in by our conventions or geometries. We see it there.

Grünbaum's central argument against congruence recognition involves a figure produced by two line segments at right angles, one horizonal and the other vertical, such that the vertical is recognized to be greater than the horizontal. He challenges Whitehead's sense recognition of incongruence with the concept of an Euclidian space that embodies an infinity of incongruences, as above, which by some function along one dimension are really congruent (AGr 1963, 54). But Euclidian space is direction independent, while the example depends on direction, the vertical direction or dimension being defined by a function not shared by others (99). Geometry will not cause the rotated rod to change its length.

Geometry means "earth measurement" and deals with *schemata*, the shapes of things, at the level of *morphe* in formal allegories. But there are many such formal allegories, each self-consistent, categorial, and fertile in deductive consequences. At the risk of repetition, I will be combining two senses of *schema*, meeting as if in the middle ground between phenomenological description and the *schema* expressing the "sensibilization" of the deductive consequences of a formal system, a model-theoretic way familiar in van Fraassen. The phenomenology is prior, both historically and in the order of knowing. Mathematics originates when a formal allegory arises and comes to have a life of its own; but just in case one is swept away by the sheer beauty of formal and rationalistic considerations, we must do for mathematics what Cartwright suggests should be done for physical theory. In founding mathematics on the things that arise, react, act, and pass away, I hope to eliminate the ontological priority of permanent presence with which philosophy, in aping mathematics, too often begins. What do we see in a synopsis of the various geometries in the light of recognitions within our oriented, motile spatiality? We need to see how our claims on behalf of Euclid stack up against some of the other possibilities for measuring lines and angles. This can be done in the plane geometry of Euclid, the elliptical geometry of Riemann, and the hyperbolic geometry of Bolyai and Lobachevsky. These are metric and they share axioms of congruence. Minkowski's is also a metric geometry, rather like Euclid's plane geometry, except that a line can be at right angles to itself; and this is often used in the special theory of relativity, for example, by Whitehead. If we drop the axioms of congruence, keeping only those other axioms common to all metric geometries, projective geometry (Veblen and Young) results. Affine geometry, like absolute geometry, is non-metrical and can be derived from Euclid by dropping the claim that all right angles are equal and the postulate permitting one to describe a circle with any radius and diameter. The unique parallel is also retained. On the other hand, one could begin, as in Whitehead's *Process and Reality*, with projective geometry and add axioms of order; if these are serial, the geometry is absolute, and if cyclical, the geometry is elliptical. Given congruence, the other metrical geometries are special cases of absolute geometry.

Guided by our experience of manipulable things set up for this or that, we will want a non-phenomenological measure of distance. A non-egocentric answer to "how near" is required in many common contexts. An ancient Egyptian surveying a field or an engineer building a bridge could tell others how to get the same data when "about here" or "over there" won't do. One needs a metric geometry, but which shall I choose? Euclid; only he gives a non-egocentric measure of distance and an arbitrary unit of measure. In elliptical geometry there are no parallels to a given line through a given, non-collinear point and the sum of the interior angles of a triangle is greater than two right angles. In hyperbolic geometry there are many distinct parallels and the angles of a triangle do not add up to the 180 degrees of Euclid's right line, which would now look like a hyperbola. In neither would distance be measured by Pythagoras' formula. Do we need to recall that this simple rule does not hold on the surface of the earth? If I walk three miles west and four miles north, I am not five miles from the origin. The earth is not a Euclidian plane. Euclid alone admits a unique parallel in a homogeneous, isotropic space which, as in Pythagoras' theorem, is the simplest rule for calculating or approximating distances, determining equivalence classes of similar shapes not of the same size, grids, and the like. The practical advantages are enormous. Since distance is independent of origin and orientation, the unit of measurement is arbitrary. This supports Duns Scotus' claim that "the same measure can be applied to a nearby object of vision as well as a distant object." As Lucas says, only here can we operate with a concept of shape and length that is independent of orientation, distance, and size, where distance entails orthogonal transformations independent of vectors (1973, 111, also 185).

Just as we were willing to pay a price for featureless time, so too this advantage must be sought in geometry if it too is to interpret our measurements. Convention has a role to play: "In our ordinary and scientific thinking, we rule that spatial differences, like temporal differences and, in certain circumstances, differences in personal attitudes, are per se irrelevant—else no two situations, events or things could be regarded as qualitatively identical and fully comparable. If spatial differences are per se irrelevant, then space must itself be undifferentiated, indifferent" (JRL 1973, 167).

If the laws of nature describe the manner in which natural things participate inter se, as well as the manner into which processes are controllable in order to understand and influence their outcome, then conventions and stipulations should not legislate congruence. It was a bad day when Kant let understanding take up the legislative task for transcendental apperception, but it is appalling when such distinguished philosophers as Reichenbach and Grünbaum legislate on behalf of idolatrous formal models. Lucas continues: "Any differences there are between one place and another are to be attributed to something other than the bare fact of their being the places they are—to climatic differences, the sun's rays, to historical influences, to some factor in the one that is absent in the other. . . . Space must be featureless because we have peeled away all its features" (166). If there is to be interplay and meaningful dialogue with beings, we must let them speak. This is an appealing possibility in Euclidian intuitions: "The Euclidian [transformational] group has practical as well as formal virtues. It is the natural group for men to adopt who are motile agents, who see things from different points of view, and move them around from one position to another" (183). Kant's case has been made; Euclid's geometry is synthetic *a priori* where "synthetic" refers to the recognition of congruence.

Mathematics and the Human Soul

1. A Backward Glance

OUR ITINERARY HAS LED through methodology to the *arché* of the Critical Philosophy, the atemporal expressive self, and its quasi-Pythagorean matrix, but we also saw that these could not account for the life world. Something even more basic than being underway with others among spatial and temporal things forced itself upon us as we penetrated the methodological core to the medial imagination; the root lies not in crossing the transcendental imagination with sense and understanding but rather in the possibility of interpretation, significance and recognition. Kant founded recognition and significance on the expressivistic veritative synthesis whose reflective form insured that temporality, and thus transcendental synthesis, thematizes time as permanently present. With Plato's aid, we moved beyond private apperception to the soul, that is, life, within whose participatory structure world worlds from a similar gap or slot. The *arché* first manifest itself under the rubric of Kant's productive imagination and then in both Kant and Husserl in time constitution which, thanks to Jacques Derrida's proto-writing, could be appropriated as the appearing of signifiers. This led us into the presencing of language, the heir to the categories as the transcendental condition for a world, by the soul's chiasmatic X-like crossing of the medial slot or *arché*.[1] Heidegger has let us see how crossing generated these conditions of significance and recognition, while dwelling among things gave access to a world.

This account of crossings is, I trust, a hermeneutical, truth-preserving translation of Kantian themes into a language purged of onto-theological assumptions. I have proposed that the groundless hypostatic self, always already involved with others, with its participatory linkage to being (*peras*) and becoming (*apeiron dynamis*) constitutes an Open which is an alternative to transcendental apperception and its generation of meaningful space and time. Most important was the discovery that Kant's imagination is medial; on being crossed by sensibility and understanding, it generated a world of accessible and connected things. This generative function and its constituted world have been taken over by a more original creativity associated with dwelling that, given self, things, and world, makes experience possible. We must find an alternative account of mathematics that respects Kant's basic insights and, at the same time, does justice to non-constructive, realistic intuitions. We are wayfarers within a tradition, not angels posited by eternity, who must found mathematics in the hermeneutics of common experience. An attempt to understand mathematics as a linguistic tradition creating and renewing itself in texts has implications for understanding any tradition. But the textual metaphor is also disclosive. Plato locates mathematics on the third level of his divided line as a reflective condition for *dianoia;* it then is a matrix, that is, a pool (*Rep.* 516A), in which ideas are imaged as hypotheses. Since pure mathematics is self-referential, this mode of representation harbors the *Ge-stell*, the objectless world of disposable energy linked as a standing reserve in information networks that allows it to be switched about, as in a power grid, and transformed. This image, appropriate to the dynamical *apeiron*, ignores the ideas into which energy is collected and through which, counter-entropically, the living creature stands out. Perhaps we can learn from Husserl and Plato how to preserve our tradition against polemical genealogies as a dwelling place for reason and being. We will begin by reviewing what we have learned about Kant through his methodology.

The Analytic, Kant says, is a "logic of truth . . . without considering specifically whether cognitions which belong to it are analytic or synthetic" (*Prol.* 31 n.). *Cogitare* means, St. Augustine says, "to collect" and "to order" (*Conf.* X,11). Analysis unconceals the condition for the conditioned (*Logic* 149). Synthesis reverses this movement so that this *arché* condition, either a grounding presence, "principle," or groundless presencing, "origin," gives truth conditions for the conditioned. This is the route of Plato's downward dialectic from principles or "ideas through ideas . . . ending with ideas" (*Rep* 511C), where the term is the conditioned. Its analogue, transcendental synthesis, presences or constitutes through the *arché* the truth condition linking thought and being, making knowable whatever can be known. Though Kant, like Plato, begins with the condition as a principle rather than as an eventual origin, our inverted account must look to his as its only paradigm.

Kant understood the synthetic method as the "movement from principles to consequents" (*Logic* 149). These "principles" are the categories of the understanding whose "consequents" will be empirical science. After Hume, however, sense no longer grounds the nomological ties science expresses in its empirical judgments. Therefore the movement from reason to sense will have to be mediated by arbitrarily constructed (142) "distinct objects" (70) in which thought can meet up with itself in self-instanced Principles. This constitution results from synthesis, in the second sense of "synthesis," which gathers and unifies a coordinate multiplicity into an objective unity. Synthesis, in its primary sense, employs this constituted "distinct object" to mediate the descent of thought through this object as an intuited *schema* to intelligible consequents, where the object is a Parmenidian "same for thinking and being."

The philosopher must look to mathematical synthesis for his constructivist paradigm. Mathematics makes or constructs its concepts (*Logic* 141) by presencing their objects *a priori* through an arbitrarily constructed intuition (A 716/B 744). Through the intuition one may further determine the mathematical concept in synthetic *a priori* judgments. By drawing lines as a *schema*, we intuit that two straight lines cannot enclose a space. This intuited *schema*, constructed shapedness, would be the middle term between thought and its formal object. Through such "archetypal" concepts, pure space and time can be generated under a mathematical synopsis as quantitative manifolds arbitrarily connectible in intuited *schemata*; for that reason, mathematical synthesis is said to be arbitrary. Aside from mathematics, the synthetically *a priori* determinable "thing in general" is the exception to the rule that finite thought cannot construct concepts, that is, can not exhibit its object in an *a priori* intuition. Its synthesis must arbitrarily connect space and time in an intuited *schema* analogous to that of mathematics, except that the manifolds will be empirically determined rather than pure. No empirical concepts are made since their constitution through synthesis of a sense manifold is anything but arbitrary. The "concept that represents *a priori* the empirical contents of experience is the concept of the thing in general" (A 720/B 748). This particular concept would be a categorially saturated or schematized concept of "the thing in general" and the latter would be its correlative truth condition. *Schemata* empirically synthesized to instance or intend it will be, as in the Principles, determinable in synthetic *a priori* judgments. This intelligible or "metaphysical" object is schematized by the mediating empirical object, as the line being drawn *schema*tizes "the line," the intelligible object of the schematized mathematical concept being synthetically explicated. Granted sensibility in which it is schematized, "the thing in general" can be archetypally presenced by transcendental apperception in an arbitrary construction, analogous to the drawing of the line, which orders or forms sensibility, its matter, into the *schema* of this intelligible condition for objectivity. The categorial synthesis of space and time gives them, *qua schema*, the form of an empirical object through which this "thing in general" is intended. Any experimental intention, will therefore find its empirical object schematized under the rubric of the second Analogy. This *a priori* presencing "framed from concepts alone" (A 719/B 747), that is, from categories of the understanding, constitutes the "thing in general" met up with and articulated in the Principles.

If sense is to be empirically significant, which according to Kant's "Copernican Revolution" means that thought will meet up with itself in its constituted objects, then pure thought's correlative "thing in general" will be the intended formality in the empirical synthesis of its object. This metaphysical "thing in general" or "object in general = *x*" (A 104), is "a mere rule of the synthesis of that which perception may give *a posteriori*" (A 720/B 748). This object, like a dance, is a determination of the manner in which some empirical determination of space and time, as such generated *a priori*, can be self-affectively taken up in judgment and thought as an objective unity, where that unity schematizes one or more of the Principles. In transcendental synthesis, apperception, the ground or principle, presences space and time as connectable manifolds for mathematical synthesis and, given empirical content, articulates these as possible forms for experiencing this content objectively under the rubric of the Principles of the Pure Understanding. The Principles secure the application of number, the morphology of succession or inner sense, and geometry, the morphology of space or outer sense, to 'conditioned' experience and thus constitute Parmenides' "same for thought and being."

If mathematics is primarily choragraphy, it must articulate the schematic structure of origins rather than determine itself by principles. Language, like play or life, is a medial phenomenon which presences (*gignesthai*) presences (*onta*), graphemes or phonemes, without itself being founded on a presence. The converse relation holds; speaking constitutes the speaker, as the play plays the player. Our venture into a Transcendental Analytic showed mathematical objectivity originating from its foundationless foundations, its *arché*, in linguistic *schemata*. If we can no longer found mathematics on a presence, its *arché* must be an originary presencing that, not being a presence, cannot as such be named; the *logos* in which it is articulated must be a *mythos*, a story, and not, as in Euclid, a principle generating deductive "consequents." Kant attributed this synthetic *arché* of the understanding to the imagination (A 78/B 103). Having only an originary and few principles, imagination must be our guide.

The mythic form taken by this account will seem less bizarre when it is seen that the contrary ideal of literal, proper, and discursive thought is founded on a metaphor, Plato's image of the sun. With the presumption that sense needs a supplement in thought, one says that just as the shining thing is to sense, so the clear and distinct intelligible thing is to mind. Plato took over *idea*, the radiance of the visible, and by the Good transformed it into the intelligible radiance that made sense of sense. This transform is effected by the trope of the sun (JD

1982, 235–52). Aristotle psychologized seen quality as a "mental affection" (*De Int.* 16a 3) expressed in a name. One could bring a thing into mind and convert its image (*phantasma*) by various faculties into an intelligible presence so that, unlike the sun, it would always be present in its *estin*, "being what it is" or "essence." This "mental affection" (Stoic *conceptus*) can be expressed in a formula, a *logos*, which is a principle or ground for demonstrative truth and the univocal discourse that it makes possible. Aristotle made "science" uniquely his own by identifying the allegorical "is" with that of equality, identification, attribution, or predication and then, except within given theological limits, banished metaphor from the text of philosophy. The univocal has a metaphorical root.

Even as Heidegger rejects metaphor, he points to something new; now that sense is already meaningful, it does not require supplementation from the intelligible domain. Plato allows us to make the same point through his rejection of the disjunction between the world of common experience and the separated ideas (*Par.* 133B–35A). There is nothing behind the text, no transcendental clue, no supplement. In the perceptual paradigm for participation in events (*Theaet.* 152Dff.), the idea is the immanent relatum of receptive and interpretative perception; the reflexive aspect, without which there could be no consciousness, does not appear until *Timaeus.* The soul, after being compounded from the transcendentals and articulated according to the musical scale (35C–36D), is divided and formed into two circles, that of the same and that of the other "intersecting like the letter *x*" (36B). In participation, the same crosses and assimilates alterity; but if it is to be conscious, this return must be reflexive. Because participation is also interpretative, the return will be self-affective. We are same ("which makes it possessor to be a rational being" [44B]) for ourselves through alterity in a crossing that "turns in on itself" (37E).

The ideality of a mathematical text derives from the animation of its indicative, non-arbitrary signifiers, which are then marginalized. Then one assumes that its objects are "real." When "real" no longer bears traces of the metaphors which found it on the thing's inseparable formalities *a parti rei,* then to speak of realism is already to forget that mathematics comes to be and lives only in and through the others which lie outside its formal objects in fortuitous notational *schema*tic expressions. Having come to see its linguisticality, the sense of the text must be founded in its disclosive language rather than presumed to lie without the text in a "real" or "anti-real" supplement.

2. *From* Schema *to* Morphe

PIERRE DUHEIM DESCRIBES a tangent galvanometer which I would see as an "assemblage" consisting of a circular frame around which is wrapped a silk insulated wire; a steel bar, suspended by a thread, hangs in the center which is attached to a needle that can move over a circle divided into degrees. As a current is passed through the wire, the needle moves and the degrees of its deflection are read off (PD 1962, 126–27). On the other hand, a physicist sees this as set up to measure the intensity of current by the angular deflection of the needle, a value that can then satisfy a variable in an electromagnetic formula. The formula is an allegorical idealization expressing characteristics of the instrument, such as the radii of the coil, the wire, and electric "currents." Intensive magnitude is measured by a *theoria* who understandingly sees the significance of the apparatus.

Prior to Duns Scotus' introduction of the concept of *intensio*, Kant's "intensive magnitude" was unknown (GW 1961, 124–25). Through schematic Euclidian projections, a *theoria* understandingly reads this apparatus and discerns the 'fact' of the current's intensity. Like Kant's plate *schema*tizing the circle (A 137/B 176), wires and coils are seen as 'round' in a metric allegory all too often mistaken for a prepredicative fact. "Facts" are artifacts of the regions (cultural, conceptual, or extentional), through which they are demonstrated.

Though I have been critical of Kant's bizarre proposals for founding mathematics, I am persuaded by his argument from incongruent counterparts, which involves recognition and not phase space, that geometry is founded in intuition. Kant thought that the mathematical object was constructively presenced *a priori* through the image or *schema*, the basis for the synthetic enlargement of concepts in predicative determinations. This procedure is understood by intuitionists as a constructive proof. But, and this is my first thesis, this object is present in an intuition which terminate a speculative demonstration and not as the conclusion of a deductive proof. Through the play of signifiers, truth is something that happens to us "over and above our doing" (HG 1975, xiv).[2] That event of *aletheia* is, like Spinoza's "knowledge of the third kind" (intuitive science), often marked by a radical break with customary and conventional modes of proceeding, and what is seen transcends naturalistic accounting. Plato celebrated this mystery with "recollection" and a myth about the soul's eternal life. While, for example, the transcendentals, perhaps depth grammar, and certain forms appertaining to all sentient life hermeneutically predispose intuition, much that would fall under the recollection thesis is a function of language. Plato misses this constitutive function of language by assigning it, as in the Seventh Epistle, an instrumental rather than disclosive role. If naturalism is equivalent to mechanism (Peirce's secondness), all life transcends mechanism in interpretative thirdness, the irreducible meanings that give point to the lowly dung beetle's continuing motility even as its legs are progressively cut away. Language, introducing narrative and spiritual dimensions, is the necessary and sufficient condition for the existence of objects disclosed in historical, not eternal, horizons. In the second thesis, I shall argue that an imaginative play involving "some third thing" (A 138/B 177), the signifiers, makes this object present to mind. We will then see with Wittgenstein that mathematics is "a mode of representation" and that it expresses the morphology of the *metaxu,* the "between." Lovers, the keepers of the between, also express themselves in the measures of poetry and song.

Language, not Kant's figurative, productive, or even reproductive imagination, is the "some third thing" mediating, at times creatively, passive and active participation, the Platonic analogues of receptive sensibility and spontaneous understanding. In a series of Heideggerian reflections that began with "household" (*oikos*-words), with "belonging" and "dwelling," which culminated in the disclosure of neighboring nearness, a way was prepared for thinking that retains, without grounding itself on, presence (MH 1971b, 94). Since we are dealing with forms of significance and have the resources of Platonic analysis and Husserl's context-forming intentionality as principles and can effect a relative closure on "infinite" chains of signifiers, we might welcome Derrida's observation that the "play of synthesis and referrals forbid, in any moment or in any sense, that a simple element be present, referring only to itself. . . . No element can function as a sign without referring to another element which is not itself present" (1981, 26). If, as Derrida says, "nothing, neither among the elements or within the system, is anywhere ever simply absent or present," does this also hold for mathematical signifiers that, like icons, schematize *morphe?* Do we not see form, not in some variant of a categorial intuition, but rather by manipulating these signifiers? Here again we transcend Husserl; following Kant, intuition is less evidential that interpretative.

Distinctions do not always displace one another; dwelling together in the same neighborhood, they can cross and engender. "Neighborhood," Heidegger says, "originates in that distance where earth and sky, God and man reach one another . . . 'face-to-face with one another' not only with respect to human beings but also with respect to things of the world. Where this prevails, all things are open to one another in their self-concealment; thus one extends itself to another, and thus all remain themselves; one is over the other, over it is as its guardian watching over the other, over it as its veil" (1971b, 104). "Thus one extends itself to another, and thus all remain themselves" is a variant of a participation metaphor, *metalambano:* "the beyond dwells in the midst of." Language calls us into this neighborhood, defined for us by proximity to the Good, thus deepening Plato's ontological insight that "discourse is one of the kinds of things that are" (*Sop.* 260A). The being about which we speak is the same *qua* (participatory) being as the (participatory) being of the speaking that may solicit a dwelling and the gift of being. The *arché* of language, the activity or productivity associated with the silent *a* of *différance*, for example, "refers to the generative movement in the play of differences" that gives and discloses structure in a language. With the proviso that this is a play of signs, I will explore the generation of mathematics from this basis.

All explanation finally appeals to an intuition which may take us in the direction of archaic experience and the natural languages in which understanding is first articulated. In the almost imperceptible gap between archaic experience and what is instituted as a spiritual formation through language, such as science or poetry, the human world as such first emerges. How does this new institution draw on what was always already there? A good metaphor is natural. What it creates, its artifact, already and always dwelt in things present. In this connection, Heidegger speaks of art, especially poetry (which shares its metaphoric roots with mathematics), as the "setting-into-work of truth. It is due to art's poetic nature that, in the midst of what is, art breaks into an open place, in whose openness everything is other than usual" (1971b, 72). The metaphor through which both poetry and mathematics break into the open and set truth working creates the possibility it then discloses. Nevertheless, *aletheia* poses itself as if disclosing something that was already there. Citing Durer's remark, "For in truth, art lies hidden within nature; he who can wrest it from her, has it," Heidegger refers to the "rift" or slot and continues:

> "Wrest" here means to draw out the rift and to draw the design with the drawing pen on the drawing board. . . . How can the rift-design be drawn out if it is not brought out into the Open by the creative sketch as a rift, which is to say, brought out beforehand as a conflict of measure and unmeasure. True, there lies hidden in nature a rift-design, a measure and a boundary, and, tied to it, a capacity for bringing forth—that is art. But it is equally certain that this art hidden in nature becomes manifest only through the work, because it lies originally in the work. (70)

Can we wrest the rift-design of mathematics from the materiality of a color? I will show how truth is set to work through Plato's *Meno*. The shapes (*schemata*) that emerge through playing with children's colored blocks will demonstrate the *morphe* of mathematical objects. It is as if the "rift-design," the projected sketch of an analytic proof, were already there in the *schema,* the monstrative signs of a mathematical language, the discovery of which is an historical accident. "By virtue of the projected sketch set into the work of the unconcealedness of what is, which casts itself toward us, everything ordinary and hitherto existing becomes an unbeing. This unbeing has lost the power to give and keep being as a measure. . . . The working of the work does not consist in the taking effect of a cause. It lies in a change, happening from out of the work, of the unconcealedness of what is, and this means, of Being" (MH 1971b, 72). One sees *morphe* through a schematic notation, a non-arbitrary (contra Saussure) set of graphematic differences lying outside the text of mathematics. If we replace "philosophy" with "mathematics," our task "is to think, in the most faithful, interior way, the structured genealogy of philosophy's concepts, but at the same time to determine—from a certain exterior that is unqualifiable and unnameable by philosophy—what this history has been able to dissimilate or forbid, making itself into a history by this somewhat unmotivated repression" (JD 1981, 6). The material signifiers are repressed. Derrida has broken the "as if" *a priori* tie between signifier and signified in the structuralist concept of sign and given us a decentered and dynamical account of the generation of structure; for "the theme of *différance* is incompatible with the static, synchronic, taxonomic ahistorical motifs in the concept of structure . . . [Differences] have not fallen from the sky nor been inscribed all at once . . . but it goes without saying that the motif *différance* is not the only one that defines structure and that the production of differences, *différance,* is not astructural; it produces systematic and regulated transformations that are able . . . to leave room for a structural science" (28). Mathematics must be counted among the "legitimated exigencies of structuralism" Derrida accepts, while his thesis about the priority of writing finds a ready home in this text concerning the graphematic foundations of mathematical thinking. This is possible only through a *Sagen,* "saying," that shows. The differential and arbitrary field of graphemes and phonemes will have to be left over for natural languages.

This then is yet another proposal concerning the (foundationless) "foundations" of mathematics. Having identified mathematics with proof and proof with formal logic, it would be counterintuitive to seek for its nature outside of these "metamathematical" parameters. There is, however, good reason to believe that these conceal its true nature; our task is to set free and let appear what has been concealed. Phenomenology can overcome the distinction between form and content, between fact and interpretation, and the like, by paying attention to what is seen rather than to sedimented opinions. For example, Hilary Putnam says in an argument against non-contextual realism that a line may be (1) a dense set of points, (2) a line segment with rational end points, or (3) a sort of linear extension from which points may be derived by the convergence of its segments (HP 1981, 489-91). The context determines what I see, but contexts are ordered inter se and non-arbitrary. In the first case, the line is idealized by Cantor-Dedekind's number theory. In the second case, the line is being used as a *schema* or allegory to demonstrate something about points and rational numbers. Finally, segments are being used as *schemata* for demonstrating points. How what is seen is said, or set up by saying to be seen, opens up possibilities, horizons of possible operations and structures that show themselves when one says that this is a line. But the line represented in the act of drawing is presentified or commemorated in the *schema*tic segment. In other words, the represented cannot be that disjoined from its representation, since what is demonstrated may be used, as in the third example, to demonstrate something else, namely points. Though I hesitate to defend realism, I believe that the line I draw is continuous, not a dense set of points, even if the line represented is detached from its originating *schema* to open new allegories *pace* Cantor.

Recognition does not require an existing stock of concepts. If concepts are involved, they are not always learned. Even such naturalists as Hume cite the recognized, though never seen, missing shade of blue, while Quine speaks of color recognition through certain privileged retinal irradiations. But surely not every recognition is in a concept. Recognizing significances through a field of differences is not always based on something learned nor is any concept involved, for otherwise E. coli would have long since been extinct and we would have been left with even more miserable bowel disorders than their presence occasions. When transported to a new substrate, E. coli grows new receptors. Recognizing a new concept in a "conceptual" field need entail no prior concept.

We always already find ourselves in a world; the word is the condition for our being there. The priority of concepts is a Cartesian malaise which, however, he mitigated by subordinating them to the self-showing of "clear and distinct" ideas. Ian Hacking has shown that this priority began in an epistemological crisis to which Cartesian analysis offered one solution and Leibnizian "proof theory" another (IH 1984, 211-24). Descartes distrusted logical proofs; even after the elimination of the malign genius, the absence of real relations between the moments in his punctal theory of time caused him to doubt the veracity of memory and to be suspicious of long proofs. His algebraic geometry enabled Leibniz to dismiss images and to focus on the now familiar non-intuitive model of truth which, as Hacking remarks, is virtually equivalent to provability. Descartes stayed with the "natural light." In following Leibniz, whose theory was better than his proofs, the tradition has lost its appreciation for the possibilities in analytic methods and placed its money on deductive or "synthetic" proof theory. With the elimination of the *res cogitans* and the promise that meaning is to be found only in non-instrumental, material *schemata*, it would be wise to rethink the foundations of mathematics in Plato's analytic dialectic through which most of what Euclid proved synthetically was already known. Hacking invites us to "consider the sterility of the modern philosophy of mathematics—not the collection of mathematical disciplines now called the foundations of mathematics, but our conflicting theories of mathematical truth, mathematical knowledge, and mathematical objects. The most striking feature of work in this Century is that it is very largely banal" (1984, 222). These suggestions and demonstrations are offered as an alternative, though they too could be banal.

This account commemorates the origin of mathematics as a pure science and its first physical interpretation by Pythagoras. He discovered the rational numbers and their proportional relationships (analogy, metaphor), defining the soul by placeless and timeless knowledge, and the first physical theory by mapping musical notes into and onto number. "Everything is number"; then a relation between physical objects, a twig and a string, is seen to be same as a relation between integers, unity and x. Thereafter this language of timeless, if not eternal, truth would be philosophy's paradigm.

Plato's *Timaeus* account of the soul is the apotheosis of Pythagoreanism. Though its *morphe* is expressed in arithmetical and harmonic proportions, by which, through measurement and metaphor, alterity can be assimilated as same, *psyche* is a temporal ordering, not a mathematical order, that stands out to assimilate things through ratios without being reducible to them. Mathematical reality is not eidetic even though it represents and may model even ideas. To be rational is not just to fix things in ratios; it is to assimilate the ratio of an other and make it same, for instance, $a\backslash b = c\backslash d$. Life is participatory and hermeneutical, where "interpretation" reflexively discerns or elicits a same in or through crossing otherness. Interpretations characterize both poles of human experience, sense and thought. Receptive sensibility interprets the causal or dynamical conditions in Berkeley's universal language of nature. This language is then interpreted through the mapping of what is given or presumed to be signified onto a mathematical or narrative domain which discloses its meaning. While receptive interpretations may be physical, such as E. coli's interpretations of the state of its DNA prior to replication, we are most familiar with those that are linguistic. It is usually impossible to draw a sharp line between what is received and what is contributed by sense-giving intentionality.

Language, like Pythagoras' measurement, is also founded on a metaphor. This transformation of language from habituation in a causal nexus (Peircian secondness) to the level of intentionality (irreducible thirdness) can be experienced, to a point, through Helen Keller. Prior to the episode at the well, Helen has formed some twenty word associations, though to both "drink" and "cup" she responded by miming drinking from a cup. Then there was that April day at the well-pump when Miss Sullivan again moved her fingers over the back of Helen's hand, doubtless soliciting from this matrix a pattern of expectations; suddenly these markings became the signifiers "w-a-t-e-r" and the "cool something or other" became water. Helen discovered with indescribable excitement that "everything had a name . . . the living word awakened my soul, gave it light, hope, joy, set it free . . . and for the first time I experienced repentance and sorrow."[3] That afternoon she learned thirty new words. The birth of signifiers was the birth of a world of things. This "unmotivated" disclosure in a contingent symbolization is the *arché* of mathematics (LS 1962, 16–22).

Plato thought that the condition for our active interpretations, that is, erotic propositions soliciting the world to show itself as _____, was a gift to us from a previous life with the gods. Kant understood them to be the *a priori* conditions for (active) experience (*Erfahrung*), and Husserl saw them as functions of a teleology of reason that runs through all things (1970a, 378).[4] This possibility of generating intentional objects through language and its often fortuitous use of certain symbolic or "presentifying" devices to extend its range is the work of genius; Michelangelo exploited the flawed and thus rejected stone, making of it his David.

3. Foundations

MY THESIS THAT MATHEMATICS has no foundations except in the contingent historical fact of signification originates with Kant's discovery of the method of setting out and setting up *schemata* that lets something be and be seen. The resulting symbolic presentations, however, are non-constructive and non-finitistic and disclose, as in realism, quasi-Platonic mathematical entities. Alvin Plantinga, in discussing creative anti-realism, says that its core is "the idea that objects in the world owe their fundamental structure—and if they couldn't exist without displaying that structure, their existence—to our creative activity."[5] Would mathematical objects exist without language? No. But if we are to look for traces prior to its linguistic unconcealment, these would lie in the structure of participation which it articulates. Participation, neither real nor anti-real yet partaking of both, articulates crossings which, as we have seen, are creative and interpretative. The soul, being defined by its root in each, mingles being *qua peras* and the dynamics of the place-granting *apeiron* receptacle. In a Kantian synopsis, for example, a linear *apeiron* manifold can be divided and, *pace* Dedekind, various number classes generated. Mathematics does not pertain to eternity, as Plato well knew, not is it the result of Aristotelian abstraction. The transcendental terms, being, same, other, one, many, which provide mingling with its *logos* also define how life and mind gather and order. Mathematics is the morphology of ordering gatherings, the language of the between. The paradigm remains Kant's act of drawing that lets the line be seen.

Mathematics is usually understood as synthetic and, as such, concerned with either constructive or logistic proof. I shall argue that, contrary to Hilbert, synthetic proof has little to do with the discovery of mathematical truth and everything to do with its deductive extensions. For example, the relation between the several geometries can be shown only if they share some of the same axioms. Only then can one appreciate the generality of topology and its relation to non-metric projective geometry and the relation of the latter through different order types to Euclid or Riemann. That vast monument to reason is discerned and released by a bricolage of schematic methods in playful analysis.

Even in this anti-foundational era, it is fashionable to speak of the "foundations of mathematics." As in Kant's "transcendental" arguments, it is not as if the truth status of a discipline such as mathematics were in doubt and so required a ground in the absolutely indubitable; rather the request is for something ontologically or epistemologically more basic or more simple, such as Plato's one and the indefinite dyad, upon which mathematics might be said to be founded. Like truths about God, mathematical knowledge seems to bear on its face the claim to transcend empirical fact, even if it is the indispensable instrument for understanding such facts; partaking of temporality, even if it is not changing, and eternity, even if it is neither consistent nor complete, makes mathematics of special interest to the philosopher. Foundations rest upon a sacred place. Like Parmenides' gates of paradise that they so strangely resemble, they are openings to the between of gods and humans in which the earth brings forth and unconceals in the Good's lighting. What they found supports what is first in the order of empirical knowing, physics, and in the order of knowing per se, metaphysics. Kant's suggestion that the philosopher alone is in a position to ask and answer such questions (A 719/B 747) has kept many in business during most of this century.

Kant says that only through synthesis which, in the spirit of

Leibniz, gives reasons can a condition be shown to be true. He found it in apperception's original presencing; I will find it is *psyche*. But that condition can be established only through a synthetic argument, an original positing or presencing. The method of synthesis is employed in the first *Critique* around the theme of the transcendental object. My application of demonstrative analysis shows that something embarrassingly trivial is involved as a "presupposition," the ability to point and make something presumed to be "there" ostentatious to another, the root sense of "demonstration"; while my synthetic argument will take me, as it took Kant, to the role of the soul in presencing.

Kant invokes the constituting apparatus of transcendental synthesis to account for intentionality. Pointing is perhaps the very paradigm of realism. Since E. coli, Aesop's dog who mistook his reflection and even bats can in fact recognize without concepts, isn't sense significant prior to thought? We don't have to account for the presencing of intelligibility. Thanks to Husserl and the "naturalization" of the *epoché* by metaphor and even language, as given to a motile being, sense makes sense. Thus pointing operates within a language that discloses world in its truth. Granted the relative priority of pointing (or "referring," *Bedeutung*) to "sense" (*Sinn*) as established in Kripke's or Putnam's familiar arguments, it can be said that languages express things, not Frege's "thoughts" or concepts. Frege's Platonism is appropriate only within the separated ontology that is superseded after *Parmenides* by the *Sophist* and *Philebus*.

4. The Origin of the Mathematical Tradition

WHAT IS POINTED TO usually survives through its being-sense as a candidate for further monstration. Apart from the usual rubric of identification or reidentification, this public and durative characteristic is attached in veritative judgements by *einai*, "to be." By virtue of the copula's durative and nominalizing force, objectivity is posited as repeatable public accessibility to determinables. We presumably speak of eternal truths and objects. Kant avoids realism by assuming that these objects are the ejects of constructive and iterative rules which, as logical, propose a propositional interpretation to reality. By recursively generating numbers in a timeless rule-governed act in accordance with the unchanging form of time, succession, he hoped to retain the timelessness of mathematical entities. Husserl remarked that even in its ideality, mathematical truth survives only because it is written down. How mathematics stands to certain forms of writing, or at least symbolization, and not how it stands to a transcendental apperception "generating time" in the synthesis of a homogeneous manifold in counting (A 143/B 182), will have to be our clue as to its timelessness. What keeps the horizon open, Husserl notices in "The Origin of Geometry," is the survival of written texts: "The persisting existence of ideal objects . . . their continuing to be where no one has [consciously] realized them in self-evidence, [lies in] written, documenting, linguistic expression" (360). "The sensible utterances have spatiotemporal individuation in the world like all corporeal occurrences, like everything embodied in bodies as such; but this is not the true spiritual form itself, which is called an 'ideal object.' In a certain way ideal objects do exist objectively in the world, but it is only in virtue of these two-leveled repetitions and ultimately in virtue of sensibly embodying repetitions" (1970a, 257). Husserl thought that "some words and propositions should be unambiguously correlated with certain essences [mathematical objects] that can be intuitively apprehended" in order to "constitute their completed 'meaning' (1982, 175–76). Ideality is pre-linguistic (DW 1989, 41).

It is said that mathematics is like chess. It is a game-like medial way of thinking that carries one along in a process within horizons that generate their own moves and activities. One never knows what will happen in a game; the engendering between is after all chaos, unpredictable. One never knows what will show itself as a symbol. But there is the predictable other side. *Logos,* like the Latin *cogitare,* means to collect and order; its Latin cognate is related, as Augustine says, to *ago,* "I do" (*Conf.* X, 11). We learned from Kant that thought is intrinsically spatial and temporal. The cognitive project collects and orders in order to *schema*tically disclose *morphe,* as we earlier showed when generating the integers from punctal manifolds. What is synoptically potentiated by this "I do" can then be interpreted as a potential for sets and classes; when crossed in a perspicuous notation, idealities are generated. The emergence is not from whole cloth but rather from a potentiated slot, as it were, which allows us to go beyond the already said. Clearly mathematics is a closed, highly structured language; nevertheless, its *arché* lies in writing that is monstrative, not in the privacy of transcendental synthesis.

While a concern for beginnings could lead to the "genetic fallacy," we may understand "origin" as the Greek *arché,* that from which something begins its development and, like the birth trauma, remains with it as a control, a limit (*peras*) and, unless creatively dealt with, can become institutionalized and exercise a despotic rule. Returning to the *arché* frees one from the tyranny of familiarity and opens the possibility of a new birth. Husserl says that "there is a distinction, then, between passively understanding the expression and making it self-evident by reawakening its meaning. But there also exist possibilities of a kind of activity, a thinking of things that have been taken up merely receptively, passively, which deals with significations only passively understood and taken over, without any of the self-evidence of original activity" (1970a, 361). "In this connection it must also be noted that sentences give themselves in consciousness as reproductive transformations of an original meaning produced out of an original activity, that is, in themselves they refer to such a genesis" (365). The *Meno* provides this "possibility of complete and genuine reactivation in full originality . . . in the case of geometry and the deductive sciences so-called" (365). We may look there for the *arché* that founds and gives the being sense, almost sacramental, to a written and "living tradition of the meaning formation of elementary concepts . . . the essential presuppositions upon which rests the historical possibility of a genuine tradition, true to its origins, of a genuine science like geometry" (367). The horizon of geometry is not eternal being; it is a historical product that offers the possibilities of rebirth that Plato found in beauty. But isn't mathematics beautiful? Reappropriating the empowering Good in a return to a mediating institution in the *arché* through pilgrimage, rite, or festival is the prototype of hermeneutics by which a tradition lives and continues to develop. Does returning to the instituting origin of mathematics in *Meno* show mathematics to be hermeneutical? I proceed on that assumption.

Since the *Meno* is the earliest written statement about the method and nature of mathematics and since later antiquity tended to associate its development with Plato and his Academic colleagues, Theaetetus, Euclid, and Eudoxus, I propose to let the *Meno* do proxy for whoever, "be he Thales or some other" (B xi), set mathematics on the sure path of science. Kant said this was "the true method . . . [which was] not to inspect what he had discerned either in the figure or the bare concept of it, and from this read off, as it were, its properties; but to bring out what was necessarily implied in the concepts he had himself formed *a priori,* and had put into the figure in the construction by which he presented it to himself" (B xii). But is this not the method of analysis implicit in the conversation between Socrates, Meno, and his young slave in the *Meno?* That written conversation to which we can always return which makes present, as if for the first time, the intention to *morphe,* pure form, through drawn *schemata,* the shapedness of concrete things, is the *arché* of our mathematical tradition; and since it marks the first occurrence of idea as a technical term (72B), it forever thereafter links the *aletheia* of Being disclosed by philosophy with mathematical demonstration.

By returning to the "origin" in which things showed themselves in self-givingness, which he does not identify with any particular event, Husserl maintains that we can reactivate the being-sense of a tradition which through countless generations has explicated what is passively received and produced its own innovations yet, nevertheless, has lost its ontological depth and spiritual sense. What was seen by the slave, as Husserl says of the *arché* event, "has from its establishment an existence which is peculiarly supertemporal and which is accessible to all men"(EH 1970a, 356) ". . . that we can live through in a quasi-new and quasi-effective manner . . . so as to experience in original fashion what is self-evident" (360). This is not a return to the axioms as "primal premises" in the usual understanding of synthesis but rather to the original synthetic unconcealment and recognition of *morphe*. Playing about with shapes can be an eidetic reduction that opens one to these "primal premises." Most of what Euclid proved had already been discovered by analysis. This event of *aletheia* can be reexperienced only within our own historical horizon, where its implications and possibilities have been worked out, not as if one were a contemporary of Socrates and the slave; the task for hermeneutics is to fuse these horizons.

In demonstrating the linguisticality of pure mathematics, its dependence on its *schemata,* I will show how the truth of a mathematical expression does not depend on a proof, contrary to formalism; that mathematical statements do not express ideas or concepts, contrary to the logistic tradition; and finally that mathematical objects are present only through a disclosive symbolism, contrary to constructivism or intuitionistic foundations. A symbolism or *schema* is a presentification, that through which the signified is present. They are quasi-symbols, and like sacred symbols, these participate in and so bear something of the character of that which they signify. The *schema*tic round, like Kant's dinner plate (A 137/B 138), is not a circle, and yet when drawn is seen as such. But take care: do not mistake the finger for the moon. The iconic character of some signifiers that are assumed to correctly picture nature can lead to grave errors, as in the Curie principle of symmetry or the wrong icons led Hamilton into error.[6] This is the reason for my perhaps unhappy choice of "quasi-symbols" to designate mathematical signifiers.

In the *Meno* example which we are about to examine, imagine Socrates pointing to the square he is drawing on the sand and saying:

> "You recognize this as a square, don't you?" [It isn't a plane figure, and surely what closes it are not four congruent straights at right angles to one another. This square (figure, *schema*) will become the primal premise on which all mathematical presences are founded.]
> "Yes."
> "And of course you know that each of these four sides will be equal?" [But are they, these fleeting images in the sand, really instances of the square itself?]

"Yes." [The correct answer, for *morphe,* i.e., squareness,
is seen (noesis) through this *schema.*]
"Now," Socrates says pointing at the *schema,* "show me
how to make a square twice the size of this one."

What had been the *schema*tic language of shape and number is now,
on the boy's acknowledgment that he understands, a shareable historical horizon within which whatever shows itself as an extended *schema*
"which always accompanies color" (75B) instances *morphe.* Something like the animation of Husserl's indicative signs occurs in this
epoché or "conversion" and lightens when seen in its intelligibility. It
may help to return to our disclosive model of analysis in which each of
a K-set of demonstrative phrases, A, B, C . . . , points out a corresponding element in a K'-set of over-lapping regions through the metaphors of the K regions, even if obscurely. What these convergent
regions point to transcends the regions through which it is elicited, as
the invisible and simple point transcends the nesting squares or circles
that converge to it. The point exists only through its defining regions.
The point, not the inscription, is now a possible element in a K-set for
further monstration, for example, a line connecting any two. With
Socrates' successful monstration, the K-set of demonstrative phrases,
e.g., "square" and "four sides being equal" will be stabilized and
serve as descriptions of the problematic *morphe,* the double square.
This illustrates Jacques Derrida's point that metaphor is the *arché* of
the univocal ideal of logocentric discourse.

The slave can, unlike Meno, recognize what lies there before him.
He sees the intelligible form in the drawn *schema.* This *aletheia,* quite
literally released from concealment through Socrates' questions and
actions, is the solution to the problem raised when one asks, "How
does one double the area of an arbitrarily given square?" Introduction
into the new *schema*tic language which lets him see the answer is parasitic on the boy's prior linguistic skills; he must speak Greek and count
if he is to follow Socrates and, unlike Meno himself, be able to "look
and see" what it says (82B). Meno himself is blind, the captive of
Gorgias' habits of questioning (70B-C) and Empedocles' learned jargon (76D). He cannot recognize what color is unless it is defined in
terms about which nothing can be known: "an effluence of shapes
commensurate ["fitting into some of the passages" of the eye] with
sight and perceptible to it" (76D). A *schema,* the shape of the drawn
lines "that always accompanies color" (75B), shows a *morphe* to the
slave, through Socrates' gesturing demonstrations, in which "these
sides are equal" (82B).

Though the slave tries to discover the *morphe* of the double
square as if that were the drawn *schema* by extending its roots or sides,

playfully running through these *schematic* signifiers as they are variously set up, the answer comes from seeing the solution in the diagonal of the original square. If seen aright, these *schemata* exhibit the "primal premises . . . [which lie] in the precultural world" of Socrates, perhaps in his workshop (EH 1970a, 376). Like the worker with stone slabs in Wittgenstein's first language game, both he and the boy were familiar with shapes (LW 1968, secs. 19–21). We will visit them, taking with us the indispensable, if pedantic, Husserl. While there we will pick up a few cubical *schemata*, like the alphabet blocks with which we played as children, and use them in the demonstrations to follow.

Returning to this world with Socrates and the slave, Husserl says, will "awaken the total problem of the historicity of the correlated manner of being of humanity and the cultural world and the *a priori* structure involved in this historicity" (1970a, 376).

Action is an *epoché*. The "primal premises" arise in this work-world

> through an activity of free variation [the method of the eidetic reduction], and in running through the conceivable possibilities [the various arrangements suggested to the slave by his understanding of the *schema*] . . . there arises with apodictic self-evidence, an essentially general set of elements [the square formed on the diagonal rather than on an extension of the root] going through all the variants. . . . We have removed the bond to the factually valid, historical world and have regarded this world itself as one of the conceptual possibilities . . . which can be made originaliter at any time, can be fixed in univocal language. (375)

Playing with *schemata* opens a "play-space," a between, which could occasion the event of *aletheia*, the truth that happens over and above our doing.

> Even if we knew nothing about the surrounding world of the first geometers, this much is certain as an invariant, essential structure: That it is a world of things . . . , that all things necessarily had to have a bodily character—though not all things could be mere bodies. . . . What is also clear . . . is that these bodies have spatial-temporal shapes and "material" qualities related to them. Further it is clear that in the life related to practical needs certain particularizations of shape and a technical practice always [aims at] the production of particular preferred shapes and the improvement of them in the direction of gradualness—surfaces, more or less smooth, more

or less perfect surfaces; edges, more or less rough or fairly
even; in other words, more or less lines, angles, more or less
perfect points. (376)

Beginning in his stone mason's shop with Socrates would lead one
beyond the circumspective grasp of shapes to their discernment as instances, more or less perfect, of *morphe* and thus to a "general set of
elements going through all the variants. . . . Only if the apodicti-
cally general content, invariant through all conceivable variation, of
the spatial-temporal sphere of shapes ["*schemata*"] is taken into account can an ideal construction arise which can be understood for all
future time and all coming generations of men and thus be capable of
being handed down and reproduced with the identical intersubjective
meaning" (377). The space of these *schemata* is Euclidian. Sophus Lie
showed that this is the only metric geometry which is isotropic and
homogeneous and so permits "playful" manipulations with the blocks
involving rotations, mirror imaging, and translations.

Demonstrative *schemata* show but do not express sense, do not
say anything; if we are to express the truth laid open to us, in addition
to the stabilizing name we require a characterizing notation which,
like the *schema*, enable us to "see" as we think about what must be
the case with things that are. In mathematics, as in a novel, one does
not describe things that are, even though Dickens's Uriah Heep or one
of Miss Murdoch's academic types seems to have its own intrinsic
reality. Elicited reality (*res*) is ideal, that is, typical; like mathematics,
it has something of the power of a concrete universal to collect and to
define others as being of its kind. It is then a paradigm standing as a
truth condition for assertions: have you not seen Uriah in obsequious
individuals? Even more important, objects (*objekts*) contextually generated by quasi-symbols have internal truth conditions. This is rather
like what we mean when we say something is "according to character"; deed and thought must match up and form a coherent story. The
logic of entailments may rest on the intuitions that justify the literary
critic. Kant says of such objects that we know them already ahead of
ourselves—but why then the need for a deduction?—because we constituted them, presenced them through our concepts. Insofar as mathematics is projective, he was correct. But we can express concepts only
after intuition, the work done by signifiers; these he neglected for fic-
tive "concepts" and allegories he failed to recognize as such.

The pure intentional objects represented in mathematical *schemata* are generated by being represented; through this recognition of
form in the facts, these *schemata* have disclosive and constituting
power. As "primal premises," these shapes are "more or less straight,

more or less identical, more or less plane," etc. *Schemata* interpret the spatiality of the workshop. Imagine Socrates and the slave playing with cubical blocks; concern with its manipulable products fosters Euclidian interpretations. "Primal premises" lie with the signifiers, not the workshop. On the other hand, Dickens found his "primal premises" in London's courts, hovels, poor houses, and the like. Signifiers in a novel are arbitrary. Uriah was not called "Uriah" because he was to the type "Uriah." By some other name he would have answered to the same descriptions. This is definitely not the case with a "stabilized" mathematical signifier. One looks at what is drawn or set up before us (*Vorstellung*). One plays about with it. One comes to see through it. That *schema* is the primal name and "square" is a rule for setting it out. We confront the mystery of human creativity, the mystery of the *logos*, the word that becomes logic, by which whatever is is. Can we explain it? I think not. We can only give examples that will narrow its scope.

One is reminded of Leibniz's search for a language which, like the "natural signs" of the Tarot deck of cards would, by having a real relation to its objects, do our thinking for us. The things unconcealed are expressed, not—as Kant or Frege would have it—just our concepts. We have used William Weedon's method of pointing to let *aletheia* happen. If we look at the exchange between Socrates and the slave, the *schema* recognized as the *morphe* "square" is the only region covered by the other K' elements. The slave's *schema*tic four unit square is an element, a "phrase," in a K-set, is not schematically present in the nine and sixteen unit *schemata*. With the recognition of the diagonal, which required something like a conversion in which one no longer moves back and forth along the root, searching for some integer greater than two and less than four, but must look back to the square itself, one may generate homologous K and K'-sets. Like its close relative, Husserl's eidetic reduction, analysis presupposes a *morphe*-preserving primary recognition that is the measure of its success or failure. All the monstrative attempts depend on the primary recognition which the "person interrogated is willing to grant" (*Meno* 75D-E); the primal premise of the argument lies given by the recognition of *schemata* through seen color (75C), which Meno himself was unwilling to grant. The primary recognition facilitates demonstration of the same entity situated in K-sets that, however, do not cover one another. Once we see in this the *morphe* square, then this, not the enabling *schema*, is the invariant upon whose diagonal the solution lies. We move dialectically back and forth between *schema* and *morphe;* what is an element in a K'-set in one movement can be a region in another; Wittgenstein somewhere says concepts are regions. Every monstrative act, a member of the set generating the K'-set, associates with its disclosive region one or more descriptive phrases from characterizing K-set, A, B, C. . . . These are "animated" in the "seeing," if there is anything to be seen. In a successful monstration these phrases provide a descriptive language, a supply of predicates, satisfying the univocal ideal in which the sign is the unity of the binary pair, signified-signifier. Whatever is dialectically disclosed is the truth condition for the set of descriptions, and these stabilized descriptions resulting from successful monstration, univocally instituted in the presence of their object "all at once," e.g., "square . . . these sides being equal," point to something which transcends natural language and its metaphors of circumspective seeing through which these mathematical objects were released. The premises are then propositions to be explicated or handed over to computers for computational ends.

5. Speculative Demonstration

GREEK NUMBER THEORY was geometrical. That meant that, as in Kant's synthetic method, one saw the solution, just as one may see it today in computer models. Can we set up some of the squarish blocks picked up in Socrates' shop to speculatively demonstrate some truths in number theory, as in Socrates' example of the double square? It is immediately evident that, given a square made from four blocks, none can be made from eight. The "line which extends from corner to corner in the figure of four units . . . which the learned call the diagonal" (*Meno* 85B) divides the square into two equal parts. The diagonal is incommensurable. The classes of rational and irrational numbers have now been introduced. The variable had to await the Stoics. We can now *schema*tically unconceal additional number theoretic formulae. What is the sum of the first n odd numbers, for any value of n? Restricting ourselves to $n=4$, can we see through this array of blocks the solution for any n? One might arrive at a variety of K

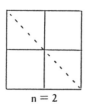

n = 2

figure 1

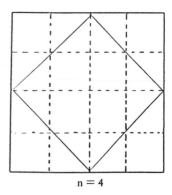

n = 4

figure 2

sets that show nothing. Should one come up with the square *schematic* arrangement in Figure 3, it will be seen to have the form of the gnomon, as in Figure 4, and the addition of any successive odd number will be *morphe* preserving: the resulting square will have the value n^2. To see in sense a virtual infinity of form is a staggering achievement sedimented in familiarity. This rather restricted instance of a *morphe*

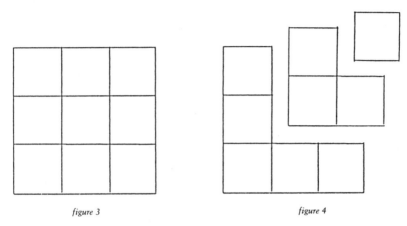

figure 3   figure 4

preserving *schema* unconceals the value of *n* for any *n*. Playing about with *schemata* lets truth happen. The model is phenomenological and not formal. Could number theory have begun in any other manner? The fact that there is no consistency proof suggests that foundations belong to analysis, not deductive synthesis.

Let's try two more examples. What is the sum of the first *n* integers, for any value of *n*? Be sure you have enough blocks for the case where $n=3$. Play about and let truth happen. This is a more difficult problem. If one comes to the arrangement in Figure 5, add its reflection to it, as in Figure 6. Then look! The area of this new rectangle is

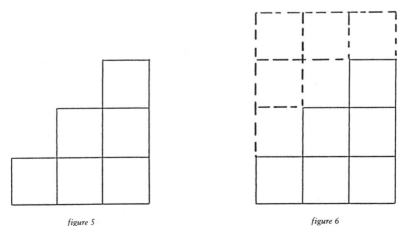

figure 5   figure 6

$n(n + 1)$. But the original (Fig. 5) is one half of this area (Fig. 6); therefore the solution is $\frac{1}{2}n(n + 1)$. If you saw it for three, you saw it for 10 billion. No wonder number has always been understood as the form of the soul's transcendence.

As a last example, try the solution to the following: "What is the sum of the squares of the first n integers, $1+ 2+ 3+ \ldots$?" This is even more difficult and one will have to play around with lots of the blocks, piling them this way and that, before one sees the solution. A promising schematic image appears in Figure 7. If then we add a block to each end of the bottom row, so that its length is $2n + 1$ and complete the rectangle, as in Figure 8, then the area of the enclosed ziggurat is to the rectangle as one is to three. Since the height of the

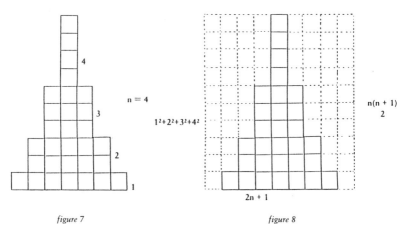

figure 7   figure 8

rectangle is $\frac{1}{2}(n(n + 1))$, its area will be given by the formula $\frac{1}{2}(n(n = 1)(2n + 1)$. The desired solution will be $\frac{1}{6}(2n^3 + 3n^2 + n)$. The *schema* is *morphe*-preserving. To see the solution is to see how a recursive rule generates the sameness of shape in different sizes, and this is possible only on a Euclidian interpretation. Given an algebraic notation, the *schema* can be ignored and answers can be arrived at by calculation. Nevertheless, it appears that mathematics has its origin in *doxa* as appearing rather than as opinion. Though the thesis concerning analytic foundations is independent of that concerning signifiers, the disclosive role given the latter builds this account into analysis as a method of coming to see (noesis) through *schemata.* In an intuitive account, rhetoric, not logic, provides intuitions, but not an absolute ground; and since none can claim that status, all we can do is to try to describe how we see mathematical objects.

The fortuitous discovery of signifiers which, for all their novelty, are fit to be characters in the same unitary, narrative history of the origins of mathematics entails the attendant and compatible intuitions of new objects and their object horizons. How we are able to say something determines both what can be seen and what can be said about it. In mathematics style is everything! For example, what is clear in one notation may be obscure in another. Divide MDCLXVI by XLIV; though one might find that the answer is XXXIV, thanks to the Arabs, isn't it easier to divide 1666 by 49? Newton had a better understanding of what is involved in the calculus than Leibniz, though his notation was a disaster when it was adopted by English mathematicians for chauvinistic reasons; not until Hamilton turned to Leibniz's symbolism was further progress made in England. Following on his interest in a Tarot-like symbolism, Leibniz produced a notation that, it has been said, enabled him to develop the integral and differential calculus in a single day. We cannot say in a natural language what these signs on being seen say, though they do carry with them a *schema*tizing history of mathematical experience that prepares one for them. For example, the way to the calculus had been prepared through a tradition concerned with the rectification and quadrature of curves, the analytic geometry of Descartes, concern with the rates of increase of certain functions, and the like. With the "discovery" of the infinitesmal, this history becomes irrelevant; if one continued to think the new objects through this older schematized experience, the results could be disastrous. Though the line between the necessary *schema,* which can be iconic, and the discerned *morphe* is difficult to draw, we must insist on the necessary role of *schema*tic signifiers in mathematical truth and the danger of mistaking these 'pointers' for what they make significant. This is a dialectical point; there is no *a priori* cartography showing the way through this Symplegades. It may help to recall that determinate objects are transparently given for or constituted by thought, while self-manifesting things give themselves.

Newton and Leibniz provide an interesting and instructive example of the confusion between *schema* and *morphe.* They were concerned with rates of change and assumed that the calculus pictured this situation. Although Leibniz's notation gave correct results that Newton obtained by an inconsistency, neither had an adequate idea of limits. Since instantaneous velocity or acceleration made no sense, they spoke directly or by implication of temporal intervals greater than 0 but less than any assigned magnitude, for example, 1. At 0 the system would be at rest and the function would have no value. From the value of the "infinitesimal" magnitude a (acceleration), one wishes to know the value of the increase in distance as its magnitude tends toward 1. Plato would eliminate talk of "increasing" and "tending." Given Weierstrass' new concept of a limit, Plato's ideal is realizable: a function $f(x)$ has a limit *1* at a value a of its argument x if its values in the neighborhood of a approximate to 1 within every standard of approximation. An Occamist reduction eliminates the infinitesimals (ANW 1958, 162–75).[7] If this is too convoluted, then recall that the metaphoric extensions of space as finite dimensional vector spaces or phase spaces has little to do with space or that extensions of conic sections and trigonometry are often equally remote from geometrical figures.

Like characters in a picaresque novel, mathematical objects enter the tale as if from nowhere, form a coherent part of the story and take on a life of their own. For example, though apparently Diophantus knew that "the product of minus multiplied by minus is plus" (Def. IX) and could express a negative number by a μ prefix, it was not until 1496 that Lucia Paciuolo used the arabic numbers and 0 as something more than place markers, as in 10, 100, 1000. Algebraic number theory, in distinction to its earlier geometrical, Pythagorean form, awaited only the zero as origin, as if *ex nihilo*, and the introduction of the prefixes $+$ and $-$. Signed numbers were first noted on warehouse goods in a book published in 1489 indicating that they were more or less than some assigned weight. They were first used mathematically in the *Deutsch Arithmetica*, published in Nuremberg in 1549, by Luther's friend Stifel. He was interested in biblical numerology and by its means twice predicted the end of the world. Later in the century, Harriot gave birth to algebraic form when he saw that $x + y = 1$ could be expressed as $x + y - 1 = 0$. What had been a place marker became an integer—with special dispensations. Descartes brought these together in his algebraic interpretation of coordinate geometry. One could now abandon the Greek's geometrical and analogical intuitions for the algebraic intuitions of the moderns. New notations and disclosures do not appear to come about through a teleology of reason, as Husserl's "Origin of Geometry" had it, nor is this an inevitable Heideggerian "sending" or "destining," *Geschichte;* its *arché* is the between, the rag and bone shop of archaic experience.

Harriott's discovery and its subsequent development by Descartes and others represents the transformation for a geometrical to an algebraic tradition which appears to have little to do with the mathematics whose foundations we have been proposing. Kant seems to ignore the apparent incompatibility between the "ostensive" foundations of geometry and the constructions of "symbolic" algebra, both of which were supposed to share the same synthetic *a priori* root (RW 1975, 22). Is algebra a phenomenon in which, as Kant said in his *Dissertation,* "ideas received from the intellect cannot be followed up in the concrete and converted into intuitions?" (389). Arithmetic has been accommodated to geometry through the gnomon; but since, as will be seen, mechanics could not really get beyond its Aristotelian, geometrical roots without algebra, can we find a clue in Kant that facilitates this transformation? As early as the 1763 *Enquiry* Kant was saying that in arithmetic "symbols are first of all supposed, together with special notations of their increase or decrease and their relations, etc. Afterwards one proceeds with the signs, according to easy and certain rules, by means of substitution, combination, or subtraction and many other kinds of transformations so that the things symbolized here are completely ignored until, at the end, and in conclusion, the meaning of the symbolical conclusion is interpreted. . . . Visible figures or signs express either the thought or their relations" (278–79). How is the meaning interpreted? Geometry constructs its object in an *a priori* intuition, but what concretely shows in a symbol? "Mathematics, in its inferences and proofs, examines its universal knowledge concretely, under signs, but philosophy always examines its knowledge, *in abstractio*, alongside the signs. . . . Mathematical signs are sensuous epistemological tools" (291). Sensuous epistemological tools?

Mathematical description tends to transcend its sensuous origin; the language of the workplace contained "square" and "four" long before Socrates or Pythagoras came upon it. But then try to say within the resources of a natural language what these formulae express and describe: $ax + by = c$ and $ax + by = 0$. When read correctly, we see as by a Cartesian *inspectio* that they describe parallel lines. In a similar manner, Socrates introduced his square by the construction of a square gnomon. One shows that the area of the whole is to a side as x^2 is to x. Pythagoras' theorem, $a^2 + b^2 = c^2$, of which the *Meno* demonstration is a special case, may have been introduced to solve problems about *schema*tic squares but, borrowing Kant's analytic jargon, the arbitrary (by anything whatsoever) satisfaction of any of the "conditioned" variables in the Pythagorean formula will be seen to determine the "condition" of the solution (which will be true under suitable interpretations of that "anything whatsoever"). A fortuitous discovery of a transformation introduced algebra and new number classes which can be given a geometrical interpretation. The introduction of variables and constants enabled a possible geometrical structure, such as those expressed in Cartesian coordinates, which is true of this phenomenon, for example, velocity, to be also true of any other having a similar form, e.g., growth in money supply. The clue to algebra lies in a roportional root it shares with metaphor, the primordial vehicle for transformations.

6. Interpretations

MATHEMATICS RESULTS FROM INTERPRETATIONS in which one can express the structure of (neither real as *schema*tically given nor anti-real as a created projection) participation. Allowing for the exceptional experience of a Leibniz, whose occult concern with efficacious symbols led him to successfully search for new ones, that is, base two for the number system, one happens upon a symbolism and, as with Michelangelo and the rejected marble, those that work disclose what seems to be always already there. For example, Claude Shannon saw a relation between the two constants of Boolean algebra and open and closed switches and the modern computer was born. A curious blend of the fortuitously contingent and the atemporality of Parmenidian presence, is it not? How can this be?

According to Jacques Derrida, Husserl thought that the possibility of history had its necessary condition in the language of objectivity, in logic and its literal use of language (1977, 66–67). As long as we restrict ourselves to natural language, its objects are "bound" and existence is never neutralized, even in a reduction. "Lion" is still bound to its empirical origins after its bearer has become extinct in its natural habitat, even if, as Hegel observed, the implicit *epoché* performed in naming "annihilated them in their existence (as existents)" (GH 1892, sec. 462; cited by JD 1977, 67). In translation from one language to another, from "lion" to *löwe,* one and the same meaning *(Sinn)* intended in these significations elicits a higher sense of ideal objectivity than is the case within a single natural language. Still these universals are founded on empirical contingencies while those of mathematics are pure in the Kantian sense. Husserl contended that the ideal "objectivity of geometry is absolute and without any kind of limit. . . . It is not that of the expression or ideal content: it is that of the object itself . . . the possibility of translation, which is identical with that of tradition, is opened ad infinitum (EH 1970a, 72). Now we are beyond bound and among free idealities. Once this intuition is secured, which is through a reduction "not only of all de facto language, but of the fact of language in general," then Husserl proposes to "redescend towards language," to reinstate it (75). How can we "redescend" towards that which we never transcend? Like Plato, Husserl makes language a disposable instrument in the face of the pure presence of the form. He also fails to recognize that metaphor is the condition for articulating both the possibility of and the conditions for the Open and that, in its earliest stage, mathematics is the form of metaphor, which is also the form of measurement and reflection. But Husserl recognized something of great importance; in bound discourse the sense of the assertion can be distinguished from the form of the assertion, but this is not the case in geometry—or presumably in all mathematical language. There is no translation problem as such; what might pass for translation are equivalence classes and transformations. Since Gadamer has made the case that "translation" characterizes hermeneutical understanding, instituted mathematics is not, though its institution is, hermeneutical. It is rather the *logos* that gathers science or logic into historical horizons. The universality and necessity of this form of expression is constitutive of transcendence.

What do mathematical *schema* constitute? That is like asking, "What do we see when we 'see' (noesis) *morphe?*" Something about ourselves and something about things. Understanding lightens an Open in which the happening of truth takes a certain form. Though apparently proven, surely Fermat's last theorem is true or false prior to a proof and it is counterintuitive, as Plantinga has remarked, to assume otherwise. This form belongs to the subjective, though not narrative, interpretative species; mathematical objects (*objekts*) are real, in Kant's sense, and are disclosed through *schema*tizing. In the sense that these objects are posited by *schemata* as real, anti-realism is also true. Moreover, if knowing is for us largely a matter of mapping and modeling, then this too comes to us in metaphor, whose mathematical form was given through the "isomorphisms" discovered in the earliest Greek mathematics (CB 1963, 8–13). We have the power to map and thus to represent or make images of all things which, according to *De Anima*, we already potentially are. In Plato's image of the divided line, this same for being and thinking is expressed as the congruence between its second and third levels. Thanks to Pythagoras and his discoveries in music and number theory, we can map or find an image of one set of elements in another. Metaphor is the single root of the soul's power. These demonstrations could be extended to establish the possibility of recognizing self-congruent objects and so the possibility of the theory of measurement. Since this theory is contingent on the possibility of metaphor, it appeals to the priority of rhetoric, the theory of disclosive tropes and their models, over logic, the theory of synthetic proof and predicative form.

What does a morphological, mathematical intuition tell us about itself? As eidetic, if not an *eidos,* it will be closed to any explanation by *schema*tic operations and temporal conditions, such as "squaring" or psychologism. In the former case, Plato thought that change might contaminate the purity of mathematics and is said to have rejected Hippias' solution of the trisection problem. What turns the mind towards genesis and away from the good and objects of pure knowledge is inadmissable; talk of "squaring and applying and adding and the like" is "ludicrous" (527A). Yet in the *Sophist* the argument against "the friends of the forms" (248A–49B) moves far beyond these ascetic prohibitions. By then the task is to express the dynamical form of the cosmos and to characterize the formal changes it occasions. Not only do all creatures participate in form, but by the principle of the relativity of the transcendentals form also participates in creatures. The form of the universe is also the form of each of its creatures; life is like the doctor doctoring himself (*De Gen. Anim.* 199b 20), is it not?

Why did Kant turn to mathematics as the paradigm example of synthesis? Synthesis was intended to secure the nomic tie between what I intend to do, draw a line, and the presencing to me of the expressed concept, "the line itself," through the auto-affective, perceived drawing. Implicit in this, if one can now understand the drawing example as an act of signifying, is the so-called logocentric unity of signified and signifier. I accept the unity in mathematical discourse and deny logocentricism. I propose this disclosive and linguistic version of Kant as a foundation for mathematics.

Formalism invites the assignment of objects to an uninterpreted language. The conceptualist expresses concepts while the intuitionist presences objects in constructive proofs. The text speaks of the concepts or the use of rules which are the anti-realist's stock in trade or the transcendently existing objects of the realist. The former seeks to ground mathematics in the expressive or rule-governed self, in its proofs or rules, forgetting that the language is instituted by what is seen in its being seen, while the latter forgets the metaphors and the institution of notation that makes his seen possible. Truth happened to Meno's slave. He could not have arrived at a solution by striving or intending, since the root required was incommensurable. The rules he understood spoke of extending a root or side. In the sense demonstrated by Socrates and the slave, the supplement lying outside the text making unconcealment possible is what makes the language a language, not what outside the language, as a preexisting, available, grounding presence makes it "true." In Plato's dialectical usage, *morphe* was seen through the questions and assemblage that freed the *schema* to unconceal and, through the mathematical language fixed monstratively, truth could now be expressed propositionally. But we are invited as participants into the text, brought to see with the slave the truth conditions for the text, and share the self-evidencing results. The formal language given and fixed as a univocal notation through analysis, through looking and seeing, that is, recognizing this figure as a square and "having these sides equal," also articulates what is seen in propositions that are true for any number.

If we are to begin with a myth which relates life to world through number, we must look closely at this strange *a priori* language that seems not to be about anything, though it makes everything of which being can be said intelligible. Is it about nothing, about something like the transcendental object which is also nothing? About the very possibility of appearing? Once signs are "animated" and one is gathered into their horizons by its *epoché*, mathematics plays through and carries one along, not by will, but as St. Paul says of grace, by a "necessity laid upon me." Does it thematize, as in the old distinction between continuous and discrete quantity, that which *qua apeiron* and *peras* the *arché* lets gather into being? Mathematics ranges over the entirety in its making and being made. How? Not because mathematics gives us, as it gave Augustine, the archetypal standpoint of the God who is "beyond finding out" (*Tim.* 28C), but rather because of the *epoché* Hegel found in names. Through naming, a factor in the general becoming of nature is prescinded to become a determinate or determinable entity, an intentional object, for thinking. Husserl noted a further level of generality when he said mathematical signs, unlike such signs as "lion," were not bound to localizable existences and thus release free idealities. These idealities, rather than being F. H. Bradley's "wandering adjectives," have as existential correlatives pure potentials, determinable and determinate. Mathematical objects, like quasi-symbols, seem to gather beings into their formality and let them be unconcealed.

The "anything whatsoever" of universal quantification refers to potential aspects of things, not to their actuality. Except in metaphor, the actual features of the world should never be assimilated to geometry, such as the belief that time is really the expressed in the "spatial" tensors in general relativity. Why? In the first place, mathematics is pure, constituted (as "lion" is not) to operate over potentials, those of determinable *peras* (Aristotle's discrete quantity or, as applied, Kant's mathematical Principles) and those of the *apeiron* determinable (continuous quantity or, as applied, Kant's dynamical Principles). These potentials, which Plato identifies with being (*peras*) and becoming (*apeiron*), define the gap, the *arché*, within which the creature arises (*Tim.* 27D–28B) as an event in being through a gift of Being.

We have to do for mathematics what Plato did for politics. The demythologization of the chthonic, female deities seems to have led Thales and Anaximander into philosophy. Oceanus, said by Homer to be the mother of the gods, was Thales' water, while Gaea, Hesiod's originary, or Cybele is surely Anaximander's *apeiron*. After Anaximander and Heraclitus, the logic of Parmenides dominated and the clearing or gap between earth and sky become less prominent, only to reemerge in Plato's *Timaeus* in a divine procession. Plato does not derive the gods from Gaea but from Oceanus (*Tim.* 40E). What had begun as a purely uranian explanation *schema* in which being lay on the side of the separated ideas with their instantiated likenesses was, even at the height of Plato's Apollonianism in the *Republic* giving way to an erotic and procreative ontology allegorized in the role assigned to woman in instituting a new ethos in which aggressive, homoerotic agon is replaced with a family structure based on sharing. Play, not warfare, became primary; and all played together—under the censor's watchful eye—in naked innocence? By *Timaeus* the chthonic elements come into their own, perhaps even surpassing the role of the sky-god or father. The Mother and the Father, necessity and suasive, not constituting, reason, are given equal or supplementary, not bifurcated status. The Open becomes thematic, a non-dualistic analogue of Cartesian consciousness is spanned by participation. Sense is born from the interpretative crossing (active crossing passive motion of *Theaet.* [157A] and the *Phaedrus'* exemplary or paradigmatic projections, [252B–57A]) of the received powers from the thing (*Theaet.* 156D–57A).

The hermeneutical dialectic between receptivity and interpretation establishes the readiness for being a self through interpretations of the sensitive field (EB 1983, 9–14). If I differ from Edward Ballard, the first to position Kant and Husserl within the context of Gaea and Plato, it is because I see this not as a single but as a dual field: elements are mingled from the differential field of *peras* with the extentional possibilities and dynamical necessities of the *apeiron* through directed power. The Open, to repeat, is the field of possibility for horizons of meaning and sense from this place (*chora*) that opens towards the being I am to be through the possibilities of world and the sometimes conflicting call of the Good. This *da,* "there," in which "becoming" and being mingle is the dwelling from which one emerges into the Open.

The condition for this Open is language. Mathematics is a technical or instituted language which expresses the form by which creatures are interpreted and thus known; but since interpretation is only an instance of participation, it follows that mathematics offers us these beings as patient for further interpretation in terms of those potentials, dynamical and formal, by which they come to be and be definite: "all things have in their nature a conjunction of limit (*peras*) and unlimited (*apeiron*)" (*Phil.* 16D). Kant thought things were given in schematized form by original construction. We attain these results by the peculiar nature of mathematical signifiers within which things can be seen. These interpretations often defy restatement in a natural language or, as in modern particle physics, yield a world quite disjoined from the everyday world in a unique language that, as Kant saw, posits objects which are its truth conditions.

A "language" disclosive of every potential, formal and extentional, and of their participatory possibilities must also express the formal structure of their mingling. Soul is this gap spanning structure that actuates potentials which mathematics describes and whose synoptic morphology it articulates. Participation is the interpretative assimilation of alterity, vital and noetic, through which a creature is a same for itself. Some "alterities" are Others, persons with whom we hold open this creative matrix. This assimilative structure of same, being, and other describes the activity of *psyche* (CB 1968, 116–56), if not the deconstructive participation of the Other in me.

Mathematics is a liberating art. Here, and perhaps nowhere else, there is an intentional bond, first ostensive and then stipulated, between signifier and signified. Put otherwise, mathematics is without any trace of a local habitation and a proper name. It knows nothing of the rift between the constituting and constituted, between thought and self-determining things. Its signs are never bound; its objects never have a place. Granted its *schematic* and instituting text, what is seen is indifferently available at all times and places; but this does not mean that its *arché* is in something that transcends all loci.

The clue to understanding this apparently "eternal" possibility lies, I think, in a peculiarity in the K-set of descriptive predicates standardized in demonstrative abstraction. What is initially a demonstrative phrase or gesture can also, when monstration is fixed, become descriptive. When Socrates points and says "That's a square, isn't it?" he is trying to demonstrate something to the slave; when the *schema* becomes a *morphe*, the property saturated "square" is descriptive. Description is introduced through the nominalizing, omnipresent and quite impersonal third person singular present tense of "to be," the linguistic artificer of eternity implicit in the answer to a "What is . . . ?" question. This nominalizing and objectifying role is apparent in Kant: "I find that a judgment is nothing but the manner in which given modes of knowledge are brought to the objective unity of apperception. That is what is intended by the copula "is." It is employed to distinguish the objective unity of given representations from the subjective" (B 142). If we are to understand the essence of mathematics, the same *epoché* by which the *schema* converts to "the square itself" must also contain the material and contingent signifiers by which it was seen. Language and its connection to the world is taught ostensively. Before Helen Keller could recognize "w-a-t-e-r" as water, some habituated bond between markings and entities was ostensively fixed. Helen had learned about twenty words; the relation was conditioned rather than intentional. On the fateful April day she learned thirty new words—"everything had a name." Ostensive conventions, prominent in indicative signs, and demonstrative force are both parts of language; this *arché* is lost to the ideal horizons disclosed, while pure thought seems to move in abstraction from its own signs. "Square" and "these four sides being equal" describe the mediation of *schemata* in which the *eidos* is intuitively given.

This metaphor in which something drawn on the ground is an eternal object is an *epoché* which closes mathematical noema to any supplements from history. The *epoché* also closes mathematics to expressivist metaphysical or mentalist foundations (ANW 1921, 3).[8] Recognizing the solution to the problem of doubling the square required of the slave a sort of 'conversion' experience in which he came to see rules as expressing *morphe* rather than as rules for manipulating *schemata.* Until that new sense of rule can be synthetically generated from other rules in Euclid's manner, the slave's solution was only "right opinion" (*Meno* 85C-D). Right opinion, the rectitude of the directedness to the thing itself, becomes *episteme* only when it is tied down—so that its does not run away from us—by a logistic synthesis (97D–98B).

Plato's disclosive analytic is prior to Kant's expressive approach; but Kant saw in Plato's dispensable *schema* the ineliminable condition for disclosure. Kant would agree that one can express in empirical concepts only what has been seen, but transcendental synthesis expresses ontological conditions for this "seen" *a priori*. The self-showing that marks the telos of playful and fortuitous disclosure, *aletheia*, results from interpretative *schema*tic and not constituting projection. But could we have so understood Plato without the fortuitous presence of Kant?

In the Kantian sense, a mathematical *schema* is a rule of constructivity, familiar enough in the modern ideal of the constructive proof apart from which, Michael Dummett says, "there is no such thing as indirect evidence for the truth of mathematical statements as well as direct evidence" (1980, 153). Dummett later admits that a demonstration is "an effective means of finding a canonical proof . . . as cogent a ground for the assertion of its conclusion as a canonical proof" (260). Analysis proves nothing and surely does not constitute nor provide a way towards a canonical proof, but analysis unconceals, makes truth manifest as an epiphany. Kant thought that by expressing the concept *schema*tically, one discovers its possibility. The emphasis is on constructive "act," "the generation of the representation" and not with "the outcome" (A 103).

Plato and Kant are concerned with representing, but Kant and not Plato is concerned with the rule-governed acts whereby an object comes to be present rather than with the object being given as a rule-governed unity through its idea, which by the way is Kant's manner of distinguishing a "concept" from an "idea" (A 103-5). What if the rule is non-constructive? Though speculative demonstration may be vacuous, it requires that something be seen, not step by step, but as if all at once through an infinite series of regions. Except where the roots or sides are equal or, if an oblong figure with roots like 3 and 4, yield a rational solution to Pythagoras' formula, the solutions are non-constructive or irrational. But there is no *a priori* reason for rejecting the infinite on intuitive grounds. Can't we "see" infinities? Isn't the point, a nothing, "seen" or demonstrated through a set of circular K' regions such that each region covers another and there is no least region? The rule of analysis generates non-constructive infinites.

Kant wisely assigned the mystery of number to the soul, if indeed transcendental apperception can claim for itself the dignity of *psyche*. Expressively generated number was for him the very life of mind and its worldly sway. Plato, closer to *theoria*'s participation in the sacred, saw that mathematics is interpretative, not real, and that it unconcealed form in trope; soul and its proportions articulate the musical form of life, binding it into harmony with cosmos and polis. Mathematics, like *psyche* and *eros*, mediates between the two great potentials, formal and extentional. Oddly enough, these define the terms of its mediation; as dynamical and self-transcendingly appropriative (*eros*), this demiurgos of life interpretatively makes alterity same through *analogia*, equality of *logoi* (ratios), with itself. *Psyche*, in which consciousness is a flickering episode, resolves the bifurcations which give these regions as thought and extension a substantial home.

The object (*objekt*) showing itself within mathematical language in self-evidencing *aletheia* often transcends the descriptive resources of a natural language. In playful, unmotivated events of unconcealment, "truth," the object and the notation are born at the same time, just as the marks on Helen Keller's hand suddenly meant and made water intuitively present. Plato explicitly recognizes the epistemological importance of this "as if" self-presencing role of mathematical language in his account of *dianoia*, "understanding"; on the third level of the divided line mathematics is a necessary condition for the analytic dialectic to the idea (*Rep.* 510B–11C) and seems to be the pool outside the cave in which the ideas are reflected (516A). Long before Galileo and his generation took Plato's advice and sought "to measure what is measurable and to render measurable what is immeasurable" and rediscovered the implications of these ways of seeing beings through the power of mathematics gather and uncover their *morphe*, the earliest mathematicians, Pythagoras and Plato among them, found mathematics to be the language through which *psyche* is itself disclosed. Only when soul is already understood mathematically would it be possible for a Galileo and Descartes to come to their remarkable discoveries.

7. The Soul and the Horizon of Universal Mathematics

MATHEMATICS SPEAKS TO US of Being, of permanent and unchanging presence in every present, and so has been the paradigm and vehicle of eternal and absolute truth. Being understood as sempiternal presence is misleading if not false, and it is advisable to establish mathematics within a historical ontology in order to destroy its charm for those, among whom I must often count myself, tempted to construe Being in its terms. If there are eternal squares, there are eternal laws, eternal centaurs, possible men in possible doorways and the like to which things in this world stand as pale, changing images. My protest is against separationism on behalf of the self-creative primacy of creatures. The old archetypal-image theory of Aquinas and Kant fell with evolution. I have shown mathematics to be an historic and linguistic phenomenon but have yet to show how it articulates the morphology of the open and participation.

In the middle dialogues soul had been more or less identified with noesis and understood through its eternal objects, the ideas. It is generally agreed that the *Phaedo* shows that Socratic self-understanding through the ideas cannot account for the life that seeks to account for itself. The *Sophist* gives a verdict on this separationism: "Can we ever be made to believe that motion and life and soul and mind are not present with perfect being? Can we imagine that being is devoid of life and mind, and exists in solemn unmeaningness an everlasting fixture?" (248E). The dynamical conditions, for life moves itself, must also be admitted. "The philosopher, who has the truest reverence for these qualities, cannot possibly say that the whole is at rest . . . and he will be utterly deaf to those who assert universal motion. As children say entreatingly 'Give us both,' so he will include both the movable and immovable in his definition of being and all" (249C-D). If we understand the clearing between being and becoming as formed and articulated by soul, then these are abstractions from what is most fully real, the living creature, the form of the cosmos (*Tim,* 30B). Life requires reference to two sorts of potentialities (powers, *dynamis*), those of the space-time continuum, the *apeiron* power of the receptacle, and the formal potentials, the limits, by which this continuum can become a gradient and given direction, meaning, value, and definiteness.

The possibility of transcendence through recognized significance also belongs to soul, since the motile animal must recognize in order to act. It too is duratively same through otherness by recognizing a same through others. The human soul reaches out by language to all beings and by mathematical means brings them as known into the ambience of its same, where its same is its own being to be. In speaking of motion and rest, Plato says they are different and yet "each itself the same for itself" (*Sop.* 254D). The living creature's "sameness for self" is not the simple positivity of identity but marks an aim and an achieved being-for-self. Identity is a property of the form (*Tim.* 52A) and the receptacle (50B), not life. Language is this world-constituting condition, and its proper form will be this modular, scale-preserving, disclosive mathematics. This is the point of the ratios by which soul, human life, is articulated.[9]

In the "Origin of Geometry," Husserl says geometry deals with "unbound" intentional objects. These are relatively independent of natural language; it is otherwise with most cultural objects, for Shakespeare is contingent on English, or de facto contingencies, since "lion" is contingent on the existence of lions. Thus geometry opens for us the horizons of objectivity and science, the horizons of Western man, and endlessly extends them around the theme of "truth." Indeed, with more than a faint echo of Hegel, Husserl says that the "essential structure of what is essentially human, through which a teleological reason running throughout all historicity announces itself, is provided by this scientific ideal" (1970a, 378). To return to the evidence is not to be persuaded that it should be read in the light of this nihilistic rational ideal.

Unquestionably, mathematics is a free ideality, omnitemporal and omnispatial; it constitutes the possibility of any object horizon in the sense that it is a transparently *a priori* condition for sameness, the chief exemplar of objectivity as such, and the medium of truth. Doubtless I have poisoned the wells by making mathematics the child and articulator of metaphor. But if the evidence and argument I have been presenting makes sense, and surely as a first presentation that hope may be unwarranted, the horizon that mathematics opens is that of the possibility of nature as a text for the hermeneutics of life. Life is hermeneutical? Of course. Hermeneutics is the very form of interpretative disclosiveness (*aletheia*) and its proportions generate propositional truth. Of course that ideal is implicit in its allegorical foundations, but it pertains to hypothetical, not categorical, conditions and is parasitic on metaphor. Mathematics, as Plato saw, never surpasses its foundational if's, its analogue to the allegory's "Once upon a time . . ."

I have demonstrated that mathematics is the morphology of participation, articulating the clearing between the flux and the separated forms in such a way as to enable us to know, in the model-theoretic sense, whatever appears. As the morphology of all eidetic possibility manifest through the *epoché* occasioned by the playful appropriation of *schemata*, mathematics offers assurance that all horizons within the Open will always be already understood in their possibility. Mathematics is a *logos* that gathers, lays out, and secures mathematical objects for the formalism of classes or sets, propositions, and proof. But this sense of knowing will never be absolute, certain, beyond doubt; we arrive here through Descartes' "romances of nature" and Plato's "likely stories." Metaphor lies at the heart of any linguistic achievement, and metaphor is the root out of which mathematics grows.

Plato's own example entitles one to take some liberties with dates. Immediately after making his discovery of the *nomos,* law, of musical harmony, Pythagoras wrote Plato, telling him what he had discovered (roughly the material in Euclid VII). Immediately after receiving the letter, Plato wrote *Timaeus.* He told how the god divided the soul by the ratios making up two tetrachords and how he then measured out these intervals by arithmetical and harmonic proportion in the form of the diatonic scale so that man, the creature of metaphor, can reach out and represent every being, make it present in an image, and finally come to understand it through the form of number, the number of points, lines, planes and so forth.[10] In this musical model, life is an eventual epochal becoming on the model of dance. This proposes that the things themselves be understood in an arithmetical formality. Plato arithmetizes the structure of process, that of the heavens that measure out time as a calendar and that of the events which are the really real beings. Moreover, as Taliaferro remarks,

> Just as dialectic must find the mean terms between one and many to reduce Necessity to order so arithmetic seeks to fill in the octave with as many mean terms as possible. For if strings are arranged in lengths approaching a continuous change from one to two as in a siren, they give the impression of chaos, just a noise. But in the solutions to the problem of the scale, Necessity shows itself again and again: in the Pythagorean chromatic by the comma and the approximations to the semitone; in the diatonic by the relatively smaller number of perfect fourths and fifths and the approximations to the semi-tones. Such is the nature of the ratio 2:1, whatever order is introduced, a disorder is also introduced. . . . Curiously enough the thresholds of the senses can be used to insinuate order; the imperfection of hearing allows a ratio between very large numbers to produce the sensible order rightly belonging to very small numbers. (CRT 1944, 28–29).

Such is the "conflict of measure [peras] and unmeasure [apeiron]" that sets truth working. (MH 1971b, 70). Taliaferro's deconstructive account shows that, even as it proposes an order and grasps becoming by interpretatively proposing differential conditions, life releases other necessities, the theme of Derrida's "trace" and *différance*. Sense itself deconstructs its evidence by providing interpretative fictions, diatonic or chromatic or even euchromatic.

Plato's arithmetization of geometry, which could have produced a science of becoming, did not survive Aristotle. Aristotle's merits were not inconsiderable, but scientific progress has passed him by. Plato's understanding of time was superior to Newton's and very close to that of special relativity. In particular, if time is the moving image of eternity, then any motion may be taken as uniform. If it is cyclical, then we can number it with whole numbers. Again, to turn to Taliaferro:

> Instead of keeping absolute time as the mediating principle in the light of which any motion could be taken as its measure, Newton tried to realize it as a hypothetical absolute motion

to which all other sensible motions could be referred
. . . because of his particular formulation of the laws of
mechanics. Since the vector of mass acceleration is for him the
essential entity to be measured and since it changes with the
frame of reference, it is necessary to postulate an absolute
frame of reference to which all observers can refer themselves
if they are to have a common science . . . [Since the laws]
do not hold for any frame of reference . . . and cannot be
found . . . , that sensible frame has been chosen which saves
most accurately the Newtonian laws of mechanics in their application to the appearances . . . one arrived at no principle
at all. (32–33)

Aristotle, a geometrical physicist, thought that geometry is an abstraction from sensible shapes. At least he attempted to treat time as a
quantity, even if he believed that it could not stand in a ratio to any
other species, as it must in acceleration and dynamics. Even if he did
not get it right, that took some doing.

Cezanne wanted to "do Poussin over again after nature" which he
saw in terms of cylinders, cones, and cubes; but what was for him a
principle of interpretation was for Galileo a simple identity: "Philosophy is written in this grand book, the universe, which stands continually open to our gaze. But the book cannot be understood unless one
first learns to comprehend the letters in which it is composed. It is written in the language of mathematics, and its characters are triangles,
circles, and other geometrical figures without which it is impossible to
understand a single word of it."[11] Reading nature geometrically, even
with the assistance of the Merton school and in the light of Brawar-
dine's Book of Proportions, could never let Galileo into the secret of
kinetics. Nature too defers. The soul can use proportions to measure
and to order its time, for it is alive; but geometry and algebra know
nothing of time. If one understands mathematics as Galileo (and
Kant) understood it, one is caught up in the non-causal formalism of
hypothetical-deductive explanation. Alexander Koyre remarked that
until Galileo abandoned his excessive geometrization and let his imagination play with time, he could not deal with the time rate of change:
"The renunciation of causal explanation reinforces the tendency to
geometrization and spatialization." Thus in trying to understand the
law of falling bodies, "he sees the line, the space traversed, as the argument of the function, velocity," rather than time. In fact, neither he
nor Descartes were able to successfully represent acceleration.

Aristotle, to whom so many turn for an alternative realism, is certainly a cul de sac. If the intellectual soul is the form of forms, these are
only contingently related to the things that are. Didn't he deny that we
can have proper knowledge of perishable things, and even eternal things

like the sun if they are unique (*Meta.* 1039b 31–1040a 7; 1040a 27–1040b 1)? An idea is, on the other hand, a potential for presence. Consider the economy of Plato's account: the soul is both the how of participation and, giving him the benefits of a non-instrumental view of language, the interpretative *logos* of all *logoi*. In these metaphors there is present an understanding of the interpretative and truth-making character of mathematical discourse. Again Pythagoras can help.

In measuring Pythagoras acted on a rule that gave him a *logos* (*ratio*) between unity and a member of the set of integers. Whether or not he measured correctly, the harmonic proportion obtained was *qua* mathematical *morphe* true of a discrete order. If the analogy of measurement is correct, then this form is in turn the truth of the heard sounds, a *nomos*, "law," that gathers these others into unity. A truth of numbers is then a truth of things. However, Pythagoras forgot that univocal signs are given in and through metaphor, which is clearly prior. Like many reductionists he crudely identified the things measured with numbers: "Everything is made of numbers." In forgetfulness of the manner in which these formulae are introduced through interpretative metaphor, he took mathematical objects to be fully real and thus either founded or gave powerful impetus to that metaphysics of permanent and pure presence to which Kant did not, unfortunately, erect the last cathedral. Measurement is metaphor wherein both ratios interpret each other, opening as by an *epoché* a clearing in which numbers become as if things and things become as if numbers. Were this not the case, we would have neither science not technology. In interpreting one another, they bear a truth relation, a partial identity of structure, inter se and either participate in one another or in the same eidetic structure. Mathematics makes mapping or allegory possible, the syntax of a rhetorical form that "enables one to discern a likeness of everything to which a likeness could be found and to draw into the light of day the likenesses and disguises that are used by others" (*Phaed.* 261E). Mathematics, aside from its beauty, provides as such no ideals towards which nature strives or defectively images. We do not need to explain nature's failure to conform to a geometrical ideal by ceteris paribus clauses. One might, on introducing Plato to elementary students, image or produce a spherical shape and say that this is a likeness of the sphere itself; but as a myth this is appropriate only to technology. An engineer might want to image the sphere itself in a critical bearing, but we would think him mad were he to say that a successful bearing is defectively spherical. In taking on spherical forms in droplets of water or in blastula, natural beings geometrize themselves for physical or biological reasons that have nothing to do with a striving to be spherical. Just as we might wish to store a hot liquid in a spherical tank to keep it hot, since relative to volume a sphere has the smallest surface area, so for reasons of surface tension or thermody-

namics nature often shows itself spherically. We would then give theoretical explanations in physical or biological allegories and rightly call
upon the ceteris paribus principle to mark this fact.

I have fulfilled my promise to return to the *arché* of mathematics
and found it with the help of Plato in Socrates' workplace. This uncovered an eidetic horizon, the form grasped as same in an assemblage of
schemata. It offered itself to us in perspicacious notation as an openly
endless object horizon. While any empirical object therein interpreted
would be contingent, the horizon carries within it eidetic necessity.
The move from shape to form was eidetic in Husserl's sense, an ideal
objectivity founded on language. Identity in variation, first with shapes
and then with proportionality, is the rigorous basis for this eidetic reduction. Since this variation is the condition for the reduction of continuous and discrete quanta to mathematical reality, I could—but
won't—claim to have established the *arché*, with more than a little
help from Plato. According to a Greek proverb, wherever we go, we
meet him coming back. The horizon established is that of formal objects generated by rules. New notations develop new objects or interpretations and correlative rules. After Gôdel, we are assured that
mathematicians will never be replaced by technology.

The "successful realization of a project is, for the acting subject,
self-evidence." By Husserl's mark, I am not persuaded that I have been
successful. But I have returned to the primal establishment of the tradition of mathematics and its attendant philosophy and have found

> an existence which is peculiarly supertemporal and accessible
> to all men, first of all to the actual and possible mathemati-
> cians of all people, of all ages; and this is true of all its par-
> ticular forms. And all new forms produced by someone on the
> basis of pre-given forms immediately take on the same objec-
> tivity. This ideal objectivity . . . is proper to a whole class of
> spiritual products of the cultural world, to which not only all
> scientific constructions and the sciences themselves belong but
> also, for example, the constructions of fine literature. Works
> of this class do not, like tools or architectural and other pro-
> ducts, have a repeatability in many examples. . . . All geom-
> etry exists only once, no matter how often or in what language
> it may be expressed. . . . Within the same language it is
> again the same, no matter how many times it is uttered.
> . . . In a certain way ideal objects exist objectively in the
> world, but it is only in virtue of these two leveled repetitions
> and ultimately in virtue of sensibly embodying repetitions
> (EH 1970a, 356–57).

These remarks are offered as a commentary on the sense of *arché* as the
founding originary in Husserl's "Origin of Geometry." If I have suc-

ceeded in showing that mathematics has a hermeneutical origin, that it is interpretative rather than constative, and have retained something of the spiritual sense that appertains to the *Logos,* then justice will have been accorded Kant and the tradition he lovingly served.

Deo Gratia

ENDNOTES

....

INTRODUCTION

....

1. See Charles M. Sherover (1971, 170–81) for an explanation of this "recoil" and its relation to the first and second editions of the *Critique* and to Heidegger himself. He concludes that Heidegger's retreat is not binding on us (179); seen within the context of the analytic and synthetic methods, the differences between the two versions will be less glaring and the possibilities of access to the *arché* are more evident.

2. Emmanuel Levinas suggests that Derrida's "deconstruction" is a continuation of Kant's attempt to bracket out the transcendent from metaphysics in which, nevertheless, there is still a trace of its presence "operating within intuition itself" (EL 1991, 3).

Robert Bernasconi mentions several strategies for breaking away from this closure on a metaphysical text. While there may be a "beyond" metaphysics, which would thus be without an essence or definition, metaphysics cannot be left "unambiguously behind" since there is no stand "unequivocally outside it" (RBr 1993, 190). On the one hand, we can show that in certain metaphysical oppositions, e.g., presence and absence or inside and outside, one term—a "quasi-transcendental"—is privileged over and governs the others. Derrida draws attention to these differences which were, Bernasconi notes, "allowed to play according to a logic we do not associate with metaphysics" (190). Let me add that there cannot be a play, which requires difference or alterity, if the same "slippage" effects "same" and "other" that befalls other differences; unless there is to be a senseless mingling of "all with all," there must be an other which is the condition for sames.

The trace of a beyond metaphysics is found within metaphysics itself. In the "Ends of Man," Derrida says this possibility is motivated by a "radical rumbling that can only come from outside"—which the friends of Plato have already heard in the solicitations of the receptacle by the Good (*Tim.* 52E–53A)—that suggests two "escape" strategies. First, "we can attempt an exist by deconstruction without changing terrain; but then there is the "risk of confirming, consolidating or subsuming what we claim to be deconstructing." Second, we can "change terrain in a discontinuous and irruptive manner by brutally placing oneself outside and affirming an absolute break and difference" (JD 1976, 135). Since we have no lexicon and no language outside the metaphysical text in which they are inscribed, this would, Bernasconi notes, reinstate the new terrain on the "oldest ground" (RBr

1993, 191). Since "beyond" is, like phono-centricism, experience, origin, property and unity, a metaphysical concept, the going beyond must employ these strategies, "perhaps in a new writing that will weave and interweave these two motifs of deconstruction" (JD 1976, 135). We have the beginnings of such a language in the middle voice, which Kant rather unwittingly introduced through his use of the imagination.

　　3. The ontological thematic governing Kant's account of perception restricts meaning to verification criteria. The only sense that an empirical object may have is that given in the schematized categories. The lack of this restraint seems to be to Husserl's advantage, for objects of any type, e.g., cultural and historical and not just scientific objects, can be taken up into various noetic modifications, i.e., imagined, fantasized, perceived, etc. The ontological determinate, given by the transcendental object, nevertheless facilitates the rather violent "retrieval" from Kant of alternative ontological possibilities, such as those explored by Heidegger and made available to hermeneutics by Gadamer. When this retrieval is effected via Husserl rather than Heidegger, who remained indifferent to Husserl's grounding of phenomenology in perceptual synthesis, and when it is conducted within the restraints of an understanding of analysis that focuses on intuition, then perception and time formation become available to phenomenology. Thanks to Kant's implicit ontological grounding, his insights into the "abyss" will lead beyond Husserl and even Heidegger to an alternative version of time formation and the Ontological Difference.

　　4. The flame metaphor is Nicholas Berdyaev's. "Desacralization" refers to a world that has lost the sense of the holy, while "disengagement" refers to the self-defining, punctal self, themes Charles Taylor's *Sources of the Self: The Making of the Modern Identity* (1989), has made distinctly his own.

　　5. Earnest Moody's *The Logic of William of Ockham* (1935) is the indispensable guide to the problems in terminist and judgmental approaches to Aristotle's *Categories*. Was Aristotle concerned with terms or with judgments? Kant followed Porphyry in the judgmental interpretation which has two important consequences. First, it disposes one towards a phenomenology of judgments in which being takes the form of the logical or epistemological subject. Second, and this is Moody's point, it disposes one towards Duns Scotus and the immanent Platonism espoused in this text. Unfortunately, Kant saw himself as an Aristotelian, not a Platonist, and adopted the prevailing judgmental approach to the *Categories*.

　　6. For a judicious account of the status of form in the early and middle dialogues and its relation to Aristotle's *Peri eideon,* see the text, translation and commentary by Gail Fine, *On Ideas: Aristotle's Criticism of Plato's Theory of Forms* (1993). She shows that great care must be taken in applying Aristotelian terms, such a universal/particular and its realist or nominalist interpretation to Plato (20-29). My own reading of Plato is inspired by Whitehead who taught me to see form in the facts (1978, 20) by his method of extensive abstraction (1919, Pt. 3) which will appear in this test as the analytic method. My applications of the method began in *Participation: A Platonic Inquiry* (1968) and continues through this text.

　　Whitehead employed extensive abstraction to define certain ideal elements, points and lines, in terms of phenomenological relations pertaining to regions such as part-whole and overlap. A point may be defined in terms of a set of squares such that every square contains another and there is no least square. We could define it by a similar set of circles. The point elicited is not the ideal entity at the center or even the limit of this approximation, but is rather the sense of the whole set. Plato's analytic method, interpreted in this scheme, will contain constitutive ideas having a similar ontological status. In the final chapter of this study, I will show that this is the method of the *Meno*. I know of no other way of eliminating the separationist doctrine that haunts middle Plato while retaining what is abidingly true and deeply appealing in this greatest of philosophers.

7. Pairing Plato and Kant seems to be oxymoronic; one is a conceptualist who limits understanding to experience, and the other is the chief architect of that transcendent realm from which Kant seems to be in full retreat. The contention of this study is that Kant's conceptualism extends through his constructive or synthetic moments; this delivers the world, as seen in analysis, to an empirical realism. On the other hand, the Kantian *schema* and the imagination greatly enhance a similar theme in Plato. Husserl, Gadamer, and, especially, Heidegger will allow us to see Plato within a phenomenological-hermeneutical context. Whitehead found a route to his cosmology through Plato and, as he told William Weedon, Kant's influence was decisive. There are essential congruities that the text itself will have to demonstrate.

8. Though Kant says "this faculty of apperception is the understanding itself" (B 154, n.), this should not preclude the self-conscious "I" from encountering others, e.g., in moral obligations as ends in themselves. This possibility removes the other from the understanding's appropriative, i.e. categorial, structure. The I that thinks, which is distinct from the I that intuits itself (B 155), can think the moral law.

9. With the assistance of Irving Polonoff's indispensable *Force, Cosmos, Monads and Other Themes of Kant's Early Thought* (1973), this methodological concern can be traced through his pre-Critical period. Even if the distinction between analytic and synthetic concepts that Kant makes in his *Logic* does not clearly appear in the first *Critique*, this account of concept formation through synthetic and analytic methods is implicit. Were Kant always consistent with what I take to be his methodological bias, one could say that the synthetic method produces synthetic *a priori* concepts, the analytic method analytic concepts through *a priori* synthetic and analytic judgments respectively. On the other hand, this would neglect the role of synthetic *a posteriori* judgments, which are employed to form hypotheses, if not concepts.

10. Platonic analysis begins with an hypothesis, i.e., something sought treated as if known, in a matrix of other assumptions or hypotheses and has, according to Pappus, a problem-solving form. In "The Heart of Mathematics," Paul Helmos, the distinguished editor of the *American Mathematical Monthly*, asks: "What does mathematics consist of? Axioms (such as the parallel postulate)? Proofs (such as Gödel's proof of undecidability)? Concepts (such as sets and classes)? Mathematics would surely not exist without these ingredients . . . [but] none of them is at the heart of the subject . . . mathematics really consists of problems and solutions" (PH 1980, 519).

11. This passage may suggest how to reconcile the judicative or Husserlian and *aletheia* or Heideggerian approaches to Kant's phenomenology. Analysis is the method of unconcealment and concept formation, where the former is intuitive and the latter judicative. One recognizes something *in* a concept (A 103). This suggest the priority of the concept. Nevertheless, sensible intuition is logically prior, since its constructive resources allow it to distinguish between knowledge and illusion. Imaginative synthesis constitutes intuition's sense-making structure; the relatum, though intuited, is already interpreted in virtue of this prior or "second order" structure of categorial synthesis. In the transcendental sense, pure concepts are prior, in the empirical sense, this priority appertains to intuition. Granted the priority of intuition and a disclosive model of language, it may be possible to eliminate this "labyrinth of mental fictions," Duns Scotus' characterization of conceptualism. Recognition is coextensive with life; E. coli recognizes, though it has no concepts.

12. The elements in a formal system are apparently eternal, but this is a function of Husserl's distinction between the unbound or contextually unsaturated character of their signs. "Lion" is bound to a habitat and "triangle" is placeless.

13. One should take notice of the scathing critique of Heidegger's exemplary model of hearing that Derrida gives in "Heidegger's Ear: Philopolemology" (1993b 172–77).

14. I offer a footnote for what, were it not written in the shadow of Derrida and Hegel, would be in a preface. This gap, which conditions my understanding of Being, originally appeared as the clearing between such chthonic gods as Ti'amat or Gaea and those of the sky, Uranus or Ap'su. My account of Being therefore differs in two major respects from Heidegger's and, I think, Derrida's. As a transcendental "being" articulates the relational structure of possible appearing, i.e., participation, and is never a predicate, at least as understood by formal or transcendental logic. Though I will justify these statements in the sequel, as a preliminary assume that as a transcendental or omnia-sayable "being" can refer to either side of the gap. Plato, under the spell of the separationist ontology of the middle dialogues, will usually apply "being" to the ideas or determinates, but it also refers to determinable "becoming," the divisible being of *Timaeus* 35A, and to the determined-determining emergent creature. Then it is a power, a receptive and reflective directedness (*Sop.* 247E). My second point has to do with the matrix or receptacle. It is not quite the dynamical and oppositional structure Foucault and Derrida seem to derive from Nietzsche, even if this does provide the context, the general text, within which creativity must be thought. It is a creative and dynamical *apeiron*, a field or matrix; insofar as it is diversified by forces, it partakes in intelligibility; for these *apeiron* forces are channelized, in Bergson's term, by the receptacle's elementary gradients or forms (*peras*), an archewriting or spacing. With this, the matrix begins to approximate Levinas's *il y a*, Heidegger's *es gibt*, or the *mouvance* of *différance*. This groundless ground is like language, disseminated and without an *arché*, either as speaker (a grounding principle) or attachment to a source. Through all this we see traces of the Good. Creativity requires transcendence, the novel introduction of

form; otherwise entropy rules. The alterity that will break this "circle of the same," Plato's description of *chora,* the immanent generative origin, must be, in Derrida's words, an "impossible possibility" (JD 1989, 60) which can never be defined in terms of the actual or its synthetic powers.

Forces do not have the stability that hierarchies of dominance, like that of the master-slave in Hegel, might be thought to provide. Like the waters of Gaea and Uranus or Ap'su and Ti'amat, they mingle. I understand this mingling or engendering as erotic, in terms of life, and thus I invoke the image of the Virgin Mary as she appears in the Byzantine icon, the Zoodochos Pege, the life-giving source, where she is represented in the receptacle imagery of *Timaeus.* In *Of Grammatology* (JD 1976, 19) Derrida suggests that Nietzsche may be open to an interpretation that differs from Heidegger's in which the "will to power" is the end of metaphysics. Though both are autochthonic and deny the role of a transcendent alterity, the Good or the ideas or "transcendental signified," Derrida differs from Heidegger in that he sees Nietzsche as close to having effected metaphysics' closure and pointing to a way beyond from within, a theme he develops with, for example, "trace" or *différance.* Nietzsche "liberates the signifier from its derivation and dependence on the *logos* and the related concept of truth or primary signified" (32). Nietzsche thought every idea arises through "equating the unequal" and that truth is "metaphor" in which illusion, dissimilarity, has been effaced. In stressing the arbitrariness of these "equations" he misses the distinction between effective metaphor as *aletheia* and as creative and the incongruities of Dada. Yet in a more profound sense he points to the Other beyond the assimilative powers of metaphor.

Nevertheless, Derrida's playful crossing of these differences is often productive, e.g., *Glas.* He is sensitive to the distinctions or differences engendered by metaphysics and the necessity of staying within the metaphysical language he deconstructs. He shows that some of these differences, e.g., the Ontological difference or the intelligible and sensible, can be more appropriately dealt with in *différance* than by a direct concern with Being. Thinking Heidegger in his term shows why. Within the tradition of Aristotle, Being is a transcendental, a predicate, and it refers primarily to the content or subject of an assertion; but the predicative or non-relational *ens* heard by Heidegger through all determined significations and in all categories is neither irreducible to and nor identical with the determinations of the *logos,* epochal or otherwise, it makes possible. "Being," the precondition of thinking, cannot be defined by thinking. Though something must be transcendentally signified as being "for the difference between *signans* and *signatum* to be somewhat absolute and irreducible," being is not transcendental signified (JD 1976, 22) and escapes the movement of the sign it commands and yet, to risk absurdity for the sake of simplicity, nothing can escape this movement. The *a-phonic* "voice of Being" is silent and there is a rupture between this "call of conscience," a theme from *Being and Time,* and the voice, i.e., articulated sound. Nothing separates signifier and signified. Being, as in *The Question of Being* (MH 1958), is "read only as it is crossed out," recognized as inappropriate yet necessary, and by destroying the transcendental signified "makes visible the sign." Signs can function within the deferring and differing field of forces, which escape any taint of presence, which we know as *différance*. To bring this long story to a close, Derrida holds that all the differences thought in Being and in the later Ontological Difference are "derivative with regard to *différance*" (JD 1976, 23). I hope to restore this autochthonic origin of language to the status of a between, a *metaxu*, that gives beings being and place.

15. Levinas says that "God cannot appear as the cause or creator of nature . . . he is other than this world. He is other than being" (1986, 24–25). Doesn't religion require nature; if Hegel is correct, nature is wedded to the moral order through religion and the latter is empty without this connection. In the words of St. Maximus the Confessor, the Creative *Logos* "wills to effect in all things the mystery of his embodiment" by embedding his words, *logoi,* in all things. Thus words and things are not, as in the Copernican Revolution in Philosophy, expressions of the self; "their voices go throughout all the earth" (*Psalms* 19:4).

16. John Llewelyn remarks that the middle voice exceeds the distinction between active and passive verb forms and is still heard, for example, in Heidegger's *lassen,* as in "I get myself hit" and "I let myself get hit" and is "less of causing than enabling" (1991, 87). This will infect *Seinlassen,* a letting be in which we are. We can even hear the deconstructive aspect of the medial voice in "to dwell" in *bin,* an archaic form of "been," whose traces infest such nouns as *Heimlichkeit,* which refers both to what makes dwelling protective and secure or anxious and uncanny. Because I am concerned to associate the middle voice with dwelling, I will give that which is neither male nor female a sometimes unwarranted feminine emphasis.

17. A cautionary note: following the example of the spontaneous understanding, we tend to think of most interpretations as active. Plato, who approached perceptual interpretations from the side of the object, spoke of "passive motion," a change that remains with the subject as the object "actively" moves about.

18. This entails showing that from any arbitrary here and now there are access, recognition, and connectedness conditions that will enable us to think any here and how. Knowing what we now know about chaos, this more or less LaPlacian thesis is probably false.

CHAPTER ONE

1. Unless it is taken nominally as something's property, the Greek *dynamis* suggests a medial process rather than "faculty." The fact that most intentional verbs were originally medial, i.e., processes which may precipitate agents, suggests that traces of this middle voice are retained in some of the active/passive forms that replaced it.

2. In the natural sciences it is often possible to vary the experimental conditions and, at least ideally, close them to environmental influence even if,

as in recent particle physics, some elicited entities may be artifacts of the experimental context. This is less feasible in the life sciences, where ecological contexts make a difference in gene expression.

3. In *Participation: A Platonic Inquiry,* I suggested that the receptacle was what Heidegger must have meant by Being in *Being and Time* (1968, 170). I now know otherwise. However, Levinas, in spite of using Being (existence) for the *il y a* rather than Plato's preferable "becoming" (*gignomenon, Tim.* 28A), convinces me that this should have been Heidegger's intention. Nietzsche also entertained the priority of becoming, which he diversified by a play of forces in the dynamics of the will to power. Platonists usually reserve "being" for its determinates, the ideas as *peras*. In deference to Levinas, I have identified the grant of place with his *il y a*, becoming, rather than, with Plato, to the receptacle which is diversified by becoming to then be gathered into place by the grant of the feminine. This must always be thought through the gift of time to Being, the durative character already found in *einai*.

Both the Good and the receptacle are beyond being and are accessible only within an "abductive" catachresis. C. S. Peirce's "abduction," an imaginative leap to a hypothesis beyond the data that explains it, is the procedure behind Plato's idea theory, according to *Phaedo:* "I'm assuming the existence of absolute beauty and goodness and all the rest of them. If you grant my assumption and assume they exist, I hope with their help to explain causation to you" (100C ff:).

4. For a revealing analysis of Heidegger's relation to biological phenomena, see David Krell, *Daimon Life* (1993).

I will be making Levinas out to be more of a Platonist and a Christian Platonist at that, which he would, quite rightly, find objectionable. For instance, I have situated the *il y a* in a Platonic receptacle diversified by an *apeiron gignesthai* and have made this, together with the Good, the supplements which give being and generate the text of philosophy. I see the receptacle in a rather heretical Mariological light, thanks to a series of Byzantine icons which represent her standing in a bowl of self-generating waters (a myth associated with Theodora and the monastery of the Zoodochos Pege in Istanbul). My Messianic hope has been fulfilled, and I, like Hegel, am likely to see Spirit in the World. Thus my face-to-face encounters will tend towards naturalism, e.g., mother and child, and a theology of Grace.

5. Experience is "inscribed within onto-theology . . . by the value of presence" (JD 1976, 22).

6. James H. Oliver, *The Civilizing Power* (1968), shows how *chora* is thematized in Panathenic discourse. Athens is allegorized, as Dante allegorized Jerusalem, in political and moral terms. In his funeral oration, Thucydides' Pericles celebrates "the *dynamis* of the city" (9) and how this becomes in its ironic successor, the Melian dialogue, contrasted with *arete*. Plato's *Menexenus* repudiates the *dynamis* of the city and, anticipating a movement we shall have to undertake with respect to Foucault and Derrida, proposes that Athens is the place of justice (10). Attica is the mother whose children are always capable not just of modeling but of surpassing the dead. Aristides, who composed his oration in Smyrna in 167 A.D., sees Athens as mediating between (*metaxu*

as matrix) time and eternity. Through its gift of the *logos*, Athens is the "visible image of, and standard for, human nature" (sec. 274) uniting the race of men with the cosmic order (39). Having elevated place to the conceptual order, it can then be transformed into Ionia and then into the *chora* Mediterranean (42). Such is the civilizing power of place. Aristides apparently saw the analogous mediation in Christ as a barbaric threat which his discourse sought to counter.

Oliver sees this transform, I believe mistakenly, as leading to Cyril of Alexandria's Encomium of Mary as *chorion tou achoretou* (Hom. XI) (42). I would trace the route to Cyril's insight back to myths of the earth mother that leads to Anatolia, "the land of the mother" and then through Plato to Ephesus and Mary. Artemis is a mediating goddess and as such particularly instructive. She is the virgin, protector of wild things; the presider over birth and, at Ephesus, takes on the demonic and orgiastic aspect of Cybele. This latter aspect may have been recognized in Sparta. Mary is also celebrated at Ephesus, the burial place of St. John and perhaps her final dwelling. In Jung's terms, the archaic, orgiastic mother of the primal waters is the shadow archetype, sometimes faintly seen in the "Black Madonna," integrated and transformed into life-giving and healing Mary. If she is the symbol of the Good's supplement, then her Lethe aspect that conceals has to be respected. This incarnational thematic, contrary to the cosmopolitan epiphany offered by Aristides, particularizes or apportions the *logos* to a place which is otherwise *unheimlich* or, as Levinas might say, elemental.

7. These comments, which reflect my own journey in search of the Mother in Greece and Turkey, were inspired by Vincent Scully's magnificent *The Earth, The Temple and The Gods* (1969).

8. Situating oneself beyond Being for the sake of coming to understand it is not easy; one may well be involved in presumptions of "presence" even as one assume one is beyond it, as may be the case with "proximity." In so far as it is to be approached via the "originary," "Being" has both a "hither" and "yonder" side. Levinas often directs us to the saying, the presencing, rather than the "said," the nominal *ens*, and speaks of this as the "hither side." This way through the appearing, which is directed towards the Good, may on Derrida's approach involve various linguistic artifacts. The archeology of the originary is the dominant theme of the "yonder side," if I may posit a new difference, which Derrida has made his own.

Derrida often approaches the "hither side" with a literary text. For instance, he has used Ponge's "Fable," a short poem, to set up a medial process (JD 1991, 201–20). It appeared in the collection, *Psyché: Invention de l'autre*, in an essay of the same name. In French, *psyché* can mean mirror. The "Fable" bends self-reflectively back on itself and resists assimilation as a "presence" in philosophy's general text. This self-reflection entails a play of differences which deconstructs such differences as inner/outer, and yet shows that one term, e.g., outer, has the priority claimed for it in a transcendental philosophy. It then becomes a "quasi-transcendental." I will follow this lead in introducing the I of the "hypostasis" as the quasi-transcendental "I" from medial becoming in chapter 5, below.

An important and suggestive effort to break through the closure of metaphysics is to be found in the Heideggerian/Derridian theme of the gift by time to life of "what it does not have" (a durative presence), i.e., being. For a marvelous discussion of this gift, which deconstructs "the vulgar" notion of circular time, which is hardly time since Aristotle's cosmology has shown it to be a form of eternal presence, see Jacques Derrida, *Given Time* (JD, 1992b). This circular motility is thematic in Plato (participation and recollection), Kant (self-affective return of the same), Husserl (the monadic ego), Hegel (the possibility of presuppositionless knowledge), Nietzsche (the eternal return of the same), and Heidegger (the hermeneutical circle). The instant that breaks this circle is an "impossible possibility." Though perhaps Derrida is too parasitic on French and English idioms, this is his most compelling account of the originary and situates it more effectively beyond being than even Plato's account of the receptacle and *chora*. Since we return again and again to this theme, some preliminary remarks may be helpful.

Since Plato defined the soul in terms of the circle of the same which crosses and appropriates alterity, thinking has been understood as the anamnestic (or constituting, expressivist, projective, or constructive) circular motion involving first an egress to the other, a giving, and then return with it, a taking, as same. Heidegger proposed that intentionality is temporality, that being is time. Derrida notes that "time begins to appear as that which undoes this distinction between giving and taking, therefore also between receiving and giving, perhaps between receptivity and activity . . ."(1992b, 3). This giving and taking is economical, in all its senses, and supposes a reciprocity and, since "the law of economy is circular, a return to the origin, the point of departure, also home (7)." However the *gift* must not be a part of this circle, "must not come back to the giving (let us not say to the . . . donor). It must not circulate, must not be exchanged. . . . If the figure of the circle is central to economics, the gift must remain *aneconomic* . . . foreign to the circle" (7). Wherever there is time, "the gift is impossible" (9). This means that the gift cannot even be acknowledged as a gift, and thus represented or symbolized, which would reduce it to a same. Gift, in this sense, breaks the triadic formula, "the gift of A by B to C." There is in giving neither a giver nor given—for this instant, which is Kierkegaard's paradoxical instant that is not part of time, isn't anything and has no being to give. Derrida continues: "A gift could be possible, there could be a gift only at the instant of an effraction in the circle will have taken place, at the instant all circulation will have been interrupted. . . . What is more, this instant of effraction would no longer be a part of time . . . the paradoxical instant tears time apart (9)." finally, "there is a gift . . . only in what interrupts the system as well as the symbol, in a partition without return and without division, without being-with-self of the gift-counter-gift" (13).

9. The explication of procreation, the medial gift of life, requires a variety of images, such as grace, play (of forces), speaking a language, perceiving, crossing and the like. I now focus on grace, though I hope to do justice to other approaches in the chapters ahead. Grace is a gift that transcends the circle of metaphysical economy and, as a medial power, through which one willingly works without willing, a doing without being what one does, given without merit and no one's due and the like. Grace avoids the usual meta-

physical distinctions, such as subject/object, action/passion, activity/receptivity. Medial phenomena are close fits to Derrida's account cited from *Given Time* in the previous note. Thus the giving constitutes the giver, who gives, not being, but the possibility of gathering—through the solicitation of the *logos*—the formless powers (*apeiron gignesthai*) of the "receptacle," the elemental "mater," a place to the emergent creature. On my interpretation, the receptacle image (*Tim.* 49A) is the condition which, as diversified by the "becoming that never really is" (27D), grants beings a place, *chora* (52B).

In the recommended Christian imagery, the elemental mother is transformed into the hypostasis, Mary. She is a woman, not a mere elemental container or spatial envelope, an image implicit in the Aristotelian biology of Pope Sextus IV's bull, *Cum praecelso* (1477), which established her veneration as the *habitaculum Dei*, "house of God." She is the house only because she, contrary to Sextus and Heidegger's "Building Dwelling Thinking" (MH 1971b, 158-60), grants place, dwelling and being through her more primordial role as the diversified receptacle. Unlike Aristotelian matter that merely receive masculine form, she gathers these elemental powers into the life forming within. Said in the later Latin tradition to be co-creator with Christ, the earlier Byzantine image of the Zoodochus Pege shows her as giving through the waters both life and healing, where life has its place in the body, the "mater" we all bear and from which all live.

This entails that we translate the inscription, *chora tou achoretou*, on *The Virgin Blachernitissa and Angels* or *The Virgin Hodegetria* (c1315) mosaics in St. Savior, the *Chora* church in Istanbul, not as "the container of the uncontainable" but as "the place of the placeless." The church also contains a fragment of the Zoodochos Pege, named after a monastery founded by Justinian and said to be curative on Theordora's discovery of the healing powers of the self-generating waters it was said to contain. I was told by the Bishop of Samos that she commissioned the first Zoodochos Pege icon. This icon represents an early, deeply Platonic and even Anatolian ("Land of the Mother") strand in Byzantine iconography.

Through the gift of form, in the erotic, propositional sense, Mary—the prototype of the mother—provides the womb in which nature collects itself into the form of the uncontainable *Logos*. This is a debt which, on other occasions, Derrida has said cannot be repaid within the general economy. On this Platonic model for a Christian theology, the giver, the Good that solicits this response, is not a being—except as a consequence of the donation. Unfortunately, Plato tends to construe his ideas through Being and not the Good, and I am condemned to follow the tradition; but at the same time I invoke the mother and her contextualization or relativization of form. Thus the Good, the father, can give only because the Mother will receive; his gift is contingent on her receptivity. The contextual relativization of the goddess (restricted to the case of Artemis) determines how the form is received and expressed.

10. "Thought as a point of departure. There is not only a consciousness of localization but a localization of consciousness which is not reabsorbed into consciousness, into knowing. There is something that stands out against knowing, that is a condition for knowing . . . [which] somehow emerges

from a material density, a protuberance, a head. Thought, which spreads instantaneously spreads into a world, retains the possibility [in sleep] of collecting itself into the *here* from which it never detached itself. . . . [Consciousness] is not first thought and then *here*. . . . This localization does not presuppose space. It is the very contrary of objectivity. It does not presuppose a thought behind it, which would first have to grasp the *here,* which is an objective *here* . . . the localization of consciousness is not subjective; it is the subjectivization of the subject" (EL 1988, 68–69). Levinas, in denying that *here* is subjective or objective, marks it as the gift of a body through the dynamics of medial becoming that makes possible its conscious hypostasis.

11. Structural anthropologists have discovered that in archaic cultures everything has a name embedded in a code, a totalizing plot that determines life's drama. Naming places things, sets them up, "represents" them, within a nexus of relations, if only those of kinship.

12. In philosophies in which the nominal sense of being dominates, power will be bound to something as its power, while in a more dynamical cosmology, power will be free and will define things. Philosophies of the former type will be corpuscular, while free forces form fields. If you read Kant's Principles backwards, you will see that he defines nominal entities by verbal processes, a move progressively refined by Hegel, Nietzsche, and Whitehead.

13. This phenomenological account of world is based on discussions with the late Edward Ballard. He generalized from idioms referring to horizonal structures of meaning, e.g., "world of music," "world of finance," "world of fashion." These are often institutionalized in shared forms of life such as churches, stock exchanges, etc. World as such, if there is one, is the overall enduring structure of meaning, i.e., reference, and value whose possibilities elicit transcending interests that take us beyond ourselves into this or that context of "worlding," i.e., where the action is, and into what really matters. Transcendence towards is intended to express Heidegger's redescription of intentionality as ecstatic temporality. World is thus the context of any setting forth. This use of "world" originates in Kant's discovery that world (in the physical or moral sense) is the correlative of the self. These worlds presuppose the life world, the minimal structure of shareable things in space and time which are variously invested with meaning.

14. If "being" is identified with power and its transcendental status as sayable of determinate *peras* graded by the Good is ignored, then it signifies a compulsive *apeiron* term. Heidegger saw something of this in the *Ge-stell,* but not enough to avoid the disasters of the ontological difference and the nihilism which follows for making it, as in Nietzsche and in his own "Anaximander Fragment," the giver of order and reck (1984, 44–48).

15. The dialectical paradigm is Platonic dialogue in which one maintains and elaborates an idea by bring to bear the tools of skepticism and logic, example and counter-example, monstration and proof through the Good's lighting amid all the strife and struggle, the sophistries and flatteries, lying along the way. Characteristically, this is the way of negation through a hypothesis, metaphor, or image which leaves neither interpreter nor interpretant unchanged.

In order to illustrate this meaning of dialectic, let me borrow an example, not its interpretation, from Hans Gadamer's *The Idea of the Good in Platonic-Aristotelian Philosophy* (1986). In the *Republic*, Socrates proposes to replace the nuclear family with the communal family where the being of each lies in the good of all. This sets in high relief the corruption of Athenian family life; Plato's extended family includes Charmides and Critias. But the negated, nuclear family isn't taken up into the interpreting predicate, i.e., the common family, but as its antithesis also interprets it. *Philia* and procreative *eros*, not *agon*, is the bond. The nuclear family also interprets the common family; contrary to Plato's socializing intentions, the latter is better at producing autism than persons able to open to and love beauty in the stranger in his or her shocking alterity. The family must socialize, take its place as an instrument of civic virtue. The inculcation of this virtue and the struggle against hereditary advantage neither required by nor founded on one's *arete* is a public responsibility. This negating dialectic defines through its antithetical *eidetic* possibility a way, that of *oikos* as "dwelling thinking," which avoids the entrapments of theoretical reason where a negation is an invitation to even more radical antithesis, e.g., as in Marx, and conventions that have become demonic.

16. I take liberties beyond permissible German usage with *Vorstellung;* no one would take it literally as describing something "set up before us." I also borrow from "representation" the theme that a *Vorstellung* is a necessary, if not sufficient, condition for something appearing, i.e., showing itself. In that sense, representing is the noesis which may unconceal something. I then argue that if Kant is to be understood as supplying transcendental grounds for empirical realism and if his epistemic terms admit of a phenomenological rather than an epistemological interpretation, e.g., *doxa*, then this transcendental *schema* will have an empirical analogue. Since mathematical intuitionism derives from Kant's constructive methods, I can also claim Kant's authority for this usage.

Representations are participatory forms, like a ritual in which the sacred appears, a painting that lets truth appear, or an experimental set-up that permits one to actively participate in some process and what it may or may not unconceal. *Theoria* names not a mere spectator but the active participant in disclosure.

That representation can impose a closure on phenomena is especially significant. For instance, the experimental set-up concretely embodies categorial conditions that let something happen, play out, within its categorial controls. A question or hypothesis in which causality is implicit presupposes apparatus, i.e., set-ups, that control the phenomena in order to determine its necessary conditions and isolate it (an impossible ideal of reason) in order to determine its sufficient conditions. Physical closure, necessary to determine sufficient conditions, is the analogue of an *epoche*. Playing out is a medial phenomena. So too is the imagination in which a procedure is born, even if few have been as skilled as Galileo in giving science dialectical and dramatic form.

On the subjective or phenomenological side, the experimental question is also an *epoché*, a closure that lets meanings appear. Its implicit "let us assume that . . . ," with its narrative analogue, "once upon a time . . . ," are shared forms of life rooted in what Kant called the "productive" or "figurative" imagination. The *logos*, logic or *mythos*, gathers us into the truth.

17. *Chaos*, the Greek term for the "gap" which lies between Gaea and Uranus is that in or from which creatures arise. Crossing *chaos* is dangerous; like the sea, it posits monsters even as it generates order, e.g., the rational interval creates surds or the well-tempered scale creates discords. *Chaos* theory is now well advanced and its unpredictabilities are known to characterize the processes of living systems, e.g., heart beats. For a readable introduction, see James Gleick, *Chaos: Making a New Science* (New York: Viking, 1987). The Kantian crossing between sensibility and understanding bridges chaotic imagination.

18. Charles Bigger, 1961, 785–96; and 1968, 15–40, 197–215. My account originated from a lecture by Jacob Klein on the *Meno* and William Weedon's method of pointing (1963) described in the following note. The possibility of extending these methodological studies to Kant was suggested by Jaakko Hintikka (1969), an essay that awoke me from my dogmatic, neo-Kantian study of Kant.

19. W. S. Weedon (1963) bases his theory of pointing, a way of describing analysis, on A. N. Whitehead's method of extensive abstraction. Whitehead was concerned to bring one to see by articulating the non-metrical and topological connectedness of space and time, or any other demonstrative elements underlying discourse, and how ideal elements, such as points, lines, and event-particles, entailed in connectedness could be phenomenologically aduced. This formalization analysis owes much to Dedekind, Weierstrass, and Cantor. Weedon applied this scheme to Plato's analytic dialectic. The element elicited in monstration may differ in ontological type from the regions in which it is shown to inhere; as is often the case in dialectic, it could also be a wind-egg. Let there be, Weedon says,

> a set K of demonstrative phrases, A, B, C, D . . . each of which points out a corresponding element in the set, K', which itself consists of the regions A', B', C', D'. . . . The regions of K' are such that, of any two, one includes the other as a part. By the relation of "inclusion" I intend only the topological property that if X and Y are regions, then all the parts of X are parts of Y, but not conversely. Every part of any region is a region, and every region has parts and is itself a part of other regions. I now stipulate that for the set K' there is no region that is included in every member of the set. In virtue of this and the property that of any two regions, one includes the other, the set K' is convergent at one end [towards a punctal entity not an element of the set] and diverges at the other. [The punctal entity] represents an ideal of exactitude in respect of its situation in every member of the set.

The element elicited is presumed, not always justly, to transcend the conditions through which it is seen.

The K-set of descriptions associated with these K' regions, e.g., models, measurements, or allegories, provide a language in which the limit may be described. The disclosive movement may be maximal, as in Eudoxus' demonstration of the circle as the limit of a regular polygons whose sides approach infinity, or these regions may converge, or as a point is the limit of a class of circles such that there is no least circle and no circle is covered by every other. But it is also possible to think of these regions as imaginative variations in Husserl's sense, and the K descriptive phrases will be theories, allegories, and the like that can be so ordered as to be eidetically disclosive. If I say my love is ice cream, candy, apple pie, etc., I show her to be sweet. To borrow an example from Bishop Ian Ramsey, "Almighty" said of God is a quantified model. We could begin with models of military and civil power, go on to the power of poetry and music, and then describe the might of duty. Beyond that is the power of love. The stories we might tell to illustrate each region, military, civil, aesthetic, moral, and spiritual, manifest something true, though conditional, about power as they progressively spiritualize it. God, to whom the set points, transcends these descriptions and gives them their ascending hierarchical order. K-sets of phrases can be almost anything that express a covering convention, such as narratives, allegories, models, and the like, through which the desired convergence is presumed to obtain.

20. For Pappus' description of Plato's methods, see Sir Thomas Heath (1947, 138). "Analysis then takes that which is sought as if it were admitted and passes from it through its successive consequences to something that is admitted as the result of synthesis [*sic*]. In analysis we assume that which is sought as if it were already done [*genosos*], and we inquire what it is from which this results, and again what is the antecedent cause of the latter, and so on, until by retracing our steps we come upon something already known or belonging to the class of first principles. . . . But in synthesis, reversing the process, we take as already done that which was last arrived at in analysis. . . . Now analysis is of two kinds, the one directed toward searching for the truth and called theoretical, and the other directed toward what we are told to find and called problematical. In the theoretical kind, we assume what is sought as if it were existent and true [and pass from it] to something admitted. . . . In the problematical kind, we assume that which is propounded as if it were known [passing through these] to something admitted." These are the upward and downward ways of the dialectic described in *Republic* VI.

21. This discussion of the epistemological and phenomenological meanings of *doxa* is largely based on Alexander P. D. Mourelatos, *The Route of Parmenides* (1970, 194–221). The translation of *aletheia* as the alpha-privative of *lanthanein*, "un-concealedness" or, as Mourelatos suggests, "non-latency," tunes us into the many disputes occasioned by Heidegger's translation of *aletheia* as Being's *Unverborgenheit*, "unconcealment." Mourelatos, who has no desire to sharpen Heidegger's axe, says that in archaic usage *aletheia* has a strong adverbial force, as if showing itself was its doing. Of course this is disclosed "to us;" but that is hardly "in us," i.e., truth as being in a right relation to things. Plato was supposed to have transformed this *de re* usage into *de dicto* "correctness." However that may be, Socratic dialectic works to uncon-

ceal those who would actively conceal themselves, e.g., Critias in *Charmides*. If successful, mere opinions, *doxa*, are converted into knowledge through a systematic, logistic deployment.

22. There is a justified tendency to associate *dianoia* or *Verstand* with the third level of the divided line. This image of the line suggests that the idea of the Good crowns a dialectic that uses the mathematical sciences as "springboards." As their cause, the Good seems related to other ideas as an axiom, e.g., Nicod's single axiom for the sentential calculus, is related to theorems. Hans-Georg Gadamer's refutation of this position in the *Idea of the Good in Platonic-Aristotelian Philosophy* is unsurpassable.

The mathematical ideal of truth measuring opinions was a counterthrust against the sophists; but its implicit separationism, if pushed, leads to the disjoined worlds, the ideas and the gods and things and humans. There is no science of sciences even though that unitary ideal, an idea in the Kantian sense, has great heuristic value. The good, which always has as its context Heideggerian thrownness, appears in an unassimilable and singular other which, thanks to the various writings of Emmanuel Levinas, we know to make a moral demand on us, the demand of the widow or the orphan.

In a more theoretical vein, Nancy Cartwright in *How the Laws of Physics Lie* (1983) shows how theoretical physics entails only an ideal or, as I call it, allegorical separation which facilitates fixing relations that can serve as premises in a formal model. In the real world, however, no law—and certainly no two laws concurrently efficacious—yields predictions that are perfectly instanced. Where there are various forces at work, such as Coulomb's and Newton's gravitational laws, the deductive resultant has little relation to reality and the truth can only be experimentally determined. Idealizations offer the advantages of rigor within a limited sector; without this, we would never really know the import of theoretical claims. An *idea* is an iterable structure, a whole of parts standing to one another in logical relations, some of which can stand as keys to the pattern and be used to deduce the others. If I neglect this aspect of theory, it is only because the more central role of *theoria* has been too long concealed.

23. Let me take this opportunity to call attention to the relation between reflexivity, writing, objectivity, and the correspondence theory of truth. The disengagement of the said from the physical graphemes of phonemes in writing and saying, especially in indirect discourse, is an *epoché* that transforms what was an element in a complex sense-making event into an object. The resulting distantiation characterizes the movement from *theoria* to theory. The gain is immense. The danger is that we overlook the model-theoretic or metaphoric nature of analytic practice and subsume everything under a univocal, literalistic logic. The growth of knowledge is then a mystery. I have discussed these matters at some length in relation to biology with Anita Bigger in "Biological Recognition," *Philosophy and Archaic Experience* (1982, 122-49).

24. See my "Kant and the Infinite, Potential and Actual" (1975, 95-103), and in "Kant's Constructivism" (1981, 279-91).

25. Kant's receptive sense and spontaneous understanding has its root

in the imagination which, as has been suggested, is medial. He supports the distinction between immediate sensory awareness and mediated perception. Awareness may be what Kant means by "apprehension" in which the synoptically given "manifold is run through and held together" (A 98–99) in "inner sense." This awareness will, on "recognition in a concept" (A 103), erupt into an "apperceived" perceptual object in veritative synthesis. Though it is not clear that Heidegger himself distinguishes between sense and perception, Husserl does. This will reveal a meaning of being prior to intentionality.

My use of "solicitation" suggests imagination's infusion into sense. Sense awareness is the primary form of receptivity in which one is already disposed to accept something to be constituted as significant. Solicitude marks this readiness for the acceptation of meaning and results from the imagination's quasi-spontaneity. That sense must receive the gift of sense if it is to make sense marks the medial character of imagination. Plato expressed these medial roots of receptivity in describing the dynamical shaking of the receptacle in *Timaeus*, not unlike the belly dancer's "solicitation," which invites in its ripeness for information an erotic proposition, e.g., Whitehead's "impure" propositional lures.

26. My debt in these pages to Georg Henrick von Wright, *Explanation and Understanding* (1971, 64) for an understanding of action as bracketing a system is considerable.

27. My comments on play were inspired by Wittgenstein, Huzinga, Heidegger and, especially, Gadamer. For the importance of play in the sciences, see Manfred Eigen and Rutheld Winkler, *The Laws of the Game* (London: Allen Lane, 1982).

28. Heidegger (1990, 83) says that what Kant calls the "object of an intuition in general" (A 125) is "something-in-general $= x$" (A 104) or "the object $= x$" (A 105), which is in turn the "transcendental object $= x$" (A 109). This "something of which we know nothing . . . is a Nothing . . . which according to its essence is pure horizon." The transcendental object as such is the correlative of pure apperception and has "a quality in which it appears, a *causality* which is not appearance" which then allows it to have a noumenal and phenomenal role (A 538/B 566–A 540/B 568). The logician's logical object $= x$ is also a nothing, but here the operative term is *Objekt* and not, as in the other citations, *Gegenstand*. It will, however, be more useful to restrict the *Gegenstand* as "something in general $= x$" to the reduced phenomenal object which, considering its locus in the medial imagination, might be said to be a nothing (that things).

My position, as developed in chapter 3 below, is closer to Gerd Buchdahl's in "Science and God: The Topology of the Kantian World," (1991, 1–24), in which the various sorts of objects are related by a quasi-Husserlian reduction-realization scheme, so that the object-in-general is a reduction of the phenomenal object and, in realization, reciprocally "viewed as" the empirical object. It too is a Nothing, "an ontological nullity," which when realized is the thing in itself. The transcendental object, on his account, is an alternative reduction of the empirical object. Buchdahl's account captures the sense of passages most commentators neglect, e.g., transcendental matter and *Sachheit* (A 143/B 182).

Chapter Two

1. In Chapter 4, "Metaphysical Foundations of Phenomenology," of his *Metaphysical Foundations* (1786), Kant says phenomenology shows how appearances, inherently subjective, can have an objective ground in motion. Motion is "the fundamental determination of something that is to be an object of the external senses . . . for thereby only can these senses be affected" (*MF* 14–15). He remarks that subjectively "either the body is moved and space is at rest or vice versa." When, however, the moving body is considered dynamically, i.e., phenomenologically, then "this disjunction is to be taken with an objective meaning" (126) and doubtless settled by the Foucault pendulum. Kant's phenomenology, which we will explore in great depth, thematizes a dynamical world that is closer to Leibniz than to Descartes, Galileo, or Newton. Unfortunately for us and for Kant, he tends to nominalize his dynamics.

2. The word in the Septuagint for this "joining," *harmozousia*, has the sense of espousal or marriage.

3. "Concept" is ambiguous; on the one hand, it is used in conceptualism to do proxy for Plato's "idea" as objective and beyond the reach of most. Less rigorously, it is also used to refer to something that every user of a language might be expected to have, i.e., being able to identify and count entities in its extension. In this latter sense, the object and the concept in which it is reflectively recognized are simultaneous products of the productive or figurative imagination. Thus, it is misleading to say, unless we are giving a conceptualist account, that there are objects which are then recognized in concepts, but this more usual locution is less confusing.

4. A series is completely ordered if, for any two elements a and b and an ordering relation R, either aRb or bRa but not both. Time is well ordered if I must do a before doing b. Though this point will be developed in more detail later, one must keep in mind this "hands on" activity context—the ground of transcendental affinity—in which events are ordered with respect to before and after throughout Kant's discussions in the Analytic. If like Hume we stand to the world as spectators and pay attention only to what sequentially appears without acting upon it, even imaginatively, then the order of the sequence will be contingent. As a result of his neglect of how causal ascription functions within the methodological context of experimental practice and accepting Hume's empirical affinities, Gerd Buchdahl shows that Kant must turn to reason for a ground for the order injected into causal laws in the higher reaches of reflective judgment, i.e., theory formation, to "tie down" the sequence objectively (1969, 353). Granted well-ordering acts, I think that Kant gets these results from his mathematical matrix by something like the Universal Generalization rule in predicate logic.

5. The object-in-general is the eidetically reduced empirical object or, alternatively, a realization of the transcendental object about which, Kant says, nothing can be known (A 250). In describing how we stand towards something from out of ourselves, Heidegger speaks of a nothing, *ein Nichts,*

that allows us to stand against. One holds oneself in the nothing in order to let the empirical not-nothing be encountered. Kant would appear to under-stood this nothing, an open crossed by sense and understanding, as "the object-in-general $= x$", the contextually appropriate designation for the transcendental object.

6. According to James G. Hart (1992), Husserl's mental acts cover the range of directed modalities, such as a believing, seeing, imagining, fearing, etc., which may modify the noema but hardly let it be interpretatively "seen as ____." Prof. Hart argues that consciousness of primal time is not totally and completely diaphanous but is already self-present, e.g., "translucent." That I am being appeared to is implicit in the most self-conscious acts. This "being appeared to" is more prominent in Kant than in Husserl. Husserl's time con-stitution does not rely on activity in the world, however shadowy participa-tion in its worlding may be, and is more spectatorial; all noetic modes except the epistemic would be, on my reconstruction, ignored.

7. Oliver Sacks's experience with "Virgil" and the evidence he cites from the twenty-odd cases in which sight was restored to those born blind or blind since infancy which have occurred during the last two hundred years is an im-portant contribution to the phenomenology of perception ("Seeing Yet Not Seeing," *The New Yorker*, 10 May 1993: 59–73). There is a rather strong dis-junction between the "habituated" succession in tactile space, which is a space of events or features, and that of coexistent or spatial visible worlds, the space of things, to which his subjects remain quite alienated. Prof. Richard Gregory (1987, 95) notes that in these reports there is some carry-over, especially when the seen object can be felt. The synoptic unity of space and time seems to re-quire a "hands on" or experimental approach, which suggests that the space and time of personal encounter, e.g., Winnicott's play space between mother and child in which the infant learns to associate visual language with the tac-tile experiences, is prior to Kant's descriptions in the Aesthetic. Sacks's pa-tient, Virgil, could not visually distinguish his dog from his cat, both of which remained quasi-Humian assemblages of successively experienced parts. Sacks cites Valvo's patient, HS, who during the first five weeks could not count his fingers: "I had the feeling that they were all there but I could not pass from one to the other while counting" (OS 1993, 64). One is able to describe only after something is touched (68). These results are reflected in our discussion of the synopsis, the condition for any higher-order interpretative synthesis, in Kant's construction of the world.

8. Disjunctive transcendentals, such as finite/infinite or passive/recep-tive, were introduced by Bonaventura and elaborated by Duns Scotus. These terms in which one of each pair is predicable of anything were then picked up by Suarez who passes them on to Kant through Leibniz and Wolff.

9. Aristotle says that if an axe had life, its first act would be the capac-ity to cut and its second act would be cutting. The uncut wood would be potential relative to this act; as cut, it would be a second potency.

10. Maximal and minimal principles are teleological; but this issue may now be moot, since Ernst Nagel has shown that all mechanistic laws may be expressed in this form (1961, 401). Leibniz is mainly concerned with the heuristic role of teleology in the order of discovery, not explanation.

11. Kant held that an inertial system can undergo no change in its non-relational predicates except through "physical influx" from other proximate bodies (ND, 246).

12. The pair of terms "realization" and "reduction" were introduced into the Kantian literature by Gerd Buchdahl. The transcendental object is the eidetically reduced object, one and the same in all contexts, which is then given further content, e.g., as noumenal or empirical, in "expanded" contexts. One must be careful not to be more precise than Kant. I tend to use the "object-in-general" in empirical contexts, one of the expressions of the transcendental object, i.e., object as transcendental.

13. This parallelism, and the implicit *natura naturans/natura naturata* distinctions, that seem to crop up in discussions of the causality of reason or ideas and caulality as used in the Analogies, reflects the Spinozism that comes into the open in the *Opus Postumum:* "Transcendental Idealism is Spinozism, to posit the object in the whole of one's representations" (64, 6; cf also 64, 8; 78, 9; and 87, 29).

14. The "transcendental matter" (A1 43/B 183) of an object is its aptitude for further realization in an object perhaps differing in ontic type. Sensation, Kant says, is not *hyle;* what organizes it is the transcendental object, which is of a higher order. Contrary to Hume, objects can only be reduced to objects, not to sensa.

15. My concern with the receptacle and its variants that gives us finite, connected truth was occasioned by a desire to avoid Bradley's claim that "in the end we assert something of a reality qualified by the whole universe" (1928, 630). On the other hand, something like this may be true of a novel, e.g., *Ulysses.*

16. This synthesis, insofar as it is, like mathematics, concerned with pure space and time will be creative.

17. The relation between contingent descriptive laws, inductively ascertained, and their *a priori* conditions on the one hand and, on the other, regulative laws or ideals has attracted the attention of many since it was raised by Gerd Buchdahl in *Metaphysics and the Philosophy of Science* (1968) and "The Kantian Dynamic of Reason" (1969, 340-74). He says that though the "cointention to the concept of an object as such, corresponding to the general concept of a cognitive experimental judgment, *contains* as a necessary presuppositional ingredient of its *possibility,* the various categorial concepts," Kant's characterization of causality as a "determined sequence under a universal rule" is Humian. The sequence "*must* be regarded as an altogether *contingent* event; not only contingent in the sense that empirical laws (and their instances) are contingent (a fact that Kant assumes throughout), but contingent also in being an individual particular happening. . . . The question whether some observed event or change of state is an instance of some universal law can be determined only by those inductive procedures distinctive of all scientific inquiry." (1968, 500) He goes on to say that Kant is invoking a regulative principle of reason when he says we should seek "for every member in a series of conditions . . . an empirical condition" (A 562/B 590). For an appreciative disagreement, see Michael Friedman, "Causal Laws and the Foundations of Natural Science," (1992, 161-99).

18. The fiction of context indifferent particles in his mechanics enables Newton to subsume Kepler's descriptions under his laws.

19. The first arguments for both space and time in the Transcendental Aesthetic are forms of the argument Plato employs at *Phaedo* 74E. For an enlightening commentary, see Gottfried Martin, *Kant's Metaphysics and Theory of Science* (1961).

20. Levinas, claiming a deep affinity with Kant, finds even in desire, as described in the last pages of *Republic IX*, an unassimilable alterity that marks something with the sign of the Good. Levinas usually attributes the mark of the latter's unassimilability, which is beyond being, to its presumed infinity. Can't we see the beginning of such a movement in Kant which, were it carried out, would make the second *Critique* prior to the first *Critique*, founding the world-theme of the latter, e.g., significance, on the moral order? One will find its traces in the pages that follow.

21. Kant's important discussion of the nature and role of symbols is found in section 59, *CAJ*.

22. Ingrid Stadler, "Perception and Perfection in Kant's Aesthetics," (1968, 339–84). In this excellent essay, however, Stadler fails to recognize the methodological constraints in the first *Critique*.

23. Richard Rorty, *Philosophy and the Mirror of Nature* (1980, 147–55), understands Kant's problem as that of getting from inner to outer space through the syntheses involved in the concept/percept distinction. While there is much that arouses sympathy in his account, the primacy of private, incorrigible sense is not Kant's initial datum. Kant's faculty psychology confuses matters which this methodological approach places in a more acceptable perspective.

24. There is a considerable gulf between the world available to Helen Keller and that required by an analytic methodology. As Locke and Berkeley argued, color alone will not yield a spatially objective world. Clinical evidence suggests that those whose sight is restored recognize motion and colors but are unable to synthesize objects and have no perception of depth. They sense without being able to judge. Except for letters already identifiable by touch (but not words), they are apparently unable to recognize molar shapes and have no concept of distance. Valvo's H. S. described a fearful world in which "street lamps were luminous stains stuck to the window panes and the corridors of the hospital were black holes" (cited in OS 1993, 63). Sacks's patient Virgil wondered if the dog seen at different times is the same dog. It is far more difficult for these people to traverse a room by sight (and then only by well-defined, invariant routes) than, as blind, by touch. It is difficult to relate a shadow to an object and to recognize the same object in variant perspectives. Visual memory is almost non-existent. Apparently the ability to visually construct a perceptually constant world in the language of sight must be learned in the first months of life (66). Such persons are agnostic, mentally blind, and are unable to make sense of what they see (62). Heidegger's "present-at-hand" would be unavailable to one unable to focus; even with vision, one would act as a blind man for whom looking is unnatural. Does Hume's account reduces experience to such a phantasmagoria?

25. Since perception is a medial process, its sensory relatum may be assigned to either the objective or subjective pole of experience.

26. For a more exhaustive discussion of these topics, see Bigger and Bigger, "Biological Recognition," (1982) and our "The Non-Reductive Molecular Basis of Life," *Proceedings of the 16th World Congress of Philosophy* (Dusseldorf, 1978), 91–93. A confirmation of Hans Jonas's ascription of proto-intentionality to living systems, e.g., E. coli, may be found in D. Koshland (1978, 1055–63).

27. The citations in the pargraph are from A. S. Byatt's remarkable essay, "Van Gogh, Death and Summer" (1993, 265–392).

28. Martin Heidegger reads *apophansis* as "exhibiting something from its own self" (1982, 209).

29. For Husserl's celebrated descriptions of perception, see 1982, secs. 41 and 97 or 1970, sec. 17.

30. Since this selectivity comes down to the medial imagination, Plato's image of the receptacle as a winnowing basket that lets some things pass and separates off others is especially appropriate.

31. These points are discussed in a commentary on the *Gorgias* by my late colleague, David Cornay, in our *Eros and Nihilism* (1967, 187–217).

32. In the pre-critical *Beweisgrund* Kant said that existence is not a conceptual determination but is the "absolute positing" of the thing. As Cassirer shows (1981, 64), this undercuts the ontological proof, but it was only in 1772 that Kant became aware of the import of his own remarks. One should see Heidegger's critique of Kant's thesis (1982, 27–76).

33. By rooting this quest for the infinite within man, Kant opens the doors for an important Romantic theme to appear as Hegel's "bad infinite," Schopenhauer's will, Kierkegaard's "sensuous-erotic infinite," and the like. For a further discussion of these roots, see my "Kant's Constructivism," (CB 1981).

34. This passage interprets Plato's *Philebus* 25C–27B.

35. The following discussion is based on Mourelatos (1970, 74–114). In modern logic the tenselessness of the copula, the "is," entails that the variously described subject *x* is timeless. Parmenides first discerned this sense of *estin*, even if its predicative role remained hidden until Aristotle.

CHAPTER THREE

1. Martin Heidegger, *Kant and the Problem of Metaphysics* (1990), and H. Heimsoeth, "Metaphysische Motive in der Ausbildung des kritischen Idealismus," *Kantstudien* 24 (1924) effected the transformation discussed in Gottfried Martin's excellent *Kant's Metaphysics and Theory of Science* (1961).

2. Oliver Sacks reports that the first thing visually recognized by the blind who have been given sight is the face because it is the place of the voice (OS 1993, 64). The gift of language that makes possible a human world be-

gins with the childs encounter with the mother (or her substitute) in the context of Winnicott's triad—the playing, talking mother, object-related play, child—which makes possible object orientation and reference, i.e., the transition to object-cathexis from the interjective or labinal cathexis. This seems to be the event that originates Levinas's face-to-face. However, this orientation is egological and, though mediated by objects, hearing the mother speak is primary. In "Ethics and Spirit," *Difficult Freedom* (1990, 7-8), he ties the face, i.e., encounter, with reference or significance:

> To speak, at the same time as knowing the Other, is at the same time making oneself known to him. The Other is not only known; he is *greeted*. He is not only named, but also invoked. To put it in grammatical terms, the Other does not appear in the nominative, but in the vocative. I not only think of what he is for me, but also and simultaneously and even before, I *am* for him [i.e., the substitution that opens the possibility of reference]. In applying a concept to him, in calling him this or that, I am already appealing to him. I do not only *know* something, I am also a part of society. This *commerce* [participation as *koinos*] which the word implies is precisely action without violence: the agent, at the very moment of his action, has renounced all claims of domination or sovereignty and is already exposed to the action of the other as it awaits a response. Speaking and hearing become one rather than succeed one another. Speaking therefore institutes the moral relationship of equality and consequently recognizes justice. One looks at a look. To look at a look is to look at something that cannot be abandoned or freed, but something that aims at you; it involves looking at the face . . . which is not a mere assemblage of a nose, a forehead . . . but takes on the meaning of a face [Gr. *prosopon,* "face," became through Lt. *persona* to mean "person"] through the new dimension it opens up in the perception of a being. Through the face, the being is not only enclosed in its form and offered in its hand, establishing itself in depth in this opening . . . somehow in a personal way. The face is an irreducible mode in which being can present itself.

This "something aimed at you" breaks down intentionality, the appropriative or assimilative form taken by Plato's participation and Heidegger's *Sorge,* care. The temporality to which this dialogic model points is not that of the reflexive hypostasis, the ecstatic standing out toward possibility which returns to the present in the perceived past, but is that of a diachronic time in which you do not return to me as assimilated.

3. Kant's distinguishes, though not firmly, *Objekt,* which has the ideality of an *ens rationis,* and derives from the Scholastic "objection," and *Gegenstand,* something intuitively given as standing over against a being that brings him to a stand. The former has the sense of "thrown before" and, in my usage, is sometimes contrasted with "eject," "thrown out from," even if the operative term in Kant is projective *Gegenstand* in which, thanks to Heidegger, we hear a reciprocal standing against.

Charles Sherover proposes that, in general, *Objekt* is used as the "internal correlate to the *Gegenstand* apprehended as in outer sense; the pure concept of transcendental *Gegenstand* then seems to be the categorial description of "somethingness" which meets the internal requirements of objectivity" (CS 1981, 258). Tentatively, then, I suggest that *Gegenstand* refers to the mind's directedness to outer experience, while Objekt seems to be Transcendental Apperception's ground for such projection onto and assimilation of that which is apprehended in intuition.

4. My "Speculative Demonstration" (1961) give a more satisfactory, but still sketchy, account. I am grateful to Prof. W. De Pater for his 1992 LSU lectures and subsequent discussions of Ian Ramsey's use of a similar formalism in his theory of disclosive metaphor. The lectures were based on Fr. de Pater's essays in *Handbuch der Sprachphilosophie*, ed. K. Lorenz (Berlin: De Gruyter, 1989) and led to this revision of my account of analysis. Ramsey also appreciated the relation of his demonstrative method to the analytic dialectic and applied it in Plato's *Symposium* to ascend to the beautiful— from one fair body to the beauty of all through institutions and laws to the science of order everywhere and, finally, to the birth in beauty.

5. I have ignored the Good which propositions the receptacle, which is also, like the Good, beyond being to grant place and let appear. I understand these to be supplements, in Derrida's sense, to the text within which Being is unconcealed. We are underway towards a "dwelling thinking" which, though inspired by Heidegger, does not define *chora,* place, in terms "raising locations by joining spaces," i.e., building (MH 1971b, 160). Place lets buildings (the feminine as interiority in proximity to the Good) and world gather each into and express one another. In "Judaism and the Feminine" (EL 1990a), Levinas says that there would be no place except for the "essential moderation of feminine existence living there, which is habitation itself" (33). Corn and flax wrenched from nature by the work of man are made into bread and clothing by this original manifestation of the perfections of the Good that subsists in itself. Can what is seized upon in nature in analysis manifest the Good?

6. David Stern reminds me of Hegel's point that either the self knows itself prior to reflection and self-consciousness presupposes what it is to explain or it does not; but then how does it know that the I that knows is the I that is known: "The motionless tautology I=I is not self-consciousness" (GH 1977, 105).

7. Though both Kant and Locke share the punctal self-defining thesis, Kant is aware of rational and empirical limits which restrict this power. Though one would never give up the self-definition thesis nor the version of expressive projection which it founds, we propose to think "thrownness" as communal and thus the non-punctal self as already within limits.

8. Gerd Buchdahl reminds me that, given this context, I should in strictness speak of the "object-in-general" rather than the "transcendental object."

9. For a critical account of Porphyry's judgmental interpretation of Aristotle's Categories which, thanks to Duns Scotus and the tradition that leads through Suarez to Leibniz and Wolff, becomes Kant's, see Earnest Moody's excellent *The Logic of William of Ockham* (1935, 66–117).

10. In a letter from Hamann to Herder cited by Cassirer (1981, 194).

11. In virtue of judgment's (groundless) ground in the medial imagination, we see *X* in the representation as we assert *X* of it. The thing's unconcealment, a sort of objective genitive, is in the act of judging a subjective genitive.

12. David Stern called my attention to the important footnote in the second edition which reconciles the intentionality of the transcendental object in the first edition with its apparent suppression in favor of judgment in the second.

> Space, represented as an *object*, (as we are required to do in geometry), contains more than the form of intuition; it also contains [*qua* synopsis] *combination* of the manifold, given according to the form of sensibility, in an *intuitive* representation, so that the *form of intuition* gives only a minifold, the *formal intuition* [intending its correlative transcendental object] gives unity of representation. In the Aesthetic I treated this unity as belonging merely to sensibility, simply in order to emphasise that it precedes any concept, although as a matter of fact, it presupposes a synthesis which does not belong to the senses [but to the productive imagination] through which all concepts of space and time become possible (B 160).

We understand ourselves to perceive objects. Since Hume made this problematic, the burden of our more naive beliefs is carried by "representation," setting something up by a rule, e.g., with language in a concept, by which something else is intended or present. First order representation, e.g., perception or perceptual judgment, presupposes a "formal intuition" of the manifold given in a "form of intuition." The formal intuition constitutes the possibility of representing, a "determination of the sensibility by understanding," the transcendental object through the sense manifold such that "the unity of this a priori intuition belongs to space and time." By the thesis of empirical realism, this is the ordinary perceptual object or, as further determined, the empirical object; and as a unity it is experienced as belonging to the receptive forms of intuition, though it is in fact the synthetic result of the imagination being crossed by a formal intuition. The forms of intuition as a combinatorial potential "presuppose a synthesis which does not belong to the senses but through which all concepts of space and time become possible." The very possibility of this sort of *a priori* attribution, e.g., "spatial object," suggests that through this ontologically prior concept space (and time) is constituted or "given as intuitions."

May one not say that the givenness of the extensive conditions (manifolds) of sense to apperception are reflexive results of a prior apperceptive act by which that manifold is constituted (B 68)? That prior act intends the manifold as meaningful or significant of empirical objects and so as latent with the possibility of knowledge. That we experience what we have put into the picture by our intentions is the by now well-worn and familiar theme of projection (in Jung or more confusedly in Freud) or objectification (Feuerbach or Marx). That which is expressively given by and to a formal intuition is a "manifold" and presupposes a recursive or iterable rule through which it can be taken up and combined. This synoptic constitution of a manifold is developed in the first edition, where the rule, like the theme of a plot, is the schematized category in which the transcendental object intended by original apperception is thought. This intention generates the prior conditions of combinability, the forms of intuition as manifolds.

13. Prof. Buchdahl has called my attention to the counter-factual sense of the transcendental object, "the subject of thoughts" (A 538), in an objection to Kemp Smith's translation, "the subject of our thoughts." This object, the paradigm of impersonal objectivity, relates to thought alone. Adickes suggests the reading, *"Subjekt von Gedanken"* rather than the usual *"Subjekt der Gedanken."* "Thought," *Gedanken,* has something of the absoluteness of Greek *nous.*

To borrow a line from the 1770 *Dissertation* (389), the noumenal object, like the actual infinite, cannot be understood but can be thought. Aside from its constitutive role in the moral life, the *Critique of Aesthetic Judgment* (sec. 59) confirms the relevance of the noumenal to expression through "symbolic presentation . . . a mode of the intuitive." Categorially disposed, i.e., schematized, sensibility can, lacking a concept, symbolize or present, i.e., realize, the supersensible in a transcendental object and gain transcending significance.

14. The Aristotelian genus is "matter" to the specific form. "Transcendental matter" would be world, rather than genus, specific.

15. This Kemp-Smith sentence masks Kant's distinction between (in B) *Objekt* and (in A) *Gegenstand.*

CHAPTER FOUR

1. Would Kant have accepted Cantor's diagonalization *schema* in which the infinite is "seen"? DeMorgan also provides an intuitive image of the infinite.

2. My debt to Martin Heidegger is more evident here than elsewhere; especially important is his discussion of time in Aristotle and Kant in Part 2, *The Basic Problems of Phenomenology* (1982).

3. This statement of the relations of successors to an origin, zero counted as first, is a common way of introducing ordinals and capturing the point, to be developed later in the text, that the now from which one addresses the manifold and the now addressed are other; the now having been is addressed from and present to the present, but the present is never self-present.

4. Kant's affinity with Aristotle is not always appreciated, yet two editions of Aristotle in Greek and Latin were among the relatively few philosophical texts in his personal library.

5. J. R. Lucas's *A Treatise on Time and Space* (1973) is a noble and delightfully idiosyncratic monograph that deserves to be more widely known.

6. Some years ago Charles Hartshorne pointed out to me a similar thesis in Peirce, where the ideas were potentials for the definition of fact which

are generated by Dedekind-like cuts. He also reported that Mary Calkins had a similar approach. I have never followed up these attractive suggestions, though I did mention them in *Participation* (1968, 151–53).

7. With *Sachheit* it would be appropriate to remark that the project of transcendental idealism deconstructs itself. Interiority is already defined by exteriority, a line, and the simple present is what it is only through difference, the conceptual difference of recognition or the retained difference of reproductive synthesis. The mathematical model makes it clear that interiority is a parasite of exteriority and that, moreover, transcendental phenomenology is also being deconstructed even as it is being founded. This Pythagorean approach, in which geometry, the form of exteriority or outer sense, is seen to be necessary for arithmetical operations, the "spacings" of inner sense should recall the more complete but less direct argument of Derrida's *Speech and Phenomena* (1973).

8. The following axioms define the order type of the rational numbers with which Kant must work. Given a discrete now series A, B, C, . . . , satisfying the identifying or objectivity conditions as represented through the line, Kant's temporal order will satisfy the following axioms:

Distinct: If there are two moments such that one is earlier than the other, then the now series is distinct.

Transitive: If A is later (or earlier) than B, and B has this relation to C, then A is later (or earlier) than C.

Completely ordered: Given any two nows, A and B, A is either earlier or later than B but not both. These will establish the series as having the order type of the ordinals.

Open: Given any now A, there is a now B which is earlier or later than A. Kant's own preference for the regressive synthesis, which is the temporal form of explanation by covering laws, suggests that the series is open with respect to "earlier than."

Continuous: If A and B are distinct nows, there is a now, C, such that it is later than one and earlier than the other. Time will have the order type of the rational numbers.

Linear: A series is linear if it is Archimedean. In this constructive context, this would mean that the isochronic intervals marked out by ordinal nows are such that if any has a denumerable subset of nows, then between any two there is another. In this rational continuum, these may serve as a mesh for time measurement. A non-denumerable and metrically amorphous subset, being featureless, would be desirable. The non-constructive Dedekind axiom would accomplish this result:

If K_1 and K_2 are any two non-empty subsets of the set K such that every element of K belongs either to K_1 or K_2, and every element of K_1 precedes every element of K_2, then there is an element X in K such that any element that precedes X belongs to K_1 and any element that follows X belongs to K_2.

9. In his classic *Individuals* (1963), Peter Strawson proposes a "feature-placing" language in which spatial/temporal entities characterized by universals such as "a fall of rain" or "a lump of gold" and the like, replace basic particulars and their sortal predicates. An event ontology is a feature placing ontology and is worthy of closer study by those of us interested in *chora*.

10. The continuum K is linear if it contains a denumerable sub-set R such that between any two of its elements there is an element of R.

11. G. N. Lewis, the distinguished British chemist, once proposed that the directionality of time, Eddington's "time's arrow," is a phenomenon of consciousness and should be purged from the physical sciences as anthropocentric (*Science* 71 [1930]). In response, Karl Popper notes that spherical waves will not close in isotopically to a precise point of annihilation and are therefore irreversible (*Nature* 177 [1956]; 538; 179 [1957]; 1, 297; 181 [1958]; 402).

CHAPTER FIVE

1. This 1954 essay, "The Ego and Totality," already sets Levinas apart from an epistemic bias. Seeing things as goods to be enjoyed approaches temporality medially. This differs from the structure of time which is thematic in voluntaristic phenomenology. In fact, action is founded on enjoyment, a medial phenomenon. I have formulated the self-individuating "me" so as to avoid Levinas's questionable exclusion of animal life as faceless from the ethical relation ("Philosophy and the Idea of Infinity," EL 1987, 55).

2. Four intersecting four-dimensional time-systems define one dimensional event-particles, abstractive elements in a relativistic analogue of absolute space.

3. Alan Wolter (1946) has provided a most illuminating study of these terms in Scholastic philosophy.

4. In Plato something is same, *auto*, through alterity. Heidegger calls attention to the following passage in the *Sophist* (254D); "each is same for itself," where the "same for itself" in not an indifferent unity (1969, 24). As he notes in the essay "Poetically Man Dwells, "The same never coincides with the equal, not even in the empty indifferent oneness of that is identical. The equal or identical always moves towards the absence of difference so that everything moves to a common denominator. The same, by contrast, is the belonging together of what differs, through as gathering by way of the difference. We can only say 'the same' if we think difference" (MH 1971b, 218).

5. Even after deconstruction, "I" is "quasi-transcendental," a term first used by Rodolphe Gasché and then picked up by Derrida. This means that while what it designates cannot claim the status of Kant's Transcendental Apperception, the term or concept will still occupy a privileged place. I find the concept of the hypostasis more directly relevant since it can be formed without use of the predicative transcendentals with which Derrida continues to operate, which is fair enough since the texts he works with do not use "transcendental" in the Platonic sense. For a fuller account, see Geoffrey Bennington (JD 1993a, 276–81).

6. Representation is the relation between a principle or origin and something that makes it present and effective, but this difference, however stated, seems to be a victim of deconstruction. The original turns out to be as

much a function of its representation as conversely. I will grant this mutuality in my account of participation but shall preserve a contextual possibility of asymmetry with the help of Levinas by defining the possibility of communion from beyond being through proximity to the other.

7. Though not without its faults, my "St. Thomas on Essence and Participation" (1988) gives a more complete discussion of these issues and citations from the relevant literature. The point of apportionment, described in *the Liber de Causis* attributed to Proclus, is the reception of form "according to the capacity of the recipient." Fr. Norris Clarke, reflecting Thomas' position as he understands it, describes apportionment as "a receiving subject limiting a higher plentitude" or, in the words of the title of his essay, "The Limitation of Act by Potency," *New Scholasticism* 26 (1966, 91). As Cornelio Fabro formulates it, "every essence, though a act in the formal order, is created as a potency to be actualized by the participated *esse* which it receives," in "The Intensive Hermeneutics of Thomistic Philosophy: The Notion of Participation," *Review of Metaphysics* 27 (1974, 470).

8. These concepts are intended to be suggestive only. If we recall that *ens*, like *on*, is a participle, verbal and nominal, then a medial reading can be given if being is hypostatically gained in or through process and "essence" is verbal, like a scenario. In such a verbal world adjectives become adverbs. The verbal formula I have proposed adjusts forms to life and time, the time of a life, and the adverbial form of intentional acts lets us see the "nature" as *haecceitas* or contracted, as we see the game contracted in a player. I am persuaded that Duns Scotus offers this possibility.

9. The relation between same and other, and all differences arising from and expressed in participation, is dialectical or deconstructive.

10. I would now add Effemination to the Principles, Relativity, Ontological and Mingling.

11. For an illuminating discussion of Derrida's thesis that life is the gift of time see John Protevi, "*Given Time* and the Gift of Life" (1993).

12. Aron Gurwitsch remarks that hyletic data are amorphous, "devoid of meaning or intentionality in themselves" and serve "as materials to [intentional] operating factors by which they are animated and receive meaning" (1964, 268). Structure is brought about by noetic factors, and examples flow from gestalt psychology in which "the same complex may receive different interpretations" (270). This is rather more promising as an approach to original receptivity than that suggested by some of Husserl's examples.

13. The hyleic datum white, if it can be said or spoken, is already saturated with the universal. When the primal datum becomes an adumbration of a noema, a redly seeing of, or thematic in its own right, e.g., seeing red, conscious acts, e.g., reflection and recognition, are implicated. Is this universal quality intuited because, as Adorno might insist, recognition is already a function of a transcending social reality, e.g., language, its classifications and hierarchies, or is it an original showing? The evidence of animal life suggest that *hyle* is the appearing of the universal in the singular, that the universal is not conferred by but rather disclosed in an act. Since, however, Husserl said hyleic data is non-intentional, I will adapt the thesis that objectification is linguistic and, to that extent, social.

14. Levinas's descriptions refer back to his own account of the *il y a* which was in turn inspired by Heidegger's effort to bring us to experience being through nothing (MH 1961, 23-24). Let me quote for the record from his most illuminating account:

> Let us imagine all beings, things and persons, reverting to nothing-ness. One cannot put this return to nothingness outside of all events. But what of this nothingness itself? Something would happen, if only night and the silence of nothingness. The indeterminateness of this "something is happening" is not the indeterminateness of a sub-ject and does not refer to a substantive. Like the third person pro-noun in the impersonal form of the verb, it designates not the uncertainly known author of the action, but the characteristic of the action itself that has no author. This impersonal, anonymous, yet "indistinguishable consummation" of being, which murmurs in the depths of nothingness itself we shall designate by the term *il y a, there is.* The "there is," inasmuch as it resists a personal form, is "being in general." (EL 1988, 57)

15. My interest in *hypostasis* began, not with its use in Emmanuel Lev-inas, but with Patristic thought. The most useful text is that by G. L. Prestige, *God in Patristic Thought* (1952). *Hypostasis* refers to that which settles out or precipitates to the bottom from a flow and was first used in place of the par-ticiple *ousia* and then in the sense of "person." *Ousia* is close to *physis*, "na-ture," which Aristotle says is an immanent *arché* of motion and rest. Thus *hypostasis*, derived from the medial *hyphistamai*, is a catachresis in which nominal being, *ens* (as in entity) precipitates out of the medial process of be-coming (*gignesthai*) and, like Aristotle's self-doctoring *physis*, controls it. The Fathers are cited from Henry Bettenson (1991a,b).

16. Though Emmanuel Levinas does not reintroduce the term "hypos-tasis" which he employed in *Existence and Existents* in his discussion of the self in *Totality and Infinity,* it is implicit in his use of enjoyment, rather than intentionality as such, to establish the primal reflexivity involved in need satisfaction. I must bypass this more profound development of the con-cept of hypostasis which allows us to define subjectivity in terms of separa-tion from totalizing structures rather than substantively.

17. Like its distant cousin, Aristotle's *hyle, chora* is systematically am-biguous. By defining the *hypostasis* in terms of the medial receptacle and its gift of place, we incorporate biological, social, and personal parameters, some or all of which may operate in other contexts. This, like the Derridian "text," is the context of all contexts. Moreover, it should have normative dimensions, analogous to Heideggerian authenticity or the Latin *persona,* used as Jung uses it, for example, to mark a fall into average everydayness.

18. David Wood (1989) defines "appropriation," with an eye to Levi-nas, as an opening to the other, "onto what may never be appropriated, made identical, brought back." This deconstruction of the egocentric self requires a less radical treatment in this ontology. The *hypostasis* is always already so-cial, through others, and *qua* medial not a presence. Nevertheless, I would

want to retain this radical alterity, the Good. The reference to the eternal return, the being of this becoming, is intended to invoke Wood's magisterial discussion of Nietzsche's elusive concept (20–35).

19. The Platonic birth is creativity (*Sym.* 207D) and ranges from sexual procreativity to the love of others as beautiful and thus to making institutions and laws that do them justice (209C).

20. The idea of a placeless, context free law is a fundamental illusion. Laws express a placing of things; the inertial law, formulated for an isolated system, points to the way models prescind from relational complexities. The receptacle and place are supplements and show that every statement, except those concerning the logic or formal possibility, is place-relative, though not always relative to particular places, e.g., Galileo's law as applicable to the surface of the earth. One must argue as if a law were eternal and thus contextless in order to discover exceptions and negative instances. In metaphysics' likely stories one also accepts the pretensions of the synthetic *a priori*, accepting a context-free discourse about the possibility of contexts.

C H A P T E R   S I X

1. This distinction between a text and a book is not to be confused with Derrida's similar distinction in *Of Grammatology*. His text is "a nexus . . . a field whose marks are related by *différance*," as John Protevi says in his admirable essay "Derrida and Hegel: *Différance and Untershied*," (1993a, 59–74). This general text retains "discursive practices, institutions, and so forth" and makes possible a contextual and historic reading of the forces and powers of Plato's receptacle, "the place of the trace," in which meaning is inscribed. Can the Derridian text accommodate, in general, what Hegel assigned to Spirit, justice and freedom, within a Nietzschian economy of forces? The image Derrida invokes seems to descend from Foucault's "statements," discursive formations and strategies; but one wonders if textuality is not itself a historical formation. In the Renaissance, language becomes an object and the relation of this text to the world is further exacerbated in the last century when, with expressivism, meaning is disassociated from things. Moreover, has Derrida's effort to eliminate the ontological priority of consciousness also eliminated the gap we have traced from Kant's imagination to the Open beyond Being? Are we not within the reductive precincts of Gaea? This place of the trace provides a radical alterity, a difference beyond Hegelian difference and identity, for any spatial or temporal mark or inscription and, in virtue of its marginal status, traces that operate within the text to deconstruct expression. No, for the text contains the trace of the Other (Levinas), which constitutes the possibility of the text and yet cannot be assimilated (*pace* Hegel) to it. But there is always such a danger.

A somewhat reductive version of the matrix is deploy by Derrida in his discussion of Francis Ponge's poem, "Fable," in "Inventions of the Other" (JD 1989). Ponge's text begins with "*By the* word *by commences then this text / Of which the* first line states the truth / But this silvering [tain] *of the one under the other / Can it be tolerated."* Derrida says this medial matrix generates "a sort of poetic performance that simultaneously describes and carries out, on the same line, its own generation." Though not all performatives are reflexive, "this constative description is nothing other than the performative itself. Its beginning, its invention, or its first coming [advent] does not come about before the sentence that precisely constitutes this event. The narrative is nothing other than the coming of what it cites, recites, points out or describes. It is hard to distinguish the telling and the told faces of this sentence that invents itself." He then notices how the text folds on itself [like the hypostasis?] so that the first "by" is quoted by the second in an "originary reflexivity that, even as it divides the inaugural event, [is] at once the inventive event and the archive of an invention . . . and mixes up two heterogeneous functions, use and mention, but also heteroreference and self-reference, allegory and tautology" (33). The said never makes an egress from the saying, never becomes a creature, but as a quasi-transcendental, proposes and dissipates its own performance.

We can admit this and welcome the fact that power has been taken away from the sun and given to the earth, the mother, but what of the alterity of the Good? Note, however, that it is not just a matter of maintaining the receptacle and the Good as beyond being. Otherwise, as Derrida suggests in "The White Mythology," the Good is a catachresis whose proposed term is to be thought through Aristotle's sun and its seeds (*De Poetics* 1457b 25-50) as a being, a neo-Platonic "Authentic Existent." This catachrestic Good, together with the catachrestic receptacle, can have those demonic implications noted in our discussion of van Gogh in the second chapter. The receptacle is incarnate in the hypostasis who, as absolutely Other, bears the stigmata of the Good.

2. In his commentary on Hugh of St. Victor's *Didascalicon* (1993, 25), Ivan Illich calls attention to the correlative emergence of person (as a unique psyche) and the text (within which he discovers himself) from the page. The journey Hugh proposes does not require that one leave home in order to travel the road to the Supreme Good that "motivates the pilgrims of the pen." The Derridian text metaphor is quite useful and I will continue to employ it, but here again with Berkeley I must return to the older "Book of Nature," which will carry its more conventional sense as something to be read and thus as something already significant—even if we must first know mathematics to read it, e.g., Descartes. This contrasts with the older doctrine of signatures, e.g., Augustine or Boehme, whose sense was transcendent.

3. In the *Phenomenology* (chapter 3) Hegel argues, I think successfully, that force, rather than being reductive (as in Nietzsche) is already an other in which the self reflectively discovers itself. With this Hegel can overcome the formal, judgmental role of categories and transform their use into speculative propositions, as if these were forms of the mind's life. This is especially true of those pertaining to "reflection" which, in thinking thought, uses categories employing and sublating difference, i.e., identity, difference, and contradiction (*Science of Logic,* v. 1, sec. 1, chapt. 2). John Protevi speaks of this as a modalization of thought thinking through the implications of each catego-

rial thought pattern. This reflects the experience we have in dialectic in which the other and her objections appear as an opposing force. Derrida proposes that we no longer "interiorize difference as contradiction" and that we speak instead of "conflicts of forces rather than contradiction" (JD 1981, 101). Though this is a misreading of Hegel, it serves us well. Since the *hypostasis* is a historical and linguistic phenomenon, then it is already inscribed in the non-discursive text of forces which logo-centric metaphysics has generated and ordered. One could turn to Deleuze's work on Nietzsche (1983) to see how this ordering and the resulting hierarchy is produced.

4. Whitehead says "the awareness of an object as some factor not sharing in the passage of nature is what I call "recognition." It is impossible to recognize an event because an event is essentially distinct from every other event. Recognition is an awareness of sameness. But to call recognition an awareness of sameness implies an intellectual act of comparison combined with judgment. I use recognition for the non-intellectual relation of sense-awareness which connects the mind with a factor in nature without passage . . . [it] is the relation of the mind to nature which provides the material for the intellectual activity" (ANW 1921, 143).

5. Significance, Whitehead continues, is "that quality of relatedness possessed by the part which is immediately under observation . . . there is essentially a beyond to what is observed . . . every event is known as being related to other events which it does not include. This fact . . . shows that exclusion is as positive a relation as inclusion" (ANW 1921, 186).

6. Contrast, a differential structure, plays a similar role in Whitehead's version of this principle. I have borrowed his distinction between relational and intrinsic essence. Charles Taylor's remarks on these fields are illuminating: "things only have meaning within a field, that is, in relation to the meanings of other things. This means that there is no such thing as a single, unrelated meaningful element; and it means that changes in the other meanings in the field semantic, conceptual, or sensory can involve changes in the given element. Meanings can't be identified except in relation to others, in this way resembling words. The meaning of a word depends on those words with which it contrasts, on those which define its place in the language (e.g., those defining 'determinable' dimensions, like color or shape), and so on" (1971, 11–12).

7. This discussion of signification derives from Jacques Derrida's criticism in *Speech and Phenomena* (1973) of Husserl's distinction between indicative and expressive signs in the first of his *Logical Investigations* (1970, v. I , 269–333).

David Wood's *Deconstruction of Time* (1989) is unsurpassable in its grasp of the nexus of originary issues in Derrida, Heidegger, and Husserl. I should also acknowledge the great value of John Protevi's "The Economy of Exteriority in Derrida's *Speech and Phenomena*" (1993, 373–88).

8. Derrida's thesis that language is proto-writing colors the following account of the movement in writing towards distantiation and objectification. My discussion has been shaped, though doubtless still wanting, by John Llewelyn's excellent *Derrida on the Threshold of Sense* (1986).

9. Plato's separationist ontology and his own expressivism is evident in

Frege's distinction between thought (the objective thought of so-and-so), ideas (subjective), and their bearers. As might be expected, the existence of these bearers becomes very problematic.

10. In *Speech and Phenomena*, Derrida shows how Husserl's position on indicative and expressive signs eliminates exteriority, first by the *epoché* in which common space becomes the space of phenomenological consciousness; second, this conscious space becomes the space of meaning, which in turn leads to the final reduction, original intuition as "spacing." John Protevi (1993b, 384) notes that the condition for the possibility of the reductions, the distinction between exteriority and interiority, is the condition for their impossibility because the temporal flux, Husserl's "absolute subjectivity," is "a spacing [the becoming space of time] . . . an interweaving of inside/outside, or "the dialectic of identity and difference in the same."

11. Plato has no concept of predication and thus no place for a universal. Obviously it cannot be something expressed that determines reference. One can extract elements from a complex, and thus "constitute" them as intentional objects, treating some as paradigms. Some of these elements will be "real," some fictions, and others will be artifacts (Socrates' "wind-eggs") of dialectic. In defending Kant's representations I am not stating my position, but rather opening the way for its effective presentation.

12. "Violence and Metaphysics" appeared in 1964 (JD 1978, 79–162) and was the first recognition by an important thinker of Levinas's *Totality and Infinity* (1961).

The *arché*, which is systematically ambiguous, is always medial. This is implicit in Plato's descriptions of Eros in the *Symposium* (203C) and of Levinas's descriptions of sexuality, e.g., "the tender is a *way*, the way of remaining in the *no man's land* between being and not-yet-being . . . an amorphous non-I sweeps away the I into an absolute future where it escapes itself and loses its position as a subject" (259). Those puzzled by the movement from physical to moral beauty in the *Symposium* (210B) in which passion "gives way to noble discourse" may find Levinas suggestive. Plato slips back and forth between beauty (passion) and the desire for the good (201C) which, to invoke a distinction from the *Republic*, is not appropriative or assimilative (585A ff.). Levinas agrees that even in sexuality the Other remains an inassimilable Other and obligates me.

13. Derrida plays down intentional acts, especially speech acts, as onto-theo-logical paradigms of self-certain self-presence. As William Cobb notes, he starts with written speech, which we recognize as containing no finality or context dependence, and thinks of spoken language as its image. What Plato says about "living speech" in the *Phaedrus* "does not suggest that it contains any final, context-independent statements that do not require continuing explanation and interpretation" (*Plato's Erotic Dialogues* [Albany: State University of New York Press, 1993], 166). Moreover speech acts are not always expressive; they are often monstrative, showing and letting another see, and assertive, i.e., truth-making, on the basis of what is disclosed. The ideal of self-responsibility characterizing Husserl and its existentialist offspring should be secondary to the response to the other, responsibility to the other for what is said.

14. What appears to be a way into the Open beyond being is like a Klein bottle, which has no inside/outside, or an Escher drawing, where the way up is the way down.

15. This Aristotelian thesis is strongly and convincingly defended by Nancy Cartwright, *How the Laws of Physics Lie* (1983).

16. Umberto Eco, *A Theory of Semiotics* (1976, 69). See his image of the entropic disorder characteristic of self-referring or closed systems in the burning scriptorum in his fine novel, *The Name of the Rose*.

17. John Llewelyn reminds me that there is nothing very generous about Levinas's "there is;" its gift is more like the German *Gift*, "poison." My reading of Levinas is distorted by a desire to introduce elements from Plato and Mary which compete the story. For instance, the amorphous, medial *il y a* is the rather more cosmological "becoming that never really is" (*Tim.* 28A) which diversifies the receptacle; thus "there is," when solicited or propositioned by the Good, grants a being a place, "here." I will read Levinas, perhaps unjustly, within these extended parameters.

18. Miss Sullivan said in a letter of 31 March 1887 that Helen knew twenty words, but could not distinguish between cup or drink and responded to both by lifting the cup to her mouth in pantomime. On 5 April, the day of the discovery that everything has a name, Helen learned thirty new words (1965, 23).

Walker Percy, *The Message in the Bottle* (1975) made this event the focus of several important studies. I have discussed the importance of this physician-novelist-philosopher for a phenomenology of language in "Logos and Epiphany" (1977, 196–206), and "Walker Percy and the Resonance of the Word," (1980, 43–54).

19. David Wood points out the difficulty in distinguishing the primal datum from retention, both of which are said to be perceived, in Husserl's internal time consciousness (DW 1989, 93-97). Once we begin the question protention, then there is a place both for possibility and a valuation on the matrix, the present as originary. The matrix gives time to being. This is clearer in self-affective activity, speaking or writing, in which the present is in some measure a function of the represented future. Getting behind the given to the giving is phenomenology's limit. *Zazen,* the Zen technique of meditation, promises the possibility of a medial experience of giving without temporal horizons, i.e., intentionality, or other analogues of Kantian synthesis. Life follows from the gift of time by the matrix to being.

20. "Crossing over into" is intended to express the experience of grace, or some medial and even naturalistic analogue thereof, in which I am through the other. Plato uses the language of birth while John Llewelyn, thinking of Levinas, speaks of the "deconstruction" of the self.

21. Though Levinas denies that one can participate in the Good, granted the Christian concept of "economy," He can dwell in us and we in Him. In this sense, the regulatives which, as Kant recognized, partake of the infinite also have a vital sense. Though it is usually constitutive or transcendental, "Being," as in "Be a man!" may have a regulative or measuring role. Regulatives, like Kantian "ideas," solicit spirit but have no constitutive force and are not forms of domination.

22. This version of perception as a participation paradigm differs from my previous accounts(1968, 135–41, and 1973, 27–53). I now see the hermeneutical force in the "active motion" of *Theaetetus* (156C–57C) or the "visual current" that passes from the eye to the object in *Timaeus* (45C–D). From the point of the physicalism of the *Theaetetus* itself, the object actively conditions the passive motion of the subject. Peirce tells us how to think this through symbols which "may, with Emerson's sphinx, say to man, 'Of thine eye, I am eyebeam'"(2.203). My appreciation of these interpretative dimensions owes much to Edward Ballard (1983); he demonstrates how to generate categories of interpretation from the transcendentals (Being, same, other, motion, rest, one, and many) which I used in *Participation*.

The thesis that sensory intuition is itself interpretative seems to have first been made by Peirce. He argued that even at the physical and psychological levels, interpretation is involved (5.213–24) and that the Kantian intuition-cognition distinction cannot be sustained. We are never immediately present to an object. This was probably inspired by Hegel: "the fact is that experience contains identity of union with difference and is the immediate refutation of the assertion that abstract identity as such is something true, for the exact opposite, namely identity in union with difference, occurs in every experience" (GH 1977, 415). This "difference" will recur in our text as a field of differences ranging over sense, semantics, and concepts. In this text I therefore speak of the sense object in a field as a physical interpretation of those events involved in passive motion.

23. Given the Russell and Whitehead symbolism, one may express the conditions of the participation of some form Ψ as a parameter in n-tipple predicates, $\Psi(x_1, x_2, \ldots , x_n)$, where $n \geq 2$. Any x_i can itself be a subparameter in the superparameter Ψ and determine a range of variables, subjective (being appeared to Ψ-ly) and objective (appearing Ψ-ly). Since that which gives being, the *receptacle* as engendering *arché*, is not itself a being, this formal approach is limited. The relational formalism avoids the monadic predicate paradigm with which it is too often confused.

Participation is not the simple relation between a form, Ψ, and an instance, α, i.e., $\Psi(\alpha)$, even if instantiating notation is often convenient and justified. It concerns the belonging together of a transcending multiplicity in the one as determinates of determinable power, is a relational structure through which a form is engendered (*Theaet.* 156B). In this first statement of the Ontological Principle, being refers primarily to this nexus of active and passive powers: "Nothing is one thing just by itself . . . all the things we are pleased to say *are* [that come to be] really are in a process of becoming (152C). . . . There is no such thing as an agent until it meets with a patient . . . from whose intercourse all things arise in the variety of their motion . . . in the process of coming to be for someone" (157A). This notion that to be is to be for another in the coming to be of something definite is the Ontological Principle. The Principle also establishes the phenomenality of participation. The transcendentals explicate this process. Being in its primary sense can be further characterized as applicable *in quid* to any determinable and *in qual* to any determinate within the scope of the ontological principle. Though this *Theaetetus* account is perfectly general and can apply to partici-

pation of fact in forms, to forms participating inter se, and to forms participating in fact, I follow Plato's perceptual model, in which the form of the
relation expresses the participation of the subject in the object.

It is helpful to think of an idea as a parameter, a constant, that determines a variable range. For example, the seen white of the snow is an *eidos* or
parameter satisfied only if other conditions, expressible in physical, biological, atmospheric, lighting, psychological, etc., subparameters, are also satisfied. The white is, like many sense objects, a constant of externality, not a
secondary quality; not only is it same under various conditioning events, e.g.,
differing conditions of lighting, but as located on the stone, however the
stone is interpretatively seen, e.g., as a weapon, geological specimen, or doorstop, it is also a same that gives access to *it as* this or that. The more appropriate formalism is $\Psi(\Sigma[x_1,x_2, \ldots ,x_n], \Omega[y_1,y_2, \ldots ,y_n])$, where Ψ is
such a constant or superparameter ranging over subparameters, the interpreta-
tive and receptive Σ (together with its own cultural, psychological, etc. subparameters x_i) which is conditioned by the "active motion" of Ω and its
physical and biological subparameters, y_j, to engender the perceptual event
characterized by Ψ. Ψ belongs neither to the "subject" Σ nor the object-
nexus Ω but is their unity, the "white" in "I see a white stone." That one
sees a white "stone" rather than doorstop or geological specimen depends on
the *schema*tizing forestructure of Σ, the beam of the helios-like eye (*Rep.*
508B). In this general sense the form Ψ results from the mingling of forms
Φ_Σ and Λ_ω more or less successfully drawn from the thing O, where Φ may
be an inseparable *a parte rei* formality of Ω interpretatively "seen as" a constant of externality Ψ in Σ. The truth relation between O, the object parameters and events, and Σ, the subjective conditions, will be satisfied if they are
isomorphic, if there is some pattern Ψ interprets that both Λ and Φ (partially)
illustrate.

Put slightly otherwise, ψ is the parametric *eidos,* and each subparameter
Σ_i and Ω_j, respectively subjective and objective, represents some factor or
condition jointly sufficient for Ψ and illustrating another of the transcendentals. Moreover there will be among these subparameters at least two differing
in ontological type, i.e., causal conditions associated with the active motion
of Ω and interpretative and receptive parameters associated with Σ, whose
crossing defines or iterates ψ. With the exception of one-many, these terms
are drawn from the list in the *Sophist* of the "greatest kinds," same, other,
being, motion, and rest.

In the *Theaetetus,* Plato speaks of perceiving a white stone, where the
sense object or *eidos* "white" is engendered by the participation or "crossing" of the object in the subject (153D–157C). Borrowing from the sexual
metaphors of *Theaetetus* and *Timaeus,* we can say $\Psi(\Sigma, \Omega)$ interprets the
"father," the objective conditions (Ω) from the place of the mother (Σ) to
her offspring, the event $\Psi(\sigma, \omega)$. Minimally, participation is a triadic relation, Peirce's "thirdness," where the form ψ, instanced as $\Psi(\sigma, o)$, is also
the form of a process, σ's Ψ-ly interpretation of o, the physical object, i.e.,
"The stone appears to me whitely." Depending on whether or not we are
interested in the "subjective" (152B) or "objective" (154B) conditions, we
could express this idealistically as pertaining to the subject, $\Psi(\sigma)$, or realisti-

cally as pertaining to the object, $\Psi(\omega)$. "White" is both the sensed object and as affective, the "whitely" sensing lived.

The white could be an immanent form and content of consciousness, the whitely as medially lived which is neither objective nor subjective since it is non-intentional. Linear time is the form of this medial "whitely" consciousness which can then break apart into reflexive noematic, "being appeared to by white," and noetic, "whitely appearing," components. In the latter case, linear time becomes reflexive time, the intentional form in which "white" protentively and retentively appears. Though participation respects the truth in realism and anti-realism, the manner in which variables governing presentification are divided up among "subjective" and "objective" components and defined is a matter for empirical science and not conceptual analysis.

Let me illustrate by a naive example of a "white" event-phase that will engage the transcendental terms. In seeing the white snow I participate in a nexus of bio-physical events in such a way that the apparent conditioning region, where the white is seen to be situated, is also the causal event, the snow, whose white is whitely illustrated. According to Whitehead,

> This interfusion is effected by those aspects of those eternal objects, such as colors, sounds, scents, geometrical characters, which are required for nature and are not emergent from it. Such an eternal object will be an ingredient in one event under the guise or aspect of qualifying another event. There is a reciprocity of aspects and there are patterns of aspects. Each event corresponds to two such patterns; namely the pattern of aspects which it grasps into its own unity, and the pattern of its aspects which other events severally grasp into its own unities. (ANW 1978, 44)

The situation of the white may be disjoined from its casual conditions, as in reflections in a mirror or an illusion. In veridical cases, this "whitely" manner of appearing is attributed *in qual* to a (common) nature which is itself *in quid* "whiteness." To say of an event, A, that it participates in Ψ relative to the nexus X is to say that its attributive *being* A is *same* with Ψ, which in turn is *other* than A, namely, a possibility for the characterization of an indefinitude of events B, C, . . . , that may also in the order of singularity individuate Ψ.

Moreover, A is a linear route of genetically linked events A', A'', A''', . . . , and may, as A, be said to be in *motion* and so is Ψ-ly *one* and *same* in *being* through its *other*, Ψ. In this A'-series of other(ing) and other(ing), this A-like epochal *plurality* is as a succession at *rest* relative to Ψ. If we allow the participle, a verbal adjective, to be a verbal adverb, which is possible in Latin, then there is a slim grammatical warrant for this interpretation. But the *haecceity* A Ψ-ing ψ-ly determines a possible range of others of each type, dynamical and formal, in which it participates in order to be a same under the parameters of the trace of its past. In Platonic terms, the whiteness appearing "whitely" participatorily interprets a vast array of events and processes in overlapping and coordinate physical, psychological, and physiological systems and subsystems and their background of more or less steady-state conditions. A region appearing whitely (a factor in sense perception) is given as white (a comparative, and thus an entity for thought) on the satisfaction of certain process variables; white as an entity is then a parameter or constant defining a possible range of variation. When what is supposed to appear whitely fails to do so, we know that some variable conditions "contracting" whiteness are lacking. Is life that different? Is our humanity anything but a parametric product of a variety of causal and interpretative systems, infinitely complex, to make the causal case? But it is also a clearing that is sustained as such, unlike the *in qual* "whitely" therein appearing, by its interpretative or spontaneous control on metabolic and other processes through "reading" nature's book. The individuating activity by which we are a clearing in which beings appear depends on the *in qual* apportioning of essence to the dynamics of becoming.

24. The concepts of projection and objectification suggest the social, psychological and historical aspects of interpretation, e.g., Plato's helios-like eye or Whitehead's phase of conceptual supplementation; but these terms should refer to subjectivity as a matrix, as a dwelling in which experiences are born under these conditions. Plato's term "passive motion" aptly expresses this interpretative or medial receptivity. Mathematics arises from and schematizes a matrix condition.

25. Lest we lose ourselves in the endless reflections precipitated by this term in Paul de Mann and Jacques Derrida, we should first recall that Derrida neither denied intentionality nor the disclosive nature of the text. The text is a metaphor about the matrix-patrix, not the world given through it.

26. Charles Taylor proposes some necessary conditions for being a sign (1971, 15–16) which I have modified with the text metaphor in mind; they are probably neither necessary and certainly not sufficient:

1. There is a field of objects about which we can speak coherently or incoherently, sensibly or senselessly.
2. Elements in the field signify in virtue of their differential relations and relative transparency. One doesn't see red, a differential in a sense field, and infer *apple* any more than one sees "red" and infers *red;* we see the apple through the "registered" but unnoticed red.
3. Significance cannot be completely context-relative, as if an artifact of demonstrative conditions, but will be a possible same in differing contexts.

The last two conditions are only imperfectly satisfied:

4. This meaningful same can be non-synonymously expressed in different "carriers and signifiers." One expression may make better sense, be more coherent that the other, as in Verdi's v. Shakespeare's *Othello,* but these distinctions frequently depend on conventions of performance, production, and the like, and are not absolute. The fields are formal. What they say can be said in other ways. Different bits of DNA, in the interests of protective redundancy, carry the same message. Just as Bach's fugues are relatively independent of the instruments on which they are played, e.g., Gould on the piano, Rugg on the organ, Segovia on the guitar and Wandowska on the harpsichord, or just as the same music appears in an analogue form on an LP record or a tape and in a digital form on a CD, these meanings also survive

particulars of expression. Meaning, like a festival, is iterable as this or that interpretation in particular expressive contexts.
5. Meaning is for an interpreter.

1. Any doubts as to murder as the alternative in a face-to-face encounter should be resolved by the last pages of Flannery O'Conner's remarkable story, "A Good Man is Hard to Find."

2. Though tempted to use the medial "essance" (-ance is medial), Levinas continues to translate *Sein* by "essence" which will then be thought temporally in an active or process, rather than nominal or static, sense (EL 1981, xli, 187).

3. For a more complete examination of Levinas's moves to avoid the closure of metaphysics, see Robert Bernasconi, "Levinas and Derrida: The Question of the Closure of Metaphysics" (EL 1986, 181–202).

4. The persons of the Trinity conjugate the transcendentals, Being, Truth, and Good. Except for Hegel, the third person has not received a primary role and even there was introduced under the rubric of reason and power. Moreover, given the Good and an adequate understanding of *homoiousia,* perhaps it would be possible to evoke the Being of Goodness, to define and articulate its enabling power, in rather more conventional ways that do not require such a radical break as Levinas requires.

5. My use of Plato's visual metaphors, which I associate with the energetics of Robert Grosseteste's *On Light* (1939) and not presence, do not fit easily into Levinas's program which is thus retrieved with a certain violence.

6. The phrase is Emmanuel Levinas's and suggests Heidegger's *andenkendes Denken,* "commemorative thinking." It also refers to the presence of the other to herself that is never present to us. We will be placing ourselves, in Robert Bernasconi's elegant phrase, within this medial arrival or "entry into the word's own rule" (1985, 11), with the speculative proposition in the final section of this chapter. In the cases in question, "being" sets up events, like rites or festivals, in which each renewal is an original presencing. Archeology is existential, not pre-historic.

7. Prof. Reiner Schürmann remarks that the "origin," the medieval God or the Kantian noumenon, had always been absent, for they can "impart their measure to our thinking and living because they escape our grasp." This radical phenomenology "takes away from absence the aura of authority. . . . Not so [for the non-authoritative] *Es gibt*" (1987, 147). It must be stressed that the Good beyond being is neither an origin nor principle, an absence with the "aura of authority" with mitigates some of Schürmann's anarchical consequences.

8. This is a "phenomenology of phenomenology" which Derrida thinks deconstructs phenomenology, a position which has found a powerful support in John Protevi (1993b).

9. Kantian retention is always related to intentional acts which well-order time in a way foreign to mere reproductive memory. I am drawing the appearing line and know that I began a moment ago at the end point rather than in the middle. The Kantian reproductive synthesis should be read retentively. The directedness of its act-content insures that apprehension will be given as meaningful. In this sense, the Kantian matrix is furrowed by the trace of a telic past and will secure the iteration of its act form.

10. In this limited context it would be impossible to do justice to Levinas's demonstration in the early pages of *Otherwise than Being or Beyond Essence* (1981, 5–16) that a saying which responds to the nakedness and destitution of the Other can never fall into the nominalized, Parmenidian said. It entails taking up a responsibility for the other. This saying as the primal datum in Husserl's pure flux "of Absolute subjectivity" is a new creation. The medial aspect of this receptivity is virtually acknowledged by Levinas; it is like the prayer in which the worshipper "asks that his prayer be heard [and] the prayer as it were precedes and follows itself" (10). This is the status of the responsibility whose prisoner I am.

11. For a discussion of the Romantic effort to mitigate Kant's mechanism, may I again recommend Charles Taylor, *Hegel*, 11–29.

12. The common pathos articulated by the word expressed at the right time and place that constitutes what Heidegger will call "nighness," depends on a more primordial condition which I, following Plato, identify as the receptacle. This, like the Good, is beyond being and is its correlative supplement. Heidegger comes very close to recognizing this medial phenomena in his late reflections on language. Nevertheless, his "face to face," unlike Levinas's, is that of "two equal and upright men." Levinas founds this possibility, as Derrida says, on the "man with bent neck and eyes raised towards the God on high" (JD 1978, 107).

13. Iin this version of a speculative predication and contrary to Hegel, the "is" does not take the subject up into the predicate but crosses over to dwell in and and reflexively interpret the subject, which retains it integrity. In the metaphor, "man is a machine," "'man' is seen as or within the semantic space of mechanics; the converse relation also obtains, and then machines, e.g., Lager, will be humanized. As such, these propositions express the form of participation, metaphor and hermeneutics.

14. For a discussion of the important Orthodox concept of the hypostasis that is sensitive to Patristic thought and both Heidegger and Levinas, see Bishop John Zizioulas (1988).

15. The autonomy of language is facilitated by the theory of universals; a logic of terms understood as names and the resulting problem of their ontological status suffers from the same lexical defect as in the classical theory of metaphor. Plato's point that the first giver of names is a God would be more to the point; the infinity of the giver who discloses things to us, to any I, through words assures that these things have the requisite objectivity; but the words are likely to be in a mathematical language that maps structure and not in an Aristotelian language that classifies substances.

16. The *Ereignis* cannot be explained; there is nothing from which it can be derived or represented. For an elegant presentation, see John Llewelyn, *Beyond Metaphysics?* (1985, 18–29).

17. Poetry is an autochthonic formation of language. The therapist awaiting the patient's word that will explain, for example, her drawing places the *"event of Being"* within the dialogic model.

18. The words by which the unsayable is said are, as that old word-monger Augustine discovered in the *Psalms,* themselves a gift.

19. I speak of creative metaphor that goes beyond the settled to create a same in the crossing of others, e.g., Faraday's use of fluid and its mechanics to characterize electricity.

20. For an introduction to chaos theory and other topics relevant to this medial phenomenon, see Ivar Ekeland, *Mathematics and the Unexpected* (Chicago: University of Chicago Press, 1988).

If I am correct, this feminine slot is as much determinate as determiner and is the complement of, not subordinate to, form. Aristotle also wants to make form a complement to *hyle,* matter, but only after it is denatured; e.g., the status of the ovum in phylogenesis.

21. Does Heidegger confuse the medial power of becoming and its determinates with Being and thus confuse what should be the role of the Good with that of Being in the "ontological difference"? The history of being conceals *gignesthai* and the receptacle. This is not "to turn our back on what has gone before," for being as durative presence is commemorated in its gift of *Wesen* to eventual beings by which they linger for awhile and in our efforts to speak them in dwelling thinking. Gendlin will soon show how this old word, Being, can come newly into "the ringing of stillness" in the fecund slot in which we await the "emerging emergent."

22. Derrida's account of Hegel's "Preface" to the *Phenomenology* in "Outworks" addresses that which can neither be inside or outside of philosophy, neither a pure form nor empty, since it "announces the path and semantic production of the concept, nor a content, a moment of meaning, since it remains external to the logos of which it infinitely feeds the *Critique,* if only through the gap between ratiocination and rationality, between empirical history and conceptual history? . . . But in thus remaining, does a preface exist? . . . Its spacing (the preface to a rereading) diverges in the place of the *chora* (JD 1982, 16). Hegelian logic, in its effective history if not in the *Logic,* negates and gathers what can't be taken up. Strictly, then, the logic dwells in the preface; crossing it should have unconcealed what Gendlin describes as the implicative intricacy, the *logos,* of the Open. Much of what passes as deconstruction, like certain forms of mystical theology, is a reduction that drives us to see this possibility. In Tibet, I am told, one responds to pointing by looking back from the finger along the arm to the elbow.

23. Wendell Kisner persuades me in his impressive, *"Erinnerung, Retrait,* Absolute Reflection: Hegel and Derrida," to appear in the *Owl of Minerva,* Spring 1995, that such forms of "domination" are really confined to the section on "Essence" in the *Logic,* "a kind of subsuming movement, taking up into itself everything that is, and might be viewed as a kind of domination in its bringing about the demise of opposition. . . ." It is unfair to attribute this overcoming to the entire corpus of Hegel's writings.

24. Mourelatos discusses this use of *eon,* "being," in B8 in *The Route of Parmenides* (AM 1970, 74).

25. H. G. Gadamer suggests a metaphorical interpretation of the spe-

culative proposition (1977, 36). Metaphor allows me, with some injustice to Hegel, to conflate his "speculative proposition" with Mourelatos' "speculative predication" and these with my efforts to articulate the method of analysis as "speculative demonstration."

26. Catesby Taliaferro (1944) gives significant examples of the way order posits disorder.

27. *Exergue* is Derrida's term in "The White Mythology" signifying that metaphor is outside the work (*ex ergon*) which founds the distinction between the sensuous and sense; the latter exists only by the elimination and thus effacement of the sensuous upon which it is founded.

28. According to Hegel's *Aesthetics*, 404–5, the metaphorical, sensuous origins of a term are effaced when it is transported into the spiritual realm: "the metaphorical element disappears [e.g., *begreifen*, "to grasp with the hand"] and by custom the word changes from a metaphorical to a literal expression . . . in the spiritual sense, it does not occur to us to think of *begreifen* as a perceptible grasping by the hand" (GH 1975, 40–05). This effacement, Derrida's *usure*, frees the term to mean as we wish, for meaning does "not depend on the first origin of a word or linguistic development generally." The question is "whether a word that looks pictorial, descriptive, and illustrative has not already, in the life of language, first lost its sensuous meaning, and the memory of it, in the course of its use in a spiritual sense and been *aufgeheben* [superseded] into a spiritual sense" (JD 1982, 202).

29. Hölderlin's fragment cited is: "Departing I left a token of friendship,\The flower of the mouth behind . . ."

30. The "conceptual network in the country of origin" may have been assembled by more phonic differences and resemblances, as in a semiotic field, so that the projective interpretation verges on conceptual pathology, as in various forms of scientific realism.

31. My debt to John Llewelyn goes far beyond this citation from *The Middle Voice of Ecological Conscience* (A Chiasmatic Reading of Responsibility in the Neighborhood of Levinas, Heidegger, and Others) (London: Macmillan, 1991), 89.

32. Hans Jonas, *The Phenomenon of Life*, is the source of the analogy between mechanics and the life sciences.

CHAPTER EIGHT

1. The force of this thesis is amplified in John Caputo's *Demythologizing Heidegger* (1993, 209–14) Once the receptacle is granted a supplementary role, then the feminine principle becomes divine. We have these resources in Mary, rather more evident in the Orthodox than in the Latin tradition.

2. Robert Brumbaugh has also shown in, for example, *Plato's Mathematical Imagination*, how the often hidden use of mathematical structures, e.g., set theory, is relevant to humanistic contexts.

3. Hermeneutical interest in allegory has been largely inspired by Walter

Benjamin, *The Origin of the German Tragic Drama* (1977). In contrast to the romantic sense of the symbol with its promise of immediate presentation of the transcendent, "In allegory the observer is confronted with the *faces hippocratic* of history as a petrified, primordial landscape. Everything about history, from the very beginning, has been untimely, sorrowful, unsuccessful, is expressed in a face—or rather a death's head" (166). But this waste land bears testimony to the sacred. "It will be unmistakably apparent, especially to anyone familiar with allegorical textual exegesis, that all the things that are used to signify derive, from their very fact of pointing to something else, a power which makes them no longer commensurable with profane things, which raises them unto a higher plane, and which can indeed sanctify them" (175).

4. Prof. Cartwright says that the laws of nature "isolate and describe the causal powers bodies have" (1983, 61). Van Fraassen agrees with Cartwright that explanation is always in answer to a contextual why, but he is as an empiricist uncomfortable with causality because of its appeal to unobservables and more at home with model-theoretic substructures. I tend to agree with Cartwright's object-related realism and her anti-realistic view of theory, but I do allow allegory a role that both might find unattractive. I would also modify her talk of bodies in the direction proposed by Whitehead: "The laws of nature are the outcome of the character of the entities which we find in nature. The entities being what they are, the laws must be what they are." The converse relation, which he also endorses, introduces a mutuality difficult to explicate in this context (1921, 142).

5. Sir Peter Strawson's "self-ascriptive" account of the objective unity of consciousness, especially the view that memory is inferential, is the most important contribution in recent analytic philosophy to Kant studies (1966). How easy it is to confuse what one has heard with a remembered event is illustrated by Piaget's vivid recollection of an early kidnapping attempt which turned out to be a story told him by his nurse.

6. My comments are based on David Cornay (1967, 188).

7. To Gadamer is due a considerable debt for making us aware of the importance of Aristotle's *phronesis* to the human sciences (HG 1975, 20 ff, 278 ff, 36 7 f, and 490).

8. Whether or not the past can be changed, e.g., Dummett's "backwards causation," was also the subject of an important medieval debate on God's power to restore virginity. St. Augustine and St. Thomas thought God could not, but St. Peter Damian argued that even this would be possible with God.

9. For some of the reasons why intentional issues will not submit to an objectivist approach, see Thomas Nagel, "Subjective and Objective," in John Rajchman and Cornel West, *Post Analytic Philosophy* (New York: Columbia University Press, 1985), 31–47; and Charles Taylor (1971).

10. Reiner Schürmann's *Heidegger on Being and Acting: From Principles to Anarchy* issues a serious challenge to the traditional view that action is founded on theory, on timeless principles that order and make praxis intelligible.

11. Nelson Goodman (1978, 88) supports Plato's view on the perception of shape through color. "Consider a solid black square moving at moderate speed from left to right against a white background. At each moment

the left edge flicks from black to white, merging with the background, while the white bordering the right edge of the black flicks to black. There are no perceptible spatio-temporal gaps between immediate successive changes at each edge—they make up a continuous process. But the component color changes are leaps between black and white—there is no passing through intermediate greys. This constitutes the motion perception . . . Only so is the continuity of contour preserved; the black square remains throughout the same black square."

12. Heidegger's break with Husserl's transcendental phenomenology came through his discovery that intentionality is founded on time, on *Dasein*'s ecstatic transcendence towards Being. Unlike Kant's continuity forming three-fold synthesis, however, the signifying present is never the perfect image of its father, memory. Ballard describes the import of this for Husserl as follows: "If intentionality should turn out to be founded on something other than consciousness, then a description of the ego's intentional performances will not be an exhaustive description of its being, nor would the ontology of consciousness be identical with the whole of ontology" (EB 1971, 2).

13. I have used metaphor to establish a biological model wherein non-conceptual recognition and significance are seen to be coextensive with life (CB 1982, 122-49).

C H A P T E R   N I N E

1. Heidegger says in the 1954 "Building Dwelling Thinking" that building, e.g., a bridge, gives "location" and articulates space, allowing a "site for the fourfold" (MH 1971b, 151). Location is not place, *chora*. "That for which room is made is always granted [sic] and hence is joined, that is, gathered, by virtue of a location, that is, by such a thing as a bridge" (154). By avoiding the mystery of *chora*, which grants being, Heidegger seems to stay within the ontology of technology, of the builder's "sighted presence." The bridge does not necessarily "gather the fourfold in such a way that it allows a site for it" (*ibid.*). It may fail "to bring us before the haleness of the divinities." The place may be wrong. Do the Bosphorus bridges in Istanbul let Europe and Asia gather one another into their neighborhoods? Or do they promote more traffic jams and the commercial wasting and desolation of the earth? In an earlier era, e.g., the founding monastery of the Zoodochos Pege, the God in a dream proposed a place. Place, not location, lets dwell and gives spaces their origin, their being.

2. "Supplement" is Derrida's term for something that lies outside the text of metaphysics that makes it possible. In Plato the Good and the receptacle are both beyond being and make participation, i.e., dwelling, possible.

3. I shall take for granted John Sallis's definitive account of Heidegger's interpretation of *aletheia* as "unconcealment" in "At the Threshold of Metaphysics" (1985, 180-85). This is also important because he shows how *idea*, in the context of "idea of the Good," cannot have the sense of "sighted pres-

ence." *Aletheia* cannot be assimilated to *idea* and thus to a permanent presence. In fact, *aletheia* "can be assimilated neither to knowing [*nous*] or the known [*ortha*] but rather cuts across this distinction [*nous* as correctly related to *idea*], crossing in the direction of what would precede and yoke together knowing and the known." (182). One consequence is that *idea* will itself no longer have the sense of permanent presence, as in neo-Platonism, where entities are as if its shadowy clones. Nor is the Good self-present; it is sustained by *lethe*. Sallis says *lethe* is to be understood, not as that which conceals by blocking, standing in the way of, but is to be thought through the "plain of concealment" in the myth of Er as counter to *physis* (*Rep.* 621A), i.e., "withdrawing and concealing it counters all emerging into presence" (184). Insofar as *lethe*, in which Heidegger finds traces of *cheutho*, preserves and shelters, it bears the sense of Plato's receptacle, the Good's supplement; the shadow of the maternal, she destroys what she shelters and conceals.

In commenting on this section of the text, John Llewelyn suggests that a medial phenomenon is neither masculine nor feminine. The feminine receptacle contains the life-giving, medial becoming that is neither masculine or feminine. I try to respect the available images of what finally is beyond imaging.

4. D. W. Winnicott, *Psycho-Analytic Explorations* (Cambridge: Harvard University Press, 1989). In his posthumous *Human Nature* (New York: Schocken, 1988), Dr. Winnicott expressed doubt about the details of Freud's ego theory, especially the birth trauma, though he fails to confront Lacan's thesis that the ego is probably a linguistic construct.

5. The concept of place, Plato's *chora,* is so foreign to our spatial, mostly Euclidian, intuitions that a preliminary word may help. Kant would like to think of his nomological laws as applying always and everywhere over homogeneous and isotropic spaces. Strangely, Euclidian space, the only space permitting rotation, translation, and transformation, is the space of *praxis,* the only interpretation of space in which the same shape can be recognized in these manipulations. To discover a nomological law, one must manipulate a system, move it about so as to isolate it. Apparatus must be so placed as to determine necessary and sufficient conditions; the placeless is the gift of place. Since the law is itself an evolutionary phenomena and therefore relative to place(s), I prefer to express it, with Descartes, as "a romance of nature," a likely story or allegory.

The bugaboo of relativism should not concern us. As evolutionary, if not historical, our world survives as a result of the interpretations made in these law-like contexts that leave their furrow in our own, like the big bang that has left its trace in background radiation. Formulating the law relative to places, even with respect to all places, allows more or less uniform conditions to account for the law, rather than conversely. Things in place explain, not laws.

If the conditions internal to these places change, then other communities can inherit from them and laws evolve. Group theory, the mathematical analogue of metaphor, could show that in their transformations these worlds are isomorphic, i.e., how a same can be intuited in variations. The model of change suggested by Feyerabend as a succession of discrete world views will not do. It is not as if worlds perish and are done with; they are either superseded or disseminated. Feyerabend argues that since Newtonian mass is not relativistic mass, gravity in each world (view) is different. Aren't we talking about this Protean *it* which can be named "Gravity?"

We need not fear relativities in hermeneutical contexts. Traces of the past always, if ambiguously, furrow the present. Tradition is a medial process from which we inherit in so many ways, perhaps in archetypes as Jung suggests. Those who wish to relativize Aristotle's ethics to a world view in the belief that essence has also gone out the window with Darwin will find no support here. Even if our understanding of the virtues will change as we come to understand ourselves in different contexts and perhaps even better or as ontological understanding changes, e.g., "Being is time," what is unconcealed as human nature survives in the transforms of dialectical interpretation. There is a human *physis* even when *phronesis* becomes hermeneutics or population genetics replaces Aristotelian cloning. Courage will still be called for even if barbaric warfare becomes passé.

6. Levinas's phenomenology of creativity to which we have access in welcome is central to the medial theme of birth. I highly recommend Tina Chanter's sensitive and appreciative sketch of these stages in "Feminism and the Other" (1988, 38–44).

Less confidently, I offer the following notes to *Totality and Infinity*. Welcome is set over against the insomniac's "uncontrollable stirring of the elemental" (160), the unstructured and non-intentional *apeiron dynamics* "between being and non-being" (258) of the *there is*. This *il y a* (190, 197, 258, 261, 280), like Heidegger's *es gibt*, situates the *arché* beyond presence and absence. In virtue of certain erotic solicitations this *chaos* welcomes. Welcome is also medial and undergoes a series of thematizations, first as "paradisal enjoyment" (163) that stills the "anonymous rustling of the *there is*" (160), as non-intentional enjoyment of sensations in which there is no separation of I and not-I (188), as caress (258), as medial tenderness between being and non-being (259), and finally in fecundity, where the actual is the vestibule of the future.

7. Many of these thoughts were inspired by John Llewelyn with whom, through a chance meeting, Edward Ballard and I shared an afternoon at St. Apollinaire (JL 1991, 109–111).

8. In the first *Critique* Kant noted that "there is no contradiction in the concept of a figure which is enclosed in two straight lines" (A 220/B 268). Given his close friendship with Lambert and his probable knowledge of the latter's discoveries, which entail an elliptical or Riemannian geometry, Kant can be understood as asserting, contrary to current thought, that we can think but not represent or *schematize* non-Euclidian geometries.

9. In the Leibniz-Clark correspondence, Clark defends Newton's choice of absolute and infinite space and time, God's sensoria, as necessary to God's sovereignty. This intuition about setting things up in their integrity is oddly justified when Euclidian space is seen as the correlative of *chora*, the place of dwelling and emergence.

10. Speaking of Descartes' and Berkeley's tower which is ambiguously round or square, Ballard notices that what we mean by "near" is the removal or elimination of ambiguity: "distance and closeness are not just functions of

the object, presentations, intentions, perceived, or perceiver taken separately" (1983, 31). This phenomenological understanding of distance, which presupposes the between, is prior to metrical assignments or measurements.

CHAPTER TEN

1. I shamefully neglect the world-soul in *Timaeus*. I assume that the demiurge is a myth about worlding that, in virtue of the isomorphism between the world and its proper parts, applies equally to the individual soul. Whitehead's panpsychism, which represents this possibility is too generalized; one hesitates to say that chaos has any psychical analogue. Nevertheless, something like the dialectic between his consequent nature and the world might yield an interpretation of the world soul. I have tried to remain within a phenomenological context. This has already been stretched quite far enough by Husserl when he presumes to found intentionality a non-intentional primal datum. Levinas's similar use of the *il y a* to mark hypostatic emergence also confounds phenomenological description. I have let the appearing signifier, or word, play a founding role. I can find no phenomenological analogue for the world soul as such.

2. This "upward" movement marks the transition from the second to the third level and then, more properly, to the fourth level of Plato's divided line and rightly became a standard in classical epistemology. "Recognition" represents the installation of the intelligible thing itself before mind through signs, where what is recognized is of a different ontological order from the physicality of the signs and marks the transition from the visible to the intelligible. This transition which is hardly our doing is central to most rationalisms. I recall the incredible light that dawned when I finally understood the fundamental theorem of the calculus.

In St. Augustine's *De Magistro* this non-natural "'seeing" is said to be a kind of natural grace conferred by Christ, the interior *Logos* who illuminates the inner man so that he is taught "by the things themselves within the soul." In its eventual and non-voluntary aspects, Aristotle's agent intellect, "in a certain sense like white light that makes all potential colors visible," confers a similar unmotivated illumination. We seem almost compelled to speak of this as "lighting" and as "lightening," both in the sense of the blinding flash and the alleviation of a burden. Husserl recognized the radicality of this transition: "As a philosopher proceeding from the practical, finite surrounding world (of the room, the city, the landscape, etc. and temporally the world of periodical occurrences: day, month, etc.) to the theoretical world view and world knowledge, he has the finitely known and unknown spaces and times as finite elements within the horizon of an open infinity. But with this he does not have mathematical space, mathematical time, and whatever else is to become a novel spiritual product out of these finite elements which serve as material; and with his manifold shapes in their space-time he does not yet have geometrical shapes, the phoronomic shapes; [his shapes as] formulations developed out of praxis and thought of in terms of [gradual] perfection, clearly serve only as a basis for a new sort of praxis out of which grow similarly named new constructions" (1970a, 376).

If, as in Plato's recollection or Augustine's illumination, I can be taught by the things themselves, then signs are instrumental and dispensable. But in the case of disclosive, not rule-governed, schemata, i.e., schemata that themselves give the rule, am I not taught as by things when the signs are significant? Theology may dictate to the Christian the virtuality of the *verbum*, but Plato, having written the *Meno,* can hardly have that excuse. I believe that the non-naturalness of linguistic signifiers and the play with notations, which *qua* signifiers form differential fields, is sufficient to account for unmotivated, eventual illumination. Mathematics happens through perspicacious symbols and notations; and what happens is an understanding that gathers into itself and articulates the structure of whatever is seen, if anything, through it. In its axioms there is a key to any such pattern. The separationism attributed to Plato's ideas really belongs to the full variety of mathematical systems which, as conditions for the possibility of and possible forms for allegorization, take the ordinary "life world" into physical theory in which we know, as Whitehead puts it in *Science and the Modern World,* "that if any group of entities enjoy any relationship among its members satisfying this set of abstract conditions, then such and such additional abstract conditions must hold for any such relationship" (1927, 36).

3. For a non-reductive description and defense of a non-natural interpretation of this event of epiphany, see Walker Percy, "The Delta Factor," (1975, 35). To his account we need to add the focus given Helen by the task of hand washing and its familiar patterns and expectations. Action and habituated context must not be ignored.

4. Husserl's most important contribution to this study is his belief that mathematics survives through a textual or written tradition. I will have more to say about schematic writing in the text, but I should clarify his thoughts on the sense of a tradition as an historical alternative to Hegel's *Geist:* "For a genuine history of philosophy, a genuine history of the particular sciences, is nothing but a tracing of the historical meaning-structures given in the present, or their self-evidences, along the documented chain of historical back-references into the hidden dimension of the primal self-evidences that underlie them" (1979, 372–73). This regressive inquiry ends in the "primally established functions" in which a tradition originates: "The whole cultural world, in all its forms, exists through tradition" (254). One's return to this *arché,* "origin," "originary event," is not as a Greek but as a modern; analytic of the *arché* is not classical archeology. Our concept of geometry is not limited to Euclid, but "this forward development understood as the progress of knowledge being built into the horizon" presupposes that its being sense constitutive of the horizon as such lies in these primal experiences; and if these are lost, mathematics and every other form of the spirit becomes nihilistic, the mere computational explication and generation of texts. I certainly share Husserl's sense of the moral dignity of the liberal arts which will be lost if one restricts oneself to logistic exercises. Philosophy is the love of Wisdom.

Husserl's concept of tradition is useful in defusing Platonic mathematics from within of its claims of access to a transcendent and eternal realm of being and so can help to overcome the mathematical ideal that has been the chief bastion of the metaphysics of onto-theo-logico eternal presence in the sciences and the human disciplines. On the other hand, nothing in Platonic mathematics is eliminated. We can "see" infinities; my Dedekind model for analysis is infinitistic. If one wishes further evidence, see DeMorgan's models. We should also recall that religion welcomes the ideal of a tradition founded on a (sacred) test and requires the sacramental ideal of the ontophanies (Eliade) of the *arché* as something always formally one and the same to which we can return. I remain a friend of the forms.

5. For a characterization of real and anti-real, see the excellent discussion of the creative possibilities of anti-realism and a strong defense of mathematical realism—for example, Fermat's last theorem is true or false independent of any proof—in Alvin Plantinga, "How to be an Anti-Realist" (1982, 50).

6. The difficulties are elegantly set out in Simon Altmann, *Icons and Symmetries* (Oxford: Oxford University Press, 1992).

7. My comments on notation were inspired by Whitehead's excellent discussion (1975, 39–48).

8. Mathematical objects can be thought about without reference to the fact that they are thought about. The only possible reference we could make to mind is that they are given to it like any other thing (res). Whatever is for us a "thing" in a human world is already the eject of an active interpretation of what is receptively given. Mathematical objects are in this sense interpretations of *schema,* that by which these are seen as instancing ideality. Receptively given physical inscriptions as *schemata* disclosively presence mathematical objects that belong in turn to the active, interpretative side of experience and, in that restricted sense, can be said to be anti-real. On the other hand, to side with Plantinga, within the horizon opened by the theory of equations, by its notation and forms of understanding, there is the analytic methodological possibility disclosed by Fermat whose truth or falsity does not depend on any sort of proof.

9. In his fine introduction to Thomas Taylor's translation and commentary on *Plato's Timaeus and Critias,* Catesby Taliaferro offers indispensable insights into the mathematical constructions of *Timaeus* which are more suggestive than anything to be found in either A. E. Taylor or Cornford.

10. Theon, according to Cornford's summary (1956, 67–68), said that in his construction Plato was not concerned with music per se but was "looking to the nature of things. The soul must be composed according to an harmonia and advance as far as solid numbers [to the third power] and be harmonized by two means, in order that, extending throughout the whole solid body of the world, it may grasp all the things that exist."

11. "The Assayer," in Stillman Drake, *Discoveries and Opinions of Galileo* (New York: Doubleday, 1957), 237–38. Marx Wartofsky (1968, Appendix A, 419–73) gives a relevant summary of the history of velocity and acceleration which is sensitive to the problems of geometrization and arithmetization. The Koyre citation is from Wartofsky.

ABBREVIATIONS USED IN BIBLIOGRAPHY

....

AB	A. S. Byatt	FB	F. H. Bradley
AG	Aron Gurwitsch	FC	F. Chimok
AGr	Adolf Grünbaum	FdS	Ferdinand de Saussure
AL	Alphonso Lingis	FN	Friedrich Nietzsche
AM	Alexander Mourelatos	FNC	F. N. Cornford
ANW	Alfred North Whitehead	GB	Guiseppe Bovini
AP	Adriaan Peperzak	GB	Gerd Buchdahl
APl	Alvin Plantinga	GD	Gilles Deleuze
AW	Allan Wolter	GEM	G. E. Moore
BR	Bertrand Russell	GF	Gail Fine
BvF	Bas van Fraassen	GG	Galileo Galilei
CB	Charles Bigger	GH	Georg Hegel
CJ	Carl Jung	GL	G. W. F. Leibniz
CK	Charles Kahn	GM	Gottfried Martin
CP	C. S. Peirce	GP	G. L. Prestige
CRT	R. Catesby Taliaferro	GS	Gregory Schufreider
CS	Charles M. Sherover	GW	G. J. Whitrow
CT	Charles Taylor	HB	Henry Bettenson
DC	David Cornay	HG	Hans-Georg Gadamer
DH	David Hume	HJ	Hans Jonas
DKo	D. E. Koshland	HK	Helen Keller
DP	DePater, Fr. W.	HL	Henri Lefebvre
DPa	Derick Parfait	HP	Hilary Putnam
DS	John Duns Scotus	HW	Herman Weyl
DW	David Wood	IH	Ian Hacking
DWW	D. W. Winnicot	II	Ivan Illich
EAH	E. A. Havelock	IN	Sir Isaac Newton
EB	Edward Ballard	IP	Irving Polonoff
EC	Ernst Cassirer	IR	I. A. Richards
ED	Eugenio Donato	IS	Ingrid Stadler
EdC	Edward Casey	JB	Jonathan Bennett
EG	Eugene Gendlin	JC	John Caputo
EH	Edmund Husserl	JD	Jacques Derrida
EL	Emmanuel Levinas	JG	Jan Gonda
EM	Earnest Moody	JH	J. G. Hart
EN	Ernst Nagel	JHi	Jaakko Hintikka
EV	Eugene Vance	JL	John Llewelyn
EVH	E. V. Huntington	JM	John E. M. McTaggart

JO	James Oliver	PR	Paul Ricoeur
JP	John Protevi	PS	Sir Peter Strawson
JRL	J. R. Lucas	PU	P. A. Underwood
JS	John Sallis	RB	Robert Brumbaugh
JW	Joseph Weizenbaum	RBr	Robert Bernasconi
JZ	John Zizioulas	RC	Roderick Chisholm
KS	Kenneth Sayre	RG	Richard Gregory
LI	Luce Irigaray	RGC	R. G. Collingwood
LS	Claude Levi-Strauss	RH	Ray Hart
LW	Ludwig Wittgenstein	RoG	Robert Grosseteste
MB	Max Black	RR	Richard Rorty
MD	Michael Dummett	RS	Reiner Schürmann
ME	Mircea Eliade	RSo	Robert Sokolowski
MF	Michel Foucault	RW	W. H. Walsh
MFr	Michael Friedman	SA	St. Augustine
MH	Martin Heidegger	SB	Scott Buchanan
MN	Martha Nussbaum	ST	Shirley Turkle
MP	Maurice Merleau-Ponty	TC	T. Cajetan
MW	Marx Wartofsky	TCh	Tina Chanter
NC	Nancy Cartwright	TH	Thomas Heath
NG	Nelson Goodman	UE	Umberto Eco
OS	Oliver Sacks	VW	G. H. von Wright
PD	Pierre Duheim	WB	Walter Benjamin
PdM	Paul De Man	WM	Werner Marx
PE	Parvis Emad	WP	Walker Percy
PH	Paul R. Helmos	WR	William Richardson
PM	P. Maupertuis	WW	William Weedon

LITERATURE CITED

....

Citations from Aristotle, St. Augustine, St. Thomas Aquinas, and Plato, though from specific editions, are cited in the standard conventions. Kant is cited by abbreviations of the title or text in the pagination of the *Gesammelte Schriften*, 1724–1804, *hersg.von der Koniglich Prevssischen Akademie der Wissenshaften*, Berlin, 1902 ____. Other authors are cited within the text by their initials, publication date and pages of the edition used.

Aquinas, St. Thomas
        ST   *Summa Theologica*, English Dominican Fathers, trs. London: Sheed and Ward.
Aristotle
                The Complete Works of Aristotle: The Revised Oxford Translation, ed. J. Barnes (Princeton: Bollingen Series LXXI—2, Princeton University Press, 1984). Individual works are cited in the following abbreviations:

De Anima	*On the Soul*
Post. Anal.	*Posterior Analytics*
Meta.	*Metaphysics*
Cat.	*Categories*
De Int.	*On Interpretation*
De Phys.	*On Nature*
E. N.	*Nicomachean Ethics*
De Gen. Anim.	*The Generation of Animals*
De Poetics	*Poetics*
Pol.	*Politics*

Augustine, St. (SA)
                De lib. arb. On the Freedom of the Will, in *Augustine: Early Writings*, J.H.S. Burleigh, tr. London: SCM Press, 1953.
                De Magistro Concerning the Teacher, in *Augustine: Early Writings*, J.H.S. Burleigh, tr. London: SCM Press,1953.
     / *Conf.*   *Confessions*, J. J. O'Donnell, tr. Oxford: Oxford University Press, 1992.
Ballard, Edward (EB)
        1971   *Philosophy at the Crossroads*, Baton Rouge, Louisiana State University Press.

1983   *Principles of Interpretation,* Athens: Ohio University Press.

1989   *Philosophy and the Liberal Arts,* Dordrecht: Kluwer.

Benjamin, Walter (WB)

1977   *The Origin of the German Tragic Drama,* London: New Left Books.

Bennett, Jonathan (JB)

1966   *Kant's Analytic,* Cambridge: Cambridge University Press.

1974   *Kant's Dialectic,* Cambridge: Cambridge University Press.

Bernasconi, Robert (RBr)

1985   *The Question of Language in Heidegger's History of Being,* Atlantic Highlands, N.J.: Humanities Press.

1993   *Heidegger in Question: The Art of Existing,* Atlantic Highlands, N.J.: Humanities Press.

Bettenson, Henry (HB)

1991a   *The Early Christian Fathers,* Oxford: Oxford University Press.

1991b   *The Later Christian Fathers,* Oxford: Oxford University Press.

Bigger, Charles (CB)

1961   "Speculative Demonstration," *Journal of Philosophy* 58.

1963   "Models and Maps," *Southern Journal of Philosophy* 1. no. 1.

1968   *Participation: A Platonic Inquiry;* Baton Rouge: Louisiana State University Press.

1969   *Eros and Nihilism,* Charles Bigger and David Cornay, eds. Dubuque: Kendell Hunt.

1973   "Objects and Events," *Southern Journal of Philosophy* 11.

1975   "Kant and the Infinite, Potential and Actual," *Southwestern Journal of Philosophy* 6.

1977   "Logos and Epiphany," *The Southern Review,* NS 13.

1980   "Walker Percy and the Resonance of the Word," *Walker Percy: Art and Ethics,* J. Tharp, ed. Jackson: University of Mississippi Press.

1981   "Kant's Constructivism," *Southern Journal of Philosophy,* xix

1982   "Biological Recognition," Charles and Anita Bigger, *Philosophy and Archaic Experience,* John Sallis, ed. Pittsburgh: Duquesne University Press.

1988   "St. Thomas on Essence and Participation," *The New Scholasticism* 63.

Black, Max (MB)

1962   *Models and Metaphors,* Ithaca: Cornell University Press.

Bovini, Guiseppe (GB)

1957   *Ravenna Mosaics,* London: George Rainbird.

Bradley, F. H. (FB)
   1928   *The Principles of Logic,* Oxford: Oxford University
               Press.
Brumbaugh, Robert (RB)
   1954   *Plato's Mathematical Imagination,* Bloomington: Indi-
               ana University Press.
Buchanan, Scott (SB)
   1975   *Poetry and Mathematics,* Chicago: University of Chi-
               cago.
Buchdahl, Gerd (GBu)
   1968   *Metaphysics and the Philosophy of Science,* Oxford:
               Blackwell.
   1969   "The Kantian Dynamic of Reason," *Kant Studies To-
               day,* Lewis Beck, ed. LaSalle: Open Court.
   1982   "Reduction-Realization: A Key to the Structure of
               Kant's Thought," *Philosophical Topics* 12.
   1991   "Science and God: The Topology of the Kantian
               World," *Southern Journal of Philosophy 30,* Spidel
               Conference Supplement.
Byatt, A. S. (AB)
   1993   *Passions of the Mind,* New York: Vintage.
Cajetan, T. (TC)
   1953   *On The Analogy of Names and the Concept of Being,*
               E. A. Bushinski and H. J. Koren, trs. Pittsburgh: Du-
               quesne University Press.
Caputo, John (JC)
   1993   *Demythologizing Heidegger,* Bloomington: University
               of Indiana Press.
Cartwright, Nancy (NC)
   1983   *How the Laws of Physics Lie,* Oxford: Oxford Univer-
               sity Press.
Casey, Edward (EdC)
   1993   *Getting Back Into Place: Towards a Renewed Under-
               standing of the Place-World,* Bloomington: University
               of Indiana Press.
Cassirer, Ernst (EC)
   1972   *The Philosophy of Symbolic Form, v. 2,* New Haven:
               Yale University Press.
   1981   *Kant's Life and Thought,* New Haven: Yale University
               Press.
Chanter, Tina (TCh)
   1988   "Feminism and the Other," *The Provocation of Levi-
               nas,* Robert Bernasconi and David Wood, eds. London:
               Routledge.
Chimok, F. (FC)
   1987   *Cora,* Istanbul: A Turizm Yayinlari.
Chisholm, Roderick (RC)
   1957   *Perceiving: A Philosophical Study,* Ithaca: Cornell Uni-
               versity Press.

Collingwood, R. G. (RGC)
    1932   *An Essay on Method,* Oxford: Clarendon Press.
    1947   *Principles of Art,* Oxford: Clarendon Press.
Cornay, David (DC)
    1967   "Plato's *Gorgias,*" *Eros and Nihilism,* Charles Bigger and David Cornay, eds. Dubuque: Kendell Hunt.
Cornford, F.N. (FNC)
    1956   *Plato's Cosmology,* London: Routledge and Kegan Paul.
Deleuze, Gilles (GD)
    1983   *Nietzsche and Philosophy,* London: Athlone.
    1988   *Foucault,* Sean Hand, tr. Minneapolis: University of Minnesota.
De Man, Paul (PdM)
    1982   "Sign and Symbol in Hegel's *Aesthetics,*" *Critical Inquiry* 8.
Derrida, Jacques (JD)
    1973   *Speech and Phenomena,* David B. Allison, tr. Evanston: Northwestern University Press.
    1976   *Of Grammatology,* Gayatri Spivak, tr. Baltimore: Johns Hopkins.
    1977   "Introduction" to *Edmund Husserl's Origin of Geometry,* J. P. Leavey, tr. Stony Brook, N.Y.: N. Hays.
    1978   *Writing and Difference,* Alan Bass, tr. Chicago: University of Chicago Press.
    1981   *Positions,* Alan Bass, tr. Chicago: University of Chicago Press.
    1982   *Margins of Philosophy,* Alan Bass, tr. Chicago: University of Chicago Press.
    1987   "*Chora,*" in *Poikilia; Etudes offertes à Jean-Pierre Vernant,* Paris, EHESS.
    1989   "Psyche: Inventions of the Other," *Reading de Man Reading,* Lindsay Waters and Wlad Godzich, *eds.* Minneapolis, University of Minnesota Press.
    1990   *Glas,* J. P. Leavey and Richard Rand, trs. Lincoln: University of Nebraska Press.
    1991   *A Derrida Reader: Between the Blinds,* Peggy Kamuf, ed. New York: Columbia University Press.
    1992a   *Acts of Literature,* Derek Attridge, ed. London: Routledge.
    1992b   *Given Time: I. Counterfeit Money,* Peggy Kamuf, tr. Chicago, University of Chicago Press.
    1993a   *Jacques Derrida,* Jacques Derrida and G. Bennington, Chicago, University of Chicago Press.
    1993b   "Heidegger's Ear: Philopolemology," in *Reading Heidegger,* John Sallis, ed. Bloomington: University of Illinois Press.
De Pater, Fr. W. (DP)
    1968   "Sense and Nonsense in Talking About God," *St. Louis Quarterly* 6, Baguio, Luzon.

de Saussure, Ferdinand (FdS)
    1959   *Course in General Linguistics,* New York: McGraw Hill.
Donato, Eugenio (ED)
    1979   "The Museum's Furnace: Towards a Contextual Read-
                ing of Bouvard and Pecuchet," in *Textual Strategies,* J.
                Harapi, ed. Ithaca: Cornell University Press.
Duheim, Pierre (PD)
    1962   *The Aim and Structure of Physical Theory,* New York:
                Atheneum.
Dummett, Michael (MD)
    1980   *Truth and Other Enigmas,* Cambridge: Harvard Uni-
                versity Press.
Eco, Umberto (UE)
    1976   *A Theory of Semiotics,* Bloomington: University of In-
                diana Press.
Eliade, Mircea (ME)
    1960,   *Myths, Dreams and Mysteries,* New York: Harper and
                Row.
Emad, Parvis (PE)
    1993   "Thinking More Deeply into the Question of Transla-
                tion: Essential Translation and the Unfolding of Lan-
                guage," in *Reading Heidegger: Commemorations,* John
                Sallis, ed. Bloomington: University of Indiana Press.
Fine, Gail (GF)
    1993   *On Ideas: Aristotle's Criticism of Plato's Theory of
                Forms,* Oxford: Clarendon Press.
Foucault, Michel (MF)
    1970   *The Order of Things: An Archeology of the Human
                Sciences,* London: Tavistok Press.
    1972   *The Archeology of Knowledge,* London: Tavistok Press.
    1984   *The Foucault Reader,* Paul Rabinow, ed. London: Pere-
                grine Press.
    1990   *The History of Sexuality,* v. 1, New York, Vintage.
Friedman, Michael (MFr)
    1992   "Causal Laws and the Foundations of Natural Science,"
                The Cambridge Companion to Kant, Paul Guyer, ed.
                Cambridge: Cambridge University Press.
Gadamer, Hans-Georg (HG)
    1975   *Truth and Method,* New York: Seabury.
    1977   *Hegel's Dialectic: Five Hermeneutical Studies,* New
                Haven: Yale University Press.
    1980   *Dialogue and Dialectic,* New Haven: Yale University
                Press.
    1986   *The Idea of the Good in Platonic-Aristotelian Philo-
                sophy,* New Haven: Yale University Press.
Galilei, Galileo (GG)
    1957   "The Assayer," in Stillman Drake, *Discoveries and
                Opinions of Galileo,* New York: Doubleday.

Gendlin, Eugene (EG)
    1983   "Dwelling," paper presented at 17th Annual Heidegger Conference.
    1987   "Thinking After Distinctions," paper presented at 21st Annual Heidegger Conference.
Gonda, Jan (JG)
    1960   "Reflections on the Indo-European Medial I," *Lingua* 9.
Goodman, Nelson (NG)
    1978   *Ways of Worldmaking*, Indianapolis: Hackett.
Gregory, Richard (RG)
    1987   *The Oxford Companion to the Mind*, Richard Gregory, ed. Oxford: Oxford University Press.
Grosseteste, Robert (RoG)
    1939   *On Light*, C.G. Willis, tr. Annapolis: St. John's College Bookstore.
Grünbaum, Adolf (AGr)
    1963   *Philosophical Problems of Space and Time*, New York: Knopf.
Gurwitsch, Aron (AG)
    1964   *The Field of Consciousness*, Pittsburgh: Duquesne University Press.
Hacking, Ian (IH)
    1984   "Leibniz and Descartes: Proofs and Eternal Truths," in *Philosophy Through the Past*, T. Hondreich, ed. Middlesex, England: Pelican Books.
Hart, James G. (JH)
    1992   "Time and Consciousness: Husserlian Reflections on the Diaphaneousness of Mind," paper delivered at 1992 Meeting, Society for Phenomenological and Existential Philosophy, Boston.
Hart, Ray (RH)
    1979   *Unfinished Man and the Imagination*, New York: Seabury.
Havelock, E. A. (EAH)
    1963   *A Preface to Plato*, Cambridge: Harvard University Press.
Heath, Sir Thomas (TH)
    1947   *Euclid: The Element*, 3 vols., Annapolis: St. John's College Press.
Hegel, Georg W. (GH)
    1975   *Aesthetics*, 2 vols. T. M. Knox, tr.; Oxford: Oxford University Press.
    1977   *Phenomenology of Mind*, J. N. Findlay and A. V. Miller, trs. Oxford: Oxford University Press.
    1892   *Encyclopedia of the Philosophical Sciences*, W. Wallace, tr. Oxford: Oxford University Press.
Heidegger, Martin (MH)
    1957   *Der Satz von Grund*, Pfullingen: Neske.

1958   *The Question of Being.* William Kluback and Jean
            Wilde, trs. New York: Twayne.
1961   *Introduction to Metaphysics,* R. Manheim, tr. New
            York: Anchor Doubleday.
1962   *Being and Time,* J. Macquarrie and J. Robinson, trs.
            London: SCM Press.
1967   *What is a Thing?* W. Barton and V. Deutsch, trs. Chi-
            cago: Regnery.
1969   *Identity and Difference,* Joan Stambaugh, tr. New York:
            Harper and Row.
1971a   *On the Way to Language,* Peter Hertz, tr. New York:
            Harper and Row.
1971b   *Poetry Language, Thought,* Albert Hofstadter, tr. New
            York: Harper and Row.
1975a   "What is Metaphysics?" (1929), in *Existentialism from
            Dostoevsky to Sartre,* Walter Kaufmann, ed., New York:
            Meridian.
1975b   "The Way Back into the Ground of Metaphysics"
            (1949), in *Existentialism from Dostoevsky to Sartre,*
            Walter Kaufmann, ed. New York: Meridian.
1977   *The Question Concerning Technology,* William Lovitt,
            tr. New York: Harper and Row.
1981   *Nietzsche: The Will to Power as Art,* 4 vols. David
            Krell, tr. London: Routledge and Kegan Paul.
1982   *The Basic Problems of Phenomenology,* Albert Hofstad-
            ter, tr. Bloomington: University of Indiana Press.
1984   *Early Greek Thinking,* David Krell and Frank Capuzzi,
            trs. San Francisco: Harper and Row.
1990   *Kant and the Problem of Metaphysics,* Richard Taft, tr.
            Bloomington: University of Indiana Press.
Helmos, Paul R. (PH)
1980   "The Heart of Mathematics," *American Mathematical
            Monthly* 87.
Hintikka, Jaakko (JHi)
1969   "Kant and the Mathematical Method," *Kant Studies
            Today,* Lewis W. Beck, ed. LaSalle: Open Court.
Hugh of St. Victor
1128   *Didascalicon,* in *Patrologiae Latine,* vols. 175–77, J.P.
            Migne, ed. Paris, 1844–1864.
Hume, David (DH)
1894   *An Enquiry Concerning Human Understanding,* in
            Hume's Enquiries, L.A. Selby Bigge, ed. Oxford: Cla-
            rendon Press.
Huntington, E. V. (EVH)
1917   *The Continuum,* Cambridge: Harvard University Press.
Husserl, Edmund (EH)
1960   *Cartesian Meditations,* Dorian Cairnes, tr. The Hague:
            Nijhoff.

1969   *Formal and Transcendental Logic,* Dorian Cairnes, tr.
              The Hague: Martinus Nijhoff.

1970a   *The Crisis in the European Sciences and Transcendental
              Phenomenology,* David Carr, tr. Evanston: Northwest-
              ern University Press.

1970b   *Logical Investigations,* J. N. Findlay, tr. London: Rou-
              tledge and Kegan Paul.

1982   *Ideas Pertaining to a Pure Phenomenology and Phenom-
              enological Philosophy:* First Book; *General Introduction
              to a Pure Phenomenology,* F. Kersten, tr. Dordrecht:
              Kluwer.

1989   *Ideas Pertaining to a Pure Phenomenology and Phe-
              nomenological Philosophy:* Second Book, *Studies in
              the Phenomenology of Constitution,* Richard Rojce-
              wiez and Andre Schuwer, trs. Dordrect, Holland: Klu-
              wer.

1991   *On the Phenomenology of the Consciousness of Inter-
              nal Time,* John Bennett, tr. Dordrecht: Kluwer.

Illich, Ivan (II)
1993   *In the Vineyard of the Text,* Chicago: University of
              Chicago Press.

Irigaray, Luce (LI)
1984   *Éthique de la différence sexualle,* Paris: Les Éditions de
              Minuit.

1991   "Sexual Difference," in *Irigaray Reader,* Sean Hand, tr.
              Cambridge, Mass: Blackwells.

Jonas, Hans (HJ)
1966   *The Phenomenon of Life;* New York: Dell.

Jung, Carl (CJ)
1977   *The Archetypes and the Collective Unconscious: The
              Collected Works of C. J. Jung,* vol. 9, Princeton: Prin-
              ceton University Press.

Kahn, Charles (CK)
1966   "The Greek Verb 'To Be' and the Concept of Being,"
              Foundations of Language 2.

Kant, Immanuel
Ak   *Gesammelte Schriften,* 1724–1804, *hersg. von der Ko-
              niglich Prevssischen Akademie der Wissenshaften,* Ber-
              lin, 1902 ———.

A or B   *Critique of Pure Reason,* Norman Kemp Smith, tr. Lon-
              don: Macmillan, 1973.

Anth.   *Anthropology from a Practical Point of View,* Victor
              Dowell and Hans Runet, trs. Carbondale: Southern Il-
              linois Press, 1978.

Beweis.   *Der einzig m oglich Beweisground,* N. Y.: Arbis Books,
              1979.

CAJ   *Critique of Aesthetic Judgement,* J. C. Meredith, tr.
              Oxford: Clarendon, 1911.

CPR   *Critique of Practical Reason,* Thomas Abbott, tr. London: Longmans, Green, 1948.

CTJ   *Critique of Teleological Judgement,* J. C. Meredith, tr. Oxford: Clarendon , 1928.

Cor.   "Selections from Correspondence with Beck, Herz, Lambert, Sulzer, and Mendleson," in *Kant: Selected Pre-Critical Writings and Correspondence with Beck,* G. B. Kerford and D. E. Walford, trs. Manchester: Manchester University Press, 1968.

Diss.   *The Inaugural Dissertation,* in *Kant: Selected Pre-Critical Writings and Correspondence with Beck,* G. B. Kerford and D. E. Walford, trs. Manchester: Manchester University Press, 1968.

Enq.   *Enquiry Concerning the Clarity of the Principles of Natural Theology and Ethics,* in *Kant: Selected Pre-Critical Writings and Correspondence with Beck,* G. B. Kerford and D. E. Walford, trs. Manchester: Manchester University Press, 1968.

Grund.   *The Moral Law: Kant's Groundwork of the Metaphysics of Morals,* H. J. Paton, tr. London: Hutcherson, 1968.

LK   *Gedanken von der wharen Schätzung der lebendigen Kräfte,* 1747.

Logic   *Logic,* Robert Hartman and Wolfgang Schwartz, trs. Indianapolis: Bobbs Merrill, 1974.

MF   *Metaphysical Foundations of Natural Science,* James Ellington, tr. Indianapolis: Bobbs Merrill, 1970.

ND   *Nova Dilucidatio,* in England, F. E. *Kant's Conception of God;* London: Allen and Unwin, 1928.

NG   *Versuch den Begriff der negativen Grössen in der Weltweisheit einzuführen,* 1763.

OH   "On the Idea of a Universal History," in *On History,* Lewis Beck, ed. Indianapolis: Bobbs Merrill, 1974.

Op. Post *Opus Postumum,* Eckert Foster and Michael Rosen, trs. Cambridge: Cambridge University Press, 1993.

OP   "On the Proverb: What May be True in Theory, But Is of No Practical Use," in *Perpetual Peace and Other Essays,* T. Humphrey, tr. Indianapolis: Hackett, 1983.

OQ   "An Old Question Raised Again: Is the Human Race Constantly Progressing?" in *On History,* Lewis Beck, ed. Indianapolis: Bobbs Merrill, 1963.

Prol.   *Prolegomena to Any Future Metaphysics,* P. G. Lucas, tr. Manchester: Manchester University Press, 1966.

Keller, Helen (HK)
    1965   *The Story of My Life,* New York: Dell.

Koshland, D. E. (DKo)
    1978   "A Response-Regulator Model in a Simple Sensory System," *Science* 196.

Lefebvre, Henri (HL)
1991   *The Production of Space,* D. Nicholson-Smith, tr. Oxford: Blackwell.

Leibniz, G. W. F. (GL)
1890   *Philosphischen Schriften,* 7 vols., C. J. Gerhart, ed. Biblithek Hannover.
1945   "Discourse on Metaphysics," George Montgomery, tr. LaSalle, Open Court.
1956   *The Leibniz-Clarke Correspondence,* H. G. Alexander, tr. Manchester: University of Manchester Press.

Levinas, Emmanuel (EL)
1973   *The Theory of Intuition in Husserl's Phenomenology,* A. Lingus, tr. Evanston: Northwestern University Press.
1981   *Otherwise than Being or Beyond Essence,* A. Lingis, tr. The Hague: Nijhoff.
1985   *Totality and Infinity,* A. Lingis, tr. Pittsburgh: Duquesne University Press.
1986   *Face to Face with Levinas,* Richard Cohen, ed. Albany: State University of New York Press.
1987   *Collected Philosophical Papers,* A. Lingis, tr. Dordrecht: Martinus Nijhoff.
1988   *Existence and Existents,* A. Lingis, tr. Dordrecht: Kluwer.
1990a   *Difficult Freedom: Essays in Judaism;* Baltimore: Johns Hopkins.
1990b   *Nine Talmudic Studies,* Bloomington: University of Indiana Press.
1991   "Wholly Otherwise," in *Re-Reading Levinas,* Robert Bernasconi and Simon Critchley, eds. Bloomington: University of Indiana Press.

Levi-Strauss, Claude (LS)
1962   *The Savage Mind,* London: Weidenfeld and Nicholson.

Lingis, Alphonso (AL)
1994   *The Community of Those Who Have Nothing in Common,* Bloomington: University of Indiana Press.

Llewelyn, John (JL)
1985   *Beyond Metaphysics?* Atlantic Highlands, N. J.: Humanities Press.
1986   *Derrida on the Threshold of Sense,* New York: St. Martin's Press.
1991   *The Middle Voice of Ecological Conscience,* London: Macmillan.

Lucas, J. R. (JRL)
1973   *A Treatise on Time and Space,* London: Methuen.

McTaggart, John E.M. (JM)
1927   *The Nature of Existence,* 2 vols. Cambridge: Cambridge University Press.

Martin, Gottfried (GM)
    1961   *Kant's Metaphysics and Theory of Science*, Manchester: Manchester University Press.
Marx, Werner (WM)
    1975   *Hegel's Phenomenology of Spirit*, New York: Harper and Row.
Maupertuis, P. (PM)
    1746   *"Les lois du movuvement et du repos déduite d'un principe méyaphysique,"* *Mémoires dw l'Académie des Sciences et Belle Lettrees de Berlin*, Berlin, 1748.
Merleau-Ponty, Maurice (MP)
    1964   *Signs*, Evanston: Northwestern University Press.
    1969   *The Visible and the Invisible*, Evanston: Northwestern University Press.
Moody, Earnest (EM)
    1935   *The Logic of William of Ockham*, London: Sheed and Ward.
Moore, G. E. (GEM)
    1962   *Commonplace Book*, London: Allen and Unwin.
Mourelatos, Alexander (AM)
    1970   *The Route of Parmenides*, New Haven: Yale University Press.
Nagel, Ernst (EN)
    1961   *The Structure of Science*, London: Routledge and Kagen Paul.
Newton, Sir Issac (IN)
    1952   *Optiks*, fac. 4th ed. New York: Dover.
Nietzsche, Friedrich (FN)
    1954   *The Portable Nietzsche*, Walter Kaufmann, tr. New York: Viking.
    1965   "Truth and Falsity in an Ultramoral Sense," *The Philosophy of Nietzsche*, G. Clyde, ed. New York: Mentor.
    1966   *The Will to Power*, Walter Kaufmann and R. J. Hollingdale, trs., New York: Vintage.
Nussbaum, Martha (MN)
    1986   *The Fragility of Goodness*, Cambridge: Cambridge University Press.
Oliver, James (JO)
    1968   *The Civilizing Power*, Tr. Amer. Phil. Soc., 58.
Parfait, Derick (DPa)
    1971   "Personal Identity," *Philosophical Review*, LXXX.
Peirce, C. S. (CP)
    1931   *Elements of Logic, Collected Papers of C. S. Pierce*, v. 2, Charles Hartshorne and Paul Weis, eds. Cambridge: Harvard University Press.
Peperzak, Adriaan (AP)
    1993   *To the Other: An Introduction to the Philosophy of*

Emmanuel Levinas, West Lafayette: Purdue University Press.

Percy, Walker (WP)
  1975   *The Message in the Bottle*, New York: Farrer, Straus and Giroux.
Plantinga, Alvin (APl)
  1982   "How to be an Anti-Realist," *Presidential Address, Eqastern Division, Proceedings of the Amer. Phil. Ass. 56*
Plato
  1953   *The Dialogues of Plato*, 4th edition, rev., tr. Benjamin Jowett., ed. Oxford: Clarendon Press. Individual dialogues are cited by the following abbreviations:
          Char. Charmides   *Crat. Cratylus*
          Euthy. Euthydemus   *Gor. Gorgias*
          Par. Parmenides   *Phaed. Phaedrus*
          Phil. Philebus   *Pol. Statesman*
          Rep. Republic   *Sop. Sophist*
          Sym. Symposium   *Theaet. Theaetetus*
          Tim. Timaeus
Polonoff, Irving (IP)
  1973   *Force, Cosmos, Monads and Other Themes of Kant's Early Thought*, Kantstudien Erganzungschefte 10, Bonn.
Prestige, G.L. (GP)
  1952   *God in Patristic Thought*, London: SPCK Press.
Protevi, John (JP)
  1993a   "Derrida and Hegel: *Différance* and *Untershied*," *International Studies in Philosophy* 25.
  1993b   "The Economy of Exteriority in Derrida's *Speech and Phenomena*, Man and World 26.
  1993c   "*Given Time* and the Gift of Life," paper delivered at the 1993 meeting of the Society for Existential and Phenomenological Philosophy, New Orleans.
  1994   *Time and Exteriority*, Lewisburg: Bucknell University Press.
Putnam, Hilary (HP)
  1981   "Reason and Realism," *Presidential Address, Eastern Division, Proceedings of the Amer. Phil. Ass. 50.*
Richardson, William J. (WR)
  1965   *Heidegger: Through Phenomenology to Thought*, The Hague: Nijhoff.
Richards, I. A. (IR)
  1954   *The Philosophy of Rhetoric*, New York: Oxford University Press.
Ricoeur, Paul (PR)
  1967   *Husserl: An Analysis of His Phenomenology*, Edward Ballard and Lester Embree, trs. Evanston: Northwestern University Press.

1987   *The Rule of Metaphor*, London: Routledge and Kegan Paul.

Rorty, Richard (RR)
1980   *Philosophy and the Mirror of Nature*, Princeton: Princeton University Press.

Russell, Bertand (BR)
1899   "Sur les Axiomes de la Geometrie," *Rev. de Meta.* 7.

Sacks, Oliver (OS)
1986   *The Man Who Mistook His Hat for His Wife*, London: Picador.
1987   *Awakenings*, New York: Summit.
1993   "Seeing Yet Not Seeing," *The New Yorker*, May 10, 1993.

Sallis, John (JS)
1980   *The Gathering of Reason*, Athens: Ohio University Press.
1986   *Delimitations*, Bloomington: Indiana University Press.
1987   "Twisting Free," *Research in Phenomenology* 17.

Sayre, Kenneth (KS)
1969   *Plato's Analytic Method*, Chicago: University of Chicago Press.

Sherover, Charles M. (CS)
1971   *Heidegger, Kant and Time*, Bloomington: University of Indiana Press.
1981   "Two Kinds of Transcendental Objectivity: Their Differentiation," *Philosophical Topics* 12.

Schufreider, Gregory (GS)
1994   *Confessions of a Rational Mystic*, West Lafayette: Purdue University Press.

Schürmann, Reiner (RS)
1987   *Heidegger on Being and Acting: From Principles to Anarchy*, Bloomington: Indiana University Press.

Scotus, John Duns (DS)
1962   *Philosophical Writings*, Alan Wolter, tr. Indianapolis: Bobbs Merrill.

Sokolowski, Robert (RSo)
1974   *Husserlian Meditations*, Evanston: Northwestern University Press.

Stadler, Ingrid (IS)
1968   "Perception and Perfection in Kant's Aesthetics"; in *Kant*, R.P. Wolff, ed. New York: Doubleday.

Strawson, Sir Peter (PS)
1963   *Individuals*, New York: Doubleday.
1966   *The Bounds of Sense*, London: Methuen.

Taliaferro, R. Catesby (CRT)
1944   "Introduction," *Plato: The Timaeus and Critias in The Thomas Taylor Translation*, Bollingen Series 3, New York: Pantheon Books.

Taylor, Charles (CT)
    1971   "Hermeneutics and the Sciences of Man," *Review of Metaphysics* 25.
    1978   *Hegel*, Cambridge: Cambridge University Press.
    1989   *Sources of the Self: The Making of the Modern Identity*, Cambridge: Harvard University Press.
Turkle, Shirley (ST)
    1992   *Psychoanalytic Politics*, New York: Guilford Press.
Vance, Eugene (EV)
    1979   "Roland and the Poetics of Memory," in *Textual Strategies*, J. Harapi, ed. Ithaca: Cornell University Press.
Underwood, P. A. (PU)
    1975   *The Kariye Djami*, 3 vols. Princeton: Princeton University Press.
van Fraassen, Bas (BvF)
    1980   *The Scientific Image*, Oxford: The Clarendon Press.
von Wright, Georg Henrick (VW)
    1971   *Explanation and Understanding*, London: Routledge and Kegan Paul.
Walsh, W.H. (RW)
    1975   *Kant's Criticism of Metaphysics*, Edinburgh: Edinburgh University Press.
Wartofsky, Marx (MW)
    1968   *The Conceptual Foundations of Scientific Thought*, New York: Macmillan.
Weedon, William (WW)
    1963   "A Theory of Pointing," *Southern Journal of Philosophy* 1.
Weizenbaum, Joseph (JW)
    1976   *Computer Power and Human Reason*, San Francisco: Freeman.
Weyl, Herman (HW)
    1963   *Philosophy of Mathematics and Natural Science*, New York: Atheneum.
Whitehead, Alfred North (ANW)
    1919   *An Enquiry Concerning The Principles of Natural Knowledge*, Cambridge: Cambridge University Press.
    1921   *The Concept of Nature*, Cambridge: Cambridge University Press.
    1922   *The Principle of Relativity*, Cambridge: Cambridge University Press.
    1927   *Science and the Modern World*, New York: Macmillan
    1931   *Adventures of Ideas*, New York: Macmillan.
    1938   *Modes of Thought*, Cambridge: Cambridge University Press.
    1958   *Introduction to Mathematics*, New York: Oxford University Press.
    1978   *Process and Reality*, New York: Free Press.

Whitrow, G. J. (GW)
    1961   *The Natural History of Time,* London and Edinburgh: Thomas Nelson and Sons.
Winnicott, D. W. (DWW)
    1988   *Human Nature,* New York: Schocken.
    1989   *Psychoanalytic Explorations,* Cambridge: Harvard University Press.
Wittgenstein, Ludwig (LW)
    1968   *Philosophical Investigations,* New York: Macmillan.
Wolter, Allan (AW)
    1946   *The Transcendentals and their Function in Duns Scotus,* St. Bonaventura: The Franciscan Institute.
Wood, David (DW)
    1989   *The Deconstruction of Time,* Atlantic Highlands, N.J.: Humanities Press.
Zizioulas, John (JZ)
    1988   *Being as Communion,* London: Darton, Longman and Todd.

INDEX